Cyclopedia

of

LITERARY
CHARACTERS

Cyclopedia

of

LITERARY

CHARACTERS

Revised Edition

Volume Five
Tonight We Improvise–Zuleika Dobson
Indexes

---

edited by
A. J. Sobczak

original editions edited by
Frank N. Magill

associate editor
Janet Alice Long

SALEM PRESS, INC.
Pasadena, California   Englewood Cliffs, New Jersey

Editor in Chief: Dawn P. Dawson
Managing Editor: Chris Moose
Project Editor: A. J. Sobczak
Acquisitions Editor: Mark Rehn
Research Supervisor: Jeffry Jensen
Research: Jun Ohnuki
Production Editor: Janet Alice Long
Layout: William Zimmerman

The Revised Edition includes *Cyclopedia of Literary Characters*, 1963 (first edition); *Cyclopedia of Literary Characters II*, 1990; and material new to this edition.

∞ The paper used in these volumes conforms to the American National Standard for Permanence of Paper for Printed Library Materials, Z39.48-1984.

Library of Congress Cataloging-in-Publication Data

Cyclopedia of literary characters / edited by A. J. Sobczak ; associate editor, Janet Alice Long. — Rev. ed.

 p. cm.

"This comprehensive revised edition of Cyclopedia of literary characters combines all the titles from the original Cyclopedia of literary characters and from Cyclopedia of literary characters II . . . adds character descriptions from titles included in Masterplots (revised second edition, 1996) and the Masterplots II sets covering African American literature (1994), women's literature (1995), and American fiction (supplement, 1994) . . . 3,300 titles [in all]."—Publisher's note.

 Includes index

1. Literature—Stories, plots, etc. 2. Literature—Dictionaries. 3. Characters and characteristics in literature. I. Sobczak, A. J. II. Long, Janet Alice.

PN44.M3 1998

809'.927—dc21

ISBN 0-89356-438-9 (set)
ISBN 0-89356-443-5 (vol. 5)

97-45813
CIP

CONTENTS

CONTENTS

KEY TO PRONUNCIATION

As an aid to users of the *Cyclopedia of Literary Characters, Revised Edition*, guides to pronunciation have been provided for particularly difficult character names. These guides are rendered in an easy-to-use phonetic manner. Stressed syllables are indicated by small capital letters. Letters of the English language, particularly vowels, are pronounced in different ways depending on the context. Below are letters and combinations of letters used in the phonetic guides to represent various sounds, along with examples of words in which those sounds appear.

Symbols	Pronounced As In
a	answer, laugh, sample, that
ah	father, hospital
aw	awful, caught
ay	blaze, fade, waiter, weigh
ch	beach, chimp
ee	believe, cedar, leader, liter
eh	bed, head, said
ew	boot, lose
g	beg, disguise, get
i	buy, height, lie, surprise
ih	bitter, pill
j	digit, edge, jet
k	cat, kitten, hex
[n]	bon (French "silent" n)
o	cotton, hot
oh	below, coat, note, wholesome
oo	good, look
ow	couch, how
oy	boy, coin
rr (rolled r)	guerrilla (Spanish pronunciation)
s	cellar, save, scent
sh	champagne, issue, shop
uh	about, butter, enough, other
ur	birth, disturb, earth, letter
y	useful, young
z	business, zest
zh	seizure, vision

Cyclopedia
of
LITERARY
CHARACTERS

TONIGHT WE IMPROVISE
(Questa sera si recita a soggetto)

Author: Luigi Pirandello (1867-1936)
First published: 1930
Genre: Drama

Locale: The theater itself and Sicily
Time: The 1920's
Plot: Surrealism

Doctor Hinkfuss, the stage manager (director) of an improvised dramatic presentation. Dwarfish in size yet gigantic in his assumed authority, Hinkfuss comes on stage to address the audience at the opening of the play, declaring himself, rather than the unidentified author of the play, fully responsible for the evening's performance. Instead of presenting the usual fixed, unmoving drama, he will present a living, changing theater as vital and unpredictable as life itself. Throughout the production, he interrupts scenes with comments of approval or disgust; he maneuvers light and set pieces to create the ambience he desires with no regard for the actors' needs or responses. At every opportunity, he heedlessly prattles on with his philosophy of the aesthetics of the theater, asserting the superiority of improvisation and spontaneity over fixed dialogue for the creation of the essential fluidity and passion of life on the stage. He asserts that, like life, improvisational theater allows for the unforeseen circumstances that may thwart the best-planned organization of events. Hinkfuss presents to the minds of the audience the Pirandellian conundrum: whether it is life that shapes and defines theater or theater that gives the shape of truth to life.

Leading Man, who plays the part of **Rico Verri**, a young Sicilian aviation officer, and speaks also as himself, **Mr. . . .**, the leading male performer of the troupe. He testily refuses to be introduced to the audience before the performance of the play-within-the-play, protesting that he must be nonexistent for the audience as anyone but his character part; he must live only as the character Verri for the time he is on stage. He is a temperamental and angry young man, both in himself and as the character he plays, frequently stepping out of his part to berate the stage manager or other actors in the same manner that his character scolds and belittles other characters in the play. The Leading Man is dissatisfied with improvisation, believing that there must be written parts or the actors will begin to speak out of real passions and life will take over where the stage should prevail. He criticizes Hinkfuss, demanding in the third act that he leave the stage entirely and allow the actors to continue without his manipulations and bring meaning solely through their own interactions.

Leading Lady, who plays the part of **Mommina**, the oldest daughter of the Le Croce family, and speaks also as herself, **Mrs. . . .**, the leading female performer. She too resists improvisation, claiming that she requires specific lines and actions to be certain of the quality of her performance. Through-

out the first two acts, she manipulates other cast members into following her view of the scenes. In the final act, however, after the stage manager has been forced to leave, she gives herself entirely to identification with her character, Mommina, who has married Rico Verri to prove that her family is worthy of a place in acceptable society.

Old Character Man, who plays the part of **Signor Palmiro Le Croce**, nicknamed **Penny Whistle**, and speaks also as himself to Hinkfuss and the other actors. Signor Palmiro is an ineffectual old man, harassed by his society-minded wife and made to appear foolish by the younger men of the village because he is fond of a young singer from the local tavern. In the course of the improvisational script, the character Palmiro is killed while protecting the young singer from an angry suitor.

Character Woman, who plays the part of **Signora Ignatia Le Croce** and speaks also as herself to Hinkfuss and the other actors. The signora is intent on living an urban style of life in her small country village. Because of this determination, she brings disgrace on her family by allowing her four daughters to entertain young men openly in their home, an action looked on as scandalously brazen by the gossipy villagers.

Mommina,
Totina,
Dorina, and
Nenè Le Croce, four charming and high-spirited young women who flirt with young aviation officers assigned them as their escorts by their mother. Their actions scandalize Rico Verri, and he marries Mommina to take her away from such circumstances. He then imprisons her in his home, however, to make certain she does not bring scandal on him.

Mangini,
Nardi,
Pomarici,
Pometti, and
Sarella, five young aviation officers who are guests at parties in the Le Croce home. They escort the Le Croce daughters and their mother to social affairs.

Members of the Audience, various men and women seated among the actual audience. Their purpose is to respond to and occasionally to heckle Dr. Hinkfuss in his lengthy explanations and philosophizing about the aesthetics of the theater.

— *Gabrielle Rowe*

TONO-BUNGAY

Author: H. G. Wells (1866-1946)
First published: 1909
Genre: Novel

Locale: England, West Africa, and Bordeaux
Time: Late nineteenth and early twentieth centuries
Plot: Social satire

George Ponderevo, an enterprising young scientist and the narrator. The son of the housekeeper at Bladesover House, a

large country estate, he learns about class barriers at an early age. When he is twelve years old, he falls desperately in love with a pampered young aristocrat, the Honorable Beatrice Normandy, who is eight. Two years later, he is banished when he fights with her snobbish half brother, Archie Garvell, and Beatrice, turning against her admirer, blames him for attacking Archie. After an unhappy experience in the household of one uncle, he is apprenticed to another, Edward Ponderevo, a small-time pharmacist with big dreams. Later, he wins a scholarship at the Consolidated Technical Schools in London, but he begins to neglect his studies after he meets Marion Ramboat, whom he later marries. He finds work with his Uncle Edward, marries Marion, is divorced after she discovers his infidelity, and finds material success in the patent medicine boom his uncle has created by flamboyantly advertising a product called Tono-Bungay. He then takes up the study of aircraft design, and as the result of a crash he meets Beatrice again. When the Tono-Bungay financial empire collapses, he goes on an expedition to secure a cargo of quap, a mysterious ore containing elements needed for the manufacture of a better lamp filament. The expedition is unsuccessful, and George flies his ruined uncle to France. He and Beatrice share a twelve-day romance, but she refuses to marry him. Disillusioned with himself and the degenerating society of his time, he turns to the designing of destroyers for a future war.

Mrs. Ponderevo, George's mother, the competent housekeeper at Bladesover House. Stern and unsympathetic, she shows her affection for her son only after he has been sent to live with Edward Ponderevo. She dies soon afterward, leaving her savings to George.

Edward (Teddy) Ponderevo, George Ponderevo's flashy, unscrupulous, and ambitious but likable uncle. As a pharmacist, he squanders his nephew's inheritance and goes into bankruptcy. Later, as the manufacturer of Tono-Bungay, a popular nostrum, and as the manager of a huge corporation called Domestic Utilities (familiarly known as Do-Ut), he acquires the wealth and power of which he has always dreamed, and he moves from one house to another, each more luxurious and impressive than the last, until his industrial empire suddenly collapses. He is forced to escape with George to France, where he dies of pneumonia.

Susan Ponderevo, Edward's admirable, gentle, and patient wife. She takes her husband's success calmly and handles matters with fortitude after his death. Kind and given to teasing, she shows more personal strength than any of George's loves.

The Honorable Beatrice Normandy, the girl with whom George Ponderevo carries on an innocent, childish love affair until she turns against him after he has beaten her half brother in a fight. As a grown woman, she nurses him after he has been injured while experimenting with a glider. She and George have a brief affair, but she refuses to marry him because of what she calls her spoiled character; she says that she is suited only to the life of a courtesan.

Archie Garvell, Beatrice Normandy's snobbish half brother, to whom George Ponderevo administers a sound beating when the two boys fight. Later, he toadies to George.

Marion Ramboat, the pretty, brittle woman whom George Ponderevo marries. A commonplace shopgirl, she puts off the marriage until she is certain that he can provide a comfortable living, then she makes his life miserable through her stupidity and prudery. They decide on a divorce after she learns that he has spent a holiday with his secretary.

Effie Rink, George Ponderevo's sensual, engagingly pretty secretary. Tired of his wife's coldness and nagging, George looks to Effie for passion, and he continues the affair with her after he and Marion have been divorced.

Nicholas Frapp, Mrs. Ponderevo's brother, the cloddish, bigoted baker to whom George Ponderevo is apprenticed after he has been sent away from Bladesover House. George incautiously shares with his two cousins the secret that he does not believe in religion; the boys tell their father, and at a church meeting, pious-minded Frapp accuses his nephew of blasphemy. Humiliated, George runs away and returns to his mother, who then sends him to live with Edward Ponderevo.

Cothope, George Ponderevo's assistant in his experiments with airborne craft. He shows his loyalty by continuing the work on his own time and money after the Tono-Bungay enterprise has collapsed.

Bob Ewart, George Ponderevo's school friend, later a clever, individualistic sculptor. When the two meet again in London, where George is continuing his scientific studies, Ewart has considerable influence in enlarging George's intellectual and social horizons.

Gordon Nasmyth, the wealthy man who proposes the ill-fated expedition in search of quap, a mysterious radioactive mineral.

Pollack, an associate with whom George Ponderevo becomes friendly on the expedition to bring back a cargo of quap.

The Captain of the *Maude Mary*, a cantankerous boor who must be bribed to carry a cargo of quap. He loses his ship when the radioactive mineral causes the vessel to sink.

Mr. Moggs, the president of Domestic Utilities, the corporation with which Edward Ponderevo merges his business.

Mr. Mantell, the purchaser of Edward Ponderevo's pharmacy. He employs George Ponderevo until the young man goes to London to study.

Mrs. Scrymgeour, a novelist with whom Edward Ponderevo carries on a brief, pseudo-Napoleonic affair.

Lady Drew, the mistress of Bladesover House.

Lady Osprey, the stepmother of Beatrice Normandy.

THE TOOTH OF CRIME

Author: Sam Shepard (Samuel Shepard Rogers, 1943-   )
First published: 1974
Genre: Drama

Locale: The United States
Time: The future
Plot: Allegory

Hoss, a killer intent on improving his position on the charts, aiming for a gold record. He is indisputably one of the best solo acts in the game and is well aware of the pressure that fame puts on him to continue to play that game and become number one. Hoss's problem is that he senses the futility of continuing to perform according to other people's rules instead of according to his own instincts. The isolation into which his managers have pushed him is destroying Hoss's confidence and his awareness of what is going on at the fringes of the game. He knows that the real threats to any star come not from the other acts playing within the game but from the Gypsy Markers acting outside the game who use and break the rules to fit their own purposes. This threat is realized in Crow, who is able to defeat Hoss in a shoot-out and to claim all Hoss's territory and entourage.

Becky Lou, Hoss's manager and girlfriend, a woman capable of shaping a renegade killer into a chart-topping solo marker, as she has done with Hoss. Becky, however, is also capable of destroying her creations, because she defines success as playing by the rules of the game. She is an opportunist who apparently joined up with Hoss when he was starting to make a name for himself on the circuit and who knows how to manipulate him to act against the instincts that served him well early in his career. After the fight, she leaves with Crow.

Star-Man, an astrologer, part of Hoss's management team. In advising Hoss when to kill and not to kill according to the stars, he takes away the unpredictable edge that made Hoss a successful solo marker. By advising Hoss against moving when he is ready, Star-Man helps to leave Hoss in the vulnerable, disheartened, and stagnant state in which Crow finds him at the time of the fight.

Galactic Jack, a disc jockey, in the style of Wolfman Jack, who keeps the charts on the game. He informs Hoss of his position on the charts and of movements being made by other participants in the game. Like the other people surrounding Hoss, Galactic Jack believes in the power of the game and the forces that administer the rules. He does not believe in the possibility of a serious threat coming from outside the game, that is, from the Gypsy Markers.

Cheyenne, the driver of Hoss's Maserati, a longtime companion and friend to Hoss. Because of their years as a team, Cheyenne senses the wavering of Hoss's confidence. Unlike Hoss, however, Cheyenne believes in the game because of the rewards it promises: the gold record and the stability the game has maintained. Following the fight between Hoss and Crow, Cheyenne is the only member of Hoss's management team who does not leave with Crow.

Doc, Hoss's trainer, whose main activities are preparing and dispensing drugs to Hoss and giving him advice about how to prepare for the big fight.

Crow, an arrogant, finely tuned, efficient young killer who comes from the outside to challenge Hoss to a shoot-out. He is a real threat to Hoss's position on the charts as well as to his pride. Crow is a Gypsy Marker and, unlike Hoss, is not restricted in how he plays the game. This freedom is one thing that Hoss has lost, and Crow capitalizes on Hoss's desire once again to be free to act as he wishes. Following Hoss's suicide at the end of their fight, Crow surrounds himself with all Hoss's possessions and entourage and prepares to move on his next target.

Referee, the official who scores the duel between Hoss and Crow.

— Eric H. Hobson

TOP GIRLS

Author: Caryl Churchill (1938-　　　)
First published: 1982
Genre: Drama

Locale: England
Time: Early 1980's
Plot: Social realism

Marlene, the thirty-three-year-old, recently promoted managing director of the Top Girls Employment Agency. A working-class woman who left behind her illegitimate daughter, she has achieved success in the business world by being as tough, ruthless, and aggressive as any man. Politically conservative and emotionally cold, she represents women who have "made it" by incorporating patriarchal standards of success and who are contemptuous of those who have selected more traditional paths. She left her industrial hometown and chose sales as a career because she believed she would be judged on her performance. Later, she settled into a career with Top Girls as a placement counselor, using her knowledge of the business world to help other women get a start. She is sympathetic to the agency's applicants and expects them to share her ambition and sense of individualism.

Joyce, Marlene's older sister and acting mother to Angie. She works as a cleaning woman. She stayed home to care for her parents and her husband, as well as Angie, after Marlene left home for London. Politically liberal, with a hatred for the wealthy people who employ her, she rejects Marlene's money, pity, and contempt and accepts without regret the choices she has made.

Angie, Marlene's slow-witted seventeen-year-old daughter. Driven by a murderous hatred of Joyce, she suspects that Marlene is her real mother and runs away to London to join her. She is one of those girls who will not, as Marlene says, "make it."

Pope Joan, who, disguised as a man, reigned between 854 and 856. Driven by a thirst for knowledge in philosophy, religion, and metaphysics, she had to assume the male role to achieve her goals. At Marlene's imagined promotion celebration, she is one of five historical and mythical dinner guests, all of whom are linked to present-day characters by the dramatic device of having an actress play more than one role. Louise is her contemporary physical analogue; Marlene is her emotional one.

Dull Gret, the subject of a Pieter Brueghel painting, in which she is dressed in armor and an apron, leading a crowd of women through hell to fight the devils. The only lower-class woman at the dinner who accepts her status, she has reared ten children, whom she is willing to go to any lengths to save. She is linked with Angie physically and with Joyce temperamentally.

Lady Nijo, born in 1258, a Japanese emperor's courtesan

and later a Buddhist nun, who traveled through Japan on foot. Totally dominated by the patriarchy, she has suffered through the murder of her children because they were not boys and the economic consequences of being out of favor with the court. Win is her counterpart.

Isabella Bird, a Scottish world traveler who lived from 1831 to 1904. She idolizes her sister and her late husband, admitting to having experienced great loneliness. The actress who plays her also plays Louise.

Patient Griselda, the obedient wife of "The Clerk's Tale" in Chaucer's *The Canterbury Tales*. Constantly tested by her husband, she always responds with acceptance. The actress who plays her also plays Nell and Jeanine.

Jeanine, a client who is looking for a job so that she can get married. She lacks self-confidence and direction.

Louise, a client who has devoted her life to her company, only to see men promoted over her. She has spent twenty-one years with her employer and developed a department, but her career has stagnated.

Win, an interviewer and employment counselor. She is having an affair with a married man. She realizes that she is being used, to an extent, because he is unlikely to leave his wife for her.

Nell, another interviewer and employment counselor. She is dating two men, one of whom wants to marry her. She is afraid that if she marries him, she will have to give up her career.

Shona, an applicant. She is confident and has an impressive résumé. Nell discovers that she is a gifted charlatan with no actual business experience.

— *Lori Hall Burghardt*

TORCH SONG TRILOGY

Author: Harvey Fierstein (1954-   )
First published: 1979
Genre: Drama

Locale: New York City and upstate New York
Time: The 1970's
Plot: Psychological realism

Arnold Beckoff, a female impersonator, twenty-five years old, Jewish, and gay. Arnold plays Virginia Hamn, a singer of torch songs. He is proud of his sexuality, and his life revolves around the gay culture. Arnold meets Ed, a bisexual schoolteacher, at a bar called the International Stud. He is devastated when Ed jilts him to take up with a woman. Arnold later meets a young hustler, Alan, and they become lovers. Still in love with Ed and not over his hurt, he is unfaithful to Alan, making routine trips to the back room of the International Stud for indiscriminate sex. When Arnold finally meets Laurel, the woman in Ed's life, at Ed's country home, he tells her that Ed is using her to prove his own normalcy. Arnold and Alan plan to adopt a child, but Alan is killed by a group of homophobic punks before the adoption goes through. Arnold assumes the responsibility alone, caring for David, a fifteen-year-old juvenile delinquent. Ed finally leaves Laurel and moves onto Arnold's couch until he can find another place to live. Arnold indicates to Ed that there is a good chance that they can renew their relationship.

Ed Reiss, a Brooklyn schoolteacher. He is thirty-five years old, handsome, charming, and, at times, insensitive. Ed claims that he is bisexual; Arnold labels him a closet case. Ed approaches Arnold at a gay bar and, for two weeks, sees him consistently. Confused over his sexuality, he is unable to make a commitment to Arnold or to the homosexual lifestyle. He becomes involved with a woman named Laurel and, after participating in group therapy, decides to marry her. When Arnold and his new lover, Alan, visit Ed and his wife at their farmhouse near Montreal, Ed experiences pangs of jealousy and seduces Alan. Ed eventually realizes that his relationship with Laurel is not a panacea and decides to leave her. Turning to his only gay friend, Arnold, he moves in and becomes a surrogate father to David. He wants to renew his relationship with Arnold, but Arnold will accept him only if he is willing to confront his sexuality. Ed assures Arnold that he is at least willing to try.

Alan, a former hustler turned model. He is eighteen years old and extremely good looking. When he was fourteen years old, he arrived in New York City with dreams of opening a disco. He quickly learned that the only reason men would give him money was in exchange for sex. These sexual encounters provided connections that led to his career as a model. One evening in a nightclub, Alan gets drunk, becomes involved in a fight, and is almost knifed; he is saved by Arnold, who is in full Virginia Hamn attire. As a result, he falls deeply in love with Arnold, even tolerating his infidelity. Alan remains faithful until his trip to the Reiss farm, where he is seduced by Ed. After deciding to adopt a child with Arnold, he is killed by a street gang.

Laurel, Ed's average-looking, liberal-minded wife. She has a history of falling in love with gay men and has numerous gay friends. She attends group therapy and has involved Ed in these sessions. Despite knowing that Arnold is Ed's former lover, she invites him and his new lover up to the Reiss farmhouse. When she learns that Ed has seduced Alan, she leaves him. She returns to him, however, and when Ed finally decides to withdraw from the relationship, Laurel has difficulty letting go.

David, Arnold's adopted son. He is fifteen years old, bright, handsome, and gay. Mistreated in foster homes, he lived on the streets for three years. Although skeptical and streetwise, he has been transformed in his six months with Arnold into a fun-loving prankster, comfortable with both home and school. At times, he is a typical teenager, but he displays an uncanny wisdom. Not wanting Arnold to devote his whole life to him, David would like to see Arnold and Ed back together.

Mrs. Beckoff, Arnold's mother. She is a widow in her sixties who has retired to Florida and is presented as a stereotypical Jewish mother. She loves to meddle and kvetch, or complain. She rambles constantly, saying very little. She cannot accept Arnold's homosexuality and prefers to deny it.

When she meets David, she takes a liking to him but is completely opposed to Arnold's plans to adopt him. She is insensitive to her son's feelings about the death of Alan (although the cause of death has been concealed from her) and is incensed that he would dare to compare their affair with her many years of marriage. They quarrel, and Arnold asks her to leave. Before she departs, they reconcile, and she tries to comfort Arnold about Alan's death.

Lady Blues, a blues singer employed between scenes. She sings 1920's and 1930's torch songs in the tradition of Helen Morgan or Ruth Etting.

— Steven C. Kowall

THE TORRENTS OF SPRING

Author: Ernest Hemingway (1899-1961)
First published: 1926
Genre: Novella

Locale: Rural Michigan
Time: Early 1920's
Plot: Parody

Scripps O'Neil, who claims to have published two stories in *The Dial* and one in *The Saturday Evening Post*. He also claims to be a Harvard man. O'Neil is tall and lean. Deserted by his wife and daughter Lucy in Mancelona, Michigan, O'Neil wanders down the railroad tracks to Petoskey and goes to work in the pump factory as a piston-collarer. It is mentioned that his father was a great composer, that his mother is from Florence, Italy, and that he and his mother had to beg from door to door in Chicago when Scripps was a boy, but much of what is said about Scripps in this satirical work is contradictory. He also claims that his father was a general in the Confederate Army and that his mother, with Scripps clinging to her dress, berated General Sherman as the Yankees burned the O'Neil plantation. O'Neil, who is "literary" and romantically fickle, takes many of his meals in Brown's Beanery, where he falls in love with and marries Diana, an elderly waitress. He soon rejects her for Mandy, a younger waitress. Scripps inexplicably carries a bird inside his shirt through much of the story. He finally gives the bird to Diana. Scripps is with Mandy at the story's end, but his mind is wandering.

Yogi Johnson, a World War I veteran. Johnson is of Scandinavian descent and works in a Petoskey, Michigan, pump factory. He is a chunky, well-built fellow, of the sort one might see anywhere. He claims to have been the first World War I volunteer from Cadillac, Michigan. Yogi is worried because he does not want to be with a woman; he fears that something is wrong. A philosopher, he often remarks on the decay of morality in his time. He meets two American Indians and tells them of his experiences both playing center in football and at the front, where he killed five men. Yogi speaks of the stages a soldier goes through as he becomes hard-boiled. The Indians take Yogi to an all-Indian private club, which he is forced to leave hurriedly when it is noticed that he is not an Indian. He takes the Indians to Brown's Beanery, a local restaurant, where he relates his most humiliating experience: In Paris, Yogi had unknowingly participated in a live sex exhibition. Having told his tale, he strides away into the night. Yogi is last seen walking down the railroad tracks with an Indian woman, at night, stripping off and throwing away all of his clothes.

Diana, an elderly waitress in Brown's Beanery. She wears steel-rimmed glasses, and her face is lined and gray. She claims to be from the English Lake Country and that, as a *jeune fille* on a visit to Paris with her mother, her mother disappeared. The police were unable to find Diana's mother, and it is not until the "Author's Final Note to the Reader" that it is revealed that she died of bubonic plague and that the French authorities concealed the matter so as not to destroy the financial success of the Paris Exposition. After her mother's death, Diana was forced, she explains, to go to America, and she became a waitress. Diana is a constant reader of *The Manchester Guardian*. She and Scripps "fall in love" and are married, but half an hour later she notices that Scripps is eyeing the relief waitress. She worries whether she can hold Scripps. She tries to hold him by reading and relating stories from the literary journals of the time: *Scribner's*, *The Century*, and *The Bookman*. She does lose Scripps, but she asks for and receives the bird. She goes out into the night.

Mandy, a waitress at Brown's Beanery. She is a buxom, jolly-looking girl. Scripps thinks that she is robust and vigorously lovely, with healthy, calm, and capable hands. He is "stirred" by her only thirty minutes after his marriage to Diana. Mandy likes to tell improbable literary anecdotes, the first one being about the death of Henry James and others concerning Edmund Gosse and other writers. She wins Scripps, but for how long is questionable. By the end of the story, his interest is already wandering to the Indian woman.

Two Indians, one small and one large, who had studied at the Carlisle Indian School. They are on their way, they say, to Petoskey, to join the Salvation Army. They both claim to be decorated war veterans. The smaller one won the Victoria Cross. He has artificial arms and legs but still shoots excellent pool and can climb ladders. The large one was a major and won the Distinguished Service Order. The Indians take Yogi to an all-Indian club; when they are thrown out, the small one loses one of his artificial arms. They are last seen picking up Yogi's discarded clothes to sell.

An Indian woman who carries a papoose. She enters the beanery wearing only moccasins. She is joined by Yogi, and they walk out together.

The author, clearly Hemingway, a character who speaks to the reader from time to time, discussing his progress on the book and what he has had for lunch and with whom.

A drummer, a steady customer at Brown's Beanery.

— Donald R. Noble

THE TORRENTS OF SPRING
(Veshniye vody)

Author: Ivan Turgenev (1818-1883)
First published: 1872
Genre: Novel

Locale: Frankfurt and Wiesbaden
Time: 1840
Plot: Psychological realism

Dimitry Pavlovich Sanin (DMIH-tree PAHV-loh-vihch SAH-nihn), a young Russian nobleman and the novel's aging narrator. The novel, presented as a reminiscence, gives two distinct visions of Sanin: the weak-willed, twenty-one-year-old idealist and the soul-sickened, fifty-two-year-old narrator. The youthful Sanin is a careless nobleman who is accosted by Gemma Rosselli while walking down a street in Frankfurt. She believes that her brother Emilio has stopped breathing, and when Sanin restores the young man, she and her family consider him their savior. Sanin stays on in Frankfurt and discovers that he is infatuated with Gemma. After winning her affection by fighting a duel in her honor, he meets the predatory Maria Nikolayevna and falls under her sexual spell. Sanin's betrayal of Gemma is worsened by his inability to confess his perfidy to her. After a time in Maria Nikolayevna's retinue, Sanin is cast aside. It is only as a life-sickened, aging man of the world that Sanin seeks out Gemma and is relieved of his guilt when he hears of her happy married state in the United States. The news fills him with a new sense of life, and he begins to make plans to immigrate.

Gemma Rosselli (GEH-mah roh-SEH-lee), a beautiful Italian girl living in Frankfurt. Dutiful and innocent, Gemma is willing to sacrifice herself to Klüber's loveless proposal for the sake of the financial stability of her family, but Sanin's romantic defense of her honor gives her the courage to break off her engagement to Klüber and openly express her love for Sanin. Her forgiving response to the aging Sanin's letter demonstrates her generosity and virtue.

Karl Klüber, a German businessman, Gemma's fiancé. Reflecting the author's growing disenchantment with Germany, Klüber is a complete materialist, devoid of character or sensitivity. He callously treats love as a business arrangement. When Gemma is insulted by von Dönhof, Klüber tries to ignore the incident.

Maria Nikolayevna Polozov (nih-koh-LAH-yehv-nah poh-LOH-zov), a wealthy half-Gypsy who seduces Sanin. Predatory and evil, Maria uses sex as a weapon, relishing her sexual victory over Sanin. Her greatest pleasure comes from despoiling the honorable love that was shared by Gemma and Sanin. In the context of nineteenth century Russian culture, Maria's sexual adventuring can be viewed as a sort of apolitical nihilism.

Ippolit Sidorych Polozov (ee-poh-LIHT sih-DOH-rihch), Maria Nikolayevna's phlegmatic husband. Morally impoverished, physically grotesque, and psychologically dominated, Polozov accepts his wife's sexual adventuring as the price he must pay to pursue in peace his own self-centered existence.

Von Dönhof, the German officer with whom Sanin fights a duel for Gemma's honor. A boasting drunkard, von Dönhof insults Gemma, who is defended by Sanin. He later shows little enthusiasm for the duel with Sanin.

Panteleone (pan-teh-leh-OH-nay), an aged, retired opera singer who lives with the Rossellis. At first, Panteleone's pathetic reminiscences of past operatic triumphs playing heroic roles make him a comic figure, but he is the character who effectively confronts Sanin with his unfaithfulness after he has betrayed Gemma.

Emilio Rosselli (eh-MEE-lyoh), Gemma's idealistic younger brother. Impressed by the heroism that he believes Sanin displays, he is encouraged to enlist in the idealistic fight for independence under Giuseppe Garibaldi. He is killed, and his growth from an uncertain boy into a martyr in the cause of national unification contrasts markedly with Sanin's sorry decline into corruption.

— *Carl Brucker*

TORTILLA FLAT

Author: John Steinbeck (1902-1968)
First published: 1935
Genre: Novel

Locale: Tortilla Flat, a section of Monterey, California
Time: Early 1920's
Plot: Naturalism

Danny, a *paisano* in his early thirties. His heritage is a mixture of Spanish, Indian, Mexican, and Caucasian, but, like all *paisanos*, he claims to be purely Spanish. He is small, dark, and compact in build. Danny is without conventional ambition but is intelligent and capable. He broke mules for the army in Texas during World War I. After his return from the war, Danny inherits two wooden houses from his grandfather, but property brings responsibility and worry, and security brings boredom, brooding, and restlessness: Danny likes women and fighting. He is the King Arthur of the round table of *paisanos* of Monterey.

Pilon (pee-LOHN), a *paisano* who is a tenant in one of Danny's houses. Smarter than most of the others, Pilon is a sentimentalist, though utterly without ambition. He is a cunning thief and rationalizer. Pilon also served in World War I.

Big Joe Portagee, another *paisano* tenant in one of Danny's houses. He had joined the infantry in World War I but spent eighteen of twenty-nine months in jail. He loves women, drinking, and brawling, and he is less intelligent than his friends. He has trouble concentrating and often falls asleep at inopportune times. He is nearly without morality because he has trouble remembering right from wrong.

Jesus Maria Corcoran (heh-SEWS mah-REE-ah koh-KOH-rahn), a *paisano*. Jesus is good-hearted and always tries to relieve suffering whenever he hears of it. He lives in Danny's house and brings home the needy strays he finds.

The Pirate, a huge, broad, slow-witted man with five dogs who cuts twenty-five cents worth of kindling each day and saves the quarters to buy a silver candlestick for Saint Francis. He lives in an abandoned chicken house until taken in by the *paisanos*.

Delores Engracia "Sweets" Ramirez (deh-LOH-rehs ehn-GRAH-see-ah rrah-MEE-rehs), a *paisana* who belongs to the Native Daughters of the Golden West. "Sweets" is given to fits of lust once or twice a week. Then, her figure has voluptuousness of movement and her voice has a certain throatiness, though she is lean-faced, lumpy, and not considered pretty most of the time. Sweets desires Danny and is catapulted to the top of the social heap when Danny, a property owner, gives her a vacuum cleaner, though she has no electricity in her house.

Torelli the wine-seller, a man much put upon by the *paisanos*, who try to cheat him as he seeks to take advantage of them. He can be miserly and foul-tempered.

Mrs. Torelli, his wife, a woman with a gentle nature, sus-ceptible to flattery. She is seduced occasionally by one of the *paisanos*.

Señora Teresina Cortez (teh-reh-SEE-nah kohr-TEHS), who is nearing thirty years of age and is the mother of at least nine children. Her own mother is only in her late forties. The Cortez children live exclusively on tortillas and beans, a diet on which, to the astonishment of all, they thrive. The *paisanos* generously provide this family with a year's supply of beans. Señora Cortez becomes pregnant once again and wonders which of them is responsible.

Cornelia Ruiz (kohr-NEH-lee-ah rrew-EES), a woman famous for her love of men and fighting. She is a favorite of the *paisanos*, although she is known to take money from men's pockets while they sleep.

The corporal from Torreón, Mexico, a man whose wife left him for a captain. He hopes his infant son will rise to be a general so that his son can steal some enlisted man's attractive young wife.

— *Donald R. Noble*

THE TOWER OF LONDON

Author: William Harrison Ainsworth (1805-1882)
First published: 1840
Genre: Novel

Locale: England
Time: The sixteenth century
Plot: Historical

The duke of Northumberland, the leader of forces opposing Mary Tudor. He is executed after she becomes queen of England.

Guilford Dudley, the son of Northumberland, who wishes him to become king. He is pardoned after the defeat of Northumberland but executed after failure of his own later plot against Mary.

Lady Jane Grey, the innocent and loyal wife of Dudley and claimant to the throne upon the death of Edward VI. The dupe of Pembroke and Renard, she is executed with Dudley after her refusal to become a Catholic.

Cuthbert Cholmondeley, Dudley's squire, who is in love with Cicely. Imprisoned and tortured in the Tower, he escapes and later marries Cicely.

Cicely, the adopted daughter of Peter the pantler and Dame Potentia Trusbut. She becomes a lady in waiting to Lady Jane. Imprisoned by jealous Nightgall, she is later revealed to be of noble birth and is permitted by Mary to marry Cuthbert.

Lady Grace Mountjoy, Cicely's insane mother, who dies in a Tower cell.

Lawrence Nightgall, the Tower jailer who is in love with Cicely. He is murdered by Renard after plotting with the French ambassador to kill Renard.

Simon Renard, the Spanish ambassador.

Lord Pembroke, Mary's supporter and the conspirator with Renard to assassinate Cuthbert.

Queen Mary, who is in love with Courtenay but affianced (upon Renard's advice) to Philip, king of Spain, after the discovery of Courtenay's double-dealing with Elizabeth.

Princess Elizabeth, Mary's younger half sister. She is confined because of complicity with Courtenay, released by Mary, and then reconfined for a later execution planned by Mary.

Edward Courtenay, the earl of Devonshire. In love with Elizabeth, he plots to get Mary's throne by pretending love for Mary, who promises to marry him. He is confined for later execution because of his treachery.

Gunnora Boase, an old woman, the tool of Northumberland and poisoner of the boy king, Edward VI.

The duke of Suffolk, the father of Lady Jane Grey.

Sir Thomas Wyat, the anti-Catholic leader of the revolt against Mary.

THE TOWERS OF TREBIZOND

Author: Rose Macaulay (1881-1958)
First published: 1956
Genre: Novel

Locale: Primarily Turkey and its environs
Time: Mid-1950's
Plot: Social realism

Laurie, the protagonist, the niece of Dorothea ffoulkes-Corbett. Both her name and her outlook (independent and tomboyish, with a zest for adventure and a love of solitude) keep her androgynous; no details of age or appearance are revealed. She narrates the adventures of the traveling party that includes Aunt Dot, Father Hugh Chantry-Pigg, herself, and, later, Dr. Halide Tanpinar and Xenophon. Enlisted by Aunt Dot as a sort of companion-cum-secretary on a trip to the Middle East, Laurie agrees to illustrate and contribute to the book about Turkey that her aunt plans to write, in addition to helping with the daily affairs of lodging, luggage, camping, transportation, dining, and caring for the camel. Like her aunt, she loves travel perhaps more than any other occupation, not only because she relishes new sights and experiences but also because she often thus encounters her mother (who had left Laurie's clergyman father when Laurie was young) and her mother's "protector," both of whom are cheerful, lively, generous, and easygoing. Engaged in an affair of ten years' duration with her married cousin Vere, Laurie yearns for the consolations of the Anglican Church (she comments that it is in her family's blood) but cannot relinquish the love that it condemns. Trebizond, with its rich and ancient history encompassing many religions and cultures, becomes for her a symbol of the mystery at the center of life, and after Vere's death she feels forever alienated both from its mystery and from the comfort of the church. Laurie's character is partially drawn from the author's own life: fascination with travel, enjoyment of writing and adventure, devotion to and alienation from the Anglican Church, and a lengthy affair with a married man, although in the author's case the affair endured for more than twenty years and ended with her lover's death from cancer.

Dorothea ffoulkes-Corbett, referred to as **Aunt Dot**, an eccentric feminist, adventurer, and missionary of sorts, very much her own person. She became a widow when her missionary husband tried to shoot her and himself to save them from cannibals; when he missed her, she feigned death to avoid his next shot, saw him kill himself, and then talked her way out of the stewpot by convincing the savages that she was a goddess. She spearheads the trip (taking the camel to make a good impression), greatly concerned about the plight of Middle Eastern women, whose religious beliefs contribute to their oppression. Convinced that only conversion to Christianity (specifically High Church Anglicanism) will liberate them, she takes along Father Chantry-Pigg to legitimize her travels, allowing her to be partially funded as a missionary. Traveling so near to "the curtain" between Turkey and Russia, which she has yearned for many years to visit and into which travel is forbidden because of the Cold War, she yields to temptation: She talks Father Chantry-Pigg into sneaking across the border with her for several months, thus leaving Laurie and the rest of the party to fend for themselves. She returns unscathed, ebullient, and even more notorious than before, accused by both the Russians and the British of spying. As the story closes, she is determined to publish her book and make the world aware of the suffering of Middle Eastern women.

Father Hugh Chantry-Pigg, a zealous and narrow-minded Anglican clergyman, now retired. He eagerly accepts Aunt Dot's invitation to accompany her abroad, desiring to enlighten the heathen, visit holy places, and test the miraculous powers of the relics he collects. His pomposity and self-righteousness alienate Laurie, the Muslims, and most of the various government officials with whom the party must deal. He fails to make a single convert and in fact probably sets back the missionary work of the Anglican Church by several years. A willing conspirator in Aunt Dot's clandestine trip across the

Russian border, he cares not at all about the plight of women but desires rather to visit shrines and collect or display relics. Like Aunt Dot, he returns notorious and accused of spying, still self-satisfied and inflexible.

Dr. Halide Tanpinar (ah-LEED tah[n]-pee-NAHR), a female doctor from Istanbul, attractive and strong-minded. While taking medical training in London, she had converted to Anglicanism, primarily to protest the Muslim treatment of women. Father Chantry-Pigg pressures her and doubts her motives. Aunt Dot persuades her to join their party as translator and part-time missionary. Dr. Tanpinar reveals that she loves a Muslim but will not marry him because of the Muslim oppression of women. Eventually, she comes to realize that change for the better must come from within the country and its people, and that Anglicanism is too alien to be accepted at that time. She reconverts to Islam, marries her beloved, and determines to work for the betterment of the situation of women as a Muslim herself.

Vere, Laurie's cousin and adulterous lover of ten years. He is evidently wealthy enough to travel frequently. Laurie is in love with his wit, intellect, and understanding. He never expresses any regret for betraying his wife or any interest in Anglicanism, a topic vitally important to Laurie. He dies suddenly in an auto accident when Laurie, enraged at a bus driver who is running a red light, attempts to beat the bus across the intersection.

Xenophon Paraclydes, a young Greek student. He joins Aunt Dot's caravan as jeep driver (he "borrows" the jeep from a family member) and as general assistant. After Aunt Dot sneaks into Russia, he regretfully heads back home, losing his zest for travel in the ensuing legal fray.

Charles Dagenham, a writer of travel books and probably a homosexual. He is an acquaintance of Laurie whom she encounters in Turkey. He has recently had a falling-out with his companion and fellow writer, David Langley. A few days after he insists on telling Laurie "the real story"—lest she should hear an alternate version from David—he is killed by a shark while swimming in dangerous waters. Laurie, spending the night in a hotel room where he had stayed earlier, finds his manuscript and keeps it to return to his family after his death.

David Langley, Charles's collaborator and (probably) lover. After Charles's death and Aunt Dot's disappearance, Laurie reads a London paper and realizes that David is plagiarizing from a copy of Charles's manuscript, unaware that she possesses the original, and taking full credit for the work. Short of funds and desperate to reach Alexandretta, where Vere awaits, she makes David aware of the original manuscript, thus gently blackmailing him into providing food and transportation. She eventually gives him the manuscript, but even back in England he continues to be obliging lest she should reveal what she knows. Although she maintains silence, his plagiarism eventually is discovered.

The camel, a gift from a rich Arab to Aunt Dot on one of her earlier adventures. It is a beast of pedigree, a white Arabian Dhalur, and is the means of Aunt Dot's escape into Russia. When Laurie is left almost penniless, it provides her transportation to Alexandretta, and it provides comic relief throughout the story.

— *Sonya H. Cashdan*

THE TOWN

Author: William Faulkner (1897-1962)
First published: 1957
Genre: Novel

Locale: Jefferson, Yoknapatawpha County, Mississippi
Time: 1909-1927
Plot: Psychological realism

Flem Snopes, the shrewdest of the materialistic Snopes clan. After successfully taking over the hamlet of Frenchman's Bend, Flem lets his desire for respectability master his voracious thirst for money, and he begins a systematic rise from restaurant owner to bank president in Jefferson. He marries Eula to secure Will Varner as an ally and permits an affair between Manfred de Spain and his wife to secure de Spain's aid in his rise. When the proper time arrives, he uses this affair to remove de Spain and take his place as president of the bank.

Manfred de Spain, the mayor of Jefferson. When a vacancy occurs, de Spain resigns as mayor and becomes president of the bank; he makes Flem vice president. After his eighteen-year affair becomes common knowledge, de Spain sells his bank stock and leaves the presidency vacant for Flem.

Eula Varner Snopes, Flem's wife. Already pregnant by Hoake McCarron, Eula is married to impotent Flem Snopes to save the family name. She has a long affair with Manfred de Spain but refuses to leave Jefferson with him. After exacting a promise from Gavin Stevens that he will marry Linda, she commits suicide.

Linda Snopes, Eula's daughter.

Gavin Stevens, a verbose county attorney. In his role as the conscience of Jefferson, Stevens attempts to reform Eula and later promises to marry Linda, if necessary, to protect her from Flem's schemes.

V. K. Ratliff, a garrulous, likable country sewing machine salesman, a narrator.

Charles Mallison, Gavin Stevens' nephew, one of the narrators.

Will Varner, Eula's father.

I. O. Snopes,

Byron Snopes,

Montgomery Ward Snopes,

Mink Snopes, and

Eck Snopes, Flem's worthless cousins, whom he abandons as he rises.

Ab Snopes, Flem's father, a horse thief and barn burner.

Wallstreet Panic Snopes, Flem's successful cousin.

THE TOWN

Author: Conrad Richter (1890-1968)
First published: 1950
Genre: Novel

Locale: Ohio
Time: Mid-nineteenth century
Plot: Regional

Sayward Wheeler, a typical, stout-hearted, firm, and sensible pioneer woman. She is the unquestioned ruler of her large family. She worries most about her youngest child, Chancey, and tries her best to strengthen him in every way she can. When the family moves into a large house in the town, she manages to keep up with her children socially, but she keeps her common touch and is most comfortable among homey things. She plants some trees around the house and becomes attached to them during her lonely old age. In her will, she stipulates that the trees must not be cut down.

Portius Wheeler, Sayward's husband, who hopes for a county judgeship but does not get it because he is an agnostic. He is shrewd in money matters and allows no one to get the better of him in a business deal. He is a popular lawyer and a financial success; he makes his family the richest in town.

Chancey Wheeler, Sayward's youngest child. As a boy, he is very delicate and frail and lives in a dream world of his own making. He leaves home and becomes a newspaperman.

Resolve Wheeler, Sayward's eldest child, who studies law with his father, marries a sensible woman, and becomes governor of the state.

Guerdon Wheeler, one of Sayward's children, who marries a woman of easy virtue and then runs away after killing her lover. His daughter, Guerda, becomes Sayward's favorite.

Huldah Wheeler, Sayward's daughter, who runs away stark naked to a man's house; she claims that gypsies took her clothes. Sayward goes after her and brings her back.

Kinzie Wheeler,

Sooth Wheeler,

Libby Wheeler,

Dezia Wheeler, and

Mercy Wheeler, Sayward and Portius' other children.

Jake Tench, a steamboat operator.

Mrs. Jake Tench, a former schoolmistress who has had a child by Portius.

Rosa Tench, Portius' child by Mrs. Tench. She commits suicide.

THE TRACK OF THE CAT

Author: Walter Van Tilburg Clark (1909-1971)
First published: 1949
Genre: Novel

Locale: The Sierra Nevadas
Time: Early twentieth century
Plot: Symbolism

Mr. Bridges, the owner of a ranch in Nevada. He is a drunkard who leaves the management of the ranch to his sons.

Arthur Bridges, a dreamer. He sympathizes with the pagan animistic religion of Joe Sam, the Indian hired man. He is killed by a huge cat while he sits whittling, waiting for his brother Curt to join him in hunting for the mountain lion.

Joe Sam, the Bridges' Indian hired man. He believes in "medicine" as the only way to avoid trouble from the cat who is the symbol of evil. When worried, he goes into a trancelike state, as he does when the cat appears on the scene. He recovers enough to help Harold Bridges hunt down and kill the cat.

Curt Bridges, the oldest of the Bridges' sons and the natural leader among the brothers. He always wants to do things his way. He apparently dies of fright, having left his campfire when frightened by the cat. He falls over a cliff to his death.

Harold Bridges, the youngest of the Bridges' sons. At first, he stays at the ranch house because his sweetheart is visiting. Later, he goes out with Joe Sam to hunt and kill the mountain lion that has killed his brother Arthur.

Mrs. Bridges, the boys' mother. She fears, because of a dream she has, that her family is in danger.

Grace Bridges, the sister of Arthur, Curt, and Harold Bridges.

Gwen Williams, Harold Bridges' sweetheart, an overnight visitor at the ranch.

TRACKS

Author: Louise Erdrich (1954-   )
First published: 1988
Genre: Novel

Locale: A Chippewa reservation, a convent, and the town of Argus, all in North Dakota
Time: 1912-1924
Plot: Domestic realism

Nanapush, one of two first-person narrators. He is an old and authoritative Chippewa speaking to his "adoptive" daughter, Lulu, as he tries to dissuade her from marrying one of the Morrisseys. Named for his tribal trickster figure, he is a survivor along with Fleur (whom he has saved) of the consumption epidemic of 1912 and a mythic figure in his own right. He claims to have guided the last buffalo hunt, seen the last bear shot, and trapped the last beaver with a pelt of more than two years' growth.

Pauline Puyat, a young mixed-blood woman whose unreliable narration moves from prevarication to madness in the course of the book. She is from a family of despised "skinners" of fur with no clan name. She is obsessed with Fleur Pillager, whose brief and tragic career in Argus and later troubles on the reservation (some of Pauline's making) she chronicles with increasingly vicious relish, to an indeterminate audience. Torn between fleshly desire (she bears a baby, Marie, whom she then abandons) and bizarre imagings mixing Native American and Catholic beliefs, she passes herself off as white and becomes a nun.

Fleur Pillager, rescued by Nanapush from her familial cabin on Lake Matchimanito during an epidemic. Tall, strong, and attractive, she is said to be the lover of Misshepeshu, the lake's spirit, who protects her from drowning and gives her

power over her enemies. During a summer working in Argus at Kozkas' butcher shop, she angers three male employees by winning repeatedly at cards. They rape her in revenge, and she (perhaps) calls forth the tornado that destroys them. Because these events are related only by Pauline, Fleur's character remains enigmatic, as does the parentage of her child, Lulu. With the encroachment of whites, her magic is no longer dependable.

Eli Kashpaw, the son of Margaret (Rushes Bear) and lover of Fleur. He is the father of their dead child. He is caught between the woods where, like Fleur, he feels most at home, and the assimilative instincts of his mother and his brother, Nector.

Margaret Kashpaw, the fourth wife of Nanapush, mother to eighteen children, and betrayer (along with her practical son, Nector) of both Nanapush and Fleur. She uses their combined and hard-earned money to pay late fees on Kashpaw property only, so Nanapush's property is forfeited to the encroaching lumber company.

Lulu Pillager, the daughter of Fleur, a beautiful, wild, somewhat spoiled child. Sent to government school by her desperate mother, then retrieved by Nanapush and Margaret, she listens restlessly to Nanapush's part of the tale.

— *Maureen Fries*

THE TRAGEDY OF KING CHRISTOPHE
(La Tragédie du Roi Christophe)

Author: Aimé Césaire (1913-   )
First published: 1963
Genre: Drama

Locale: Haiti
Time: 1806-1820
Plot: Historical

Henri Christophe (an-REE kree-STOHF), the king of the new nation of Haiti, a former slave, cook, and revolutionary soldier with the great liberator, Toussaint-Louverture. He is named a general and commander of the northern province and then offered the presidency of the new republic. He refuses, preferring to have himself crowned king of the northern province, and sets up a court in imitation of Haiti's former masters, the French. His throne has a gold sun emblazoned on the back to resemble that of Louis XIV, and he puts the crown on his

own head at the coronation, as did Napoleon. After fourteen years of trying to make a world power of Haiti, however, he admits defeat and commits suicide.

Pétion (pay-TYOH[N]), a mulatto who accepts the presidency after Christophe refuses. He rules the other half of Haiti as a republic. He urges the senate to refuse Christophe's offer of unification and later sends the army to destroy his rival.

Hugonin (ew-goh-NA[N]), Christophe's agent and "court jester," who insists that the nobility created by Christophe is a fine way to bestow favors and to secure the king's authority. Although he is a buffoon and scoundrel, he is appointed as minister of public morality; in this role, he is commanded to force marriage on the promiscuous natives and to reinstate respect for the family. When Christophe at last commits suicide, Hugonin declares himself ready to join the return to former ways and announces the end of the king's dream of a European-style kingdom.

Master of Ceremonies, a protocol expert sent by the European nations to set up a court in response to Christophe's request for technical aid. He oversees dress, dancing, and general etiquette at the court.

Corneille Brelle (kohr-NAY brehl), archbishop of the realm, who crowns Christophe as king, "first crowned monarch of the New World." He later displeases the king, who orders him walled up in the archbishop's palace and left to die.

Metellus (meh-teh-LEWS), a conspirator who hopes to overthrow both Christophe and Pétion because they have betrayed the revolution and divided the country.

Madame Christophe, a former servant, now the queen.

She warns her husband that he is pushing his people too hard in his drive to make Haiti a world power.

Martial Besse, a young European engineer who will oversee the building of Christophe's great stone citadel, a monument to glorify the new Haiti and to inspire its citizens to greater accomplishments.

Richard, Count of the Northern Marches, banished to distant Thomasico after dancing the Bamboola at a court ball.

Franco de Medina (FRAH[N]-koh deh meh-DEE-nah), a French diplomat who comes to Christophe's court with a proposal from the French king and is promptly put to death by Christophe.

Juan de Dios (hwahn deh DEE-ohs), the archbishop who replaces the murdered Corneille Brelle. He is forced to accommodate the king and celebrate the Feast of the Assumption at a church near Christophe's palace instead of at the cathedral in the capital city. His intoning of the Mass puts Christophe in a trance that causes him to see the ghost of Corneille Brelle and to collapse.

— *Lucy Golsan*

THE TRAGIC MUSE

Author: Henry James (1843-1916)
First published: 1889-1890
Genre: Novel

Locale: Paris and England
Time: The 1880's
Plot: Social realism

Peter Sherringham, who is in the early stages of a promising career in British diplomacy. He is stationed in Paris. He enjoys the theater and has developed a close relationship with the Parisian theatrical circle. He has no ambition to enter the profession himself, but he has a reputation as an excellent judge of the craft. He is asked to support the career of a young English woman of Jewish extraction, Miriam Rooth, who is determined to become an actress. Sherringham is not impressed by her audition performance but is open-minded about it. She works hard, and when she proves to be quite gifted, he puts money into a theatrical production for her in London. It is a great success. Sherringham keeps his distance, in part because of his work in Paris and in part because of his natural discretion and desire not to impose himself on the young girl in her early career. After she becomes established, however, he falls in love with her and wants her to marry him, as well as to give up her career. She refuses, not because she does not love him but because her career is important to her. He believes he can offer her an equally important role as his wife, because he is convinced that he will have a brilliant career as a diplomat. She suggests that he give up the diplomatic world and become her husband and her manager; that role would be important because she is destined to have a brilliant future. They cannot agree, and eventually, some time later, Peter marries his cousin, who has waited patiently for him.

Nicholas Dormer, Peter Sherringham's cousin. He is a gifted politician whom the Liberal Party in England projects as having a brilliant career if he can win a seat in Parliament. He is modest about his political skills, in part because he has some talent as a painter and would, if he had a chance, choose to be an artist. His cousin, Julia Dallow, the sister of Peter Sherringham and a rich widow, has political control over a country jurisdiction. Julia offers its parliamentary seat to Dormer, with

the promise to support him financially. She loves him, as he does her, and they have an agreement to marry sometime after he has settled into politics. Dormer wins election to Parliament, but Julia refuses to marry him immediately, suspecting his artistic inclinations. She is right. Dormer, urged on by friends in the art world, renounces his seat and becomes a full-time painter. He hopes to become a popular portrait painter, and he begins with some success with portraits of Miriam Rooth. Julia breaks off the engagement. Dormer, for all of his aesthetic enthusiasms, still loves Julia. He discovers that he is only a mildly gifted artist. Eventually, the two lovers come together in a compromise in which he will, occasionally, paint members of high society.

Miriam Rooth, a young British woman with an ambition to become an actress. She seems to have little but her natural beauty to offer when she seeks support and theatrical instruction in the inner circles of the Parisian theater. Told that she has no real talent, she stubbornly begs for instruction from an old actress, who reluctantly takes her on at Sherringham's request. Eventually, Miriam shows some promise, which turns into first-class acting. She is aware of the fragile nature of theatrical fame and is determined to have a long career that will not depend on public whim. She is true to her gift, and the offer from Sherringham to become his wife and a respected member of high society does not tempt her, despite her love for him. Eventually, she marries not for love but for her career. Her husband, a minor actor, is a good manager and will take care of her business.

Julia Dallow, who was widowed by a rich man while still young. She is beautiful, ambitious, and intelligent, but a victim of social and political convention. She is interested in politics and has the money and the connections to involve herself in that endeavor. Because she is a woman, she is not able either to vote or to run for office. She is determined to involve herself in politics, and she seems to have the perfect way to do it, through Nicholas Dormer. She has no understanding of his infatuation with art and lacks any personal appreciation of art.

Eventually, they come together in a compromise that delicately ignores their differences.

— *Charles Pullen*

TRAIN WHISTLE GUITAR

Author: Albert Murray (1916-   )
First published: 1974
Genre: Novel

Locale: Rural Alabama
Time: Primarily the 1920's
Plot: Bildungsroman

Scooter, the boyhood, nickname identity of the adult narrator of the novel. He is the protagonist of the adventures that the narrator is relating from memory. The narrator presents his boyhood self as typifying, in many ways, black boys of his time and place, as well as all boys of any time and place. Scooter is free-roaming, curious about life, appropriately naïve and mischievous but playfully learning from experience, hero-worshiping, confident, and eager to conquer the world. In certain ways, which have made the narrator what he is, Scooter is special. He always has been told that he was born to "be somebody," and this sense of himself sometimes has made him feel and act somewhat detached and superior. Possessing above-average intelligence and a wide-ranging intellectual curiosity, he is eager to learn and to please his family and teachers. He is observant and reflective, articulate, and accepting of the rightness of virtue.

Little Buddy Marshall, the best possible "riddle buddy" for Scooter and a constant companion in the pursuit of answers. Possessing many of Scooter's boyish traits, he is also a foil for Scooter's main distinguishing characteristics. Not a scholar, he does not have Scooter's knowledge of history and geography, but he has experiential knowledge of violence and death, which he is prepared to find anywhere. He is more likely than Scooter to pick up and go. He carries his father's .38 whenever he thinks he might need it.

Luzana Cholly (**Louisiana Charlie**), a fearless blues hero who plays the twelve-string guitar as well as anyone has ever played it. Exceptionally capable in everything that he is known to do, from the ordinary to the outrageous, he is Scooter's, and the townspeople's, major model of male ability and achievement. In the tradition of the wise fool, he is more than an entertainer, more than a gambler and a rambler—he is a local legend, larger than life, and a carrier and expresser of historic black experience and culture. He represents survival and, beyond that, style and grace in the transformation of raw life into the beauty that is necessary for the good life.

Miss Tee (**Edie Bell Boykin**), Scooter's favorite aunt, who showers her love upon him and strongly reinforces his tendency to be studious and to think of himself as capable of higher education and achievement. She dreamed of being a teacher and still loves and encourages many children, but Scooter receives her special favors. Eventually, he learns that she is his mother; she found it necessary to give him up for adoption.

Deljean McCray, Scooter's first, continuing, and last lover during his youth. She is the only one with whom he maintains a bond of deep affection, even beyond his youth. She gives him an honest appraisal of his personality.

— *Tom Koontz*

THE TRAITOR

Author: James Shirley (1596-1666)
First published: 1635
Genre: Drama

Locale: Florence, Italy
Time: c. 1480
Plot: Tragedy

Lorenzo (loh-REHN-zoh), the kinsman of Duke Alexander of Florence. Eager to unseat Alexander and succeed him, Lorenzo uses the ruler's lustful attraction for Amidea to lure her brothers into a plot against the duke. Foiled at first, he tries again and kills Alexander when the duke comes to visit Amidea, who is already dead. He himself is killed by Amidea's angered brother.

Alexander, the young duke of Florence. Forgetting safety of person and security of position, the young duke is absorbed by his pursuit of Amidea. When he realizes that she died rather than submit to him, he welcomes death.

Amidea (ah-MEE-deh-ah), a chaste young woman who is betrothed to Pisano and is the innocent and unwilling object of Alexander's lust. She shames the duke into repenting at first, then dies at the hands of Sciarrha rather than be shamed.

Sciarrha (skee-AHR-rah) and
Florio (FLOH-ree-oh), her brothers and avengers. Allied

with Lorenzo, Sciarrha murders Pisano and kills his own sister rather than let her be shamed. After Duke Alexander's murder, Sciarrha kills Lorenzo but is himself mortally wounded.

Pisano (pee-ZAH-noh), a young man who is betrothed to Amidea. Influenced by Petruchio and Lorenzo, Pisano breaks his marriage contract with Amidea to marry Oriana and is murdered by Sciarrha.

Cosmo, his friend. To please Pisano, Cosmo breaks his engagement to Oriana. After the bloodbath, Cosmo assumes the rule of Florence.

Oriana (oh-ree-AH-nah), who is loved by Pisano. She was formerly betrothed to Cosmo.

Morosa (moh-ROH-sah), Oriana's mother.

Petruchio (peh-TREW-kee-oh), Pisano's servant, hired by Lorenzo to help kill Duke Alexander.

Depazzi (deh-PAHZ-zee), one of Lorenzo's conspirators.

THE TRANSFIGURATION OF BENNO BLIMPIE

Author: Albert Innaurato (1948-   )
First published: 1976
Genre: Drama

Locale: The Italian section of Philadelphia, Pennsylvania
Time: The 1970's
Plot: Expressionism

Benno Blimpie, an enormously obese, physically repulsive man of about twenty-five. Although he is relatively short, he weighs more than five hundred pounds and has a splotchy, sickly complexion and greasy, unkempt hair. His shapeless clothes, too large even for him, are wet with his sweat and filthy from his slovenly habits. Although Benno undergoes no physical transformation, he is depicted at the various stages of his unhappy life in a series of scenes in which his age is indicated by gestures and changes in his voice. He otherwise remains inactive, a large, inert blob. These scenes, like flashbacks in fiction, lead to Benno's transfiguration, or his decision to eat himself to death. Once that decision is made, Benno refers to his previous self in the third person. This former Benno, further revealed through recollections and dreams, is full of longing and desperate for love, but he inspires none, not even in his own family. He is always both frustrated and brutalized by experience. In one episode, he is nearly beaten to death after being sexually abused by three teenage bullies. In another, as a prelude to biting himself on the arm, he imagines himself being cooked in an oven like a roast. Although for a time he is able to find solace in art of the Italian masters and his own drawings, and, presumably, some emotional satisfaction in his perpetual eating, he finally resigns himself to his fate. The transfigured Benno will feed upon himself and, nearing death, eat large quantities of poison so that the rats feeding on his body will die and he, in death, will have achieved some purpose.

Girl, a streetwise tease of twelve or thirteen. Her notable characteristic, suggesting her sensuality, is her red hair. She is full of erotic fantasies and uses her sexual attraction to torment Benno's grandfather, who pursues her shamelessly. Although she finds him offensive, she is willing to let him fondle her as long as he gives her his social security checks. She eventually

tires of the lurid games with the old man and stabs him to death with a broken bottle when he tries to overpower her.

Mary, Benno's haggard, middle-aged mother. She is a very coarse, ill-tempered woman who deeply resents the loss of her youth and good looks. Much of her resentment is taken out on her husband and Benno, both of whom she grows to despise. She is loveless and cruel, and her frequent tirades include extremely bitter and vicious remarks that help crush Benno's spirit.

Dominick, Benno's middle-aged father. Like his wife, he is coarse, vulgar, and able to hold his own in the furious family rows. He is a compulsive gambler who is accused by his wife of being a dismal failure both as a husband and as a father. Although greatly disappointed in Benno, he does not revile him as Benno's mother does and is more patient with him. He believes his son is a "pansy" who can never measure up to the father's conception of what it means to be a real man. Although he is less vituperative than Mary, he wounds Benno just as much as she does.

Old man, Benno's grandfather, called **Pop-Pop** by Benno. He is a lecher, more than seventy years old, with pedophilic preferences. He ardently pursues the girl, who encourages him, even though she finds him physically disgusting. He often has Benno in his care and seems to be Benno's best hope for familial affection. He, at least, is not cruel to Benno and has some protective concern for his welfare. In one of Benno's fantasies, the old man is transformed into an angelic-appearing butcher who covers Benno with a sheet and marks it like a chart used to designate cuts of meat. The old man's murder is profoundly disturbing for Benno and contributes to his alienation and withdrawal.

— John W. Fiero

TRANSLATIONS

Author: Brian Friel (1929-   )
First published: 1981
Genre: Drama

Locale: Baile Beag, in County Donegal, Ireland
Time: 1833
Plot: Social realism

Hugh Mor O'Donnell, the master of an Irish hedge school, in his early sixties, who persists in educating his charges (most of whom are adults) in the classical languages, despite his growing recognition that English is the language of the future. Fond of his pint, he has usually taken a drop too much, but he is never really drunk. Irascible and arrogant, he, more than anyone else in the play, understands that the translation of Irish place-names into English involves a transition from one world to another. Furthermore, despite his personal regret at the cultural violence done by such translation, he recognizes the inevitability of the transition if Ireland is to avoid being "imprisoned in a linguistic contour which no longer matches the landscape of . . . fact." A poet writing in a language few can

read, he understands the extent to which language shapes humankind's understanding of the world and sees clearly the forces sweeping his country from "spiritual" Irish to "commercial" English.

Manus, Hugh's eldest son, in his late twenties or early thirties. He assists Hugh in the hedge school, makes his dinner, and sees him safely through the hours of drink. For all of this, his father pays him no salary and treats him like a footman. Manus loves Maire and would like to marry her, but he has no way to support her and will not go against his father for the job at the new national school the British are building. He is lame because his father, drunk, fell on him while he was a baby. Manus somehow turns the incident into a reason for being responsible for his father. He is a gentle, caring man, hurt by what is happening to Ireland and hurt by Maire's defection but without the capacity to resist either effectively.

Owen, Hugh's youngest son, in his late twenties, who had "escaped" to England and returns now in service to the British, who need him to help remap Ireland because they do not speak Irish. The British never get his name right and call him Roland. Initially pleased to have avoided his brother's fate and to be earning a good salary, he is finally appalled by the consequences of the process of which he has been a part.

Lieutenant George Yolland, in his twenties, the officer in charge of translating Irish place-names into English. He speaks only English and relies heavily on Owen. In love with Ireland and with Maire, he longs to learn the language that will open communication with both. His courtship of Maire takes place across the language barrier and illustrates the power of love and nonverbal communication.

Maire, a lively, strong woman in her twenties, with little sympathy for Manus' reluctance to take steps to escape the dual traps of exploitation by his father and a failing Irish economy. She wants to learn English, a practical language that she knows will serve her well when she immigrates to America. When she falls in love with Yolland, she discovers that feelings are not hindered by language barriers.

Jimmy Jack, called the **"Infant Prodigy"** even though he is in his sixties, a dirty, poor student in Hugh's school who does not always distinguish clearly between the mythology he studies in Greek and the "real" world around him. He is at times faintly ridiculous, but his fluency in Greek and Latin indirectly comments on the superiority assumed by the British, who speak only English.

Sarah, in her twenties, a student in Hugh's class whose speech defect is so severe that she has always been assumed to be mute. Manus, whom she loves, is teaching her to speak.

Captain Lancey, Lieutenant Yolland's superior officer. He is a stereotypical representation of rigid, self-righteous British imperialism, convinced of his own superiority, with no sympathy or understanding of the country or the people whose land he is dominating and changing.

— *Helen Lojek*

THE TRANSPOSED HEADS: A Legend of India
(Die vertauschten Köpfe: Eine indische Legende)

Author: Thomas Mann (1875-1955)
First published: 1940
Genre: Novella

Locale: Kurukshetra, India, and environs
Time: The eleventh century
Plot: Fable

Shridaman, a merchant who is well versed in classical learning, twenty-one years old and of delicate build. His father, also a merchant in the village of Welfare of Cows in the land of Kosala, was of Brahman stock and very familiar with Vedic texts. Shridaman has all the attributes of a man of the mind. It is for this reason that he is attracted to his mental and physical opposite, Nanda. They are friends and inseparable. It is through Nanda that Shridaman is introduced to the pleasures of the flesh and the senses. It is also through him that he comes to know the identity of his future wife. By accident, he and Nanda witness Sita's ritual ablutions near the temple of Kali. Shridaman falls in love with her. Because Nanda and Sita knew each other as children, Nanda is able to bring Sita and his friend together. It is Shridaman's admiration for his friend's physical strength and uncomplicated mind, as well as his love for Sita, that finally leads him to acknowledge Sita's longing for Nanda by sacrificing himself in the temple of Kali, "the great mother." With the same loyalty and devotion, he accepts his new existence as an amalgam of his former self and that of his friend. His honesty, fair-mindedness, and love for Sita ultimately lead him to agree to a murder-suicide pact that results in a triple funeral pyre. Through this, the conflict between the friend and the couple may be resolved and their child's future happiness ensured.

Nanda, a shepherd and blacksmith who is eighteen years old. He is dark-skinned, with a big, flat nose and a strong, muscular body. His father is also a smith. Nanda has a "lucky calf lock" on his chest. Nanda is devoted to his friend Shridaman, whom he admires for his learning and slender, "elegant" physique. Nanda, although loyal to Shridaman and intent on avoiding any hint of an interest in Sita, Shridaman's wife, is nevertheless secretly desirous of her, just as Sita is of him. After his unquestioning immolation before the corpse of his friend in Kali's temple and his cheerful acceptance of a new physical identity, he also accepts willingly the hermit's verdict as to whether he has a right to Sita's affections. Because the judgment goes against him, he decides to live in self-imposed exile and seclusion. He accepts willingly Shridaman's decision that each end the life of the other by mortally wounding his heart, and he agrees to Sita's decision to die on the funeral pyre so that their unhappy union may have a happy resolution and Samadhi a happy future.

Sita, a young maiden who becomes Shridaman's wife. Her appellation is "Sita of the beautiful hips." She possesses innocence, piety, and devotion to her parents, and she obeys unquestioningly when her parents and Shridaman's agree that she should marry Shridaman. It is her husband who introduces her to the pleasures of the senses, although, over time, it is clear to her that he is more a man of the mind than of the flesh. She, therefore, develops a secret longing for Nanda's arms and body, which seem perfect to her, and she wishes for a combination of her husband's mind and his friend's body. She inadvertently reveals to Shridaman this secret longing. It is her sense of guilt that leads her to implore Kali, the goddess, to restore the friends to their former life, and it is her secret desire for a perfect husband that leads her to transpose their heads. She enjoys a night with Nanda's "husband-body" during Shridaman's absence, but, in the end, she decides to join in the friends' suicide pact by her self-immolation on a funeral pyre at the feast of burning. She does so because she rejects polyandry and out of concern for the future of her child, whom she wants to grow up not as the child of an abandoned mother but as an orphan and the son of a legendary mother, whose self-sacrifice assures her legend and commemoration through a monument.

Kali, the Hindu goddess of motherhood, destruction, sacrifice, and bloodshed. These contradictory attributes match those of her victims and followers, Shridaman, Nanda, and Sita. As a disembodied voice, she enters into a dialogue with Sita. In forceful terms, she expresses her displeasure with the disingenuous sacrifices of Nanda and Shridaman. She is willing to accede to Sita's fervent desire to see the two restored to their former existence with Sita's help.

Kamananda, a pious hermit. He agrees to settle the dispute between Shridaman, Nanda, and Sita. He has no difficulty in deciding that it is the head that is the decisive criterion in determining whether Shridaman with Nanda's body or Nanda with Shridaman's body is now the husband of Sita.

Samadhi, called **Andhaka** (the blind one), the lightskinned and nearsighted son of Shridaman and Sita. As the child of a famous mother, he is reared by "a wise and learned Brahman." His progress is reported at the ages of four, seven, twelve, and twenty. At the age of twenty, he has become reader to the king of Benares.

— Arthur Tilo Alt

TRAVELLING NORTH

Author: David Williamson (1942-   )
First published: 1980
Genre: Drama

Locale: Australia
Time: 1969-1972
Plot: Social realism

Frank, a retired construction engineer and widower, more than seventy years old, from Melbourne, Australia. He has taken his lover, Frances, north to live in a small cottage in a remote tropical area in Queensland, where he intends to escape people and examine the meaning of his life. A disenchanted former Communist and an atheist, he is an assertively self-assured man governed by his own rationality. He sees the world in terms of measurable quantities capable of explanation or analysis. Direct and opinionated, he does not relate to people easily. Estranged from his artist son, Frank still remains on good terms with his daughter, Joan. Untroubled by guilt, he dismisses the guilt held by Frances regarding her disapproving daughters, whom he sees as exploitative. His tall and athletic physique exudes an energetic vitality, which increasingly diminishes as the infirmity of a discovered heart ailment strikes. His illness causes a progressive withdrawal into himself that makes him difficult to live with, but eventually his condition makes him realize his dependence on other human beings. Frank is the initial motivator of the action as the coldly rational and dominant half of a complex love affair with a loving woman whose qualities and temperament contrast sharply with his own. When Frances leaves him temporarily, he arrives at the self-discovery that although he has "always loved mankind in general," he has been ungenerous to some of those he has been "involved with in particular." Effecting a reconciliation with Frances, who has now become the controller of the action, Frank puts aside his anticonventional prejudices for marriage. Frank, as a result of his life with Frances, has a monumental revelation about himself.

Frances, a slim and attractive woman of about fifty-five whose home has been in Melbourne. She is the divorced mother of two married daughters. With her lover, Frank, she has traveled north to distant Queensland. She is distressed that her daughters, Sophie and Helen, question her relationship with an older man who is taking her to northern isolation. Recalling her disinterested mothering of them as children, she feels guilty about their apparent domestic unhappiness. Her loyalty to Frank is in part an effort to compensate for her past irresponsibility. Gentle and reticent as well as restless by nature, Frances is a sensitive, emotional person who holds an undefined openness to life and people. For her, questions exist to be answered. Her temperament complements and contrasts with that of Frank, for she represents the warm and initially passive half of a complicated relationship whose difficult odyssey forces her to become a more complete woman. Restless in the north and dismayed by Frank's irascible self-absorption, exacerbated by his discovered infirmity, Frances returns south to her daughters only to realize that they, and all people, are responsible for their own lives. She reunites with Frank, who also has reached important self-realizations and pleases her with his decision to marry her. Reaching a final fulfillment with Frank shortly before his death, Frances gains a more defined and guilt-free concept of herself.

Helen, Frances' youngest daughter, an attractive housewife in her late twenties. She and her children have been deserted by her husband. Direct and somewhat neurotic, she has not forgiven her mother for placing her with a relative when a child and considers Frances' departure for Melbourne yet another betrayal. Helen strongly disapproves of her mother's affair with Frank and warns her of becoming an older man's nursemaid. Stimulating Frances' guilt feelings, she functions with her sister as a secondary antagonist to the two major characters.

Sophie, Frances' thirty-year-old daughter, who is a pretty suburban wife with impractical and self-absorbing career expectations that create domestic unhappiness. Gentler and better adjusted than Helen, she is more sympathetic toward her mother's relationship with Frank.

Saul Morgenstein, a disenchanted but wry Queensland physician who correctly diagnoses Frank's illness. His medical advice is vindicated after Frank's stubborn insistence on treating himself runs its course. Affectionate toward Frances and tolerant of Frank, Saul becomes a close family friend.

Freddy Wicks, a jovial widower and neighbor to Frank and Frances in the north. A World War II veteran and a nationalist who supports Australian participation in Vietnam, he proves to be a good neighbor despite Frank's trenchant opposition to his views. His acceptance by Frank, with that of Saul, indicates Frank's realization of his need for other people.

Joan, Frank's daughter. She is an intelligent woman in her early thirties whose liberal ideas support those of her father. She openly accepts Frank's liaison with Frances.

— Christian H. Moe

THE TRAVELS OF LAO TS'AN
(Lao Ts'an youji)

Author: Liu E (Liu Tieyun, 1857-1909)
First published: 1904-1907
Genre: Novel

Locale: The countryside of southern China
Time: The 1880's and 1890's
Plot: Allegory

T'ieh Pu-ts'an, known as **Lao Ts'an** (low sahn), a man who wanders through the North China province of Shantung as an itinerant physician. The nickname Lao Ts'an means "Old Vagabond" and fits his unconventional style of life. In his travels, he savors the special character of each place while encountering old friends and making new ones. He is regularly drawn into some human problem and finds wise, just solutions. Lao Ts'an, a vigorous, healthy man of about fifty, has no home but resides in plain inns; he is a person of modest means but disdains money. He has few possessions beyond simple cotton clothes, a few books, his medicine chest, and a string of bells used by Chinese itinerant healers to attract patients. Lao Ts'an's humble existence hides administrative insight, considerable learning, a cultivated aesthetic sense, and a noble character. In addition to curing his patients, he helps control Yellow River flooding, exposes a ruthless official, shows a new magistrate how to suppress banditry, and prevents a miscarriage of justice. His sagacity leads others to treat him with the highest respect. Once his solutions are set in motion, Lao Ts'an leaves before he is fully thanked, to continue his wandering care for humanity.

Kao Shao-yen, a secretary to the governor of Shantung, who seeks Lao Ts'an's treatment for his sick concubine. Through him, Lao Ts'an is brought to the attention of the governor.

Governor Chuang, the highest official in Shantung, who shows great favor to the apparently common medical practitioner Lao Ts'an by seeking advice and accepting his recommendations. This character is modeled on Chang Yao, a governor of Shantung in the 1880's and a mentor to the author.

Yü Tso-ch'en, also known as **Yü Hsien** (yew syehn), a notorious Manchu official from history who appears under his own name. In the novel, Yü Hsien is pilloried for the harsh justice he meted out as a prefect in Shantung. On his own initiative, Lao Ts'an travels to Yü Hsien's prefecture, where he confirms the reports of Yü Hsien's cruelty and enlightens the governor about Yü Hsien's deficiencies. In real life, Yü Hsien

(who died in 1901) was executed for promoting antiforeign attacks during the Boxer uprising of 1900. The author and the historical Yü Hsien were enemies.

Shen Tung-tsao, a cautious newly appointed magistrate whom Lao Ts'an encounters. Lao Ts'an advises him on how to suppress banditry without resorting to the cruel and unwise policies of Yü Hsien.

Shen Tzu-p'ing, a nephew of Magistrate Shen Tung-tsao who is sent into the mountains to locate a man whom Lao Ts'an has recommended to his uncle. During this search, the young man encounters a beautiful maiden and a middle-aged recluse who calls himself "Yellow Dragon." In a long fantasy sequence, these two figures introduce the philosophical ideas of the T'ai-chou school, a nineteenth century Chinese syncretic philosophy (combining Buddhism, Taoism, and Confucianism) favored by the author.

Huang Ying-t'u, also called **Huang Jen-jui**, an educated man from a family of high officials who had come to Shantung to offer advice on river control. Huang Jen-jui is about thirty years old and is pleasant but dissolute. Lao Ts'an encounters Huang Jen-jui while traveling and, through him, meets the courtesan Ts'ui-huan and learns of a tangled and unsolved multiple murder case.

Ts'ui-huan, a young courtesan whose name means "Green Bracelet." With a companion, she is invited to entertain Huang Jen-jui and Lao Ts'an. Ts'ui-huan relates how she fell into prostitution. Moved by her story, Lao Ts'an devises a means to free her from bondage. She later becomes his concubine.

Kang Pi, a narrow, arrogant judicial official, brought into a multiple murder case. His inhuman use of torture produces a miscarriage of justice. Lao Ts'an, however, intervenes and saves the wrongly convicted widow and exposes the real murderer, a callow nephew. Kang Pi represents another Manchu official, Kang I, who, like Yü Hsien, was a real enemy of the author.

— *David D. Buck*

TRAVESTIES

Author: Tom Stoppard (Tomas Straussler, 1937-   )
First published: 1975
Genre: Drama

Locale: Zurich, Switzerland
Time: 1917-1918 and the 1970's
Plot: Play of ideas

Henry Carr, an elegantly attired character who appears both as a very old man and as his youthful self. The character is modeled on a minor official by the same name who was in the English consulate in Switzerland during the turbulent years of World War I. The events of the play mirror history. As young Carr, this character is involved in a quarrel with James Joyce over money for clothes in a production of Oscar Wilde's *The Importance of Being Earnest*, in which Joyce is closely

involved. As an old man, Carr narrates the events of the time, and it is his erratic recall of events through which the playwright filters the events of the play, including a fictional meeting in the Zurich library among Tristan Tzara, James Joyce, and Vladimir Ilich Lenin.

James Joyce, an inelegant dresser, thirty-six years old, who mixes jackets and trousers from two different suits. At work in the Zurich library on his famous novel *Ulysses*, he comes in conflict with Tzara and Lenin on the nature of art. As the play's *raisonneur*, he argues that art is its own excuse for being and that whatever meaning is to be found in history is what art makes of it. He uses Homer's poems about the Trojan War to illustrate his theory that art re-creates the shards of history into a "corpse that will dance for some time yet and leave the world precisely as it finds it."

Tristan Tzara, a Romanian Dadaist artist. He is short, dark-haired, charming, and boyish, and he wears a monocle. He argues his theories of history and art as pure chance. In demonstration, he tears up a sonnet by William Shakespeare, letting the words fall where they will, in the process arranging themselves into a new poem. Tzara is in love with Gwendolen, and, despite a mix-up of names and identities that parallels the plot of *The Importance of Being Earnest*, he does end up with her. His role unites the two major plot components: the debates on art and the romantic intrigues.

Vladimir Ilich Lenin, a forty-seven-year-old revolutionary. Writing in the Zurich library, he sees art as a means to change the world for the good of the masses. In contrast with

the brilliantly parodic language of Tzara and Joyce, that of Lenin is pedestrian and pedantic.

Gwendolen, the attractive younger sister of Carr. She is secretary to Joyce but in love with Tzara. With Cecily, she forms the double romantic interest in the plot. Their mix-up of briefcases causes Joyce's latest chapter of *Ulysses* to fall into the hands of Tzara and Lenin's political treatise to come into Joyce's possession, thus creating occasions for romantic complications, as well as for Tzara to criticize Joyce and for Carr to impress Cecily with his pretended admiration of Lenin's views.

Cecily, a young, attractive librarian who appears also as her eighty-year-old self. She is deeply devoted to Lenin's philosophy and is in love with Carr. With Gwendolen, she falls farcically into and out of the mistaken-identity confusion, eventually ending up with her Algernon, Henry Carr.

Nadya (Nadezhda) Krupskaya, the forty-eight-year-old wife of Lenin, a minor character in the play who converses with Lenin about their impending journey to Russia.

— *Susan Rusinko*

TREASURE ISLAND

Author: Robert Louis Stevenson (1850-1894)
First published: 1883; serial form, 1881-1882
Genre: Novel

Locale: England and the Spanish Main
Time: The 1740's
Plot: Adventure

Jim Hawkins, the principal narrator, a bright, courageous boy. His father owns the Admiral Benbow Inn, where Billy Bones hides. In Bones's sea chest, Jim finds a map of Captain Flint's buried treasure.

Dr. Livesey, who treats Jim's dying father and later the wounded mutineers on Treasure Island.

Squire Trelawney, who finances the treasure hunt and outsmarts the pirates.

Captain Smollett, the captain of the expedition's ship, the *Hispaniola*.

Captain Bill Bones, who steals the map and sings, "Fifteen men on a dead man's chest." He dies of fright when the pirates bring him his death warning.

Black Dog, who discovers Bones's hiding place and is almost killed in a fight in the inn parlor.

Blind Pew, a deformed pirate who delivers the Black Spot death notice. He is trampled to death by the mounted revenue officers who attack the pirate gang searching for Bill Bones's sea chest.

Long John Silver, a one-legged ship's cook who owns a pet parrot called Captain Flint. He gathers a crew for the *Hispaniola*, from pirates whom he can control. Once, he saves Jim from their fury. He manages to get back to the West Indies with a bag of coins.

Ben Gunn, a pirate marooned by Captain Flint on Treasure Island. He moves the treasure and thus can keep it from the pirates and turn it over to Squire Trelawney.

Israel Hands, a pirate shot by Jim after he tries to kill Jim with a knife.

THE TREE CLIMBER
(Ya tali' al-shajarah)

Author: Tawfiq al-Hakim (1898-1987)
First published: 1962
Genre: Drama

Locale: Zeitoun, a suburb on the outskirts of Cairo, Egypt
Time: The 1960's
Plot: Absurdist

The husband, Bahadir Effendi, a retired train conductor ("ticket inspector"), sixty-five years of age, who has been married for nine years to Madame Behana. During that time and especially since his retirement on a modest pension five years ago, he has devoted exclusive attention to an orange tree in the garden of their home. Underneath his precious orange tree resides a lizard called Lady Green, whom only he can see and for whom he professes love. Bahadir and his wife appear

to have no relatives or social acquaintances. He seems content to care for his tree, never disagrees with his wife, and says he has lost the habit of being worried and perturbed. His philosophizing, hypothesizing, and inattention to his wife (he admits to the detective that he has thought about killing her) lead to his arrest at the end of act 1 for the murder of his wife, who has disappeared. After Behana returns home, a philosophical motive leads him at the end of act 2 to kill her for real. He feels no guilt thereafter and decides to risk ultimate arrest and possible execution for the sake of his tree, which can be much nourished by burying her corpse under it.

The wife, Madame Behana (or **Bihana**), Bahadir's wife, a woman sixty years of age. She has white hair and always wears a green dress. Bahadir is her second husband. Behana thinks and talks constantly of Bahiyya, the daughter she can never have. As a young woman of nineteen, she acceded to her first husband's request that she have an abortion. She had named the anticipated girl Bahiyya early in that pregnancy. Later, when their circumstances improved and they wanted children, Behana discovered that she could not get pregnant again. At the death of her first husband, who was a real estate broker, she inherited the house in the Zeitoun suburb of Cairo where she and Bahadir live. When talking with Bahadir, she speaks only of Bahiyya, and he only of his orange tree. Behana has been gone for three days when the play begins and returns shortly after the beginning of act 2. As oblivious to Bahadir's needs and character as he is to hers, she refuses to respond to his insistent queries about where she was during her absence from home. Bahadir grabs her by the throat to force words out of her, and she dies. Before Bahadir can bury her under his orange tree, however, her corpse disappears.

The maid, a day servant for nine years to Madame Behana and Bahadir Effendi. She returns to her own home each evening to care for her old and blind husband. The play opens with her conversation with the detective, who is investigating Madame Behana's disappearance. The maid recalls for the detective a conversation between Bahadir and Behana, which, when acted out for the detective, gives a sense of the curious relationship of mutual inattention and self-centered misunderstanding between the married couple. In act 2, the maid answers a knock on the door and is startled to see her mistress, Madame Behana, back home after everyone, including the maid, had assumed that Bahadir had killed her.

The detective, a plodding police investigator who reaches conclusions on the basis of suspicions and circumstantial evidence. After conversations with the maid and with Bahadir Effendi early in act 1, he concludes that Bahadir must have found his missing wife unbearable and, consequently, killed her. Led further by Bahadir's hypothesizing, a mode of thinking with which he cannot deal, he assumes that Bahadir has buried his wife's corpse beneath the orange tree in their garden. When Bahadir subsequently does kill his wife and calls the detective to inform him of the crime, the latter again misconstrues the ambiguous statements he hears and advises Bahadir to continue with his gardening and to expect his wife to return sooner or later.

The conductor's assistant, a lazy young man from Bahadir's past who used to sleep on the job at every opportunity. He appears in a scene recalled by Bahadir when describing his railway conductor's career for the detective. The assistant tells Bahadir of the latter's own sleeping or fixed gazing on the job. Bahadir used to stare out of the train window and count the trees rushing past, saying that he wanted this tree and that.

Children's voices, a hundred schoolchildren on the train described by Bahadir to the detective. They sing: "Oh tree climber, bring me a cow with you./ Milk it and feed me with a silver spoon." Bahadir also sings, but changes the second line to "Bring me a tree with you."

The dervish, a wise and prescient man on the train whom the conductor's assistant reports to Bahadir as not having a ticket. When Bahadir accosts him, he presents his birth certificate as his "ticket for the journey." When threatened with arrest, he produces ten valid tickets out of the air. Then, when Bahadir conjures him up in the present while talking with the detective, the dervish states that Behana's fate is to suffer death one day at the hands of her husband for a philosophical reason. The dervish later appears just as Bahadir is about to bury his wife's body beneath the orange tree. He will not turn in Bahadir, however, because he can act, he says, only when Bahadir wants him to.

Lady Green, a beautiful green lizard (unseen by the audience) that Bahadir says he has known for nine years, ever since he set foot in his wife's house and garden. According to Bahadir, she disappeared when his wife did and reappears when his wife does. After killing his wife, Bahadir discovers Lady Green dead, in a hole under the orange tree.

— *Michael Craig Hillmann*

A TREE GROWS IN BROOKLYN

Author: Betty Smith (1896-1972)
First published: 1943
Genre: Novel

Locale: Brooklyn, New York
Time: Early twentieth century
Plot: Bildungsroman

Francie Nolan, a sensitive and intelligent Brooklyn girl, growing up in grinding poverty. Because of her high values and her strength of spirit, she is able to make the most of her environment. She acquires self-reliance and is never crippled by a sense of defeat and deprivation. As the novel ends, she is making preparations to go to college.

Neeley Nolan, Francie's younger brother, a sympathetic but less intelligent and less interesting figure. His importance in the story is secondary to hers.

Johnnie Nolan, their father, a Saturday-night singing waiter. He is charming, sensitive to his children's needs, and an affectionate father but also is an alcoholic and a bad provider. He dies of pneumonia just after Francie's fourteenth birthday.

Katie Rommely Nolan, Johnnie's wife. Married early, she knew by the time Neeley was born that she could not count on Johnnie for support. She works as a janitor in their tenement. As the novel ends, her life is to be easier: She is married again, this time to a retired policeman.

Mr. McGarrity, at whose saloon Johnnie did most of his drinking. After Johnnie's death, he helps out by giving the children part-time jobs.

Ben Blake, Francie's fellow student, with whose help she prepares for her college examinations.

Lee Rhynor, a soldier who is Francie's first real date. Believing his offer of marriage sincere, she promises to write every day. Although she is not seriously in love, she does feel wounded on receiving a letter from the girl he married during his trip home.

Officer McShane, a retired policeman who has long been fond of Katie. He at last persuades her to marry him, with the full agreement of the children.

Laurie Nolan, Katie's youngest child, born a few months after Johnnie's death.

THE TREE OF KNOWLEDGE
(El árbol de la ciencia)

Author: Pío Baroja (1872-1956)
First published: 1911
Genre: Novel

Locale: Madrid and several provinces of Spain
Time: The final decades of the nineteenth century
Plot: Impressionistic realism

Andrés Hurtado (ahn-DREHS ewr-TAH-doh), a medical doctor. A permanent feeling of loneliness that became more acute after his mother's death has made Andrés withdrawn, melancholy, and sad in appearance. He defines himself as a partisan of the Republican Party and as an upholder of the cause of the poor, but his true commitment is to literature and things intellectual. His main concern is to find a rational explanation for the formation of the world and, at the same time, for life and humankind. At the beginning of the novel, Andrés is attending his first medical classes at the Institute of San Isidro in Madrid. Despite the fact that Andrés does not show a profound calling for medicine, he continues his studies, completing his internship in the hospitals of Madrid, where he witnesses all forms of abuse and misery. Finally, he is graduated. After two disappointing and weakening experiences, one as a rural doctor and the other in a public hospital in Madrid, he weds an old friend, Lulú, and begins a new job as translator of technical papers for a journal. Later, other personal experiences lead him to the extreme decision to commit suicide.

Lulú (lew-LEW), Andrés Hurtado's wife. Lulú is unattractive and has a caustic disposition, but she is intelligent, noble, and progressive in her thinking. Julio Aracil, Andrés' friend, introduces him to Lulú. From the very first moment, she falls in love with Andrés, but they do not talk about marriage until several years have passed. They are finally married and, after a period of peace and contentment, she becomes pregnant, changing both her mood and the family stability. Her child is stillborn, and, three days after delivering it, she dies of internal injuries.

Dr. Iturrioz (ee-tew-rree-OHS), Andrés' uncle and mentor. Iturrioz is a medical doctor with a pragmatic attitude toward life. Several times, Iturrioz helps Andrés to succeed, approving his exams and obtaining professional positions. He is one of the few people to whom Andrés can talk about various far-reaching topics, in particular, his personal observations on people and everyday life. They discuss not only the meaning of life but also Andrés' personal preoccupations concerning his future.

Montaner (mohn-tahn-EHR), one of Andrés' classmates. Montaner is lazy and quiet. He belongs to the monarchist party, and he supports the aristocratic and wealthy classes. At the beginning, he is out of step with Andrés, but, after concluding their first courses together, they become friends.

Julio Aracil (HEW-lee-oh ahr-ah-SEEL), one of Andrés' old friends and now his classmate at the university. Aracil is opinionated, selfish, and incapable of doing anything for others. Because his family has no means to support him, he has to support himself by gambling. His interest in pleasure and luxuries, even false and cheap ones, results in a constant need for money. Aracil seems finally to succeed in life because he is able to do whatever is necessary to obtain what he wants.

— *Daniel Altamiranda*

THE TREE OF MAN

Author: Patrick White (1912-1990)
First published: 1955
Genre: Novel

Locale: Australia
Time: The twentieth century
Plot: Parable

Stan Parker, an ordinary, hardworking, twentieth century Australian farmer. He is the son of a blacksmith and an educated mother. After his parents' deaths, Stan leaves the bush town where he grew up and moves to a piece of property he had inherited in an unsettled area near Sydney. He carves out a home and the beginning of a farm in the wilderness, then marries Amy, whom he meets at a dance in a nearby town. They settle into a humdrum life centered on domestic chores and rearing children. They live uneventfully for the next fifty or so years. Although Stan's relationship with his wife is a close one, it is never demonstrative or charged with passion. Service in France during World War I marks the only time Stan leaves the farm for an extended period. This experience has little effect on his outward life, which continues in its set pattern. What makes Stan an intriguing character is his inner life, at which the narrative only hints. The author reveals early on that Stan is no interpreter of his feelings and aspirations. Later, the reader learns that Stan harbors a desire that had never been fulfilled, to express himself in substance and words. This would-be visionary and interpreter lives to be an old man. Shortly before he dies, he manages to say "I believe," because it had at last become clear to him "that One, and no other figure, is the answer to all sums."

Amy Fibbens Parker, a simple, industrious woman who on the surface appears to be an ideal wife and loving mother. Until she marries Stan, Amy lives on the fringes of conventional, small-town Australian society, with an aunt and uncle who have too many children and lack ambition. Once settled with Stan, she learns to love and respect her silent and thoroughly good husband. She takes pride in her household chores and in the role of wife and mother, even though her son eventually disappoints her because she cannot possess him. The desire to possess emerges as Amy's flaw. She reveals a mean streak when her will is thwarted in family relationships, even with her calm, patient husband. Convinced that there is more to life than what she has discovered, she explores the possibilities of passion in a brief affair with a traveling salesman, but that fails. Present at her husband's death and still alive at the end of the novel, Amy is last seen whimpering a little for remnants of love and habit.

Thelma Parker, Stan and Amy's daughter. Cold and calculating as a child, Thelma dreams of leaving the farm and fulfilling her desire to be cultured and sophisticated. Her parents provide her with the means to reach this goal by sending her to business college in Sydney. Eventually hired as a secretary in a law office, Thelma sees her efficiency and ambition work in her favor when one of the lawyers—equally sterile and cold—marries her and provides her with financial security and social prestige. Thelma emerges at times as a caricature of a pretentious woman determined to be cultured and tasteful, but she remains faithful to her parents and their needs as they grow older. By no means a bad woman, Thelma—though hardly aware of it—seeks inward meaning in spite of her outward success.

Ray Parker, Stan and Amy's wayward son. Adored by Amy and ignored by Stan, Ray early on shows a tendency toward violence and cruelty. Like the rest of the family, he longs for something beyond the ordinary and desires something indefinable. Stan apprentices him to a saddle maker in a nearby village, but Ray soon leaves to seek a fuller, richer life. Thereafter, he appears only occasionally, mainly to borrow money. Following years of wandering across Australia, at times serving prison sentences for various crimes, Ray turns up in Sydney and marries a simple but decent woman. Unable to settle, he deserts his wife for a prostitute and is eventually murdered. It is Ray's son who offers hope at the end of the novel by pledging to put into poetry the things his grandfather knew but was unable to express.

Mrs. O'Dowd, a neighbor. Of all the minor characters who pass through the lives of the Parkers, Mrs. O'Dowd emerges as the most colorful and memorable. The first settlers in the area after the Parkers, Mrs. O'Dowd and her drunken husband are in part comic and in part pathetic. She relishes carrying bad news to her neighbors, takes pleasure in pointing out others' shortcomings, and enjoys reporting other people's misfortunes. An ignorant and crude woman who tolerates her husband's drinking, even joining him at times, and who lives in a state of filth, Mrs. O'Dowd does not question life, does not look beyond its surface, and faces living and all the accompanying misery without complaint. In this way, she serves as an antithesis to her friend Amy.

— Robert L. Ross

THE TREE OF THE FOLKUNGS
(Folkungaträdet)

Author: Verner von Heidenstam (1859-1940)
First published: 1905-1907
Genre: Novel

Locale: Sweden
Time: The eleventh and thirteenth centuries
Plot: Historical

Folke Filbyter, a peasant freebooter, founder of the Folkung family and builder of the hall called Folketuna. He has three sons by the daughter of Dwarf Jorgrimme, a Finnish sorcerer.

Ingemund and

Hallsten, Folke's two sons who become sea-rovers and, later, members of King Inge's guard.

Ingevald, Folke's other son, who stays at home with his father.

Holmdis, Ingevald's wife, carried off by force from the house of her father, Ulf Ulfsson.

Folke Ingevaldsson, Ingevald's son and old Folke's heir. He becomes a Christian and an adherent to Blot Sven, the king of Sweden.

Old Jakob, a begging friar who brings Christianity. He becomes the foster father of Folke Ingevaldsson.

Earl Birger, a descendant of Folke Filbyter. He is the real ruler of Sweden, though his son wears the crown.

Valdemar, a weak king of Sweden, the son of Earl Birger.

He loves pleasure and women, and he is no warrior. After his father's death, he allows confusion to spread over Sweden. He is finally overthrown by his brother Magnus.

Sophia, Valdemar's queen, a jealous woman who has Yrsa-Lill thrown into a cage filled with snakes. Sophia is a princess of Denmark.

Lady Jutta, Sophia's sister. She has a son by Valdemar.

Yrsa-Lill, a goat-girl in whom Valdemar takes an active interest.

Junker Magnus, Valdemar's knightly brother. He becomes king and restores order to Sweden after defeating his brother.

Gistre Härjanson, a minstrel. He rescues Yrsa-Lill from a cage of snakes.

Sir Svantepolk, a Swedish knight. He becomes a henchman of Junker Magnus.

Archbishop Fulco, the prelate of Uppsala. He becomes foster father to the child of Valdemar and Lady Jutta.

Lady Luitgard, Valdemar's last friend and his mistress.

THE TREES

Author: Conrad Richter (1890-1968)
First published: 1940
Genre: Novel

Locale: Old Northwest Territory
Time: Late eighteenth and early nineteenth centuries
Plot: Regional

Worth Luckett, a pioneer woodsman who has real wanderlust and cannot stay in one place very long. He feeds his family by shooting game; when the game runs out, they must move on. He is a simple man and loyal to his wife and family, but he is somewhat irresponsible. He starts to build a cabin for his family to live in, but he is gone so much of the time that his wife has to prod him to finish the building before the winter snows come.

Jary Luckett, Worth's wife. She is rather sickly and has the slow fever. She does not like to move about so much but realizes that Worth can support his family only if he can kill game. She says nothing about the unfinished cabin until one day when the leaves fall from the trees and she sees the sky through the branches. She then decides that she must have a house in which to live. She finally dies of fever.

Sayward (Saird) Luckett, Worth and Jary's eldest child. She is a big, strapping girl who takes most of the responsibility for the care of the other children. She is very strong, both physically and mentally. She marries Portius Wheeler after

offering herself as his wife when another woman turns him down.

Wyitt Luckett, Worth and Jary's son, who grows up to be a "woodsy" exactly like his father.

Genny Luckett, Worth and Jary's daughter, who marries a no-good man named Louie Scurrah.

Louie Scurrah, a woodsman who immediately charms Genny and Achsa. Sayward does not like him from the first. When she finds him in the woods with Genny, she demands that he marry her. He does so but later runs away with Achsa.

Achsa Luckett, Worth and Jary's daughter, who is as brown and tough as an Indian.

Sulie Luckett, Worth and Jary's youngest child, who is lost in the woods and never returns.

Portius Wheeler, a lawyer who marries Sayward while he is drunk. She offers him the chance to leave her if he likes, but he chooses to stay. He treats Sayward well, and she is happy with him.

Jake Tench, the man who tries to find a bride for Portius. The woman he picks decides that the match is not for her.

TREMOR OF INTENT

Author: Anthony Burgess (John Anthony Burgess Wilson, 1917-1993)
First published: 1966
Genre: Novel

Locale: Bradcaster, London, aboard the *Polyolbion*, Yarylyuk, Istanbul, and Dublin
Time: The mid-1960's, with flashbacks
Plot: Spy

Denis Hillier, a British secret agent in his mid-forties. His final assignment before retirement is to travel to Yarylyuk, in the Crimea, where he is to persuade or compel the defector Edwin Roper to redefect. Coincidentally—or perhaps not—Hillier and Roper were schoolmates at a Roman Catholic public school, continued to correspond during World War II, and remained friends afterward. As a secret agent, Hillier is sophisticated, capable, and skeptical; he is also overtly sexual and combative. Unlike most spy heroes, however, he keeps discovering his limitations. Traveling aboard the *Polyolbion*, a Black Sea cruise ship, for example, his cover is penetrated by a thirteen-year-old whiz kid, he is seduced and drugged by a Eurindian sexual prodigy, he loses a stupid eating contest, and he discloses major secrets to a double agent. Furthermore, in his attempts to regain the initiative and realize his objective, he keeps learning that things are not as they seem and that dividing the world into "us and them" is a reductive absurdity. By the end of the novel, having "disappeared" himself, he has become a priest.

Edwin Roper, Hillier's former friend, a rocket-fuels scientist who has defected to the Soviets. From the beginning of their friendship, Roper is a doubter of conventional explanations. He begins by rejecting the orthodox Catholic doctrine of his public school chaplain, progresses to questioning the innocence of German culture in the atrocities of World War II, and ends in finding the Cold War a convenient political contrivance for both sides. Although assertive in intellectual confrontations, Roper is hopeless socially. In Germany, after the war, he falls in love with Brigitte, a prostitute by nature. Led apparently by his hormones, he pliantly accepts her excuses for German complicity and marries her, only to find her continuing her trade. When Hillier succeeds in separating them, Roper

temporarily adopts the platform of the Labour Party; however, he defects to the Soviet Union in the hope of being reunited with Brigitte. When he finally is liberated by Hillier, he demonstrates that repatriation would have absolutely no effect on anything but the reputations of certain intelligence operatives and administrators. He remains in Russia.

Theodorescu, a double agent and intelligence broker. A man who makes positive virtues out of obesity and consumption, he seems simply a gourmand and polysophisticate on first acquaintance; however, he proves to be the most sinister of sensualists, deviants, and amoralists. This is disclosed first in his conscienceless seduction of the thirteen-year-old Alan Walters. He defeats Hillier in a bet on gluttony, then uses Hillier's own sexual appetites to gain control of and neutralize him. He thus becomes the truly evil element in the political world of the Cold War, one who catalyzes existing tensions solely to profit from them and who believes only in himself and his own gratification.

Richard Wriste, also called **Rick** and **Ricky**, a steward aboard the cruise ship *Polyolbion*. He apparently is quite willing to provide any service for the appropriate gratuity. In this respect, he inhabits a moral universe parallel to Theodorescu's: Anything can be bought or sold, regardless of right or wrong. It nevertheless is shocking when it is revealed that he is a hired assassin, a hit man for a neutral agency, assigned to kill both Hillier and Roper. He was hired by Hillier's own superiors, who believe that he has learned too many Allied secrets during his career. Still, whether as an obsequious Cockney waiter or as a contract murderer, Wriste, like Theodorescu, is one of the soulless neutrals, indifferent to good or evil.

Miss Devi, the seductive and inscrutable companion-assistant of Theodorescu. A stunning, dark, exotic beauty with an encyclopedic repertoire of sexual techniques, she confronts Hillier directly, almost impersonally, before he has time to determine his own sexual objectives. She practices sex expertly but indifferently, as a means of gaining control of men. When Hillier later expresses a preference for sex as a simple exchange of intimacy, she immediately disengages.

Alan Walters, a precocious thirteen-year-old game show expert. He is aboard ship with his sister; his self-indulgent father, who suffers a fatal stroke on the voyage; and his indifferent, gold-digging stepmother. Left essentially to rear himself, Alan embarrasses Hillier by breaking his cover, then lets himself be seduced by Theodorescu so that he can get a gun. Ultimately, he proves indispensable in saving Hillier. In return, Hillier gives him the direction his father failed to provide.

Clara Walters, Alan's eighteen-year-old sister, an amazingly beautiful blond, abandoned like her brother to her own devices. At the beginning of the novel, though still a virgin, she spends most of her time studying sex manuals. After her father's death, Hillier takes on the necessity of comforting the survivors; in Clara's case, this leads at first to sexual initiation but finally to a kind of spiritual fatherhood.

— *James L. Livingston*

THE TRIAL
(Der Prozess)

Author: Franz Kafka (1883-1924)
First published: 1925
Genre: Novel

Locale: Germany
Time: The twentieth century
Plot: Symbolic realism

Joseph K., an employee in a bank. He is a man without particular qualities or abilities, a fact that makes doubly strange his "arrest" by the officer of the Court in the large city where K. lives. K.'s life is purely conventional and resembles the life of any other person of his class. Consequently, he tries in vain to discover how he has aroused the suspicion of the Court. His honesty is conventional; his sins, with Elsa the waitress, are conventional; and he has no striking or dangerous ambitions. He is a man without a face; at the most, he can only ask questions, and he receives no answers that clarify the strange world of courts and court functionaries in which he is compelled to wander.

Frau Grubach, K.'s landlady. She has a high opinion of K. and is deeply shocked by his arrest. She can do nothing to help him.

Fräulein Bürstner, a respectable young woman who also lives in Frau Grubach's house. She avoids any close entanglement with K.

The Assistant Manager, K.'s superior at the bank. He invites K. to social occasions that K. cannot attend because of his troubles with the Court. He is also eager to invade K.'s proper area of authority.

The Examining Magistrate, the official who opens the formal investigation of K.'s offense. He conducts an unruly, arbitrary, and unsympathetic hearing.

The Washerwoman, an amiable but loose woman who has her dwelling in the court building. She is at the disposal of all the functionaries of the system.

The Usher, the subservient husband of the Washerwoman. His submission to official authority is, like his wife's, a sign of the absorption of the individual into the system.

The Clerk of Inquiries, a minor official who reveals court procedures to newly arrested persons.

Franz and

Willem, minor officers of the Court who must endure the attentions of The Whipper because K. has complained to the Court about them.

Uncle Karl (**Albert K.**), Joseph K.'s uncle, who is determined that K. shall have good legal help in his difficulties.

Huld, the lawyer, an ailing and eccentric man who is hand in glove with the Court. He keeps his great knowledge of the law half-hidden from K., who finally dismisses the lawyer as a man whose efforts will be useless.

Leni, the notably promiscuous servant at the lawyer's house. Full of kind instructions to K., she tells him how to get along with the erratic Huld.

Block, a tradesman who has been waiting for five and a half years for Huld to do something for him. He lives at the lawyer's house so that he can be ready for consultations at odd hours.

The Manufacturer, one of K.'s clients. He expresses sympathy for K.'s plight and sends K. to an artist acquaintance, Titorelli, as a means of influencing the Court in K.'s favor.

Titorelli, an impoverished painter who lives in an attic just off the courts of justice. He paints many a magistrate in uneasy and yet traditional poses. He explains in great detail to K. the different kinds of sentences an accused person can receive. He also reveals the contrast between what the law is supposed to do and how it actually works.

The Prison Chaplain, whom K. encounters as the preacher at the cathedral in the town. The Chaplain tells K. a long story about a door guarded by a Tartar; it is a door that somehow exists especially for K. Despite his sympathy, the Chaplain finally reveals himself as merely one more employee of the Court.

THE TRIAL BEGINS
(Sad idzie)

Author: Andrei Sinyavsky (as Abram Tertz, 1925-1997)
First published: 1959
Genre: Novella

Locale: Moscow
Time: Late 1952-March, 1953
Plot: Political

Vladimir Petrovich Globov (vlah-DIH-mihr peh-TROH-vihch GLOH-bov), a public prosecutor during Soviet tyrant Joseph Stalin's last round of purges. These purges were aimed at Jewish citizens, who were referred to as "rootless cosmopolitans" and "enemies of the people." A man with a "large spreading trunk" and "hands as heavy as oars," Globov is an unquestioning follower of the Master's (Stalin's) will. He discovers that Dr. S. Y. Rabinovich, a Jewish physician he has prosecuted for alleged activities against the Soviet state, had performed an abortion for Marina, Globov's wife, who is having an affair with Yury Karlinsky, a public defense attorney. Globov is severely bothered by this deprivation of his embryonic "daughter," yet he does not protest when his adolescent son, Seryozha, is arrested and sentenced to Siberia for an innocent involvement in political idealism.

Marina, the second wife of Prosecutor Globov. She is an "ideally constructed" woman who spends much of her time trying various cosmetics to stop time's inexorable erosion of her beauty. She seeks the attention of her husband's colleagues as a means of assuring herself of her powers of attraction. In a moment of spite, she announces to him that she has had an abortion. Without any real passion, she submits to Karlinsky's seduction. The arrest of her stepson, Seryozha, does not concern her, although she does later send a box of candy to him in Siberia.

Yury Karlinsky (kahr-LIHN-skee), a public defense attorney whose brilliance is frustrated by the Soviet state's prosecutorial bias. He rationalizes his continual failure by philosophizing that "one man's justice is another man's injustice." To show himself that his words can have an appreciable impact, he sets about to seduce Marina, the prosecutor's wife. At the moment of his success, he is unable to perform. It is Karlinsky who interprets Seryozha's immature notes about a communist utopia to be antistate "Trotskyism" and denounces the youth to the authorities.

Seryozha (sehr-YOH-zhah), the teenage son of Prosecutor Globov. In his classes, he questions whether "the end justifies the means" and disquiets his father with discussions of "just and unjust wars." He confides his doubts about the wisdom of the prevailing political system to his grandmother, Ekaterina Petrovna, and to his admiring schoolmate, Katya, who shows his notes outlining "a new world, communist and radiant," to Karlinsky. To his father's embarrassment, he is arrested and sentenced to prison in Siberia.

Dr. S. Y. Rabinovich (rah-BIH-noh-vihch), a Soviet gynecologist of Jewish extraction who is sentenced to Siberia for being a "rootless cosmopolitan." The fact that he had performed an abortion on his prosecutor's wife probably explains his continued confinement in Siberia after the "rehabilitation" of others in his plight. In the epilogue, his mind deteriorates, and he rambles on about "God, history, and ends and means."

Ekaterina Petrovna (yeh-kah-teh-REE-nah peh-TROHV-nah), the mother of Prosecutor Globov's first wife and the grandmother of Seryozha. She is a Communist of the old school who is proud of her revolutionary activity. Globov indulges her daily visits to his office and calls her "mother," but he is frightened by her insistence that he intervene in Seryozha's unjustified arrest and tells her not to visit him again.

Katya, a young girl and a schoolmate of Seryozha. She shares Seryozha's dream of a new and just communist society, naïvely reporting the matter to Karlinsky. After Seryozha's arrest, she writes a note to Karlinsky protesting his denunciation of Seryozha. She is trampled to death by the crowd surging to view the body of the Master, lying in state after his death.

The narrator, a Soviet writer whose room is searched by two police agents, who subsequently discover torn-up drafts of this novel in his sewage. He was instructed to write the text that eventually incriminates him by a supernatural vision of Stalin, who requires him to "celebrate" the Master's "beloved and faithful servant," Prosecutor Globov. He is arrested for failing to depict Globov and the others "in the fullness of their many-sided working lives" and sentenced to Siberia, where, as he relates in the epilogue, he encounters Seryozha and Dr. Rabinovich.

— *Lee B. Croft*

TRIAL BY JURY

Author: W. S. Gilbert (1836-1911)
First published: 1875
Genre: Drama

Locale: England
Time: The nineteenth century
Plot: Comedy

The Learned Judge, an eminent jurist who rose to the top of his profession by first wooing, then jilting a rich attorney's elderly, ugly daughter. A good judge of beauty, he ends the case by offering to marry the plaintiff.

The Plaintiff (Angelina), a lovely young woman suing Edwin for breach of promise. She wins the love of the jury and the Judge, whom she accepts in lieu of Edwin.

The Defendant (Edwin), a fickle lover who would be glad to marry Angelina if it would not deprive so many other girls of happiness. He would marry her today if he could marry another tomorrow. The jury considers him a monster.

The Usher, a careful and conscientious instructor of the jury. He urges the jurors to be free from all bias, to listen to the Plaintiff with sympathy, and to pay no attention to anything the vile Defendant says.

The Foreman of the Jury, a tenderhearted man who wishes to be like a father to the Plaintiff. He offers his manly bosom for her to recline on if she feels faint and gives her a fatherly kiss.

The Counsel for the Plaintiff, a sympathetic lawyer. He, too, offers his bosom for her to recline on. He is horrified at the Defendant's proposal of plural marriages, for to marry two wives at a time is "Burglaree."

The First Bridesmaid, a lovely young woman who captivates the Judge before the Plaintiff appears.

THE TRICK OF THE GA BOLGA

Author: Patrick McGinley (1937-   )
First published: 1985
Genre: Novel

Locale: Garaross, County Donegal, Ireland
Time: 1942-1943
Plot: Detective and mystery

Rufus George Coote, an English expatriate and engineer, a thirty-year-old man with prematurely gray hair and a black beard. He has purchased a farm in the remote village of Garaross in County Donegal, Ireland, to wait out World War II. Ironically, he bears the name of one of Oliver Cromwell's generals and believes that he is living a double existence without control of his destiny. After several sexual affairs and minor social triumphs, he believes that he has become an integral part of the village life. In death, however, he learns that he has always been an outsider, both to himself and to others.

Hugh "The Proker" Donnelly, a farmer and one of Coote's neighbors. Tall and thin, with an odd, permanently closed eye, he constantly feuds with Salmo and vows revenge for the death of his dog. The original source of his quarrel with Salmo dates to their teens, when they both desired and lost the affections of a village girl. When he believes that Coote is trying to take advantage of him, he provokes a fight and is killed inadvertently. Coote arranges his corpse to appear like the remains of some strange mystery.

Manus "Salmo" Byrne, another bachelor neighbor, with a bald, egg-shaped head fringed by fair, curly hair. Although he is large and imposing, he is actually a gentle soul who enjoys lying in a field simply observing nature. Arrested and jailed for Proker's murder, he is innocent but feels oddly responsible for having wished the man dead. Once in jail, he deteriorates markedly, putting up no defense and wishing for his death. He has prescient powers and predicts the nature of Coote's eventual demise.

Imelda McMackin, another neighbor. She is large, buxom, and sensual; she seduces Coote, who is overwhelmed by her sexuality. Although he is warned to avoid her, Coote succumbs to her schemes. She operates as a quietly malevolent force in the village world.

Denis McMackin, a soldier in Africa who suffers from nervous exhaustion and is sent home. He is tall and heavy, with a pallid, triangular face topped with thick, curly hair. He takes an instant dislike to Coote and repeatedly attempts to provoke him. At the novel's close, he kills Coote for kissing his daughter.

Helen McMackin, a bony child with red hair, wide eyes, and taut, pale skin. Her appearance is often referred to as otherworldly. Coote saves her from drowning, and the solitary child visits his farm to sweep his floor and listen to stories. When he affectionately kisses her, however, she is horrified, runs out of the house, and is drowned in bog water. Coote soon learns from her father that her parents have never kissed her.

Consolata O'Gara, another neighbor who takes an interest in Coote. Twenty-six years old, pleasant looking, and commonsensical, she becomes Coote's lover and boon companion. One night, she inadvertently finds him with Imelda and then hangs herself without explanation. She warns Coote against involvement with the McMackins.

Master "Timideen" O'Gara, a retired schoolmaster. He is a short, thin man with a flat head. He is intent on marrying his daughter to a man of substance. Garrulous and agreeable, he befriends Coote and seriously misleads him with a spurious account of the trick of the Ga Bolga, a tale with origins in Irish mythology.

Father McNullis, the village priest. Short, jowly, round-headed, and gray-haired, he has a narrow body and a self-confident manner. With the three hundred pounds that he finds on a corpse, he finances the building of a bridge, which he persuades Coote to engineer. As their unlikely friendship grows, Coote confesses to killing Donnelly, but Father McNullis refuses to believe him. Although initially he appears to be an unscrupulous schemer, the priest is actually wise and understanding of human fallibility.

Sergeant Blowick, the village policeman. He is a tall, thin man obsessed with the disappearance of his official caps. When he finds one on the Proker's corpse, he is convinced that it is incriminating evidence of Salmo's guilt, despite Coote's confession. Although well-intentioned, he is largely ineffectual and comical.

— *David W. Madden*

A TRICK TO CATCH THE OLD ONE

Author: Thomas Middleton (1580-1627)
First published: 1608
Genre: Drama

Locale: London, England
Time: The first years of seventeenth century
Plot: Comedy

Theodorus Witgood, a dissolute young spendthrift. He conspires with the courtesan, his former mistress, to deceive his avaricious old uncle and regain enough of his wasted and confiscated fortune to marry Joyce. Once successful, he swears that he will give up all the vices that have nearly ruined him.

Pecunious Lucre, his uncle, a greedy old man who leaps at the thought of adding to the family fortune by Witgood's proposed marriage to a wealthy widow. He is not above a little flirtation with his nephew's bride-to-be, but he expends most of his energy in his feud with his equally ill-tempered contemporary, Walkadine Hoard.

A courtesan, Witgood's accomplice, a witty woman with a genius for taking advantage of situations that will result in her own advantage. She plays her part of wealthy widow so convincingly that she wins a proposal from old Hoard. When her profession is revealed, she pacifies her new husband with the somewhat specious assurance that, having sinned in her youth, she will be faithful in maturity.

Walkadine Hoard, her miserly suitor, who is attracted primarily to her four hundred pounds a year. He crows over his old enemy, Lucre, when he thinks he has successfully cheated his rival by carrying off Witgood's rich widow. He realizes finally that he has been gulled and reluctantly admits that he must keep his bride to save his reputation.

Joyce, Hoard's niece, Witgood's pleasant, amenable sweetheart, who plays very little part in the schemes of the others.

Taverner, Witgood's ready accomplice in fleecing the greedy Lucre.

THE TRICKSTER OF SEVILLE
(El burlador de Sevilla)

Author: Tirso de Molina (Gabriel Téllez, c. 1580-1648)
First performed: c. 1630
Genre: Drama

Locale: Naples, Italy, and Seville, Spain
Time: Seventeenth century
Plot: Social morality

Don Juan Tenorio (WAHN teh-NOH-ree-oh), the protagonist, the typical depiction of the legendary Don Juan figure, whose main mission in life is to seduce as many women as possible. He achieves this end through trickery and sweet talk. In Naples, he steals into Isabela's room under cover of darkness, disguised as Duke Octavio, her lover. When Isabela calls for light after their sexual encounter, his true identity is revealed. He is immediately arrested, only to be permitted to escape through the connivance of his uncle, Don Pedro Tenorio, the Spanish ambassador to Italy. Don Juan next seduces Tisbea, a fisherman's daughter. Upon arriving in Seville, Don Juan discovers that the king has arranged his marriage to Doña Ana, who is in love with her cousin, the Marqués de la Mota. Don Juan, using trickery, insinuates himself into one of their nightly trysts, but when Doña Ana screams, her father, Don Gonzalo de Ulloa, enters the room and engages in a duel with Don Juan, who kills the old man. Don Juan makes hasty tracks from Seville to a small village where Aminta is planning to marry Batricio, but Don Juan steals into Aminta's bed before the nuptials. Meanwhile Duke Octavio, having learned of Don Juan's defiling of Isabela, presses Don Juan to marry her, to make her an "honest woman." Don Juan comes to the tomb of Don Gonzalo and reads the inscription: "Here the most loyal knight waits for the Lord to wreak vengeance upon a traitor." Affronted by the inscription, Don Juan completely forgets that in seducing Aminta, he had promised that if he did not marry her, God would kill him, by means of a dead man, for treachery and deceit. After two bizarre dinners with the statue of Don Gonzalo, Don Juan meets his end and all the other principals marry save for Tisbea, who never finds a husband.

Catalinón (kah-TAH-lee-NOHN), Don Juan's servant, who always has horses at the ready for his master's escapes. Cata-

linón continually warns his master about the possible consequences of his profligacy, but Don Juan brushes his admonitions aside by repeating, "That is a long way off."

Isabela (ee-sah-BEHL-ah), an aristocratic young woman of Naples, in love with Duke Octavio, whom she eventually marries. She is tricked into having sex with Don Juan, who appears in her bed under cover of darkness and whom she mistakes for Duke Octavio.

Don Pedro Tenorio (PEH-droh), Don Juan's uncle, Spanish ambassador to Italy, who arranges for his nephew's escape after his arrest for seducing Isabela.

Marqués de la Mota (MOH-tah), Doña Ana's lover and cousin. Don Juan intercepts a letter from him to Doña Ana and, changing the time of their meeting, impersonates the Marqués in order to seduce Doña Ana.

Don Gonzalo de Ulloa (gohn-ZAH-loh deh ew-LYOH-ah), Doña Ana's father, who catches Don Juan in his daughter's bed and challenges him to a duel, in which Don Gonzalo is killed. The statue of this nobleman at his tomb then brings about Don Juan's downfall.

Tisbea (TIHS-bay-ah), a simple fisherman's daughter, who rescues Don Juan after he is shipwrecked on the Spanish coast following his escape from Naples. Don Juan seduces her by promising marriage, but at his master's command, Catalinón already has horses standing by to assure Don Juan's escape as soon as he has had his way with Tisbea. In the end, Tisbea is the only one of Don Juan's seductees who does not marry.

Aminta (ah-MIHN-tah), betrothed to Batricio when Don Juan, escaping from his deadly encounter with Don Gonzalo, arrives in her small town and insinuates himself upon the unsuspecting woman, who awaits her lover's arrival in her bed.

— *R. Baird Shuman*

TRILBY

Author: George du Maurier (1834-1896)
First published: 1894
Genre: Novel

Locale: Paris and London
Time: The nineteenth century
Plot: Sentimental

Trilby O'Ferrall, a Scotch-Irish artist's model. Very tall, well developed, and graceful, she lacks classical beauty, having freckles, a large mouth, and eyes set too wide apart, but she has a simple, amiable charm and astonishingly beautiful feet. She sings wretchedly except when hypnotized by Svengali, under whose spell she comes after going out of Little Billee's life. Traveling with Svengali as his wife, she attains

fame as a singer. After his death, she wastes away and dies.

Svengali (svehn-GAH-lee), a middle-aged Jewish musician from Austria, tall and bony, with long, heavy black hair; brilliant black eyes; a thin, sallow face; and black beard and mustache. Conceited, derisive, and malicious, he alternately bullies and fawns in a harsh, croaking voice. He is a dedicated and expert player of popular and light classical music. Although Trilby is repelled at first by his greasy, dirty appearance and regards him as a spidery demon or incubus, she becomes completely his creature under his hypnosis.

Talbot "Taffy" Wynne, an art student and former soldier, a Yorkshireman, handsome, fair, blue-eyed, big, and brawny. He wears a heavy mustache and drooping auburn whiskers.

Sandy McAllister, called "**The Laird of Cockpen**," another art student, a burly Scotsman who becomes a noted artist.

William Bagot, called **Little Billee**, an art student, a Londoner, much younger than his friends Taffy and Sandy, whom he idolizes. Small, slender, black-haired, blue-eyed, and delicate-featured, he is graceful and well built and dresses much better than his friends. He is also innocent of the world and its wickedness. Infatuated with Trilby, he is shocked at her posing nude, and he becomes hysterical and very ill following her disappearance after her promise to his mother. Although he recovers after a fashion, there is a return of his severe illness following Trilby's pathetic death several years later. Little Billee himself dies shortly afterward.

Gecko, a young fiddler, small, swarthy, shabby, brown-eyed, and pock-marked. Although he loves Trilby, he helps Svengali train her to sing so that Svengali may exploit her.

Mrs. Bagot, Little Billee's mother, who persuades Trilby not to marry her son.

Alice, a parson's pretty daughter with whom Little Billee falls in and out of love.

Dodor and

Gontran (**Zouzou**), soldier friends of Taffy, Sandy, Little Billee, and Trilby.

Jeannot, Trilby's young brother, whose death deeply saddens her.

Marta, Svengali's aunt, a fat, elderly woman, grotesque looking but kind to Trilby.

Blanche Bagot, Little Billee's sister, who marries Taffy.

TRIPMASTER MONKEY: His Fake Book

Author: Maxine Hong Kingston (1940-   )
First published: 1989
Genre: Novel

Locale: San Francisco, California
Time: The 1960's
Plot: Magical Realism

Wittman Ah Sing, a presumptive Chinese American poet and playwright, a recent graduate of the University of California, Berkeley. Wittman is a tall, skinny, long-haired, black-clad, manic storyteller with a beatnik penchant for attacking establishment values in favor of experimenting with personal visionary states sometimes augmented by drugs and music. After being fired from his job as a toy department clerk in a large retail store, throughout most of the novel Wittman is devoted to a double quest: acquiring unemployment compensation and putting on a marathon play incorporating characters from two Chinese classics, the war epic *The Romance of the Three Kingdoms* by fourteenth century author Lo Kuan-chung and the equally monumental narrative *Journey to the West* by sixteenth century writer Wu Ch'eng-en. In the second of those works, a Buddhist priest named Hsuan-tsang and his supernatural companion Monkey, the most famous comic figure in Chinese literature, survive a number of fantastic adventures on their travels from China to India. Similarly, Wittman's large-scale stage production as well as his entire narrative take on, through the power of his imagination and the magic of his wordplay, aspects of the real and the fanciful. Like the legendary Monkey, Wittman is a trickster who, through the agencies of roleplaying and verbal dexterity, transcends social rules and restrictions to tap into what psychologist Carl Jung referred to as the collective unconscious. In this case, Wittman examines ethnic stereotypes and, in so doing, redefines for himself and his audience—like his namesake, the nineteenth century American poet Walt Whitman—the nature of both individual and group identity.

Tana Chloe De Weese, an assistant claims adjuster who wants to be a painter. Wittman is attracted to her golden blond beauty. After one night of lovemaking, they are "married" by a draft dodger named Gabe, who carries a card proclaiming himself to be a minister in the Universal Life Church. Tana subsequently is introduced to Wittman's parents, and the young couple decide to live together, although each tells the other that theirs is not a true, romantic love. Tana informs Wittman that she wants him to be the "wife" and do the housework.

Lance Kamiyama, a Japanese American government worker and Wittman's erstwhile best friend. As a career-conscious conformist, Lance is a foil to Wittman. Hosting parties for other ambitious young Asian Americans, whom he calls "Young Millionaires," Lance lives in an impressive Victorian house with his blond wife, Sunny. He tends to underplay the consequences of his ethnicity, having blocked out memories of his childhood in a relocation camp during World War II.

Ruby Ah Sing, sometimes called **Ruby Long Legs**, Wittman's mother. Ruby, a retired vaudeville song-and-dance performer, spends more time with her female friends than with her eccentric husband. Skeptical of the value of Wittman's college education, Ruby calls him *moong cha cha*, or spacy.

Zeppelin Ah Sing, Wittman's father, a former huckster of cure-all potions and sidewalk organ grinder whose exotic appearance often makes others think that he is not Chinese but of Italian, Mexican, or gypsy descent. When Wittman was a child, Zeppelin often dressed him as a monkey to collect money from passersby. Now, in retirement, he spends his time with his male cronies at a makeshift fishing camp near the Sacramento River.

PoPo, an elderly theater wardrobe mistress. Wittman thinks of her as his grandmother despite the fact that she is not related to the family by blood. On the pretense of picnicking in the high Sierras, PoPo is abandoned by Ruby and Zeppelin, who have come to see her as a financial burden, but she somehow manages to hitch a ride from a wealthy property owner named Lincoln Fong, who marries her in Reno and bankrolls the production of Wittman's play.

— *S. Thomas Mack*

TRIPTYCH
(Triptyque)

Author: Claude Simon (1913-   )
First published: 1973
Genre: Novel

Locale: A farm valley, a Riviera beach resort, and a city in northern France
Time: The 1970's
Plot: Antistory

Corinne, a middle-aged actress. She spends her time in bed reading about a young man and woman who have recently been married. She is worried about her son, who has problems with drugs and who is under investigation by the police. She asks her friends Brown and Lambert to secure the release of her son.

Lambert, an Englishman who has made love to Corinne with the apparent understanding that he will intervene with the police authorities to secure her son's release from jail.

Brown, an overweight, middle-aged friend of Corinne. He has a conversation with a man in a bar, where he exchanges money for little packages of powder. He later assures Corinne that her son will be freed. He also completes a jigsaw puzzle that represents the boys in the fishing scene and then scatters it.

A clown, who is pictured on a circus advertisement hanging on a barn. He participates in a dumb show with a monkey and another man who torments him. His performance is staged against a background of music that is frequently interrupted by the lion tamer's animals.

Two young boys, who are fishing and take time to examine some film strips that they try to arrange in the proper sequence. Some of their film relates the story of Corinne at the beach. They notice a young mother leaving her child to meet her lover in a barn. They then head toward the barn to spy on the lovemaking.

Young men, who are part of a boisterous wedding celebration. They accompany the groom into a bar.

Man, who appears in a bar wearing a leather jacket and a cap and has a swarthy complexion. After talking with one of the women there, he leaves and finds Lily with the young husband on the street. He continues his ride into the country, where, after meeting the young married woman in the barn, he repeatedly makes love to her.

Lily, a barmaid. She has a conversation in the bar with a young groom on his wedding day. She apparently has known him for some time. While his friends noisily celebrate the

marriage with much drinking and loud music, she leaves the bar to rejoin him in an alley, where the two make love. He has vomited, and she tries to clean him with her rolled-up underwear. She unsuccessfully tries to keep him from leaving her.

The groom, who abandons his wife to return to a bar, at the entrance of which he had earlier seen Lily and another woman. Once he has become inebriated and has made love to Lily, he returns to his hotel room in clothes now soiled with vomit and dirt. He goes to bed without undressing and falls into a deep sleep.

The young bride, still in her wedding clothes, who has been crying because she has been left alone. When her inebriated husband returns and she finds him asleep in bed, she undresses him and then herself.

An adolescent, who is studying geometry and drawing triangular figures. He is interested in a photograph of a naked woman that he intermittently takes out from his desk drawer.

A young boy, with tow-colored hair, who herds cows in a pasture. Nearby, two other young boys are fishing.

An elderly woman, who crosses the field with a rabbit in hand and walks past the barn where the couple is making love. She had been feeding several rabbits and has just chosen the one that she eventually kills and skins. She belongs to the household of the young woman whose child is missing.

A young married woman, who goes on a walk with her little girl and leaves her with the boys who are fishing when she sees a motorcyclist ride by. She crosses the field to join him in a barn, where they make love. She later discovers that her little girl is missing.

Two young girls, who take a walk in the countryside. They take care of the little girl, who has been turned over to them by the boys who were fishing. They, in turn, abandon her, and she drowns in the river.

Young boys, who try to slip into a barn where a motion picture is being shown. The film features the story of Corinne.

— *Peter S. Rogers*

TRISTAN AND ISOLDE
(Tristan und Isolde)

Author: Gottfried von Strassburg (fl. c. 1210)
First transcribed: c. 1210
Genre: Poetry

Locale: Northern Europe, Ireland, and England
Time: The Arthurian age
Plot: Romance

Tristan (TREES-tahn), the courtly son of Rivalin and Blanchefleur. Orphaned at birth, he is reared by Rual the Faithful until he joins King Mark's court after his escape from Norwegian kidnappers. He serves his lord well by killing Duke Morolt and winning the hand of Isolde the Fair for Mark. Tristan and Isolde drink a love potion by accident and fall helplessly in love. The two lovers deceive Mark until Tristan is forced to flee. Later, he marries Isolde of the White Hands, but

it is a marriage in name only.

Isolde the Fair (ee-ZOHL-deh), the wife of King Mark and lover of Tristan.

Mark, the vacillating king of Cornwall, uncle of Tristan, and cuckolded husband of Isolde the Fair.

Rivalin (ree-VAH-lihn), a lord of Parmenie. On his travels, he marries Blanchefleur and fathers Tristan before his death in battle against Duke Morgan.

Blanchefleur (blahnsh-FLOOR), the sister of King Mark and wife of Rivalin. Shortly after learning of Rivalin's death, she dies giving birth to Tristan.

Brangene (BRAHN-gay-neh), the companion of Isolde and her substitute in Mark's wedding bed.

Rual the Faithful (rew-AHL), the foster father of Tristan.

Duke Morolt (moh-ROHLT), the brother of Queen Isolde.

He is killed by Tristan when he demands tribute from Cornwall for Ireland.

Duke Morgan, the enemy of Rivalin, later killed by Tristan.

Isolde of the White Hands, the wife of Tristan in name only.

Queen Isolde of Ireland, the mother of Isolde the Fair.

TRISTRAM

Author: Edwin Arlington Robinson (1869-1935)
First published: 1927
Genre: Poetry

Locale: England and Brittany
Time: Arthurian period
Plot: Arthurian romance

Tristram, the prince of Lyonesse, nephew to King Mark of Cornwall. An attractive and talented youth, blessed by fortune in every way, Tristram heedlessly enjoys life until the moment that he realizes he is in love with Isolt of Ireland, the bride whom he had fought to bring back for his uncle. He has a chivalric sense of the demands of honor, from which the only escape is death. His healthy instinct to live means accepting extreme mental anguish, with physical suffering seen as a welcome relief. He is a Hamlet-like figure in his willingness to see the tragedy of his situation and to blame himself.

King Mark, who is calculating, selfish, and ignoble, the opposite of his nephew Tristram. Mark can detect the nobility and generosity of others, and he does not hesitate to take unfair advantage of them. After a lifetime of dissipation, his face is marked by a "sad craftiness" rather than the wisdom that should come with his years. He is loved by no one, except for his creature, Andred, a subhuman flunky whose joy is to anticipate Mark's wishes.

Isolt of Ireland, the princess taken away to Cornwall. She is a proud and fiery beauty, as uncompromising as Tristram. Her fate is to endure years of mental and physical agony, as the king's "shuddering toy," rather than to escape through suicide. Strong by nature, she is resigned to a long life of misery. She is broken only after being reunited with Tristram, then snatched away from him again.

Isolt of the White Hands, the princess of Brittany, a gentle soul who provides a foil to the fiery passions of the other Isolt and of Tristram. Her eyes are gray and always looking to the gray sea and the white birds above it. She represents faithful, undemanding, childlike love. She becomes Tristram's wife after he decides that the other Isolt is lost forever. Since child-

hood, she had lived for Tristram, and she would gladly have healed him even after losing him to Isolt of Ireland a second time. When Tristram is treacherously slain by Andred, the gentle survivor, Isolt of Brittany, is the one hurt most of all.

Howel, the king of Brittany. He is fond of Tristram, his son-in-law. He cherishes his only child, Isolt, and shares with her a quiet, intuitive wisdom. Howel's misgivings about whether his quiet child can hold Tristram must be put aside, as he recognizes that despite all gentle advice and persuasion, she cannot be brought to love anyone else.

Andred, King Mark's reptilian flunky, reminiscent of dead creatures spewed up from the sea after storms. A perpetual spy and slanderer, his supreme moment comes when he sneaks up on the grieving Tristram and murders him, in ultimate homage to his master. Even then, Mark views his flunky absentmindedly and only mumbles that perhaps Andred has done right, after all, in giving Tristram peace.

Gouvernail, Tristram's attendant and friend, worldly and well-meaning. He shows Tristram fatherly kindness and support but has no authority over him. A brave knight himself, he helped to rear Tristram and developed his chivalrous qualities and ideals. Tristram compliments him for not having more of a dark side.

Queen Morgan, a sorceress and temptress who recurs throughout the Arthurian legends. Ever the consummate opportunist, she tries to tempt Tristram on the night of King Mark's wedding to Isolt. After the banished Tristram is found delirious in a forest, she tries more wittily to seduce him, quoting him worldly wisdom while caring for him in her castle.

— *D. Gosselin Nakeeb*

TRITON

Author: Samuel R. Delany (1942-   )
First published: 1976
Genre: Novel

Locale: Neptune's moon Triton and Earth
Time: 2112
Plot: Science fiction

Bron Helstrom, a metalogician from Mars. Bron is an attractive, tall, blond, curly-haired man, with one gold-inlaid eyebrow; the other eyebrow is the normal hairy type, though it grows so constantly that it has to be trimmed regularly, giving it a rough, rumpled look. As a youth, Bron was a prostitute on Mars, and he has always been highly sexed. He is an indifferent socializer, "emotionally lazy"; people become his friends almost by default, with Bron not really playing an active role

in developing the relationships. When he meets The Spike, however, he meets his match. Her rejection of him completely undermines his emotional world. His life changes radically as he undergoes a sex change and as he develops the capacity to care about other people's feelings.

Gene Trimbell, also called **The Spike**, a director and producer of, and actress in, "microtheater for unique audiences." The Spike is a big-boned, thirty-four-year-old woman with whom Bron falls in love after seeing one of her shows. It is her bluntness in a letter to Bron that motivates him to change his life, though he at first denies the validity of her criticisms of him.

Lawrence, one of Bron's only real friends. Lawrence is a seventy-four-year-old homosexual originally from South Africa, which he left because of the repression of human rights there. Lawrence helps Bron after he becomes a woman, finding for Bron a place to stay and new clothes. Ultimately, Lawrence joins a musical commune and becomes a singer.

Sam, a big black man who has also had a sex change, having formerly been a blond, sallow waitress. At first, Bron claims to dislike Sam, perhaps out of jealousy, and though Bron originally dismisses Sam as an average, handsome, friendly man, after a while he realizes that "under that joviality there was a rather amazing mind." After Bron has his sex changed, "she" runs into Sam in a bar and propositions him, but Sam refuses, perhaps realizing Bron's unstable emotional state.

Audri, one of Bron's bosses. Audri is a lesbian mother with three children. Although she likes Bron, she is never sexually interested in him. After Bron becomes a woman, however, Audri falls in love with Bron and asks her to move in with her and her family. It is at this point that, for the first time in his/her life, Bron tries to spare someone's feelings. Not wanting to hurt Audri, Bron makes up a story about already being involved with another woman.

— *T. M. Lipman*

THE TRIUMPH OF DEATH
(Il trionfo della morte)

Author: Gabriele D'Annunzio (1863-1938)
First published: 1894
Genre: Novel

Locale: Italy
Time: The nineteenth century
Plot: Psychological realism

George Aurispa (ah-ew-REES-pah), a wealthy young Italian independent of his family. He takes the beautiful Hippolyte as his mistress but comes to distrust her and his love affair with her as leading him into the same kind of gross sensuality that had ruined his father. His distress leads him to consider suicide and, later, the murder of the woman who has overpowered his emotions. Finally, he leaps to his death on a rocky coast, taking his mistress with him in his embrace.

Hippolyte (eep-POHL-ee-teh), a beautiful married woman who falls in love with George Aurispa. She leaves her husband and returns to her family to take George as her lover, but she is disturbed many times by the thought of her mortality, a thought frequently suggested to her by an inclination toward epilepsy. From being almost frigid, she becomes, through George Aurispa's lovemaking, a passionately sensual woman.

Signor Aurispa, George's father. He is a worldly man who leaves his wife to take up with a mistress, by whom he has two illegitimate children. He squanders his fortune, though he refuses to help his wife and their daughter. He is regarded by his wife and son as a gross sensualist.

Signora Aurispa, George's mother. As a woman deserted by her husband, she has her son's deep sympathy. It is partly her unenviable position that enables her son to see that he is slipping into the same kind of sensuality that ensnared his father.

TROILUS AND CRESSIDA

Author: William Shakespeare (1564-1616)
First published: 1609
Genre: Drama

Locale: Troy
Time: During the Trojan War
Plot: Tragedy

Troilus (TROY-luhs), the heroic young son of Priam. An idealistic and trusting young lover, he first wins Cressida with the aid of Pandarus, then loses first her presence and afterward her faith. He becomes bitter in disillusionment. He is a good fighter, showing no compassion toward his enemies.

Cressida (KREHS-ih-duh), the daughter of Calchas. She is a beautiful woman but not gifted with the power to say "no." She yields to Troilus after a certain amount of coyness, and she shows real regret when she has to leave him to go to her father with the Greeks. She swears eternal truth to him, but in her fickleness she soon accepts Diomedes as her lover. William Shakespeare's Cressida is much less complex and less appealing than Geoffrey Chaucer's Criseyde. Ulysses in the play finds her contemptible, and audiences do not greatly disagree with him.

Pandarus (PAN-duh-ruhs), the uncle of Cressida and the go-between for Troilus and Cressida. Much simplified and considerably degraded from his complex original in Chaucer's fine poem, he is an off-color jester, especially in the presence of the lovers. He speaks a particularly unpleasant dirty epilogue, which a number of scholars have ascribed to some unknown play-dresser instead of to Shakespeare.

Hector (HEHK-tohr), the greatest of Priam's sons and chief defender of his country. He has better judgment than most of his fellows, but he yields to pressure and consents to Helen remaining in Troy instead of being sent back to the Greeks. Troilus accuses him of excessive clemency to fallen foes. In keeping with the medieval tradition of Hector as one of the Nine Worthies, he is given great prowess. His death at the hands of Achilles and his Myrmidons is depicted as the murder of an unarmed man by numerous opponents.

Achilles (uh-KIHL-eez), the most famous of the Greek champions. Painted from the point of view of the legendarily Trojan-descended English, he is a most unpleasant character, self-centered, stupid, arrogant, and ruthless. He avoids combat partly because of pique and partly because of desire for Polyxena, one of Priam's daughters. He returns to combat partly out of jealousy of Ajax but perhaps chiefly because of the death of his friend Patroclus. Although allowed a respite by Hector when they first meet, he has Hector murdered while he is unarmed. He instructs his men to run through the Grecian camp shouting, "Achilles hath the mighty Hector slain."

Thersites (thehr-SI-teez), a cowardly, foul-mouthed Greek. He ranges through the play as a sort of chorus, making impudent or vile comments on all whom he sees. When Hector, meeting him on the field of battle, asks him if he is a worthy opponent, he characterizes himself truthfully as "a rascal, a scurvy railing knave, a very filthy rogue," thereby saving his life. He seems to be accepted by his cohorts as an "all-licens'd fool."

Ulysses (yew-LIHS-eez), the shrewd Greek hero. He delivers a much-admired speech on order. He and Nestor are usually in agreement and are experienced practical psychologists. Despising Cressida, during a truce he conducts Troilus to a spot from which he can see and hear Cressida and Diomedes making love.

Nestor (NEHS-tohr), the venerable old man of the Greek forces. He confers frequently with Ulysses and represents with him the rational outlook.

Diomedes (di-oh-MEE-deez), or **Diomed**, the unprincipled warrior sent to escort Cressida to the Greek camp. After seducing her, he fights an indecisive match with Troilus.

Ajax (AY-jaks), a Greek champion related to the Trojan royal family. Slow and bearlike, he is as stupid as Achilles and as much filled with self-love, but he is a much less unpleasant character. He meets Hector in single combat but agrees to call off the battle because of their kinship.

Priam (PRI-am), the king of Troy. He appears very briefly to preside over the council to determine the fate of Helen and to try to dissuade Hector from tempting fate.

Paris, the son of Priam and lover of Helen. He insists on keeping Helen instead of returning her to her husband; his selfishness, having caused the War of Troy, continues it. He is supported heartily by Troilus, the lover, and very reluctantly by Hector, the warrior.

Helen, the wife of Menelaus and mistress of Paris, fair outside but hollow within. She and Paris are guilty of causing the Trojan War. Pandarus exchanges ambiguous pleasantries with her.

Andromache (an-DRO-muh-kee), Hector's wife. She pleads piteously, but in vain, for her courageous husband to remain inside the walls on his fateful day.

Cassandra (kuh-SAN-druh), the daughter of Priam, a prophetess. Considered mad by all her family, she prophesies Hector's death but is unable to prevent his going into combat.

Calchas (KAL-kuhs), a Trojan priest, taking part with the Greeks. He insists on having his daughter Cressida sent to the Grecian camp in exchange for a Trojan captive, Antenor.

Agamemnon (a-guh-MEHM-non), the Greek general. He is a royal figure of great dignity.

Menelaus (meh-nuh-LAY-uhs), Helen's husband and Agamemnon's brother. He and Paris meet on the battlefield with Thersites as a scurrilous cheerleader, but the combat is indecisive.

Patroclus (pa-TROH-kluhs), the youthful companion of Achilles. Hector kills him.

Aeneas (ee-NEE-uhs), a Trojan commander. He delivers the message to Troilus that Cressida is to be sent to the Greeks. In the battle, he is rescued by Troilus.

Antenor (an-TEE-nohr), another Trojan commander. After being captured by the Greeks, he is exchanged for Cressida.

Deiphobus (dee-IH-fuh-buhs) and
Helenus (HEHL-eh-nuhs), sons of Priam.

Margarelon (mahr-GAR-eh-lon), a bastard son of Priam. In the final battle, he frightens Thersites into flight.

Alexander, the servant of Cressida.

TROILUS AND CRISEYDE

Author: Geoffrey Chaucer (c. 1343-1400)
First transcribed: c. 1382
Genre: Poetry

Locale: Troy
Time: During the Trojan War
Plot: Love

Troilus (TROY-luhs), a young prince of Troy. He scorns love until he falls in love with Criseyde, who then becomes his mistress until she is traded to the Greeks for a Trojan warrior. When Criseyde fails to return to Troy as she has promised, Troilus is grief-stricken. He is killed on the battlefield by Achilles, the great Greek warrior.

Priam (PRI-am), the king of Troy during the Trojan War. He is Troilus' father.

Criseyde (KREHS-ih-duh), a beautiful young widow. She fears that Troilus' love is dishonorable, but she becomes his mistress so he will not die of unrequited love. Although she loves him and vows to return to Troy, she falls in love with Diomedes, a young Greek, and remains in the Greek camp with him.

Calchas (KAL-kuhs), Criseyde's father. A soothsayer and prophet, he runs away from Troy to join the Greeks, who are

fated to win the war. He arranges to have his daughter exchanged for Antenor, whom the Greeks have captured.

Pandarus (PAN-duh-ruhs), Criseyde's uncle. He arranges the details of the affair between Troilus and Criseyde.

Deiphobus (dee-IH-fuh-buhs), Troilus' brother. He enables the lovers to meet by inviting Troilus and Criseyde to dinner at his home.

Antenor (an-TEE-nohr), a Trojan warrior captured by the Greeks and exchanged for Criseyde.

Hector (HEHK-tohr), Troilus' brother. He does not wish to make the exchange of Criseyde for Antenor.

Diomedes (di-oh-MEE-deez), a handsome young Greek. Criseyde falls in love with him and hence fails to return to Troilus.

Achilles (uh-KIHL-eez), the mightiest of the Greek warriors. He slays Troilus on the battlefield.

THE TROJAN WOMEN
(Trōiades)

Author: Euripides (c. 485-406 B.C.E.)
First published: 415 B.C.E.
Genre: Drama

Locale: Outside the ruined walls of Troy
Time: After the fall of Troy
Plot: Tragedy

Hecuba (HEH-kyew-buh), the queen of Troy. Aged and broken by the fall of the city, she is the epitome of all the misfortune resulting from the defeat of the Trojans and the destruction of the city. She is first revealed prostrate before the tents of the captive Trojan women, with the city in the background. Her opening lyrics tell of the pathos of her situation and introduce the impression of hopelessness and the theme of the inevitable doom that war brings. The Greek herald enters with the news that each of the women has been assigned to a different master. Hecuba asks first about her children, Cassandra and Polyxena; then, when she finds that she has been given to Odysseus, she rouses herself to an outburst of rebellious anger. Cassandra appears and recalls the prophecy that Hecuba will die in Troy. After Cassandra is led away, Andromache, who appears with news of the sacrifice of Polyxena, tries to console Hecuba with the idea that Polyxena is fortunate in death, but Hecuba, in reproach and consolation, points out to Andromache and the younger women of the Chorus the hope of life. Her attempts to console those younger than herself, here and elsewhere, are her most endearing feature. The other important aspect of her character, the desire for vengeance against Helen, who has caused her sorrow, is shown in her reply to Helen's plea to Menelaus. Hecuba's reply is vigorous: She points to Helen's own responsibility for her actions and ends with a plea to Menelaus to kill Helen and vindicate Greek womanhood. Hecuba's last action is the preparation of the body of Astyanax, the young son of Andromache and Hector killed by the Greeks out of fear, for burial. Her lament over the body is profoundly moving. At the end of the play, she is restrained from throwing herself into the ruins of the burning city.

Cassandra (kuh-SAN-druh), the daughter of Hecuba, a prophetess chosen by Agamemnon as a concubine. When she first appears, wild-eyed and waving a torch above her head, she sings a parody of a marriage song in her own honor, but she soon calms down and prophesies the dreadful end of Agamemnon because of his choice and of the suffering of the Greeks. She views aggressive war as a source of unhappiness for the aggressor. As she leaves, she hurls the sacred emblems of her divine office to the ground and looks forward to her triumph in revenge.

Andromache (an-DRO-muh-kee), Hector's wife, allotted to Neoptolemus, the son of Achilles. She brings Hecuba news of the sacrifice of Polyxena and compares her fate in accepting a new lord to Polyxena's escape through death. When she learns of the Greeks' decision to kill Astyanax, her son by Hector, she gives expression to her tortured love as a mother. Unable to condemn the Greeks because they would refuse Astyanax burial, she curses Helen as the cause of misfortune.

Helen, the beautiful and insolent queen of Sparta abducted by Paris. Her pleading before Menelaus is an attempt to place the blame for her actions on others: on Priam and Hecuba because they had refused to kill Paris at the oracle's command, on the goddess Aphrodite because she promised Helen to Paris at the time of the judgment, and on the Trojan guards who had prevented her return to the Greeks. She departs, proud and confident.

Menelaus (meh-nuh-LAY-uhs), the king of Sparta and the husband of Helen, who has been returned to him, the man she wronged, to kill. It is evident that he will not do so. His eagerness to assure others that Helen has no control over him and that he intends to kill her becomes almost comic.

Talthybius (tal-THIH-bee-uhs), a herald of the Greeks. He appears three times: to fetch Cassandra, to execute Astyanax, and to bring back the body of Astyanax for burial and set fire to the remains of Troy. A kindly man, he is unable to carry out the execution of Astyanax personally.

Astyanax (as-TI-uh-naks), the infant son of Andromache and Hector. He is flung from the highest battlement of Troy because the Greeks believe that a son of Hector is too dangerous to live.

A Chorus of Trojan women, whose odes express a mood of pity and sorrow for the Trojans.

Poseidon (poh-SI-duhn), the god of the sea and patron of Troy. He appears, at the beginning of the drama, to take official leave of the city; he had favored it, but the gods aiding the Greeks had proved too strong, especially Pallas Athena. His monologue also gives the necessary background for the play.

Pallas Athena (PAL-uhs uh-THEE-nuh), the goddess of wisdom. She confronts Poseidon as he bids farewell to Troy and proposes a common vengeance against the Greeks, though she had favored them earlier. Because their impious behavior at the capture of Troy has alienated the gods, the Greeks are to be punished as they go to sea. This threat of retribution looms over the entire play.

TROPIC OF CANCER

Author: Henry Miller (1891-1980)
First published: 1934
Genre: Novel

Locale: Paris and Dijon, France
Time: 1930-1931
Plot: Autobiographical

Henry Miller, the narrative consciousness of the novel, a somewhat transformed, semiautobiographical elaboration of the author. He is a man of indeterminate middle age, an indigent, aspiring writer who is visiting Europe to escape from the conditions of life in the United States, which he believes are responsible for his artistic and economic failures. After trying to conform to the conventional rules and requirements of middle-class society in America, he is struggling to survive as a kind of underground man in the bohemian realms of Paris. Convinced that his true nature has been suppressed by his failed attempts at various mundane jobs and two marriages, he has recast himself as an artist/hero, a rebel, and a kind of gangster of erotic aggression. He is mostly appetite, for both sex and food. Although it is not as immediately apparent, he is also a man of feeling and sensitivity. He is essentially an observer; he demonstrates his kinship with the historical tradition of great art in Paris through his extremely inventive use of language, employing verbal styles of expression charged with the energy of the anger and joy with which he confronts everything. His spirit remains strong in the midst of conditions that crush nearly everyone else with whom he associates. His heartfelt tributes to the subtle beauties of the city, its architecture, and its rivers and streets register his deeper, more humane and more gentle side. As he progresses through the eighteen months or so that the novel covers, the manner in which he skips from one incident, episode, and location to another suggests entries in a journal, a record of the final phases of his development as the artist who will write the book.

Van Norden, a newspaperman of sorts, also American, who represents the worst aspects of the society from which Miller is trying to escape and who also exhibits the author's worst traits carried to excess and with no redeeming qualities. He is vain, stupid, consumed by self-pity, and completely oblivious to the extraordinary features of the city in which he feels trapped. His only interest seems to be the seduction of women, whom he regards as little more than versions of sexual mechanisms and to whose human qualities he is completely blind. He "wakes up cursing" and tries to obliterate his psychic numbness with the gratification of sensory demands. Ultimately, he is a homicidal monster, though not in the conventional sense. He is a killer of the soul, and his murderous tendencies destroy every life he touches, including his own. Miller uses him as a powerful contrast to the life to which he aspires, a life that is animated by the "spark of passion" Van Norden lacks. Other characters named Carl, Boris, and Moldorf are variations of Van Norden.

Fillmore, a relatively young American trying to live in the style of the carefree bohemians of legendary Parisian society. Like Van Norden and Carl, he is a case of arrested development, an adolescent who has no real sense of himself. Also like Carl, he is forced into a pitiable retreat from life. At the conclusion of the novel, Miller helps Fillmore onto a boat headed back to England and then to America. Fillmore is a beaten man whose defeat is presented as a contrast with Miller's survival.

Germaine, a prostitute, who is praised by Miller for her lack of pretense and is admired for exhibiting some of the same characteristics that the narrator relishes in himself: guts, fire, stamina, courage, and cunning. Although she is primarily presented as another version of the members of an essentially nondistinct conglomerate of women named Tania, Llona, and Irene, some aspects of personality and singularity emerge, suggesting an individual more than a sexual device.

Mona, a beautiful, dark young woman who had been involved with the narrator prior to his arrival in Paris and who spent some time with him in Paris during his first days there. She is a characterization of Miller's second wife, Jane Smith, and represents a mysterious and valued woman who is still a factor in the narrator's existence.

— Leon Lewis

TROPIC OF CAPRICORN

Author: Henry Miller (1891-1980)
First published: 1939
Genre: Novel

Locale: Brooklyn and New York City
Time: c. 1900-late 1920's
Plot: Autobiographical

Henry Miller, the narrator, who tells about his life in mixed order, including long descriptions of events in his childhood. The narration is stream of consciousness and includes philosophical asides. Even as a child, Miller wanted to die. He recalls his childhood and reflects that he has not gained from enlargement of his world as an adult. He sees no sense in struggling against inevitable failure. He has no ambitions, nothing he wishes to do that he could just as well not do. He has no desire to become a useful member of society. He does not believe in doing things just to earn a living; it is better to starve to death or kill someone else. He thinks people work only because they do not know any better. He takes menial jobs, rather than learning a profession, because they keep his mind free. He claims his whole aim in life is to get near to God and that music is the "can opener of the soul." He links music to sex and is obsessed with women, even though he seems indifferent (at best) to his wife. He lets his wife support him for a while right after getting married. He has had many jobs; he was fired from them because he inspires distrust. He finally needs a job and applies as a messenger for the Cosmodemonic Telegraph Company of North America. He is rejected but reapplies and is given a job as a manager, responsible for hiring and firing messengers. Miller is berated for having too big a heart; he gives things away, using company funds as well as his own possessions. He goes into debt to be able to give things away, and he constantly looks for sources of loans to him that he never intends to repay. He works hard at his job, trying to give jobs to all the people who need them. The vice president of Cosmodemonic suggests that Miller write a Horatio Alger type of book about the messengers. Miller realizes that the book he writes is bad, and everyone says it is, but he is in love with it. He recognizes that he attempted to do too much, to make it a terrific book even though he is not yet capable of such a thing. He sometimes feels compelled to either write or run away; those are the only choices. In the coda, he admits to walking out on his wife and child at the age of thirty. This begins his new life.

Gottlieb Leberecht Müller, who has lost his identity. He is an alter ego of Miller and narrates the interlude near the end of the book. Things he does under this name are regarded as crazy. He plays the piano madly, improvising incredible music.

Lola Niessen, Müller's piano teacher, a woman in her late twenties with a sallow complexion, bilious-looking eyes, warts, and a mustache. She is very hairy, which excites Müller. He loses his virginity to her when he is fifteen years old.

Mara, a woman whom Miller visits in the dance hall in the coda to the book. She is perhaps eighteen years old or perhaps thirty, with a full body, blue-black hair, and a white face. Miller sees her as the embodiment of America.

Valeska, one of Miller's many girlfriends. Miller relates that she committed suicide. She has some black blood and makes people aware of it. Miller hires her as his secretary. She is "promoted" to a job in Havana because the bosses do not want a mulatta in the office. She says she will fight the decision, and Miller says he will quit if they fire her. They make love in his house while his wife is out having an abortion.

Hymie Laubscher, the Jewish Cosmodemonic employee who rejected Miller from employment, though he had no authority to do so. When Miller is made a manager, Laubscher works under him. He participates in Miller's trading of jobs for sex with female applicants. He always seems to have a lot of money, even though he is one of the lowest-paid employees. He is absorbed in his wife's "rotting" ovaries and speaks of the problem every day.

Steve Romero, a "prize bull" Miller keeps around in case of trouble. He is a clean man, inside and out, as Miller describes him, in contrast to Laubscher, who keeps himself immaculate but talks filth incessantly. Romero finds it difficult to lie so has a more difficult time than the others in getting women.

O'Rourke, a company detective. He accompanies Miller on walks at night and insistently tells Miller stories. The stories concern murder, theft, other crimes, love, and human nature.

Kronski, a young Jewish medical student interested in the pathological cases on staff at Cosmodemonic. His wife dies. Even while she was alive, he pursued some of the same women as Miller. He tells Miller that Miller could be something big.

MacGregor, a friend of Miller who is always worried about his penis. He washes it so frequently that it gets red and inflamed, making him worry about it and wash it more. He also worries about dandruff and his cough. He picks up women in bars with Miller. MacGregor is always trying to improve his mind. Miller likes him because of all of his idiosyncrasies, which are like those of his childhood friends. MacGregor berates Miller for trying to be independent; he thinks it important to have a network of friends. MacGregor was the one who introduced Miller to his wife. He does not understand how a man can stay attached to one woman, even if he womanizes. He recommends that Miller run away.

Maxie Schnadig, another friend of Miller. He has an attractive sister, Rita, and a deranged brother. Miller visits them only for amusement; Schnadig thinks Miller is genuinely concerned about the brother. Miller finds Schnadig boring. He tolerates him only because Schnadig loans money readily and buys Miller things he needs.

Curley, a seventeen-year-old whom Miller has known for about three years and whom he gave a job as a messenger. Miller likes Curley because Curley has no morals or shame. He lives in Harlem. His parents, in South America, sent him there to live with an aunt. His aunt seduced him, and he sometimes blackmails her for that; when it is easier, he simply takes money from her. He gets lots of women, including Valeska.

Grover Watrous, a childhood acquaintance of Miller on whom Miller reflects. He is a filthy boy with rotting teeth, a running ear, and a clubfoot. He is a piano prodigy. He reappears later, looking tidy and having given up his boyhood habit of smoking. He has found religion, though he belongs to no particular church. In hindsight, Miller is convinced that Watrous is a great man, though at the time he thought him crazy; Miller considers him great because he realized that the one certainty in life is death and acted on his certainty.

— *A. J. Sobczak*

TROUBLE IN MIND

Author: Alice Childress (1920-1994)
First published: 1971
Genre: Drama

Locale: New York City
Time: 1957
Plot: Problem

Wiletta Mayer, a veteran actor beginning rehearsals of a play. She is an attractive, middle-aged African American woman with an outgoing personality. She made a career out of playing stereotypical black roles but aspires to be cast in parts more deserving of her rich talents. Initially, she readily gives advice to John Nevins, a novice actor, on how to ingratiate oneself, to stay on good terms with the management no matter how loathsome the production may be. When rehearsals begin, however, she cannot adhere to such a strategy. Her white director uses tactics that humiliate her, and the script calls for the black characters to make statements and perform actions that offend her racial pride. Consequently, Wiletta becomes an outspoken critic of the production.

Al Manners, a theatrical director in his early forties, working on his first Broadway show. He is an energetic, confident man with a patronizing manner. He unknowingly triggers Wil-

etta's critical evaluation of the production by demanding that she find a sense of integrity about her work. Although he considers himself to be a liberal, he treats black and white cast members differently and is insensitive to the objections the black members have concerning the script. As the racial strife becomes more intense, he exposes his own deep-rooted racial biases.

John Nevins, a novice actor. He is an African American college graduate aspiring to rise to the top of his profession. Although he believes his formal training and performances in Off-Broadway plays to be superior to Wiletta's experience, he condescendingly listens to her advice out of deference to her age and her acquaintance with his mother. As the conflict between Wiletta and the director heightens, he becomes embarrassed by her, viewing her as too racially sensitive and ignorant of contemporary acting methods. Aligning himself with the director and the white cast members, he attempts to appease Wiletta without fully considering the validity of her complaints.

Millie Davis, a veteran actor. She is a well-dressed thirty-five-year-old African American woman. Like Wiletta, she has spent her career performing black stock characters, and she readily voices her dissatisfaction concerning dialogue and actions that demean black people. Unlike Wiletta, she stops short of pursuing her objections with the director even when he chooses to ignore her opinions or provides a patronizing response. She is willing to sacrifice her dignity for the job she needs.

Sheldon Forrester, a veteran actor. An elderly, poorly educated black man, he embodies the Uncle Tom stereotype. He fawns on the director and criticizes Wiletta for disrupting rehearsals with her racial complaints. He has held such an obsequious posture for so long that he is numb to the indigni-

ties he and other African Americans suffer in the profession. He may be more than he appears; he may be only playing a role that pleases white people as a means of survival.

Judith (Judy) Sears, a novice actor. She is a young, energetic white woman of a privileged background. Thrilled to be in her first professional production since her training at Yale, she is eager to please the director. A liberal, she becomes uncomfortable with some of her dialogue, which uses offensive terms in reference to African Americans. She befriends John, to the dismay of the director and several black cast members.

Bill O'Wray, an old white character actor, the only cast member who has steady work. He insists that he is not prejudiced but is reluctant to have lunch with the black actors. At best he is insensitive, and at worst he is a bigot.

— *Addell Austin*

TROUBLES

Author: J. G. Farrell (1935-1979)
First published: 1970
Genre: Novel

Locale: Ireland
Time: 1919-1921
Plot: Comic realism

Major Brendan Archer, the protagonist, a shy, well-bred British major who witnesses the fall of the British empire in Ireland at first hand. Tired, disoriented, and shell-shocked, Archer goes to Kilnalough to investigate his uncertain engagement to Angela. As he patiently awaits some personal response from her, he becomes fascinated by the uncertainty, decay, and general Irishness of her surroundings, and he experiences the frustrations and lunacies of Anglo-Irish life and the troubles that provide the satiric edge of the book. Valuing propriety, reason, and detachment, he is amazed at the eccentricity and the vulgar excesses of the Anglo-Irish. As he seeks to bring order to the chaos about him, he gradually takes on hotel responsibilities. He provides a liberal outsider's view on the viciousness of reprisals and a pro-Irish perspective in debates with his host. Except for occasional rather vague sexual fantasies, he is brusque, judicious, and responsible: a peacemaker. For his trouble, the Sinn Féin bury him neck-high in sand to let him drown with the tide. Only rescue by the small, elderly ladies of the Majestic Hotel allows him to flee Ireland with his life and with the only reward for his efforts: the hotel's much-abused statue of Venus.

Angela Spencer, Archer's Anglo-Irish fiancée. A straightforward mine of trivial gossip in letters, Angela is a remote, untouchable model of decorum in person. She finessed a slight acquaintance with Major Archer into an engagement, and her detailed letters provide a graspable reality at odds with the confusion left by the war. She soon disappears into her room, however, only to exit in a coffin, having slowly succumbed to leukemia. Her deathbed letter is as long-winded and embarrassing as her personal presence. It is her tenuous relationship with Archer that motivates his observations on the Anglo-Irish troubles.

Edward Spencer, Angela's eccentric and volatile father, the owner of the Majestic Hotel. He is "a fierce man in flannels" with a stiff, craggy face, rugged brow, and clipped mustache, along with a broken nose and flattened ears that testify to his career as a boxer. The stony set to his jaw suggests his

hot temper as he fights—with impatience, irascibility, and resignation—a losing battle against decay. A sportsman and dog lover, at times he is overbearing, opinionated, and tyrannical, at times weak and sentimental. He provides an Anglo-Irish view of the reprisals, of mixed marriages (religion and race), and of the Irish (a subhuman and superstitious rabble composed of criminals and fanatics). His hate-filled desire to avenge the English loss of Ireland leads him purposely to shoot a Sinn Féiner for tampering with his provocatively displayed statue of Queen Victoria. He is Archer's opposite, his rival for Sarah, and his burden.

Ripon Spencer, Angela's roguish brother. Compelled by his glands rather than his mind, Ripon is a lazy, ill-mannered bumpkin who spends his days tossing jackknives and romancing village women. He finally elopes with the chubby but winsome Maire, the Roman Catholic daughter of the wealthiest man in Kilnalough, to the consternation of both families.

Sarah Devlin, a temperamental Roman Catholic flirt. Charming and cruel, she becomes the second unattainable object of Archer's affection, not only because of her youth, her gray eyes, and her attractive sunburn but also because of her sharp-tongued, aggressively Irish wiles. She is catty, rude, self-pitying, and self-deprecating, yet men continue to pay her court, even before she jettisons her wheelchair. Her biting letters of local life and her London visit lure Archer back to Ireland, while the smitten Edward Spencer pays her medical bills. She spurns them both for a brutish British soldier who scorns her race and beats her regularly. Her scandalous behavior and shocking comments suggest the irrationality of the love/hate relationship between the British and the Irish.

Evans, a prototype of Irish rage, the venomous tutor to Spencer's two frolicsome and mischievous daughters, Faith and Charity. Evans nurses his explosive sense of outrage and injustice. Belligerent and aggressive, he deals the grandmother's attacking cat a crippling blow and then, in an ecstasy of violence and with a "savage rictus in his white pocked face," hurls it against the wall. Later, at the Majestic's final ball, he displays open antipathy for guests and hosts alike.

Murphy, a prototype of Irish deceit, the sullen, two-faced, aged hotel butler. His face is wrinkled and wizened, with his few teeth discolored. Murphy hides his mad hatred of anything English and his malevolent joy at English suffering behind a façade of loyal subservience. Despite his long years of service, he abuses the defenseless and chuckles at their discomfort. Ultimately, he ignites the hotel, its multitude of cats, and himself in an orgy of hate.

— *Gina Macdonald*

TROUT FISHING IN AMERICA

Author: Richard Brautigan (1935-1984)
First published: 1967
Genre: Novel

Locale: San Francisco, California; various trout streams; and elsewhere in the Northwest
Time: Fall, 1960, through fall, 1961, with flashbacks
Plot: Picaresque

The narrator, who is unnamed though possibly identified with the author, because he is a writer and has had similar life experiences; that is, he had a fatherless, rather lonely childhood, living in poverty with his mother first in Great Falls, Montana, then later in Portland, Oregon, and Tacoma, Washington. In his late teens, he moves to San Francisco, which becomes the center of his life as a writer. A more spiritual element is provided by certain trout streams and lakes in the mountains to the north and east, such as Grider Creek, Graveyard Creek, Paradise Creek, Lake Josephus, and Hell-Diver Lake. The narrator tends to describe the people and settings in his brief collection of sketches with an inventive, sometimes even magical poetic surrealism. For example, the narrator recalls having seen, as a child, a distant, beautiful waterfall. As he draws closer to it, however, he sees that his vision was only a flight of white wooden stairs leading into some trees. Such disillusionment is an important element in the narrator's worldview. He continually seeks escape from reality yet retains the integrity to be able to admit to doing so.

The narrator's wife, who is unnamed but usually referred to as "my woman" or "the woman I live with." She corresponds to the author's wife of this period (that is, his first wife), Virginia "Ginny" Adler. Little of the woman's personality is revealed. Her role is simply to cook, have sexual intercourse, conceive and bear a child, and tend it as it grows. Once, the narrator and his wife have sexual intercourse in the warm water of Worsewick Hot Springs, in the midst of green slime and dead fish. This is a typical juxtaposition by the narrator of the beautiful and the profane (or of life and death).

The narrator's daughter, an unnamed child called only "the baby." She corresponds to the author's daughter, Ianthe, born in 1960. The child, as she grows older, affords a perception of the passage of time.

Trout Fishing in America, a personification that talks and writes but has no corporeal existence. The figure sometimes evokes the distant past, such as the time of the American Revolution, or the day that Meriwether Lewis discovered Great Falls. It acts on the whole as a positive or even romantic vision of America.

Trout Fishing in America Shorty, a legless wino in San Francisco who demands even of strangers that they push him everywhere in his wheelchair. Once, he falls face first, drunk, right out of his chair. The narrator and his acquaintances decide to mail him to Nelson Algren, in honor of the latter's character "Railroad Shorty." He disappears, however, before they can get around to doing this.

Statue of Benjamin Franklin, a statue in Washington Square, San Francisco. This statue is mentioned frequently throughout the book, beginning in the first chapter, in which it is the central figure. In addition, it is an important feature of the cover photograph. It is presented as a symbol of welcome. Beatniks and hippies sit before it and drink port wine.

— *Donald M. Fiene*

TRUE GRIT

Author: Charles Portis (1933-   )
First published: 1968
Genre: Novel

Locale: Arkansas and the Indian Territory
Time: Late 1870's
Plot: Adventure

Mattie Ross, the narrator-protagonist, a fourteen-year-old girl who has been an adult since birth. Mattie is narrating the story fifty years after her grand adventure. She has never married. Her most intimate contact with a man has been her warm, but chaste, relationship with Rooster Cogburn, the grizzled lawman whom she hired to catch her father's killer. Mattie is proud, rigid, and self-righteous. She can also be imperious. More important, however, she is bright, resourceful, tenacious, loyal, and exceedingly brave.

Reuben J. "Rooster" Cogburn, a U.S. deputy marshal for the western district of Arkansas. He has a questionable past, having fought as a guerrilla rather than as a regular soldier during the Civil War. He is approaching middle age, has lost an eye, has grown fat, and drinks too much. Mattie needs a man with grit, however, to run down her father's murderer. Cogburn appears to possess that commodity in abundance, as he has killed twenty-three men in the past four years.

LaBoeuf (lah-BOOF), a Texas Ranger on detached service, seeking the same quarry as Mattie and Rooster. The fugitive, known by another name in Texas, has killed a state senator in Waco. The senator's family has hired LaBoeuf to find the killer and bring him to justice. Mattie, both as a woman and as an Arkansan, immediately develops a strong prejudice against the swaggering Texan; she finds him flashy, conceited, and condescending.

Tom Chaney, the murderer of Mattie's father, Frank Ross, and (under his original name of Theron Chelmsford) of at least one other man in Texas. After killing Ross in Fort Smith, Chaney flees across the Arkansas River into the Indian Terri- tory. There, he joins Lucky Ned Pepper's band of desperadoes, with whom Mattie, Rooster, and LaBoeuf eventually have a thrilling confrontation.

A TRUE HISTORY
(Alēthōn diēgēmatōn)

Author: Lucian (c. 120-after 180)
First transcribed: The second century
Genre: Short fiction

Locale: The universe
Time: The second century
Plot: Satire

Lucian, the author and narrator, who says in the introduc- tion that readers should not believe a word of what follows. He is going to make fun of historians and travel writers who tell fantastic tales about exotic places and unbelievable peoples and creatures. He then becomes the narrator of his own fantas- tic story and strives to convince readers that he is telling the truth. He reports events and details in a matter-of-fact manner, presenting himself as a curious yet rational observer. The narrator is a typical Greek intellectual: He wants to discover the unknown and to understand it. He is well versed in Homer and the literary tradition, and he has more than a passing interest in philosophy. Although occasionally vulnerable to fear and feelings of homesickness, he is resolved to continue his journey to the continent on the other side of the ocean, and beyond. Lucian is also a reincarnation of Odysseus: His voy- age is a process of discovery and self-knowledge. The rela- tionship between Lucian the author and Lucian the narrator is like that between Homer and Odysseus; in each case, the storyteller manages to outdo the author in imagination and fabrication.

Endymion (ehn-DIH-mee-ehn), the King of the Moon, a human being who, as a handsome young shepherd, was car- ried off while asleep by the moon goddess, Selene. She gave him eternal sleep. He is hospitable and kind to the travelers. Endymion has been at war with his rival Phaethon ever since Phaethon tried to thwart Endymion's attempt to colonize the Morning Star. In the battle, Endymion's army is initially victo- rious but is unexpectedly routed at the last minute. Endymion agrees to a peace treaty that gives Phaethon equal participation in the colonization. The King of the Moon is eager to get the travelers to stay with him, even offering Lucian his own son in marriage. When Lucian insists that they must return to the sea, he sends them off with an escort and gifts of tunics and armor. Endymion represents the immortal soul, in accordance with the belief that the moon was a resting place for souls on their way to reincarnation.

Phaethon (FAY-eh-tehn), the King of the Sun, a more shad- owy figure than Endymion, described only in secondhand reports. He is the son of Helios, the Sun god, and is depicted in mythology as an impetuous youth. In this story, he is a skilled general, clever enough to defeat Endymion by building a wall of clouds that cuts off the sunlight from the moon. Phaethon probably represents the light of knowledge, which the Greeks frequently symbolized as the sun. Phaethon and Endymion represent opposing positions in philosophical arguments: The battle of the solar and lunar forces is, on one level, a satirical depiction of the contentious disputes between different philo- sophical schools.

Scintharus, an old man whom the travelers encounter in the belly of a whale. He escapes with Lucian and his friends and becomes their new helmsman. Scintharus is a resourceful man and apparently is a good soldier. He has a son, Cinyras, who carries off Helen from the Isle of the Blessed: They are in love with each other. Scintharus is bald, but he magically acquires long hair after the encounter with the giant kingfisher in the second book. His name may be connected with Spin- tharos, one of Socrates' disciples. He represents the type of the "wise old man"—like Homer's Nestor—or the spiritual guide.

— *David H. J. Larmour*

THE TRUE STORY OF AH Q
(Ah Q cheng-chuan)

Author: Lu Hsün (Chou Shu-jên, 1881-1936)
First published: 1923; serial form, 1921
Genre: Novel

Locale: Wei, a village in China
Time: Early 1900's
Plot: Satire

Ah Q, an impoverished, homeless man in his late twenties who loafs around the village where he lives and earns his living by working at various odd jobs. Lean and weak, he has a bald spot on his head, a physical blemish caused by scabies that often makes him the butt of jokes among the people of the village of Wei. Whenever he suffers humiliation, however, he is always able to find solace and even triumph through his imagination. He leads a relatively quiet, though obscure and insignificant, life in the countryside until one day when the entire village rejects him as a result of his proposition to a maidservant, Wu Ma. Because of this incident, people avoid him and refuse to give him any work. To continue his liveli- hood, he leaves for the city. After returning to the village, he is later falsely accused of robbery and eventually is executed.

Chao T'ai-yeh, an influential country squire. Somewhat educated and in middle age, he is greedy and unkind, espe- cially in his treatment of Ah Q, whom he sometimes employs for odd jobs. When the revolution of 1911 breaks out, he safeguards the money of Pai Chü-jen, a gentleman from the city. In the end, some people break into Chao's house and steal

Pai's money. Chao has to pay a small fortune to the local official to clear his name so as to avoid being accused by Pai of swindling his money.

Pai Chü-jen, a well-educated man of the gentry class living in the city. After leaving the village of Wei, Ah Q serves in his house for a short period of time. Because of his uncertainty about the revolution, Pai sends some of his property to the Chao family for safekeeping when the revolutionaries enter the city. He becomes a high official in the city shortly after the revolution. To his chagrin, his property safeguarded by the Chao family is never retrieved.

Ch'ien Shao-yeh, also known as the **Imitation Foreign Devil**, a son of a gentry family in the village of Wei. Because of the loss of his queue while pursuing his studies away from home, he wears a false queue after his return to the village. Different from the other villagers, he studies in Western schools, first in a neighboring city, then later in Japan. His Western education causes him to support the revolution, in the name of which he, along with Chao T'ai-yeh's son, steals an antique incense burner from a Buddhist temple. When Ah Q expresses his interest in becoming a revolutionary, Ch'ien rudely rejects him.

Chao Mao-ts'ai, the son of the country squire, Chao T'ai-yeh. He beats Ah Q and chases him away after Ah Q proposes to sleep with Wu Ma. Later in the story, he becomes a revolu-

tionary and, along with Ch'ien Shao-yeh, steals an antique incense burner from a local Buddhist temple in the name of the revolution.

Wu Ma, also called **Amah Wu** in some translations, the maidservant for the Chao family. She reacts violently to Ah Q's proposition and tries to hang herself to prove her chastity as a widow. On the day of Ah Q's execution, she appears in the watching crowd.

Ti Pao, the local policeman, who takes advantage of Ah Q's misfortunes by extorting money from him.

Hsiao Niku, a nun in the local Buddhist temple. Young and docile, she is the only one whom Ah Q can insult without fear of retaliation. Ironically, after maliciously pinching her face in public, Ah Q becomes conscious of his sexual desires, which lead to his proposition to Wu Ma.

Wang Lai-hu, another impoverished, homeless man of Ah Q's class, characterized by a full beard and scabs also caused by scabies. He insults Ah Q at the beginning of the story. After Ah Q returns from the city to the village of Wei, Wang regards him with awe because of his experience of living in the city.

Pa Tsong, the commander of the local troops, who has Ah Q arrested and eventually executed as a scapegoat for the theft of Pai's property.

— *Vincent Yang*

TRUE WEST

Author: Sam Shepard (Samuel Shepard Rogers, 1943-   )
First published: 1981
Genre: Drama

Locale: A suburb forty miles east of Los Angeles
Time: The 1980's
Plot: Psychological

Austin, a self-deprecating but aspiring screenwriter in his early thirties. Somewhat romantic, he works by candlelight in his vacationing mother's house, creating a "simple love story" to complete a film deal with producer Saul Kimmer, toward whom he is respectful and sycophantic. Conventionally educated at an Ivy League college, Austin inhabits a neat world constructed of middle-class values of rationality, self-discipline, and hard work. This world is threatened by the arrival of his brother Lee, the object of Austin's sibling envy and repressed hostility. As Lee insinuates himself into Austin's territory, Austin becomes increasingly insecure. Adopting Lee's behavior, speech, and profession in a complete character transformation, he abandons his film project and becomes roaring drunk, thereby unleashing an inventiveness previously stifled by his intellectuality. With a burst of bravado, he steals every toaster in the neighborhood in an attempt to outperform Lee's nefarious activities. Now uncertain of his identity and believing himself unable to exist in modern society, he bargains to return to the desert with Lee. When Lee reneges on the promise, Austin's civilized veneer shatters, exposing a murderous violence beneath.

Lee, Austin's menacing older brother. He is in his forties and scruffily dressed. He has just returned from several months of nomadic existence in the desert with only a pit bull dog for company. Austin's opposite, he is a natural man, lacking education and goals. Lee is without visible morality or scruples (except in the matter of their absent father), but his behavior reveals a jealousy of his brother's lifestyle; he sys-

tematically usurps Austin's time, space, and identity. He is not without insight, and he possesses an imagination unfettered by education, but he lacks discipline and cannot tolerate frustration. What he wants he takes, whether it be a neighbor's television set, Austin's car, or, ultimately, Austin's work, as he gambles with Saul Kimmer for the acceptance of his scenario in preference to his brother's. When he discovers that he lacks the skills necessary to transform his imaginative ideas into art, or his lifestyle into one of legitimacy, he becomes destructive.

Saul Kimmer, a Hollywood producer in his late forties. Shallow and superficial, dressed in loud flowered shirts and polyester pants, he is a caricature of the Hollywood parasite who, lacking talent himself, survives by marketing the talents of others. His amorality matches Lee's; he is seduced by Lee's manipulations and rejects Austin's script without a qualm. Lee's insistence on calling him "Mr. Kipper" labels him accurately as a cold fish.

Mom, a woman in her sixties, the mother of the two brothers. Mom is characterized by Lee as not liking "even a single tea leaf in her sink," but she is strangely indifferent to the destruction of her home and plants when she returns suddenly in the last scene from her vacation in Alaska. More concerned about what she has interpreted as a visit of Picasso to the local museum than about the primal contest occurring before her eyes, she seems unable to grasp the fact that Picasso is dead, and she is blind to her sons' hatred, thus displaying an inability to distinguish life from art.

— *Joyce E. Henry*

THE TRUTH SUSPECTED
(La verdad sospechosa)

Author: Juan Ruiz de Alarcón (1581-1639)
First published: 1630
Genre: Drama

Locale: Madrid
Time: The seventeenth century
Plot: Comedy

Don García (gahr-SEE-ah), a young noble. A congenital liar, he is himself faced by a confusion of facts as he woos the veiled Jacinta, thinking that her name is Lucrecia. The lies that he tells during the courtship constantly involve him in difficulty. Enraged by his lies, Don Beltrán arranges for his son's marriage to Jacinta, but Don García invents a wife in Salamanca to avoid marrying Jacinta, little realizing that she is the girl he is wooing. His lie is discovered too late, and a rival marries Jacinta. Don García must be content with Lucrecia.

Juan de Sosa (hwahn deh SOH-sah), who is in love with Jacinta. Rejected by her uncle until he attains knighthood, Juan must stand by while Don García courts his lady. Juan challenges Don García to a duel because of one of his lies and later reveals that his rival has lied about the supposed wife in

Salamanca. Finally, Juan becomes a knight and marries Jacinta, much to Don García's chagrin.

Don Beltrán (behl-TRAHN), Don García's father, who despises lying.

Tristán (trees-TAHN), Don García's shrewd and cynical servant, who gives his master lectures about lying peppered with quotations from Roman and Greek authorities.

Jacinta (hah-SEEN-tah), the niece of Don Sancho, thought by Don García to be Lucrecia.

Lucrecia (lew-KREH-see-ah), her friend, who later marries Don García.

Don Sancho (SAHN-choh), Jacinta's uncle, who forbids her to marry Juan de Sosa until that young man attains knighthood.

TUBBY SCHAUMANN: A Tale of Murder and the High Seas
(Stopfkuchen: Eine See- und Mordgeschichte)

Author: Wilhelm Raabe (1831-1910)
First published: 1891
Genre: Novel

Locale: A town in Germany and a farm overlooking the town
Time: Probably the 1880's
Plot: Social realism

Heinrich "Tubby" Schaumann (HIN-rihk SHOW-mahn), the owner of Red Bank Farm after his father-in-law's death. As a boy, he was very overweight and a slow student, and therefore subject to ridicule. He comes to be called Tubby by the local townspeople. His dream is to live at Red Bank Farm, which he views as a kind of refuge from the cruelty of the world outside. Because he understands the feelings of an outcast, he is able to befriend young, lonely Valentina and her bitter father. Although he tries to please his parents by going away to school, Schaumann is not suited for that venture. Instead, he finds his true place and a philosophy of peaceful acceptance of his life by marrying Valentina and taking over Red Bank Farm. From this safe haven, he wants to take in the whole of human experience: His fossil hunting represents his look at history in all its depth, and his outsider position gives him a wider perspective on the community. At the end of the story, his capacity for forgiveness and humane understanding allows him to wait until after Störzer's death to reveal that man's identity as the true murderer of Kienbaum.

Edward, a boyhood friend of Schaumann and narrator of the story. Although he was Schaumann's closest friend at school, he, too, was often involved in the cruel taunting that the boys aimed at Schaumann. A man who desired travel and adventure, Edward has made his fortune and settled in South Africa. Returning to his boyhood town, he visits his old friend Tubby and comes to admire and appreciate him.

Andreas Quakatz (KVAY-kats), the owner of Red Bank Farm. He is falsely blamed for the murder of Kienbaum. At first a bitter old man, he is helped by Schaumann to become

somewhat reconciled to the unfair situation that made him an outcast. He dies without seeing his name cleared.

Valentina, the daughter of Andreas Quakatz and later Schaumann's wife. As a child, she often bears the brunt of her father's bitter anger against the community. Finding love and compassion in Schaumann, she blossoms into a loving, compassionate woman herself, in spite of her difficult childhood. Her care and devotion to Schaumann make Red Bank Farm a true refuge for them both.

Friedrich (Fritz) Störzer (FREE-drihk STEHR-tsehr), a country postman who often told young Edward stories about exotic places. A mild-mannered worker who never missed a day's work during thirty-one years of service, he is tormented by Kienbaum, until one day he accidentally kills him. Afraid to confess even after Quakatz is unjustly accused, he carries a burden of guilt with him until his death.

Kienbaum (KEEN-bowm), a prosperous livestock dealer and bully who constantly mocked and tormented Störzer on his mail route. His death brings the community to label Quakatz a murderer.

Meta (MAY-tah), the barmaid who listens to Schaumann's story about how Störzer happened to kill Kienbaum and then spreads the information to the community, as Schaumann had intended.

Schoolmaster Blechhammer (BLEHKH-hahm-mehr), who is a leading part of the cruel, judgmental force of the community that mocks Schaumann for personal characteristics outside the societal norm and that judges Quakatz guilty without sufficient evidence, using rumor to make him an outcast.

— *Susan L. Piepke*

TUNG-CHOU LIEH-KUO CHIH
(Hsin lieh-kuo chih)

Author: Fêng Mêng-lung (1574?-1645?)
First published: After 1627
Genre: Novel

Locale: China
Time: 770-220 B.C.E.
Plot: Historical

King Yu of Chou, a cruel and foolish man. He is ungrateful and impassive, as well as unscrupulous in political intrigue. He spends much of his time eating, drinking, and engaging in lechery. Ignoring the difference between a wife and a concubine, he degrades his consort and elevates his favorite concubine, Pao-ssu. He attempts to make her child his heir and sends another of his sons, the heir apparent, into exile. His foolish effort to amuse his concubine by tricking his vassals with misleading signal fires results in his death and the downfall of his regime.

Kuan Chong, or **Kuan I-wu**, a master archer, philosopher, and outstanding statesman who becomes prime minister under Duke Huan of Ch'i. He is a close friend of Pao Shu-ya, who recommends him to the duke. He becomes a model of the later idealization of the Chinese ministry.

Duke Huan of Ch'i, originally named **Hsiao-po**, the first forceful leader to emerge in China during the Ch'un-ch'iu period. He and his brother Chiu are sons of Duke Hsi by concubines, and they contend the succession between themselves, with Hsiao-po winning. He appoints Kuan as prime minister on Pao Shu-ya's advice even though Kuan tried to assassinate him.

Duke Hsiang of Sung, an ambitious man with a delusional concept of reality. He attempts unsuccessfully to bring various princes together in a covenant respecting him as leader. He loses a battle with the army of Ch'u State because he refuses to take the advice of his minister of war regarding tactics; he believes that the minister's tactics violate Confucian principles of love and duty.

Duke Wên of Chin, originally named **Ch'uang-êrh**, a fugitive for nineteen years after he declines to take a dukedom because he considers the terms dishonorable. He performs a service for a duke and is himself confirmed a duke by imperial decree. He tries to smoke an old friend out of a forest by setting fire to it and inadvertently burns his friend to death.

Po-li Hsi, a native of Yü State. He becomes prime minister in the Ch'in court under Duke Mu.

Duke Mu of Ch'in, a feudal ruler. His fame rests on subjugation of the Jung barbarians who live along the border of China.

King Chuang of Ch'u, the aggressive but conciliatory brother of King Ting of the Chou line. He invades Chêng repeatedly and defeats the Chin State in the Battle of Pi in 597 B.C.E.

Wu Tzu-hsü, also known as **Wu Yüan**, a native of Ch'u. His father and brother are executed by Prince P'ing, and he flees to Wu State, where he becomes a general.

Prince Shên Pao-hsü of Ch'u, the grandson of ruler Prince Liao. He helps Wu Yüan avenge his relatives' deaths at the hands of Prince P'ing.

Prince Kung-tzu Kuang of Lu, an unscrupulous and ambitious man who hires Chuang Chu to assassinate his sovereign, Prince Liao. After the assassination, he takes the throne under the title of **Prince Ho-lu**.

Kung Fu-tzu, also known as **Kung Chiu** and **Confucius** (the Latinized form of his name), a government official whose principles clash with the behavior of the ruling class. He goes into exile for thirteen years, teaching and acquiring disciples.

King Kou Chien of Yüeh, who is at first immature but who acquires maturity through experience and spiritual self-training. He attacks Wu State unsuccessfully, failing to heed the advice of his minister. He later gets his revenge by having an ambassador send a concubine to the ruler of Wu State. She so distracts the ruler that he neglects his duties, allowing Kou Chien to conquer Wu State.

Ho Po, Count of the Yellow River, a deity depicted as having a man's head and torso but the tail of a fish. The river is important to commerce and to many people's livelihoods, so Ho Po is worshiped.

Wei Yang, also known as **Shang Yang** and whose real name is **Kung-sun Yang**, a statesman. His talents go unrewarded in Wei State, so he becomes a minister for Duke Hsiao of Ch'in State. He executes reforms in law, military affairs, agriculture, taxation, and family life. He helps to combine the forces of Han and Ch'i to defeat Wei State.

Sun Pin, also known as **Sun Tzu** or **Sun Wu**, a native of Ch'i State and a professional soldier, one of the world's greatest military strategists. He plans two major victories over Wei State.

Su Ch'in, who at first is a political failure but who later conceives the idea of forming a federation of Chinese states.

King Nan of Chou, the last true Chou ruler. His reign is characterized by warfare among the feudal states. He seeks to unite the states in league against Ch'in. In response, the Duke of Ch'in invades Chou, forcing Nan to surrender most of his land, his army, and himself. Nan is freed but dies soon afterward.

Ching K'o, an adventurer and hired assassin who is killed in an attempt to kill Prince Chêng.

Shih Huang-ti, ruler of Ch'in State for twenty-five years and of all of China for twelve years. He abolishes nobility of birth, substituting nobility based on gifts and services. He creates the Great Wall by unifying defensive barriers.

— *Richard P. Benton*

TURCARET

Author: Alain-René Lesage (1668-1747)
First published: 1709
Genre: Drama

Locale: Paris, France
Time: The seventeenth century
Plot: Social

Frontin (froh[n]-TA[N]), the knight's valet, later M. Turcaret's valet. A master of fraud, he ably shows that he is better at trickery than his masters. Replacing M. Turcaret's valet, he keeps funds flowing from the financier to the baroness, from her to his knight, and secretly from the knight to himself. By the end of the play, Frontin has accumulated enough money for Lisette to marry him.

M. Turcaret (tewr-kah-RAY), a duped financier who is in love with the baroness, a charming widow. Deeply enamored, he lavishes gifts on her, little realizing that she is passing on his funds. He is dropped by the coquette shortly before he is arrested for a pay-officer's default of two hundred thousand crowns.

The baroness, a young widow and a coquette. Madly in love with the knight, she is duped as she herself has duped M. Turcaret. Sensing M. Turcaret's fiscal embroilments, she lets him go only to cast off the parasitic knight when she discovers his duplicity.

The knight, a coxcomb who loves the baroness only for the crowns she can get from gullible M. Turcaret.

Marine (mah-REEN) and

Lisette (lee-ZEHT), the baroness' maids. Annoyed by her mistress' gullibility, Marine leaves her post and is replaced by Lisette, who aids Frontin in keeping funds flowing to the knight.

Mme Turcaret, the financier's estranged wife.

The marquess, her coxcomb.

Mme Jacob (zhah-KOHB), M. Turcaret's sister, a dealer in toilette necessaries.

Flammand (flah-MAH[N]), M. Turcaret's first valet.

THE TURN OF THE SCREW

Author: Henry James (1843-1916)
First published: 1898
Genre: Novella

Locale: England
Time: Mid-nineteenth century
Plot: Ghost

The governess, from whose point of view the story is told. Employed to look after his orphaned niece and nephew by a man who makes it clear that he does not wish to be bothered about them, she finds herself engaged in a struggle against evil apparitions for the souls of the children. There has been a good deal of the "Is-Hamlet-mad?" sort of inconclusive speculation as to whether *The Turn of the Screw* is a real ghost story or a study of a neurotic and frustrated woman. Probably both interpretations are true: The apparitions are real, the children are indeed possessed by evil, and the governess is probably neurotic.

Miles, a little boy, one of the governess' charges. At first, he seems to be a remarkably good child, but gradually she learns that he has been mysteriously corrupted by his former governess and his uncle's former valet, whose ghosts maintain their evil control. Miles dies in the governess' arms during her final struggle to save him from some mysterious evil.

Flora, Miles's sister and feminine counterpart. The governess finally sends her away to her uncle.

Miss Jessel, the former governess, now dead. She appears frequently to the governess and to the children, who refuse to admit the appearances.

Peter Quint, the uncle's former valet, now dead. Drunken and vicious, he was also Miss Jessel's lover. The governess sees his apparition repeatedly.

Mrs. Grose, the housekeeper of the country estate where the story is set. Good-hearted and talkative, she is the source of what little concrete information the governess and the reader get as to the identities and past histories of the evil apparitions. Allied with the governess against the influence of Peter Quint and Miss Jessel, she takes charge of Flora when the child is sent to her uncle.

TURTLE MOON

Author: Alice Hoffman (1952-   )
First published: 1992
Genre: Novel

Locale: Verity, Florida, and Great Neck, New York
Time: The 1980's
Plot: Detective and mystery

Lucy Rosen, a divorced woman in her late thirties, the mother of Keith and neighbor of Bethany Lee. Lucy's parents died when she was a teenager, and she lived with relatives in Great Neck, New York, where she became a successful, popular student. After divorcing her high school sweetheart, she moved to Verity, where she writes obituaries for the local newspaper. Her primary concern is her son Keith's increasingly delinquent behavior. She loves him intensely but does not understand him and cannot communicate with him. When Keith disappears with Bethany's baby after Bethany is murdered, Lucy joins Julian Cash in the investigation.

Julian Cash, a police detective who trains and owns tracking dogs. Although he grew up in Verity, he maintains a distance from others in the community. Abandoned as an infant,

Julian later established a close friendship with his cousin, Bobby. When he was seventeen, Julian's car crashed into a tree, killing Bobby. His guilt over this incident still haunts him, and he cannot come to terms with his own past. Julian's closest relationships are with his two dogs, Loretta and Arrow, and with Miss Giles, the woman who reared him. He takes Loretta with him everywhere, but Arrow is too wild to be let out of his pen except when his talent at sniffing out dead bodies is needed.

Keith Rosen, who is referred to as "the meanest boy in Verity." As he enters adolescence, Keith is angry and confused. He has started skipping school, drinking, and committing petty crimes. He dislikes Verity intensely and wants to return to Great Neck to live with his father. Despite his rebellious attitude, Keith establishes close connections with Bethany's baby and with Julian's dog, Arrow.

Bethany Lee, Lucy's neighbor. She has moved to Verity and taken on a false identity to escape her former husband, Randy, who wants to claim custody of their daughter. Her murder initiates the central plot of the novel.

The Angel, the ghost of Julian's cousin, Bobby. In part because Julian has never returned to the scene of the fatal crash, Bobby has never been able to forgive his cousin, and he remains waiting in the small area around the tree into which they crashed.

— *Sherry Lee Linkon*

TURVEY: A Military Picaresque

Author: Earle Birney (1904-1995)
First published: 1949; revised, 1976
Genre: Novel

Locale: Canada, England, Belgium, and Holland
Time: 1942-1945
Plot: Satire

Thomas Leadbeater "Tops" Turvey, the somewhat befuddled, persistently cheerful hero of this satire of Canadian military life. He is backward and painfully lacking in sophistication. He was born in Shookum Falls, British Columbia, on May 13, 1922, went to school only through the ninth grade, and has an employment record that leads nowhere (cucumber pickler, worker in a hat factory, popsicle coater, assistant flavor manager in a candy factory, and oiler in a mosquito-control gang). Lured by a spirit of adventure, he desires to become a soldier. His first attempts to enlist in the army and in the air force are unsuccessful. When the national need for manpower increases with the outbreak of war, he is finally inducted. The character of this army seems clear: If it can take Turvey, it will take anyone. Turvey hopes to fight in a good regiment, specifically the Kootenay Highlanders, in which his best friend, Gillis MacGillicuddy, serves. This determination propels him through a series of situations in which his incompetence and bumbling depict the military and its leaders in an increasingly nonsensical light. Turvey's army jobs are just as dead-end as those in civilian life. His routine infraction of rules and petty lawbreaking earn for him constant company punishment. He is a Parsifal, incapable of understanding any world that does not coincide with his own. An eternal bumpkin, he is readily gulled by others, most of these more misguided than himself, to whom he looks for guidance and leadership. Thus, he is court-martialed for being absent without leave because he impulsively follows a friend to Buffalo to spend the Christmas holidays with two women. He is sentenced to forty-five days detention, but this, as with the punishment he receives from further escapades, is not sufficiently onerous to destroy his good humor. Other characters in the book serve to set the stage for Turvey's purposeless, live-for-the-moment existence. Only when his best friend, Mac, is killed does Turvey begin to realize that only through his own efforts can he bring order to his life and achieve resolution.

Gillis MacGillis "Mac" MacGillicuddy, Turvey's best friend and object of his quest. He runs into Turvey by chance in St. James Park in London. Mac is a con artist who affects an upper-class accent to twist the Canadian army's confused social and hierarchical system to his advantage. Thus, through

his wits and a little chicanery (he cheats on the officer candidate examination), he successfully rises from an enlisted man to a lieutenant. As such, he arranges Turvey's transfer to him as his batman and jeep driver. Mac fulfills Turvey's idea of success, a factotum and operator who can challenge the system and win. War is difficult to control, however, and Mac is killed by artillery fire.

Peggy, Turvey's girlfriend and, later, fiancée, introduced to him by Mac. She is a plump and charming young woman who makes Turvey feel like a man of romance and adventure. Their courtship seems a product of the same nonchalance that characterizes most of Turvey's associations. A letter that she writes to Turvey—reaching him three months late for Christmas (when he is a patient in a military hospital in England)—brings them more closely together. Peggy, a force for order and common sense, characteristically tells Turvey that she cares about him by reminding him to change his socks when they get wet. Ensuing visits lead to a promise of marriage, which implies that Peggy will become a steadying influence in Turvey's life, helping him to end the nutty confusion and chaos that heretofore had bedeviled his existence.

Horatio Ballard, a private with the complexion of a celery root, strikingly adept at wheeling and dealing. He induces Turvey to take off to Buffalo, which leads to the charge of being absent without leave. Later, in England, the irresponsible Ballard takes Turvey on another escapade on a stolen motorcycle, and Turvey is arrested again.

Sanderson, the alcoholic lieutenant charged with defending Turvey on the charge of being absent without leave. He does so in a drunken stupor.

Archibald McQua, a gloomy New Brunswicker who leads Turvey into a field full of land mines.

Captain Airdale, a shy army psychiatrist who believes that the best way of diagnosing personality is through word association tests. He is aroused by suggestive words. He says that Turvey is suffering from temporary hysteria with a possible latent father-rivalry: Turvey had machine-gunned his own overcoat because it looked like a German paratrooper.

— *Wm. Laird Kleine-Ahlbrandt*

TWELFTH NIGHT: Or, What You Will

Author: William Shakespeare (1564-1616)
First published: 1623
Genre: Drama

Locale: Illyria, a region on the east shore of the Adriatic Sea
Time: The sixteenth century
Plot: Comedy

Viola (VEE-oh-luh), who, with her twin brother Sebastian, is shipwrecked on the coast of Illyria. The twins are separated, and a friendly sea captain helps Viola to assume male clothes and to find service as the page Cesario, with Orsino, the duke of Illyria. Her new master is pleased with her and sends the disguised girl to press his suit for the hand of Countess Olivia, with whom the duke is in love. Olivia, who has been in mourning for her brother, finally admits the page and instantly falls in love with the supposed young man. Cesario, meanwhile, has been falling in love with Orsino. So apparent is Olivia's feeling for Cesario that the countess' admirer, Sir Andrew Aguecheek, is persuaded that he must send a challenge to the page, a challenge Cesario reluctantly accepts. Antonio, a sea captain who is a friend of Sebastian, chances on the duel and rescues Viola, mistaking her for her brother, whom he had found after the wreck and to whom he had entrusted his purse. In the ensuing confusion, Olivia marries the real Sebastian, thinking him to be Cesario. Viola and her brother finally are reunited. Viola marries Orsino, and all ends happily.

Sebastian (seh-BAS-tyehn), Viola's twin brother. Separated from her during the shipwreck, he makes his way to Duke Orsino's court, where he is befriended by Antonio. He is involved in a fight with Sir Andrew Aguecheek, who mistakes him for Cesario. When Olivia interferes and takes Sebastian to her home, she marries him, also thinking him to be Cesario. Thus, he and Viola are reunited.

Orsino (ohr-SEE-noh), the duke of Illyria, who is in love with Olivia. He sends the disguised Viola to press his suit, not realizing that Viola is falling in love with him. When Viola reveals herself as a woman, the duke returns her love and marries her.

Olivia, a rich countess, living in retirement because of the death of her brother. Orsino courts her through Cesario, but she rejects his suit and falls in love with the disguised Viola.

When Sebastian, whom she mistakes for Cesario, is brought to her after the fight with Sir Andrew, she marries him.

Malvolio (mal-VOH-lee-oh), Olivia's pompous steward. Considering himself far above his station, he dreams of marrying the countess. He so angers the other members of her household by his arrogance that they plan a trick on him. Maria, imitating Olivia's handwriting, plants a note telling him that to please the countess he must appear always smiling and wearing yellow stockings cross-gartered, affectations that Olivia hates. The countess considers him insane and has him locked in a dark room. He is finally released and leaves the stage vowing revenge. Some critics have seen Malvolio as the playwright's satiric portrait of the Puritan, but this interpretation is disputed by others.

Maria, Olivia's lively waiting woman. It is she who, angered by the vanity of Malvolio, imitates Olivia's handwriting in the note that leads him to make a fool of himself. She marries Sir Toby Belch.

Sir Toby Belch, Olivia's uncle and a member of her household. His conviviality is constantly threatened by Malvolio, so that he gladly joins in the plot against the steward. Sir Toby marries Maria.

Sir Andrew Aguecheek (ay-GYEW-cheek), a cowardly, foolish drinking companion of Sir Toby and suitor of Olivia. He is forced into a duel with Cesario but mistakenly becomes involved with Sebastian, who wounds him.

Antonio, a sea captain who befriends Sebastian, though at great risk, for he has been forbidden to enter Illyria. Having entrusted Sebastian with his purse, he is involved in the confusion of identities between Sebastian and Cesario. When he is confronted with the twins, Antonio helps to clear up the mystery of the mistaken identities.

Feste (FEHS-tuh), a clown. He teases Malvolio during his confinement but brings to Olivia the steward's letter explaining the trick that has been played on him.

THE TWELVE
(Dvenadtsat)

Author: Aleksandr Blok (1880-1921)
First published: 1918
Genre: Poetry

Locale: Petrograd, Russia
Time: 1917
Plot: Ballad

Vanka, one of the revolutionaries marching through the streets of Petrograd. At the time the marchers are depicted in the poem, he is seen only in the distance, prancing with Katka, the girlfriend of another revolutionary, Petrukha. By eloping with Katka, he betrays not only his friend but also the revolutionary cause. His former comrades accuse him of defecting to the enemy and becoming a bourgeois, a soldier in the enemy camp, and an enemy to the Red revolutionaries. He clearly possesses, in his speech, qualities of a seducer that others lack. His army coat symbolizes his betrayal in comparison with the ragtag and even prison garb of his former comrades. He has somehow gained superiority over them, as illustrated by his miraculous escape from Petka's avenging bullet.

Katka, or **Katya**, a pretty girl involved with the only two named revolutionaries, Vanka and Petka. By abandoning Petka in favor of a more dashing and richer Vanka, she shows that

she is interested primarily in pleasures and a better life. She dances and frolics in the evening snow and flashes Vanka a pearly smile, indicating that the two of them complement each other. She shows no remorse for betraying Petka because she is not generally faithful, as indicated by the knife scars on her neck and under her breasts received during another, most likely equally faithless, affair. She owns lacy attire and has plenty of money, received for her amorous services (or whoring, as Petka calls it).

Petrukha, or **Petka**, the aggrieved party in the triangle, stricken by jealousy and by the loss of his love. The extent of his grief is such that he almost forgets the cause for which he is fighting. In this sense, he shows himself to be a credible human being, wallowing in his sorrow rather than pursuing the loftier, abstract goal of his comrades. He shows that he is capable of resolute action when he tries to kill his rival; that he kills his beloved instead only underscores the depth of his personal tragedy. The intensity of his love is measured by his willingness to take back Katka even though he is fully aware of her shoddy character and infidelity. In fact, it is through him that the reader discovers the extent of her promiscuity. He trudges under the burden of his sorrow throughout the poem, despite the admonitions of his comrades that the times are too serious for such trifling personal concerns as unhappiness in love. Petka acts as most people in his position would act. The fact that the author gave all three characters common Russian names underscores the popular nature of both the love triangle and the revolution.

Jesus Christ, who appears at the end of the poem not as a person but as an apparition. For that reason, he cannot be termed a true character despite the important role the poet gives him.

Bystanders, who include an old woman, a bourgeois, a writer, a priest, an aristocratic lady, and a prostitute. They are not presented as individual characters. Like Jesus Christ, they contribute substantially to the overall plot of the poem as types, each symbolizing a segment of the society opposing the revolution.

— *Vasa D. Mihailovich*

TWENTY-SEVEN WAGONS FULL OF COTTON: A Mississippi Delta Comedy

Author: Tennessee Williams (Thomas Lanier Williams, 1911-1983)
First published: 1945
Genre: Drama

Locale: Blue Mountain, Mississippi
Time: The 1930's or 1940's
Plot: Tragicomedy

Flora Meighan, the young wife of Jake Meighan. Blonde, buxom, seductive, and mindless, Flora is childish and childlike, behaving like a petulant, demanding, spoiled child while exuding a vulnerability and dependence that make her a stereotypical female victim. Flora enjoys her husband's physical abuse and willingly accepts the role of baby to Jake's "big daddy" role; theirs is clearly a sadomasochistic relationship. Flora agrees to lie for Jake and provide him with an alibi when the neighboring cotton gin is destroyed by fire. She quickly reveals the lie under the questioning of Silva Vicarro, the superintendent of the gin. Once Vicarro realizes Jake's guilt, he takes his revenge out on Flora, and she quickly becomes the victim of his sexual advances and physical abuse.

Jake Meighan, the owner and operator of a cotton gin. A large, fat, greedy, and ambitious sixty-year-old man with all the mannerisms and class consciousness of a hardworking, lower-middle-class Southerner, Jake proudly possesses his voluptuous young wife as a sign of his own power and sexuality, abusing her while he indulges her. As the play begins, he finds his business threatened by a rival cotton gin owned by the neighboring Syndicate Plantation. Jake sets fire to the rival cotton gin, forcing the superintendent, Silva Vicarro, to bring his cotton to Jake's gin. This brings together Vicarro and Flora, who begin their adulterous relationship as the unwitting Jake supervises the ginning of Vicarro's cotton. So absorbed is Jake by the success of his plot that he fails to notice that although his cotton business has been saved, his wife, on whom he dotes, has been lost to the younger man.

Silva Vicarro, the superintendent of the Syndicate Plantation. Vicarro is of Latin descent, small, dark, intense, and intelligent. More clever than Flora, Vicarro quickly surmises from her conversation that Jake is the arsonist. His quick-tempered nature causes him to seek revenge on Jake, who has treated him with conspicuous condescension. Motivated by anger and a desire for revenge, he seduces Flora, who responds to his powerful physical aggression and abuse.

— *Jean McConnell*

TWENTY THOUSAND LEAGUES UNDER THE SEA
(Vingt mille lieues sous les mers)

Author: Jules Verne (1828-1905)
First published: 1869-1870
Genre: Novel

Locale: At sea
Time: 1866-1867
Plot: Science fiction

Captain Nemo (NEE-moh), a mysterious man who designs and builds the submarine *Nautilus* on a desert island. It provides its own electricity and oxygen, and the sea supplies food for its crew. Nemo hates society but uses gold recovered from sunken ships to benefit the unfortunate.

Professor Pierre Aronnax (pyehr ah-roh-NAKS), of the Paris Museum of Natural History, who heads an expedition aboard the American frigate *Abraham Lincoln* to track down a mysterious sea creature that has attacked and sunk ships all over the world.

Ned Land, a harpooner taken along on the theory that the killer is a gigantic narwhal. An explosion aboard the *Abraham Lincoln* tosses him, along with Aronnax and Conseil, aboard the *Nautilus*, where he and Nemo save each other's lives.

Conseil (koh[n]-SEHY), the servant of Aronnax, who shares their adventures aboard the *Nautilus* in the Atlantic, Pacific, and Polar Oceans. After a maelstrom overcomes the submarine in Norwegian waters, Aronnax, Land, and Conseil recover consciousness on an island, in ignorance of the fate of Captain Nemo and the *Nautilus*.

TWENTY YEARS AFTER
(Vingt Ans après)

Authors: Alexandre Dumas, *père* (1802-1870), with Auguste Maquet (1813-1888)
First published: 1845
Genre: Novel

Locale: France and England
Time: Mid-seventeenth century
Plot: Historical

D'Artagnan (dahr-tahn-YAH[N]), the clever and resourceful hero, a lieutenant in the Musketeers. He succeeds in almost all of his pseudohistorical adventures, even against Cardinal Mazarin's final treachery.

Porthos (pohr-TOHS), one of the original Three Musketeers. He joins D'Artagnan in serving Cardinal Mazarin and the king. He is noted for his great strength.

Athos (ah-TOHS) and

Aramis (ah-rah-MEES), the remaining two of the original Three Musketeers. In this novel, Athos and Aramis are allied with the Fronde, against their former comrades, but they end by sharing their English adventures with D'Artagnan and Porthos. Athos is the saintly member of the group, and the dandy Aramis is living in luxury despite his monastic vows as the novel begins.

Cardinal Mazarin (mah-zah-RA[N]), the French minister of state. He engages D'Artagnan to protect him and the king against the Fronde, political opponents endeavoring to overthrow the king.

Mordaunt (mohr-DOH[N]), a monk, the son of Milady. He is Cromwell's agent. He is the musketeers' sworn enemy and ultimately is defeated by Athos.

King Louis XIV (lwee), of France, now ten years old.

Queen Anne, the mother and protector of Louis. She is under Mazarin's control.

King Charles I, of England, whom the four musketeers almost save from execution. In aiding Charles, D'Artagnan offends Mazarin.

Lord de Winter, an Englishman in the service of King Charles.

The duke de Beaufort (deh boh-FOHR), Cardinal Mazarin's escaped political prisoner, in whose pursuit D'Artagnan and Porthos encounter Aramis and Athos.

Oliver Cromwell, the Puritan leader, to whom Cardinal Mazarin sends D'Artagnan and Porthos as messengers. The cruelty of the Puritans leads D'Artagnan to help Charles.

Henrietta Maria, King Charles's wife, now in France.

Raoul (rah-EWL), the adopted son of Athos, in reality his illegitimate son.

TWO FOR THE SEESAW

Author: William Gibson (1914-   )
First published: 1959
Genre: Drama

Locale: New York City
Time: Late 1950's
Plot: Tragicomedy

Jerry Ryan, an attorney from Nebraska. A melancholy man of thirty-three, he fled Omaha and an unhappy marriage to start over in New York City. Jerry owes much of his success to the intervention of others, especially his father-in-law, but he is now determined to do things for himself and for others. After meeting a young woman named Gittel at a party, the unlikely duo begins a nine-month-long rocky romance that is complicated by Gittel's unwillingness to let Jerry help her financially and by Jerry's emotional ties to his wife, which remain even after their divorce is granted. In the end, Jerry realizes that he still loves his wife and returns to Nebraska for another chance at life with her on his terms, not hers or her father's.

Gittel Mosca, a twenty-nine-year-old aspiring dancer who lives on unemployment insurance and income from various temporary jobs. She has spent much of her adult life as a victim, playing that role in a failed marriage and numerous doomed relationships. At first, she resists Jerry's willingness to help her, including his offer to pay rent on a loft Gittel wants to use as a rehearsal hall for a dance recital that could be her big break. Jerry eventually changes her mind about accepting help from others, and he makes her think, for the first time, about setting specific goals. When Jerry suspects her of sleeping with another man, they almost break off their relationship. Gittel's bleeding ulcer acts up, however, and Jerry nurses her back to health. Even though Gittel loves Jerry, she knows that he will never love her as he loves his former wife, so she decides that they should go their separate ways.

— *Gregory McElwain*

THE TWO GENTLEMEN OF VERONA

Author: William Shakespeare (1564-1616)
First published: 1623
Genre: Drama

Locale: Italy
Time: The sixteenth century
Plot: Comedy

Valentine (VAL-ehn-tin), a witty young gentleman of Verona. Scoffing at his lovesick friend, Proteus, he goes with his father to Milan, where he enters the court of the duke and promptly falls in love with Silvia, the ruler's daughter. He plans to elope with her but finds his plot betrayed to the duke. He flees to a nearby forest to save his life. There, he joins a band of outlaws and becomes their leader, a sort of Robin Hood. His concept of the superior claims of friendship over love is uncongenial to the modern reader, who finds it hard to forgive him when he calmly bestows Silvia on Proteus, from whose clutches he has just rescued her, to testify to the depth of his renewed friendship for the young man.

Proteus (PROH-tee-uhs), his friend, a self-centered youth who fancies himself a lover in the best Euphuistic tradition. He forgets his strong protestations of undying affection for Julia when he meets Valentine's Silvia in Milan. No loyalties deter him from betraying his friend's planned elopement to the duke, then deceiving the latter by trying to win the girl for himself while he pretends to be furthering the courtship of Sir Thurio. When Silvia resists his advances, he carries her off by force. Stricken with remorse when Valentine interposes to protect her, he promises to reform. The constancy of his cast-off sweetheart, Julia, makes him recognize his faithlessness and her virtue, and they are happily reunited.

Julia, a young noblewoman of Verona. She criticizes her suitors with the humorous detachment of a Portia before she confesses to her maid her fondness for Proteus. She follows him to Milan in the disguise of the page Sebastian, and with dogged devotion she even carries Proteus' messages to her rival, Silvia, to be near him. She reveals her identity almost unwittingly by fainting when Valentine relinquishes Silvia to Proteus as a token of his friendship. She regains the love of her fiancé by this demonstration of her love.

Silvia (SIHL-vee-uh), the daughter of the duke of Milan. She falls in love with Valentine and encourages his suit. She asks him to copy a love letter for her—directed to himself, although he does not realize this fact at first. Proteus' fickle admiration annoys rather than pleases her, and she stands so firm in her love for Valentine that his generous offer of her to Proteus seems almost intolerable.

Speed, Valentine's exuberant, loquacious servant, cleverer than his master at seeing through Silvia's device of the love letter. He is one of the earliest of the playwright's witty clowns, the predecessor of Touchstone, Feste, and the Fool in *King Lear*.

Launce (lahns), Proteus' man, a simple soul given to malapropisms and social faux pas, in spite of his excellent intentions. His presentation to Silvia, in Proteus' name, of his treasured mongrel, Crab, a dog "as big as ten" of the creature sent by his master as a gift, does little to further Proteus' courtship. Inspired by his master's gallantry, he pays court to a milkmaid and gives great amusement to Speed by his enumeration of her virtues.

The duke of Milan, Silvia's father, a strong-willed man who attempts to control his rash impulses. He welcomes and trusts Valentine, although he suspects his love for Silvia, until Proteus reveals the proposed elopement; he then cleverly forces Valentine into a position in which he must reveal his treachery. He finally consents to his daughter's marriage to Valentine as gracefully as possible, but one cannot forget that he is at this time the prisoner of the prospective bridegroom's men.

Sir Thurio (TEW-ree-oh), a vain unsuccessful suitor for the hand of Silvia, who despises him. Although he is willing to follow Proteus' expert instruction in the manners of courtship, he has no desire to risk his life for a woman who cares nothing for him, and he hastily departs when Valentine stands ready to defend his claim to Silvia's hand.

Lucetta (lew-SEHT-uh), a clever, bright young woman who delights in teasing her mistress Julia, for whom she is friend and confidante as well as servant.

Sir Eglamour (EHG-luh-mewr), an elderly courtier. He serves as Silvia's protector when she prepares to flee from her father and marriage to Sir Thurio.

Antonio, Proteus' father, a domineering man convinced that "What I will, I will, and there's an end."

Panthino (pan-THEE-noh), Antonio's servant, who advises him to send Proteus to join Valentine at the court of the duke of Milan to learn the gentlemanly skills of "tilts, and tournaments, and sweet discourse."

THE TWO NOBLE KINSMEN

Authors: William Shakespeare (1564-1616) and John Fletcher (1579-1625)
First published: 1634
Genre: Drama

Locale: Athens and Thebes
Time: Antiquity
Plot: Tragicomedy

Palamon (PAL-uh-mon), a young knight, the nephew of Creon, the king of Thebes. Palamon sees and abhors the corruption of his uncle's government. With his cousin and closest friend, Arcite, he plans to leave Thebes, but when he learns that Theseus, the duke of Athens, is marching against the city, he sees it as his duty to stay and defend it. Imprisoned by the Athenian ruler, he responds with enthusiasm to Arcite's eager insistence that their friendship will make even lifelong captivity palatable. A few moments later, he shatters this friendship with one brief glimpse of Emilia, who is walking in the garden beneath their window. He will not tolerate Arcite's professions of love and claims the preeminence of his affection on the grounds that he saw the lady first. He rages with jealousy when his cousin is sent into the country, and he insists on fighting a duel to the death when Arcite comes on him in the woods where he is wandering, hungry and still in chains after his escape from prison. Arcite's kindness wins from him grudging recognition of his cousin's nobility in all matters but love, but he begs Theseus to allow their combat to take place. He prays before the fateful battle to the goddess of love, and his prayer is answered, rather deviously, by Arcite's untimely death. He laments life's painful irony, which allows him to win his lady through the loss of his dearest friend.

Arcite (AHR-sit), his cousin, an equally worthy young man. He seems, on occasion, a little more forceful than Palamon; it is he who suggests that they leave Thebes and he who comforts his cousin during their imprisonment. Resourcefully disguising himself as a country yeoman to obtain a place in Emilia's household, he wins favor with the whole court until he is discovered fighting with Palamon. He is never so violently jealous as Palamon is, and, refusing to take advantage of his cousin's weakness after he has escaped from prison, he offers Palamon first food, then honorable combat. He achieves the victory for which he prayed to Mars, but he is brought down by fate in a freak riding accident.

Theseus (THEE-see-uhs), the noble duke of Athens, a staunch defender of right. His first impulsive decision is generally an absolute one, but he is amenable to the suggestions of his friends and advisers. He yields to the pleas of his Amazon bride and her sister and agrees to delay his wedding to avenge the wrongs of the widowed Theban woman against their tyrannical ruler, Creon. Although he condemns Palamon and Arcite to death when he discovers them in a forbidden duel, he is persuaded to allow them to fight a tournament for the hand of their beloved Emilia, for he hates, as much as his wife and sister do, to lose either of the valiant young men.

Hippolyta (hih-POL-ih-tuh), Theseus' wife, the former queen of the Amazons, a wise and sympathetic wife and sister. She urges Theseus to postpone their wedding when she recognizes the great need of the Theban women. Later, she pleads for the lives of Palamon and Arcite.

Emilia (ee-MIHL-ee-uh), her younger sister, loved by the two young Theban princes she has never met. She tells Hippolyta that she does not intend to marry; no man could ever win from her as much love as her friend Flavinia, who died when she was twelve years old. She is at first overwhelmed by the intensity with which the unknown knights fight for her. She then finds herself in love with both of them and can only pray that the one who loves her best will win her.

Perithous (PEHR-ih-thuhs), Theseus' friend and adviser. He joins Hippolyta and Emilia in pleading for the lives of Palamon and Arcite.

The jailer, Palamon's keeper, a devoted father who is distressed by his daughter's madness.

His daughter, a young woman who pines away for the love of Palamon. She frees Palamon from prison, hoping to make him return her affection. His disappearance and the death sentence placed on her father for his negligence drive her into a deep melancholy, and she wanders distracted through the woods around Athens, raving like Ophelia. The kindly dissembling of her father and of her wooer, who pretends to be Palamon, restore her to health.

A wooer, her gentle suitor. He is filled with pity for his mad sweetheart and agrees to do all the doctor advises to bring about her recovery. He plays his role as Palamon well, treating his bride with great tenderness.

A doctor, a rather cynical gentleman who suggests that the wooer masquerade as Palamon.

A schoolmaster, a pompous pedant who prepares entertainment for Theseus and Hippolyta on a May morning.

TWO SOLITUDES

Author: Hugh MacLennan (1907-1990)
First published: 1945
Genre: Novel

Locale: The Saint Lawrence River valley, Montreal, Nova Scotia, and Maine
Time: 1917-1939
Plot: Regional

Athanase Tallard (ah-tah-NAHZ tah-LAHR), an elderly French Canadian aristocrat, seigneur of Saint-Marc-des-Erables, and member of Parliament. As a federal politician, he is in an invidious position: Elected by French-speaking Catholic Quebec, he must work with English-speaking Protestants in Ottawa and is supporting national conscription, to which Quebec is opposed. A Catholic, Tallard is more intellectual, less biddable, and less religiously observant than the local priest desires—but Athanase knows the bishop. Tallard's second marriage has alienated him from his elder son. Attracted by the vision of industrial development and employment for Saint-Marc, Tallard mortgages his property to join a consortium headed by Huntly McQueen. The local priest, fearing change, quarrels with him and orders the parish to boycott him. Athanase moves to Montreal, defiantly becomes Protestant, and sends his younger son to an English school. Having offended French Canadians, Tallard is useless to McQueen. Ruined, he dies, returning to the Catholic faith on his deathbed.

Kathleen Tallard, Athanase's second wife, a young Irish Catholic beauty and former hatcheck girl, Paul's mother. Kathleen cannot share her husband's political life, hates rural Quebec, and longs for urban distractions and male admiration. Nine years after Athanase's death, Kathleen marries an American businessman. Her character stresses the gap between Anglophones and Francophones even when religion is not an issue. She also contributes an English component to Paul.

Marius Tallard, the son of Athanase and Marie Adele, Athanase's first, pious, Québécois wife. Marius Tallard is attracted to his stepmother, detests his father's remarriage, and goes into hiding to escape conscription. He later becomes a lawyer, but his first concern is French Canadian politics.

Paul Tallard, the son of Athanase and Kathleen, a brilliant student. His father's death and the Depression force Paul to play professional hockey and become a sailor. He returns to Canada determined to become a writer. Always an admirer of Captain Yardley, he loves Heather Methuen and marries her. The product of a French English marriage and the husband of an English wife, as well as bilingual himself, Paul embodies the ideal of an integrated Canada.

Father Émile Beaubien (ay-MEEL boh-BYAH[N]), a local priest in Saint-Marc, embodying the religion, culture, and antagonism to change characteristic of rural Quebec. Although he contributes to Tallard's destruction, Father Beaubien cannot stop McQueen, so Saint-Marc becomes a secular, modern community in spite of him.

John Yardley, a retired Nova Scotian sea captain, the father of Janet, grandfather of Daphne and Heather, and mentor to Paul Tallard after his father's death. Captain Yardley fulfills an old dream by buying land in Saint-Marc. Unprejudiced, intelligent, and sensitive, he is accepted by all even though he speaks no French and is not a Catholic. Only his daughter Janet is ashamed of his unpretentious style. Paul and Heather love him and appreciate his wisdom. Captain Yardley retires to Nova Scotia, where he dies. Heather and Paul marry two days after the funeral. The captain epitomizes the human values that run counter to all barriers of status, religion, and culture.

Janet Methuen (meh-TWA[N]), Yardley's daughter. A limited, insecure woman, resembling her English mother rather than her father, she is delighted to marry into the Methuen tribe, an old moneyed family in Montreal, pseudo-British and snobbish. Widowed by the war, Janet becomes socially ambitious for her daughters; however, she is stupid and unscrupulous. She betrays Marius Tallard to the authorities, seeks McQueen's help in separating Heather and Paul, and fakes a heart attack. She embodies all the pettiness, prejudice, and traditional English privilege that antagonize French Canada.

Heather Methuen, the younger daughter of Harvey and Janet, a tomboy, independent thinker, and her grandfather's favorite. Always in rebellion against her mother's values, Heather wishes to be useful. She has socialist ideals, loves Paul, believes in his writing, and marries him, knowing that war is coming.

Huntly McQueen, a self-made man, creator and head of a powerful conglomerate. He admires the Methuens, especially Janet. Huntly has private foibles (communing with his dead mother, for example), but his unremarkable appearance and his refusal to court publicity are protective coloration. Secretive, ruthless, pragmatic, and visionary, he is at the center of the Canadian power elite.

— *Jocelyn Creigh Cass*

2001: A Space Odyssey

Author: Arthur C. Clarke (1917-   )
First published: 1968
Genre: Novel

Locale: Prehistoric Africa, the Moon, and near Saturn
Time: Three million years B.C. and A.D. 2001
Plot: Science fiction

Moon-Watcher, a "man-ape" of the Pleistocene geologic era, hairy and muscular. At almost five feet in height, he is unusually tall for his dying race of cave-dwelling hominids and weighs more than one hundred pounds in spite of his tribe's usual lack of nourishment. Of the first creatures to take notice of the Moon, he is the only hominid in the world to stand erect and one of the few having a glimmer of intelligence. He discovers the New Rock, which is in fact a monolithic probe of an extraterrestrial intelligence. It studies him in particular and inspires him to use a stone to kill a warthog, then to kill another hominid. Moon-Watcher's tribe members become hunters to begin the evolution of humanity.

Dr. Heywood Floyd, the chairman of the National Council of Astronautics. A widower of ten years and father of three, he completed one voyage to Mars and three to the Moon before returning to the lunar crater Tycho to see a recently uncovered monolith there.

David Bowman, the first captain of the spaceship *Discovery*. At thirty-five years of age, unmarried, and holding a Ph.D., he is a veteran astronaut with the curiosity of a generalist and an almost photographic memory who reads avidly and enjoys many styles of classical music. A caretaker of the ship and its three hibernating scientists until the planned rendezvous with Saturn, he has to disconnect the rebellious HAL, a

computer, to complete the mission as he understands it. Once in orbit, he exits the ship in an exploratory pod to examine a free-floating monolith, then enters a Star Gate and is swept across time and intergalactic space until being transformed by extraterrestrials into the Star-Child.

Frank Poole, the deputy captain of the *Discovery*. He is unmarried, like all the astronauts; experienced in his work; careful; and conscientious in sharing on-board duties with Bowman. Poole is murdered by HAL during an extravehicular activity.

HAL 9000, an acronym for Heuristically programmed ALgorithmic computer, the brain and nervous system of the *Discovery*. Faster and more reliable than the human brain, HAL "thinks" intelligently, speaks, navigates the ship, and monitors the life-support systems of the three hibernating scientists. Unlike Bowman and Poole, HAL alone knows the true nature of the mission: to locate the source of the radio signals to the monolith in Tycho. Created to be innocent and incapable of making errors, HAL tries to murder the humans on board when they threaten to disconnect HAL's brain, the equivalent of death. HAL fails to kill Bowman, however, who then disconnects HAL.

— *Clark G. Reynolds*

TWO THOUSAND SEASONS

Author: Ayi Kwei Armah (1939-   )
First published: 1973
Genre: Novel

Locale: Western Sudan, Ghana, and elsewhere in Africa
Time: 1000-1900
Plot: Epic

The narrator, an omnipresent griot (poet-historian) and the voice of traditional African culture, specifically that of Ghana. Masculine in tone but speaking in the first person plural ("we"), the narrator is confident in his remembrance and in his interpretation of Anoa's prophecies as he traces the migration of his people from the deserts of western Sudan to present-day Ghana. In recalling the collective experience and the principles of "the way," reciprocity and compassionate

mutual respect, he also offers vivid, intimate, and detailed descriptions of "connectedness" among the people and with the land. Clearly charting the growth, decay, and transformation of cultural practices and values, he frequently employs rhetorical questions that reveal an obvious disdain for fragmented consciousness and religious dogmatism.

Anoa (ah-NOH-ah), the second prophetess bearing the name, living around 1000. She prophesies five hundred years (a thousand seasons) of cultural decline toward death and five hundred years of return to principles affirming life. Slender, supple, and of stunning beauty, she has a grace that embodies her skills as a hunter. Her "deep" blackness reveals both physical strength and spiritual understanding. Although gentle in manner, Anoa speaks in "two voices," one that is harassed and shrieking in her knowledge of impending doom for her people and one that is calm and encouraging, seeking to explore causes for the decline and creating hope for survival after the people's long suffering.

Isanusi (ee-sah-NEW-see), a learned counselor to Koranche, later exiled for his challenge to the king's authority. A master of eloquence and honest in his assessment of leadership, he refuses to flatter Koranche, who declares him mad when Isanusi reveals the king's secret alliance with the Europeans. Tired from suffering despair and loneliness resulting from the people's loss of values, the slender teacher becomes rejuvenated by serving as mentor to and leader of a small group of young revolutionaries. After the revolt is in full force, Isanusi is betrayed by a messenger from the king and is killed.

Idawa (ee-DAH-wah), the companion of Isanusi during his exile. Slender and graceful, the beautiful black woman is the ideal of physical strength and endurance as well as of compassionate, intelligent strength of mind and soul. She chooses to marry Ngubane, a farmer, whom she loves, to avoid being coerced into marriage with Koranche. The king kills her husband within the year. Articulate and courageous, Idawa confronts Koranche with his own inferiority and rejects him with public contempt. After Isanusi has been exiled, she joins him in the forest.

Abena (ah-BAY-nah), a young woman who becomes the principal voice for the young rebels. Eloquent, beautiful, and brilliant, Abena is quick to grasp the various skills of initiation rituals. She is the most skillful dancer in the village. In the ceremonial dance to choose mates, she dances her way to freedom, joining the rebels and rejecting Koranche's command that she marry his son Bentum. When the rebels are betrayed and enslaved, her comprehension of Isanusi's wisdom helps the rebels endure their suffering before their escape. After the rebels return to Anoa, she leads them to victory over the colonists at Poano; at Anoa, she persuades Koranche to confess his crimes publicly and then executes him.

Koranche (koh-RAHN-chay), the king of Anoa who betrays African values to remain in power by allying himself with European slave traders and colonialists. He was born an idiot in an incestuous dynasty. Koranche's sole skill consists of an uncanny ability to undermine the achievements of others, often destroying the fruits of their labor. As a child, he does not smile or cry, expressing himself in a dull, flat, constant stare. Breast-fed for five years and then vomiting at the sight of naked breasts thereafter, he does not walk until he is seven years old and does not talk until he is nine. Because he cannot complete the initiation rituals, he changes them for his son when he becomes king. Possessed by a numbing inner despair and emptiness in the self-knowledge that he is an utter fraud as an adult, Koranche learns to stay in power through mystification and pompous ceremony while surrounding himself with self-serving flatterers. He relies on the Europeans to enslave any who oppose him. Entirely dependent on the people's gullibility, he continually betrays the Anoans, who come to fear his fraudulent power. As he ages, he becomes a very fat, deluded alcoholic, eventually executed by Abena.

Bentum (BAYN-tewm), later renamed **Bradford George**, the son of Koranche and prince of Anoa. Reared by Europeans in the colonized village of Poano and educated in Europe, Bentum is married to an older, physically disabled white woman to strengthen Koranche's alliance, but he lusts for Abena, who rejects him. Fat and stupid, he oversees the slave trading in Poano, marching children around the ground while he wears a blue cloak and a yellow wig. After his father is executed, Bentum, as Bradford George, becomes the colonial puppet king of Anoa.

— *Michael Loudon*

TWO TRAINS RUNNING

Author: August Wilson (1945-   )
First published: 1991
Genre: Drama

Locale: A restaurant in a ghetto of Pittsburgh, Pennsylvania
Time: 1969
Plot: Psychological realism

Memphis Lee, whose restaurant forms the play's only set and who has struggled to build a life in Pittsburgh after whites forced him off his Jackson, Mississippi, farm in 1931. Intelligent and determined, he has fought a valiant, if unsuccessful, battle to maintain his establishment amid grinding poverty and urban decay. Although his marriage of twenty-two years has foundered and his restaurant faces the wrecking ball, he still yearns for the financial success that would enable him to reclaim his farm. The sale of his restaurant at the play's end makes the fulfillment of his wish at least possible.

Wolf, one of Memphis' customers, a numbers runner. He is a roving peddler of dreams; his illegal trade allows a few fortunate winners to purchase coveted material goods. Although he relishes the reputation his occupation fosters, he is disappointed in love: His relationships with women are limited to brief physical encounters. His interest in Risa never develops into anything substantial.

Risa (Clarissa) Thomas, Memphis' lethargic employee, who is mentally stable despite having disfigured her shapely legs. She has scarred them so that she can build a relationship on more than a physical basis. Like Sterling, with whom she falls in love, she recognizes Hambone's value and tries to befriend him.

Holloway, another of Memphis' few remaining regular customers. He has coped all his life with the ravages of injustice. Noteworthy for his role as the play's resident philosopher, he is a keen observer of the other characters and the economic system that holds them in bondage. It is his faith in Aunt Ester's prophetic power that enables him to survive.

Hambone, a retarded man in his late forties and another

frequent visitor to the restaurant. He is dissociated from reality. For nine and one-half years, this dysfunctional character has repeated the lines, "He gonna give me my ham. I want my ham." The ham is the unpaid debt of Lutz, the white owner of a meat market. This pathetic character dies without attaining his goal.

Sterling Johnson, a thirty-year-old former convict who has been out of prison for only one week. He was jailed for five years on a bank robbery conviction. His dismal prospects seem destined to land him back in prison. He sees the inner beauty that lies beneath Risa's scars and begins a romantic relationship with her. Moreover, he recognizes that Hambone's sense of purpose makes him "lucky."

West, the funeral director, who has devoted himself solely to the acquisition of money since his wife's death. A schemer who has profited handsomely from the deaths of his neighbors, he tries and ultimately fails to cheat Memphis out of a fair price for his restaurant. Lacking Holloway's spiritual vision, he once rejected Aunt Ester's command to consign twenty dollars to the river.

— *Cliff Prewencki*

TWO WINGS TO VEIL MY FACE

Author: Leon Forrest (1937-1997)
First published: 1983
Genre: Novel

Locale: The Deep South
Time: The Civil War era to the mid-twentieth century
Plot: Magical Realism

Nathan Witherspoon, a young black man born in 1937. He has a college education. He transcribes the family reminiscences of Sweetie Reed Witherspoon. Nathan has a special relationship with Sweetie Reed, who helps him gain a new perspective on his family heritage. The tragedies, antagonisms, and triumphs of I. V. Reed, Angelica Reed, Jericho Witherspoon, and the Rollins Reed plantation are written down by Nathan as his grandmother talks. As the precocious child of a failed marriage between a black man and his light-skinned wife, Nathan forms a new appreciation of his African American heritage as the story unfolds.

Sweetie Reed Witherspoon, who is ninety-one years old and is the great storyteller of the novel. The death and funeral of her estranged husband J. W. Reed inspire her to narrate the complex tale of her past. Sweetie Reed was once a minister and has a special relationship with God as well as possessing the oral history of her clan. She is also mystical and often has dreams within dreams. Her recollections of slavery, the Civil War, and Reconstruction form the basis of the novel. Her memories chronicle the Witherspoon family from slavery into the twentieth century. Lying on her bed, coming in and out of reveries and memories, Sweetie Reed is the last in a long line of oral historians who maintained the continuity of the African American spirit through difficult times.

Aunt Foisty, a black conjure woman, who is more than one hundred years old. She retains a perfect memory that stretches back to Africa. She was wet nurse to almost everyone on the plantation, including Rollins Reed, the master. She possesses ancestral conjuring skills, speaks an African language, and is able to revive Rollins Reed from near death with her magic rituals and incantations.

I. V. Reed, the father of Sweetie Reed. He worked as a slave in the plantation house of Rollins Reed and was the illegitimate son of his master. I. V. Reed, who died in 1906 at the age of seventy-six, is presented as a crafty old man with a thousand voices and myriad identities. He is unscrupulous and self-serving, yet he knows the old-time whooping cries that gave birth to praise tunes, spirituals, and the blues.

Jericho W. Witherspoon, who died in 1944 at the age of 117. Sweetie Reed refused to attend the funeral and quarrels with her son Arthur. Jericho Witherspoon is an archetypal character from the African American past. He escaped slavery in 1850 and went north to become a lawyer and a judge. He was a large, reddish-yellow man, six feet, five inches tall and weighing 250 pounds. His initials were branded on his left shoulder by his owner.

— *Stephen F. Soitos*

TWO WOMEN
(La ciociara)

Author: Alberto Moravia (1907-1990)
First published: 1957
Genre: Novel

Locale: Sant'Eufemia, Italy
Time: 1943-1944
Plot: Social realism

Cesira (cheh-ZEE-rah), the narrator. Readers learn about her not only from her direct descriptions of herself but also from all she has to say about others. Her ability to articulate her feelings and her impressions of landscape and characters are remarkable; critics have objected that the author blurs the line between what a woman of little formal education would be capable of and his own intensely literary and intellectual powers. The times when the author takes Cesira out of character with an inappropriate figure of comparison or piece of knowledge are few; and readers come to accept Cesira's inner monologue as authentic and her vocabulary as one of an inner life that can make itself known through means other than words. At her most primitive and undifferentiated Cesira is a peasant from a region noted for its sturdy, feisty stock, steeped in tradition. At a more sophisticated level, she is a Roman shopkeeper, meticulous about property and money. Much that a reader is likely to find unpleasant about her—as small-minded, mean, or snobbish—results from these layers of her personality. Cesira is much more than this, and the depths of her understanding and her ability to reconcile herself with devastating hardship give her impressive stature as a kind of Everywoman. Certain values endure in her, including her standards of decency and her sense of justice.

Rosetta, Cesira's daughter. Much of the book appears to be about one woman (Cesira), rather than the two women of the title. Cesira narrates the novel, so all of its information is filtered through her. Bit by bit, however, Rosetta becomes known to the reader, at first as the object of her mother's love and concern, but then increasingly as a person in her own right who can influence Cesira's actions and be credited by her mother, in the penultimate paragraph of the book, with having inspired Cesira's newborn confidence. Rosetta's growth in importance parallels her growth as a person as well as Cesira's removal by war from other persons she had come to depend upon for company. Although she is an adult, Rosetta in some ways remains childlike, in part because of her mother's over-protectiveness. She is deeply and simply religious. All of this appears to have changed following her rape by a band of Moroccan soldiers (nominally liberators of Fascist Italy) in front of a statue of the Virgin Mary in a country church. Driven to repeat some elements of this experience, but in situations in which she can feel more in control, Rosetta acts promiscuously, at one point having sex, it is implied, with three young gangsters at once. Cesira has said that her daughter is a kind of saint, by which she means someone given to absolute goodness. After the rape, Rosetta appears to be devoted to being wicked. Challenged on this, Rosetta offers no defense, other than to say that the war has created a new morality—one that her mother, for one, finds indistinguishable from amorality. After her boyfriend Rosario is murdered by highwaymen, Rosetta regains her ability to sing, together with her ability to grieve. It is implied that she will be able to forgive herself for all that she has done or has happened to her as a result of the war that is now at an end.

— *David Bromige*

TYPEE

Author: Herman Melville (1819-1891)
First published: 1846
Genre: Novel

Locale: The Marquesas Islands
Time: Mid-nineteenth century
Plot: Adventure

Tom (Herman Melville), an American sailor on the whaler *Dolly* who, with his friend Toby, jumps ship at Nukuheva and immediately contracts a disease that makes his leg swell and become very painful. When their food runs out, they give themselves up to the Typee tribe of natives on the island. They are treated kindly, and Tom is given a native servant to take care of him. Toby leaves to seek medical aid and never returns, leaving Tom alone with the natives, who, the friends had discovered, are cannibals. Tom is allowed a fair amount of freedom but is always attended by Kory-Kory, his servant, and Fayaway, a beautiful native girl. Tom finally is allowed to go down to the beach to see a boat from an Australian vessel. Although the natives watch him carefully, he manages to break away from his guards and is taken on board by the Australians.

Toby, Tom's friend, who leaves the whaler with him and shares his adventures on the island until he goes to find medi-cal help for Tom and is tricked into boarding a vessel that leaves the island the next day. Years later, he meets Tom and is happy to learn that his friend escaped and is well.

Kory-Kory, Tom's faithful native servant, who is always by his side. Tom very much regrets having to leave him behind when he escapes.

Fayaway, the native girl who is Tom's constant companion while he is among the Typees.

Marnoo, a native taboo man who is free to move among all the tribes on the island without danger. Tom asks Marnoo to help him escape, but Marnoo cannot do so without arousing the natives' anger. He does, however, tell the captain of the Australian vessel of Tom's situation.

Mehevi, the Typees' chief, a stereotypical relaxed Polynesian.

TYPHOON

Author: Joseph Conrad (Jósef Teodor Konrad Nałęcz Korzeniowski, 1857-1924)
First published: 1902
Genre: Novella

Locale: The China Seas
Time: The 1890's
Plot: Adventure

Tom MacWhirr, the captain of the steamer *Nan-Shan*. Dutiful, calculating, mechanical, mature, and effectual, the main character of the story does his job correctly although he does so without any manifest confidence from the men serving under him. His job is to take two hundred Chinese coolies to their destination of Fu-Chau and to do so directly and without delay. The obstacle to this plan is the typhoon, presenting MacWhirr with the central dilemma of the novella as he must decide whether to proceed straight into the hurricane or run from it. This latter choice would be a relinquishment of duty, which he cannot accept. In confronting the typhoon and surviving it, MacWhirr somehow comes to terms with all of life's adverse universal forces.

The typhoon, a hurricane that Captain MacWhirr must confront. Violent, strong, forceful, and controlling, the typhoon represents not only the power of nature but also all the adverse conditions that humanity must face and struggle against. The typhoon does not succeed in destroying the *Nan-Shan* and the men on board; however, it does not surrender the battle to MacWhirr so much as it simply ceases to struggle.

Young Jukes, the chief mate. Innocent and inexperienced in the evils of life and the violence of nature, Jukes rightfully depends on Captain MacWhirr for guidance, and he exactingly follows the orders of his superior. The central sections and the major portions of the plot are told from Jukes's perspective, though he is not the narrator. In following Captain MacWhirr's cold and calculating orders, Jukes realizes that he must be functional and mechanical to survive.

Solomon (Sol) Rout, the chief engineer, the tallest man on each of the ships on which he has served. Old Sol's towering height accounts for his "habit of a stooping, leisurely condescension." As engineer, Rout is perhaps the most mechanical of the men on board; his ability to follow MacWhirr's orders and to maintain a rather automaton-like existence helps ensure the preservation of the ship.

The second mate, a secretive loner who is "competent enough." He has failed to master the subservience to duty, responsibility, and effectuality possessed by MacWhirr. He is an older, shabby fellow, one who is a ghost of what MacWhirr would become were he to fail. During the typhoon, the second mate loses his nerve and is unable to carry out his responsibilities.

The boatswain, the first in charge of the crewmen on deck. Once described as an "elderly ape" and in another place as a "gorilla," the boatswain embodies raw strength, gruffness, and stupidity in human nature. Surprisingly, Captain MacWhirr likes the boatswain, presumably because he knows he controls him and can put his strength to good use.

The steward, a personal attendant to Captain MacWhirr. Unable to mind his own business, the steward reads Captain MacWhirr's personal mail to his family. Consequently, the reader is informed about the contents of these letters and MacWhirr's character is further revealed.

Two hundred Chinese coolies, who exist in the story literally as cargo; they are returning to China after working several years abroad. They represent the thoughtless, purposeless mass of humanity toward which MacWhirr feels his duty and responsibility as well as his contempt. Several of the coolies die as the typhoon proceeds.

— *Carl Singleton*

TYPICAL AMERICAN

Author: Gish Jen (1956-   )
First published: 1991
Genre: Novel

Locale: China and the United States
Time: Late 1940's to early 1970's
Plot: Social realism

Ralph Chang, originally known as Yifeng (Intent on the Peak) in China but given the name Ralph (which he discovers means "a kind of dog") in America. He is a professor of mechanical engineering. He is portrayed as having mediocre talents, pathetic beginnings, and modest aspirations. Ostensibly, he is a male chauvinist. He becomes obsessed with financial success and positive thinking, leading him to open a fried chicken restaurant with the help of a Chinese American businessman (Grover Ding). In the process, he miscalculates and plunges his family into misery. He is an allegorical figure of unbridled freedom and greed.

Theresa Chang, Ralph's sister. She saved Ralph when he was down and out and helped him complete his education. She also made it possible for him to get married, rear some children, and own a house. Having struggled quietly to become a medical doctor, she falls in love with a patient, a married man who happens to be her brother's colleague. She acquires a larger-than-life stature as she falls victim to her brother's sanctimonious abuses. She is fond of cats.

Helen Chang, Ralph's wife, who was reared in an affluent family in Shanghai. Too intent on conforming to American standards of the good life, she finds herself seduced by Grover Ding, thus incurring the vengeful anger of Ralph when her secret is discovered. Helen epitomizes the desires of a woman and her limits in a world manipulated by men.

Grover Ding, a Chinese American businessman who was born in the United States. Sly, greedy, and arrogant, he induces Ralph to pursue a business of his own, seduces his wife, and hastens Ralph's financial ruin by withholding vital information about the restaurant. As the villain of the novel, Grover is the agent of negative change. Grover is also the name that Ralph gives, in commemoration of Grover Ding's trickery, to a dog he is raising; the dog is trained by Ralph to attack cats.

Henry Chao, Ralph's colleague and department chair. He has an ongoing extramarital affair with Theresa and is genuinely concerned about her. Rejuvenating Theresa's life and enabling her to live for herself rather than merely for others, he can be seen as an agent of positive change.

— *Balance Chow*

TZILI: The Story of a Life
(Kutonet veha-pasim)

Author: Aharon Appelfeld (1932-   )
First published: 1983
Genre: Novel

Locale: Eastern Europe, from Poland or Russia to Yugoslavia
Time: Late 1930's to the 1940's
Plot: Allegory

Tzili Kraus, a young, provincial Jewish girl, plain, quiet, and not very bright. Tzili is disliked by her family for her lack of intelligence. When the Nazi troubles begin, her family decides that she is so simple that no one will bother her, so they leave Tzili behind when they try to make their escape.

Although she is simple, Tzili has an innate sense of survival (such as saying that the town prostitute Maria, who is not Jewish, is her mother) that other Jews lack; no matter what troubles befall her, she goes on living in her undemanding, almost heedless, way—even when, near the end of the book, she sees Jewish survivors of concentration camps committing suicide around her. The novel follows her journey as she seems to survive accidentally, her pregnancy that ends in a stillborn child, and finally her decision to go to Palestine.

The old blind man, who sits in the fields all day. He gives Tzili some food but then tries to rape her.

The religious teacher, a Jewish tutor who is brought in by Tzili's family to teach her religion because they believe she is too stupid to learn anything more worthwhile. Although he did not feel affectionate toward Tzili, he was not cruel to her, so she remembers him as a kind man. The prayers she learned from him serve to comfort her while she is hiding in the countryside.

Katerina, a dying old prostitute, once a friend of Maria, Tzili's "adopted" mother. Katerina takes Tzili in for the winter. When Katerina becomes too ill to entice men, she tries to turn Tzili into a prostitute.

The old man and

the old woman, a couple who take Tzili in after she runs away from Katerina. The old woman beats Tzili, and the old man tries to rape her, so she flees them.

Mark, a Jewish man who has escaped from a concentration camp and who is hiding in the countryside. He and Tzili hide together in a bunker that he has dug. As Tzili matures, Mark is attracted to her, and Tzili becomes pregnant by him. The hiding takes a mental toll on Mark, and one day he leaves and never returns, presumably having been captured by the Nazis.

Linda, a fat Hungarian woman who was a cabaret performer. Linda helps keep up the spirits of the fatally depressed and guilt-ridden Jews who have survived the Holocaust. At one point, she forces the group of wanderers that Tzili has joined to go back for Tzili and carry her, when Tzili is heavily pregnant and unable to continue walking. At the end of the book, she joins Tzili for the voyage to Palestine.

The merchant, another Holocaust survivor. He helps to organize the men to carry Tzili on a stretcher when she can no longer walk, and he brings her milk. When Tzili starts having a problem with her pregnancy, the merchant goes from place to place trying to get her help. He is left behind, however, when the military ambulance finally arrives to take Tzili to the hospital.

The nurse, a young gentile Czechoslovak woman. She is Tzili's nurse in the hospital in Zagreb after Tzili's dead baby is surgically removed. With the nurse, Tzili strikes a chord of solidarity for the first time. Tzili is moved away to make room for the sicker patients.

— *T. M. Lipman*

UBU ROI

Author: Alfred Jarry (1873-1907)
First published: 1896
Genre: Drama

Locale: An imaginary Poland
Time: Unspecified
Plot: Absurdist

Père Ubu (par EW-bew), the former king of Aragon, captain of the Dragoons, count of Sandomir, and, later, king of Poland. He is an obese, smelly grub, with an enormous paunch, who carries a walking stick in his right-hand pocket and uses a toilet brush as his scepter. As a grotesque parody of a petty official who usurps a position of power, he is vulgar, gluttonous, rapacious, untrustworthy, greedy, sadistic, cowardly, and stupid. His actions are impulsive, and his speech is a mixture of vulgar expressions, oaths, and repetitive phrases. He ruthlessly obtains the Polish throne, then recklessly abuses his power by killing off the nobility, usurping the power of the judiciary, and overtaxing the peasants. Unsuccessful in defending his kingdom against the Russians, he escapes to France.

Mère Ubu (mar), Ubu's wife, a repulsive, unattractive, foulmouthed woman who cooks her food in excrement. She goads Ubu into assassinating the Polish king and usurping the throne. Although just as vicious as Ubu, she knows the limits to which power can be wielded and is more practical than he in matters of politics. She tries to act independently of Ubu in stealing the royal gold, but her scheme is thwarted by Boggerlas.

Captain Macnure, an officer in the Polish army who agrees to assassinate the king. He is a parody of the honorable soldier who would rather split the king in half with his sword than poison him. Betrayed by Ubu, he joins the Russian czar to wage war on Ubu, who eventually tears him to pieces in combat.

King Wenceslas (van-TSEH-slahs), the good king of Poland who provides for his subjects. Rash and imprudent, he becomes an example of foolish credulity and heedless obstinacy when he attends the Grand Review unarmed and unprotected and is assassinated by Ubu's henchmen.

Queen Rosamund, the queen of Poland. Cautious and wary, she warns her husband not to attend the Grand Review. After he is assassinated, she dies of grief in her son's arms in a scene that parodies a melodramatic death scene.

Boggerlas, the fourteen-year-old son of King Wenceslas, wise to Ubu's schemes. He vows to avenge himself on Ubu for causing the death of his family. Fighting with great courage, he eventually reclaims the throne.

Tsar Alexis, the noble czar of Russia, who will not use treachery to win a victory. He joins forces with Macnure to defeat Ubu.

General Laski, a foolish general of the Polish army. He is more interested in the formality of parading than in battle tactics.

Heads,

Tails,

Gyron, and other

Palcontents, Ubu's henchmen, who kill King Wenceslas and his sons. Heads and Tails kill a wild bear without the help of Ubu, who watches and prays. After this incident, they desert him. Gyron, a black man, is killed while helping Mère Ubu rob the crypt of the Polish kings.

— *Paul Rosefeldt*

THE UGLY DUCHESS
(Die hässliche Herzogin Margarete Maultasch)

Author: Lion Feuchtwanger (1884-1958)
First published: 1923
Genre: Novel

Locale: Central Europe
Time: The fourteenth century
Plot: Historical

Duchess Margarete (mahr-gah-RAY-teh), Heinrich's daughter, fat, shrewd-eyed, and apelike but intelligent and learned. She attempts to compensate for her ugliness by ruling her lands with strength and skill. She romantically idealizes the double-dealing Chrétien. Discovering his perfidy, she has him killed, as she later arranges the death of Karl Ludwig and

Aldrigeto. Long rivaled by Agnes, she is defeated at last. Margarete, despoiled of her power and most of her possessions, abdicates and lives in self-imposed poverty.

Prince Johann (YOH-hahn), her tall, strong, cowardly, and ill-humored husband, who sulkily avoids his ugly wife until the strong-minded Margarete has the marriage annulled.

Chrétien de Laferte (kreh-TYAY[N] deh lah-FEHRT), a lean, brown-faced aide to Prince Johann. A close friend of Margarete but a treacherous one, he plans to marry Agnes. Margarete's discovery of this leads to his death.

Margrave Karl Ludwig (LEWT-vihkh), the widowed son of Ludwig. Acceding to his father's will, he becomes Margarete's second husband. He is poisoned.

Prince Meinhard (MIN-hahrd), the easygoing, stupid son of Margarete and Karl. He is a leader of the Arthurian Order of Bavarian Chivalry, a gang of pillagers. He is murdered by Konrad.

Konrad von Frauenberg (KOHN-rahd fon FROW-ehn-burg), Margarete's unscrupulous adviser, a repulsive albino who poisons Karl, throws Meinhard from a cliff, and poisons Agnes. From his villainies, he at last reaps rich rewards.

Agnes von Flavon (AHG-nehs fon FLAH-fohn), Margarete's beautiful, vain, mocking, and popular rival, the daughter of Heinrich's mistress and Chrétien's intended wife. For plotting against Margarete, she is imprisoned and is poisoned by Konrad.

Heinrich (HIN-rihsh), the duke of Carinthia, count of Tyrol, and king of Bohemia, a widowed, aging, fat, and financially reckless ruler. He dies worn out by his dissipations.

John (yohn), the king of Luxemburg, the glittering, brilliant, and promiscuous father of Prince Johann. He anticipates getting Heinrich's territories by inheritance through the marriage of Johann to Margarete. He becomes blind before he dies in battle.

Albert (AHL-burt), the tough, far-seeing king of Austria with whom Margarete signs a treaty.

Ludwig, the slow-witted king of Wittelsbach.

Princess Beatrix (BAY-ah-trihks), the shy, anemic young wife of Heinrich. Shocked at his lavishness, she becomes grasping and tries in miserly fashion to save something for the son she never has. She dies some months after her marriage.

Albert von Andrion (AHN-dree-ohn), the gay and good-natured illegitimate half brother of Margarete. After an abortive plot, he is tortured, despoiled of lands, and made a lifelong captive.

Mendel Hirsch (MAN-dehl hihrsh), Margarete's fat, fidgety, and obsequious Jewish confidant. He is killed in a pogrom.

Jacob von Schenna (YAH-kob fon SHOO-nah), Margarete's serious, kindly friend from youth, now a wealthy man of cultured tastes with a love of poetry. Long faithful, he finally turns against Margarete and gets some of the rich spoils when her conniving enemies defeat her.

Duke Stephan (STA-fahn), the brother of Karl Ludwig.

Baron Aldrigeto (ahl-dree-GAY-toh), a handsome youth who falls in love with Margarete. After a brief affair, she orders that he be killed.

ULTRAMARINE

Author: Malcolm Lowry (1909-1957)
First published: 1933; revised, 1962
Genre: Novel

Locale: Tsjang-Tsjang harbor, China, and Merseyside, England
Time: c. 1927
Plot: Social realism

Eugene Dana Hilliot, the novel's center of consciousness, an upper-middle-class youth, half-Norwegian and half-English, taking his first voyage as a deckhand. Sensitive, creative, out of place, and out of his class among the crew, Hilliot is the only character to be described in any detail. He has an identity problem that mirrors that of the author himself, whose own 1927 voyage to China Hilliot takes. Even his name is a compendium of references to the author's literary influences: Eugene O'Neill, Richard Henry Dana, and T. S. Eliot (the crew pronounce Hilliot's name "Illiot"). Hilliot wants both to be accepted as an "ordinary seaman" and to be extraordinary; at the age of nineteen, he has left boyhood behind but has yet to enter into adulthood. The voyage, his all-night "binge" ashore at Tsjang-Tsjang, his challenge to Andy, and his acceptance as part of the group will allow him to come to terms with the bourgeois Merseyside past of which he has freed himself, his schoolboy love, and his sexual urges, and to forge for himself an identity as a spinner of yarns and an expatriate (like his creator). Much of the novel is occupied with his interior monologues and dreams.

Andy, the "chinless wonder," the ship's cook and focus of its social life, a dominating personality. The most memorable of the novel's sketchily drawn supporting players, tattooed and sensual, working-class Andy is important not for what he is but for what he represents: a rival and alter-ego (he spends the night ashore with the prostitute Hilliot had fancied), a model for selfhood, and a father figure (he calls Hilliot "son" at the close of the novel) who can be left behind and surpassed.

Norman, the cabin boy, another rival and model. Easygoing, plucky, and eminently "normal," Norman performs the bathetically "heroic" act of rescuing a pigeon from atop the mainmast that Hilliot feels he should have attempted, the prize being the crew's applause and acceptance. He accompanies Hilliot on his binge and tour of the port sights: the cinema, the anatomical museum, and the bars. Concern for Norman (he loses his pigeon) draws Andy and Hilliot together.

Janet, Hilliot's innocent schoolboy love, to whom most of his monologues are addressed. Something of a cardboard cut-out (the hometown madonna to the whore with whom Hilliot had contemplated losing his virginity), Janet is a soft, sweet, idealized representative of Hilliot's childhood values. His good-bye to her in Merseyside, finally related near the novel's close, has proved a decisive moment in Hilliot's life. He receives a letter from her only to lose it in a bar to an uncomprehending German, Popplereuter, who later forwards it. At the novel's close, Hilliot is mentally drafting his reply: an account of himself and his changes.

— *Joss Lutz Marsh*

ULYSSES

Author: James Joyce (1882-1941)
First published: 1922
Genre: Novel

Locale: Dublin, Ireland
Time: June 16, 1904
Plot: Psychological realism

Stephen Dedalus, a proud and sensitive young Irishman. He is a writer and teacher called **Kinch** (from "kinchin," meaning "child") by one of his friends. In his search for the nature and meaning of life, Stephen examines all phases of his existence. History, he says, is a nightmare from which he is trying to awake. As he looks back to his childhood, he can remember only his family's poverty and his father as a patron of taverns. His devotion to Ireland is not the answer to his search; she is an old sow, he believes, that eats her own young. His religion is not enough to make life purposeful. Stephen cannot dismiss his mother's deathbed prayer that he avow his belief, and his inability to comply causes him to fret with remorse. Symbolically, Stephen is Telemachus, the son in search of a father. In effect, he finds a symbolic father in Leopold Bloom, an older man who takes care of Stephen after the young man has been in a street fight with British soldiers. Declining Bloom's invitation to live with him and his wife, Stephen goes out into the darkened street to return to the Tower where he is staying and to his dissolute life among the young men and students he knows.

Leopold Bloom, a Jewish advertising salesman who is, symbolically, Ulysses, the father of Telemachus. Bloom's yearning for a son stems from the long-past death of Rudy, his eleven-day-old son. A patient husband, he is cuckolded by his wife's business manager, but he is carrying on a furtive flirtation of his own. Bloom is Any Man, plodding through the daily routine of living—visiting bars, restaurants, newspaper offices, hospitals, and brothels of Dublin—because he hopes for something out of the ordinary but must be satisfied with the tawdry.

Malachi "Buck" Mulligan, a medical student and the friend of Stephen Dedalus. He points up Stephen's attitudes and philosophies, the two young men being opposites, the scientific and the philosophical. Buck says that death is a beastly thing and nothing else; it simply does not matter. According to Buck, Stephen's religious strain is all mockery; if it were not, Buck says, Stephen could have prayed with his mother. Buck is doubtful that Stephen will ever produce any great writing. The model for Buck Mulligan was Oliver St. John Gogarty, an Irish physician and poet.

Marion "Molly" Tweedy Bloom, whose background differs greatly from her husband's. Brought up in the atmosphere of a military post in Gibraltar, Molly, a lush creature and second-rate concert singer, finds life with her husband and life in Dublin dull. Her escape from the reality of the humdrum comes through love affairs with other men. Her latest lover is Blazes Boylan, a virile younger man. Bloom's suggestion that Stephen Dedalus come to live with them gives Molly a momentary tingle as she contemplates the pleasure of having a still younger man in the house. Molly's thoughts and reverie make up the final section of the book, as she considers the present but finally lapses into reminiscences of a sexual experience of her girlhood. She is Penelope to Bloom's Ulysses.

Blazes Boylan, Molly's lover and the manager of a concert tour she is planning. The business aspect of their meetings does not delude Bloom.

Haines, a young Englishman who lives in the Tower with Stephen Dedalus, Buck Mulligan, and other students and artists. His indulgence in drinking orgies alienates the more ascetic Stephen. Because Haines has considerably more money than the other young men, he is frequently the butt of their sarcasm. Haines is an anti-Semite who fears that England may be taken over by German Jews.

Paddy Dignam, Bloom's friend, who dies of a stroke.

Father Coffey, who performs the funeral rites over the body of Paddy Dignam.

Mrs. Breen, a neighbor to whom Bloom gives the account of the funeral.

Mrs. Purefoy, another neighbor, who, Mrs. Breen reports, is in a maternity hospital. Bloom's visit to the hospital to inquire about her leads to his meeting with Stephen Dedalus.

Davy Byrnes, a tavern owner whose establishment attracts all types of people who discuss many subjects.

Barney Kiernan, the owner of a bar where Leopold Bloom gets into an argument with a patriotic Irishman and is ejected.

Mr. Deasy, the headmaster of the school where Stephen teaches. Deasy probably assesses Stephen's aptitudes rather exactly when he tells the younger man that he is more a learner than a teacher. In lamenting the influx of Jews in England, Deasy points out to Stephen that Ireland is the only country where Jews have not been persecuted—because it never let them in.

Talbot,
Cochrane,
Armstrong,
Comyn,
Edith,
Ethel, and
Lily, some of Stephen's pupils. Their indifference and ineptness are discouraging to their young teacher, giving rise to Deasy's prognosis of Stephen's career.

Milly, the Blooms' daughter. Her existence does not mitigate Bloom's longing for a son, nor does it lessen Molly's desire for romance and release from tedium.

Gertie MacDowell, a young girl who exhibits herself to Leopold Bloom on Sandymount shore.

Myles Crawford, a newspaper editor.

THE UNBEARABLE BASSINGTON

Author: Saki (Hector Hugh Munro, 1870-1916)
First published: 1912
Genre: Novel

Locale: London, England
Time: Early 1900's
Plot: Satire

Francesca Bassington, a heartless, scheming society matron of London who has an attractive home and a Van der Meulen painting. She wants her son Comus to marry Emmeline Chetrof, heiress to her house, and to go into politics. The news of his death in Africa and of the falsity of her painting reach her at the same time.

Comus Bassington, a young man with a casual attitude toward the world and indifference to his mother's ambitions. Although he is attracted to Elaine de Frey, he ruins his chances by borrowing money from her and being boorish about a silver tray at her tea. He dies at an unwanted political post in Africa.

Emmeline Chetrof, the heiress to a considerable fortune, including Mrs. Bassington's home.

Lancelot Chetrof, Emmeline's brother and a schoolmate of Comus, whom he treats badly because of Mrs. Bassington's matrimonial suggestion.

Elaine de Frey, an heiress who invites both her suitors to a tea, to choose between them. She marries Courtney and discovers her mistake during their honeymoon.

Courtney Youghal, a young member of Parliament whose scurrilous attack on Governor Jull is signed by Comus to escape a political appointment.

Suzette, a cousin of Elaine and the first to hear of her engagement to Courtney.

George St. Michael, a gossiping member of the fashionable world of Mayfair and Ascot.

Sir John Jull, the governor of a West Indian island. He needs a secretary.

Henry Greech, the brother of Francesca and a man of political influence.

THE UNBEARABLE LIGHTNESS OF BEING
(Nesnesitelná lehkost bytí)

Author: Milan Kundera (1929-   )
First published: 1984
Genre: Novel

Locale: Czechoslovakia and Switzerland
Time: The 1960's and 1970's
Plot: Political

Tomas (TAW-mahsh), a noted Czechoslovak surgeon and indefatigable philanderer. At the novel's pivotal chronological moment (the summer of 1968, when the Russians invade and occupy Czechoslovakia), Tomas is forty years old. He and his wife, Tereza, flee to begin a new life in Switzerland. After several months in Zurich, Tereza abruptly returns to Prague. The fact that Tomas follows Tereza suggests the depth of his love for his wife and homeland. There is, however, no corresponding commitment to fidelity. One of the keys to Tomas' character, to the pattern of his life, is his firm belief that love and sexuality have nothing in common. Thus, although he returns to Tereza, and truly loves her, his promiscuous womanizing continues. He also loves his country but will not participate in its destruction by the police-state apparatus. He twice refuses to retract a political essay he had published before the crackdown, he resigns his position at the clinic before the police have him fired, and he becomes a window washer. This job presents him with a certain freedom, or blissful indifference, and with many new opportunities to practice his avocation: epic womanizing. There is a stubborn integrity at the core of his personality. Finally, when Tomas and Tereza choose to settle in the countryside and work at a collective farm, a kind of happiness settles over them. They are killed in a highway accident.

Tereza, a small-town waitress and autodidact who yearns for "something higher." Through a sequence of fortuities, she meets Tomas, follows him to Prague, and becomes his wife. Pursuing her new career as a photographer, she is caught up in the Soviet invasion, taking daring photographs, risking arrest, and experiencing a happiness she has not known before. She initiates their move to Switzerland, just as she chooses to return. However insecure Tereza may feel, she does make choices, and she lives up to the consequences of them. The mainspring of her character is her longing for beauty, for a world in which the soul will manifest itself and take precedence over the promiscuous and immodest flesh and over the view of the world—instilled in her by her mother—as a grim concentration camp of bodies. Driven and haunted by jealousy, and compelled by and committed to fidelity, Tereza feels unhappiness that is centered on her husband's sexual encounters with other women. Finally, when they have settled in the country and there is no longer a wide range of women for Tomas to pursue, Tereza knows the happiness for which she has longed, the satisfaction of her vision of "weight" through responsibility and fidelity.

Franz, a Swiss university professor. A gifted and successful scholar, he feels suffocated by his vocation. He has a "weakness for revolution" and a fascination with leftist causes, and he remains intoxicated with the kitsch of the "Grand March," the author's name for the fantasy joining leftists and revolutionaries of all times. His personal life parallels his political life: His relationship with his wife is superficial, as is his affair with Sabina, his mistress, from whom he is separated by an abyss of misunderstanding. In Sabina's eyes, Franz, though he has physical strength, is a weak person. In the schematic presentation of character that drives the novel, Franz is an exemplar of "lightness."

Sabina, a Czechoslovak painter. Like Tomas and Tereza, Sabina flees her homeland, but she remains in a permanent state of exile in both a physical and a spiritual sense. She is a strong, liberated, and sophisticated professional woman. A central figure in spite of her limited presence, she is mistress to both Franz and Tomas. She serves as a foil to define her lovers, yet she remains mysteriously superficial and profoundly unattached. The essence of her character is projected by her fascination with betrayal: She longs to betray everything, even her own betrayals. In the novel, she is the most sophisticated exemplar of "lightness"; she continues her drift westward until she ends up in California, alone, unattached, still living on the surface of things, successful and content with her life "under the sign of lightness."

The narrator, the central presence and voice. The narrator is probably the most engaging character. Whether regarded as the author's direct voice or as a compelling fictional device, the narrator delivers the rich and paradoxical political, philo-sophical, and erotic speculations that shape the novel and define each of the characters.

— *H. R. Stoneback*

UNCLE SILAS: A Tale of Bartram-Haugh

Author: Joseph Sheridan Le Fanu (1814-1873)
First published: 1864
Genre: Novel

Locale: England
Time: The nineteenth century
Plot: Gothic

Austin Ruthyn, a wealthy recluse and widower. He is a Swedenborgian who devotes his time to scientific and literary studies. When he dies, his will appoints several men as trustees for his estate and places his daughter Maud under the guardianship of his brother Silas.

Maud Ruthyn, a wealthy heiress. She goes to live with her uncle Silas, believing she is to vindicate her uncle's good name. She is disturbed by her uncle's idiosyncrasies but even more by the attentions of her coarse cousin, who wishes to marry her. She is tricked into being made a prisoner, and her cousin and uncle try to murder her to inherit her wealth. The attempt fails. Later, she marries Lord Ilbury, one of the trustees of her estate.

Silas Ruthyn, Maud's uncle. According to rumor, he has killed a Mr. Charke, to whom he owes a large sum of money. When his attempt to marry Maud to his son fails, he and the young man attempt to murder Maud to inherit her wealth. The attempt fails, and Silas commits suicide.

Dudley Ruthyn, Maud's cousin, a coarse, cruel man. He courts Maud but fails to win her. When he tries to murder Maud, he kills Mme de la Rougierre by mistake. After the murder, he disappears. His attempts to court Maud end following his marriage to a lower-class woman named Sarah Mangles.

Mme de la Rougierre, Maud's governess. She becomes an accomplice of Silas and Dudley in their attempted murder, only to be killed herself.

Dr. Bryerly, Austin Ruthyn's doctor and friend. He is one of the trustees of Maud's estate.

Lady Monica Knollys, a cousin of Austin Ruthyn, who tries to warn him and Maud against Mme de la Rougierre.

Lord Ilbury, also known as **Mr. Carysbrook**. He is one of the trustees of Maud's estate and marries Maud.

Milly Ruthyn, Maud's cousin. She is a loud, good-humored girl who becomes Maud's friend. She grows up to marry a minister.

Sir William Aylmer and
Mr. Penrose Cresswell, other trustees of Maud's estate.

Mary Quince, Maud's maid.

Meg Hawkes, a miller's daughter who befriends Maud.

Tom Brice, a servant who loves Meg Hawkes and saves Maud from her uncle and cousin.

UNCLE TOM'S CABIN: Or, Life Among the Lowly

Author: Harriet Beecher Stowe (1811-1896)
First published: 1852
Genre: Novel

Locale: Kentucky and Mississippi
Time: Mid-nineteenth century
Plot: Social realism

Uncle Tom, a slave. Although he is good and unrebellious, he is sold by his owner. After serving a second kind but improvident master, he comes under the ownership of brutal Simon Legree and dies as a result of his beatings.

Eliza, a slave. Learning that her child is about to be sold away along with Tom, she takes the child and runs away, crossing the Ohio River by leaping from floating ice cake to floating ice cake.

George Harris, her husband, a slave on a neighboring plantation. He also escapes, passing as a Spaniard, and reaches Ohio, where he joins his wife and child. Together, they go to freedom in Canada.

Harry, the child of Eliza and George.

Mr. Shelby, the original owner of Eliza, Harry, and Uncle Tom. Encumbered by debt, he plans to sell a slave to his chief creditor.

Haley, the buyer, a New Orleans slave dealer. He shrewdly selects Uncle Tom and persuades Mr. Shelby to part with Harry in spite of his better feelings.

George Shelby, Mr. Shelby's son. He promises to buy Tom back one day but arrives at Legree's plantation as Tom is dying. When his father dies, he frees all his slaves in Uncle Tom's name.

Mrs. Shelby, Mr. Shelby's wife. She delays the pursuit of Eliza by serving a late breakfast.

Marks and
Loker, slave-catchers hired by Haley to track Eliza through Ohio. Loker, wounded by George Harris in a fight, is given medical treatment by the Quakers who are protecting the runaways.

Augustine St. Clare, the purchaser of Tom after Tom saves his daughter's life. He dies before making arrangements necessary to free his slaves.

Eva St. Clare, his saintly and frail daughter. Before her death, she asks her father to free his slaves.

Mrs. St. Clare, a hypochondriac invalid. After her husband's death, she sends Tom to the slave market.

Miss Ophelia, St. Clare's cousin from the North. She comes to look after Eva and is unused to lavish Southern customs.

Topsy, a pixie-like black child bought by St. Clare for Miss Ophelia to educate; later, he makes the gift legal.

Simon Legree, the alcoholic and superstitious brute who purchases Tom and kills him. He is a Northerner by birth.

Cassy, Legree's slave. She uses his superstitions to advantage in her escape. Her young daughter, who was sold years ago, proves to be Eliza, and mother and daughter are reunited in Canada.

Emmeline, another of Legree's slaves. She escapes with Cassy.

Madame de Thoux, whom Cassy and Emmeline meet on a northbound riverboat. She proves to be George Harris' sister.

Aunt Chloe, Uncle Tom's wife, left behind in Uncle Tom's cabin on the Shelby plantation.

Senator Bird, in whose house Eliza first finds shelter in Ohio.

Mrs. Bird, his wife.

Simeon Halliday and
Rachel Halliday, who give shelter to the fugitive slaves.

UNCLE VANYA
(Dvadya Vanya)

Author: Anton Chekhov (1860-1904)
First published: 1897
Genre: Drama

Locale: Russia
Time: Late nineteenth century
Plot: Impressionistic realism

Alexander Serebrakov (ah-lehk-SAHN-dr seh-reh-brah-KOHF), a retired professor who takes up residence with his young wife at their small estate in the country. After many years of writing books about art, his life is deemed a failure. Success and fame have eluded him; he is a gout-ridden, whining, testy, and complaining old man incapable of generosity or kindness. Presumptuous and full of self-conceit, he is a trial to all those around him.

Helena Andreyevna (eh-LEH-nuh ahn-DRAY-ehv-nuh), the professor's beautiful young wife. Disillusioned by her husband, whom she married in the belief that he was famous and learned, she spends her life in idleness and indolence, infecting those about her with her absence of direction and values. She holds a fascination for men, but in doting on her, they themselves are corrupted. She remains true to her husband but in the process destroys her own spirit.

Sonya Alexandrovna (SOH-nyuh ah-lehk-SAHN-drehv-nuh), the professor's daughter by a previous marriage, an innocent, plain young woman hopelessly in love with the local physician, who does not return her love. She learns to endure her pain by helping others, by work, and by a deep faith in a better afterlife.

Ivan Voitski (ih-VAHN VOYT-skih), called **Vanya** (VAH-nyuh), the brother of Serebrakov's first wife and manager of his country estate. After having worked diligently for the professor for years, editing and translating his manuscripts, caring for his business affairs, and making it possible for him to lead a comfortable life, Vanya discovers that the professor is a fraud, that his own sacrifice has been for nothing, and that he has lost a lifetime. Despairing over his false trust in the professor and his unrequited love for Helena, he unsuccessfully attempts to kill his brother-in-law. At the end of the play, knowing that he can find no new life, Vanya mechanically works over the account books while trying to endure the life remaining to him.

Mihail Astrov (mih-hah-IHL ahs-TROHF), the local physician, overworked and discouraged by the tediousness of human existence. Claiming to be a misanthrope, he nevertheless falls in love with Helena and lets his practice and estate fall into ruin. Helena, because of her affection for him, takes her husband and leaves the country. Astrov remains to reassume his old life. The most intelligent and visionary of the characters, he sees his own life only as preparation for the better life of future generations.

Marya Voitskaya (MAHR-yuh VOYT-skah-yuh), the widowed mother of Vanya and of the professor's first wife. Obsessed with the emancipation of women, she spends her life reading revolutionary pamphlets and dreaming about the dawn of a new life.

Ilia Telegin (ih-LYAH teh-LEH-gihn), called **Waffles** because of his pockmarked face, an impoverished landowner. He is sentimental, obsequious, and simpleminded.

Marina (mah-RIH-nuh), an old family nurse. Representing the traditional ways of an older generation, she kindly offers tea or vodka to console any suffering.

UNDER FIRE: The Story of a Squad
(Le Feu: Journal d'une escouade)

Author: Henri Barbusse (1873-1935)
First published: 1916
Genre: Novel

Locale: France
Time: 1914-1915
Plot: Political

Volpatte (vohl-PAT), a square-faced, jaundiced-looking, broken-nosed man who is hospitalized after almost losing his ears but returns bitter about the men in the hospital, both the malingering patients and the arrogant staff members.

Eudore (ew-DOHR), a pale, pleasant-faced former keeper of a roadside café. Ironically, the one night of furlough he spends with his wife is spoiled by the presence of four soldiers taken in because of a heavy rain. He is later killed on patrol.

Poterloo (poh-tehr-LEW), a pink-faced, blond former miner who accompanies some friendly German privates to an Alsatian village to see his wife and is shocked to see her enjoying herself with a German sergeant. He is later killed.

Joseph Mesnil (zhoh-SEHF meh-NEEL), one of six brothers, four of whom already have been killed by 1915. Almost maddened by the death of his last remaining brother, Joseph is later wounded and is taken by the narrator to a dressing station.

André Mesnil (ahn-DRAY), Joseph's brother, a former chemist, who is killed on patrol.

Corporal Bertrand (behr-TRAH[N]), a leader who is soldierly, serious, and friendly to and respected by his squad. He is killed.

Lamuse (lah-MEWZ), a fat, ruddy-faced peasant, killed on patrol.

Paradis (pah-rah-DEE), a plump, fat-cheeked, baby-faced former carter. He often discusses war with the narrator.

Cocon (koh-KOH[N]), a slight, desiccated ironmonger. He is killed.

Tirloir (teer-LWAHR), the former manager of a traveling circus, sent back from the trenches with dysentery.

Bicquet (bee-KAY), a squat, gray-faced, heavy-chinned Breton, killed on patrol.

Barque (bahrk), a Parisian porter and tricycle messenger, killed on patrol.

Fouillade (fwee-LAHD), a middle-aged, tall, long-jawed, and goateed soldier from southern France.

The narrator, apparently the author, who remembers his friends, grieving for those who have died and brooding on the filth, brutality, and nausea of war experience.

UNDER MILK WOOD: A Play for Voices

Author: Dylan Thomas (1914-1953)
First published: 1954
Genre: Drama

Locale: Llaregyb, also called Llareggub, a mythical seaside village in Wales
Time: Indeterminate
Plot: Domestic realism

The Reverend Eli Jenkins, the town's minister, whose love for the fishing village of Milk Wood is expressed by his prayers and poetry as well as his life's hobby, writing a book about every aspect of the town. His poems articulate what he loves in the little town—its humble beauties in the midst of the grandeur of Welsh landscapes that surround it. His prayers remind God that "We are not wholly bad or good/ Who live our lives under Milk Wood," a theme the play seems to endorse. The play, presented as a day in the life of the town, is somewhat formless but is given some structure by Jenkins' speeches, which begin and end the town's day.

Captain Cat, a retired sea captain, now blind, who spends his days dreaming in his room at Schooner House. He is the most important of several old people who seem to watch over the town. He dreams of his travels on the seas and of the young men who sailed with him, some of whom apparently drowned at sea. Most of all, he dreams of long-dead Rosie Probert, a prostitute who was loved by Captain Cat (and many other seafarers) and who speaks to him in his dreams. Her speeches suggest her essential innocence.

Polly Garter, the town washerwoman and the subject of much local gossip. Her fatherless babies appear yearly, to the horrified interest of more respectable women. Polly is alluring and very accessible to men. Her monologues make clear, however, that although many men have loved her, she herself has loved only Little Willy Wee, who died long ago.

Mog Edwards, who is described as "a draper mad with love." He keeps a dry goods store and courts Myfanwy Price. Their courtship is carried out through letters. Mog's contain equal parts of local gossip, dry goods news, and love talk. His love for money and her fondness for her tidy life mean that their love will never go beyond letters.

Mrs. Ogmore-Pritchard, who is twice widowed and keeps a house for paying guests. She spends her days in a whirlwind of vacuuming and polishing, carrying on a conversation with the ghosts of both of her dead husbands. She ruled their lives with the same methodical ruthlessness with which she attacks dust in her home. In the morning, she makes the hapless ghosts recite a litany of their daily tasks, which include drinking herb tea and removing fleas from the family Pekingese.

Mr. Waldo, who is one of Milk Wood's many eccentrics. His occupations include rabbit catcher, barber, herbalist, cat doctor, and "quack." He lives alone, haunted by dreams of his several dead wives, his dominating mother, and favorite foods of his childhood.

Cherry Owen, a newly wed man who shares the local weakness of having too much to drink at the local pub, the Sailor's Arm. His wife is forgiving, however, and they spend mornings in their one-room apartment laughing at his drunken antics of the night before.

Gossamer Beynon, the town's beautiful young schoolmistress. Her schoolteacher's demure propriety is belied by her own sexuality and her secret passion for the rough Sinbad Sailor, who dominates her passionate fantasies. She imagines a variety of intimate encounters with him but is unaware that he loves her; he thinks that she is too proud for him to approach her.

Mr. Pugh, who is miserably married and is a would-be poisoner. Like many of Milk Wood's citizens, Mr. Pugh finds his fantasies more powerful than his actual life. He spends his days imagining himself in a laboratory, mixing poisons with which he would like to murder his ill-tempered wife.

Nogood Boyo, Milk Wood's delinquent. He spends his days fishing in the bay and fantasizing about the town's women.

Dai Bread, the town's baker, who divides his time between his two wives. Mrs. Dai Bread One is a figure of blowsy respectability, and Mrs. Dai Bread Two is a gypsy, alluring in her bangles and dirty yellow petticoat. They vie for the attention Dai divides between them.

— Ann Davison Garbett

UNDER THE GREENWOOD TREE

Author: Thomas Hardy (1840-1928)
First published: 1872
Genre: Novel

Locale: Rural England
Time: The nineteenth century
Plot: Pastoral

Richard (Dick) Dewy, a young carter with musical inclinations and talent. One Christmas season when he goes caroling with the church choir, for whom he plays accompaniment on his violin, he falls under the spell of Fancy Day, the new schoolmistress in the parish. When his companions look for him after he disappears from the group, they find him under the girl's window, already in love. Dick Dewy begins courting Fancy at the Christmas party held in his parents' home, but he soon finds he has a rival for her hand. Although she favors his courtship and reciprocates his affection, his hopes are somewhat dashed for a time by her father's refusal to consent to a marriage. The father claims that his daughter is too well-educated for the young carter. The girl herself overcomes her father's objections and wins his consent. A little more than a year after he sees her for the first time, Dick Dewy weds Fancy Day beneath a great tree near her father's home.

Fancy Day, the young schoolmistress at Mellstock, a pretty young woman well educated as a teacher and a musician. Her beauty and talent immediately attract admirers, including Dick Dewy, who later becomes her husband. Fancy is a pleasant young woman, almost guileless, whose only fault, if it is that, is the pleasure she takes in her appearance and her clothes. Her obvious concern about her appearance twice creates courtship problems, for Dick Dewy resents her love of apparel. Once Fancy is tempted into jilting her fiancé. This temptation occurs when the local vicar, Mr. Maybold, appears suddenly at the schoolhouse and proposes marriage. Fancy, taken by the idea of marrying higher than her station, says yes. The next day, upon consideration, she writes to the vicar and withdraws her answer; she is also wise enough to keep this incident a secret from her husband after their marriage.

Mr. Shiner, a farmer of means and Fancy Day's admirer. Although his courtship meets with no particular favor from the girl, it does create some problems for his rival, Dick Dewy. As a churchwarden, Mr. Shiner introduces an organ to replace the church choir, with Fancy Day as the organist. Dick Dewy's problem then is one of conflicting loyalties, his loyalty to his beloved and his loyalty to the church choir. Mr. Shiner's suit is favored by Fancy's father, but Mr. Day's approval fails to change his daughter's mind.

Geoffrey Day, Fancy's father and agent for a great landowner. Pleased with his daughter's beauty and talent, he wants her to marry well. He opposes her marriage to Dick Dewy as being beneath the girl and favors her marriage to Mr. Shiner, a well-to-do farmer. When Fancy goes several weeks without apparent appetite, Mr. Day becomes concerned about her health and is thus tricked into consenting to her marriage with the young carter.

Mr. Maybold, the local vicar, a good-looking bachelor. Admiring Fancy Day and not knowing that she is engaged to marry Dick Dewy, he proposes to her. She accepts his proposal, but the very next day the vicar learns, to his sorrow, of her previous engagement to Dick Dewy. As an honorable man, Mr. Maybold writes a courteous letter to the girl asking to withdraw his proposal. In the meantime, Fancy has written him a note breaking their engagement. He later advises her to keep the incident a secret. Mr. Maybold creates a disturbance in the parish life by supplanting the choir with an organ, at the request of Mr. Shiner, one of the churchwardens. His innovation is at first highly resented, but it is finally accepted by the choir because of his sympathetic attitude toward them and their displacement.

Reuben Dewy, Dick Dewy's father. As a member of the parish choir, he is the spokesman when the men go in a group to the vicarage to protest their being turned out of service.

William Dewy, Dick Dewy's grandfather and leader of the parish choir. He is upset when his lifelong service to the church is ended by the introduction of an organ.

Mrs. Day, Fancy Day's stepmother. She is an odd woman whom her husband regards as a cross he must bear. Her behavior, that of a person suffering from mental illness, is entirely humorous.

UNDER THE SUN OF SATAN
(Sous le soleil de Satan)

Author: Georges Bernanos (1888-1948)
First published: 1926
Genre: Novel

Locale: The rural northwestern area of France
Time: Early twentieth century
Plot: Religious

Germaine "Mouchette" Malorthy (zhehr-MEHN mew-SHEHT mah-lohr-TEE), a sixteen-year-old murderess and suicide. Small, nymphlike, and intense, she unashamedly sets out to seduce both Dr. Gallet and Jacques de Cadignan. Pregnant by the latter, she threatens to expose him to public scorn and to the police if he does not agree to marry her. After Mouchette tells him that she is also the mistress of Dr. Gallet, however, he violently rapes her. She then shoots him in the throat, and it looks as though he committed suicide. She also attempts to blackmail Dr. Gallet into performing an abortion, but he refuses. She lies for the sake of lying and enjoys watching others suffer; she will do anything to get her own way. Her final attempt at seduction is with the saintly Father Donissan, who immediately recognizes her demoniac powers and offers her pity and forgiveness. She is so outraged by his generosity that she goes home and slits her throat.

Antoine Malorthy (ahn-TWAHN), the middle-aged father of Mouchette. A brewer by trade, he possesses all the manipulative cleverness of a northern French peasant. Although disturbed by the marquess of Cadignan's sexual exploitation of his teenage daughter, he attempts to find ways by which the family can benefit financially from it. Antoine convinces the marquess that unless he makes some kind of monetary reparation for violating Antoine's daughter, Antoine will make the marquess' crime public.

Jacques de Cadignan (zhahk deh kah-deen-YAH[N]), Mouchette's lover, an impoverished nobleman, a forty-five-year-old pleasure-seeking member of a dying nobility. He relentlessly pursues the young women of his area of the Artois. Although somewhat paunchy, he is a charming gentleman, with soothing manners and pale, icy blue eyes. He has been seduced by the nymphette Mouchette, who tells him that he has impregnated her. She insists that he marry her and rear the child as his own, but he refuses.

Dr. Gallet (gah-LAY), a middle-aged physician and member of the local Chamber of Deputies. He has become Mouchette's lover but is fearful of being found out. After Mouchette becomes pregnant, she insists that Dr. Gallet perform an abortion. He refuses on ethical grounds, but she threatens him with blackmail if he does not do as she wishes. After she commits suicide, he successfully keeps the facts of the situation quiet, thus protecting her family and himself. Everything he does is self-serving.

Father Donissan (doh-nee-SAH[N]), the saintly Curé of Lumbres. He is a powerfully built, intellectually dull, inarticulate, and awkward priest who is totally devoted to his parishioners. Because his natural instincts frighten him, particularly aspects of his bleak and violent nature, he flagellates himself, wears a hair shirt, and practices other techniques of self-mortification. To gain complete control over his feelings, he fasts and sleeps only a few hours each night. He is most fearful of the joy that spiritual pride may create within himself and leans heavily toward Jansenistic spiritualism. He is tempted by Satan himself when lost on a dark road late at night. He resists the consolations that Satan offers him and, as a result of his victory, attains the ability to read the souls of his parishioners, particularly in the confessional. He becomes a new Curé of Ars and spends the remainder of his life ministering to the souls of sinners. Mouchette commits suicide after he reveals the secrets of her soul to her.

Father Menou-Segrais (meh-NEW-seh-GRAY), an aging canon of the parish of Compagne and spiritual director of Father Donissan. He is a clear-sighted and practical, though spiritual, guide for Father Donissan. Although he is heir to a huge fortune, he has chosen the priestly life and devotes himself to the needs of his flock and to the younger priests in the diocese. He believes that Father Donissan has confronted Satan and urges him to seek temporary refuge in a monastery for further prayer and contemplation. He is in many ways responsible for Father Donissan's growing sainthood, urging him to pursue his spirituality in less masochistic ways, thus opening his heart to his parishioners.

Father Sabiroux (sah-bee-REW), a priest in his fifties who is the pastor of the parish at Luzarnes. He befriends Father Donissan and believes in his miraculous powers, although he is skeptical at first. He is a former professor of chemistry in the minor seminary at Cambrai and leads a well-ordered and sober life.

Satan, or **Lucifer**, a figure who appears as a normal-looking, short, cheerful horse dealer who emerges out of the dark to guide Father Donissan to his destination. Father Donissan is immediately attracted to him and confides the secret of his soul to him. As Satan embraces him and declares his love for him, the young priest becomes violently aware that he is being kissed by Lucifer himself. The priest resists Satan's temptation and is empowered thereafter to read the souls of sinners. His victory over Satan comes as a result of the pity and love he expresses toward him.

Antoine Saint-Marin (sah[n]-mah-RA[N]), a middle-aged, wealthy intellectual. He is a famous author whose book, *The Paschal Candle*, is a scathing indictment of the mystical practices of the Catholic Church. He has come to see the now-famous, aging Father Donissan and to prove to himself that his agnosticism is correct. Although he never meets the aging saint, his rationalistic skepticism is damaged somewhat by the moving stories he hears about the holy pastor. He discovers the priest dead in his confessional at the conclusion of the novel.

— *Patrick Meanor*

UNDER THE VOLCANO

Author: Malcolm Lowry (1909-1957)
First published: 1947
Genre: Novel

Locale: Quauhnahuac (Cuernavaca), Mexico
Time: November 1, 1939
Plot: Psychological realism

Geoffrey Firmin, formerly the British consul to Quauhnahuac, Mexico. He has resigned from the consular service and attempts to find a way not to return to England. When Geoffrey's mother died, Geoffrey's father remarried, and shortly following the birth of Hugh, Geoffrey's half brother, the father walked away from the family. Geoffrey tried a career in the military prior to joining the consular service, but that, too, fell through. Geoffrey finds himself always forcing himself out of personal relationships. During the one day covered by the novel, Geoffrey demonstrates his inability to come to terms with his personal relationships with his wife, Yvonne; his half brother, Hugh; and his friend, Jacques Laruelle. Geoffrey's one escape is his drinking. His greatest distress is that his

brother, Hugh, and friend, Jacques, have committed a sin greater than one against marriage, one against blood. Geoffrey is executed by Mexican officials who accuse him of espionage.

Yvonne Firmin, Geoffrey's wife. Yvonne appears after a one-year absence, during which she secured a divorce from Geoffrey. Like Geoffrey, she is unable to come to terms with her relationship with her spouse and Hugh and Jacques, two men with whom she has had affairs. Prior to her death by being trampled by a runaway horse, Yvonne is the force that brings the three other major characters together.

Hugh Firmin, Geoffrey's half brother and Yvonne's former lover. A leftist journalist who has returned to Quauhnahuac to write an article for the *London Globe*, he also appears to be a gun runner for the Spanish loyalists. Hugh shows his personal makeup when he discloses that he has long been bothered by leaving Quauhnahuac without ever experiencing Yvonne's agony for betraying Geoffrey. Not knowing of the couple's separation, Hugh has returned to Mexico as much to see Yvonne as to see his brother.

Jacques Laruelle, a French film director. His role is to recount the story of the day of Geoffrey and Yvonne's deaths. Jacques spent a period of his youth with Geoffrey and Hugh; therefore, he is considered one of three brothers. Like Hugh, Jacques commits adultery with Geoffrey's wife. His aim is to make a French version of the Faustus story, similar to the version he witnesses in the life of Geoffrey Firmin. During his conversation with Señor Bustamente in the cinema, Jacques reacquires the copy of Elizabethan plays Geoffrey loaned to him and finds a letter Geoffrey had written to Yvonne, imploring her to return, but that he never mailed.

Señor Bustamente (bews-tah-MEHN-tay), the manager of the cinema. During his conversation with Jacques, he discloses that he suspects that Geoffrey may be more than he is; he may, in fact, be a spy. He gives Jacques the copy of Elizabethan plays Geoffrey had loaned to Jacques.

Dr. Arturo Diaz Vigil (ahr-TEW-ro DEE-ahz VEE-hihl), who met Geoffrey only once. During their meeting, Dr. Vigil recognized that of all the people with whom he came into contact, Geoffrey was the only one who had absolutely no one waiting or caring for him.

— *Thomas B. Frazier*

UNDER THE YOKE
(Pod igoto)

Author: Ivan Vazov (1850-1921)
First published: 1893; serial form, 1889-1890
Genre: Novel

Locale: Bulgaria
Time: 1875-1876
Plot: Historical

Ivan Kralich (ih-VAHN KRAH-lihch), a Bulgarian patriot who has escaped after eight years of imprisonment by the Turks. He eludes pursuit and, having changed his name, finds a job teaching school. He is still a revolutionary, however, and after suspicion forces him to flee again, he leads a revolt that is soon crushed. Once more a fugitive, he takes refuge in a mill, where his sweetheart and an old comrade join him. All three are killed after a valiant struggle during an attack on the mill.

Rada (RAH-duh), a gentle orphan who teaches school. She and Kralich fall in love, and she goes to a nearby village to join him, but a misunderstanding and a crushed revolt force them to part. Rada, learning that Kralich is hiding in the mill, goes to aid him. There, she is killed in the Turkish attack.

Sokolov (soh-koh-LOHF), an eccentric Bulgarian. He is the village doctor, though without formal training, and a patriot.

He is often a fugitive from the Turks. He dies in the attack on the mill with Rada and Kralich.

Marika (mah-RIH-kuh), the miller's young daughter. Kralich, hiding in the mill, is able to save her from attack by two Turkish policemen. She and her father then aid the fugitive.

Marko (MAHR-koh), a Bulgarian patriot who aids Kralich and Sokolov.

Mouratliski (mew-raht-LIHS-kih), Kralich's friend and fellow patriot, also a fugitive from the Turks. He poses as an Austrian photographer.

Ivan, called **Kill-the-Bear**, a giant, one of the members of Kralich's group.

Kandov (KAHN-dof), a student who makes Rada miserable by following her about. His attentions and pursuit are the cause of a misunderstanding between Kralich and Rada.

UNDER TWO FLAGS

Author: Ouida (Marie Louise de la Ramée, 1839-1908)
First published: 1867
Genre: Novel

Locale: London and environs, the Continent, and Algeria
Time: Mid-nineteenth century
Plot: Sentimental

The Honorable Bertie Cecil (behr-TEE seh-SEEL), a young nobleman and an officer in the Life Guards who travels in fashionable circles. Although he is deep in debt, he is a gallant young man, loved by ladies and admired by men. When he is accused of forgery, he lets the accusation stand to save a woman's honor. He flees to Africa and joins the Foreign Legion, serving gallantly. He is condemned to death for striking a superior officer who insulted a noblewoman, but he is saved from a firing squad by a camp follower who loves him and takes the bullets in her own body.

Cigarette (see-gah-REHT), an entertainer who is also a patriotic Frenchwoman, though a camp follower. She falls in love with Bertie Cecil, though she hates the English and is jealous of the woman Bertie loves. She saves Bertie's life by dashing between him and the firing squad so that the bullets intended for him hit her.

Princess Corona d'Amagüe (koh-roh-NAH dah-mah-GEW), a beautiful English widow loved by Bertie. He risks death to defend her honor by striking Colonel Chateauroy. Knowing that Bertie has been exonerated of forgery charges and has the right to his father's title and estates, the princess agrees to marry him.

Lord Rockingham, known also as **The Seraph**, Bertie's best friend and the brother of Princess Corona. He tries to save Bertie from the firing squad.

Berkeley Cecil, Bertie's young brother, who inherits the family title and estates after it is assumed that Bertie is dead. He is so selfish that he fears Bertie may return to England to claim what is rightfully his.

Colonel Chateauroy (shah-toh-RWAH), Bertie's commanding officer in the French Foreign Legion. Jealous of Bertie and hating him, he is glad for an opportunity to sentence Bertie to death.

Rake, Bertie's faithful, intelligent servant, whom Bertie rescued from a bad situation. He is killed while serving in the Foreign Legion with his employer.

Lady Guenevere (GWEH-neh-veer), the woman whose honor Bertie protects by not defending himself against charges of forgery.

Lord Royallieu (rwah-yahl-LYEW), Bertie's father, who dislikes his son because Bertie looks like his mother's lover.

UNDER WESTERN EYES

Author: Joseph Conrad (Jósef Teodor Konrad Nałęcz Korzeniowski, 1857-1924)
First published: 1911
Genre: Novel

Locale: St. Petersburg, Russia, and Geneva, Switzerland
Time: Early twentieth century
Plot: Psychological realism

Kirylo Sidorovich Razumov (kih-RIH-loh sih-DOH-roh-vihch rah-ZEW-mov), an idealist and a student at St. Petersburg University. His background is strange and unknown; he has a mysterious benefactor but no family. Returning to his rooms one night, he finds Victor Haldin, a fellow student and casual acquaintance, who confesses that he has assassinated a minister of state. Haldin confidently asks Razumov's help in making his escape, and Razumov promises it. Instead, he secretly betrays the assassin to the police. Because his name is now linked with Haldin's, the dead man's friends accept Razumov as a revolutionary. He is sent to Geneva as a police spy to report on the activities of the revolutionists there. He falls in love with Haldin's sister. After he has received information that makes him safe from detection, he confesses his true role to Miss Haldin and to the revolutionists, who beat him and destroy his hearing. Deaf, he is struck by a tram car that he cannot hear. Crippled for the rest of his life, he is cared for by a compassionate young woman named Tekla.

Victor Haldin, the ardent young revolutionist who kills the minister of state with a bomb. Betrayed by Razumov, he is captured and executed.

Ziemianitch (zeh-MYAH-nihch), the cab driver who was to carry Haldin to safety. He is drunk when Razumov finds him. Later, he hangs himself, supposedly in remorse for having betrayed Haldin.

Nathalie Haldin, the sister of the dead revolutionist. Although she remains free of revolutionary activities, she has a mystical vision of human concord. Later, she returns to Russia to devote herself to social work.

Mrs. Haldin, Victor and Nathalie's mother. Grief over the loss of her son and lack of information as to what happened to him hasten her death.

Peter Ivanovitch (PYOH-tr ee-VAH-noh-vihch), a Russian refugee who has escaped from Siberia and made his way to Geneva. An author and an advocate of feminism for the purpose of elevating humanity, he becomes the leader of the revolutionists and a companion to Madame de S———.

Tekla, the compassionate former secretary of Ivanovitch. Because she feels a compulsion to help the punished and the broken, she cares for Razumov after he is crippled.

Sophia Antonovna, an older, dedicated, and trusted revolutionary who is called to Geneva to verify an identity.

Nikita (nih-KIH-tah), an anarchist, a man so grotesque as to set town dogs barking. He is a famed killer of gendarmes and police agents. He brutalizes Razumov and destroys his hearing after Razumov makes his confession of betrayal. Later, Nikita is revealed as a police informer.

Yakovlitch (YAH-kohv-lihch), a revolutionist whose missions take him to America. He and Sophia Antonovna were once lovers.

Laspara (lah-SPAH-rah), a subversive journalist suspected of complicity in revolutionary plots.

Madame de S———, a legendary figure who presides over a "revolutionary salon."

Prince K———, Razumov's mysterious benefactor, an influential czarist official and Razumov's unacknowledged father.

General T———, the protector of autocracy, to whom Razumov first reports when he decides to betray Haldin to the police.

Councilor Mikulin (mih-KUH-lihn), the government official who sends Razumov to Geneva as a police spy.

Father Zosim (ZOH-sihm), the priest-democrat who gives Razumov a letter of introduction to Peter Ivanovitch.

The tall student, a hungry fellow who works on the fringes of the revolution. He suspects that Razumov was Haldin's accomplice.

Mad Cap Costia, a rich, reckless student, impressed by Razumov's reputation, who wishes to help him.

The narrator, an Englishman and an old language teacher to whom Miss Haldin entrusted Razumov's diary, which supplied the details of the story.

THE UNDERDOGS
(Los de abajo)

Author: Mariano Azuela (1873-1952)
First published: 1915
Genre: Novel

Locale: Mexico
Time: 1914-1915
Plot: Historical

Demetrio Macías (day-MAY-tree-oh mah-SEE-ahs), a Mexican Indian who fights against government forces in the Mexican Revolution. Demetrio rebels against the government as a result of the treatment he receives at the hands of Federalist troops. He has no personal ambition, but his bravery and leadership eventually earn him the rank of general. Still, he is not a student of the rebel cause. His reasons for fighting at the outset are simple, even personal; later, he does not know why he continues to fight. His men wreak havoc on the many towns they enter, but Demetrio, in general, is not the sociopathic thug that so many of his men are, and he often steps in to keep their behavior in check. Demetrio is successful at defeating his enemy in battle but rejects several chances to kill those who have wronged him. He will not consider im- migrating to the United States. He is an essentially peaceful man who has reacted to his circumstances. His only wish is to return home and to a peaceful life. He does return home, but the revolution does not provide him with a peaceful end.

Luis Cervantes (lew-EES sehr-VAHN-tehs), a pseudointellectual who joins Demetrio's troupe, claiming to be a former journalist who has just deserted from the Federalist forces. He has deserted in part because he has come to see the truth about the government's side, and he sympathizes with the poor and oppressed, represented by the rebels. How much of Cervantes' story and, more important, his stated beliefs about the revolution is true is often difficult to discern. It takes some time for Demetrio and his men to trust him. He has the ability to intellectualize the revolution in all the ways in which Demetrio cannot, and it is Cervantes who encourages Demetrio to take his rightful place in history. Cervantes, however, looks out for himself. He always keeps himself out of harm's way during battle, he collects booty when the opportunity arises, and he finally immigrates to Texas, from where he invites another of Demetrio's men to come so the two of them can open a Mexican restaurant together.

Solís (soh-LEES), a true intellectual who has become disillusioned with the rebel cause. Solís appears only briefly, but his conversation with Cervantes provides an important view of the revolution, one probably similar to the author's view. Solís began as an idealist and supported the rebel cause, but he has come to see the revolution as a hurricane and its participants like leaves in the wind, simply swept up by circumstances. He still appreciates the revolution on an ideal, theoretical level, but in the hands of the thugs who have executed it, he recognizes that it has become nothing more than an arena for robbery and murder. Solís is killed by a stray bullet as he and Cervantes talk.

Blondie (or **Whitey Margarito**, depending on the edition of the translation), a rebel who exhibits outrageous, even sadistic, behavior. Virtually all of Demetrio's men display repugnant, criminal behavior (and in fact share criminal pasts), but Blondie's behavior borders on the criminally insane. For example, he tortures a prisoner by dragging him down a road with a rope around his neck, and he makes an innocent person he meets in the street dance by shooting at his feet.

Camilla (kah-MEE-yah) or **Camila** (kah-MEE-lah), depending on the edition of the translation, a young woman who helps nurse a wounded Demetrio back to health. Her interests lie in Cervantes, who ignores her. Later, Cervantes tricks her into coming to join Demetrio, who has expressed an interest in her. She comes to care for Demetrio, but her criticism of the barbaric behavior of Blondie lands her on the wrong side of War Paint, who brutally murders her later.

War Paint or **La Pintada** (lah peen-TAH-dah), depending on the edition of the translation, a camp follower and armed female thug who accompanies Demetrio's men. At first, she expresses interest in Demetrio, but soon she is back at Blondie's side. She is jealous of Camilla on many levels, and when Demetrio orders the women not to accompany the men—an order instigated by Camilla—La Pintada, already enraged by Camilla's comments about Blondie's behavior, stabs Camilla to death in front of Demetrio and his men. Her attitude and actions are surpassed in their criminal nature only by those of Blondie.

— *Keith H. Brower*

THE UNDERGROUND MAN

Author: Ross Macdonald (Kenneth Millar, 1915-1983)
First published: 1971
Genre: Novel

Locale: California
Time: The 1960's
Plot: Detective and mystery

Lew Archer, the narrator, a private detective and former police officer who is middle-aged and divorced. Not a typical violent hard-boiled detective, Archer is more a questioner than a doer, humane and sensitive to clients, victims, and even criminals. He works by understanding and analyzing psychological states and family histories rather than by collecting physical evidence.

Jean Broadhurst, his client, whose son apparently is kidnapped during a visit with his father to his grandmother's mountain cabin.

Ronny Broadhurst, her six-year-old son, who witnesses the death of his father, Stanley, in the same place that Stanley aurally witnessed his own father's shooting fifteen years earlier.

Stanley Broadhurst, Jean's twenty-seven-year-old, newly estranged husband, Ronny's father. Stanley was deeply affected as a child by the disappearance of his father, Leo, and has become obsessed with the need to search for him, neglecting his family as a result. He has recently stirred up interest in that search by putting an advertisement in the paper and offering a reward for information about Leo. His murder by pickax at his family's mountain cabin near the beginning of the novel leads eventually to the discovery that Leo was killed fifteen years earlier in the same place.

Elizabeth Broadhurst, the wealthy wife of Leo Broadhurst, mother of Stanley, and grandmother of Ronny. A cold-hearted daddy's girl, she is proud of her family's history. She shot Leo out of jealousy fifteen years earlier and believed that she had killed him.

Leo Broadhurst, a man who vanished fifteen years earlier, supposedly leaving his family to elope with Ellen Strome Kilpatrick and subsequently deserting her as well. In fact, Leo had been murdered the night before his planned departure. A chronic womanizer and the father of Susan Crandall, he blamed his infidelities on his wife's lack of attention to him. He had gone to the mountain cabin with Martha and Susan, was shot (but not fatally) by Elizabeth, and then was stabbed to death by Edna as he lay unconscious.

Edna Snow, Elizabeth's former housekeeper. She murdered Leo in revenge for the trouble he had caused Fritz and also in judgment of his infidelities, then murdered Stanley fifteen years later as he was about to discover his father's body and Edna's crime. A quick-moving gray-haired woman, she is accustomed to making excuses for Fritz and is overprotective of him.

Frederick (Fritz) Snow, Edna Snow's son and Elizabeth's gardener, in his middle thirties, with a moon face and a scar resembling a harelip. Fritz, along with Albert, took the blame and was punished for Leo's statutory rape of Martha Nickerson. Fritz suffered a nervous breakdown as a result and has been "emotionally immature" ever since. He lives with his mother and is both afraid of and dependent on her.

Albert Sweetner, a former convict who was once a foster child of Edna Snow. He responds to Stanley's advertisement but is murdered by Edna before he can reveal the information that he and Fritz buried Leo's body for her.

Brian Kilpatrick, a real estate agent and the partner of Elizabeth Broadhurst in the Canyon estates development. He is a dangerously emotional man about forty-five years old. Out of jealousy caused by his wife's affair with Leo, he called Elizabeth to tell her that Leo and Martha would be in the cabin that night. He has been blackmailing Elizabeth ever since.

Ellen Strome, Brian's former wife and the former mistress of Leo Broadhurst. She went to Reno to obtain a divorce from Brian and wait for Leo, who never arrived. She has become a lonely woman who is content with her loneliness and spends her time painting. A former high-school teacher, she has stayed friendly with Martha, a former pupil.

Jerry Kilpatrick, a lanky boy of about nineteen, with long hair and a beard. He is hostile and emotional. He flees with Susan Crandall and Ronny Broadhurst after Stanley's murder.

Susan Crandall, the eighteen- or nineteen-year-old illegitimate daughter of Leo Broadhurst and the then-underage Martha Nickerson. Susan accompanies Stanley and Ronny to the mountain cabin, panicking and fleeing with Ronny after Stanley is murdered. She was present, as a three-year-old child, at Leo's murder. Although basically a good girl, she is confused and suicidal.

Lester Crandall, a shrewd and wealthy sixty-year-old man. He married Martha Nickerson when she was pregnant with Leo's child, Susan, and reared Susan as his own daughter.

Martha Nickerson Crandall, an attractive middle-aged woman who felt that she and her family did not belong in the wealthy world in which her husband wanted them to live. She has never told anyone that she was with Leo when he was shot.

— *William Nelles and Lori Williams*

UNDINE

Author: Friedrich de La Motte-Fouqué (1777-1843)
First published: 1811
Genre: Novel

Locale: Austria
Time: The Middle Ages
Plot: Symbolism

Undine (EWN-dee-nuh), a water spirit, daughter of a Mediterranean water prince and foster daughter of a poor fisherman and his wife. Fifteen years earlier, she appeared, as a child of three or four, at the fisherman's cottage shortly after the disappearance of his young daughter. She is now a beautiful young woman but rebellious, mischievous, and wildly capricious. When Huldbrand mentions Bertalda in telling his adventures, Undine bites him out of jealousy. After she and Huldbrand are married and the priest tells her to attune her soul to her husband's, she becomes a submissive, loving wife. She generously consents to have the rejected Bertalda live at Ringstetten. On a trip down the Danube, when Huldbrand angrily calls her a sorceress, she disappears into the water. After Huldbrand's marriage to Bertalda, Undine appears to him and embraces him until he dies. Following his burial, she becomes a spring that almost encircles his grave, thus embracing him forever.

Sir Huldbrand von Ringstetten (HEWLD-brahnd fon RIHNG-sta-tan), a knight, wealthy, handsome, and a model of all knightly virtues except that of constancy of heart. Though

forewarned against marrying Bertalda, he does so. His spirit wife, released from the fountain in which she lives, then claims him eternally.

Kuhleborn (KEW-luh-bohrn), Undine's uncle, a water spirit who appears sometimes to mortals as a tall man dressed in a white mantle and in various other disguises. He warns Huldbrand to protect Undine and reveals to Undine the secret of Bertalda's birth. He mischievously interferes many times in the lives of Undine, Huldbrand, and Bertalda.

Bertalda (bahr-TAHL-dah), a beautiful but haughty lady loved by Huldbrand. She is the foster daughter of a powerful duke and his duchess but the real daughter of Undine's foster parents, who lost her shortly before Undine came to them. Bertalda is shocked and angry to learn of her humble origin. After she has been turned out by her foster parents, she acquires some humility, but her haughtiness occasionally returns.

Father Heilmann (HIL-mahn), an old priest who marries Undine and Huldbrand, refuses to unite Huldbrand and Bertalda, and administers the burial service for Huldbrand.

THE UNFORTUNATE TRAVELLER: Or, The Life of Jack Wilton

Author: Thomas Nashe (1567-1601)
First published: 1594
Genre: Novel

Locale: England and the Continent
Time: Mid-sixteenth century
Plot: Picaresque

Jack Wilton, a page to Henry VIII of England. Bored with his life, he leaves King Henry's service to become a soldier of fortune. Because he is a bright and merry lad, he has all sorts of adventures and scrapes. He travels with the earl of Surrey as a companion throughout Europe. Finally, he returns to England and the service of Henry VIII.

The earl of Surrey, Jack's friend, benefactor, and traveling companion. He is a gallant courtier.

Tabitha, a Venetian prostitute who meets Jack and the earl of Surrey. She and her pander try to kill the earl but are caught and executed.

Geraldine, a beautiful woman of Florence loved by the earl of Surrey. The earl fights all comers in a tourney to prove his love for her.

Diamante, a goldsmith's wife suspected of infidelity by her husband. She takes Jack as a lover to punish her husband for his suspicions. After the goldsmith's death, Diamante travels with Jack, and the two share many adventures, including being bondservants in the household of one of the pope's mistresses.

Johannes de Imola, a citizen of Rome with whom Jack and Diamante live for a time. He is unfortunate enough to die of the plague during an epidemic.

Heraclide de Imola, Johannes' wife. She commits suicide after being raped by a band of cutthroats, and her death is blamed on Jack, putting him for a time in danger of hanging.

Cutwolfe, a famous brigand whose execution Jack witnesses. Cutwolfe confesses to murdering the bandit who led the assault on Heraclide and Diamante.

UNHOLY LOVES

Author: Joyce Carol Oates (1938-   )
First published: 1979
Genre: Novel

Locale: Woodslee, New York
Time: The 1970's
Plot: Stream of consciousness

Brigit Stott, a professor of English and the only novelist at the relatively prestigious Woodslee University, 256 miles north of New York City. Thirty-eight years old, thin, sharp-featured, and attractive in a mysterious way, Brigit has written two novels that have attained minor success, but her current work remains a tumble of notes and sketches. Separated from her abusive husband, whom she married when she was twenty-two years old, she begins an intense love affair with a musician on campus, just when she had hoped to fall in love with the great visiting poet in residence, Albert St. Dennis. Her introspection, self-respect, and overwhelming desire to write novels, however, keep her from destruction in the painful romance; victoriously, she realizes that nothing in her life is inevitable.

Alexis Kessler, a thirty-two-year-old composer and pianist on the faculty at Woodslee University. Blond and beautiful, he has had numerous love affairs with both men and women. He is attracted to the mystery in Brigit and, while they are together, wants to possess her and transform her into a beautiful woman. Most of his peers feel intense animosity toward him, and it is only the dean of humanities' support that allows him to remain on campus. Meretricious and frustrated by an unrealized career, Alexis is pursued by unwarranted scandal and has an almost childlike inability to handle responsibility.

Albert St. Dennis, a seventy-year-old English poet in a one-year residence at Woodslee University. Known as the greatest living English poet, he has recently become a widower and looks and behaves like a confused and feeble old man. At his first poetry reading on campus, he is a critical success. Faculty members covet his attention and seek his opinions and insight, but his comments are often garbled and sententious, even though his career is based on impressive creativity and scholarship. His death, caused by a fire ignited from a cigarette he dropped when he passed out in a drunken stupor on his sofa, brings chaos and disorder to the entire English department.

Oliver Byrne, the attractive dean of humanities. Ambitious and egotistical, he views his current position as a stepping-stone on the path of an extremely successful career in academe. He regularly lists to himself the brilliant victories he has had, the latest and best of which was arranging the yearlong residency of Albert St. Dennis. Considering his wife, at best, to be a necessary inconvenience, he arranges a social life that will lead to the presidency of Woodslee or another major university.

Marilyn Byrne, the troubled wife of Oliver Byrne. She tries to create proper parties and a proper persona, but, as the year progresses, she fails more and more miserably, until she finally seeks divorce and hospitalization.

Warren Hochberg, the chairman of the English department. His one scholarly book, on John Dryden, belongs to the far distant past, and now he seems devoted to his administrative position. A dull man, he operates successfully in academic middle management.

Vivian Hochberg, the attractive and sophisticated wife of Warren Hochberg. Vivian, it is rumored, was in love with another member of the department, Lewis Seidel. For mysterious reasons, the relationship ended, but an emotional intimacy remains between the two of them.

Lewis Seidel, an influential faculty member and sometime rival of Oliver Byrne. Lewis had hoped to resurrect his flagging scholarly reputation with a book about St. Dennis' work. Locked into a loveless marriage, but affable and social, he has liaisons with other women, but he is suffering increasingly from an unnamed pulmonary condition.

Faye Seidel, Lewis' wife, who rightly feels unloved and out of place in the social group in which she is forced to remain.

Gladys Fetler, an older and very popular professor who is forced into retirement though remaining well-liked by students and members of the department, particularly Brigit.

Gowan Vaughan-Jones, the most highly acclaimed critic in the department. He gains the greatest benefits for his career from the visit of Albert St. Dennis. Although eccentric and ingenuous, he is likable and unpretentious.

Leslie Cullendon, a James Joyce scholar who is dying from a mysterious degenerative disease that has forced him into a wheelchair. He is vitriolic, drunken, and insulting to everyone, including his wife; as a result, he is unliked and avoided by all.

Babs Cullendon, the long-suffering wife of Leslie. At parties, she either remains silent or complains of what she must endure in her life with Leslie.

Ernest Jaeger, a twenty-eight-year-old newly hired professor. Hardworking and grateful for his position, he still suffers the anguish associated with possible termination.

Sandra Jaeger, the beautiful, blond, twenty-four-year-old wife of Ernest. At first idealistic about her husband's bright future, she later becomes the lover of Lewis Seidel to combat boredom.

— *Vicki K. Robinson*

THE UNICORN

Author: Iris Murdoch (1919-   )
First published: 1963
Genre: Novel

Locale: A remote region in western Ireland
Time: The early 1960's
Plot: Love

Hannah Crean-Smith, nominally the mistress of Gaze Castle, a large and forbidding nineteenth century house situated near the black sandstone cliffs of western Ireland's coastline. Hannah, a lovely golden-haired woman who is no longer young nor yet middle-aged, is restricted to the castle because of an indiscretion that she committed almost nine years before the story begins. Having married Peter Crean-Smith before she was twenty years old, she then had a two-year affair with Philip "Pip" Lejour, a neighbor. After being discovered by Peter, who was more frequently absent than present, she is said to have tried to kill him by pushing him over a cliff, after which she was imprisoned in the house and her husband left for New York. She has not seen him since, but he is rumored to be returning soon. Pampered and indulged for their own selfish purposes by the staff and a few other persons, Hannah nevertheless is a prisoner, arrested in time, fearful of the world outside the castle, and apparently content to live in an alcoholic haze, childlike and unchanging, like an enchanted princess.

Marian Taylor, who is in her late twenties, recently a schoolmistress and now a companion and tutor to Hannah Crean-Smith. Having decided that her relationship with Geoffrey would never go beyond affectionate friendship, Marian answered an advertisement that suggested change and adventure. She is astonished to learn that instead of a child her charge is a beautiful woman of about her own age. Marian quickly overcomes her initial apprehension and is soon as devoted to this appealing, unusual person as everyone else in the household seems to be. The other household members, however, all play a role in keeping Hannah quietly content, dependent, and totally deprived of freedom. When a rescue attempt fails miserably, Marian, shaken by grief and acceptance, decides to return to the world of reality.

Gerald Scottow, the head keeper of the castle and of Hannah. Once Peter Crean-Smith's lover, he now holds young Jamesie Evercreech in a similar thralldom. In his early forties, he is a big, handsome man, with a powerful, domineering manner slightly disguised by a courteous, reserved exterior. A local man, he is reputed to have supernatural powers commonly ascribed to the "fairy folk" of the region. His dominion over Hannah and the staff is absolute, even during his frequent and unexplained absences. Marian is both attracted to and repelled by him. Having incurred the hatred and anger of everyone through his cruel and brutal strength, Gerald threatens to take Hannah away with him after the aborted escape. Before he can do so, she kills him with Pip Lejour's shotgun and then shortly thereafter takes her own life by drowning.

Denis Nolan, the clerk of Gaze and the most devoted of those who serve Hannah. Formerly, he was employed at Riders. Like Gerald Scottow, he is a local man, thought to have fairy powers. He is thirty-three years old, short, watchful, and taciturn. He performs services that cheer and entertain Hannah, such as singing in an astonishingly beautiful voice, dexterously cutting her hair, and bringing live creatures from outside for her to see. She never leaves the house, except on three disastrous occasions. He and Marian are united in their protective love for Hannah and their fearful hatred of Gerald, against whom Denis warns and advises Marian. Slowly, Marian begins to comprehend the strange circumstances surrounding life at Gaze. Only Denis seems to be single-mindedly and selflessly concerned for Hannah; when she dies, he leaves the castle, as does everyone else.

Jamesie Evercreech, a distant relation of Hannah, the chauffeur and Gerald's current lover. Five years ago, Jamesie tried to help Hannah escape but was stopped by Gerald, who whipped him and completely subjugated him to his own will.

Violet Evercreech, Jamesie's sister and the housekeeper of Gaze. Of an indeterminate age somewhere between forty and sixty, she is much older than Jamesie. She is thin and intense, and she is perhaps a little mad, like everyone else at Gaze.

Effingham Cooper, a governmental department head, a frequent houseguest at Riders, where he visits his former tutor, and an egotistical pretender to Hannah's love, though he is essentially more curious and intrigued than truly concerned about her. Marian enlists Effingham in her plot to release Hannah from her prison. He experiences an analogous adventure when he is almost drowned in a bog, from which he is magically rescued by Denis. At the end of the novel, Effingham leaves the area, relieved to be released from the spell that has held them all for a while and to which so many of them succumbed.

Alice Lejour, a horticulturist who once accused Denis of having tried to rape her, after which he was compelled to leave Riders. Later, she confesses that she had lied and that, as a matter of fact, it was she who tried in vain to get Denis to make love to her. She becomes a dear and solid friend to Marian during the turbulent and tragic events at the end of the novel.

Philip "Pip" Lejour, a journalist and poet, the owner of Riders. He is the brother of Alice and the son of Max Lejour. Pip figures in the novel primarily as an important person in Hannah's life when the two had an affair and were discovered by Peter Crean-Smith, then later, at the end of the novel, when

he comes armed with a shotgun to rescue Hannah. She refuses to leave with Pip, however, and he is reported to have killed himself accidentally while cleaning his gun.

Max Lejour, an elderly, weary classics scholar, the father of Pip and Alice. Although he takes no part in the action of the story, Max is significant in his revealing conversations with several of the characters, particularly Effingham Cooper, his former pupil. He is the only person who seems to understand the whole mystery of Gaze, but his wisdom is of no help to anyone. He has remained aloof from Gaze all this while, yet it is to him that Hannah leaves her entire property in a will that is a surprise to all the survivors except Alice, who realizes that it was only Max, who did not prey on or interfere with Hannah, whom she really loved.

— *Natalie Harper*

UNION STREET

Author: Pat Barker (1943-   )
First published: 1982
Genre: Novel

Locale: A depressed inner-city neighborhood in northeastern England
Time: Winter, 1973
Plot: Social realism

Kelly Brown, an eleven-year-old schoolgirl who lives with her older sister Linda and their mother. "Uncle" Arthur, the latest in a succession of her mother's male friends, also lives with the family for a while. A latchkey child who frequently skips school, Kelly has grown accustomed to deprivation and to using deception to survive. Although proud of her independence, Kelly still unconsciously clings to her mother, seeking her love and approval. When Kelly is raped, she is too afraid to tell anyone at first; her reactions emerge later, in a screaming fit. Kelly cuts her hair as an act of self-mutilation and of aggression, and she retreats into an obstinate isolation. Kelly also acts out her pain and anger through petty crime but is increasingly afraid of herself and what she might do.

Joanne Wilson, an eighteen-year-old bakery worker who wants for herself something different from what she observes around her. When she finds herself pregnant and unmarried, however, she gradually realizes that she is caught in the same trap. The pregnancy alienates her from her mother. Moreover, although communication with her resentful boyfriend, Ken, is never good, the couple feel themselves doomed to marry. Joanne is different enough from others to stand up for a co-worker, but her conformity is revealed through her relationship with the midget Joss. Joss is handsome and offers hospitality, a refuge, advice, and respect, but Joanne cannot imagine more than friendship because of his size.

Lisa Goddard, a young married woman with two boys (Kevin and Darren) and a third child on the way. She is often forced to cope alone because her unemployed husband, Brian, is always out drinking. He is often abusive when he does return home. Lisa is frequently tired and desperate, and she takes her anger and frustration out on the children. Although this reaction horrifies her, she is unable to stop herself. The discovery that Brian has stolen money she was saving for the new baby finally gives Lisa the courage to take a stand, but it is short-lived, causing Lisa resentment and bitterness. The

birth of her daughter in the new hospital does little to free her from this situation.

Muriel Scaife, a woman who works as a school cleaner while her husband John is on disability leave because of prolonged illness. The couple have a twelve-year-old son (Richard) and an older daughter (Sharon). Richard is clever, studious, and protective of his mother. Muriel's happiness is cut short by John's death. Coming to terms with this loss proves difficult for Muriel, who must continue to defend John to her mother and also support the family financially. In addition, Richard, who is also mourning his father, lapses into sullen uncooperativeness. Muriel's love, fortitude, and almost religious optimism finally effect a reconciliation, however, and she and Richard face an uncertain future together.

Iris King, a middle-aged worker for a home health service. She lives with her husband, Ted; her daughter Brenda, who is sixteen years old; and her schizophrenic aunt, Laura. Two other daughters, Sheila and Lindsey, already have families of their own. Solidly built, Iris survives on tea, cigarettes, and adrenaline. To some, she appears vulgar, and she is quick to judge and gossip, but she can be counted on in a crisis and is a good neighbor to everyone. Although she works full-time, she keeps her own house spotlessly clean and cares about her reputation above all. Born in the worst part of town, Iris remains emotionally scarred for life by her childhood and is subject to fits of black depression. Because of these experiences, Iris is overprotective of her own children. When Brenda's pregnancy presents a crisis, Iris arranges for an illegal abortion to save face.

Blonde Dinah, a sixty-year-old prostitute who picks up men in pubs for whatever they can afford to pay. Although Dinah is physically run-down and lives in a sordid rented room, for men like George Harrison, a retired blast-furnace worker, sex with Dinah is a revelation.

Alice Bell, a widow in her mid-seventies who lives on social security. A staunch socialist, her two main fears remain the workhouse and a pauper's funeral. To avoid these supreme indignities, Alice clings to her independence and forgoes heat and food to save for her funeral. The double shame of poverty and her emaciated appearance at first isolate her from others, but, in time, she comes to trust and depend on the help of caring neighbors such as Iris King, her home health worker. In turn, Alice serves as a mother figure and discreet friend to many. After a stroke makes Alice even more helpless, her son decides to transfer her to the dreaded nursing home (formerly the workhouse), causing Alice to make one last gesture of independence.

— *Melanie C. Hawthorne*

THE UNIVERSAL BASEBALL ASSOCIATION, INC., J. HENRY WAUGH, PROP.

Author: Robert Coover (1932-   )
First published: 1968
Genre: Novel

Locale: An American city
Time: The 1950's and the "UBA Years LVI and CLVII"
Plot: Psychological

J. Henry Waugh, a fifty-six-year-old accountant for the firm of Dunkelmann, Zauber & Zifferblatt (German for "Obscurantist, Magic & Clock-face"). He is the creator ("J. Henry Waugh" is a play on "Jehovah") of a dice-and-paper game involving the Universal Baseball Association, Inc., a baseball league consisting of eight teams, with twenty-one players each. Play is controlled by the throws of three dice, with various combinations representing hits, errors, strikeouts, stolen bases, and other (fifty-six in all) standard activities and strategies of a baseball game. Waugh plays out full seasons of the league. He keeps complete records (earned-run averages, most valuable players, and so on) for each season. In what is now Year LVI of the UBA, he has some forty volumes of records dating from Year IX. Henry's ballplayers, managers, owners, and chancellors become real people to him, and his creation takes over his life. Year CLVII represents either Henry's complete departure from his ordinary existence or the UBA's survival of its creator.

Lou Engel, Henry's coworker. He is a devoted but inept friend whose corpulence attests his love of good food. He spends every Sunday evening at the cinema. He is the only person with whom Henry tries to share the UBA. During the single occasion on which they play, Lou is much more interested in recounting a film he has just seen than in playing Henry's intricate and highly detailed game. True to his name, which is a play on "Lucifer Angel," he messes up Henry's creation by spilling beer on the score sheets and record charts.

Hettie Irden, an aging B-girl. She is Henry's earthy (German *irden*) hetaera. Her lovemaking with Henry is described in the vocabulary of baseball, for example, "pushing and pulling, they ran the bases, pounded into first, slid into second heels high, somersaulted over third, shot home standing up, then into the box once more, swing away, and run them all again."

Horace Zifferblatt, the director and sole surviving member of the firm of Dunkelmann, Zauber & Zifferblatt. As Henry's employer, he is exacting and intolerant of laxity but not without some patience and consideration. Well aware of Henry's valuable competence, he puts up with Henry's tardiness and absenteeism as long as he can; ultimately, however, as Henry's preoccupation with the UBA causes him to neglect his work completely, Zifferblatt fires him.

Pete, a bartender, whom Henry calls **Jake** in his imposition of the UBA world on the actual world. Jake Bradley is a UBA second baseman who retires to barkeeping.

Mitch Porter, a suave and stylishly competent restaurant owner who serves Lou and Henry a gourmet meal of duck.

Benny Diskin, the son of a delicatessen owner. He makes regular deliveries to Henry.

Damon Rutherford, a rookie UBA pitcher for the Pioneers team. He is cool, gracious, and superbly talented. After he pitches a perfect game against the Haymakers, his creator (Henry) assumes the Damon Rutherford identity in a night of lovemaking with Hettie. In a game against the Knickerbockers, Damon is fatally beaned by pitcher Jock Casey in accordance with Henry's having thrown three consecutive triple ones with the dice.

Jock Casey, a rookie UBA pitcher for the Knickerbockers. He is gaunt and emotionless. After fatally (and, to all appearances, deliberately) beaning Damon Rutherford, he is killed in a subsequent game by a line drive to the mound, as Henry manipulates the death by deliberately setting up a third consecutive dice throw of triple sixes.

Royce Ingram, a UBA catcher for the Pioneers. He hits the line drive that kills Jock Casey.

Brock Rutherford, all-time great UBA pitcher and father of Damon and Brock II. He is fifty-six years old in Year LVI and is in the stands on Brock Rutherford Day when his son Damon is killed by a pitched ball.

Sycamore Flynn, the UBA manager of the Knickerbockers and ancestor of Galen Flynn.

Barney Bancroft, the UBA manager of the Pioneers. He is murdered after he becomes the ninth chancellor of the UBA.

Raglan "Pappy" Rooney, the UBA manager of the Haymakers, who lives to the age of 143.

Melbourne Trench, the UBA manager of the seventh-place Excelsiors and ancestor of Paul Trench.

Hardy Ingram, a descendant of Royce Ingram. In Year CLVII of the UBA, he plays the role of Damon Rutherford (equated with good) in the ritual Damonsday celebration.

Paul Trench, a descendant of Melbourne Trench. In Year CLVII of the UBA, he takes the part of Royce Ingram in the Damonsday rite.

Galen Flynn, a descendant of Sycamore Flynn. In Year CLVII of the UBA, he appears to have been assigned the role of Jock Casey (equated with evil) in the Damonsday rite.

— *Roy Arthur Swanson*

THE UNLIT LAMP

Author: Radclyffe Hall (1880-1943)
First published: 1924
Genre: Novel

Locale: Seabourne, on the southern coast of England
Time: Near the beginning of the twentieth century
Plot: Bildungsroman

Joan Ogden, the protagonist. The oldest daughter of a retired British colonel and his pretentious wife, Joan has one sister and few friends. Her life is circumscribed by the domestic confines of the small, economically strapped family home in an obscure seaside resort. Short-haired Joan is willful, unconcerned with stereotypical feminine pursuits, and uncommonly intelligent. Encouraged by her beloved governess, she aspires to attend university and become a physician. Joan's mother, however, struggles against all such plans. Joan's development as a person, as a typical unmarried woman of her historical moment, is the novel's focus.

Mary Ogden, Joan's mother and her antagonist. Part of a once-notable family line, Mary sees her diminished existence as a military wife being measured by anniversaries of her forebears' accomplishments. She consistently defers to her demanding husband and has difficulty managing her household. Inclined to neurotic, psychosomatic illnesses, she apparently loves her daughters but manipulatively maintains a life-long iron grasp on Joan's doting attention. Mary is a maddening, monstrous presence in the novel.

Elizabeth Rodney, Joan's governess and friend. An exceptionally bright, well-educated woman, Elizabeth moves from Cambridge to Seabourne to live with her unmarried brother, a banker. She energetically undertakes the education of Joan and her sister, Milly, remaining in her position even when Ogden finances are failing. Devoted to Joan, she presses her toward a university education despite her sex, for she perceives the girl's great intellectual potential. Elizabeth and Joan also develop profound personal affection, which sets Elizabeth and Mrs. Ogden at odds, as unequal and bitter rivals. Elizabeth is the third leg in a volatile female triangle that forms the novel's main conflict.

Richard Benson, the "sensitive" son of a prominent local family, Joan's alter ego. He loves Joan and respects her intellect, but Joan disregards his love. He leaves Seabourne to attend university and reappears only near the novel's end, reemphasizing the consequences of Joan's choices.

Milly Ogden, Joan's sister, a pretty, self-centered, musically gifted child. She escapes her mother's control, leaving home to pursue a violin career. Dutiful Joan enables Milly's rebellion, but Milly dies young of consumption.

James Ogden, Joan's despised father, a retired officer who served in India. James bullies his wife and daughters and secretly squanders the girls' inheritance, left in trust by his Americanized sister. James resists female independence and resents the terminal illness that reduces him to an invalid.

—Penelope J. Engelbrecht

AN UNSUITABLE JOB FOR A WOMAN

Author: P. D. James (1920-   )
First published: 1972
Genre: Novel

Locale: London and Cambridge, England
Time: The 1970's
Plot: Detective and mystery

Cordelia Gray, the protagonist, a twenty-one-year-old detective on her first case. She inherited Pryde's Detective Agency when her senior partner, Bernie Pryde, committed suicide. Reared in a succession of foster homes and a convent until her father, an itinerant Marxist poet, called her to leave school and assist him as a party organizer, Cordelia has become an extremely self-reliant young woman, accustomed to making her own way in the world. Ironically, this case takes her to Cambridge, the university she was preparing to attend when her father took her from school. This awareness informs her investigation, as does the instruction of her late partner. Most of all, however, she is moved by her increasingly powerful sense of identification with the subject of her investigation, Mark Callender.

Sir Ronald Callender, a noted scientist who directs a private laboratory. He displays a cool demeanor and single-minded interest in his work. Sir Ronald hires Cordelia to investigate the motives for the recent suicide of his son Mark. It quickly becomes clear that he and Mark have shared little contact and less affection, so his concern seems surprising to Mark's friends. At the novel's conclusion, he dies in what seems to be a suicide.

Elizabeth Leaming, Sir Ronald's beautiful secretary and housekeeper. She is obviously unhappy at the prospect of Cordelia's investigation into Mark's death. When her interest in Mark finally is revealed and explained, she conspires with Cordelia to conceal the circumstances of Sir Ronald's death.

Lunn, Sir Ronald's sinister young lab assistant, whom he took from an orphanage and trained. He obviously dislikes Elizabeth and Cordelia.

Sophia Tilling, a Cambridge student, Mark Callender's former lover. She likes Cordelia but—along with her brother Hugo, Hugo's girlfriend Isabelle, and her own current lover Davie Stevens—seems intent on concealing information about Mark's death.

Isabelle de Lingerie, a beautiful but rather stupid exchange student from France. She visited Mark on the night of his death.

Miss Markland, who lives with her brother and her sister-in-law. They employed Mark as a gardener when he suddenly decided to leave Cambridge. Of the three employers, only Miss Markland seems interested in Mark's death and Cordelia's investigation of it. She gives Cordelia permission to stay in Mark's cottage.

Mark Callender, the subject of Cordelia's investigation. A few months before his death, Mark suddenly left Cambridge, where he had been a promising history student, and took a job as a gardener. Although he is not alive during the novel's action, Cordelia comes to feel very close to him while she stays in his cottage. She reads his books, sleeps in his bed, and admires traces of his orderly habits. Her growing attachment to him is instrumental in her understanding of his death and becomes a theme of the novel.

—*Ann Davison Garbett*

DER UNTERGEHER

Author: Thomas Bernhard (1931-1989)
First published: 1983
Genre: Novel

Locale: Wankham, a village in Upper Austria
Time: 1981
Plot: Psychological

The narrator, an Austrian writer and former pianist from a well-to-do family, suffering from pulmonary disease. As the novel begins, the narrator has just attended the funeral of Wertheimer, one of his two best friends. He stops on the spur of the moment at an inn in the vicinity of his deceased friend's hunting lodge in Upper Austria. Feeling lonely, vulnerable, and somewhat guilty because of his recent neglect of Wertheimer, the narrator attempts to come to terms with his friend's suicide. This attempt leads him to explore the lifelong friendship and competition between him, Wertheimer, and a third pianist, Glenn Gould, and to review the consequences of that relationship for each of the men's individual biographies. The three men met at the Mozarteum in Salzburg twenty-eight years before, studying under Horowitz. The narrator instantly recognizes Gould's musical genius and, not content to be second best, gives up music and, eventually, his beloved Steinway. The narrator turns to philosophy, although he never really understands what it is, and writing, although he never publishes his work. Eventually, he flees to Madrid to escape the narrow-minded dilettantism and social corruption he perceives in Austria. The narrator is convinced that this change in locale protects him from inborn (Austrian) tendencies toward suicide and insanity, tendencies to which Wertheimer has succumbed. While in Madrid, the narrator starts a manuscript about Glenn Gould. Although he had thought it complete, he realizes now that it must be totally revised once again. The narrator's reminiscences eventually are interrupted by the landlady of the inn. From her and, later, from Franz Kohlroser, the narrator learns about Wertheimer's last few weeks of life. He proceeds to the hunting lodge, hoping—in vain—to be the recipient of Wertheimer's notes.

Wertheimer, an Austrian amateur philosopher and former pianist from a well-to-do family, the second of the three lifelong friends. Prone to failure, self-pity, madness, and despair, and suffering from pulmonary disease, Wertheimer is named the loser, or founderer (*der Untergeher*), by Gould. Wertheimer lacks a sense of his own unique identity, striving always to imitate other, more successful people. It is for this reason that his contact with Gould proves to be fatal. Like the narrator, Wertheimer recognizes the greatness of Gould immediately upon hearing him play at the Mozarteum. He follows the narrator's lead and exchanges his Borsendorf piano for a desk and his music for philosophy, jotting down aphorisms on thousands of paper scraps only to burn them all just prior to his death. He writes a book called *Der Untergeher* but revises and corrects it so frequently that only the title remains. Ultimately, and in contrast to the narrator, all such survival tactics prove ineffectual. Whereas the narrator puts both physical (Madrid) and psychological (denial of desire to be a virtuoso) distance between himself and his former life as a concert pianist, Wertheimer continues to desire the virtuosity of a Glenn Gould and despairs when he cannot attain it. The immediate reason for Wertheimer's suicide seems to be his sister's marriage, which Wertheimer perceives as personal betrayal and abandonment and which prompts him, for revenge, to hang himself on a tree in front of her new home. The marriage, however, serves only as the final release of forces that began to destroy Wertheimer the moment he first heard Gould play. Gould's death at the age of fifty-one and at the height of his musical brilliance forces Wertheimer, the same age, to see his life as the failure that it is.

Glenn Gould, a Canadian American piano virtuoso (a real person, not merely a fictional character), the third of the lifelong friends. Like the others, he is consumptive and rich. Described by the narrator as "the most clairvoyant of all fools," Gould is obsessed with making music and displays much of the eccentric behavior—for example, constant humming—typical of the actual pianist. His favorite word is "self-discipline," and he is relentless in his pursuit of perfection, which to him means total effacement of the artist as subjective interpreter. Instead of mediating between composer and musical instrument, Gould strives to be the Steinway piano. After a total of only thirty-four concerts, he withdraws to the seclusion of a recording studio so as to safeguard his performance against any influence from the audience. Gould is most famous for the execution of Johann Sebastian Bach's *Goldberg Variations*, and it is this work that is first heard by the narrator and Wertheimer at the Mozarteum in Salzburg in 1953. It is this work that destroys their aspirations to greatness; it is clear from this point on that Gould is the triumphant one and that the narrator and Wertheimer are failures. The three friends see one another only two times after their summer together: two years later, when Gould performs at Salzburg, and in 1969, when the narrator and Wertheimer visit Gould for four and a half months in New York City. Thereafter, contact is maintained only through the recordings sent by the pianist to his two European friends. At the age of fifty-one, while playing the *Goldberg Variations*, Gould dies, but for the narrator and Wertheimer he lives on in his music. The final scene of the novel shows the narrator in Wertheimer's room as he plays the record lying ready on the open stereo: Gould's *Goldberg Variations*.

Wertheimer's sister, who lived in Vienna with Wertheimer for more than two decades. During this time, he tyrannized her, forbidding her any contact with society and degrading her to a mere page turner. Finally, at the age of forty-six, she escapes her dungeon by marrying a rich industrialist named Duttweiler and moving to Switzerland.

Landlady, the owner of the desolate and dirty inn where the narrator stops on his way to Wertheimer's lodge. Although the narrator finds her to be vulgar and base, Wertheimer had an affair with the landlady. After ignoring the narrator's presence for some time, thereby allowing him extended time to reminisce, the landlady informs the narrator about Wertheimer's strange activities during the last weeks of his life.

Franz Kohlroser, one of Wertheimer's woodsmen. Franz, who has worked on the Wertheimer estate all his life, is worried now that the sister will change or even sell it. He provides the narrator a detailed account of events in the lodge during Wertheimer's final stay there. Most important, the narrator learns that Franz helped destroy the numerous notes written by Wertheimer that the narrator had hoped to acquire.

— *Linda C. DeMeritt*

THE UNVANQUISHED

Author: William Faulkner (1897-1962)
First published: 1938
Genre: Novel

Locale: Mississippi and Alabama
Time: The Civil War and the Reconstruction period
Plot: Bildungsroman

John Sartoris, a colonel in the confederate army. Sartoris, who is from Mississippi and devoted to the antebellum South, twice raises volunteers from the Jefferson area to fight in the Civil War. Although he is a widower and must leave behind an elderly mother-in-law and a twelve-year-old son, Sartoris believes it is his duty to fight for the South. Even after he realizes that defeat is inevitable, he continues to fight. After the war, he devotes his time and energy to reclaiming his land and rebuilding the city of Jefferson. Accustomed to holding power and killing, Colonel Sartoris wields his influence after the war as he builds a railroad and runs for political office. While his son Bayard is studying law, Sartoris tells him that times are changing and he would like to stop killing. He dies when his former business partner, whom he needlessly humiliated and needled, shoots him.

Rosa "Granny" Millard, Sartoris' mother-in-law. She lives on Sartoris land during the Civil War, caring for her grandson Bayard, whose mother died in childbirth, and overseeing the property and the black people who work on the Sartoris land. Despite her religious beliefs, Granny forges papers to steal mules from Yankee soldiers in order to help poor Southerners survive. She is killed by a Southern raider when she tries to make a deal to get valuable horses in order to have money to help her family and restore the Sartoris land after the war.

Bayard Sartoris, the colonel's son, the narrator and protagonist. An adolescent during the war, Bayard begins by idolizing and glorifying his father the soldier. At the age of fifteen he kills Grumby, the man responsible for his grand-

mother's death. As he matures watching the fighting and the effects of the war on Southerners, he becomes a less eager participant in the "glory." At the age of twenty-four, Bayard is studying law and refuses to avenge through violence his father's death.

Ringo, Bayard's boyhood companion, the son of Sartoris slaves. He aids Bayard in shooting at the Yankee and in tracking and killing Grumby. He takes a more active role than Bayard in the plot to swindle mules from the Yankees and resell them for profit to other Yankee regiments. Unlike Bayard, he is ready to avenge the colonel's death.

Drusilla Hawk, Colonel Sartoris' second wife. After her fiancé is killed in the Civil War, Drusilla, with short hair and men's clothing, eagerly joins Colonel Sartoris in the war, fighting beside his men. After the war, she lives with the Sartoris family and helps rebuild the land, again working with men. Her mother and the women of Jefferson soon pressure her into marrying the colonel and accepting the traditional female role. After the colonel is killed, she encourages Bayard to avenge his death. She becomes hysterical when she realizes Bayard has no such intentions, but she leaves him a sprig of verbena when she knows he goes unarmed to meet the man who killed his father. She leaves Mississippi to live with her brother.

Ab Snopes, a poor neighbor of Colonel Sartoris who aids Granny and Ringo in their plot to steal mules from the Yankees. Mainly concerned with personal profit, he switches allegiances whenever profitable and leads Granny to her death.

— *Marion Boyle Petrillo*

U.S.A.

Author: John Dos Passos (1896-1970)
First published: 1937
Genre: Novel

Locale: United States
Time: 1900-1935
Plot: Historical

Fenian O'Hara McCreary, called **Fainy Mac**, a young Irishman who learns the printing trade from an uncle. His uncle's bankruptcy puts McCreary out of a job and makes a tramp of him. Because of his skill as a printer, McCreary is able to find jobs here and there, one with a shoddy outfit called the Truthseeker Literary Distributing Co., Inc., and he travels from place to place, usually riding on freight trains. During his travels, he falls in with members of the Industrial Workers of

the World and becomes an earnest worker in that labor movement. He marries Maisie Spencer, but eventually they quarrel. He leaves his family in California to become a labor organizer in Mexico, where he lives a free and easy life.

Maisie Spencer, a shopgirl who marries Fainy McCreary. She is unable to share his radical views, and they part.

Janey Williams, a girl who wants a career in business. She becomes a stenographer and through her luck and skill is hired as secretary to J. Ward Moorehouse, a prominent man in public relations. She becomes an efficient, if sour, woman who makes a place for herself in business. Her great embarrassment is her brother Joe, a sailor who shows up periodically with presents for her.

Joe Williams, Janey Williams' brother, a young man who cannot accept discipline. He loves life at sea and becomes a merchant seaman after deserting from the Navy. Although he is in and out of scrapes all the time, he manages to qualify as a second officer during World War I. His life ends when a Senegalese hits him over the head with a bottle in a brawl over a woman in the port of St. Nazaire.

Della Williams, Joe Williams' wife. Although she is cold to her husband and claims that she is modest, she comes to believe during World War I that it is her patriotic duty to entertain men in uniform all that she can, much to her husband's chagrin.

J. Ward Moorehouse, an opportunist who becomes a leading public relations and advertising executive. He is eager to succeed in life and to have a hand in many activities. His first wife is Annabelle Strang, a wealthy and promiscuous woman; his second is Gertrude Staple, who helps him in his career. Although he succeeds as a businessman, he is unhappy in his domestic life, to which he gives all too little time because he prefers a whole series of women to his wife. A heart attack finally convinces him that the life he leads is not a fruitful one.

Annabelle Strang, the wealthy, amoral woman who becomes J. Ward Moorehouse's first wife.

Gertrude Staple, J. Ward Moorehouse's second wife, a wealthy young woman whose family and fortune help her husband become established as a public relations counselor. She becomes mentally ill and spends many years in a sanatorium.

Eleanor Stoddard, a poor girl from Chicago gifted with artistic talent. She sets herself up as an interior decorator and succeeds professionally. She becomes a hard and shallow but attractive woman. While serving as a Red Cross worker in Europe, she becomes J. Ward Moorehouse's mistress for a time. Always climbing socially, she becomes engaged to an exiled Russian nobleman in New York after World War I.

Eveline Hutchins, the daughter of a liberal clergyman, a young woman who spends her life seeking pleasure and escape from boredom. She becomes Eleanor Stoddard's erstwhile business partner. Her life is a series of rather sordid love affairs, both before and after marriage. She commits suicide.

Paul Johnson, Eveline Hutchins' shy and colorless soldier husband, whom she meets in France while doing Red Cross work.

Charley Anderson, a not very promising youth who becomes famous as an aviator during World War I. He cashes in on his wartime reputation and makes a great deal of money, both as an inventor and as a trader on the stock market. His loose sexual morality and his heavy drinking lose him his wife, his jobs, his fortune, and finally his life. He dies as the result of an auto accident that occurs while he is drunk. He has a brief love affair with Eveline Hutchins.

Margo Dowling, the daughter of a ne'er-do-well drunkard. Using her beauty and talent, she makes her own way in the world and becomes a film star after many amatory adventures. For a time, she is Charley Anderson's mistress.

Agnes Mandeville, Margo Dowling's stepmother, friend, and financial adviser. She is a shrewd woman with money.

Frank Mandeville, a broken-down vaudeville actor and Agnes' husband. A lost man after the advent of motion pictures, he spends much of his time trying to seduce Margo Dowling and eventually rapes her.

Tony de Carrida, Margo Dowling's first husband, an effeminate Cuban musician who is finally reduced to being Margo's uniformed chauffeur.

Sam Margolies, a peculiar but successful producer who "discovers" Margo Dowling and makes her a film star. He becomes her second husband.

Richard Ellsworth Savage, called Dick, a bright young man and a Harvard graduate who wishes to become a poet. He meets J. Ward Moorehouse and ends up as a junior partner in Moorehouse's firm. He is Anne Elizabeth Trent's lover for a time.

Anne Elizabeth Trent, called **Daughter**, a wild young girl from Texas who makes the wrong friends. In Europe as a relief worker after World War I, she falls in love with Richard Ellsworth Savage and becomes pregnant by him. She goes for an airplane ride with a drunken French aviator and dies when the plane crashes.

Mary French, a bright young Vassar graduate interested in social work. She becomes a radical and a worker for various labor movements sponsored by communists. She loses her lover, Don Stevens, who returns from a visit in Moscow with a wife assigned to him by the Party.

Don Stevens, a Communist organizer who for a time is Mary French's lover. In Moscow, he marries a wife of whom the Party approves.

Benny Compton, a Jewish boy from New York who drifts into labor work and becomes a highly successful labor organizer and agitator. He turns Communist and gives all his energy to work for the Party. Sentenced to the penitentiary in Atlanta for his activities, he is released after World War I. He lives for a time with Mary French.

Webb Cruthers, a young anarchist who for a brief period is Anne Elizabeth Trent's lover.

UTOPIA

Author: Sir Thomas More (1478-1535)
First published: 1516
Genre: Novel

Locale: Antwerp, Belgium, and the imaginary commonwealth of Utopia
Time: Early sixteenth century
Plot: Social morality

Raphael Hythloday, a philosophical traveler who has returned to Europe from Utopia, a far-off island adjacent to a larger land mass, somewhat like England in relation to the continent of Europe. In his account of what he saw there, which forms book 2 of the work, Hythloday never characterizes individual Utopians; the interplay of character in the narrative is between Raphael and his two companions in book 1. Hythloday is an experienced traveler who is supposed to have accompanied Amerigo Vespucci on his last three voyages. He has seen the coasts of the continents that came to be named for Vespucci, as well as countries such as Ceylon and India; later, with five companions, he visited lands even stranger to Europeans. Hythloday thus arrived in Utopia with extensive knowledge of the societies of the earth, and as a student of moral philosophy, Hythloday was well equipped to interpret what he saw. His two companions regard him as a man who desires neither wealth nor power. He is also modest, rejecting his companions' judgment that he is a man fit to advise a great prince. He understands human nature well enough, however, to know that princes are more likely to listen to a yes-man than to a wise and prudent adviser. Having scrutinized Utopian institutions such as agriculture, justice, the economy, business relations, and marriage customs, he has concluded that communal living and the utter discouragement of any attempt to accumulate property—especially money, jewels, gold, and the like—is central to Utopia's success. On the basis of his observations, he concludes that sound social and political institutions can keep human pride and dangerous ambition in check and thus maintain peace and harmony in a society.

Peter Giles, the Flemish gentleman who introduces Hythloday to his friend, Sir Thomas More. Giles is a historical personage who, in book 1, is credited with many virtues, including learning, courtesy, trustworthiness, affection, modesty, candor, and wit. He perceives that Hythloday is the kind of person More would desire to meet and converse with. Like More, Giles appears to be much more optimistic than the experienced Hythloday about human moral capacity and society as it exists. He not only agrees with the suggestion that Hythloday would make an ideal adviser to a king but also believes that he would achieve happiness in this role, an opinion at which Hythloday scoffs. Giles is also somewhat chauvinistic, admiring the political institutions of the Europe of his day until Hythloday demonstrates the superiority of the Utopian ones.

Sir Thomas More, the narrator of the encounter with Giles and Hythloday into which the latter's narrative of Utopian life is incorporated. It is important to recognize that this More is a character to be differentiated from the author. The character More tends to share Giles's optimistic view of human judgment and moral fiber, and he considers many Utopian customs "absurd." Along with Giles, the character More learns of a people whose social and moral standards are rational and tolerant rather than specifically Christian and often intolerant of those in different cultures. More finally concedes that many things about the Utopian system—he does not specify which—would be worth emulating. The use of the character More makes it difficult to determine what the author considers most admirable about the imaginary commonwealth. The things that the character specifically mentions as absurd—communal living and the downgrading of gold and items commonly regarded as precious—seem to have attracted the author. The effect of the character More is to provoke confusion in the reader as to the author's judgment on his imaginary commonwealth, but this ambiguous character also serves as an incentive to reexamine thoughtfully the entire subject of which social values and institutions are basic to the success of a real commonwealth.

— *Robert P. Ellis*

V.

Author: Thomas Pynchon (1937-   )
First published: 1963
Genre: Novel

Locale: Italy, France, Egypt, German Southwest Africa, Malta, Virginia, and New York
Time: 1898-1956
Plot: Satire

Benny Profane, a former Navy man and self-styled "schlemiel" who wanders purposelessly the streets of New York, Norfolk, and Malta. His chief activity is "yo-yoing" up and down the East Coast between New York and Norfolk. He has no goals and no value system and is incapable of loving or receiving love. Society around him is decaying, and his wandering simply keeps him continuously in motion to minimize the possibility of reaching a point of equilibrium. His last name, **Sfacimento**, means destruction or decay in Italian.

Herbert Stencil, the son of Sidney Stencil, a British spy who mysteriously lost his life near Malta in 1919. Herbert spends his life obsessively pursuing the mysterious V. He attempts to make some meaningful structure of the facts he obtains about V. as if he were a nonemotional historian. After searching in the sewers of New York, reading his father's diaries, and interviewing people about V., he avoids the possibility of actually succeeding in his quest, because to do so would end the search and leave him susceptible to the process of entropy.

V., a mysterious woman (and perhaps a place or even a fiction) who appears in various guises and in various places around the world, generally at a moment of crisis and upheaval. Some of her appearances are as Victoria Wren, Vera Meroving, Veronica, and the Bad Priest. She becomes increasingly mechanized and dehumanized, being a closed system subject to entropy with its resulting decay and disorder. She represents a dying society, personifying the forces that have sapped modern humankind's vitality and have made the world's people a "Sick Crew." She also seems to represent Henry Adams' theory of history as a mechanized twentieth century equivalent of Adams' Virgin or Venus.

Victoria Wren, a manifestation of V. as an eighteen-year-old girl in Egypt in 1898. In this guise, her innocence is emphasized, so she is seen as calm and incapable of being aroused by any emotion, as if she embodies some female principle that complements explosive male energy.

Vera Meroving, a woman about forty years old, a manifestation of V. under siege in Africa in 1921. She has a glass eye containing a watch.

Veronica Manganese, a manifestation of V. in Malta in 1919, following the end of World War I. Seen wearing an evening cape and an elaborate bonnet, she has a reputation for being in the company of various revolutionary Italians and for being a wealthy troublemaker.

The Bad Priest, a manifestation of V. in Valletta, Malta, during World War II. Pinned under a falling timber during a bombing raid, she is slowly dismantled by some Maltese children. Because V. has become more and more artificial, the children are able to remove a white wig, false teeth, a glass eye, a star sapphire in her navel, and artificial feet.

Mildred Wren, the stocky, myopic sister of Victoria Wren. Although she is plain, she is good. The sisters symbolize the terrible opposition between beauty and humanity.

Fausto Maijstral (mizh-SHTRAHL), another character who parallels Henry Adams. Both felt themselves moving toward inanimateness, both wrote journals, both recognize the futility of achieving order, and both turn to art in an attempt to save themselves from chaos. He appears in four stages. Fausto Maijstral I, before 1938, is a young man vacillating between politics and the priesthood. Fausto II emerges when his daughter Paola is born. Fausto III was born on the Day of the 13 Raids of Malta during World War II. More than any other character, he approaches being nonhuman, like a stone. Fausto IV represents a level that reveals a slow return to humanity. An Irish Armenian Jew, he claims to be the laziest person in New York.

The Whole Sick Crew, a group that includes such characters as **Charisma**, **Fu**, **Melvin**, **Raoul**, **Winsome**, **Slab**, and sometimes **Paola**. The "Crew" represents decadence, especially among the younger generation. Purposelessly, they wander from one aimless party to another, indulging in drink and promiscuous sexual relationships.

Hugh Godolphin, an explorer and discoverer of Vheissu, a mysterious polar underworld. Apparently a spy, he had engaged in a polar expedition that had been declared a failure, although he had survived. He is fifty-four years of age when he appears in Florence but is almost eighty in South Africa during a Bondel uprising. He is the father of Evan Godolphin. The two appear to represent God the Father and God the Son, focusing on the perversion and deterioration of religion in the twentieth century.

Evan Godolphin, the son of Hugh Godolphin. He is a

British agent and World War I flying ace. As a youth, he was the leader of a nihilistic group called the League of the Red Sunrise. He is now a liaison officer in his middle thirties, sent on temporary duty with the Americans for some reconnaissance missions. On one mission, he lost the top of his nose, part of one cheek, and half his chin. When all the physical attributes and his manner of speaking are brought together, there emerges a picture of a Christ figure, thus showing the kind of decadence and deterioration that religion underwent in the twentieth century.

Rachel Owlglass, a short woman with long red hair that has strands of premature gray. She is a mothering person who, though kind to the Whole Sick Crew, is aloof from its decadence. An association with Rachel in the Bible may be intended. An occasional girlfriend of Benny Profane, she urges him, as a wanderer, to come home. She often pays the way for her roommate, Esther Harvitz, who takes unfair advantage of Rachel's kind nature. At other times, her own decadence comes to the fore.

Esther Harvitz, the twenty-two-year-old roommate of Rachel Owlglass. She has plastic surgery to make her look less Jewish. Half the time, she is in control of her life; at other times, she is portrayed as a "victim" type. She habitually depends on Rachel for financial support and sometimes borrows things without permission.

Paola Hod, née **Maijstral**, a woman who is separated from her sailor-husband, Pappy Hod. She assumes several identities, including that of a barmaid named Beatrice (possibly to be associated with Beatrice in Dante's *The Divine Comedy*). She is sometimes associated with the Whole Sick Crew; she appears as Ruby, a black prostitute, and may be one of a number of Puerto Rican girls in the novel. She is the daughter of Elena Ximxi and, at one point, she seduces Melanie l'Heuremaudit.

Dr. Shale Shoenmaker, an expensive plastic surgeon. He does plastic surgery on Esther Harvitz's nose to lessen her Jewish appearance and also tries to seduce her, emphasizing a trend toward inanimateness and perversion of sex.

Dudley Eigenvalue, a Park Avenue dentist who schedules dental sessions as if there were psychological connections with one's teeth. Ironically, Eigenvalue provides a contrasting figure to Stencil when he points out that the occurrence of cavities in several teeth does not constitute a connection among them, an approach opposite to Stencil's practice of trying to find connections with everything, almost to the point of paranoia.

Hedwig Vogelsang, V.'s sixteen-year-old surrogate sister. She has white-blond, hip-length hair. She is pursued by Mondaugan.

Mafia Winsome, a New York author who preaches a theory of heroic love that reduces love to lust. Her sympathetic characters are white; her villainous or comic characters are African Americans, Jews, and southern European immigrants.

Gouverneur "Rooney" Winsome, a native of North Carolina, one of the Whole Sick Crew. He is the husband of Mafia.

Josefina (Fina) Mendoza, the sister of Angel and Kook. She urges Benny Profane, a sometime friend, to come home and to get a job. She was once something of a spiritual leader to a youth gang known as the Playboys.

Angel Mendoza, the brother of Josefina and Kook. He works under the street in the New York sewers with Geronimo.

DaConho, a Brazilian Zionist restaurant-bar chief at Schlozhauer's Trocadero in New York. He wants to fight Arabs in Israel and keeps a machine gun handy.

Mrs. Beatrice Buffo, the owner of the Sailor's Grave bar. She hosts a "Suck Hour" from eight to nine on payday.

Beatrice, one of the guises of Paola Maijstral. She is a barmaid in the Sailor's Grave in Norfolk and is "sweetheart" of the destroyer USS *Scaffold*.

Cesare, a sidekick of Mantissa. He slashes Sandro Botticelli's painting *Venus*. Sometimes, he thinks of himself as a steamboat and calls out "toot."

Clayton "Bloody" Chiclitz, a munitions king and president of Yoyodyne, a large defense contracting company that was once the Chiclitz Toy Company.

Geronimo, a friend of Angel, with whom he works in the New York sewers. He likes to "girl-watch." He is also a friend of Benny.

Melanie l'Heuremaudit (lehr-moh-DAY), a fifteen-year-old dancer whose name means "cursed hour." She is loved by V. and had a romance with her father. Representing the perversion of sex in modern society, she is killed when she is impaled on a pole while performing a dance.

Hugh Bongo-Shaftsbury, an Egyptologist who is wired, representing the increasing mechanization of humanity. He wears a ceramic hawk's head to represent an Egyptian deity.

Father Fairing, a priest, formerly of Malta, now in New York. He preaches Christianity to the sewer rats in Manhattan in the 1930's.

Kurt Mondaugan, a stout, blond engineer at the Yoyodyne plant on Long Island. He had worked in Germany developing weapons and is in South Africa in 1922 working on a project involving atmospheric radio disturbances.

Foppl, a leader in a military effort to put down the Bondel uprising against the Boers in South Africa. He had been with General Lothar von Trotha, who had led a systematic extermination effort against the Hereros and Hottentots in the Great Rebellion of 1904-1907. He held a "siege party."

Andreas, a Bondel beaten by Foppl, representing one of many kinds of destruction that have contributed to the deterioration of values in the twentieth century.

Mr. Goodfellow, a red-faced Englishman in his forties who is a British agent. He is suspected of being a spy because he looks like a street fighter but attends a consulate party.

Hanne Faherze, a stout, blond, German barmaid described in a Faulknerian manner as possessing a cowlike calm, which is a positive asset in the beer hall, where she is continuously surrounded by drunkenness, prostitution, and general immorality. She is unable to remove a triangular stain from a plate in a Pentecost-like experience. The name "Hanne" may be associated with Hansen's disease (leprosy), whose symptoms of inanimateness, paralysis, and waste parallel those of modern society.

Vernonica, a sewer rat in New York and possibly another manifestation of V. From what Benny Profane has heard, Vernonica was the only one of Father Fairing's parishioners whom the priest believed was worthy of having her soul saved.

— *Victoria Price*

THE VAGABOND
(La Vagabonde)

Author: Colette (Sidonie-Gabrielle Colette, 1873-1954)
First published: 1911
Genre: Novel

Locale: France
Time: Six months during the early 1900's
Plot: Psychological realism

Renée Néré (reh-NAY nay-RAY), the narrator, a French mime and a dancer. Intelligent and largely self-aware, she divorced her husband after eight years of his adulteries and cruelties and has been struggling to support herself as a music hall performer in Paris for the past three years. She also was a writer but rationalizes that she can no longer afford the time for writing. She is still an attractive woman at thirty-three years of age but worries that she is losing her good looks. Her bitter marriage has made her determined to keep her independence, despite her sense of loneliness and thwarted sensuality, but when she is devotedly pursued by an admirer, Maxime, she succumbs to his lovemaking and agrees to become his mistress and even wife, after completing an already planned six-week tour of the provinces. She discovers, however, that her free identity and a desire to create with words mean more to her than attachment to any man and breaks with him to remain a vagabond and pursue a career.

Maxime Dufferein-Chautel (mak-SEEM dew-feh-REH[N]-shoh-TEHL), Renée's black-haired, long-lashed admirer, with tawny brown eyes and full red lips under his mustache. He is a wealthy, idle man-about-town whose mother runs the family estate in the Ardennes, leaving her youngest son free to pursue his pleasures. Handsome and thirty-three years old, like Renée, he is much more conventional in his notions and far less quick-witted. He wants to marry Renée, settle down, and have children. Although he tolerates her tour, he disapproves of it. He would prefer to load her with luxuries and cannot understand why she wants to work.

Brague (brahg), Renée's mentor, partner, and comrade in vaudeville theater. Brague is a skilled and ambitious pan-

tomimist, swarthy but with a clean-shaven Catalan face. Although authoritative and sometimes brusque in manner, he is genuinely fond of Renée and provides her with emotional support as well as professional guidance. He arranged for the French tour and, to Renée's delight, for a South American one to follow it.

Hamond (ah-MOH[N]), Renée's old friend, a painter. A tall, thin, and sickly man, he also has been disappointed by marriage but is not so cynical about love as is Renée. He acts as the go-between who formally introduces Maxime to Renée and encourages her to form a relationship.

Margot Taillandy (mahr-GOH ti-yahn-DEE), Renée's friend, the sister of her former husband. A warmhearted woman with bobbed hair turning gray, Margot collects ailing Brabançon terriers to nurse them back to health and helps to support Renée with a monthly allowance to supplement her meager pay. Skeptical of Renée's determination to avoid love, she predicts that Renée must fall in love again because one cannot deny one's senses.

Jadin (zhah-DA[N]), an empty-headed, unkempt eighteen-year-old singer, with light brown hair. Jadin has left the streets for the vaudeville theater and has become a success with her artless contralto. She impulsively runs off with a lover, but just as casually, she returns to resume her stage career.

Bouty (bew-TEE), a slender vaudeville comic with beautiful, tender eyes. He is suffering from chronic enteritis and is gradually dying from the strain of performing while ill. He loves Jadin with silent devotion.

— *Harriet Blodgett*

THE VALLEY

Author: Rolando Hinojosa (1929-   )
First published: 1983
Genre: Novel

Locale: The Texas-Mexico border
Time: The 1920's to the 1970's
Plot: Social realism

Rafa Buenrostro (RRAH-fah bwehn-ROH-stroh), whose name means "goodface," the autobiographical narrator in many of the sketches. Rafa is a self-assured young man who has served in the military and soon will go to the University of Texas at Austin. He was born and reared in Belken County, but having been exposed to some of the world outside it, he realizes the need to make a break from its confines. He understands the people of the area, observing them carefully and presenting them with considerable objectivity. He usually reserves his judgments about others.

Jehú Malacara (heh-HEW mahl-ah-KAHR-ah), whose name means "badface," an orphan who comes of age. Jehú's parents die before he reaches puberty, so he is reared with his Briones cousins. Through Vicky Briones, he is introduced to the life of the circus. He becomes don Víctor's helper in transporting circus props from place to place.

Don Víctor (VEEK-tohr), a former revolutionary. As a lieutenant colonel in the Mexican armed forces, he married a Mexican Jew, Lía Samaniego, by whom he had a son, Saúl. After an epidemic of Spanish influenza claims the pregnant Lía and their son, don Víctor retires from the military and eventually makes his way to Belken County. There, he is connected with the circus, and Jehú goes to work with him.

Don Manuel Guzmán (mahn-WHEHL gews-MAHN), a former revolutionary who knew Pancho Villa and Álvaro Obregon. Don Manuel can trace his U.S. citizenship through his family to 1845, when a new boundary was drawn between the United States and Mexico. Despite his citizenship, don Manuel is thoroughly Mexican. Later in life, he owns three dry-cleaning establishments and part of a bakery. He is a free spirit who was once a bronco buster. He dies suddenly in his mid-forties, from a stroke that hits him when he is in the middle of telling a joke.

Baldemar (Balde) Cordero (bahl-deh-MAHR BAHL-deh kohr-DEH-roh), Gilberto's brother-in-law and friend. Balde kills Ernesto Tamez in a brawl over one of the hostesses of a local bar. He is tried, found guilty, and sentenced to fifteen years in prison. Drunk when he committed this rash act, he cannot remember what he did but has to pay the price for having done it.

Gilberto (Beto) Casteñeda (heel-BEHR-toh BEH-toh kahs-tahn-YEH-dah), the friend and brother-in-law of Baldemar Cordero. Beto is present when Balde fatally stabs Ernesto Tamez. Called on to give a deposition that details his recollection of the barroom stabbing, Beto tells the truth, although he never forsakes his friend. Beto is orphaned early, when his parents are killed with twenty others riding in a farm truck that is struck by a train. He knows the fields well and works hard in them. He dies at the age of thirty, leaving Marta Cordero as a widow.

Chedes Briones (CHEH-dehs bree-OH-nehs), Jehú Malacara's aunt, who helps to rear Jehú. Distressed when her daughter Vicky joins the circus, she is soon soothed by getting free tickets to its performances.

Juan Briones (hwahn), Chedes' husband, a stoic who, when he learns that his children have left home, drinks another beer and orders another dozen oysters.

Panchita (pahn-CHEE-tah), Rafa Buenrostro's aunt, who practices folk medicine and incantations to treat those who are ill, including Rafa.

THE VALLEY OF DECISION

Author: Edith Wharton (1862-1937)
First published: 1902
Genre: Novel

Locale: Italy
Time: Late eighteenth century
Plot: Historical

Odo Valsecca (oh-doh vahl-SEH-kah), a cousin to the duke of Pianura. Odo lives in neglect and poverty until, at the age of nine, his noble father dies and Odo is introduced to life at the duke's court. The contemplative Odo, influenced by the pageantry of the church, desires to become a bishop. When the duke's young son becomes ill, however, and the heir-presumptive (the marquess of Cerveno) dies, Odo becomes the heir-presumptive to the duke's throne. During his education as a nobleman, he learns philosophy, including the teachings of Voltaire, which are banned by the church. Count Lelio Trescorre befriends Odo, but the duchess of Pianura warns Odo that the count is really Odo's enemy and wants to discredit him.

Count Lelio Trescorre (lay-LEE-oh tray-SKOH-reh), the duke's arrogant comptroller of finance and Master of the Horse. He has made himself indispensable to the court, and his engaging personality, handsome youthfulness, and sharp intellect allow him access to every area of political intrigue. The duchess is beholden to him for paying off her debts, an act that also made him popular with the tradesmen she had ruined. He immediately wins Odo's trust by engaging him in philosophical discussions. By letting Odo openly express his views, he exposes Odo to danger from the church. If Odo is discredited, Trescorre hopes to be appointed regent of Pianura.

Maria Clementina, the duchess of Pianura since the age of fourteen, when she married the duke. The fun-loving duchess, excessively rouged and jeweled in the French fashion, is neglected by the duke. She delights in reading books banned by the church, merely to upset her religious husband. Her extravagant entertaining of all the pretty women and dashing spendthrifts of the court has led her to financial trouble. She is fond of Odo and helps him to escape Trescorre's plot against him.

The duke of Pianura (pee-ah-NEW-rah), a sickly, narrow-faced man with a slight lameness that makes his walk ungainly. The duke cannot settle on one policy for governing his people. He leans first to one religion, then to another. After three months of marriage, he ignores his wife in favor of his young, pale cousin and heir-presumptive, the marquess of Cerveno. When the marquess loses favor with the duke, through the manipulations of Count Trescorre, the duke takes Countess Belverde as his mistress. When he realizes that his son is sickly, he sends for Odo, impressing on him the necessity for strong religious beliefs rather than reform.

Countess Belverde (behl-VEHR-day), a slender and graceful woman notorious for her cruel treatment of those serving her, though she maintains a piety toward the church. At the court, on behalf of the duke, she entertains the more conservative members of the church and the nobility. The duke gives her a villa at Boscofolto, making her the marchioness of Boscofolto.

Cantapresto, a former primo soprano of the ducal theater of Pianura turned abate of the church. He is Odo's servant. Cantapresto's acting ability and countless friends reveal to Odo yet another side of life. Cantapresto follows Odo carefully, so much so that Odo thinks he is a spy.

Carlo Gamba, a hunchbacked servant at the palace, Count Trescorre's brother, and a member of the outlawed Illuminati. Found by a Jesuit priest at a foundling asylum, Gamba was educated to be a clerk. After the priest's death, the duke gave him as a servant to the marquess of Cerveno. After Cerveno's death, Count Trescorre obtains a position for Gamba as an assistant to the duke's librarian. Gamba reveals to Odo the intrigues and political structure of the court.

— Sandra Willbanks

VANESSA

Author: Sir Hugh Walpole (1884-1941)
First published: 1933
Genre: Novel

Locale: England
Time: Late nineteenth and early twentieth centuries
Plot: Historical

Vanessa Paris, the beautiful daughter of Adam and Margaret Paris. She is engaged to her cousin Benjie, but because of his wildness, their marriage is postponed for two years. Her father's death forces her to postpone it still longer. Learning that Benjie has married a woman whom he impregnated, Vanessa wishes him well and later marries a distant cousin, a respected financier. Her husband's mind fails, however, and he plots to have Vanessa declared insane. Now nearly forty years old, she turns to Benjie, whose wife has left him. They live together happily for a time, until she learns that her husband's mind has failed entirely and that he cries constantly for her. Vowing to return to her husband until his death, Vanessa goes back to London, but her husband becomes stronger and outlives her.

Benjie Herries, who is in love with Vanessa but is trapped into marriage by another woman. He alone of the Herries family remains unconventional: He loses an arm fighting the Boers; he serves with the Russians in World War I, even though he is more than sixty years old; and in his seventies, he lives a gypsy life in a caravan with one manservant.

Marion Halliday, who at her mother's instigation goes to bed with Benjie. He marries her, but she later leaves him for another man.

Tom Herries, the son of Benjie and Marion. He and Vanessa become great friends.

Ellis Herries, a financier, Vanessa's husband and distant cousin. He and Benjie meet at Vanessa's deathbed without rancor.

Sally Herries, the illegitimate daughter of Vanessa and Benjie. Returning to London, Vanessa takes Sally with her. Sally lives for a year with a young man she expects to marry, but they part and she marries a blind French veteran of World War I. He works for the League of Nations, and Sally goes with him to Berlin to aid the cause of international peace.

Arnold Young, the man with whom Sally lives. His mother objects to the match, and Arnold finally marries another woman.

Judith Paris, Vanessa's grandmother, who dies when Vanessa is fifteen years old.

Adam Paris, Vanessa's father, whose death results in the final postponement of Vanessa's marriage to Benjie.

Margaret Paris, Vanessa's mother.

VANITY FAIR

Author: William Makepeace Thackeray (1811-1863)
First published: 1848; serial form, 1847-1848
Genre: Novel

Locale: England and Europe
Time: Early nineteenth century
Plot: Social satire

Rebecca (Becky) Sharp, an intelligent, beautiful, self-centered, and grasping woman whose career begins as an orphaned charity pupil at Miss Pinkerton's School for girls and continues through a series of attempted seductions, affairs, and marriages that form the background of the novel. Unscrupulous Becky is the chief exponent of the people who inhabit Vanity Fair—the world of pretense and show—but she is always apart from it because she sees the humor and ridiculousness of the men and women of this middle-class English world where pride, wealth, and ambition are the ruling virtues.

Amelia Sedley, Becky Sharp's sweet, good, and gentle schoolmate at Miss Pinkerton's School. Although married to George Osborne, who subsequently dies in the Battle of Waterloo, Amelia is worshiped by William Dobbin. Amelia does not notice his love, however, so involved is she with the memory of her dashing dead husband. Eventually, some of Amelia's goddess-like virtue is dimmed in Dobbin's eyes, but he marries her anyway and transfers his idealization of women to their little girl, Jane.

Captain William Dobbin, an officer in the British Army and a former schoolmate of George Osborne at Dr. Swishtail's school. He idolizes Amelia Sedley, George's wife, and while in the background provides financial and emotional support for her when she is widowed. After many years of worshiping Amelia from afar, he finally marries her.

George Osborne, the dashing young army officer who marries Amelia despite the fact that by so doing he incurs the wrath of his father and is cut off from his inheritance. George, much smitten with the charms of Becky Sharp, slips a love letter to Becky on the night before the army is called to the Battle of Waterloo. He is killed in the battle.

George Osborne, Jr., called Georgy, the small son of Amelia and George.

Captain Rawdon Crawley, an officer of the Guards, the younger son of Sir Pitt Crawley. He marries Becky Sharp in secret, and for this deception his aunt cuts him out of her will. Charming but somewhat stupid, he is a great gambler and furnishes some of the money on which he and Becky live precariously. He lets Becky order their life, and even though she flirts outrageously after they are married, he does not abandon her until he discovers her in an intimate scene with the marquis of Steyne. He dies many years later of yellow fever at Coventry Island.

Rawdon Crawley, the son of Rawdon and Becky. He refuses to see his mother in her later years, though he gives her a liberal allowance. From his uncle, he inherits the Crawley baronetcy and estate.

Joseph (Jos) Sedley, Amelia's fat, dandified brother whom Becky Sharp attempts unsuccessfully to attract into marrying her. A civil servant in India, acting as the Collector of Boggley Wollah, Jos is rich but selfish and does nothing to rescue his father and mother from bankruptcy. Persuaded by Dobbin, finally, to take some family responsibility, he supports Amelia and her son Georgy for a few months before Dobbin marries her. For a time, he and Becky travel on the Continent as husband and wife. He dies at Aix-la-Chapelle soon after Amelia and Dobbin's marriage. His fortune gone from unsuccessful speculations, he leaves only an insurance policy of two thousand pounds, to be divided between Becky and his sister.

Sir Pitt Crawley, a crusty, eccentric old baronet who lives at Queen's Crawley, his country seat, with his abused, apathetic second wife and two young daughters, Miss Rosalind

2050 / *Vanity Fair*

and Miss Violet. Immediately after Lady Crawley's death, Sir Pitt proposes marriage to Becky. His offer reveals her secret marriage to Rawdon Crawley, his younger son. Later, grown more senile than ever, Sir Pitt carries on an affair with his butler's daughter, Betsy Horrocks, much to the disgust of his relatives. He eventually dies, and his baronetcy and money go to Pitt, his eldest son.

Miss Crawley, Sir Pitt's eccentric, unmarried, and lonely sister. Imperious and rich, she is toadied to by everyone in the Crawley family and by Becky Sharp, for they see in her the chance for a rich living. She finally is won over by young Pitt Crawley's wife, Lady Jane, and her estate goes to Pitt.

Pitt Crawley, the older son of Sir Pitt Crawley. A most proper young man with political ambitions, he marries Lady Jane Sheepshanks, and after his brother's secret marriage so endears himself to Miss Crawley, his rich, domineering aunt, that he gains her money as well as his father's.

Lady Jane Crawley, Pitt Crawley's wife. Like Amelia Sedley, she is good, sweet, and kind, and is, above all else, interested in her husband's and their daughter's welfare.

The Reverend Bute Crawley, the rector of Crawley-cum-Snailby and Sir Pitt's brother. His household is run by his domineering wife.

Mrs. Bute Crawley, who dislikes Becky Sharp because she recognizes in her the same sort of ambition and craftiness that she herself possesses. Mrs. Bute Crawley fails in her plans to gain Miss Crawley's fortune.

James Crawley, the son of the Bute Crawleys. For a time, it looks as if this shy, good-looking young man will win favor with his aunt, but he ruins his prospects by getting very drunk on his aunt's wine and later smoking his pipe out the window of the guest room. Miss Crawley's maid also discovers that James has run up a tremendous bill for gin at the local inn, treating everyone in one of his expansive moods. This fact, combined with his smoking tobacco, puts an end to the Bute Crawleys' prospects of inheriting Miss Crawley's money.

Horrocks, Sir Pitt Crawley's butler.

Betsy Horrocks, the butler's daughter and old Sir Pitt's mistress. She is done out of any inheritance by the interference of Mrs. Bute Crawley.

Mr. John Sedley, the father of Amelia and Joseph, a typical middle-class English merchant of grasping, selfish ways. After his failure in business, his family is forced to move from Russell Square to a cottage kept by the Clapps; the daughter of the Clapp family is a former servant of the Sedleys. Never able to accept his poverty, Mr. Sedley spends his time thinking up new business schemes with which to regain his former wealth.

Mrs. John Sedley, the long-suffering wife of Mr. Sedley and mother of Amelia and Joseph. She, like her daughter, is a sweet woman. Her only expression of wrath in the entire story comes when she turns on Amelia after her daughter has criticized her for giving little Georgy medicine that was not prescribed for him.

John Osborne, George Osborne's testy-tempered father, provincial, narrow, and mean. Never forgiving his son for marrying the penniless Amelia Sedley, Mr. Osborne finally succeeds in getting the widow to give up her adored Georgy to his care. Amelia regains her son, however, and when Mr. Osborne dies, he leaves to his grandson a legacy of which Amelia is the trustee.

Jane,
Maria, and
Frances Osborne, George's sisters, who adore their young nephew. Maria finally marries Frederick Bullock, Esq., a London lawyer.

Mr. Smee, Jane Osborne's drawing teacher, who tries to marry her. Mr. Osborne, after discovering them together, forbids him to enter the house.

Lord Steyne, Lord of the Powder Closet at Buckingham Palace. Haughty, well-born, and considerably older than Becky, he succumbs to her charms. Her husband discovers them together and leaves her.

Wirt, the Osbornes' faithful maid.

Mrs. Tinker, the housekeeper at Queen's Crawley.

Lord Southdown, Lady Jane Crawley's brother, a dandified London friend of the Rawdon Crawleys.

Miss Briggs, Miss Crawley's companion and later Becky Sharp's "sheepdog." She fulfills Becky's need for a female companion so that the little adventuress will have some sort of respectability in the eyes of society.

Bowles, Miss Crawley's butler.

Mrs. Firkins, Miss Crawley's maid. Like the other servants, she is overwhelmed by the overbearing old lady.

Charles Raggles, a greengrocer, at one time an assistant gardener to the Crawley family. Having saved his money, he has bought a greengrocer's shop and a small house in Curzon Street. Becky and Rawdon live there for a time on his charity, unable to pay their rent.

Lord Gaunt, the son of Lord Steyne. He goes insane in his early twenties.

Major O'Dowd, an officer under whom George Osborne and William Dobbin serve. He is a relaxed individual, devoted to his witty and vivacious wife.

Mrs. O'Dowd, the Irish wife of Major O'Dowd. She is an unaffected, delightful woman who tries to marry off her sister-in-law to William Dobbin.

Glorvina O'Dowd, the flirtatious sister of Major O'Dowd. She sets her cap for Dobbin, but because she is only "frocks and shoulders," nothing comes of the match. She marries Major Posky.

General Tufto, the officer to whom Rawdon Crawley at one time serves as aide-de-camp. He is a typical army man with a mistress and a long-suffering wife.

Mrs. Tufto, his wife.

Mrs. Bent, his mistress.

Dolly, the housekeeper to the Rawdon Crawleys in London. She fends off tradesmen when they come to demand their money.

Mrs. Clapp, the landlady of the Sedleys after their move from Russell Square.

Polly Clapp, a young former servant of the Sedleys. She takes Dobbin to meet Amelia in the park after the former's ten-year absence in the Indian service.

Mary Clapp, another daughter of the Clapps and Amelia's friend.

Lady Bareacres, a snobby old aristocrat who cuts Becky socially in Brussels. Later, Becky has her revenge when she refuses to sell her horses to the old woman so that she can flee from Napoleon's invading army.

Lady Blanche Thistlewood, Lady Bareacres' daughter and

a dancing partner of George Osborne when they were young.

Mr. Hammerdown, the auctioneer at the sale of the Sedley possessions.

Major Martindale,

Lieutenant Spatterdash, and

Captain Cinqbars, military friends of Rawdon Crawley who are captivated by his charming wife.

Tom Stubble, a wounded soldier who brings news of the Battle of Waterloo to Amelia Sedley and Mrs. O'Dowd. They care for him until he regains his health.

Mr. Creamer, Miss Crawley's physician.

Miss Pinkerton, the snobbish mistress of the academy for girls at which Amelia Sedley and Becky Sharp met. She dislikes Becky intensely.

Miss Jemima Pinkerton, the silly, sentimental sister of the elder Miss Pinkerton. She takes pity on Becky and tries to give her the graduation gift of the academy, a dictionary, but Becky flings it into the mud as her coach drives off.

Miss Swartz, a rich, woolly-haired mulatto student at Miss Pinkerton's School. Because of her immense wealth, she pays double tuition. Later, the Crawley family tries to marry off Rawdon to her, but he already has married Becky.

Mr. Sambo, the Sedleys' black servant.

The Reverend Mr. Crisp, a young curate in Chiswick, enamored of Becky Sharp.

Miss Cutler, a young woman who unsuccessfully sets her cap for Joseph Sedley.

Mr. Fiche, Lord Steyne's confidential man. After Becky's fortunes have begun to decline, he tells her to leave Rome for her own good.

Major Loder, Becky's escort in the later phases of her career.

VATHEK: An Arabian Tale

Author: William Beckford (1760-1844)
First published: 1786
Genre: Novel

Locale: Arabia
Time: Indeterminate past
Plot: Gothic

Vathek (VAH-tehk), an Arabian sultan, a man addicted to sensory pleasures who indulges in black magic. The Giaour gives him the key to the dark kingdom in response to human sacrifices. He makes Nouronihar his companion in the pleasures of this world and the world of magic. Vathek finds the secret lair of Eblis, Lord of Darkness, only to have his heart consumed by eternal flames.

Nouronihar (noh-ROHN-ih-hahr), the daughter of Emir Fakreddin. She is stolen from her betrothed by Vathek and becomes the favorite of his harem. She shares Vathek's discovery of the lair of Eblis and also has her heart consumed by eternal flames. She turns from a sweet young woman into an addict of pleasure and depravity.

Carathis (kah-RAH-tihs), Vathek's mother. She is a wor-shiper of evil and, by her live sacrifices, leads her son to black magic and its discoveries. She arrives at the lair of Eblis shortly after her son, who sees her heart burst into flame.

The Giaour (JAW-ur), a mysterious stranger and an emissary of the powers of evil. He brings sabers with changing inscriptions to Vathek. The inscriptions are the key to the pathway to the kingdom of darkness.

Gulchenrouz (GUHL-kehn-rowts), the betrothed of Nouronihar. He and his sweetheart are drugged and taken to a hidden retreat to save Nouronihar from Vathek.

Emir Fakreddin (fah-kreh-DEEN), the devout Muhammadan father of Nouronihar. He is scandalized by Vathek's violation of the laws of hospitality.

VEIN OF IRON

Author: Ellen Glasgow (1873-1945)
First published: 1935
Genre: Novel

Locale: Ironside and Queensborough, Virginia
Time: 1900-1935
Plot: Family

Ada Fincastle, later **McBride**, a ten-year-old when the novel opens, the daughter of John Fincastle, a defrocked Presbyterian minister. Sensitive to people and nature, she instinctively understands that her role in life is to make the best of every situation. Drawing heavily on the "vein of iron" that is the bloodline of her heritage (beginning with Great-Great-Grandmother Martha Tod, who was held captive and married to a young chief by the Indians and then returned to civilized Christianity), Ada has a deep faith in the ultimate goodness of life and in the necessity of accepting one's predestined fate. Growing up in Ironside, Virginia, she experiences disappointment, loss, and great happiness. Ada is the moral, financial, and ethical glue that keeps the family from falling into chaos. Throughout the thirty-five years of her life that the novel chronicles, Ada is faithful to her heritage, her sense of what is appropriate, and her deeply felt understanding of the strength of love. As the novel ends, she moves Ralph, their son Rannie, and herself back to the manse in Ironside, believing that if they try, they will succeed.

Grandmother Fincastle, John's mother and Ada's grandmother, who is seventy years old as the novel opens. She is the strength holding the family together in the manse during the era of family poverty after John's dismissal from the pulpit. Deeply religious and a survivor, she believes that the Lord will provide and is content with what life gives. Of her nine children, only John and Meggie survived to adulthood. Her consistency in activity and belief gives meaning to the Fincastle home. Despite her disapproval of Ada's pregnancy, she assists at the birth of Rannie. She dies after a fall in 1917.

John Fincastle, Ada's father, the fourth to carry the name. He is, a world-renowned philosopher who lost his pulpit for preaching Baruch Spinoza's god and not Abraham's. He is forty-four years old as the novel begins, unemployed, living in his family's manse, and writing his (ultimately) five-volume philosophical opus. At the suggestion of Dr. Updike, the family physician and friend, he opens a school in one room of the manse and is able to maintain periodic payments on his insurance and the mortgage. His two years of study in England, mainly in the British Museum, have driven him away from the firm Presbyterian beliefs of his ancestors and mother. A loner for much of his life, he is able to accept things as they occur, even the early death of his beloved Mary Evelyn and the necessity of abandoning the manse and moving to Queensborough. In town, he becomes a bit more human, develops friendships that were denied to him in Ironside, and even stands with others in the bread lines. When he feels his own death coming, he slips away and returns to Ironside. He dies early in 1935 at the manse, alone.

Ralph McBride, Ada's childhood playmate. Ralph is two years older than Ada. His family is even poorer than the Fincastles, but his mother has instilled in him the virtues of work and duty. Ada admires him from the beginning. When Janet Rowan's family accuses Ralph of fathering the child she is carrying and forces him to marry her, Ada is devastated. Ralph returns in 1913 for Mary Evelyn's funeral, and Ada promises to leave with him when he is free. In 1917, he and Ada spend a weekend in a cabin in the mountains, and Ada becomes pregnant. Ralph serves his time in France and comes

home a different man, quieter, more morose, and less optimistic. Janet divorces him, making him and Ada free to marry. Their time in Queensborough is a time of hardship and joy, a mixed bag of success and failure as the Depression forces him from temporary job to temporary job.

Meggie Fincastle, John's unmarried sister and the de facto keeper of the house, aged thirty-three at the beginning of the novel. Like her mother, she is a stabilizing force by virtue of her consistency and insistence on doing things as they must and need be done. Her beliefs are firm and unchangeable. A Good Samaritan by nature, she helps, whenever and however she can, anyone who needs help.

Mary Evelyn Fincastle, a woman in her early forties as the novel begins. She is from similar pioneer stock to that of the Fincastles. Bright, sprightly, overly optimistic, and publicly cheerful, she is the sunshine in an otherwise often-dulled existence. She is dying slowly of an undisclosed illness, which claims her life in August, 1913. Her marriage to John was a good marriage, and his grief at her death and after is genuine.

Dr. Updike, the Fincastle family physician and a friend of the family, forty years old as the novel begins. He takes care of Mary Evelyn in her illness, suggests to John that he start a school in the manse, and eventually buys the manse when the Fincastles have to leave.

— *William H. Holland, Jr.*

THE VELVET HORN

Author: Andrew Lytle (1902-1995)
First published: 1957
Genre: Novel

Locale: Tennessee
Time: The 1880's
Plot: Bildungsroman

Captain Joe Cree, Julia Cropleigh's husband. Cree is killed when he moves in front of a tree his crew is felling. The steady older cousin of the Cropleigh orphans, Joe married Julia to provide for her. At the time of his death, Cree was taking part in a risky business venture with Amelie Cropleigh. Cree explains to his son, Lucius, that he took part in the bargain—she sold him timber at a lower price and he agreed to cut it in half the usual time—so he could "repay" her for the death of her husband, whom he had sent on a dangerous mission during the Civil War that ended in his death.

Julia Cropleigh, the youngest child and only daughter in the Cropleigh family. When she is widowed, Pete Legrand, mistakenly believing himself to be the father of her child, Lucius, comes to ensure Lucius' inheritance. Usually strong and independent, Julia accepts his help and his courtship, eventually marrying him. First, however, she tells him that her brother Duncan, not Pete, fathered Lucius. Despite the illicit birth of her own son, Julia is enraged when she discovers that Lucius has run off with Ada Belle Rutter, the daughter of sharecroppers. She eventually accepts their marriage, even suggesting that Ada Belle be taught her letters.

Duncan Cropleigh, who was killed during the Civil War. Duncan shared an unusually strong but pure bond with his sister Julia. Their bond changed, however, when Julia became engaged to Joe Cree. One night in the woods, they slept together, at first in all innocence, but then Duncan took Julia, hoping to keep her to himself. The next day, she left her

brothers to track deer with Legrand and was discovered in his arms. Duncan cut Legrand and would have killed him had not their brother Dickie, a doctor, been there to save him. The night of Julia's wedding, Duncan ran off with his brother Dickie's girl, Amelie. Duncan was killed on a dangerous mission the night Amelie came into camp looking for him.

Lucius Cree, Julia's eighteen-year-old son. Rather than help his father cut the timber that is his inheritance, Lucius accompanies his Uncle Jack to witch a well. While with Jack, he experiences his first sexual encounter, with Ada Belle. His idyll ends abruptly when news arrives that his father is dead. Overwhelmed by guilt, Lucius has a revelation that his father realized that Lucius was not worth the inheritance he was providing for him and committed suicide. Lucius matures rapidly as he attempts to fulfill Joe's business venture. When he realizes that he cannot, he goes to Amelie to ask for an extension. His manhood in going to her rather than Legrand causes Amelie to give him the title to the lands. Staggered by the news of his illegitimacy, which Legrand blurts out on his return, Lucius winds up at Ada Belle's home, only to discover that she is pregnant with his child and about to marry someone else. After their elopement, his pride prevents him from telling their families that they are married when they find the couple at Jack's. As a result, Othel shoots Jack, who steps in front of Lucius. As the novel ends, Lucius is coming to terms with who he is and attempting to make a life for his wife and child.

Jack Cropleigh, a water witch, Julia's brother. One of five siblings orphaned when their parents were killed in a riverboat explosion, Jack has an eccentricity that shows up in his philosophical discourse, his affinity for jackasses, and his ability to divine underground currents. His life is forever changed after he falls into the open grave dug for Captain Joe Cree. Jack is shot and killed by Othel Rutter when he steps between him and Lucius, who has eloped with Othel's sister, Ada Belle. Jack is unable to resurrect himself this time.

Pete Legrand, a rich young Virginian madly in love with Julia. Her brothers married her off before he recovered from

the wound Duncan inflicted on him. Pete spent the following years amassing a fortune and is able to help Julia when she needs it. Her revelation that Lucius is not his son does not affect Pete's love for her or his protectiveness of her son.

Amelie Cropleigh, called "the witch" by Julia. Amelie gets her vengeance on the entire Cropleigh clan, first when she tells Joe Cree that Legrand is the father of Lucius and again when she does not tell Lucius.

— *Jaquelyn W. Walsh*

THE VENDOR OF SWEETS

Author: R. K. Narayan (1906-   )
First published: 1967
Genre: Novel

Locale: Malgudi, India
Time: The 1960's
Plot: Comic realism

Jagannath, called **Jagan**, a manufacturer and seller of sweets in the fictional town of Malgudi in southern India. A prosperous widower, Jagan has almost reached the age of sixty, at which Hindus are expected to enter into a life of detachment from worldly affairs. Deeply imbued with Gandhian values, he reads from *Bhagavad Gita*, lives ascetically, and engages in numerous dietary experiments. Jagan is a parsimonious and wealthy businessman who secretly counts his earnings in a daily ritual and hides his profits. He makes and sells a product that he thinks is bad for people but rationalizes that he uses the purest of ingredients. Jagan deeply loves his son Mali but is unable to understand or communicate with him. Repeatedly disappointed by Mali's behavior, he lacks the confidence to confront his son and solve the problems of their relationship. When pressed to invest in his son's business idea, he tries avoiding Mali but finally must abandon his old way of life.

The Cousin, an unemployed man-about-town who survives by sponging off of others and ingratiating himself with his benefactors by offering them advice and the latest gossip. A contemporary of Jagan, The Cousin serves as the primary channel of communication between Jagan and his son Mali, and from him Jagan learns of Mali's plans and behavior.

Mali, Jagan's restless, modernistic son, who abandons his college studies, steals ten thousand rupees from his father's hidden cash box, and flies off to America for three years to learn how to write novels. He returns to India with Grace and tries to persuade his father to invest large sums of money in a joint venture with an American firm, which will create machines that can write stories. Mali has little love or respect for his father, considers his country and countrymen backward, and behaves in a scandalously modern fashion.

Grace, Mali's half-Korean, half-American wife. She tries to be a good daughter-in-law and encourages Jagan to support Mali's business plans. Jagan discovers that it was Grace who wrote all the letters he received from America that he thought were written by his son. When Jagan learns from Grace that the couple has never married, he feels that his home has been tainted and isolates himself from both of them.

The Hair Dyer, formerly an apprentice to a master carver of temple statues, who dreams of carving two religious statues to complete his late master's unfinished work. He looks to Jagan to give him the financial support he needs to finish the project. He supplies the new challenge and phase of life that will permit Jagan to end his old way of life.

— *Joseph Laker*

THE VENETIAN GLASS NEPHEW

Author: Elinor Wylie (1885-1928)
First published: 1925
Genre: Novel

Locale: Venice, Italy
Time: 1782
Plot: Fantasy

Peter Innocent Bon, a cardinal of the Roman Catholic church who yearns to have a nephew, though all of his sisters are in holy orders and his brothers have fathered only daughters. In his naïveté, he asks a glassblower friend to make him a glass nephew and bring the creation to life.

Virginio (veer-JEE-nee-oh), the cardinal's nephew, formed of Venetian glass and given life. He is a handsome young man with a translucent complexion and golden hair. He is baptized Virginio by the cardinal and sent to receive an education at the hands of Angelo Querini, a scholar and philosopher. He falls in love with Rosalba Berni and marries her, though the

marriage to a glass man is difficult for a flesh-and-blood young woman.

Rosalba Berni (roh-ZAHL-bah BEHR-nee), known as **Sappho the Younger** because she is a splendid poet and a woman of learning. She is the ward of Angelo Querini, at whose home she meets Virginio and falls in love, despite her engrossment in the classics and philosophy. Upon knowing love, she becomes an active girl, even a hoyden, and her marriage to a glass husband has complications. After she attempts suicide in her unhappiness, her friends permit her to be transformed into Sèvres porcelain so that she can be a more suitable wife for her beloved. Rosalba, it is discovered, is the illegitimate child of Cardinal de Bernis.

M. de Chastelneuf, Chevalier de Langeist, a strange man from Bohemia who has supernatural powers. His interest in Rosalba stems from having loved her mother before the woman became Cardinal de Bernis' mistress.

Caterina (kah-teh-REE-nah), Rosalba's mother, the mistress of Cardinal de Bernis.

Alvise Luna (ahl-VEE-seh LEW-nah), a famous glass-blower of Murano who works with M. de Chastelneuf. He is accused of being a sorcerer.

Count Carlo Gozzi (KAHR-loh GOH-zee), a longtime friend of Cardinal Innocent Bon. He is a writer of fairy tales.

Angelo Querini (kweh-REE-nee), a scholar and philosopher, formerly the friend of Voltaire. As a man of great learning, he is the guardian of Rosalba and the tutor of Virginio.

VENICE PRESERVED: Or, A Plot Discovered

Author: Thomas Otway (1652-1685)
First published: 1682
Genre: Drama

Locale: Venice
Time: The Renaissance
Plot: Tragedy

Jaffier (JAF-yur), a Venetian citizen who wins the undying animosity of Priuli by secretly marrying his daughter, Belvidera. After three years of being thus disowned, Jaffier and his wife are heartbroken and penniless, their only joy being in their deep love for each other and for their baby son. When their household is seized at the father-in-law's vindictive order, Jaffier is most amenable to a suggestion that he avenge the abuse to his wife by joining a conspiracy against the Senate of Venice. Revolted by the crudity of the conspirators, he informs the council of their plans and thus incurs the scorn of his noble friend Pierre. Jaffier has woven a tangled web by abusing his wife and betraying his friend. He can regain his self-respect only by stabbing his friend and himself.

Pierre (pyehr), a gentle philosopher and an honored citizen of Venice. By his own candid estimate, he is a villain; though he sees how the government is enslaving the people, he remains passive and does little to correct the situation. Intrigued by the conspirators' plot, Pierre concludes that he is as free to be a foe as to be a friend of Venice. His decision is inspired as much by his desire for personal vengeance as by any sense of altruism. Sensing his contempt for the bullying cowardice of the conspirators as they imply Jaffier's disloyalty to the conspiracy, he nevertheless continues with the cause. Complex circumstances conspire to shatter the friendship of Jaffier and Pierre, but in the end the men reunite. In a gesture of mutual forgiveness, Pierre, on the executioner's stand, asks Jaffier to stab him. This act saves Pierre from the wheel; more important, it serves to deceive the Senate.

Belvidera (behl-vee-DAY-rah), Jaffier's beautiful, noble, and sensitive wife. Even though she suffers the hurt of Jaffier's abuse, to prove his honor to the conspiracy, she forgives him and begs to be informed of the revolutionary scheme. She is loyal to Jaffier when he reports to the council and swallows her pride when she seeks her father's aid in saving Pierre. Visited by the ghosts of Jaffier and Pierre, she dies of grief.

Priuli (pree-EW-lee), a leading senator of Venice and the father of Belvidera. He so bitterly despises his daughter's marriage to Jaffier that he wishes her dead. After Belvidera's death, Priuli condemns himself to self-exile with the closing lines "bid all Cruel Fathers dread my Fate."

Renault (ray-NOH), a reformer. Scheming and relentless, he is the chief of the conspirators against Venice. He reveals his contemptible character by his attempts to compromise the lovely Belvidera when Jaffier, at first convinced of the rightness of the conspiracy, gives his wife over to Renault as a token of his loyalty. Such is Renault's compelling power that Jaffier, learning of his conduct, says he will endure personal indignity for the success of the plot against the council. Execution on the wheel, after the conspiracy is discovered by the Senate, seems a suitable end for Renault. The other conspirators are willing to be led by Renault, but they question his pressing Pierre so hard concerning Jaffier's honor. They, too, are executed for treason.

Antonio (ahn-TOH-nyoh), a leader and eloquent speaker of the Senate. In his contemptibleness and senility, he lends an aura of satire to the play. Bitter rivalry and mortal jealousy exist between Antonio and Pierre because of their various interests in a common mistress. Antonio is a weak character in his childish adoration and preoccupation with the mistress, who threatens to kill him as a way to make him promise to save Pierre, whom she loves and who loves her. Antonio consents but, like Priuli's, his decision comes too late.

Aquilana (ah-kwee-LAH-nah), the exciting and exotic Greek courtesan whom Pierre loved but lost to lecherous Antonio. In her effort to save Pierre, Aquilana shows a noble strain of character.

A friar, who tries to comfort Pierre before his death. He is alternately scorned and ignored by Pierre because of his sanctimonious prating.

VENUS AND ADONIS

Author: William Shakespeare (1564-1616)
First published: 1593
Genre: Poetry

Locale: Greece
Time: Antiquity
Plot: Erotic

Venus (VEE-nuhs), the goddess of love and beauty. Voluptuous and fierily passionate, she is greedy for the love of young Adonis and immodestly thrusts her attentions on him.

His shyness and sullenness increase her desire. She is a master of Renaissance rhetoric and delivers a stream of oratorical debate to convince Adonis of the importance of fertility. Her knowledge of the English countryside and hunting makes for particularly graphic and poetic descriptions. Her grief at the death of Adonis is as passionate as her love. There have been some scholarly arguments that hold her to be an allegorical Platonic figure rather than the erotic creation she appears to most readers to be.

Adonis (uh-DON-ihs), a shy, handsome young hunter. Venus' lavish wooing drives him into sullen obstinacy. He too is well trained in rhetoric and carries his side of the debate with rebukes for her lustful behavior. He is, however, tenderhearted and softens considerably when she swoons. He does not yield completely to her importunities and stubbornly goes ahead with his plans to hunt the boar. His death results. Those who hold that the poem is an expression of the Renaissance ideal of love compare Adonis with the fair young man of the sonnets and indicate that his death is justly the result of his rejection of love and beauty and his consequent failure to reproduce his kind.

VENUSBERG

Author: Anthony Powell (1905-   )
First published: 1932
Genre: Novel

Locale: London and an unnamed Scandinavian country
Time: Mid-1920's
Plot: Love

Lushington, a young British journalist, intelligent but inexperienced, assigned to a nameless Baltic country on the eve of its political upheaval, which may result in revolution. He is sorry to leave Lucy, with whom he is in love, but he is nevertheless vulnerable to the attractions of Ortrud Mavrin, whom he meets on the boat. He and Ortrud begin an affair that lasts throughout his stay in the Baltic. Lushington's approach to life is detached and uninvolved, which may explain why he is always at the furthest edges of the news stories he would like to cover. The deaths of Ortrud and his friend da Costa seem to jolt him into consciousness, and, at the novel's end, he may be ready to court Lucy more actively.

Lucy, Lushington's attractive young mistress, a sometime actress. Although Lucy has been married twice, she is not particularly interested in men until, as Lushington's mistress, she meets da Costa, whom she finds attractive. Most of her letters to Lushington urge him to remind da Costa of her existence. Her disengagement is fully as great as Lushington's, however, and, at da Costa's death, she seems passive but willing to accept Lushington as a substitute.

da Costa, Lushington's friend and Oxford schoolmate. Somewhat livelier and more social than Lushington but no less disengaged, da Costa is an honorary attaché at the British legation of the Baltic state where Lushington is assigned. His death as a bystander during an assassination attempt on a military leader leaves Lushington and Lucy once more together.

Ortrud Mavrin, the beautiful and coolly flirtatious woman with whom Lushington falls in love during his foreign assignment. Dissatisfied in her marriage to a distinguished professor of psychology many years her senior, Ortrud has had a series of lovers. She is perfectly aware, however, that she will never leave her husband and child.

Panteleimon Mavrin, Ortrud's complacent but likable husband. Mavrin's knowledge of psychology has done little to attune him to his wife's restless state of mind; when he imagines that she may be in love with someone else, he confides to Lushington that he suspects da Costa.

Count Scherbatcheff, a Russian émigré who is vaguely in love with Ortrud. The numerous maladies from which he suffers at first seem only one more level of agony in an already painful life, but at last those illnesses cause his death, an event that begins to make Lushington and da Costa confront the reality of pain and loss.

Count Michel Bobel, a fraudulent Russian count. He surfaces at every turn, accompanied by disreputable women, borrowing money, and constantly trying to insinuate himself into society. Ironically, Lushington must share a cabin with him on his return voyage to England.

Pope, a valet shared by da Costa and Lushington. Pope is talkative, self-centered, and fond of platitudes. He uses his employers as a captive audience for his dull reminiscences. After da Costa's death, he goes to work for Cortney.

Curtis Cortney, the third secretary at the American legation. Cortney has a puppyish enthusiasm for what he conceives to be the "old world" and an adolescent eagerness to believe every cliché concerning Europe and its quaintness; he thus contrasts with his blasé friends Lushington and da Costa.

— *Ann Davison Garbett*

THE VICAR OF BULLHAMPTON

Author: Anthony Trollope (1815-1882)
First published: 1870; serial form, 1869-1870
Genre: Novel

Locale: England
Time: The nineteenth century
Plot: Domestic realism

Frank Fenwick, the vicar of Bullhampton. He is involved in an altercation with the marquis of Trowbridge, in part over the vicar's standing by a young man the marquis thinks should be in jail. The vicar is also concerned about the lack of progress made by his friend, Squire Gilmore, in courting Fenwick's wife's guest, Mary Lowther.

Harry Gilmore, the squire of Bullhampton and the chief landholder after the marquis. The woman he loves, after much reluctance and hesitation, becomes engaged to him. He is crushed when she breaks her engagement to marry the man she loves.

Mary Lowther, Janet Fenwick's friend and guest. Prevented by lack of money from marrying her cousin, whom she loves, she finally becomes engaged to devoted Squire Gilmore. Her cousin's sudden acquisition of wealth, however, enables her to break her engagement to the squire and marry her cousin.

Janet Fenwick, the vicar's wife. In her sympathy for the squire after he is thrown over, she wishes that Mary had never come to Bullhampton.

Walter Marrable, Mary's cousin, a soldier home from India. He is trying to regain an inheritance from his father, who has cheated him of it. He and Mary become engaged but are forced to break their engagement when it is discovered that Walter's father has spent the inheritance. Subsequently, Walter is made heir to his uncle, a wealthy baronet. On the uncle's death, Walter is united with Mary.

The marquis of Trowbridge, a wealthy landholder and owner of most of Bullhampton, though he has no residence within ten miles of it. Disliking the vicar personally as well as for his leniency to ne'er-do-wells, he complains of the vicar to the bishop. His complaint proving ineffectual, he conspires with the Methodist minister to build a Methodist chapel across the street from the vicarage. Both the Methodist minister and the marquis are greatly upset to learn that the land on which they are building is really the vicar's and that their chapel will have to be removed.

Jacob Brattle, a crabbed, hardworking mill owner. With two exceptions, his many children have turned out well.

Sam Brattle, his son, who consorts with low companions. His association with a known former convict leads to his being suspected of a murder and robbery. The vicar defends him, and Sam is at last proved innocent.

Carry Brattle, Jacob's daughter. Her father is heartbroken because she has become a prostitute. She is living with the former convict, but the vicar befriends her and finds her a home with a farm family. Later, through the vicar's intercession, she is received at her old home, and at last even her stubborn father is reconciled to her.

Miss Marrable, Mary Lowther's unmarried aunt, with whom she lives.

Colonel Marrable, Walter's profligate father.

THE VICAR OF WAKEFIELD

Author: Oliver Goldsmith (1728 or 1730-1774)
First published: 1766
Genre: Novel

Locale: Rural England
Time: The eighteenth century
Plot: Domestic realism

Dr. Charles Primrose, the vicar of Wakefield, "a priest, an husbandman, and the father of a family." He is generous, kindly, honest, and given to strong opinions (as on monogamy). A homely philosopher, he admonishes his wife and daughters on their vanity, warns them against Squire Thornhill (who later takes him in), urges them to be temperate, and frequently delivers himself of wise saws and modern instances, all the while remaining a good-hearted fool who is easily duped by villains. His fortitude is amazing during his train of calamities. He is so completely a good man that he is lovable despite his frequent gullibility and his occasional absurdity.

Deborah Primrose, his wife, an ambitious woman whose chief interest is in getting her daughters well married. She is vain and, through George, she seeks vengeance on Olivia's betrayer.

George Primrose, the oldest son. Bred at Oxford for one of the learned professions, he (somewhat like the author himself) tries various occupations, succeeding at none. Through Squire Thornhill, he obtains an army commission. George at long last marries Arabella.

Sophia (Sophy) Primrose, the younger daughter, soft, modest, and alluring, a girl whose beauty increases upon better acquaintance. She marries Sir William Thornhill.

Olivia (Livy) Primrose, the older daughter, strikingly and luxuriantly beautiful, open, sprightly, commanding, and coquettish. Deceived by Squire Thornhill, she elopes with him and is deserted shortly afterward. She suffers remorse, especially when she learns that her marriage apparently was false. Later, learning that she is not the fallen woman she thought herself, she recovers and even offers to consider forgiving her betrayer if he reforms.

Mr. Burchell, in reality Sir William Thornhill, the uncle of Squire Thornhill. Sir William is famed for his great generosity and whimsicality. An experienced observer and judge of people, he is a self-admitted humorist and eccentric. Fond of children, he is very popular with them. After aiding various members of the Primrose family several times, he reveals himself, helps to bring happiness to the whole family, and marries Sophia.

Squire Thornhill, Dr. Primrose's landlord and Olivia's betrayer. He is a handsome, unscrupulous rake. Guilty of multiple villainies, he is exposed before he is able to bring utter ruin on the Primrose family and also before he is able to marry Arabella and gain control of her fortune.

Arabella Wilmot, who is betrothed to George. She is the daughter of a neighboring clergyman. After Olivia's seduction and desertion and George's long absence, Arabella plans to marry the squire, who convinces her that George has married and gone to America. She learns of the deception just in time and becomes George's wife.

Mr. Wilmot, Arabella's thrice-married father.

Mr. Williams, a farmer neighbor of the Primroses who plans to marry Olivia and is dismayed when she runs away.

Moses Primrose, the fourth child and second son of the Primroses. Being intended for business, he received a miscellaneous education at home. He is talkative, naïve, and as gullible as his father.

Dick and

Bill Primrose, the two youngest Primrose children.

Solomon Flamborough, a neighbor who loves to hear himself talk and who talks too much and too repetitiously. Moses is interested in one of the two Flamborough daughters.

Lady Blarney and

Miss Carolina Wilhelmina Amelia Skeggs, two strumpets, friends of the squire posing as town ladies.

Ephraim Jenkinson, a venerable old man (under his disguise, he is many years younger), a spouter of bogus learning who cheats Moses out of money and Dr. Primrose out of a horse. He and Dr. Primrose later meet in jail. A crony of the squire, Jenkinson tricked him by bringing a real priest to perform the marriage ceremony for Olivia and the squire.

Mr. Symmonds, a keeper of a public house who informs Dr. Primrose of the squire's unsavory reputation as a seducer. Dr. Primrose learns that Olivia has been staying at the public house after her desertion by the squire.

Timothy Baxter, the squire's hireling and the abductor of Sophia, who is saved from him by Sir William.

THE VICOMTE DE BRAGELONNE

Authors: Alexandre Dumas, *père* (1802-1870), with Auguste Maquet (1813-1888)
First published: 1848-1850
Genre: Novel

Locale: France and England
Time: The seventeenth century
Plot: Historical

Raoul (raw-EWL), **vicomte de Bragelonne** (vee-KOH[N] deh brah-geh-LOHN), the son of Athos, the comte de la Fère, who was one of the famous Three Musketeers. Raoul becomes the rival of Louis XIV for the love of Louise de la Vallière. Disappointed in love, he goes to Africa, where he is killed.

Louise de la Vallière (lweez deh lah vahl-YEHR), a beautiful young woman. Though betrothed to the vicomte de Bragelonne, she becomes the mistress of Louis XIV.

Louis XIV (lwee), the king of France and vicomte de Bragelonne's rival for Mlle de la Vallière.

The comte de la Fère (deh lah fehr), formerly known as **Athos**, one of the Three Musketeers. He helps Charles II regain the throne of England. He dies of shock when told of the death of the vicomte de Bragelonne, his son.

Charles II, the English king, who took refuge in France while Cromwell ruled England.

Cardinal Mazarin (mah-zah-RA[N]), the chief minister to Louis XIV.

D'Artagnan (dahr-tahn-YA[N]), the famous Musketeer. He is loyal to Louis XIV and supports the king against those who plot against the monarch. He dies in battle shortly after having been made a marshal of France.

General Monk, the leader of the English Parliamentary forces. He is seized by D'Artagnan and taken to France, where he agrees to put Charles II on the English throne.

Planchet (plah[n]-SHAY), a wealthy merchant who was formerly D'Artagnan's servant. He helps finance his former master in the effort to put Charles II on the English throne.

Fouquet (few-KAY), the finance minister under Louis XIV. He plots against the king.

Colbert (kohl-BEHR), an intendant under Louis XIV.

M. du Vallon (dew vah-YOH[N]), formerly **Porthos**, one of the Three Musketeers. A plotter against the king, he is killed in battle at Belle-Isle.

The bishop of Vannes (vahn), formerly **Aramis**, one of the Three Musketeers. He is also known as **M. D'Herblay**. Although he plots against the monarchy, he is pardoned at the request of D'Artagnan.

Mlle de Montalais (moh[n]-tah-LAY), a lady in waiting at the court and a plotter against Louis XIV.

Philippe (fee-LEEP), Louis XIV's twin brother. He is the mysterious prisoner in an iron mask.

M. Saint-Aignan (sah[n] teh[n]-YAH[N]), who is killed in a duel over Mlle de la Vallière by de Bragelonne.

THE VICTIM

Author: Saul Bellow (1915-   )
First published: 1947
Genre: Novel

Locale: New York City
Time: Probably the 1940's
Plot: Moral

Asa Leventhal, who works as an editor of a trade paper. He finds his life turned upside down in a matter of days. While Asa's wife, Mary, is out of town visiting relatives, Asa receives a call from his brother's wife, Elena, who is also alone. Her husband, Max, has gone to Texas for a better job. Elena's son Mickey is sick, and she asks Asa for help. Over the next few days, Mickey grows worse and dies. At the same time, Asa meets a seedy alcoholic, Kirby Allbee, who blames his downfall on Asa. Years before, using Kirby as a reference, Asa had a job interview with Kirby's employer, Mr. Rudiger. During the interview, Asa had argued rudely with Rudiger. Shortly afterward, Kirby was fired, and he thinks that Asa's outburst with his boss started his problems, which also include the death of his wife in an accident. Asa is at first irritated with Kirby's constant appearances and requests for help, but he is gradually overwhelmed by a growing sense of responsibility for Kirby. When Kirby is thrown out of his rooming house, Asa takes him in. Kirby wants to reverse his fate by the same device that

caused it; he asks Asa to introduce him to an acquaintance in the hope of landing a job. Asa catches Kirby in his bed with a woman and throws him out, but Kirby sneaks back in and tries to gas himself while Asa is sleeping. Gradually, Asa becomes crushed by the weight of his guilt—guilt over what he did or Kirby imagines he did, guilt over his distant relationship with his brother, guilt over his inability to prevent the death of his nephew, and guilt about his Jewish heritage. All these elements combine to make Asa a severely chastened person. In a surprise ending months after Kirby's suicide attempt, Asa and his wife meet Kirby in the company of a beautiful actress, at a theater. Kirby is doing quite well, and Asa is completely bewildered. Now it is unclear who is the victim.

Kirby Allbee, who at first appears to be the victim of the title. He is adept at manipulating people, particularly Asa. He tries to get Asa to arrange a meeting with Shifcart, the man he hopes will get him a job, even though he knows nothing about the man—he found Shifcart's business card in Asa's belongings. Kirby thinks that Asa will have special influence with Shifcart because both men are Jews. Asa begins to think of Kirby as a kind of double or as an agent of the dark, failure-ridden side of his personality.

Stan Williston, a mutual friend of Asa and Kirby. He deepens Asa's sorrow when he tells Asa about Kirby's history and

reveals that Asa's argument with Rudiger did indeed contribute to Kirby's firing.

Daniel Harkavy, a friend of Asa who serves as a sounding board for him and takes care of him when Asa drinks too much at a child's birthday party.

— James Baird

VICTORIA

Author: Knut Hamsun (Knut Pedersen, 1859-1952)
First published: 1898
Genre: Novel

Locale: A small Scandinavian village
Time: Late nineteenth century
Plot: Love

Johannes, the miller's son, later a poet. At the age of fourteen, Johannes is immersed in nature. Birds, trees, and stones are all his friends. Imagination peoples his small realm with dwarfs, giants, kings, and princesses. Emotional and sensitive, he suffers the misery of being the poor boy and servant when Ditlef and Victoria, children from the local manor house, wish to play. Even at the age of fourteen, he adores the ten-year-old Victoria, who enchants him with her pretty appearance and gestures. His love for Victoria inspires him to write a series of successful books of love poems. His success, however, cannot clear away the misunderstandings, doubt, and pride that continue to bar his way to Victoria.

Victoria, the daughter of the master and lady of the castle. At ten years of age, Victoria is irresistible to Johannes, and as she grows older she becomes more lovely, graceful, and slender. Her deep blue eyes and wide, slender brows lure the miller's son. As her childish affection for Johannes matures, Victoria disguises her love to save her mother. Although the great success of Johannes and the death of Victoria's wealthy fiancé, Otto, might have freed the two lovers, a lack of frankness prevents their union. Hurt by Victoria's actions, Johannes

proposes to Camilla hours before he learns of Otto's death. Misperception continues until Victoria's death, which comes not long after a tubercular attack. Death frees her not to call to him but to write him a letter and admit the depth and constancy of her love.

Camilla, the young child rescued from drowning by Johannes, later his fiancée. Where Victoria is complex, Camilla is simple and childlike. Cheerful, fair, and naïve, she holds no surprises for Johannes. Despite her engagement to Johannes, she falls in love with the uncomplicated and friendly Richmond.

Otto, a chamberlain's son. Wealthy and thoughtless, the young lieutenant is not someone Victoria can love. His snobbish actions begin in childhood. The evening before he dies in a hunting accident, the jealous Otto strikes Johannes in the eye "by accident."

Master of the Castle, an improvident, party-loving man who allows the manor house to decline. Dependent on his daughter's good marriage to restore his fortunes, the master destroys himself and the castle by fire when Otto dies.

— Marlene Youmans

VICTORY: An Island Tale

Author: Joseph Conrad (Jósef Teodor Konrad Nałęcz Korzeniowski, 1857-1924)
First published: 1915
Genre: Novel

Locale: The East Indies
Time: Early twentieth century
Plot: Psychological realism

Baron Axel Heyst, a man who has deliberately attempted to stand aloof from life, an effort that has made him a pathetic man if not a tragic one. He is innately and fastidiously virtuous, but by detaching himself from the entanglements and consequences of experience he has made himself incapable of coping with evil. Consequently, when he is forced to defend Lena, the only person he has ever dared or tried to love, he fails miserably and destroys himself. He is characterized aptly by epithets: His apparent willingness to drift forever within a "magic circle" in the East Indies earns him the name "Enchanted Heyst"; his naïve optimism, the "Utopist"; his attempt to establish organized trade in the islands, "the Enemy"; his isolated retirement on Samburan, "the Hermit"; and his alleged exploitation of Morrison, his former partner, "the Spider." After Lena dies as the result of a wound inflicted by Mr. Jones, Heyst sets fire to his bungalow and burns himself and her body.

Lena, the new name Heyst gives to **Alma**, a young entertainer in Zangiacomo's orchestra, after he meets her while she is performing at Wilhelm Schomberg's hotel in Sourabaya. He quixotically thinks that the new name symbolizes her break with her sordid past. It is to Lena that the "victory" of the title applies. Realizing that Heyst is completely incapable of meeting evil with action, she resolves, out of love and gratitude, to save him, if necessary by committing murder. She is a foil to Heyst in that she has been forced since childhood to confront and resist the evil in life, and she is prepared, instinctively, to challenge and defeat it. Mr. Jones shoots Lena when he finds her and Martin Ricardo together in Heyst's bungalow.

Mr. Jones, "a gentleman at large" who embodies the evil intelligence and calculating wickedness that threaten and finally destroy Heyst. Outlawed by his perversity from the genteel society of which he was once a member, Jones travels with two companions among the outpost islands and obtains his living through gambling, theft, and murder. After shooting Lena and Martin Ricardo, Jones falls from a wharf and drowns.

Martin Ricardo, Mr. Jones's henchman. Although he is dedicated to performing dirty work for Jones, whom he considers a gentleman, he does not conform to his leader's misogynist principles. Characterized as a cat, he symbolizes instinctive savagery. Believing that Ricardo has betrayed him by concealing the fact of Lena's presence in Heyst's bungalow, Jones shoots him after fatally wounding Lena.

Pedro, the third of the evil trio threatening the lives of Heyst and Lena on Samburan. Symbolizing brute force, this apelike creature, formerly an alligator hunter in Colombia, has attached himself to Jones out of gratitude for having spared his wretched life. Wang shoots him with a pistol stolen from Heyst.

Wilhelm Schomberg, the brutal owner of a hotel in Sourabaya. His obsessive hatred for Heyst increases after Heyst carries off Lena, whom Schomberg had desired for himself. To get rid of Jones and Ricardo, who have been operating a gambling den in his hotel, Schomberg sends them to Samburan in search of a treasure Heyst is supposed to keep hidden on the island. His hope is that Jones and his followers will kill the man he hates.

Mrs. Schomberg, who is still in love with her brutish husband, even though he has reduced her to a condition of domestic servitude and spiritual degradation. To keep him for herself, she helps Lena escape with Heyst.

Wang, the inscrutable Chinese houseboy who deserts Heyst after seeing Ricardo's attempt to attack Lena. Before his flight to a native village on the other side of the island, Wang takes Heyst's gun; thus, Heyst and Lena are left defenseless, at the mercy of Mr. Jones and his henchmen.

Morrison, Heyst's former business partner in maintaining a coaling station on Samburan. After Morrison died in England, Schomberg circulated reports that Heyst had cheated his partner. Except for Lena, Morrison was the only person with whom Heyst had ever become involved. In return for a loan at a time of need, he had secured Heyst's appointment as a manager of the Tropical Belt Coal Company, now liquidated.

Captain Davidson, the skipper of a trading vessel. He is in the habit of sailing his schooner close to Samburan so that Heyst will not be completely isolated. He appears shortly after Mr. Jones has shot Lena. Later, he explains to the authorities the violent affair that for Lena and Heyst ended in a spiritual victory snatched from circumstances of physical defeat and death.

Zangiacomo, the leader of the ladies' orchestra in which Lena performs. His wife arouses Heyst's sympathy for Lena by pinching her.

Julius Tesman, a partner of Tesman Brothers. He backs Heyst in the coal company venture.

VIENNA: LUSTHAUS

Authors: Martha Clarke (1944-   ), Charles L. Mee, Jr. (1938-   ), Richard Peaslee, and Robert Israel
First published: 1987
Genre: Drama

Locale: Vienna
Time: Late nineteenth century
Plot: Surrealism

Vienna, a city at the turn of the century, the "character" that emerges from this group of tableaux, which are arranged so as to overlap, fade in and out, and even to take place simultaneously. The first one opens in a café, with a couple waltzing while Hugo and Magda converse about a friend who, it seems, can fly through the air. There follows the description of the toilette of an elderly lady, then a woman's memory of an erotic encounter in India. A mother gives a lecture on deportment, and a speaker tells of his daughter being drenched by an ornamental fountain. In an "Orchard Scene," a man carrying a tree branch has a homosexual encounter. A "River Scene" gives an impression of the Danube in the rain. In a return to the first tableau, the same couple speak "out of sync" about a visit to the Hofoper to see *Fidelio* and of the flying friend; the scene is taken from Sigmund Freud's *The Interpretation of Dreams*, according to the notes. There follows a woman reciting a list of

"I don't likes" beginning with Johann Strauss. An elderly mother contemplates suicide. An anecdote follows of an eccentric aunt who always wanted to be dusted. A speaker describes a black-and-white butterfly. Another tells of a rat seen in his lodgings: He unsuccessfully tries to strangle it. The drama ends with a discussion with a soldier on death. It is accompanied by music and mime: An old woman throws herself at a young man, nudes pose, and a soldier in red is both himself and his horse. The purpose of the whole is to evoke the unconscious world of Vienna, the subterranean world that informed life in that time and place. Freud is omnipresent in the sexuality, in patriarchal figures, and in the association of sex and death. Notes refer to Freud's *Five Letters on Psychoanalysis*.

— *W. Gordon Cunliffe*

VILE BODIES

Author: Evelyn Waugh (1903-1966)
First published: 1930
Genre: Novel

Locale: England
Time: Between the two world wars
Plot: Social satire

Adam Fenwick-Symes, a young writer. He returns from Paris to England to marry his fiancée but is forced to postpone his wedding because the manuscript of his autobiography is confiscated and burned by customs officials. Winning a bet of

a thousand pounds, he renews his marriage plans, only to postpone them again when a drunken major, to whom he has given the money for a horse-race bet, disappears. His fiancée's father gives him a thousand-pound check to enable the couple to marry. After they happily spend a night together, Adam learns that his fiancée's father has absentmindedly signed Charlie Chaplin's name to the check, and the wedding is postponed again. Adam takes over a newspaper gossip column, loses his job, and permits another man to marry his fiancée in exchange for a small loan. Later, in the war, during a lull in the fighting, he meets his drunken major again on a battlefield. The major, now a general, offers to pay Adam the thirty-five thousand pounds (the horse won) on the spot, but Adam thinks the money will be useless. They find champagne in the general's car, and Adam drinks some of it and falls asleep.

Nina Blount, Adam's fiancée, whose marriage is repeatedly postponed. She marries the man who lent money to Adam, but after he is called up for military service, she takes Adam along, as her husband, to spend Christmas with her father.

Colonel Blount, her father, an absentminded film fan. He makes a film about the life of religious leader John Wesley and is too preoccupied with it to notice that his supposed son-in-law is a young man he had previously met as Fenwick-Symes.

Agatha Runcible, a leader of the Bright Young People. Returning to England, she is mistaken for a notorious jewel smuggler, stripped, and searched. After escapades that include a party at No. 10 Downing Street, she goes to the auto races and takes the wheel of a car, the driver of which has been disabled. Having established a course record for the lap, she leaves the track and drives across country until she crashes into a monument. Still thinking she is driving in a spinning world of speed, she dies in a nursing home.

Miles Malpractice, another leader of the Bright Young People. Thrown out of Throbbing House when his brother, Lord Throbbing, returns from Canada, Miles needs money and takes a job as successor to Adam as gossip columnist on the *Daily Excess.*

Lottie Crump, the proprietress of Shepheard's Hotel, where Adam stays. She bullies kings, advises members of Parliament, and is careless about bills if she likes her guests.

Captain Eddy (Ginger) Littlejohn, who is in love with Nina. He lends money to Adam in return for Adam's promise that he be allowed to marry Nina. Shortly after the honeymoon, Ginger is called up for military service.

Mrs. Melrose Ape, a female evangelist who travels with her troupe of singing angels. She confirms a sensational but false gossip-column account of scandalous confessions made by aristocrats whom she has converted, then departs with her angels to pep up religion at Oberammergau.

Baron Balcairn, Adam's predecessor as Mr. Chatterbox, a gossip columnist. Refused an invitation to Lady Metroland's party for Mrs. Ape, Balcairn goes in disguise. Suspected of spying on a secret conference, he is exposed. He gives his paper a false story of aristocratic scandal, then goes home and kills himself.

Lord Metroland,
Father Rothschild, a Jesuit, and
Mr. Outrage, the new prime minister. These three hold a secret political conference, on which Balcairn is suspected of spying.

Lady Metroland, at whose party for Mrs. Ape the uninvited Balcairn shows up in disguise.

Miss Brown, the daughter of Prime Minister Sir James Brown. Agatha Runcible, after staying overnight at No. 10 Downing Street after a party, appears the next morning wearing a grass skirt, to the delight of waiting photographers.

Sir James Brown, Miss Brown's father and Mr. Outrage's predecessor as prime minister. Reports of his daughter's wild parties result in a change of government.

Archie Schwert, whose costume party is responsible for Agatha wearing her grass skirt.

Judge Skimp, an American guest at Lottie Crump's.

Lord Throbbing, the brother of Miles Malpractice.

A drunken major, later a general, who fleeces Adam of thirty-five thousand pounds won on a horse race. Their paths cross fleetingly several times, but Adam never collects the money.

Chastity, one of Mrs. Ape's singing angels. She appears along with the champagne in the general's car, after Adam and the general meet on the battlefield. Falling asleep, Adam leaves Chastity and the general to entertain each other.

THE VILLAGE
(Derevnya)

Author: Ivan Alexeyevich Bunin (1870-1953)
First published: 1910
Genre: Novel

Locale: Russia
Time: Early twentieth century
Plot: Social

Tikhon Ilitch Krasoff (TIH-khon ihl-YIHCH krah-SOHF), a dram-shop keeper and an entrepreneur. He is bitter because his illegitimate child is killed accidentally and his wife cannot bear him any children. When his crops fail because of bad weather, he turns to drink. Little better than a brute, he is sensually aroused by The Bride, who does not respond but who finally impassively endures his crude seduction. He believes all people are like himself and judges them accordingly.

Rodka (ROHD-kuh), one of the peasants on Tikhon's estate. He beats his wife cruelly, causing his master to fear him.

The Bride, Rodka's beautiful wife. She poisons her brutal husband and later becomes Kuzma Krasoff's housekeeper. Her employer feels sorry for her because of the life she has led. Later, she marries another peasant, but without expectation of any happiness.

Kuzma Ilitch Krasoff (kooz-MAH), Tikhon's brother, a poet. He and Tikhon work together as peddlers but eventually quarrel and go their separate ways. After many years, Kuzma returns and becomes overseer of his brother's estate at Durnovka. Although he is uneducated, he fulfills a lifelong dream by seeing a volume of his poetry published. He regards his life as a failure because he has not devoted it entirely to poetry. He believes Russia's troubles are all caused by a lack of education.

THE VILLAGERS
(Huasipungo)

Author: Jorge Icaza (1906-1978)
First published: 1934
Genre: Novel

Locale: Ecuador
Time: The twentieth century
Plot: Social realism

Andrés Chiliquinga (ahn-DREHS chee-lee-KEEN-gah), an Indian who dies defending his *huasipungo* (a small plot of ground given workers on an estate) against the greedy whites.

Cunshi (KEWN-shee), his wife, who is wronged by Pereira.

Alfonso Pereira (ahl-FOHN-soh peh-RA-rah), a debt-ridden Ecuadorian landowner who cheats the Indians and sells timber rights on his estate.

Blanca (BLAHN-kah), his wife, who uses Cunshi as wet nurse for their baby.

Lolita (loh-LEE-tah), their seventeen-year-old daughter, in love with a mestizo.

Don Julio (HEW-lee-oh), Pereira's uncle, who demands repayment of a ten-thousand-sucre loan.

Policarpio (poh-lee-KAHR-pee-oh), Pereira's overseer, who is somewhat sympathetic toward the Indian tenants.

Padre Lomas (LOH-mahs), the avaricious, lustful village priest. He overcharges for masses and burials and tricks the Indians into building a road to open their territory.

Mr. Chapy (CHA-pee), a North American promoter interested in timber and oil.

Jacinto Quintana (hah-SEEN-toh), the proprietor of the village store and saloon.

Juana (HWAH-nah), his wife, who is forced to accept the attentions of Pereira and the priest.

Juancho Cabascango (HWAHN-choh kah-bahs-KAHN-goh), a prosperous Indian, cursed by the priest and killed by the Indians.

A captain, who burns out and machine-guns the rebellious Indians.

VILLETTE

Author: Charlotte Brontë (1816-1855)
First published: 1853
Genre: Novel

Locale: Belgium
Time: Early nineteenth century
Plot: Bildungsroman

Lucy Snowe, a quiet, intelligent, and hardworking young English girl whose grave demeanor covers a deeply passionate nature. Orphaned at an early age, she spends her childhood in the homes of distant relatives and with her godmother, Mrs. Bretton. Later, through a varied chain of circumstances, she goes to Villette, a city on the Continent, where she becomes a governess in the household of Madame Beck, the mistress of a boarding school for girls. Before long, Madame Beck gives her a post as a teacher of English in the school. Eventually, with the help of Monsieur Paul Emanuel, another teacher at the school, she secures a school of her own. At the end of the novel, she anticipates marrying M. Paul.

Dr. John Graham Bretton, called Dr. John, the son of Lucy's godmother, now living in Villette. He is the kindhearted, handsome young physician who attends Madame Beck's children. Lucy had known him earlier in her life as a mischievous boy who had little time for girls. His recognition of Lucy comes when he is summoned to revive her after she has fainted while leaving a church. For a time, romance seems about to flower between Lucy and Dr. John, but when Paulina de Bassompierre once more appears in the lives of the Brettons, Dr. John's heart goes to her. At the end of the novel, Pauline and Dr. John marry.

Mrs. Bretton, John's mother and Lucy's godmother, a handsome and vivacious widow. She cares for Lucy after the child has been orphaned. Mrs. Bretton is most attentive to the details of domesticity, and her home and life testify to this interest. In Villette once more, she and her son care for Lucy.

Monsieur Paul Emanuel, Madame Beck's cousin, the instructor in music and French at her school. Hot-tempered and passionate, he falls deeply in love with Lucy and hates to see her in the company of Dr. John. At the beginning of his interest in Lucy, he constantly admonishes her and tries to draw her out with his discussions. Later, his manner becomes less abrupt, and because of the consideration and tenderness he shows, she finally falls in love with him. Before he leaves for a three-year journey abroad, he makes arrangements to establish her in a school of her own. The two plan to marry when he returns.

Madame Beck, a cold, dumpy looking, and self-controlled headmistress of a school for girls in Villette who hires Lucy Snowe to teach English. Always in possession of herself, Madame Beck is an outrageously curious person, snooping in Lucy's desk and drawers whenever she feels the occasion warrants it and restlessly prowling, ghostlike, through the school at night. She, together with her relatives, tries to block the romance of Lucy and M. Paul, but her efforts are thwarted.

Paulina Mary Home de Bassompierre (hohm deh bah-sohm-PYEHR), also called **Polly Home**, a beautiful and poised young lady who marries Dr. Bretton. She first appears in the story as a lonely, small girl called Paulina Home. Because her father, Mr. Home, is forced to leave her for a time with the Brettons, she falls into a state of depression broken only by the attentions of young John Bretton. She transfers all her affection for her father to the schoolboy and ignores Lucy Snowe's efforts to help her. She grows into a charming young woman and marries her old playfellow, who is now known as Dr. John.

Mr. Home, also known as **Monsieur de Bassompierre**, a distant cousin of Mrs. Bretton and the father of Paulina Home, to whom he is completely devoted. Because his wife was a giddy, flirtatious woman who never gave her husband the warmth and love he bestowed on her, he became very close to his daughter, and he is quite reluctant for her to marry anyone. Finally, he is reconciled to her marriage with Dr. John and looks forward to becoming one of their household.

Miss Marchmont, a woman of fortune, a rheumatic cripple when Lucy goes to care for her after living with the Brettons. Miss Marchmont's lover had died when she was young, and the old woman has turned into a firm, patient, and sometimes morose person who cares a great deal for Lucy. When Miss Marchmont dies, Lucy is once more forced to go into the world to make her own living.

Mrs. Barrett, the old servant of Miss Marchmont, also fond of Lucy Snowe.

Mrs. Leigh, an old schoolmate of Lucy, a comely, good-natured woman. Her French maid suggests to Lucy, after Miss Marchmont's death, that there are many English girls living on the Continent and that perhaps Lucy can find a position abroad.

Ginevra Fanshawe (zhih-NEH-vrah FAN-shah), a vain and proud but attractive girl, Paulina Home's cousin. She is a passenger aboard the *Vivid*, the ship on which Lucy crosses the channel, and is a student at Madame Beck's school. She carries on a flirtation with Dr. John while at the same time meeting Alfred de Hamal secretly on Madame Beck's premises. Spoiled and unscrupulous, Ginevra torments Lucy with constant demands for attention. Eventually, she elopes with Alfred de Hamal, and the two are married.

Colonel Alfred de Hamal, one of Ginevra's suitors and eventually her husband, a dandified figure in fashionable society. He disguises himself as a nun to hold many rendezvous with Ginevra in Madame Beck's establishment.

Mrs. Cholmondeley (CHUHL-mo[n]-deh-lay), Ginevra's chaperon at many parties, a woman of fashion in Villette who has attached herself to court circles and enjoys a prominent place in society.

Mademoiselle St. Pierre (sah[n] pyehr), a fellow teacher in Madame Beck's school, a prodigal and profligate woman whose chief achievement is the ability to keep order among the students.

Rosine Matou (roh-ZEEN mah-TEW), the portress at Madame Beck's school, a pretty, airy, and fickle young woman afraid of M. Paul's temper tantrums.

Fraulein Anna Braun, a worthy, hearty woman of forty-five. She instructs Lucy Snowe and Paulina Home in German.

Mademoiselle Sauver (soh-VAY), Monsieur Paul's ward, who adores him.

Vashti, a complex and beautiful actress who entrances Lucy Snowe when Dr. John takes her to one of Vashti's performances.

Désirée (day-zee-RAY), the oldest daughter of Madame Beck, a vicious child who smashes things and steals from the servants. She is overindulged by her mother.

Fifine (fee-FEEN), Madame Beck's middle child, an honest, gleeful little girl.

Georgette (zhohr-ZHEHT), Madame Beck's youngest daughter, attended during her illness by Dr. John. Her sickness introduces him to the Beck household.

Mrs. Sivinc (SIH-vihnk), the whiskey-drinking nursery governess to the Beck children, replaced by Lucy Snowe.

Mademoiselle Blanche (blahnsh),

Mademoiselle Virginie (veer-zhee-NEE), and

Mademoiselle Angélique (ahn-zhay-LEEK), three obstreperous pupils at Madame Beck's school. They plague Lucy Snowe on the first day of her teaching.

Dolores, another unusually willful student whom Lucy Snowe punishes by locking her in a closet.

Madame Walravens (WAHL-ray-vehnz), a hideous little woman, the grandmother of M. Paul's dead sweetheart. He supports her after the death of Justine Marie, his betrothed.

Père Silas (pehr see-LAHS), the priest who hears Lucy Snowe's confession. The cleric is supported by M. Paul because he is a kinsman of the dead Justine Marie. He tries in vain to change Lucy to a Catholic.

Monsieur Boissec (bwah-SEHK) and

Monsieur Rochemonte (rohsh-MONT), professors who attempt to embarrass M. Paul by claiming that he has written Lucy Snowe's compositions.

VINELAND

Author: Thomas Pynchon (1937-   )
First published: 1989
Genre: Novel

Locale: California
Time: Late 1980's
Plot: Social satire

Zoyd Wheeler, a former hippie living in a Northern California community called Vineland. He earns a government pension by taking an annual dive through a plate glass restaurant window in front of television cameras to prove that he is mentally afflicted. He tries to look after his daughter, Prairie, but has little control over her or over his own life. He is driven from his home by an invasion of federal and local police who ostensibly are looking for marijuana crops but whose real target is Prairie.

Prairie Wheeler, the teenage daughter of Zoyd and Frenesi Gates. She is a groupie for a rock band called Billy Barf and the Vomitones, and she works in a New Age pizza parlor in Vineland. Her driving desire is to locate her mother, Frenesi

Gates, and to learn why her mother deserted her when Prairie was an infant. Her search takes her to Southern California, where the band has an engagement and where she meets DL Chastain. She is guided by sympathetic women, especially DL, and a number of people who want to protect her from the federal prosecutor, Brock Vond. At a huge reunion in Northern California, she finally meets her mother, and they reach a friendly accommodation.

Frenesi Gates, Prairie's mother, a member of a radical film collective during the student unrest of the 1960's and early 1970's. She met and was fascinated by Brock Vond, who seduced her and turned her into a government agent charged with subverting the student movement on a small college campus. Eventually, she was made to supply the weapon used to kill the faculty member who acted as a guru for the student uprising. Vond spirited her away to a secret government camp. Rescued by DL Chastain, she could not resist when Vond called her back, and she has spent the years since as an undercover agent for antisubversive programs. She married another agent, with whom she had a son. Her occupation is threatened by cutbacks in government spending during the Ronald Reagan administration, leading her to go the family reunion in Vineland for shelter.

Brock Vond, a government prosecutor who uses his office to harass radicals and those he believes to be subversives. He believes that he is Prairie's father, and he mounts a huge government operation with a secret purpose of abducting Prairie. Ironically, he is foiled when the Reagan administration's budget cuts terminate his operation just as he is about to succeed. He is disposed of by strange means at the end of the novel.

Darryl Louise (DL) Chastain, the daughter of an Army career man. She has been trained in the martial arts by a Japanese master, and Brock Vond has tried to use her as an assassin. At a wild wedding reception in Southern California, she takes Prairie under her wing and takes her to a women's ninja collective. Its records contain information about Frenesi.

She later protects and guides Prairie in learning about Frenesi. She was at one time a lover of Frenesi and tried to rescue Frenesi from Brock Vond, but she is now a partner of an Oriental martial arts expert.

Sasha Gates, a Hollywood film writer and old-time radical activist. She is Frenesi's mother. She distrusts Zoyd but has shared with him responsibility for rearing Prairie. She is a prime mover in the reunion of the Gates clan at which Prairie meets her mother and reaches a kind of accommodation with her, although there is no reason to believe that Sasha and Frenesi will ever be close again.

Hector Zuniga, a television-addicted agent for the Drug Enforcement Agency and sometime friend of Zoyd Wheeler. Hector is hospitalized periodically for treatment of his addiction. He warns Zoyd of the increased government activity aimed at Zoyd, in time to allow Zoyd to leave his home before it is raided.

Hub Gates, Frenesi's father, an expert in film lighting. Like his wife, Sasha, he is an old-time radical. He is a kind man and more sane than most of the other characters, but his politics have made it difficult for him to earn a living in the film industry.

— *John M. Muste*

THE VIOLENT BEAR IT AWAY

Author: Flannery O'Connor (1925-1964)
First published: 1960
Genre: Novel

Locale: Tennessee
Time: 1952
Plot: Psychological realism

Francis Marion Tarwater, a backwoods teenager who is perversely proud to have been born at the site of a car wreck in which his unmarried mother died. His father was a divinity student who later committed suicide. Kidnapped by his great uncle Mason Tarwater and taught to be a prophet, he struggles to reject his indoctrination, creating internal voices to express his own doubts and even equating strangers he meets—especially his rapist—with these voices. As much as Tarwater rejects Old Tarwater, he equally rejects the citified and superficially rational ways of his uncle George Rayber, finally simultaneously rejecting and accepting his prophetic calling when he baptizes and drowns his cousin Bishop Rayber. He consistently claims that his ability to act makes him superior to the thoughtful, talkative Rayber, but Tarwater's unconscious drives and the words he speaks to perform a baptism are crucial to his story.

George F. Rayber, a high school teacher, about forty years old, who specializes in testing. Like Tarwater, he has a strong interest in the role of prophet and the teachings of Old Tarwater. At the age of seven, he cooperated with his abduction by Old Tarwater. Rayber fights the attraction of prophecy by pouring his energies into rational methods for analyzing and changing others' lives. He is not interested in his son Bishop except as a means to draw the line on love, but he does like the idea of remaking Tarwater. He ends up as much of a bully as Old Tarwater. After he allows Tarwater to drown Bishop, he may find himself unable to recover without becoming even more like the two Tarwaters.

Mason Tarwater, called **Old Tarwater**, dead at the age of eighty-four. He was a backwoods prophet and haunts the other characters. Institutionalized for four years, he learned that he could be considered sane if he stopped talking about religion. Once released, he kidnapped children to give them a fundamentalist upbringing. His nephew Rayber's plausible theory that he called himself to become a prophet earned only his disgust. Old Tarwater resembles Rayber in his eagerness to pigeonhole other people.

Bishop Rayber, a mentally retarded child about five years old, who innocently wants to be friends with others. An old-looking child, he has white hair, and his eyes bear a strong resemblance to those of Old Tarwater, suggesting that, as he presents Tarwater with opportunities to perform a baptism by regularly rushing toward bodies of water, he is carrying on Old Tarwater's legacy. When Rayber tries to drown him and when Tarwater does drown him, his struggle to survive makes him seem a symbol of an elemental life force.

Bernice Bishop, whom Old Tarwater called the "welfare woman." She went with Rayber to recover the kidnapped Tarwater, then gave up the attempt after Old Tarwater shot Rayber and she saw the cold look on the baby Tarwater's face. Older than Rayber, she later married him and gave birth to their child Bishop, only to leave him, probably in part because she disagreed with his determination not to institutionalize Bishop.

Buford Munson, a black man who lives near Old Tarwater's house in Powderhead. Buford appears to be part of a stable community of Christians who treat one another humanely; he knows to bury Old Tarwater without being ordered. He helps bring about the crucial turn in Tarwater's life, but his own life is more conventional and comfortable than the tortured lives of the major characters.

T. Fawcett Meeks, a traveling salesman of copper flues who gives Tarwater a ride into the city. Meeks believes that the value of loving other people is that you can sell them things. He also values machines and hard work, and had he not had a rendezvous scheduled with a girlfriend, he would have pressured Tarwater to work for him.

Lucette Carmody, a child evangelist since the age of six. Now eleven or twelve years old, she has a physical disability in her legs. She travels with her parents, also evangelists. Her sermon focuses on the Massacre of the Innocents. Although Rayber thinks he can connect with her emotionally, she calls him damned. She may serve as a role model for Tarwater.

— *Marshall Bruce Gentry*

THE VIOLENT LAND
(Terras do Sem Fim)

Author: Jorge Amado (1912-   )
First published: 1942
Genre: Novel

Locale: The city of São Jorge de Ilhéus, Bahía, Brazil, and nearby plantations
Time: 1911-1912
Plot: Historical

João Magalhães (zhoh-OWN mah-gahl-YAYS), a gambler and drifter who claims to be a captain and military engineer who has participated in several revolutions. Although he won his engineer's ring at a gaming table, he agrees to survey the Sequeiro Grande (see-KAY-roh GRAHN-dee), a rich area of fiercely contested tropical forest. While working for the Badaró family, he falls in love with the only heir, Ana. João's shadowy background notwithstanding, Ana's family considers his ability to reinvent himself and adapt to his circumstances a useful asset in a land that is in the process of self-creation, and they approve the match. He agrees to change his surname to Badaró and continue the family line.

Colonel Horacio da Silveira (oh-RAH-see-oh seel-vay-EE-rah), a former mule driver who by hard work becomes the wealthiest of the cacao plantation owners. Widowed, he marries the young and cultured Ester, with whom he has one son. Like other "colonels" of the region, he employs many bodyguards and ruffians to protect his life and to forward his interests. With their aid, he launches a bloody campaign to claim the Sequeiro Grande as part of his already extensive cacao holdings, using his hired guns to assassinate those who stand in his way. He survives the fever that kills his wife, has his principal rival assassinated, and, when political power shifts to his party, even wins the legal battles related to the acquisition of the forest.

Ester Silveira, Horacio's wife and the mother of his only son. She does not adapt well to the roughness of plantation life. She falls in love with Horacio's lawyer, Virgilio, with whom she dreams of escaping the violent life of Ilhéus. After tending to Horacio during his bout with typhus, she succumbs to the fever, dying a few days later.

Juca Badaró (ZHEW-kah bah-dah-ROH), the brother of Sinhó Badaró. He is more aggressive than his brother in the struggle for the Sequeiro Grande. He is married to Olga, but they are childless. A hard-drinking, card-playing womanizer, he is assassinated by one of Horacio's henchmen.

Sinhó Badaró (seen-YOH), the widowed patriarch of the Badaró family and Ana's father. Loathe to resort to violence, he nevertheless refuses to let Horacio claim the Sequeiro Grande. He seeks guidance in his daily ritual of reading at random from the Bible. Wounded while defending his plantation from Horacio, he is forced to abandon his home to the torches of his enemies.

Don'Ana (Ana) Badaró (dohn-AHN-ah), the intrepid daughter of Sinhó Badaró and his wife Lidia, who died when Ana was very young. Ana knows the plantation thoroughly and has no desire for a more refined lifestyle. She has no interest in men or in love until she meets the adventurer João Magalhães. In the standoff with Horacio and his men, she is the last to defend the family home. Hiding in the attic after all others have abandoned the house in fear of their lives, she shoots the last bullet shot by a Badaró in the struggle for the Sequeiro Grande. Her enemies admire her courage and let her go free.

Virgilio Cabral (veer-HEE-lee-oh kah-BRAHL), a recently graduated lawyer, sent from Bahía by his political party to assist the head of the opposition, Colonel Horacio. He has a passionate affair with Horacio's wife, Ester. When she dies of typhus, he shares Horacio's grief and, as a way of remembering Ester, becomes Horacio's dedicated collaborator in the land wars. When Horacio discovers they were lovers, he has Virgilio assassinated. Though he is forewarned, Virgilio rides to meet his death, seeking union with his dead beloved.

Margot (MAHR-goh), Virgilio's lover during his student days in Bahía. She follows him to Ilhéus, where they end their relationship. She becomes Juca Badaró's mistress.

Raimunda (ri-MEWN-dah), the daughter of Risoleta, who nursed Raimunda and Don'Ana at the same time and showed every preference for her white "daughter" over her natural, black daughter. Raimunda grows up as Ana's playmate and then becomes a member of the household staff. She and Ana are married on the same day.

Antonio Victor, a young man who comes to Ilhéus in search of his fortune. Hired by Juca as a field laborer, he saves his master's life and becomes a hired hand. He courts Raimunda unsuccessfully until he is wounded while saving Juca's life a second time. As his reward, he asks for her as wife. She agrees to marry him.

— *Linda Ledford-Miller*

VIOLET CLAY

Author: Gail Godwin (1937-   )
First published: 1978
Genre: Novel

Locale: Charleston, West Virginia; New York City; and the Adirondacks
Time: The 1970's
Plot: Psychological realism

Violet Clay, the protagonist and narrator. Nine years ago, Violet left her husband and moved to New York City to make her mark as a painter. Since then, however, she has instead illustrated gothic romances. Violet is haunted by her tragic past—her mother committed suicide shortly after her father's death in World War II—and by her own apparent failure to realize her gifts. As a young artist, she particularly modeled herself on her uncle Ambrose, a writer. During the course of the novel, Violet comes to terms with Ambrose's suicide and his ambiguous legacy.

Ambrose Clay, Violet's uncle. As a young man, Ambrose spun a successful novel out of his infatuation with Violet's mother. For years after that early triumph, he made a series of halfhearted attempts at a second novel, first in New York and then in Mexico. Meanwhile, he supported himself with part-time jobs and money from his mother and the women who fell for his Southern charm. Ambrose finally retreated to Plommet Falls, where he made a last-ditch assault on his novel and then killed himself. Ambrose is a very complex character: An alcoholic, a Don Juan, and a manipulator, he is nevertheless an artist of integrity. Violet's ambivalent responses to his life shape her own artistic development.

Samantha De Vere, a poor unwed mother and Ambrose's neighbor in Plommet Falls. Proud, plainspoken, and fiercely independent, Sam is the opposite of the charming, romantic, aristocratic Clays. Despite her own tragic history, she has taught herself carpentry, plumbing, and other constructive skills. Sam is a mysterious figure until the novel's end, when she teaches Violet not to wallow in the past but to look to the future.

Georgette "Granny" Clay, who gave up a promising career as a concert pianist to marry Violet's grandfather. Even as Granny warns Violet not to repeat this mistake, she arranges a similar marriage for her.

Violet Pardee, Georgette's best friend, called "the Big V." to distinguish her from Violet Clay, her namesake.

Liza Lee Clay, Violet's mother. A nineteen-year-old war widow, she committed suicide shortly after Violet's birth.

Lewis Lanier, the Big V.'s nephew and Violet's husband. Their marriage, orchestrated by the two old friends, does not last.

Ivor Sedge, an embittered Hungarian refugee and conceptual artist. He is Violet's art teacher in New York and eventually her lover. She refuses his marriage proposal.

Jake, a musician and Violet's most recent lover, who leaves her after a bitter quarrel.

Milo Hamilton, Violet's best friend. The author of successful pulp romances under the name Arabella Stone, he is now composing a feminist gothic novel.

Sheila Benton, an editor at *Vogue* and Ambrose's lover. Sheila offers Violet a job, but Violet's career at *Vogue* ends when Ambrose marries Carol and Sheila suffers a nervous breakdown.

Carol Gruber, a tycoon whom Ambrose meets and marries in Italy. She loves both Ambrose and Violet but grows impatient with their romantic dreams. The marriage does not last.

Doris Kolb, the art director at Harrow House Publishers. Her firing of Violet, on the day of Ambrose's suicide, sets the plot in motion.

— Susan Elizabeth Sweeney

THE VIOLINS OF SAINT-JACQUES: A Tale of the Antilles

Author: Patrick Leigh Fermor (1915-   )
First published: 1953
Genre: Novel

Locale: Mitylene in Asia Minor and the Caribbean island Saint-Jacques
Time: 1902, as recalled from 1952
Plot: War

Berthe de Rennes (behrt deh rehn), the governess of the Serindan family, wealthy landowners living in Saint-Jacques. Berthe is an intelligent and independent-minded seventy-year-old Frenchwoman who is highly respected for her talents as a painter, pianist, and storyteller. At the time of the novel, she is retelling the events of her life when she was a young woman of eighteen fleeing from a poverty-stricken existence in France and settling into Saint-Jacques. As governess, she is privy to the romantic entanglements that develop between the other characters, in particular between Count Serindan's beautiful, young daughter Josephine and Governor Sciocca's son, Marcel. Berthe senses the calamity that will prevail if this love is revealed, for Josephine represents the social class of decorum and grace, while Marcel embodies the newly emerging political cry of liberation. Just as this class conflict is ready to

surface, a volcanic eruption decimates the island, leaving, as almost by chance, Berthe as the lone survivor and, hence, the narrator of the events.

Count Raoul de Serindan (rah-EWL deh sehr-a[n]-DAH[N]), a wealthy landowner whose Beausejour is Saint-Jacques' most opulent estate. At once the symbol of hedonism and decadence as he parades through the crowds invited to his lavish balls and festivals, he also provides a portrait of a compassionate and sincere man. At the end of the novel, he has relinquished his political prejudices and invited the opposing Sciocca family to the Shrove Tuesday celebration; in doing so, he has created some semblance of peace and goodwill throughout the island. His caring deeds earn for him the unofficial title of mayor of Plessis.

Sosthène de Serindan (sohs-TEHN), the count's oldest son, who is quite enamored of his governess, Berthe. While growing up under the tutelage of Berthe, he is well versed in the arts. As an adolescent, he falls in love with Berthe, or, more precisely, her charming aura. With the imagination and zest of youth, he hurls himself into the classical role of the pining lover who wails and threatens suicide, all because of unrequited love. At the end of the novel, he matures into a concerned brother stepping forward in an effort to save his sister Josephine from a doomed elopement.

Josephine de Serindan, the count's oldest daughter. Beautiful and noble, Josephine enters womanhood by falling in love with Marcel Sciocca, the son of the rival liberal governor. Undaunted by this seemingly hopeless love, she is willing to proclaim her feelings and to sacrifice even her life to preserve them. At the end of the novel, she has decided to meet covertly with Marcel and flee aboard his yacht, where the two lovers intend to marry.

Anne-Jules de Serindan, the count's youngest son. Anne-Jules is a sprightly boy who represents the very best of childhood, in all its wonder. He learns his musical lessons, tames mongooses, and entertains as a snake charmer.

Valentin Sciocca (SEE-oh-kah), the French resident governor of Saint-Jacques. He represents the liberal attitudes that are slowly surfacing and threatening to challenge the traditional customs of the island.

Marcel Sciocca, the governor's son. With somewhat wily flirtations, he awakes passion in young and impressionable Josephine. At the Shrove Tuesday ball, he recklessly ridicules a portrait of Prince Louis and is then challenged to a duel.

British traveler-journalist, who provides the introductory framework of the novel. While traveling through Mitylene, he interviews Berthe, inquiring about the almost-forgotten island of Saint-Jacques. In the process, he allows her to record her reminiscences.

— *Don DeRose*

VIPERS' TANGLE
(Le Nœud de vipères)

Author: François Mauriac (1885-1970)
First published: 1932
Genre: Novel

Locale: Calèse (an estate), Bordeaux, and Paris
Time: 1930
Plot: Psychological realism

Louis (lwee), a dying lawyer who comes to realize that his heart is a knot of vipers. Intelligent, cunning, greedy, unscrupulous, and incapable of love, Louis—as death approaches—writes a letter to be left to his wife. The letter, intended to explain his hatred for her and their children, becomes a diary of his dying days, a record of his life, and functionally an autobiography; ultimately, it becomes a confession of his spiritual journey to Christianity. The document rambles but is always coherent and organized as it records his unhappiness as a miser. In writing it, Louis comes to see his own selfish and evil nature, and he is transformed.

Isa Fondaudège (ee-SAH fon-doh-DEHZH), Louis' wife. Self-sacrificing to Louis and the children, Isa is a remarkably strong person in dealing with such a serpent as her husband. She lives with him by honoring the rule of not having conversation with him about anything important, by being subservient, and by being devoted to the Catholic church and her children. Stable, steady, and always dependable, she never does anything unpredictable in her life, except to shock everyone by dying before Louis.

Hubert (ew-BEHR), Louis' son, a stockbroker by trade. Cunning, greedy, and unscrupulous, Hubert is a nearly exact replication of his father, though perhaps not quite as smart. His main activity is to prevent Louis from disinheriting Hubert and his sister, and toward that end he contacts Robert, Louis' illegitimate son, and brings his half brother under his influence. These attempts are discovered by Louis, however, and

they are ended. At the end, Hubert reads his father's letter only to fail to comprehend it, and he is left filling his father's shoes.

Geneviève (zheh-neh-VYEHV), Louis' daughter. Geneviève is Hubert's female counterpart. She helps her brother plot against their father and is one of the little vipers in this family of serpents.

Janine, Louis' granddaughter, Geneviève's daughter. At twenty-two years of age, she is the only member of the family who comes to understand Louis and accept him. As a devout Christian, she forgives Phili, her husband, when he runs off with a music teacher. The family puts her in a nursing home, from which she escapes to be with Louis for the last three weeks of his life.

Robert, Louis' illegitimate son. A harmless store clerk by profession, Robert is too stupid to take Louis' money when it is offered to him as a revenge on Louis' legitimate children and heirs. Louis makes a lifetime settlement on him anyway, much to the dismay of Hubert and Geneviève.

Luc (lewk) and
Marie, two other children of Louis and Isa. This brother and sister died in their youth; thus, as Louis thinks back on his life, he believes that he really had loved these two. In fact, he had sent Luc off to war to die, and Marie had died, it is suggested, because when she fell ill, Louis had her treated by a cheap practitioner rather than an expensive specialist.

— *Carl Singleton*

THE VIRGIN AND THE GIPSY

Author: D. H. Lawrence (1885-1930)
First published: 1930
Genre: Novel

Locale: A rural rectory in the Midlands of England
Time: The 1920's
Plot: Psychological

Yvette Saywell, a nineteen-year-old who has just returned home from school. A proud, spoiled young woman, Yvette causes friction in the family because she does not take responsibility for her own actions. Like her sister, she is both attracted and repelled by the notion of having a relationship with a man. Because she does not like the "common" boys who are attracted to her, she decides never to fall in love. The candor of this "virgin witch" brings her both admirers and enemies. Because of her longing for freedom, she identifies more with the carefree Gypsies than with the members of her own family. After her father reprimands her for visiting the Eastwoods, she becomes hard, detached, and revengeful; only the Gypsy is able to reveal the mysteries of love to Yvette, thereby bringing her "back to life."

Lucille Saywell, Yvette's older sister and confidant. Unlike Yvette, this aristocratic-looking twenty-one-year-old not only takes care of household matters involving doctors and servants but also works at a job in town from 10:00 A.M. until 5:00 P.M. every day. Her insolence toward Granny and her belief that a girl should have flings and then marry at the age of twenty-six have much to do with Yvette's rebellion against her family and her involvement with the Gypsy.

The rector, the father of Yvette and Lucille. Heavy and inert, this forty-seven-year-old man is fanatically afraid of the unconventional, which is why he prevents Yvette from visiting the Eastwoods. Although he still worships his departed wife, he is greatly disturbed by Yvette's similarities to this woman.

The Mater, the girls' grandmother, who is the matriarch of the household. Obese, bedridden, and nearly blind, this "toad-like" creature never does any harm, but her compulsive desire to control other people's lives interferes with the plans of Yvette and Lucille. After the great reservoir bursts, she drowns in the resulting flood.

Aunt Cissie, the rector's middle-aged sister. This pale, pious woman who eats very little has dedicated her life to serving the Mater. When Yvette steals from the money that Aunt Cissie has collected to commemorate the fallen heroes of World War I, Aunt Cissie's jealousy of the girl's privileged position in the family manifests itself in a torrent of insinuations and verbal abuse.

She-Who-Was-Cynthia, the girls' mother, who ran off years before with a younger man. Her freethinking qualities and blithe carelessness have been transferred to Yvette. Whereas the Mater and Aunt Cissie regard the girls' relation to this woman as a badge of shame, Yvette views her mother as a being from a higher, immortal world.

Joe Boswell, a Gypsy who becomes Yvette's lover. Neat and dapper, almost rakishly so, he is, in Major Eastwood's words, a "resurrected man," having barely escaped death in World War I. Unlike Yvette, he is the master of himself and, therefore, is the only person who has any real power over her. At the end of the novel, he rescues Yvette from the flood and from her stifling view of love and sex. She is ultimately saved because of the Gypsy's admonition to be brave in heart and body.

Mrs. Fawcett, a rich Jewish divorcée. This thirty-six-year-old mother of two leaves her husband, a renowned engineer, for a man six years younger than she. Her nonconformist lifestyle attracts Yvette and repels the rector.

Major Eastwood, Mrs. Fawcett's lover and an admirer of the Gypsy. Like the Gypsy, he is a "resurrected" man; he was literally dug out of the ground by his fellow soldiers. This handsome, athletic man also resembles the Gypsy in his disdain for work and in his assertion that anyone who can really feel desire is a king. Because of his relationship with a rich woman who is younger than he, the major is viewed as a "sponge" by the rector.

Bob Framley, Yvette's friend and a member of the big, jolly, unruly Framley family. He accompanies Yvette on her holiday to Bonsall Head and assists in her rescue from the flooded house.

Leo, a friend of Yvette who is described by her as a "mastiff" among the "housedog" boys who court her. He proposes to Yvette, even though he is practically engaged to Ella Framley. It is Leo who honks the horn of his car and thereby brings the Gypsy to Yvette's attention.

Lady Louth, a friend of the Mater. The Mater insists that Yvette and her friends visit this awful woman during their trip to Bonsall Head.

Uncle Fred, the rector's middle-aged brother. This stingy and gray-faced man eats dinner with the Saywells periodically.

— *Alan Brown*

VIRGIN SOIL
(Nov)

Author: Ivan Turgenev (1818-1883)
First published: 1877
Genre: Novel

Locale: Russia
Time: 1868
Plot: Social criticism

Nezhdanov (nehzh-DAH-nof), a young socialist who idealistically believes in revolution as the panacea for all of Russia's ills. Born illegitimate to a wealthy aristocrat, Nezhdanov (literally, "the unexpected") received a university education, specializing in the arts. This training frustrates him because, although a basic appreciation of music and poetry has been instilled in him, he indignantly denies that aesthetics have any social value. Frustration is the key to his character. More than once, he compares himself to Hamlet, the idealist challenged to act in a practical situation. While tutoring in the home of Sipyagin, he falls in love with Marianna, who elopes with him and agrees to work for the cause of the party. Nezhdanov cannot devote himself wholeheartedly to social revolution and consequently considers himself a failure unworthy of Marianna's love. In desperation, he takes his own life, leaving Marianna to Solomin, his friend and compatriot. In Nezhdanov, the author has depicted the dilemma of a sensitive soul, basically opposed to ugliness and brutality, caught up in a social movement that demands the violent overthrow of the aristocracy.

Marianna (mah-rih-AHN-nuh), Sipyagin's niece, living in his household. Although she is of the aristocracy, her parents died in shame and poverty; her father, a general, had been detected in a huge theft from the government funds. Marianna, longing for freedom, loathes the life of a dependent in the Sipyagin family and is incensed by Valentina's remarks concerning her disreputable father and her lack of gratitude. In Nezhdanov she finds both a lover and a cause; not only does she agree to elope with him, but she also proves a ready convert to the party line. It is largely the purity and intensity of her devotion to Nezhdanov that draws the latter's frustration to a tragic climax.

Sipyagin (sih-PYAH-gihn), a nobleman who hires Nezhdanov as tutor for his young son Kolya. Wealthy and respected, Sipyagin is regarded as a liberal and progressive aristocrat who favors certain experiments in social profit sharing. As such, he is the mean between the extremes of Kallomyeitzev, who is an aristocratic tyrant, and Nezhdanov and his comrades, who ostensibly advocate annihilation of the aristocracy. He tolerates Nezhdanov and even welcomes him in his household until Nezhdanov's extreme views become offensive. Enmity between the two is sealed when Nezhdanov persuades Marianna to reject both her family and her social position.

Valentina (vah-lehn-TIH-nuh), Sipyagin's wife, a woman of beauty and poise. She is also the appropriate feminine counterpart to the moderately liberal views of her husband. Only once does her nature become wholly unpleasant, when Nezhdanov spurns her attentions in favor of Marianna.

Markelov (mahr-KEHL-lof), Valentina's brother, a violent advocate of social rebellion. When captured and exposed, he remains firm in his hatred of the aristocracy, refusing influential aid from Sipyagin, his brother-in-law.

Solomin (soh-LOH-mihn), a factory manager, a calm and taciturn man of great strength of character. Although a comrade, he recognizes the impossibility of immediate rebellion; hence, he lives amiably and profitably in the existent society, helping the party cause when and where he is able. As a manager, he is the picture of efficiency, respected by owner and worker alike. Aside from Nezhdanov, he is the most sympathetic portrait of a party member, interested more in peaceful means of social improvement than in inciting peasants to chaotic rebellion. He marries Marianna after Nezhdanov's suicide.

Kallomyeitzev (kahl-loh-MEHYT-zehf), a nouveau riche aristocrat, the inveterate opponent of Nezhdanov's social views. Essentially a fop, he takes meticulous pains to dress in the latest style and ostentatiously peppers his speech with French phrases. Politically, he believes in iron-hand control of the peasants.

Miss Mashurin (mah-SHEW-rihn), a devoted party member, plain and masculine in her features, secretly in love with Nezhdanov.

Kolya (KOH-yluh), the young son of Sipyagin, tutored by Nezhdanov.

Anna Zakharovna (ahn-nuh zah-HAH-rov-nuh), Sipyagin's aunt, a meddlesome woman.

Ostrodumov (osh-troh-DEW-mof),

Pakhlin (PAH-lihn), and

Golushkin (goh-LEWSH-kihn), party members frequently in the company of Nezhdanov, Solomin, and Markelov.

THE VIRGINIA COMEDIANS

Author: John Esten Cooke (1830-1886)
First published: 1854
Genre: Novel

Locale: Colonial Virginia
Time: 1763-1765
Plot: Love

Champ Effingham, the foppish, Oxford-educated son of a wealthy Virginia planter. Infatuated with Beatrice Hallam, he wounds his rival for her love and then flees to Europe. When he returns, two years later, he has lost his foppish ways and is a moody young man. His mental health is finally restored, and he marries his original fiancée, Clare Lee.

Beatrice Hallam, a beautiful young actress, supposedly the daughter of the manager of The Virginia Comedians, a traveling drama company. She despises Champ Effingham but loves Charles Waters. She turns out to be her beloved's cousin and not Hallam's daughter. She and Charles are married, but she lives only a few years after the event.

Charles Waters, a poor young man. He rescues Beatrice from drowning and wins her love. He recovers from the sword wound inflicted by his rival for her love and marries her. After his wife's death and the passage of the Stamp Act, he becomes a leader in the revolutionary movement in the Virginia Colony.

Mr. Hallam, Beatrice's supposed father, the manager of The Virginia Comedians. He wants Beatrice to marry Champ so that she will be rich and respected. He also sees her marriage into a wealthy family as a source of money and ease for himself.

Mr. Effingham, Champ's planter father. He is against his son's courting of Beatrice Hallam, the actress.

Clare Lee, Champ's cousin and fiancée. Though spurned for a while by Champ, she continues to love him and finally is married to him.

Captain Ralph Waters, Charles's brother. When Champ loses his foppish ways, the captain becomes his close friend. Ralph marries Clare Lee's sister.

Jack Hamilton, Champ Effingham's friend.

THE VIRGINIAN: A Horseman of the Plains

Author: Owen Wister (1860-1938)
First published: 1902
Genre: Novel

Locale: Wyoming
Time: Late nineteenth century
Plot: Western

The Virginian, a cowboy in Wyoming who is one of nature's gentlemen. He can perform his duties well and hold his own in practical jokes, drinking bouts, and poker games. When given an opportunity, he proves to be an apt leader of men and a successful ranch foreman. He falls in love with a young schoolteacher from the East and by his manly behavior proves his worth to the woman, who finally marries him, even though he is a rough-and-ready man by her standards. The Virginian believes in law and order, even if violence is required to maintain them; one of his most difficult experiences is the hanging of a friend who has turned cattle rustler.

Molly Wood, a very feminine but efficient young woman from Vermont who goes to Wyoming to teach in the grade school at Bear Creek, Wyoming. She entrances the Virginian, who almost immediately falls in love when he rescues her from a stagecoach marooned by high water. Molly acts the coquette at first with the cowboy, but she falls in love with him, even risking her life to attend him when he is wounded by hostile Indians. She tries to keep him from a gunfight by threatening not to marry him, but when he emerges from the duel unscathed, she is too happy that he is left alive to make good her threat.

Trampas, a cowboy who becomes the Virginian's enemy when the latter accuses him of cheating at cards and faces him down without a fight. Trampas turns cattle rustler and becomes an outlaw, even killing a fellow rustler to save his own life. He is killed by the Virginian in a gunfight.

Steve, a cowboy, one of the Virginian's close friends. He becomes a cattle rustler and is hanged by a posse of which the Virginian is a member. When caught, Steve refuses to speak to his friend, who feels bad about the death of Steve, outlaw or not.

Judge Henry, the owner of a cattle ranch at Sunk Creek, Wyoming, where the Virginian works. Judge Henry is impressed by the Virginian and makes him his foreman.

Shorty, a cowboy who becomes one of Trampas' fellow rustlers. He is killed by Trampas when his death will allow the other outlaw to escape justice.

THE VIRGINIANS: A Tale of the Last Century

Author: William Makepeace Thackeray (1811-1863)
First published: 1858-1859; serial form, 1857-1859
Genre: Novel

Locale: England and the Colony of Virginia
Time: Late eighteenth century
Plot: Historical

George Esmond Warrington, the older son of Madame Rachel Esmond Warrington and her deceased husband, and the heir to the Castlewood estate in Virginia. Impetuous, emotional, and introspective, George volunteers to serve in the French and Indian War under a family friend and neighbor, Colonel George Washington. George Warrington is reported killed in action, but he turns up three years later, his life having been saved by an Indian girl. A short time later, he goes to England, where his young brother, Harry, has been confined in debtors' prison. While in England, he takes up the study of literature and marries the daughter of a family friend. For a time, he tries to earn a living by writing; one of his plays is a success, the other a failure. Then his uncle, Sir Miles Warrington, dies, and George inherits his title and estate. Shortly before the outbreak of the Revolutionary War in America, he and his wife return to the family plantation in Virginia; however, having no sympathy for the cause of the colonists, he leaves Virginia and returns to England once more. There he retires to the management of his country estate.

Harry Esmond Warrington, the younger brother of George, an extroverted, gay, and athletic young man, almost the complete opposite of his brother. Motivated by a strong personal sense of honor, Harry became involved in many scrapes in England, where he goes after the report of his brother's death. Usually lucky in gambling, Harry soon becomes the center of a social group of court dandies, but after a wild, profligate career he ends up in debtors' prison. He is rescued by his brother George, who intends to share his patrimony with him. Harry, feeling that he has to justify his life, uses the money to buy a commission in the army and fights under General Wolfe at Quebec. Returning to Virginia, he marries Fanny Mountain, the daughter of his mother's housekeeper and companion. Spurred on by Fanny, an ardent revolutionist, Harry fights against the British in the Revolutionary War. Later, after his wife's death, he returns to England and marries the younger sister of his brother's wife.

Madame Rachel Esmond Warrington, the mistress of Castlewood, a Virginia plantation, a handsome and charming but snobbish woman proud of her Esmond connections in England and preferring to be called Madame Esmond. Always possessive of her sons, she cannot adjust herself to their independence in maturity, and she carries on a feud with them in her last years. A staunch defender of the British crown, she remains a Tory throughout the Revolution.

Baroness Beatrix Bernstein, Madame Warrington's older half sister in England. Cold, grasping, and aggressive, she feels little sympathy for any human being except her young kinsman, Harry Warrington. She uses every device she can think of to break up Harry's proposed marriage to her niece, Maria Esmond.

Lady Maria Esmond, a spinster who claims to be twenty-seven years old but is really forty. Still a handsome woman, she is eager to marry. She flirts with her cousin, Harry Warrington, and inveigles from him a proposal of marriage. A great gambler, she is always in debt. When it is discovered that George Warrington is alive and Harry is not the heir to the Virginia fortune, she releases him from his promise to marry her. Later, she marries a parson, Mr. Hagan.

William Esmond, Lady Maria's brother, a sour individual who dislikes Harry Warrington. Always the loser in his bets with Harry, Will tricks him by paying off his debts with a broken-down mare after he had promised his best animal in settlement.

Fanny Esmond, Maria's younger sister. She is attracted to Harry Warrington, but her mother, Lady Castlewood, discourages the affair because she wants to marry off Maria.

Lord Castlewood, another of Harry's cousins, a gentleman much given to gambling but not much good at it. In his last match with Harry Warrington, he wins the latter's remaining money but is unable to help his kinsman when he is sent to debtors' prison.

Mr. Sampson, the chaplain at Castlewood in England and Harry Warrington's good friend. Kind but foolish, Mr. Sampson is constantly in debt and depends on Harry's generosity for funds. A worldly clergyman, he is fond of the bottle.

Gumbo, Harry's black slave, popular with the domestics in England, where he marries a white maid. He brags unendingly about his master's great fortune and home in Virginia.

Colonel Lambert, the husband of an old friend of Madame Warrington. He takes Harry in and doctors him when the young man falls from a horse while on the way to Tunbridge Wells with Lady Castlewood and her daughter Maria. Fond of Harry, the colonel is greatly distressed by stories about the young man's wild ways in London, and he tries to offer him his guidance. Colonel Lambert is the father of Theo, whom George Warrington marries, and Hetty, who becomes Harry's second wife.

Mrs. Lambert, the colonel's wife, an old school friend of Madame Warrington.

Hetty Lambert, the older daughter of Colonel and Mrs. Lambert, a great beauty and an accomplished pianist. Secretly in love with Harry Warrington, she conceals her feelings because she knows that he is supposed to marry Lady Maria Esmond. At the end of the story, she becomes his second wife.

Theo Lambert, Hetty's sister. She marries George Warrington.

Fanny Mountain, the daughter of Mrs. Warrington's housekeeper. She changes from a gentle girl to a firm-minded woman, and after her marriage to Harry Warrington she domineers him in many ways. An ardent revolutionist, she imbues Harry with some of her fervor and follows him while he serves in campaigns against the British. She dies soon after the close of the war.

Mrs. Mountain, her mother, Madame Warrington's good friend and capable housekeeper. When her daughter and Harry announce that they plan to be married, Mrs. Mountain leaves Mrs. Warrington because of the latter's insults to her daughter.

Sir Miles Warrington, a baronet, one of Harry Warrington's uncles in England. Jolly, fat, and rustic in appearance and manner, Sir Miles is actually very selfish and cold. When Harry is in prison, Sir Miles makes no attempt to help his nephew, and he disparages the young man before his family. When Sir Miles dies, George Warrington inherits his estate and title.

Lady Warrington, the wife of Sir Miles and a religious addict who constantly thrusts her pamphlets on luckless friends. When Harry Warrington is in prison, she sends him a set of tracts, but that is the extent of her help to her nephew.

Dora and

Flora Warrington, the daughters of Sir Miles. Although much taken with their cousin Harry, they distrust him as a bad person because of his profligate ways and their mother's warnings.

Tom Claypool, Dora's intended husband, the village gossip who carries the news of Harry's imprisonment to the Warrington family at their country estate.

Mademoiselle Cattarina, a French ballet dancer, one of the gay charmers at Tunbridge Wells to whom Harry pays court. He breaks off the affair when she becomes too demanding.

George Washington, a neighbor of the Warringtons in Virginia, a simple, upright man of the most scrupulous gravity and good breeding. When George Warrington hears that Colonel Washington is to marry a widow, he immediately concludes that the bride will be Madame Warrington. Warrington challenges the colonel to a duel but makes a retraction when the true state of affairs is revealed by Mrs. Mountain.

Mr. Dempster, the Warrington boys' Jacobite tutor.

Lord March, one of Harry Warrington's friends at Tunbridge Wells. A young man of fashion, he lives in London, and the two meet frequently in the city.

Lord Morris, another of Harry Warrington's drinking and gambling companions.

The countess of Yarmouth Walmoden, one of Baroness Bernstein's card-playing friends at Tunbridge Wells.

Mrs. Betty, Lady Maria Esmond's maid, who takes a fancy to Gumbo and gets drunk with him and Case.

Case, Baroness Bernstein's servant.

Mr. Draper, the lawyer to the Esmond family. A patronizing man, he conducts Harry Warrington about London until the latter tires of him and asks to be left alone.

THE VISIT
(Der Besuch der alten Dame: Eine tragische Komödie)

Author: Friedrich Dürrenmatt (1921-1990)
First published: 1956
Genre: Drama

Locale: Güllen, a town in Central Europe
Time: The mid-1950's
Plot: Tragicomedy

Claire Zachanassian, one of the richest and most powerful women in the world and a former resident of Güllen. She is a sixty-three-year-old redhead smartly dressed in black, a grotesque figure with an artificial leg and an ivory hand. Eccentric and extravagant, she rides around in a sedan chair, carries a coffin with her, owns a black panther, smokes cigars, and picks up and discards husbands at will. Once a wild and vivacious young girl in love with Alfred Ill, she lost a paternity suit against him through his deceit and left Güllen in disgrace to work in a brothel, where she was found by a millionaire. Incredibly wealthy, she has sought vengeance by buying up Güllen and shutting off its progress. Cold and menacing, she offers the town a large sum of money to kill Ill.

Alfred Ill, known as **Anton Schill** in the English translation, Güllen's leading citizen and the town's next mayor. He is a shabbily dressed, overweight, sixty-five-year-old shopkeeper with gray hair. As a young man, he had a passionate love affair with Claire but failed to meet his obligation to her when she became pregnant. Having bribed two witnesses to brand her as a whore, he abandoned Claire and married Matilda to get Matilda's father's general store. When Claire offers money for his life, he feels secure that the town will support him. When he sees his townsmen spending lavishly on credit, however, he flees in panic but is stopped at the train station. Betrayed by his friends, stripped of his position of honor, and branded as a criminal, he courageously accepts the responsibility for what he has done to Claire and goes to his death with an air of tragic dignity.

The mayor of Güllen, a stodgy and long-winded man always trying to orchestrate events and create the appearance of propriety. Although he is the first to turn down Claire's proposal, on humanitarian grounds, he is later seduced by wealth. Eventually, he threatens Ill to keep silent about the bounty on Ill's life and then gives Ill a gun so that he might commit suicide and save the town the messy business of executing him. During the course of the play, he changes from an inept and bungling politician to a snide and manipulative petty official.

The schoolmaster, a small-town teacher who has turned down better offers because he has faith in Güllen's potential. The first to see Claire as a sinister figure, he is the one townsman who is truly outraged at Claire's proposal because it goes against all the cherished values of Western civilization. When reporters come to town, he wants to tell them the truth, and he urges Ill to fight for his life. Then, overwhelmed by temptation, he finds himself taking part in Ill's murder. Ironically, he gives a speech condoning Ill's murder as an act of justice, not a crime motivated by greed.

The priest, who has purchased new bells for the cathedral on credit. When Ill comes to him seeking sanctuary, he tells Ill to be concerned about his eternal life, not his earthly one.

Stricken by pangs of conscience, he urges Ill to flee, for the temptation to kill him is too great.

The policeman, the town constable. When Ill asks for protection, he uses doubletalk to assure Ill that no harm will come to him, but Ill becomes suspicious of his hedging when he discovers that the policeman has bought a gold tooth. In the end, the policeman takes a self-righteous and brutal attitude toward Ill.

Boby, Claire's eighty-year-old butler, who wears dark glasses. He was the chief justice who ruled against Claire in her paternity suit. She bought his services as a butler and lets him go after Ill is condemned to death.

Koby and

Loby, Claire's two talkative, overweight, and aging eunuchs, who constantly repeat themselves. They are the two men bribed by Ill to swear that they slept with the young Claire. She tracked them down in Canada and Australia and had them blinded and castrated.

Roby and

Toby, two husky, gum-chewing gangsters from New York who act as Claire's porters and always speak in unison. Roby plays the guitar while Ill and Claire reminisce.

Matilda Ill, Ill's thin, pale, worn-out, and embittered wife. When the money is promised, she refurnishes the general store and jubilantly buys a fur coat, thinking that everything will work out for Ill.

Ill's grown children, a daughter and a son. They diligently seek work to aid the family until Claire's proposal drives the son to buy a new car and the daughter to play tennis and study literature. Before Ill goes to his execution, his children, along with their mother, drive out of town.

— *Paul Rosefeldt*

VISITANTS

Author: Randolph Stow (1935-   )
First published: 1979
Genre: Novel

Locale: Papua New Guinea
Time: 1959
Plot: Psychological realism

Alistair Cawdor, a patrol officer in the Australian protectorate of Papua New Guinea. Called **Misa Kodo** in the local pidgin, Cawdor is responsible for all aspects of central administration. His official duties, however, only add to the personal turmoil that has eroded his skill in the islands' maze of custom and responsibility. On the island of Kailuana, he becomes obsessed with an apparent cargo cult that worships extraterrestrial visitors. Considering evidence of spacecraft sightings, Cawdor finds what he considers to be his only chance for salvation: The returning aliens, it is said, will annihilate the "Dim-dims" (whites) or will transform them into islanders; either possibility appeals to Cawdor. The one possibility unbearable to him, that the apocalyptic cult is merely part of a political upheaval of an all-too-terrestrial kind, proves to be the case. With his hope for redemption dashed, Cawdor commits suicide rather than enforce the flawed and limited kinds of order that he represents officially, culturally, and personally.

Tim Dalwood, also called **Misa Dolu'udi** (doh-lew-EW-dee), Cawdor's nineteen-year-old assistant patrol officer. Although he is hindered by inexperience and ignorance of

the local language, Dalwood has an innate generosity that makes him attractive to both whites and natives. He and Saliba begin an affair—necessarily exploitative and hopeless under the circumstances—that surprisingly develops into genuine friendship. His enthusiastic study of local customs includes depths and sensitivities that seem uncharacteristic until his self-descriptions are taken as seriously as other characters' opinions of him. At that point, Dalwood emerges as a strong figure, capable of surviving the psychological upheavals of cultural interaction and helpful in directing, along with Saliba and Benoni, the transcultural affairs of modern Pacific society.

K. M. MacDonnell, who has been given the title **MacDonnell of Kailuana** and is called **Misa Makadoneli** (mah-kah-DAHN-eh-lee), a planter who has lived on the island since 1915. The eccentric MacDonnell's cynicism and low expectations cover deep considerations of the personal and cultural interactions in which he participates. In Cawdor, MacDonnell recognizes equal intellectual range, but he is unable to argue the officer out of depression; he sees greater promise in Dalwood, whose open-mindedness and strength remind him of his own youth. At the onset of the native battles, MacDonnell withdraws: His age and position preclude involvement both in the political struggle and in his friend's sad decline.

Naibusi (nay-BEW-see), MacDonnell's housekeeper and former lover. Rumored to maintain MacDonnell's security through sorcery, she is in fact a most alert witness to the complex interactions of natives and administrators. Her comments on Cawdor's self-destructiveness and Dalwood's assumption of authority provide a good measure of the whites' situation.

Saliba (sah-LEE-bah), Naibusi's teenage assistant. She is attracted to Dalwood but realizes that her prospects lie entirely on Kailuana. Although repelled by the whites' conduct—particularly when Dalwood kisses her in public—she is even more saddened by the violence among the natives; she ends the uprising by killing Metusela. Along with Benoni, Saliba represents a new, hopeful relationship between administrators and islanders.

Benoni (bay-NOH-nee), Dipapa's nephew and rightful heir; he lost his position by having an affair with one of the chief's wives. Educated off the island in white-run schools, Benoni feels less threatened than most others by the values and customs of the whites. Although his transcultural accommodation—not assimilation—continues to bring alienation and in-

security, Benoni proves to be a capable leader in the restructuring that follows the violence.

Dipapa (dee-PAH-pah), the chief of Kailuana. Ancient and nearly immobile, yet still revered and powerful, Dipapa instigates the native violence through Metusela. His exact motive is not revealed; perhaps he desires to create proper conditions for the return of the "starmen," but he may want only a last show of force.

Metusela (may-tew-SAY-lah), the prophetic, possibly insane leader of the cargo cult and a provoker of violence. It is suggested, though not proven, that Metusela is actually Taudoga, the disappeared leader of a violent coup on another island. The spiritual basis of his nativist movement may be qualified by a simple lust for power.

Osana (oh-SAH-nah), a government interpreter. Unscrupulous and manipulative, Osana is detested by all on Kailuana. As the only character fluent in both English and the island dialect, his power lies in the ability to play one side against the other through threatened mistranslation.

Kailusa (kay-LEW-sah), Cawdor's servant. Pathetic and physically deformed, he is utterly reliant on Cawdor. He commits suicide shortly after the death of his benefactor.

— *John Scheckter*

A VISITATION OF SPIRITS

Author: Randall Kenan (1963-   )
First published: 1989
Genre: Novel

Locale: North Carolina
Time: April 29-30, 1984, and December 8, 1985
Plot: Psychological realism

Horace Thomas Cross, a sixteen-year-old adolescent of predominantly African American ancestry with one white ancestor who was a leading citizen of the community. Throughout the novel, Horace undergoes a severe psychotic episode triggered by his conflict over his homosexuality and exacerbated by his interest in the supernatural. In his desperate quest to find answers to his life problems, he has resorted to necromancy. He has a nervous breakdown. Throughout the novel, he wanders around town nearly naked and carrying his grandfather's rifle.

The Reverend James (Jimmy) Malachai Greene, Horace's cousin, a minister of the Southern Baptist Church who is in his twenties. He has gotten over his earlier homosexual conflicts but is now undergoing conflicts of religious faith. He wishes to be able to counsel people in distress but feels incompetent to do so. Although he buries himself in his work, he does not feel satisfied with what he is doing; he believes he is only going through the motions of being a preacher to please his many doting, sacrificing relatives. He is also frustrated with people's obstinate, self-destructive behavior. He encounters an extreme example of such behavior when he sees Horace Cross carrying the rifle. At first it appears that the deranged youth may have decided to kill Jimmy; eventually, it becomes apparent that Horace has decided, after his long night of wandering, to commit suicide.

Anne Gazelle Dubois Greene, Jimmy Greene's deceased wife. A beautiful, sensual woman, she destroyed his faith in himself, in his calling, and in humanity in general when he caught her in bed with a strange man. Jimmy feels guilty about

his wife's infidelity, about their divorce, and even about her death. He blames everything on his sexual inadequacy, which results from his repressed homosexuality. He has been unable to love any other woman since her death from cancer. Since adolescence, he has steadfastly refused to allow himself to contemplate sexual relations with men.

Ezekiel Cross, (ee-ZEE-kee-ehl), Horace's grandfather, who provides a home for Horace and tries to impress on him the conservative wisdom that has guided African Americans for hundreds of years. He is a crotchety old man who loves to talk about the past and obviously thinks that things were better in the old days, even though African Americans in North Carolina experienced remarkable improvements in living standards, civil liberties, education, and other areas during his lifetime. Ezekiel is a sort of spokesperson for the older generations of African Americans in this novel. He is appalled that his grandson Horace prefers to associate with white youths rather than with members of his own race.

Gideon Stone, a highly intelligent and artistic adolescent schoolmate of Horace who has displayed pronounced homosexual behavior since elementary school. He and Horace eventually have a love affair, but Horace breaks it off when he decides to resist his homosexual tendencies. An important difference between the two young men is that Gideon is not troubled by his effeminate tastes and tendencies. Gideon is the son of a bootlegger and is hypersensitive to any social slights resulting from his background.

— *Bill Delaney*

VIVIAN GREY

Author: Benjamin Disraeli (1804-1881)
First published: 1826-1827
Genre: Novel

Locale: England and Germany
Time: Early nineteenth century
Plot: Political

Vivian Grey, an ambitious young Englishman who desires a political career. His unscrupulous conduct ends that career. Traveling in Germany afterward, he learns how terrible politics can be and realizes how immoral his own conduct has been.

Mr. Dallas, the proprietor of a school from which Vivian Grey is expelled.

Sidney Lorraine, the marquess of Carabas, an incompetent who has been turned out of office. His support in politics is sought by Vivian because the man has a title and represents the aristocracy.

Mrs. Felix Lorraine, Sidney's fashionable sister-in-law. Vivian attempts an affair with her, but she falls in love with Frederick Cleveland.

Frederick Cleveland, a retired minister of state. He gives his support for a time to Vivian. After Vivian insults him, the two fight a duel, and Cleveland is killed.

Baron Eugene von Konigstein, a worldly German nobleman who becomes Vivian's friend for a time while the two are studying at Heidelberg. The baron cheats at cards.

Essper George, a conjurer. He becomes Vivian's valet. He is killed during a storm, and his death has a sobering effect on Vivian.

Lady Madeleine Trevor, a friend of Vivian's father.

Mr. St. George, Lady Madeleine Trevor's brother.

Violet Fane, a friend of Lady Madeleine. She dies of natural causes in Vivian's arms, causing him to be grief-stricken.

Mr. Beckendorff, a recluse who is host to Vivian. He conspires to become prime minister of the Duchy of Reisenberg. When Vivian falls in love with Sybilla, Beckendorff plans to kill him but relents on condition that Vivian leave the duchy.

The prince of Little Lilliput, a guest at Beckendorff's home. He becomes Vivian's friend and introduces the Englishman to court circles in Germany.

Sybilla, a beautiful young baroness. Vivian falls in love with her, but he is disillusioned when he learns that for political reasons the woman must marry a deformed, half-witted prince.

THE VIVISECTOR

Author: Patrick White (1912-1990)
First published: 1970
Genre: Novel

Locale: Sydney, Australia, and its environs
Time: c. 1900-1970
Plot: Psychological realism

Hurtle Duffield Courtney, a renowned Australian artist. He is sold at a young age to the wealthy Courtney family by his impoverished, prolific parents, the Duffields. This commerce in a human being provides the novel's main metaphor: Hurtle will be bought and sold many times more as an accomplished artist. Hurtle brings great hope to the Courtneys, who have one handicapped daughter; they throw all their energies into making Hurtle a suitable heir. Even while he is young, however, the selfish, egotistical qualities surface that will later contribute to his artistic genius. Hurtle ruthlessly uses people for his own artistic purposes: His family, friends, and lovers all provide fodder for his vision. Ironically, his quest is for purity and simplicity, a search for the color of God. As an artist, Hurtle is an iconoclast, tearing away at the pretensions and hypocrisy of the art world. To that end, he turns to the gritty, seamy, and even grotesque side of life to produce his paintings. Hurtle has many affairs with women, all of which end badly because he uses and emotionally abuses them. Still, Hurtle is never entirely despicable: His honesty, although brutal at times, is admirable.

Alfreda Courtney and

Harry Courtney, the wealthy couple who adopt Hurtle. Alfreda is a pretentious, selfish woman who insists on Hurtle calling her Maman and who exhibits incestuous tendencies toward him. Harry is a decent man and would dearly love to get close to his son but, in his blundering, male way, cannot.

Rhoda Courtney, the hunchbacked daughter of Alfreda and Harry, Hurtle's adoptive sister. Rhoda is intelligent and sensitive; as a child, she both resents and adores Hurtle. Her brother is repulsed by her, even though she fascinates him: Her deformed body becomes his first artistic victim and his earliest artistic triumph. To a certain extent, Hurtle also fears Rhoda: She is perceptive enough to understand much about Hurtle and blunt enough to make him uncomfortable. When he finally leaves the Courtneys behind, Rhoda is the one person he misses. Many years later, he comes across Rhoda by chance. She has become a bag lady, collecting stinking horseflesh by day so she can feed street cats by night. Hurtle, as if to purge himself of guilt for his earlier treatment of Rhoda, persuades her to move in with him. Because Rhoda remains the one person who is completely honest with Hurtle, and from whom he has no secrets, they develop an extraordinary relationship. Rhoda provides Hurtle with both inspiration and exasperation.

Nance Lightfoot, a simple, warmhearted prostitute. Hurtle carries on an extended affair with Nance, whose amply endowed body provides him with fresh forms for his paintings. He transforms her curves into rocks and cheeses and enters on a successful and productive period in his career. As much as he cares for Nance, however, he refuses to become attached to her. Ultimately, her accidental/suicidal death jars him into some belated self-reflection and humanity.

Olivia Davenport, formerly **Boo Hollingrake**, a wealthy woman, a patron of the arts and a friend to both Rhoda and Hurtle. She first becomes acquainted with the Courtneys when she is a girl named Boo, and she is, in fact, Hurtle's boyhood crush. She surfaces again after many years as a socialite named Olivia who throws elegant dinner parties and collects Duffields even though she secretly despises them. She rejects Hurtle as a lover but tries to procure him for her own friend and lover, Hero Pavloussi. Olivia is charming and superficial and knows it, which is why she patronizes Hurtle.

Hero Pavloussi, Hurtle's lover and Olivia's friend, the wife of a wealthy Greek shipping magnate. Hurtle is attracted to petite, dark, and exotic Hero but is also repulsed by her tragic Greek air. Theirs is a mutually destructive relationship: He uses her for his artistic needs, and she lures him into taking a futile, depressing trip to Greece. Hero is victimized by herself as much as she is by Hurtle.

Kathy Volkov, a brilliant young pianist, Hurtle's neighbor and lover. In his old age, Hurtle finds himself attracted to and seduced by the nubile young girl next door. She becomes his final source of inspiration and the one female capable of hurting him. When he first comes to know her, Kathy is all braids and limbs; still, she is not sexually shy. As she matures and achieves fame as a concert pianist, she discards Hurtle in selfish pursuit of her own goals. In Kathy, Hurtle comes up against an ego as large and ruthless as his own.

— *Susan Whaley*

VOICES IN TIME

Author: Hugh MacLennan (1907-1990)
First published: 1980
Genre: Novel

Locale: Germany and Montreal
Time: 2039-2044, with flashbacks to the twentieth century
Plot: Historical

John Wellfleet, the narrator, age seventy-six, a former hippie and teacher and the survivor of the "clean" bombs that destroyed civilization. During the rebuilding of Metro (Montreal), the Wellfleet-Dehmel papers are discovered, and André Gervais asks John Wellfleet to put them in order. The papers reveal the history of the twentieth century. Happy in his rediscovery of the past and his usefulness to a new generation, John dies in a cottage near the Gervais family.

André Gervais, a young French Canadian, discoverer of the papers, discoverer of John, and representative of the new generation eager to rebuild a civilization connected with the best the past can offer. He befriends Wellfleet, discovers his body, and narrates his death. Their friendship represents the renewed linking of the generations and the transmission of history and wisdom that results.

Timothy Wellfleet, John's older cousin, an advertising man and host of the 1970's television show *This Is Now*. The child of divorced parents and shaped by the novel *The Catcher in the Rye*, Timothy rejects his conventional suburban life and family and his success in advertising for Esther Stahr and television. Apparently criticizing the capitalist system, his abrasive show is really a safety valve for it. Unprincipled showmanship leads Timothy falsely to accuse Dehmel of Nazism, an accusation that leads to Dehmel's murder. When Timothy discovers that his show has been canceled and his victim is the husband of his foster mother, he becomes distraught and disappears.

Esther Stahr, the Jewish coproducer of *This Is Now* and Timothy's mistress. Realizing that Timothy destroys public men simply to entertain, she leaves him and the show before the Dehmel debacle.

Colonel Wellfleet, Timothy's father, a war hero and an archetypal male WASP of the Eisenhower period, rich, bewildered, and irrelevant in later decades.

Stephanie Wellfleet, John's mother, Timothy's foster mother, and the wife of Conrad Dehmel. She is a gentle, loving woman.

Conrad Dehmel, the second narrator, a German Egyptologist and historian. His narrative, written in German, is addressed to Stephanie and tells of his childhood in Freiburg with his gentle mother and grandfather, both musicians and cultured Europeans; of his father, a naval officer; and of his younger brother, Siegfried, a fanatical Nazi. Conrad foolishly marries the stupid Eva Schmidt and takes her to England, where he is studying. The marriage fails. Subsequently, he falls deeply in love with Hanna Enlich, a Jewish woman. In spite of her warnings, he returns to Adolf Hitler's Germany, where he is trapped, becoming director of an academic institute and working for an anti-Gestapo intelligence service. Finally, he joins the Gestapo to help the Enlichs escape, but Eva Schmidt recognizes him and betrays him to her husband, Heinrich. Conrad breaks under Gestapo torture. The Allies liberate Dehmel from Belsen. He goes to North America and marries Stephanie. He appears on *This Is Now* to warn Canadians that casual violence, the manipulation of the economy and the society by hidden powers, and the absence of principle and restraint signal a civilization's collapse. When Timothy accuses him of Nazism, Dehmel walks off the show, but a Jewish viewer, confusing him with Heinrich, subsequently shoots him.

Hanna Enlich, Conrad's mistress, a cellist and member of the Jewish intelligentsia. Hanna returns to Nazi Germany as a Red Cross official to help her interned father. Although Conrad arranges their escape, they are captured, and the Gestapo confronts them with Conrad. Understanding that under torture he has revealed their whereabouts, Hanna's last act is to explain that they already had been captured, so the betrayal is unimportant.

Rear-Admiral Dehmel, Conrad's father, a gunnery officer, technocrat, and unthinkingly obedient patriot. He is shattered by the defeat of 1914-1918, shamed by the Treaty of Versailles, and seduced by Nazi promises. Although he is promoted in the rebuilt navy, he becomes disillusioned with Nazism. Accused of being privy to the officers' plot against Hitler, he is killed, and his wife is taken by the Gestapo. He represents the German officer class.

— *Jocelyn Creigh Cass*

VOLPONE: Or, The Fox

Author: Ben Jonson (1573-1637)
First published: 1607
Genre: Drama

Locale: Venice
Time: The sixteenth century
Plot: Social satire

Volpone (vohl-POH-nay), the Fox, a Venetian magnifico. Delighting in foxlike trickery, Volpone scorns the easy gain of cheating widows and orphans and the hard gain of labor. He chooses for his victims Venice's leading crooked advocate, its most greedy and dishonest merchant, and its most hardened miser. The joy of the chase of gold and jewels belonging to others is keener to him than the possession. He also delights in acting, both onstage and off. To fool others with disguises, makeup, and changes of voice is a passion with him. His three weaknesses are excessive trust of his unreliable parasite Mosca, his ungovernable desire for Corvino's virtuous wife Celia, and his overconfidence in his ability to deceive. When defeated, however, he shows a humorous and sporting self-knowledge and resignation to his punishment.

Mosca (MOS-kah), the Gadfly, Volpone's malicious and witty parasite. Acting as the chief instrument of Volpone's trickery and the frequent instigator of additional pranks, he keeps the plot moving. Under cover of tormenting Volpone's victims, he often engages in annoying Volpone himself, almost always with impunity. His tantalizing of Volpone with sensuous descriptions of Celia sets in train the events that finally destroy both his master and himself. A master improviser of deceit and pranks, he becomes in love with his dear self, underestimates his master, and falls victim to his own overconfidence and greed. He whines and curses as he is dragged away to punishment.

Voltore (vohl-TOH-ray), the Vulture, an advocate. A ruthless and voracious scavenger seeking the spoils of the dead, he yearns for Volpone's wealth. He is willing to connive whenever gain is apparent. A dangerous man when thwarted, he helps Volpone achieve acquittal in his first trial; then, tormented beyond endurance by Mosca, who pretends that Volpone is dead and has left Voltore nothing, the lawyer reverses himself and causes the collapse of Volpone's plans.

Corbaccio (kohr-BAH-chee-oh), the Raven, an aged miser, feeble, deaf, and pathologically greedy. He is willing to risk his son's inheritance to have Volpone exchange wills with him.

He is also willing to have Mosca administer poison in Volpone's sleeping draft to hasten the validation of the will.

Corvino (kohr-VEE-noh), the Crow, the merchant husband of Celia. Mean-spirited, cowardly, and insanely jealous of his beautiful wife, he is the most repulsive of Volpone's victims. His greed is sufficient to counteract his jealousy, and he is willing to leave his wife in Volpone's hands to assure his future as Volpone's heir.

Celia (SEEL-yuh), Corvino's virtuous wife. Cursed with a repulsive and pathologically jealous husband, the heavenly Celia faces her slander and perils with noble fortitude.

Bonario (boh-NAH-ree-oh), the good son of Corbaccio. He is the savior of Celia when she is helpless in Volpone's clutches.

Lady Politic Would-Be, a parrot-voiced, shallow-brained Englishwoman. She grates on Volpone's sensibilities so much that he is willing to lose the financial gains she thrusts on him. At any price, he wishes to be rid of "my madam with the everlasting voice." Her unreasonable jealousy makes her a gullible tool when Mosca accuses her husband of having an affair with Celia; her resulting false testimony saves Volpone and convicts Celia and Bonario at the first trial.

Sir Politic Would-Be, a gullible, naïve traveler. Eager to be thought a member of the inner circle of state knowledge, Sir Pol has a sinister explanation for even the most commonplace actions. He furnishes the picture of the ridiculous English tourist on the Continent.

Peregrine (PEH-reh-green), a sophisticated traveler. He finds amusement, mixed with contempt, in the credulities and foibles of Sir Pol.

Androgyno (ahn-DROHJ-eh-noh), a hermaphrodite,

Castrone (kah-STROH-neh), a eunuch, and

Nano (NAH-noh), a dwarf, household freaks kept by Volpone for amusement.

Avocatori (ah-VOH-kah-TOH-ree), the four judges. The ambition of the fourth, to marry his daughter to Mosca, stirs Volpone to make his confession, which saves Bonario and Celia and brings punishment on the evildoers.

VOLUNTEERS

Author: Brian Friel (1929-   )
First published: 1979
Genre: Drama

Locale: Ireland
Time: The 1970's
Plot: Tragicomedy

George, the site supervisor. A pompous, rather unlikable man, he has the most contact with the diggers. He refuses to be entertained by their antics or concerned with their troubles. Most of the time, he literally looks down on them from a temporary office built above the excavation site. He is in constant conflict with Keeney.

Mr. Wilson, the guard. Professing a great understanding of criminal behavior, he is a no-nonsense, ostentatiously tough

man in his sixties. Despite his loudly voiced concern over issues of crime and punishment, he is not a strong presence in the play. When he does appear, he is preoccupied with his young daughter's musical examination.

Des, an archaeology student nicknamed **Dessy the Red** by the diggers. He is a serious young leftist, twenty years old. He likes to think of himself as more closely allied to the prisoners on the dig than to the professionals who supervise it. His small gestures of camaraderie—buying cigarettes and newspapers for the men—prove to be the extent of his aid to them, as he consistently fails to live up to his political and professional ideals.

Knox, a prisoner on the dig. A dirty, shambling man of sixty-five years, but looking older, he is noteworthy among the men for his smell and his ill temper. He is frequently the butt of Keeney and Pyne's jokes. Reared in a fabulously wealthy and privileged home, he was left poor and useless after his father's death. He subsequently found money and companionship as a message carrier for political subversives.

Butt, a prisoner on the dig. He is a solid, quiet man in his late forties, from the countryside. He looks after Smiler and is the only man on the dig who develops an objective, intellectual interest in the archaeological work. Throughout the play, he is a model worker and a foil to the irreverent Keeney. It is Butt who makes the most significant gesture of rebellion when he smashes a valuable jug that is the prize find on the dig.

Smiler, a prisoner on the dig, in his mid-thirties. Smiler is a harmless, childlike man, appearing most of the time in a ridiculous tasseled hat. He has been made an idiot by torture in prison. His disappearance from and later return to the dig precipitates Keeney's confession to the other diggers that they are marked for assassination by their fellow political prisoners. Smiler, on occasion, begins speaking in his former idealistic voice before lapsing into vacuity.

Keeney, a prisoner on the dig. A sharp-tongued, energetic man in his forties, Keeney—along with his sidekick Pyne—keeps up a running series of jokes, insults, and limericks through much of the play. Once a leader in the Nationalist movement, he is the man who persuaded the others to join the dig, despite the threat of retaliation from the other political prisoners. Until he makes his revelation, he is the only one who knows that they will all be killed. Keeney is obsessed with the Viking-era skeleton of a murdered man found on the dig and makes up a series of stories about the reasons for this man's death.

Pyne, a prisoner on the dig, in his thirties. He is a devoted follower of Keeney, joining him and imitating him in his bantering. Pyne is less certain of himself than Keeney, however; sometimes even he is confused by Keeney's joking. He is more confused by Keeney's outbursts of anger. Pyne has difficulty distinguishing Keeney's serious statements from his irreverent ones.

— *Heidi J. Holder*

VOLUPTÉ

Author: Charles-Augustin Sainte-Beuve (1804-1869)
First published: 1834
Genre: Novel

Locale: France
Time: Early nineteenth century
Plot: Psychological

Amaury (ah-moh-REE), the narrator, later a priest. A sensitive, melancholy youth, he engages in a platonic love affair with Madame de Couaën after putting aside Amélie de Liniers, the young woman who loves him. When the marquis de Couaën is arrested, he takes over Madame de Couaën's affairs. When she rejoins her husband at Blois, Amaury has an unrewarding affair with Madame R. until he realizes the unhappiness he has caused three women. He takes holy orders and leaves for America soon after Madame de Couaën's death.

Madame de Couaën (deh kwah-EH[N]), the Irish wife of the marquis. She truly loves her husband and can return only platonic love for Amaury, yet she feels that no one can understand her as he does. She remains with her husband and is saddened by Amaury's affair with Madame R.

Madame R., the wife of a royalist sympathizer. Lonely and disillusioned, she becomes Amaury's constant companion in Paris. Although she refuses to become his mistress, she is jealous of his love for Madame de Couaën.

The marquis de Couaën, a friend of Amaury and an influential figure in royalist circles. He is arrested in Paris and later is sent to Blois.

Amélie de Liniers (ah-may-LEE deh leen-YAY), the granddaughter of Monsieur de Greneuc. She is the unmarried woman in Amaury's life.

Monsieur R. and
Monsieur D., royalist sympathizers.

Monsieur and
Madame de Greneuc (deh greh-NUHK), friends of Amaury in his youth.

Monsieur Ploa (ploh-AH), Amaury's Latin teacher.

VOSS

Author: Patrick White (1912-1990)
First published: 1957
Genre: Novel

Locale: Various locations in Australia
Time: The 1840's
Plot: Historical

Johann Ulrich Voss, a German immigrant to Australia, a botanist with a desire to become famous as an explorer during the golden age of nineteenth century exploration. Voss possesses the will of a Nietzschean superman, and he has settled on the goal of being the first to cross the Australian continent. The character of Voss is inspired by a historical figure, Ludwig Leichardt, whose obsession with crossing the Australian desert led to his death. Voss is a humorless and passionate idealist who sees the conquest of the Australian territory as both a personal triumph and a victory for the human spirit. Despite a natural arrogance and the fanatical dedication of the truly obsessed, Voss, a slender man with enormous capacities for planning and endurance, captures the imagination of many who meet him, including the Bonner family. Laura Trevelyan, Bonner's niece, finds him fascinating while resenting his pride and self-sufficiency. He wins her respect and undeclared love, and on his expedition, he believes he communicates with her telepathically. In the desert, Voss is betrayed by some of the members of his expedition and dies a tragic death, but not before learning a humility that softens his indomitable will. After Voss's death, his tragic enterprise is gradually transformed into a heroic legend, which Laura helps to create and perpetuate in her work as a teacher.

Edward Bonner, a Sydney merchant who has made a small fortune, mainly through the sale of cloth. He is a stolid middle-class businessman who helps to finance Voss's expedition, though he does not fully understand why he is attracted by Voss's vision. Bonner enjoys being a patron and hopes that fame as well as financial advantage will result from Voss's venture.

Laura Trevelyan, Bonner's niece, who lives with the Bonners but is the family nonconformist. A beautiful young woman who is somewhat intellectual and contemptuous of conventional men, she has chosen to reject her childhood Christianity and considers herself a rationalist when she meets Voss; he perceives that she is in reality a believer with a concern for humility and compassion. Fascinated by his vision and drive, she falls in love with him, though neither she nor Voss will openly avow this passion. During his absence on the expedition, she writes long letters to him expressing her love. Like Voss, she imagines that they communicate telepathically. After Voss's death and the failure of his quest, she chooses to remain unmarried and gains fame as a schoolmistress, while helping to create the legend of his heroism.

Harry Robarts, a simple young man who follows Voss out of an inarticulate devotion and out of gratitude, because Voss treats him as a person of importance. At twenty years of age, Robarts is physically strong but rather quiet and without intellect. He is willing to follow Voss to the end, and he dies with Voss in the interior desert of Australia.

Frank Le Mesurier, another of Voss's faithful followers on the expedition, though he has seldom stuck to any purpose before he met Voss. A relatively young man, he has worked at several jobs in Australia without staying long at any, and he has even published a volume of indifferent verse. Although he has artistic ambitions, or pretensions, he has been a dilettante, lacking commitment to work or vision. Attracted to Voss be-

cause the German has an assurance of the significance of his vocation that Le Mesurier lacks, he hopes to find himself on the wilderness trek. Although he refuses to desert Voss, he is unable to sustain his courage when captured by a tribe of aborigines, and he commits suicide.

Albert Judd, a former convict, now emancipated and a respectable farmer. He is a responsible and steadying influence on the expedition. A strong and sensible middle-aged man, Judd has been tempered and humbled by his harsh years of penal servitude. Essentially, Judd is a man of material reality and common sense. Despite his kindness toward Voss, he finally mutinies after the death of Palfreyman, considering the expedition to be hopeless.

Palfreyman, a kindly but boring ornithologist who goes on Voss's expedition out of scientific curiosity. Constantly abstracted and devoid of egotism, Palfreyman practices a kind of benign Christian charity until he is murdered by an aboriginal tribesman.

Ralph Angus, the son of a wealthy landowner. He goes on the expedition seeking adventure and self-respect. Angus finds that he is ultimately a practical man and becomes a friend of Turner, a former alcoholic and the least dedicated member of the expedition. Somewhat reluctantly, Angus follows Judd when the latter rebels against Voss.

Turner, supposedly a reformed alcoholic, primarily a man of the senses who experiences life in the simplest epicurean terms. Turner joins the expedition somewhat reluctantly, hoping to find his fortune, but his gross and vulgar views often annoy the others, even when they find them entertaining. Turner readily joins Judd's mutiny and abandons Voss to his fate.

Dugald, an elderly aboriginal guide who barely understands English. Entrusted by Voss with some important letters, including a love letter to Laura, Dugald sets off for the outpost of Jildra. After meeting some other tribesmen, he is persuaded to tear the letters to pieces and scatter them to the winds.

Jackie, a young aboriginal guide who accompanies Voss and his two remaining companions to their final encounter with a tribe of cannibals. Although Jackie feels bound to Voss by some inexplicable magic, he readily allows himself to be adopted by the tribe. To show his loyalty to the tribe, he finally works up the nerve to murder Voss. Somewhat sullenly, Jackie cuts off Voss's head while the latter is sleeping.

— *Edgar L. Chapman*

THE VOYAGE OUT

Author: Virginia Woolf (1882-1941)
First published: 1915
Genre: Novel

Locale: London, the mid-Atlantic, and South America
Time: c. 1906
Plot: Psychological realism

Rachel Vinrace, the twenty-four-year-old protagonist, an intelligent and sensitive but only informally educated young woman. She plays the piano beautifully and has considerable musical talent but is socially innocent and naïve, with a weak face and a hesitant character. As an only child, she has led a sheltered life, having been reared primarily by her two unmarried aunts, her mother being dead and her father, Willoughby,

a shipping magnate, being a very busy man of affairs. She has been kept ignorant of the relations between men and women. When introduced through her aunt and uncle into the society of Santa Marina, which consists of a group of Englishmen vacationing at the local resort hotel, she meets and falls in love with Hewet after a series of encounters initiated by an afternoon climbing expedition and later a ball. They become engaged during an expedition by boat up the river into the jungle. The main plot of the novel revolves around Rachel's metaphorical "voyage out" from innocence to experience, from her initially naïve and unreflective state to a greater intellectual sophistication, her first experience of love, and finally her death from a fever, possibly contracted on the journey up the river.

Helen Ambrose, Rachel's aunt. She is forty years old, tall, and beautiful, not well educated formally but widely read and socially sophisticated. She and her husband, Ridley, a Cambridge scholar working on an edition of Pindar's odes, have left their two children with the grandparents so that they can spend a winter and spring away from England at her brother's villa in Santa Marina, a coastal resort town in South America, presumably in Brazil. Having become interested in her niece during the literal "voyage out" to Santa Marina on the ship of her brother-in-law, who has business on the Amazon, she invites Rachel to stay with them rather than continue the voyage with Willoughby. Helen sets herself the task of helping Rachel learn about life and developing her character.

Terrence Hewet, who becomes Rachel's suitor and eventual fiancé, a young man with literary tastes who is vacationing in Santa Marina with his friend Hirst and attempting to write a novel. He is twenty-seven years old, tall, and rather stout, and he wears glasses. The only son of an English gentleman, he attended Winchester and then the University of Cambridge for two terms before leaving to travel. He has an independent income (his father died when Hewet was ten years old) sufficient to allow him not to work. His role as the organizer of the climbing trip first brings him and Rachel together. Hewet is presented initially as a somewhat superficial character, but he becomes more sympathetic through his love for Rachel.

St. John Alaric Hirst, a friend of Hewet, twenty-four years old, a scholar and a fellow of King's College. He is one of the most distinguished young intellectuals in England. He is in Santa Marina trying to decide whether to continue at the university or to become a lawyer. Young but unattractive, already stooped and very thin, he is uncomfortable with women and does not seem to get along well with Rachel. Helen initially has the plan of recruiting him to help with the project of Rachel's education by recommending books to her. He is attracted to both Helen and Rachel, and for a while he imagines that Rachel has fallen in love with him. His cynical nature is softened by the novel's end by his observation of his friends' love and by Rachel's affecting death.

— *William Nelles*

A VOYAGE ROUND MY FATHER

Author: John Mortimer (1923-   )
First published: 1971
Genre: Drama

Locale: England
Time: The 1930's-the 1960's
Plot: Psychological realism

Father, a barrister in London, an antisocial man who takes refuge in his beloved garden every time a visitor threatens to disturb him. He seems sincerely to pity his son for having to go visit someone. Father collects the earwigs caught in his garden traps every evening and drowns them. His garden is his true passion, and the law is merely a way to earn a living—though he is very good at what he does. He is blinded from an accident while pruning an apple tree, but he refuses to acknowledge that he is blind. His visual blindness epitomizes his emotional blindness: He refuses to allow any emotional closeness between himself and his son or himself and his wife. He is a confusing yet fascinating character. It is not certain whether he has had several mistresses and smoked opium. He gets along with his grandchildren better than with his son.

Mother, a housewife. She caters to Father after he is blinded, taking care of him completely, even cutting up his food, but she never acknowledges his blindness overtly. She panders to her husband's every whim, including making marmalade, even though she hates doing it. She does not seem to be very sentimental or emotional; when her young son starts to cry, she apparently cannot believe or accept it. She is living in a rut, but one in which she means to stay. When she speaks about what she will do when her husband dies, she says she will stay in her home, because "someone has to see to the marmalade." Her main concern seems to be that no improper subject be discussed in general conversation.

Boy and **Son**, a character who has two physical dimensions. He is called "Boy" when he is very young and "Son" when he is an adult. As a boy, he is bewildered and hurt by his parents' emotional aloofness. When he cries, his father merely tells him to say "rats," on the premise that no one can cry when they are saying the word "rats." When the boy is sent away to school, he finds that the school world is even stranger than home—complete with shell-shocked teachers who hallucinate that enemy attacks are taking place in the classroom and throw books at their students. The main facet of the young man's character is that as he evolves from a boy into an adult, he loses his softer side. At the play's end, his wife, Elizabeth, accuses him of exhibiting the same inability to deal with seriousness that his father shows.

Miss Cox and

Miss Baker, a lesbian couple who run a bookstore. The son makes friends with them while he is home during World War II. During a conversation, the women automatically assume that the son will join the Fire Service and become a writer, because that is what all their friends do.

Elizabeth, a scriptwriter who becomes the son's wife. Elizabeth is a beautiful brunet who is married when the son first meets her. She writes film scripts as part of the war effort. Elizabeth is an honest, open person; she disapproves of the mother, son, and father's charade about not mentioning his blindness. She is unhappy about the way her husband seems to have inherited his father's lack of being able to cope with serious issues.

— *T. M. Lipman*

VOYAGE TO TOMORROW
(Rihlah ila al-ghad)

Author: Tawfiq al-Hakim (1898-1987)
First published: 1957
Genre: Drama

Locale: Earth and another planet
Time: Late 1950's and 309 years later
Plot: Science fiction

The first convict, a prominent physician and son of a physician, sentenced to death for murdering a patient, the husband of a woman with whom he falls in love. Although he has confessed to this crime of love at his trial, he later protests that the woman, misrepresenting her husband's character, encouraged him to kill the husband and, after they were married, betrayed him by establishing a relationship with his own defense attorney. He is obsessed with his wife and, he tells the prison doctor, would like nothing better than a few minutes alone with her, to strangle her. When cut off from Earth (act 2) on the rocket trip and later, when the rocket crashes (act 3) on a strange planet (where electrical charges, and not blood and hearts, energize him and his fellow space traveler), he still believes in emotions and in good and evil, and he treasures memories. Back on Earth (act 4), love remains important to him and causes his re-incarceration at the end of the play.

The guard, who talks briefly with the first convict at the beginning of the play as the latter, expecting to face execution any day, paces back and forth in his cell nervously.

The prison doctor, who is respectful of the first convict's scientific knowledge and accomplishments in medicine, although he does not believe the latter's story about his wife's collusion with the defense attorney.

The warden, who visits the first convict twice (in act 1) to announce that his wife has come to see him and then that he may have a reprieve from his death sentence if he agrees to a proposal by the representative of a scientific agency. As a condition of accepting the proposal, the first convict is thereafter not allowed to see his wife.

The representative of a scientific agency, who comes to the first convict with a top secret proposal, a scientific experiment involving a manned rocket being sent into outer space with little chance of the men on board returning or surviving the journey. The first convict agrees to participate in the experiment as preferable to his imminent execution.

The second convict, the first convict's companion on the rocket (in act 3), an engineer specializing in electrical and atomic sciences. He too feels that death on the rocket is preferable to death on Earth. He had been sentenced to death for the murder of four older wealthy wives after being caught planning to do the same with a fifth wife. He married all of them to obtain money to finance a beneficial engineering project. He also does not believe the first convict's story about his wife's collusion with the defense attorney. On the strange planet, the second convict worries about a life without work, events, and

a future, and he suggests suicide. The first convict's suggestion that they repair the rocket and attempt to return to Earth lifts his spirits. At the end of the play, he notes that the first convict has not changed in the three hundred years that they have been away and that the first convict is again going to prison because of a woman.

The voice from ground control, which announces (in act 3) to the first and second convicts, as their rocket hurtles through space, that their contact with Earth will cease at a distance of five million miles from Earth, which they will reach in three minutes.

The first convict's wife, who is on the first convict's mind throughout the play but appears only on the strange planet (act 3), a realm where mental telepathy is possible. The first convict is able to conjure up her image and show her, projected as if on a screen, to the second convict.

The blonde woman, who is assigned to the first convict when he and the second convict return (at the beginning of act 4) from outer space after three hundred years. As a member of the party of the future, she is suited to the second convict, who believes in materials and technological progress and attaches no importance to love. They will likely spend the rest of their lives together.

The brunette woman, who is assigned to the second convict. As a member of the party of the past, she is better suited to the first convict, who falls in love with her. She will likely treasure his memory once they are separated. He is sent in her stead to prison because of politically dangerous ideas stemming from a belief in the value of love.

The security man, who is sent with the robot, both in strange attire, to arrest the first convict and the brunette woman for having subversive thoughts and to give them a choice between "rays," by which their thoughts will be changed, and isolated confinement in the City of Quiet. They immediately choose the City of Quiet. The first convict grapples with the security man when the latter tries to take the brunette woman away.

The robot, who accompanies the security man on his visit to the first and second convicts and the blonde and brunette women.

The voice from headquarters, which orders that the brunette woman be taken to the City of Quiet alone but then agrees to let the first convict take her place and finish his reports on his trip in space.

— *Michael Craig Hillmann*

WAITING FOR GODOT
(En attendant Godot)

Author: Samuel Beckett (1906-1989)
First published: 1952
Genre: Drama

Locale: A country road
Time: Indeterminate
Plot: Absurdist

Vladimir (vla-dee-MEER), also called **Didi** (dee-DEE), and **Estragon** (ehs-tra-GOH[N]), also called **Gogo** (goh-GOH), two tramps. In this play, action is unimportant; the characters remain undeveloped as they wait impatiently for Godot, who remains a mysterious entity, possibly a local landowner but also a symbol of spiritual seeking. They gnaw carrots, rest their tired feet, and engage in other simple activities while their conversations reveal the helplessness of their situation. Throughout the play, there is every suggestion that the two live estranged from a state of grace that is hoped for but never realized. Often considering suicide, they are caught in a calm of inactivity between hope and despair in their longing for salvation, which is linked somehow with Godot. When the play ends, the two are still waiting for the promised appearance of Godot.

Pozzo (poh-ZOH), a materialist. A rich, boisterous tyrant,

he is obviously an expounder of Nietzschean doctrines and materialistic concepts. Pozzo admits that Lucky has taught him all the beautiful things he knows, but now his servant has become unbearable and is driving him mad. At first, he drives his servant with a rope. Later, when Pozzo reappears, blinded in symbolic fashion by his own worldly successes and romantic pessimism, he must be led by his mute servant.

Lucky, Pozzo's servant. Born a peasant, he gives the impression of a new proletarian, the symbol of modern people's belief in the promises and miracles of science. Lucky first appears driven by Pozzo at the end of a rope. Ordered to think for the group, he delivers the wildest, most brilliantly sustained monologue of the play. When he next appears, he is leading the blind Pozzo, but he is mute.

A boy, a messenger from Godot.

WAITING FOR THE BARBARIANS

Author: J. M. Coetzee (1940-   )
First published: 1980
Genre: Novel

Locale: A settlement on the frontier of an imaginary empire
Time: Late nineteenth or early twentieth century
Plot: Psychological realism

The Magistrate, the story's first-person narrator, an administrator of a territory belonging to an unnamed empire. He is an aging and somewhat decadent man who explains that he has lived in the remote settlement for decades and has haphazardly and inefficiently carried out his administrative duties on behalf of the empire. Although he admits to his laziness, his fondness for young native girls, and his satisfaction with the old ways of imperialism, he still emerges as an admirable and sympathetic character. When he comprehends the full extent of the cruelty condoned by the new regime, which is determined to save the empire at any cost, he regrets his initial compliance with the Third Bureau's orders and rebels, then becomes a prisoner himself. At the same time, he searches for some significance in his own wasted life. In the light of the novel's allegorical overtones, the character of The Magistrate represents all men and women who face not only their inherent weaknesses but the forces of totalitarianism as well. At the story's conclusion, The Magistrate simply goes on living, however uneasily, and

continues his struggle to find a clear pattern in the complexities of life.

Colonel Joll, an official in the mysterious Third Bureau, an arm of the Civil Guard that was created to protect the empire, which is threatened by barbarians. This young officer specializes in torture and interrogation. An elegant sort with affectations in dress, manner, and speech, the colonel has come to terms with the demands made by the forces of evil set loose by a desperate government. Unlike The Magistrate, Joll does not question; he only acts. Ultimately, he encounters defeat at the hands of the barbarians.

Warrant Officer Mandel, an assistant to Colonel Joll. He is a younger version of his superior officer: handsome and vain, sophisticated, cruel, spiritually vacuous, and, above all, blindly committed to the cause he serves. For The Magistrate, a man with a conscience, he feels neither sympathy nor pity. He displays his true colors by fleeing when it appears that Colonel Joll will not return from his expedition into the wilderness.

A young native woman, a victim of Colonel Joll's torture. She is stocky in build, quiet and long-suffering in nature, and an innocent amid corruption. Blinded and crippled during her interrogation, she is rescued by The Magistrate, who nurses her to health, seduces her, and attempts to use her as a kind of expiation for his own part in the activities of the Third Bureau. The young woman gains a measure of nobility in her suffering.

— *Robert L. Ross*

WAITING TO EXHALE

Author: Terry McMillan (1951-   )
First published: 1992
Genre: Novel

Locale: Phoenix, Arizona, and Denver, Colorado
Time: 1990
Plot: Social realism

Bernadine Harris, one of the four protagonists. She is thirty-six years old, black, and college educated. After a marriage of eleven years, her husband, John, leaves her for his white, twenty-four-year-old secretary. John tries to steal all of their community assets. She spends most of 1990 trying to pull herself together after the divorce and its resulting emotional drain. She accepts the lifestyle of upper-class suburbia, with its attention to material possessions, even when it gives her no personal satisfaction.

Savannah Jackson, one of the protagonists, the former college roommate and friend of Bernadine. She is also thirty-six years old. She has been living in Denver for three years, but she is dissatisfied with its cold weather. She also is dissatisfied with black men and her job, doing publicity for a gas company. She is offered a job in Phoenix and decides to take it even though her salary will decrease by twelve thousand dollars. She wants a new beginning and a chance to meet a man who is her equal. She also wants to be near Bernadine. She is level-headed and, of all the women, has the least amount of growing to do.

Robin Stokes, one of the protagonists, college educated and thirty-five years old. She is an underwriter for a major insurance company and brings millions of dollars in deals to the company. In her personal life, she is much less successful. She has a number of relationships with men; most of them are failures. She partly blames herself because she has a taste for handsome black men who exhibit sexual prowess but have little else to offer. She also has a style of her own, including a penchant for expensive hairweaves, a fondness for designer clothes, and an interest in astrology and numerology.

Gloria Matthews, one of the protagonists. At the age of thirty-eight, she has changed from the perfect size nine she was in college to a woman who derives much of her meaning in life from eating and rearing her teenage son. As owner of the best black hair salon in Phoenix, Gloria is a success financially, but personally she has put her life on hold. A consequence of her eating behavior is that it complicates a family disposition to have high blood pressure.

Russell, Robin's most important recent lover. He cheats on her, uses her financially, and makes promises he does not keep. Robin keeps coming back to him, even though she knows he is no good, because he is such a good lover.

Michael King, who works at Robin's insurance company. He is an upper-management team player, has been divorced twice, and falls in love with Robin. He is a decent, hardworking black man, but he fails to ignite sparks for Robin.

Marvin King, a fifty-year-old who moves into Gloria's neighborhood, helps her around the house, and spends time with her son. He is a warm, generous, and strong black man.

Tarik Matthews, Gloria's teenage son. Although he has been a model son in the past, Tarik's grades have dropped, and Gloria discovers that he is sexually active. Gloria gives him a lecture on safe sex, and his behavior seems to improve. At least, he seems less hostile and develops new interests.

John Harris, Bernadine's former husband, a study in self-hatred. He lives to be white and for most of his marriage to Bernadine tried to make her do the same.

— *Charles P. Toombs*

A WALK IN THE NIGHT

Author: Alex La Guma (1925-1985)
First published: 1962
Genre: Novel

Locale: District Six, a slum in Cape Town, South Africa
Time: c. 1960
Plot: Social realism

Michael Adonis, a man of mixed race; in South African racial terminology, he is "coloured." In segregated Cape Town, he must live in the notorious District Six. He works irregularly and hangs about in cheap cafés, generally unemployed and existing on the fringes of crime. Although he dresses in worn clothes, he moves with an air of jaunty, brash self-confidence. Fired for exchanging racist slurs with his white manager, he drinks himself into a mood combining bravado and self-pity. While drunk and burning with accumulated racial hate, he visits a white resident of the quarter, an old man, and murders him. Adonis rushes away, at first shocked and sobered by his horrendous yet futile crime. With a mixture of elation and hysteria, however, he soon rationalizes his deed and joins with real criminals in plans for an armed robbery. The story ends with Adonis cheerful and confident about his violent future.

Willieboy, another café lounger. In his dress and manner, he endeavors to present a smart image, taking pride in a prison sentence for assault. He is as impoverished in money and spirit as are the rest of his street acquaintances; he exists on menial jobs and small handouts. His background is commonplace: His mother beats him without provocation to vent her frustration against his father, who, when drunk, straps both of them. He accidentally finds the body of the murdered old white man. Instinctively reacting to the rule that no nonwhite, even if innocent, should ever risk being involved with the law, he runs away but is recognized by the other tenants. Following their description, the police find him. He is cornered and shot. While dying, he has a final illumination that lives such as his are doomed from the start.

Constable Raalt, a policeman. Angry, tense, and arrogantly racist, he is indifferent to police regulations and legal restraints. Constant quarrels with his wife regularly reinforce his visceral rage and indicate its neurotic origin. Even his partner fears and deplores his pathological antagonism toward blacks. With threats, Raalt forces the tenement witnesses to identify Willieboy. Searching the streets, he triumphantly encounters his suspect and drives him into an alley. His more sensible partner is horrified when Raalt deliberately draws his revolver and shoots to kill, but he fears to challenge Raalt. Even after shooting Willieboy, Raalt refuses to call an ambulance, conversing at a café while his prisoner bleeds to death in the van.

Uncle Doughty, an aging Irishman, technically white. He is married, illegally, to a nonwhite woman and is an alcoholic and a diabetic. Drink, malnourishment, and disease have ruined a once-handsome face. His skin is puffy and gray, his nose reddened, his teeth yellowed, and his head bald. Once a recognized actor who played theaters in Great Britain and Australia, he now lives from one day to the next in a tenement legally reserved for "coloureds." From his rambling memory of playing Hamlet's father comes the title of the novel. Adonis kills him by smashing his head with a wine bottle.

Joe, one of the sad young people who live on the streets. His intelligence is low, but his nature has a strange sweetness. He has run away from home and manages to survive on the scraps the fishermen leave. Adonis is his hero because he has treated Joe kindly. In his halting way, Joe perceives and articulates deep truths, and his warning against Adonis mixing with the violent criminals is both wise and well-intentioned.

John Abrahams, a tenement dweller. He is induced by Raalt to describe the man he saw running from the murder. Other tenants violently abuse him for giving away anything to the hated police. He uses the familiar self-defense, that to survive one must not provoke those in authority.

— *John F. Povey*

WALK ME TO THE DISTANCE

Author: Percival L. Everett (1956-   )
First published: 1985
Genre: Novel

Locale: Savannah, Georgia, and Slut's Hole, Wyoming
Time: The Vietnam War era
Plot: Bildungsroman

David Larson, the protagonist, an aimless young Vietnam veteran in search of a purpose in life. Leaving his native South, he settles in Wyoming, where he discovers a sense of place and redefines the concept of family. He comes to see preservation of the family as a matter of honor, of dignity, of duty, and, most painfully, of love.

Chloe Sixbury, an elderly female rancher with a prosthetic leg. She lives alone with her retarded son, thirty sheep, and some chickens. She embodies traditional frontier values.

Patrick Sixbury, Chloe's mentally impaired son, whom she says "ain't a part of me." Larson recognizes Patrick's human qualities—his "passion," however "unfortunate" and "pitiful"—only after he catches Patrick copulating with a ewe. Patrick's abduction of Butch precipitates the major crisis of the novel. He is lynched by several of the town's men, who believe he molested Butch.

Howard Dale, a veterinarian who becomes Larson's closest male companion partially because they have the shared experience of a college education. Although he is a Wyoming native, his medical training makes it impossible for him automatically to accept the code of Western justice.

Jill, David's sister, who initially rejects him after her marriage to Rodney, an antiwar activist. She later courts him to curry favor with the members of a support group that she and her husband have founded, Action for Vets.

Butch, a seven-year-old Eurasian girl abandoned by her Vietnamese family at the highway rest area where Larson works. She is consigned to his care because he was wearing his fatigue jacket when she was found and admitted to fighting in the war. She is "adopted" by Sixbury and Larson and becomes the victim of rape and the catalyst for murder.

Joshua Lowe, a local rancher who functions as Larson's surrogate father. As a fellow participant in Patrick's lynching, Lowe is regarded by Larson as a "solid, decent man with whom he had committed a premeditated murder."

The Reverend Damon Zacks, a traveling preacher who makes three stops at the highway rest area where Larson works, each time assuring the protagonist that he can live on the edge and not fall off.

Olivia, a twenty-year-old prostitute whose services Larson and Sixbury purchase on Patrick's behalf. Although the experiment does not work, Larson responds to what he sees as Olivia's childlike qualities. He buys her a doll and, despite all evidence to the contrary, persists for a time in regarding her as someone misplaced in her line of work. Olivia serves to spark certain latent, protective feelings in Larson, emotions that find their full flowering in his relationship with Sixbury and Butch.

Katy Stinson, a pretty young woman Larson meets on his flight east to visit his sister after Patrick's lynching. She becomes the focus of Larson's yearnings for a stable love life.

— *S. Thomas Mack*

A WALK ON THE WILD SIDE

Author: Nelson Algren (Nelson Ahlgren Abraham, 1909-1981)
First published: 1956
Genre: Novel

Locale: Texas and New Orleans
Time: Early 1930's
Plot: Picaresque

Dove Linkhorn, a red-haired, six-foot illiterate from Arroyo, Texas. After a brief affair with Terasina Vidavarri, he rides a freight train to seek his fortune in New Orleans. Convinced that anything can happen to someone who can make words from letters, Dove projects unsophisticated country innocence, but his principle of living is to do violence to anyone who tries to push ahead of him. On Perdido Street in New Orleans, Dove walks on the wild side with prostitutes, pimps, con artists, condom manufacturers, and petty criminals. With a pair of con artists, he joins a coffee-selling scam and a free beauty-treatment scam; later, he assists a manufacturer of condoms and peddles salves while wearing a white suit with a pink-striped shirt, yellow suede shoes, and a hat with a matching yellow feather. In partnership with master pimp Oliver Finnerty, he becomes Big Stingaree, a corrupter of supposedly innocent girls for a peep show. In Finnerty's house, Dove is scorned by Achilles Schmidt and attracted to Hallie Breedlove, both of whom figure prominently in his life. Dove is drawn to Hallie by a book; the two go away and live together during an idyllic period while he learns to read and questions her about history. His insecurity about his ignorance dissolves, and she secretly departs, carrying his child. Caught in a raid back at Finnerty's, Dove spends time in jail, where he observes that he has found only suffering and degradation, but that those with the greatest troubles are always the ones most likely to help. After his release, he is beaten and blinded by Schmidt. At the end of the novel, Dove, feeling his way with a cane, returns to Arroyo seeking Terasina.

Fitz Linkhorn, Dove's father, a wild man of Scottish descent. Widowed with two sons, Fitz is reduced to cleaning cesspools and becomes a self-styled preacher. Estranged from his older son and allowing his younger son to grow up illiterate because the school principal is a Catholic, Fitz depends for inspiration on a whiskey bottle in his hip pocket as he harangues the townspeople in the square, preaching against vice and creating dire images of damnation for an audience that considers him crazy.

Byron Linkhorn, Dove's older brother and Fitz's primary antagonist. Disillusioned, angry, and wasting from tuberculosis, Byron straddles the cannon on the town square and taunts Fitz as he preaches. He dies during Dove's absence.

Terasina Vidavarri, the thirty-year-old Mexican owner of a run-down hotel that formerly was a brothel. Terasina has held herself aloof from men since a youthful experience with a brutal former soldier, but she is overcome by Dove's innocence. She has a brief affair with Dove and shares a picture book with him before telling him to leave.

Hallie Breedlove, a prostitute who is one-sixteenth black but lives as white. Tall and aloof, Hallie is a former schoolteacher once married to a white man, who left her when their black child was born. After the child's death, Hallie turned to prostitution, but she has never accepted Finnerty as her pimp. Before Dove arrives, she is Schmidt's lover.

Achilles Schmidt, a former wrestler and carnival worker, a man with a powerful torso whose legs were severed by a train. He moves about on a wooden platform mounted on skates. As a wrestler, Schmidt retained his gentleness; as an embittered, legless man, he scorns Dove's crude performance in peep shows. Violently angry over the loss of Hallie, he beats Dove unconscious and then calls for help. Schmidt is destroyed when onlookers send him and his platform thundering downhill; he crashes into a pole.

Kitty Twist, a seventeen-year-old runaway with straight brown hair. When Dove meets Kitty on the way to New Orleans, she leads him into a robbery from which he escapes. She is caught and sent to jail. Later, when Kitty reappears in New Orleans with Finnerty, she is antipathetic toward Dove.

Oliver Finnerty, the master pimp at Mama Lucille's. Shrewd, brutal, and arrogant, he claims to be five feet tall in cowboy boots and looks like an Australian fox with enormous ears. When one of his girls displeases him, he beats her on the nape of the neck, where bruises do not show.

Mama Lucille, who actually is the madam at Finnerty's house but technically is a maid because the law forbids a black woman from managing a house employing white prostitutes.

Rhino Gross, an obese, weak-eyed former obstetrician. With his wife, Velma, Gross manufactures condoms in a back room covered with reddish dust. Dove briefly works as an errand boy for Gross and Velma and learns from their shrewdness.

— *Mary Ellen Pitts*

THE WALL

Author: John Hersey (1914-1993)
First published: 1950
Genre: Novel

Locale: Warsaw, primarily the ghetto sector
Time: November, 1939—May, 1943
Plot: Historical

Noach Levinson, a ghetto archivist and historian, the "recorder" of the events of the novel. A small man in his early forties, Levinson is a messy-haired, intense intellectual whose face is dominated by eyes made large by the magnification of steel-rimmed glasses. At times, the self-educated former shoemaker is cynical, even bitter, about his poor family background, unattractive appearance, and lack of ties to his fellow humans. He eventually finds human warmth and happiness, however, in the extended family of the ghetto. Levinson comes to serve as both the eyes and ears of the Warsaw Jewry, for he not only writes about what he sees but also listens unselfishly to those who need a sympathetic ear. With his fervor for

Jewish literature and sense of conviction, he comes to be regarded as the ghetto orator as well. As the Nazi atrocities intensify and Levinson becomes monomaniacal about preserving the archives, he finally becomes the very creator of Jewish memories and thoughts. The ultimate turnaround in the character of the scholarly Levinson comes when, inspired by dedicated young Jews, he fights as a soldier of Israel. Then, almost a year after escaping through the sewers to safety, Levinson dies of pneumonia.

Dolek Berson, a thirty-two-year-old, jovial, talkative drifter who becomes a highly responsible leader in the Jewish resistance. A big and gentle but impatient man and a gifted pianist, he has reacted against his parents' demands for his high personal achievement as a way of meeting the German threat. Instead, he has restlessly followed a number of occupations, moved for a time with a company of tramps, and finally settled down to a life of ease and prosperity with his beautiful wife, Symka, on his patrimony. As Nazi pressures increase, he works first as a bricklayer on the construction of the wall and then as a ghetto policeman. Gradually aligning himself with the radical resistance movement, he becomes firm, purposeful, and self-motivated. He proves to be a genius at finding safe routes and hiding places and at maintaining lines of communication within the ghetto. As coordinator of such networks, Berson is equally esteemed by all factions of ghetto Jews as a humane genius who meticulously serves humanity. His bold defiance of his captors with guerrilla concerts on the concertina inspires his compatriots with a will to survive even as he is inadvertently left, after their rescue, to die in the sewers.

Rachel Apt, a serene, intelligent, and well-proportioned young woman who, in spite of her ugly, parrotlike face, with its large nose and eyes set close together, rises to a position of leadership in the Jewish community because of her competence and boldness. Before the Warsaw ghetto years, she is totally overshadowed by her beautiful sister, Halinka Apt Mazur, whom their father obviously favors. After being painfully separated from her young brother, David, Rachel experiences a brief period of vacillation and moodiness before finding a housemother position, in which she can fulfill her instinct for mothering. Once she goes into underground work, she is dubbed "Little Mother" of the Jewish Fighter Organization (Z.O.B.). Admired for her modest, fearless, kind, and selfless spirit, she sets the emotional tone for the whole group. As a group commander, she plays a profound role in the resistance. Near the end of the ghetto period, she has an affair with the widower Dolek Berson that gives her a sense of freedom and happiness that, because of her ugly face, she might never have known under more pleasant circumstances.

Halinka Apt Mazur, the beautiful, fragile, and flirtatious daughter of a wealthy Jewish defector. She is attracted to men of power but marries a strong, handsome youth, Stefan Mazur, who is a Jewish ghetto policeman. After becoming a courier for the resistance and the mistress of the Hashomer leader, Zilberzweig, she suddenly ages and hardens in her will. Once dependent and submissive, she becomes obdurate in dangerous work outside the ghetto.

Mauritzi Apt, a prominent Jewish jeweler and art collector who attempts to buy favor for his children and finally escapes from the ghetto himself after undergoing plastic surgery to reverse his circumcision.

Pavel Menkes, a forty-year-old, tall, somewhat rotund, and jovial Jewish baker who devotes his services to the underground late in the resistance movement and dies fighting with the Z.O.B.

Rutka Mazur Apt, a Jewish courier on the Aryan side who gives birth to a son, Israel, in an underground bunker. A resourceful, lively, and optimistic woman, she retains hope for the survival of Jewry even after her baby is smothered in the bunker by a Z.O.B. leader because he cannot be quieted at a crucial moment.

Symka Berson, the attractive, delicate wife of Dolek Berson. She barely hangs onto life for a long period after suffering a serious case of typhus, only to be betrayed to the police by the quota-seeking Stefan Mazur, a member of her own extended ghetto family.

— *Janie Caves McCauley*

THE WALL JUMPER
(Der Mauerspringer)

Author: Peter Schneider (1940-   )
First published: 1982
Genre: Novel

Locale: West Berlin and East Berlin
Time: The 1980's
Plot: Social realism

The narrator, an author who has lived in West Berlin for the last twenty years. Fascinated by the divisions and similarities between the two Berlins, he decides to write about someone who breaks the barrier separating East and West Berlin, a "wall jumper." He moves back and forth between the two cities, visiting friends and hearing their stories of such jumpers, which he blends into various fantasies. He discovers that each government molds the thought processes of its inhabitants to suit its peculiar social system. In the end, he finds that he cannot jump the wall inside his own mind.

Robert, a poet who has immigrated to West Berlin from East Berlin. A neighbor and friend of the narrator, he adapts quickly to life in his new home precisely because he is a Berliner. He has a cynical distrust of authority, finding a subtext in every act and a plan behind what seems to the narrator to be simple chance. He tells the narrator the stories of Mr. Kabe and Walter Bolle.

Lena, a former girlfriend of the narrator. She immigrated to West Berlin from East Berlin in 1961. During her relationship with the narrator, she was suspicious of his absences and eventually became suspicious of everyone. He accompanied her on her first return visit to her family and realized she needed the security she had left on the other side of the wall. She meets with the narrator briefly in the present but talks mainly to Robert. The narrator is left to fantasize a one-sided conversation with her after she leaves.

Pommerer, an author living in East Berlin. He tells the narrator the stories of the three teenage cinema-goers and of Michael Gartenschläger. After signing a letter protesting a fine levied on a fellow author, he discovers that his telephone is often out of order and begins to think about leaving East Germany.

Gerhard Schalter, the narrator's first landlord in West Berlin. He claims that he is involved with a West German television correspondent based in Africa who wants to take her child and live with him but is prevented from doing so by her husband. As he loses hope in the future of that relationship, his appearance grows shabbier. He takes trips to East Berlin, where he discovers cheaper goods and friendlier people. Finally, he moves there.

Mr. Kabe, a welfare recipient in his mid-forties who becomes famous as a "border violator." Using a pile of rubble as a staircase up the wall on the West Berlin side, he jumped into East Berlin. He was imprisoned for three months and then returned to his home. After a vacation in Paris, paid for by the three months of welfare checks waiting for him, he returned and jumped again. The process was repeated. Following a failed attempt by the West German government to institutionalize him, he went on to jump the wall fifteen times.

Willy Wacholt,

Willy Walz, and

Lutz, three teenage boys who live close to the wall in East Berlin and jump it to see motion pictures in West Berlin. They love Westerns but not the West, at least not enough to emigrate during their twelve visits. The two Willys are apprehended at school after authorities read a West Berlin news account of their travels. By chance, Lutz escapes when a showing of *High Noon* in an East Berlin suburb is canceled and he goes to a late show in West Berlin. Wacholt is put in the army and Walz into a labor camp; Lutz becomes a lumberjack.

Walter Bolle, a border violator and spy. After being imprisoned for seven years for illegal border crossings, he was ransomed by West Germany in 1973 for fifty thousand marks. Motivated by a desire to avenge himself on East Germany and to destroy the wall, he becomes a spy for the West against the East. Later, to magnify his revenge by means of disinformation, he also becomes a spy for the East against the West.

Michael Gartenschläger, a radical wall jumper who defaced the wall soon after its erection and burned property in East Berlin in protest of the wall. His freedom was purchased by the West German government after he spent ten years in prison. He helped many people escape, but his greatest coup was dismantling two self-triggering robots that sprayed shrapnel at wall jumpers. While attempting to dismantle a third, he was shot by East German border guards.

Dora, the narrator's aunt in Dresden, a small, vivacious woman who lives in privileged, upper-middle-class surroundings. In telling the family history, she provides a link and a contrast between the old and new Germanys.

— *James W. Jones*

WALLENSTEIN

(Wallensteins Lager, Die Piccolomini, *and* **Wallensteins Tod)**

Author: Friedrich Schiller (1759-1805)
First published: 1800
Genre: Drama

Locale: Germany
Time: 1618-1648
Plot: Historical

Albrecht Wallenstein (ahl-brehkht VAHL-ehn-shtin), the duke of Friedland and the general of Emperor Ferdinand's forces in the Thirty Years' War. His experience follows the well-known pattern displayed by any overly ambitious and capable leader. Favored by the court for his military prowess in raising and leading a large army to subdue the Protestant states and to repel the Swedish invaders, Wallenstein loses his sense of perspective concerning his real function to the government. Fearful that other leaders will rise above him and greatly admired by his soldiers, he practices self-aggrandizement. Through a long series of political intrigues, involving Wallenstein's officers, and personal complications, involving various members of his family, Wallenstein's fate is precarious. Blind either to the realities of the intrigue he knows so well or to the recollection of his once strong favor with the court, he fails to heed the advice of those who would avert his downfall. Such naïveté leads to his murder on orders of one of his trusted commanders.

Prince Octavio Piccolomini (ohk-TAH-fyoh peek-koh-LOH-mee-nee), the duke of Amalfi, Wallenstein's lieutenant general and lifelong friend. Loyal to his leader, Piccolomini serves him until the general's ambitions and aims become apparent. Piccolomini's apparent scruples and the news that Wallenstein is to be deposed change the rapport between the two men. Imminence of his own promotion to the position of generalissimo completes the rift, and Piccolomini's chief task becomes the enlightenment of his own son, an officer, to Wallenstein's negotiations with the enemy. By leading Wallenstein's forces to defection through persuasion and deception, and by winning officers away from the once-powerful Wallenstein, Piccolomini completes his work and is given a princedom.

Max Piccolomini, his son, a regimental colonel who is faithful to Wallenstein in the face of evidence of the general's treachery. When Max, who is loyal to the emperor, is convinced of his leader's treason—through Wallenstein's own confession—the young man tries to get Wallenstein to retract his negotiations with the Saxons and the Swedes. Max, betrothed to Wallenstein's daughter, leaves with his forces of the imperial army, his decision to stay honorable having the concurrence of his betrothed, who says she cannot love him if he betrays his own conscience. The noble young Max is killed in a battle against the Swedes, his death being directly attributable to the man whom he had trusted and admired.

Butler, a regimental commander, an Irish soldier of fortune. He remains loyal to Wallenstein, despite the defection of the greater part of the army, until Octavio Piccolomini leads him to believe that Wallenstein has hindered Butler's promotion and insulted him. Learning of the successes of the Swedish forces to be joined by Wallenstein's remaining troops, Butler arranges the murders of Wallenstein and the officers who have remained with Wallenstein.

Count von Questenberg, the war commissioner. As the envoy from the emperor, Questenberg delivers word of Wallenstein's deposition. Through his recital of battles lost to the enemy, the reasons for the general's dismissal, Wallenstein's treachery is revealed. The scenes with Questenberg point up the fidelity of Wallenstein's officers.

Field Marshal Illo (EEL-loh), Wallenstein's confidant. He cunningly induces the officers, under the influence of wine, to sign a pledge of loyalty to Wallenstein. He has removed a proviso from the pledge, safeguarding their loyalty to the emperor. His deceptions and his allegiance to Wallenstein bring about his murder.

Countess Terzky, Wallenstein's sister-in-law, who sees the advantage of an alliance between Max Piccolomini and Wallenstein's daughter. The countess leaves no stone unturned in furthering the aims of Wallenstein. Because family and success mean so much to her, she cannot accept Wallenstein's reverses, and she poisons herself.

The duchess of Friedland, Wallenstein's wife, who admonishes her husband to temper his ambitions. She reports to him that she has heard rumors about his tactics and describes him as the despot he has become.

Thekla (TAYK-lah), Wallenstein's daughter, who through Countess Terzky's connivances becomes attracted to Max Piccolomini. Despite her real love for him, she tells him to obey his conscience and desert her father's cause. After Thekla learns of Max's heroic death, she goes to his tomb to die.

Count Terzky, the commander of several regiments. Having remained loyal to Wallenstein through the thick of the treachery, he is slain by Butler's men.

Gordon, the governor of Egra and commander of the citadel. Through Gordon, much of Butler's plan for murdering his adversaries is revealed. Gordon, a peaceful person, advocates deliberation rather than haste, especially where lives are concerned. He discourages Butler in his plans.

Devereux (deh-veh-ROH) and

Macdonald, captains under Butler who carry out Butler's plot to murder Illo, Terzky, and Wallenstein.

Colonel Wrangel, the Swedish envoy with whom Wallenstein negotiates for Swedish troops in return for the territories Wallenstein would yield to those troops in feigned battles.

THE WANDERER
(Le Grand Meaulnes)

Author: Alain Fournier (Henri-Alain Fournier, 1886-1914)
First published: 1913
Genre: Novel

Locale: France
Time: The nineteenth century
Plot: Psychological

Augustin Meaulnes (oh-gews-TA[N] MOHL-neh), a romantic, dreamily adventurous new boy at Sainte-Agathe's School who magnetically draws the other children to him. After leaving Sainte-Agathe's, he lives in Paris with Valentine, whom he angrily leaves after learning of her love for Frantz. He marries and deserts Yvonne, but later, grief-stricken when informed of Yvonne's death, he lovingly accepts the care of his young daughter.

François Seurel (frah[n]-SWAH sew-REHL), the son of M. and Mme Seurel. Prevented by a hip infection from playing with the village boys, he idolizes Meaulnes. After completing his own schooling, he joins his parents as a teacher in the school. He brings Yvonne and the wandering Meaulnes together and is saddened and puzzled over Meaulnes' later desertion of her.

Frantz de Galais (frah[n]ts deh gah-LAY), an unhappy young aristocrat who joins a gypsy band after losing his fiancée and who later remains briefly at Sainte-Agathe's.

Through Meaulnes, he finally finds his lost love.

Yvonne de Galais, Frantz's sister, loved by Meaulnes, who marries and then deserts her. She dies after the birth of a daughter.

Valentine Blondeau (vah-lah[n]-TEEN blohn-DOH), Frantz's fiancée, a peasant girl who flees from her home because she believes that a peasant girl should not marry an aristocrat. She becomes a dressmaker in Paris. She is later the mistress of Meaulnes, who deserts her when he discovers that she is Frantz's lost fiancée. Through Meaulnes, the separated lovers are at last reunited.

M. Seurel, the head of the middle school and one of the higher elementary classes at Sainte-Agathe's.

Mme Seurel, his wife, the teacher of the younger children.

Millie Seurel, their daughter.

M. and Mme Charpentier (shahr-pah[n]-TYAY), grandparents of François.

THE WANDERERS

Author: Ezekiel Mphahlele (1919-   )
First published: 1971
Genre: Novel

Locale: South Africa, Nigeria, and Kenya
Time: Late 1950's-1960's
Plot: Social realism

Timi Tabane (TEE-mee tah-BAH-nay), a black South African journalist who becomes an exile. Tabane, sensitive and idealistic, lives in the slums of Tirong, a black township in South Africa, and writes for the magazine *Bongo*. In Tirong, he meets Naledi Kubu, a young woman who is convinced that her husband has been murdered at a slave farm labor camp. Risking arrest, Tabane travels with her to investigate the case. After publishing his exposé, Tabane, discouraged by the mild public response and disheartened by the prospects of progress in South Africa, leaves the country illegally. He accepts teaching positions in Iboyoru (Nigeria) and Lao-Kiku (Kenya), but he is deeply dissatisfied with the rootlessness of his existence

and concerned by the rebelliousness of his eldest son, Felang. Ironically, Felang's death gives Tabane hope for the future, indicating to him that the younger generation may find a more assertive and effective path than he has.

Felang (FAY-lahng), Tabane's eldest son, who is killed with other African nationalist guerrillas by white farmers. Felang refuses to follow his parents' advice and runs away from home to join a rebel group that is fighting the South African government. He is murdered by white South African farmers along the border, and his body is thrown to the crocodiles. Felang shares his father's idealism but represents the new radicalism of African youth who are unwilling to wait for slow change.

Karabo (kah-RAH-boh), Tabane's wife. Beautiful, intelligent, and dignified, Karabo is unswervingly loyal to her husband, following him throughout his wandering exile, but she also demonstrates considerable independence. Her stamina, courage, and refusal to accept oppression or to allow it to beat her down make her an admirable complement to Tabane.

Steven Cartwright, the white editor of *Bongo* and a friend of Tabane. Cartwright is Tabane's white counterpart. Repelled by the racism of his country, Cartwright struggles to disengage himself from his racist heritage. His love for the black woman Naledi is a conscious rejection of the code he has been taught. Like Tabane, Cartwright becomes disenchanted with the prospect of progress in South Africa, chooses exile, and suffers from a sense of homelessness. Cartwright marries Naledi but is killed while covering the Biafran revolution in Nigeria.

Sheila Shulameth (SHEW-lah-mehth), a white novelist who has an affair with Steven Cartwright. Although sympathetic to the plight of black Africans, she is still tied to the racist heritage that Cartwright seeks to escape. She represents the materially comfortable life that he abandons.

Naledi Kubu (nah-LAY-dee KEW-bew), a young black woman whose husband dies after enforced farm labor. She eventually marries Cartwright. At first, Naledi is a simple country girl, but her struggle to discover the truth of her husband's fate, her cautious initial rejection of Cartwright's advances, and her eventual marriage and exile turn her into a strong, sophisticated woman. After Cartwright's death, Naledi decides to stay in London and pursue a degree in nutrition.

Rampa Kubu, Naledi's husband, who is forced into slave labor. Tabane and Naledi discover that Rampa has been shanghaied, beaten, and dismissed before dying. Rampa exemplifies victims of South African racism, victims so numerous that their individual stories cause little concern.

Kofi Awoonor (KOF-fee ah-woh-ohn-or), the famous African author and Tabane's mentor in Iboyoru. Awoonor is an example of Mphahlele's tendency to mix historical and fictional characters. Tabane looks to Awoonor for inspiration and guidance.

Emil, Tabane's Austrian friend in Iboyoru. Emil is a companion with whom Tabane can commiserate about the subtle torments of exile.

— *Carl Brucker*

THE WANDERING JEW
(Le Juif errant)

Author: Eugène Sue (1804-1857)
First published: 1844-1845
Genre: Novel

Locale: France
Time: 1831-1832
Plot: Melodrama

Samuel (sah-mew-EHL), the Wandering Jew, who is condemned to wander undying through the centuries after he mocks Christ on the day of the Crucifixion. He invested for a friend a small sum of money, now grown into an enormous fortune, and his friend's descendants are to claim the money on a certain day in 1832. After the last of these heirs dies, Samuel goes to a lonely spot where stands a cross on a hill. There, he gives thanks that his punishment is over at last.

Herodias (eh-roh-DYAHS), who demanded the head of John the Baptist on a charger. Also condemned to live through the centuries, she is driven by some power to the meeting place where the will is being read. There she temporarily foils a wicked Jesuit plot by producing a codicil to the will, suspending its execution for three months. At last, she joins Samuel by the cross and echoes his words.

Marius de Rennepont (mahr-YEWS deh rehn-POH[N]), Samuel's friend in the seventeenth century, whose modest wealth, wisely invested by Samuel, results in the huge fortune his ill-fated descendants gather to share.

Rodin (roh-DA[N]), the secretary to the provincial of the Jesuits. His villainous scheming is responsible for most of the tragedy. At last, he is killed by a mysterious Indian poison.

Marshal Simon (see-MOH[N]), an exiled Bonapartist hero.

François Baudoin (frah[n]-SWAH boh-DWA[N]), called **Dagobert** (dah-goh-BEHR), the marshal's faithful friend. He accompanies the marshal's daughters from Siberia to Paris to claim their share of the legacy.

Blanche Simon (blahnsh) and

Rose Simon, the marshal's daughters. Taken to a hospital during a cholera epidemic, they die of the disease.

Gabriel de Rennepont (gah-BRYEHL deh rehn-POH[N]), who is persuaded to become a Jesuit priest by evil Jesuits who intend to make sure he is the only heir. In this they are successful, but the entire inheritance is lost by fire. Gabriel then retires to live out his brief life with the Baudoin family.

Adrienne de Cardoville (ah-DRYEHN deh kahr-doh-VEEL), another Rennepont descendant. Falsely declared insane and committed to an asylum before the first reading of the will, she is later released. At last, after becoming the victim of a malicious report that results in a slaying, she chooses to die with her lover.

Prince Djalma (dzhahl-MAH), another Rennepont heir. Led to believe that Adrienne is another man's mistress, he kills a woman he mistakes for Adrienne and discovers his mistake only after he has swallowed poison.

Agricola Baudoin (ah-gree-koh-LAH), Dagobert's son. He is the man whom Prince Djalma, deceived, believes to be Adrienne's lover.

Jacques de Rennepont (zhahk), another heir, a good-hearted sensualist named **Couche-tout-Nud** (kewsh-tew-NEWD). He is jailed for debt. Later, he is separated from his mistress and dies after an orgy induced by a Jesuit agent.

François Hardy, a benevolent manufacturer and an heir. After the burning of his factory and the spiriting away of his young mistress, he is taken to a Jesuit retreat, where he accepts the doctrines of the order and dies as a result of the penances and fasts.

M. l'Abbe d'Aigrigny (lah-BAY day-green-YEE), the provincial of the Jesuits.

THE WANDERING SCHOLAR FROM PARADISE
(Der fahrende Schüler im Paradies)

Author: Hans Sachs (1494-1576)
First published: 1880
Genre: Drama

Locale: Nuremberg, Germany
Time: The sixteenth century
Plot: Farce

The Wandering Scholar, a witty, unscrupulous student from Paris. Taking advantage of the mistake of a simple-minded widow, who misunderstands his origin as "Paradise" instead of "Paris," he plays on her sympathies for her departed first husband to wheedle goods and money from her to take to the poor man in Paradise. When the widow's present husband chases him, he hides the bundle and his identifying yellow scarf, sends the husband on foot across a bog while he "watches the horse," and then rides merrily away, praising the generosity of both wife and husband.

The Wife, a simpleminded and good-hearted widow. Remembering with affection her open-handed first husband, and weary of her skinflint second, she sends goods and money to Paradise by the Scholar. The second husband chases the Scholar in anger but returns to tell her that he gave the Scholar his horse to shorten the travel to Paradise. At that news, she is carried away with affectionate rapture and expresses a hope that she will be able to outlive him and send him goods in Paradise.

The Husband, a grouchy, tightfisted farmer. His anger at his wife for being tricked by the Scholar gives way to shame when he himself is taken in and loses the horse. He accepts her affection as a balance for her stupidity.

THE WAPSHOT CHRONICLE

Author: John Cheever (1912-1982)
First published: 1958
Genre: Novel

Locale: St. Botolphs, Massachusetts; Washington, D.C.; and New York City
Time: The 1890's to the 1950's
Plot: Family

Moses Wapshot, the handsome, promising elder son of Leander and Sarah Wapshot. His quasi-idyllic life in St. Botolphs, a formerly prosperous Massachusetts river town, comes to an abrupt end when his aunt Honora discovers his affair with Rosalie Young. In the same way that earlier generations of young Wapshot males were sent to sea, Moses is sent out into a tempestuous modern America. In Washington, D.C., he loses his government job because his affair with a singer named Beatrice makes him a security risk. Immediately afterward, a chance meeting leads to a well-paying position in New York and in turn to his meeting Melissa Scaddon, a distant relation. He later marries her.

Coverly Wapshot, Moses' younger, less promising, and less manly brother. He too leaves St. Botolphs, but secretly and voluntarily, and his odyssey proves even more wayward. Ill-prepared for life outside the confines of his sleepy hometown, he tries to secure a job at a relative's factory in New York only to be judged unemployable on the basis of his emotional profile. He is hired as a stock boy in a department store and takes night classes in computer taping. He meets his future wife, Betsey, in the sandwich shop where she works. After a nine-month posting on a Pacific island, Coverly takes up residence in Remsen Park, the monotonously modern residential area attached to the rocket-launching center where he has been reassigned. Coverly's slapstick love for his "sandwich-shop Venus" is beset by troubles, but eventually the two are reunited and produce a male heir.

Leander Wapshot, the last of the seafaring and journal-keeping Wapshots. His New England roots go back to 1630. Leander's attachment to the sea is real but takes the decidedly reduced form of ferrying passengers across the bay to a local amusement park aboard the thirty-year-old *Topaze*. Boyishly enthusiastic and appealingly ceremonious and celebratory, he suffers numerous blows to his self-esteem, primarily at the hands of his cousin Honora, who holds the family purse strings and who puts the *Topaze* up for sale, and his wife Sarah, who later converts the *Topaze* into a floating gift shop. Deprived of his usefulness, Leander begins writing what he calls his autobiography or confession. Just as his sons, now seemingly secure, are about to return home and buy him a boat, Leander declares that he intends to return to the sea (as he grandly and perhaps ambiguously puts it), quits his job at the local silver factory, and soon afterward drowns, perhaps intentionally. In death, Leander gets what he rarely did in life: the last word, in the form of the "Advice to my Sons" with which the novel concludes.

Honora, Leander's cousin, born in Polynesia to missionaries and reared by her Uncle Lorenzo. She is the Wapshot clan's imperious and decidedly eccentric matriarch. Honora is childless, although she was married briefly to a Spaniard who claimed to be a marquis. The marriage disappointed her in some unspecified, presumably sexual, way. According to her long-suffering yet strangely faithful housekeeper Maggie, Honora represents "some naked human force," one that Leander would define as both financial and emasculating. Heir to Lorenzo's fortune, she in effect controls the futures of all the Wapshots, including Leander's sons, whom she has designated her heirs on a contingent basis, stipulating that they must marry and produce male heirs.

Sarah Wapshot, Leander's wife and another of the controlling forces in his life. She feminizes their younger son and transforms Leander's boat into a floating gift shop.

Betsey MacCaffery Wapshot, Coverly's wife. An orphan from Georgia, she meets Coverly while working in a New

York sandwich shop. In comically but also pathologically unfriendly Remsen, her loneliness appears at once ludicrous and nightmarishly real, and her search for a friend seems both Herculean and hilarious. Although she leaves Coverly, taking all their savings, they eventually reconcile, with more than a hint that they, or at least he, will not live happily ever after.

Melissa Scaddon Wapshot, Cousin Justina's beautiful ward, later Moses' wife. She promises to marry Moses if they can live with Justina. Following their wedding, Melissa undergoes a transformation: The sensuous fiancée is transmogrified into an asexual, emasculating wife until a fire destroys Justina's home, breaking the spell that held Melissa in thrall.

Rosalie Young, a minister's daughter whose loneliness and great expectations lead her to confuse sex with love. She convalesces at the Wapshots following a car accident and has a brief affair with Moses.

Clarissa, a girl made pregnant by a young Leander's aged employer, who then coaxes Leander to marry her. Leander quickly comes to love her, but soon after the birth of a daughter, she commits suicide. Clarissa's story is recounted in Leander's autobiography. The daughter, Helen Rutherford, later comes back to haunt Leander, mistakenly thinking that he is her father, and is indirectly responsible for his wrecking the *Topaze*.

Pancras, Coverly's boss at the rocket center. His homosexual advances shortly after Betsey's departure leave Coverly unnerved and sexually uncertain, feeling unworthy and exiled.

Justina Molesworth Scaddon, the seventy-five-year-old widow of a five-and-dime store magnate. Ensconced in her Hudson River Valley castle (a cross between Randolph Hearst's San Simeon and Edgar Allan Poe's House of Usher), she is the novel's most imperious and most comically grotesque female. She is sexless and vengeful.

— Robert A. Morace

THE WAPSHOT SCANDAL

Author: John Cheever (1912-1982)
First published: 1964
Genre: Novel

Locale: St. Botolphs, Massachusetts; Proxmire Manor, a Westchester suburb; and Talifer, site of a missile research base
Time: Early 1960's
Plot: Social satire

Coverly Wapshot, who is younger and seemingly less agreeable and promising than his brother Moses. He is also "a model of provincial virtues" and as such seems both naïve and strangely noble. He is twenty-eight years old and lives in Talifer with his wife and son. Although trained as a computer taper, he has been assigned to the public relations department at the Talifer missile site and research center. When his marriage begins to sour, he develops the habit of "talking like a Chinese fortune cookie" and pretending that nothing unpleasant has happened. Wanting to be useful as a husband, father, and worker, he is repeatedly made to feel helpless and inconsequential. Despite the blows to his fragile sense of self-esteem, he remains both hopeful and dutiful to the end.

Betsey Wapshot, Coverly's wife, who holds in her hands the raw material of his dreams. In unfriendly Talifer, the dark side of her personality emerges. As marriage to this "moon goddess" with her irreconcilable faces turns into a battleground, Coverly adopts the posture of a losing sexual combatant and Betsey seizes on every crumb of self-esteem that he drops.

Moses Wapshot, Coverly's older brother. Now in his early thirties, he works for a shady brokerage house and lives in affluent Proxmire Manor. When his aunt Honora's monthly stipend stops, Moses, deeply in debt, departs on a frantic and unsuccessful effort to raise cash. His absence is the proximate cause of his wife's adultery, which is in turn the proximate cause of his subsequent drinking and pessimism.

Melissa Wapshot, Moses' bored and lonely wife. A mysterious illness makes her fearful of death and greedy for pleasure. She takes nineteen-year-old Emile Cranmer as her lover, but instead of being reinvigorated, she comes to feel old and "morally shabby." Separated from her husband, she ends up in Rome, where she buys Emile in a beauty pageant/sex-slave auction. She lives with him unhappily ever after.

Emile Cranmer, a nineteen-year-old grocery clerk who lives with his widowed mother in straitened circumstances. Although Melissa thinks him "divine," the narrator judges him "pitiful, vain, and fair, a common young man trying to find some pleasure and adventure in life." Always hungry but never greedy, he takes what Melissa offers but remains unsatisfied and disappointed.

Gertrude Lockhart, a happily married mother of three. She suffers a series of domestic setbacks—frozen plumbing, an exploding furnace, an overflowing washing machine, and blown fuses—that take her from tears to promiscuity and drink, then to being ostracized and finally to suicide. Her comic predicament, minus her tragic end, anticipates Melissa's downfall.

Lemuel Cameron, the imperious director of the Talifer missile site and research center. He has distanced himself from his Italian heritage and retarded son. Ending his affair with his greedy Roman mistress, he is rewarded with the discovery "that there was some blessedness in the nature of things." Soon after, in a twist of irony, a congressional committee strips him of his security clearance.

Honora Wapshot, Coverly's aunt, the matriarch of the Wapshot family. When her eccentricity eventually gets her in trouble with the government, for failure to pay income tax, she flees to Rome, where she feels the full weight of homesickness. Returning to St. Botolphs, she promptly drinks and starves herself to death.

The narrator, who enters the story at several points. Near the beginning, he recalls the pleasant times he spent with the Wapshots at their home as well as their power to make him feel alone and to make it painfully clear that he was an outsider. At the end, he bids farewell to St. Botolphs, a town he loves but to which he says he will never return.

— Robert A. Morace

WAR AND PEACE
(Voyna i mir)

Author: Leo Tolstoy (1828-1910)
First published: 1865-1869
Genre: Novel

Locale: Russia
Time: 1805-1813
Plot: Historical

Pierre Bezuhov (pyehr beh-ZOO-khof), the illegitimate son of wealthy Count Cyril Bezuhov. Clumsy, stout, and uncommonly tall, he is at first spurned by the social set; later, after his father leaves him a fortune, he is much admired. He is beguiled into a marriage with Hélène Kuragina, who in turn is unfaithful to him. For long years, Pierre searches for peace of mind and meaning in life. He seeks it in philanthropy, in the dissipations of society, in wine, and in heroic feats of self-sacrifice during the war with Napoleon. Finally, he gains such an internal harmony through witnessing the horror of death on the battlefield and by learning to share the misery of the human race. Near the conclusion of the novel, he marries Natasha Rostova, whom he has long secretly loved.

Princess Natasha Rostova (nah-TAH-shah rohs-TOHF-uh), the beautiful daughter of Count Ilya Rostov. Regularly in attendance at all social functions, she is admired by a host of suitors. She becomes engaged to the wealthy and handsome Prince Andrey Bolkonsky; however, the marriage is postponed for a year at Andrey's father's request. During this engagement period, Natasha ruins the proposed marriage and her reputation by attempting to elope with the rake Anatole Kuragin. When Andrey is mortally wounded, she faithfully cares for him and receives his forgiveness. Later, she becomes the wife of Pierre Bezuhov.

Princess Hélène Kuragina (EHL-ehn KOO-ruh-gihn-uh), "the most fascinating woman in Petersburg," who becomes Pierre Bezuhov's wife. Although she has no love for Pierre, she marries him for the advantage of wealth and social position. Marriage in no way hampers her amours, and she constantly entertains and encourages prosperous admirers. Essentially, she is a superficial and shallow individual, seemingly unperturbed by the misery and suffering of the war around her.

Count Nikolay Rostov (nih-koh-LAY rohs-TOHF), Natasha's handsome older brother, who distinguishes himself as a cavalry officer in the Russian army. It is long supposed that he will wed Sonya, his cousin, who lives with the Rostov family; however, the financial ruination of his family makes necessary a more profitable match with Princess Marya Bolkonskaya. When the Russian army is in retreat, he saves Marya from the rebellious peasants on her estate.

Princess Marya Bolkonskaya (MAH-ryah voh-KOHN-ski-yah), Prince Andrey Bolkonsky's sister, who endures the eccentricities of a tyrannical father. The old prince, desirous of Marya as a nurse and companion, methodically destroys her chances of marriage by refusing to entertain would-be suitors. Resigned to her fate, she takes refuge in an intense religious conviction, entertaining and sponsoring "God's Folk," peasants who have had various mystical experiences. After the deaths of her father and brother, she desires the life of a recluse, but her admiration and love for Nikolay Rostov, whom she later marries, restore her to a normal life.

Sonya (SOH-nyah), Nikolay Rostov's poor cousin, the affectionate companion of Natasha in the Rostov family. For the sake of allowing Nikolay to make a more advantageous marriage, she releases him from a childhood pledge.

Prince Andrey Bolkonsky (ahn-DRAY vohl-KOHN-skihy), a wealthy nobleman, the son of an eccentric father and the brother of Marya. At the battle of Austerlitz, he fights valiantly, rallying the Russian troops by charging directly into the front line while waving the Russian flag. Missing in action, he is assumed dead, but he later returns after having been nursed to health by peasants of the countryside. He becomes engaged to Natasha Rostova, but the marriage is canceled as a result of Natasha's indiscretions. Although he swears never to fight again, his sense of duty compels him to enlist when France invades Russian soil. Again wounded, he dies in Natasha's arms, having been reconciled to her through her untiring devotion to him during his illness.

Princess Lise Bolkonskaya (LIH-suh vohl-KOHN-ski-yah), the beautiful, sensitive, and neglected wife of Prince Andrey. She dies in childbirth.

Nikolushka Bolkonsky (ni-koh-LOO-shkuh), the young son of Prince Andrey and his wife, Lise. Count Nikolay Rostov and his wife, Marya, adopt the child after Prince Andrey's death.

Prince Nikolay Bolkonsky, the tyrannical and eccentric father of Andrey and Marya.

Prince Anatole Kuragin (ah-nah-TOH-lihy KOO-ruh-gihn), Hélène's brother, a profligate. Although previously forced into marriage, he woos Natasha Rostova and subjects her to scandal and ridicule.

Prince Vasily Kuragin (vah-SEE-lyuh), the head of the Kuragin family and the father of Anatole and Hélène.

Prince Hippolyte Kuragin (hih-POH-liht-uh), his feeble-minded younger son.

Count Ilya Rostov (eel-YAH rohs-TOHF), a wealthy nobleman.

Countess Natalya Rostova (nah-TAHL-yuh), his wife.

Countess Vera Rostova (VYEH-ruh), their older daughter.

Count Petya Rostov (PYEE-tyuh), their younger son.

Lieutenant Alphose Berg, an officer and intimate friend of the Rostov family. He marries Countess Vera.

Prince Boris Drubetskoy (boh-RIHS droo-BEHT-skohy), a fashionable and ambitious friend of the Rostovs, a successful staff officer.

Princess Anna Drubetskaya (AHN-nah droo-BEHT-ski-yah), the mother of Prince Boris, an impoverished noblewoman.

Julie Karagina (zhew-LEE), a wealthy young woman who marries Prince Boris Drubetskoy.

Anna Scherer (SHAY-rur), maid of honor to Empress Marya Fedorovna. Her salon is a meeting place for the highest St. Petersburg society.

General Michael Kutuzov (mih-hah-IHL koo-TOO-zehf), who is appointed commander in chief of the Russian army in August, 1812. Obese and slovenly, he is disliked by his fellow officers, and his military tactics are considered obsolete. It is to him, however, that Czar Alexander I and all of Russia turn when Napoleon boldly advances onto Russian soil. Even then, however, he is viciously criticized when, after a prolonged and costly battle at Smolensk, he chooses not to defend Moscow by what he considers a useless and hopeless encounter. His wily scheme of "time and patience" proves sound after Napoleon, his line overextended and the Russian winter fast approaching, is forced to withdraw his forces, which are virtually annihilated by hunger, cold, and guerrilla warfare.

Napoleon Bonaparte, the renowned commander of the French Grand Armée. Worshiped and admired by the French, and feared by the Russians, he shatters the myth of his invincibility during his disastrous Russian campaign.

Mademoiselle Bourienne, a companion of Marya in the Bolkonsky family. In his senility, Count Bolkonsky finds her alluring and sympathetic.

WAR AND REMEMBRANCE

Author: Herman Wouk (1915-   )
First published: 1978
Genre: Novel

Locale: Sites of action in World War II
Time: 1941-1945
Plot: Historical

Victor "Pug" Henry, a career naval officer serving as a captain at the outbreak of World War II. Deprived of a battleship command when the Japanese sink his ship at Pearl Harbor, Henry commands the USS *Northampton*, a light cruiser in the Pacific fleet, and participates in the Battle of Midway. He returns to shore duty, where his close association with President Franklin D. Roosevelt leads to his assignments in various posts both in Washington, D.C., and abroad, handling sensitive political and military matters. He travels to Russia to assist Harry Hopkins in negotiating Lend-Lease matters with Joseph Stalin before returning to sea as a rear admiral in charge of a battleship division. His division participates in the historic battle of Leyte Gulf in the Philippines. During these turbulent years, Henry struggles to salvage his marriage to his wife of a quarter century and to deal with his growing feelings of love for his younger British friend, Pamela Tudsbury. Eventually, the Henrys are divorced, and Victor marries Pamela shortly before becoming naval aide to President Harry Truman.

Rhoda Henry, who has been married to Victor Henry for more than twenty-five years but is growing increasingly disenchanted with the marriage as she passes her fiftieth year. While her husband is at sea or abroad serving during World War II, Rhoda keeps house in Washington, D.C., participating in the limited social life there. For some time she agonizes over her relationship with businessman Palmer Kirby, with whom she has had an affair. She then meets Colonel Harrison Peters, whom she marries after divorcing Victor Henry.

Natalie Jastrow, an American Jew, thirty years old, living in Siena, Italy. Although she is married to Byron Henry, she stays with her uncle, noted historian Aaron Jastrow, who refuses to leave Siena despite advice to evacuate before the Nazis make it impossible to leave. Natalie finally persuades her uncle to leave, but because he is well known and she has her child with her, they are easily identified. She makes repeated attempts to engineer a return for all three to U.S. custody, but she finds herself being taken further into the Nazi circle. First, they are detained in Italy, then they land in Germany, and eventually they are assigned to the Germans' model concentration camp at Thieresenstadt. There, Natalie is coerced into working to trick representatives of the International Red Cross regarding the Nazis' real program for Jews. She is separated from her son and transferred to Auschwitz, but she is rescued when Germany surrenders. After recuperating in Paris, she is reunited with Byron.

Pamela Tudsbury, who works as an assistant to her father, a noted journalist, and later as assistant to Lord Bourne-Wilke of the British Air Corps. A woman of thirty, Pamela has fallen in love with fifty-year-old Victor Henry. She witnesses the fall of Singapore and is in North Africa when her father is killed. Unable to marry Victor, she becomes a military assistant in the British war effort. Her postings take her to both Moscow and Washington, D.C., where she meets Victor to renew her relationship. She is engaged briefly to Lord Bourne-Wilke, but his death from war injuries frees her just as Victor is divorced. She moves to Washington, where she realizes her ambition of becoming Mrs. Victor Henry.

Byron Henry, the second son of Victor Henry and a submariner in the Pacific fleet. Although he is married to Natalie Jastrow, he is separated from her and tries repeatedly to get reassigned to the European theater so that he can help her escape the Nazis. Aboard ship, he proves to be a highly competent officer, becoming executive officer and eventually commander of a boat. Prolonged separation from his wife and repeated trips to his widowed sister-in-law's home test his fidelity, but he remains committed to his wife. After hostilities end, he is able to go to Europe to locate his missing child and reunite his family in Paris.

Aaron Jastrow, a noted historian in his sixties. He believes that his status as an American will protect him from the Nazis' attempt to round up all Jews in Europe. He relies on a former student of his, Werner Beck, to protect him, only to learn that Beck is attempting to get him to collaborate with the Nazis. He is shipped to various detention areas and at Thieresenstadt is beaten into submission and made to work for his captors. When he is no longer of use to the Nazis, he is shipped to Auschwitz and sent to the gas chamber.

Warren Henry, Victor Henry's eldest son, a career naval officer. Warren's assignment aboard the aircraft carrier USS *Enterprise* places him in the thick of the action at the Battle of Midway. He distinguishes himself in combat but is killed in the final sortie of the engagement, leaving behind a widow and a young son.

Madeline Henry, the Henrys' only daughter and their youngest child. Slightly older than twenty years, she has secured a lucrative position as assistant to radio personality Hugh Cleveland, but the star's amorous advances put off her family. She eventually sees that this relationship will go nowhere; she returns home and takes up with an old beau, Simon

Anderson, a naval officer. The couple marry and are transferred to Los Alamos, New Mexico, the site of the atom bomb testing.

Berel Jastrow, a prisoner in the Nazi concentration camp at Auschwitz. Although he is more than sixty years old, Jastrow is healthy and cunning. He manages to get a job on a work crew and becomes involved in collecting evidence on atrocities at the camp. At an opportune moment, he escapes and makes his way first to the Soviet Union and then to the West, where he delivers evidence to authorities who are able to make public the horrors of the Germans' treatment of Jews.

Werner Beck, a German diplomat, formerly a student of Aaron Jastrow in the United States. Beck makes several gestures to guarantee the Jastrows their safety from persecution. He is intent on securing Aaron's services as a collaborator who can assure the world that the Nazis are not monsters; when Jastrow balks, Beck finds pressure being put on him, especially from Adolf Eichmann.

Harrison Peters, an Army colonel in his mid-fifties. Peters is a ladies' man in Washington, where he works on the top-secret Manhattan Project. He falls in love with Rhoda Henry and marries her after she is divorced from Victor. He plays a significant role in assembling the personnel and material for the successful testing of the atom bomb at Los Alamos.

Palmer Frederick Kirby, a widower in his fifties. An independent engineering consultant and manufacturer, Kirby helps the government build the successful atom bomb. After having an affair with Rhoda Henry, he sees the relationship die when she refuses to divorce her husband. He gives up his romantic interests and devotes his full attention to the war effort.

Simon Anderson, a Naval Academy graduate and former classmate of Warren Henry. Working on research projects in Washington, Anderson makes the most of an opportunity to resume his courtship of Madeline Henry; they marry, to the delight of the Henry family. At work, his talents are recognized by superiors, who assign him to projects that involve him in nuclear research. He is reassigned to Los Alamos to assist with the testing of the first atom bomb.

Janice Henry, the wife of Warren Henry and the daughter of Senator Isaac LaCouture. She and her infant son reside in Pearl Harbor, Hawaii, while Warren is at sea. She is crushed by the news of Warren's death at Midway but stays in Hawaii to help the war effort. She has an affair with Carter Aster, whom she met through her brother-in-law Byron, but keeps the news from Byron because it becomes clear to her that he needs her emotional support in his struggle to learn the fate of his wife and child in Nazi Germany.

Carter "Lady" Aster, a naval submarine officer. A fearless and clever warrior, Aster takes over the submarine from his inept commanding officer and establishes a reputation throughout the Pacific fleet for his exploits in sinking enemy ships. Ashore, he takes up with Janice Henry, Warren's widow, though he has no genuine love for her. He is killed by enemy aircraft while his submarine is surfaced in hostile waters.

Armin von Roon, a major general in the German army. His assignment on the German General Staff places him in a position to witness the exploits of Adolf Hitler from close proximity, and his account of World War II from the Germans' perspective, written while he is imprisoned for war crimes, is interspersed with the story of the Henry family to give a portrait of grand strategy and to render a retrospective assessment of the growing derangement of Hitler as the war progressed.

Alistair Tudsbury, an internationally renowned British correspondent. His radio and newspaper accounts of the war outline the demise of the British empire. He is present at the fall of Singapore and is killed by a land mine while out with the British forces in North Africa.

Leslie Slote, an American diplomat, formerly Natalie Jastrow's lover. He works to get Natalie and her uncle free from German control. As a result, he learns of the atrocities at the concentration camps and attempts to make the news public. Stymied by superiors, he becomes frustrated and quits the U.S. State Department. He joins the Office of Strategic Services and dies in France in operations incident to the D day invasion.

Sammy Mutterperl, a Jew confined to the Auschwitz camp. Because Sammy has earned the trust of his Nazi captors, he is allowed to lead a work crew. He recruits Berel Jastrow for his work party. Together, they build many of the structures that will be used as gas chambers, all the while planning a breakout. Sammy dies trying to escape, after killing several of his guards.

Branch Hoban, a naval officer and commander of the submarine on which Byron Henry is serving when he sees his first combat. Although he is a stern disciplinarian and able commander in training, Hoban cracks under the pressure of combat and is relieved at sea by his executive officer, Carter Aster.

Philip Rule, a minor U.S. State Department official. Posted in Europe when World War II breaks out, he is eventually transferred to the Far East and is in Singapore when the Tudsburys arrive for a tour of British defenses there. He attempts to rekindle his old romance with Pamela Tudsbury, almost succeeding as he catches her in a weak moment when she is sure that she has lost Victor Henry forever.

Raymond Spruance, a naval rear admiral (later vice admiral) who commands the U.S. forces at the battle of Midway and later serves as chief of staff for Pacific forces. Spruance shows exceptional courage and skill in managing naval forces at Midway, as well as prudence in the heat of battle, a trait that earns for him little respect from junior underlings but the grudging admiration of senior officers.

William "Bull" Halsey, a naval vice admiral and the hero of the American fleet in the Pacific. Sidelined with illness that keeps him from commanding the forces at Midway Island, Halsey takes the U.S. task force against the Japanese at Leyte Gulf in the Philippines. Victor Henry commands one of Halsey's battleship divisions there. Halsey's actions appear rash and chaotic to some of the senior officers, though the United States emerges victorious.

Adolf Eichmann, the Nazi officer responsible for implementing Hitler's plans to exterminate the Jews. He crosses paths with Natalie and Aaron Jastrow on several occasions, culminating in a meeting at the model camp at Thieresenstadt, where the Nazis try to convince the International Red Cross that they are treating the Jews kindly. Eichmann brutalizes both Jastrows into cooperating with his scheme.

— *Laurence W. Mazzeno*

THE WAR BETWEEN THE TATES

Author: Alison Lurie (1926-   )
First published: 1974
Genre: Novel

Locale: Upstate New York and New York City
Time: 1969-1970
Plot: Social satire

Brian Tate, a political science professor at Corinth University in upstate New York, born into a long line of social achievers. Forty-six-year-old Brian is a dissatisfied and disappointed man. Because it is clear that his greatest accomplishment is to hold an endowed chair at a second-tier university, he suffers discontent in realizing that he will never be famous and important. While working on a new book, he is seduced by one of his students, Wendy Gahaghan, who convinces him that a physical relationship with her will abet the success of the book. After his wife, Erica, discovers the affair early in the novel, Brian agrees to break off the relationship. He does not quite do so, and Wendy eventually shows up in Erica's kitchen, crying and pregnant. Brian is then kicked out of the house by his wife, with whom he is reunited at the end.

Erica Tate, Brian's wife, a homemaker, conservative, well-read, and alert. Erica's actions usually are guided by a sense of moral righteousness, a holdover from her Presbyterian childhood. Erica accepts Brian's initial affair with Wendy, but only on the condition that he break it off. A few months later, Wendy visits Erica to apologize for her crimes against Erica and blurts out that she is pregnant. Erica takes Wendy under her own care, orders Brian to leave the house, and then helps Wendy secure a then-illegal abortion. During Brian's absence from the house, Erica attempts an affair with Zed, a 1960's guru who runs a metaphysical bookstore. Her attempt fails, and at the end she invites Brian to come home.

Wendy Gahaghan, Brian's student and mistress. Truly a flower child, something of a hippie, and gullible, Wendy serves the vague and naïve idealism of the era. She convinces herself that she is sacrificing herself to the arts and to humanity by repeatedly offering herself to Brian, and she becomes pregnant by him. Acting under pressure from both Brian and Erica, she has an abortion, only to become pregnant a second time at the end of the novel. (Brian may not be the father this time.) She is last seen heading west to join a commune with a young man who is her equal in gullibility.

Danielle Zimmern, Erica's best friend. Independent and divorced, Danielle is everything that Erica can become if she maintains her separation from Brian; as such, she is not much of a figure to emulate, for she is no happier without a cad for a husband than Erica is with one. Danielle is something of a failure as a mother, because she operantly—although perhaps not finally—hates her children. She has an affair with a veterinarian and accepts his first proposal of marriage with no real thought.

Sanford "Zed" Finkelstein, a former classmate of Erica, a 1960's guru and owner of the Krishna Bookshop. Zed is a social loner and something of a pariah; he has come to town because he knows Erica is there. He meets her after she separates from Brian, and they attempt several times, unsuccessfully, to have a physical relationship. Zed stands as a counterpart to Wendy, on one hand, and to Danielle's new husband, on the other.

— *Carl Singleton*

THE WAR OF THE END OF THE WORLD
(La guerra del fin del mundo)

Author: Mario Vargas Llosa (1936-   )
First published: 1981
Genre: Novel

Locale: Brazil, primarily the backlands
Time: Late 1890's
Plot: Historical

The Counselor, whose name is **Antônio Conselheiro**, a tall, thin, and bearded man with fiery eyes, of mysterious identity and origins. He proclaims that he has been sent by God to become the lord of Canudos. This backlands mystic cloaked in a purple tunic begins to develop a following in the interior of the state of Bahia, Brazil. Predicting the end of the present world and the beginning of a new one, he gradually becomes a symbol and leader for those who remain committed to the monarchy. He preaches an errant Christian message of love, peace, and repentance, of death and judgment. He and several thousand of his followers establish a community at an abandoned cattle ranch called Canudos, where they plan to wait out the apocalyptic developments that he has predicted. Rejecting the advances of the encroaching republican civilization, they refuse to pay taxes and also shelter numerous backlands outlaws. The insecure new federal government eventually crushes this "revolt" in 1897.

Galileo Gall, the alias of a Scottish-born utopian anarchist and phrenologist. This libertarian intellectual views Canudos idealistically as a model of human fraternity, only superficially cluttered by religion. In his view, the Canudos movement is the beginning of a revolution that ultimately will end the tyranny of the state.

Epaminondas Gonçalves (eh-pah-mee-NOHN-dahs gohn-SAHL-vehz), the ruthless young leader of the Progressivist Republican Party and the ambitious editor of the *Jornal de Noticias*. He attempts to use the rebellion in the backlands to bring ultimate discredit to the remnants of the empire.

Baron de Canabrava (kah-nah-BRAH-vah), an unscrupulous politician and head of Bahia's Autonomist Party. He represents the local elite. In response to attacks from both sides, he attempts to turn matters to his own favor by accusing the republicans of inciting the entire episode.

Rufino (rrew-FEE-noh), a tracker and guide from Quijingue. A young, suspicious man with a thin, supple body and an angular, weather-beaten face, he has been hired by Galileo Gall to take the latter to Canudos.

The nearsighted journalist, an ugly, inept, and unnamed individual whose mission is to report on the campaign against Canudos. He breaks his glasses and cannot see anything during the destruction of the religious community, symbolically taking a myopic view of historical events. His character, one of the most memorable and believable in a novel devoted to the clash of monolithic social forces, performs a consistently subversive function in the narrative by indulging in self-parodying remarks. He also serves as one of Vargas Llosa's surrogate authors.

Jurema (zhew-RRAY-mah), Rufino's young wife, Gall's victim, and the journalist's lover. Considered as nothing more than a domestic animal by Gall, she is raped by him in an intense scene of physical violence. Her rape underscores the relationship between sexual and political repression in the novel.

— *Genevieve Slomski*

THE WAR OF THE WORLDS

Author: H. G. Wells (1866-1946)
First published: 1898
Genre: Novel

Locale: Woking and London, England
Time: Late nineteenth century
Plot: Science fiction

The narrator, a man of intellectual curiosity who is interested in observing Mars through a telescope. One day, he sees harmless-appearing creatures emerging from a projectile fallen to Earth. The Martians, left undisturbed because they seem helpless, set to work making curious machines. These finished, they begin to lay waste to the countryside. The narrator, after taking his wife to Leatherhead, returns home to find the area defenseless against the Martians' metal monsters. The Martians move on to London, which becomes a ruined city, but at last they fall victim to earthly bacteria, and the world is saved.

The narrator's wife, who is taken by the narrator to Leatherhead to escape the Martians' destruction. Finally, after the deaths of the Martians, the narrator and his wife are reunited.

An artilleryman, the only survivor of his outfit. He and the narrator escape together by hiding in bushes and streams.

A curate, with whom the narrator hides in a deserted cellar. The curate goes raving mad and, because silence is necessary to escape detection by the Martians, the narrator is forced to kill him. His body is taken by one of the Martians, whose diet consists of the blood of their victims.

THE WARDEN

Author: Anthony Trollope (1815-1882)
First published: 1855
Genre: Novel

Locale: London and Barchester, England
Time: Mid-nineteenth century
Plot: Social realism

The Reverend Septimus Harding, a kind and gentle man who had been a minor canon near Barchester for many years. At the age of fifty, he had become precentor of Barchester Cathedral, a position that included the wardenship of Hiram's Hospital. The latter was an almshouse for twelve old men established by the will of John Hiram four centuries earlier. Through the efforts of John Bold, a local reformer, and the *Jupiter*, a newspaper devoted to attacking the greed and power of the church, Mr. Harding is accused of receiving too large an income from his management of the hospital. The legal issue is ambiguous and the almshouse has been well managed, but Harding, distressed that others might question the justice of his position, resigns. All the legal and ecclesiastical officials, even John Bold himself, protest the resignation. After the suit is dropped, the bishop offers the warden a position as chaplain in the bishop's house, but Harding refuses this charity and lives in poor lodgings in town, supported only by his tiny living near the Cathedral Close.

Eleanor Harding, the favorite and younger daughter of Septimus Harding. She is in love with John Bold. Fully cognizant of her father's sensitivity, she understands why he wants to resign his wardenship. In a scene that reveals their love for each other, she begs John Bold to drop the suit, as he does. She marries Bold, and her father frequently visits the couple.

The Reverend Theophilus Grantly, the archdeacon of Barchester and rector of Plumstead Episcopi. He is the son of the bishop and the son-in-law of Mr. Harding. Archdeacon Grantly believes in "the sacred justice of all ecclesiastical revenues." Recognized as more worldly than his fellow churchmen, he insists that Harding take a strong stand against the lawsuit and the press, and he disapproves strongly of Eleanor's interest in John Bold.

Susan Grantly, the wife of Archdeacon Grantly and the older daughter of Mr. Harding. She joins her husband in trying to persuade her father to insist on the prerogatives of the church.

Bishop Grantly, the father of Archdeacon Grantly, more than seventy years old. The bland, kindly bishop of Barchester warmly supports Harding but leaves most of the controversial campaigning to his son.

John Bold, a surgeon and town councillor, genuinely concerned with reform. He honestly believes that John Hiram's will did not provide for the income the warden receives, and he begins the action by instituting a lawsuit. When he is persuaded that the lawsuit has created more injustice than it has ameliorated, he willingly drops the charges.

Mary Bold, the older sister of John Bold. A kindly woman, she promotes the engagement of her brother to Eleanor Harding, her best friend.

John Bunce, the oldest of the beadsmen at Hiram's Hospital. He is entirely loyal to Harding.

Abel Handy, another beadsman at Hiram's Hospital, selfishly disloyal to Harding.

Tom Towers, a reporter for the *Jupiter*. He maintains, in print, that Harding has unjustly received more money than Hiram's will intended. His attacks, originating from an anticlerical point of view, are both personal and unfair.

Sir Abraham Haphazard, an eminent queens' counsel and attorney general. He is hired to defend Harding and is a conservative adherent of ecclesiastical privilege.

Mr. Finney, the solicitor hired by John Bold to collect evidence against the warden. He gets most of the inmates of Hiram's Hospital to sign a petition protesting the management by promising them each one hundred pounds per year.

Doctor Pessimist Anticant, a Scots pamphleteer, one of whose moral and reforming pamphlets "exposes" Harding.

Mr. Popular Sentiment, a muckraking novelist whose work, *Almshouse*, depicts the clergyman as a vicious monster depriving the old beadsmen of all sustenance.

Chadwick, the bishop's steward and the man who farms John Hiram's estate.

Charles James Grantly, the oldest child of Archdeacon Grantly, an exact, careful boy.

Henry Grantly, the second and favorite son of Archdeacon Grantly, the most "brilliant" of the children.

Samuel Grantly, a sneaky, cunning child of Archdeacon Grantly.

Florinda and

Grizzel Grantly, daughters of Archdeacon Grantly.

THE WARS

Author: Timothy Findley (1930-   )
First published: 1977
Genre: Novel

Locale: Canada, France, and England
Time: 1915-1922 and the 1970's
Plot: Neorealism

Robert Ross, a second lieutenant in the Canadian Field Artillery during 1916 and 1917. As a boy, he feels somewhat distanced from his parents; consequently, he devotes himself to his congenitally deformed sister, developing very early in his life the desperate conviction that self-esteem must be measured by very personal, rather than conventionally public, standards. Inspired by Tom Longboat, an Indian marathon runner, he imposes a strict training regimen on himself, believing that his achievements in such an elemental sport will stand as a testament to his love for his sister. It is Ross's belief in his personal standards that leads to his attempts to save a group of war horses, actions that result in his disfigurement and ultimately his death.

Mr. and Mrs. Tom Ross, Robert's parents. Tom Ross is well-meaning, but he lacks the self-assurance to rally his family at times of emotional crisis. Robert's mother becomes a cynical alcoholic after her daughter Rowena is born with hydrocephalis. She views Robert's enlistment with bitter foreboding and, at one point while he is overseas, furiously leaves church in the middle of the service, disgusted by the generally accepted notion that religious fervor and patriotic zeal are compatible.

Lady Barbara d'Orsey, who is as physically beautiful as she is emotionally stunted. She ritualistically offers herself to a series of war heroes, as if believing that her fiercely sexual involvements with them function as some sort of classically symbolic corollary to their inevitable self-sacrifice in battle. Robert is one of her lovers. When he is not killed but wounded so terribly that he is incapable of further combat, she makes a practice of visiting him in the hospital, accompanied by her new lover and presenting—with a pointed silence—a bouquet that serves as a coldly formal tribute to the fallen hero.

Lady Juliet d'Orsey, Barbara's younger sister. During Barbara's affair with Robert, she becomes infatuated with him, instinctively sensing the goodness and innocence that underlie his barely repressed turmoil. After his disfigurement, she becomes his constant, platonic companion.

Marian Turner, Robert's nurse at the frontline hospital where he is taken after he is burned. When she offers to administer a morphine overdose, he manages to communicate the simple response, "Not yet." She believes that he was a hero for daring to do what no one else dared.

Rodwell, who in civilian life is an illustrator of children's books. Robert shares his dugout when he first comes to the front lines. In this dugout, Rodwell keeps a menagerie of small animals that he has rescued from the battlefield. Acutely sensitive, he writes truly touching letters to his daughter to maintain his sanity and finally to help her to cope with his death. He commits suicide after watching battle-weary soldiers set fire to a cat.

— *Martin Kich*

THE WARTIME TRILOGY
(D'un château l'autre, Nord, *and* Rigodon)

Author: Louis-Ferdinand Céline (Louis-Ferdinand Destouches, 1894-1961)
First published: 1957-1969
Genre: Novels

Locale: France, Germany, and Denmark
Time: 1944-1945 and 1957-1961
Plot: Biographical

North, 1960

Louis-Ferdinand Céline (lwee-fehr-dee-NAH[N] say-LEEN), the narrator in all three novels; in this one, he focuses on his first adventures as he flees France, threatened with prosecution for collaborating with the Germans. His training as a medical doctor serves as a passport to hoped-for safety. Embittered by misfortune, he relentlessly attacks his perceived persecutors, seeing himself as a martyr, hated because he dares to tell the truth—that humankind is depraved and doomed.

Lili (lee-LEE), Céline's wife and constant companion, carrying their cat, safe and fed, in a small case. Brave and generous, she possesses a mysterious female strength that sustains him in their journey.

Le Vigan (vee-GAH[N]), a popular French actor who accompanies Céline through Germany, acting the clown to divert hostile crowds and serving as Céline's confidant until almost the end of the journey.

Harras, a physician in the German army and Céline's friend. He gives the three exiles refuge in the town of Zornhof. Harras' jolly spirit masks a shrewd, practical intelligence, and his guidance and generosity are invaluable to Céline. Although he helps his friend get to Denmark, he himself comes to a bad end.

Count Otto von Simmer, an irascible old veteran of World War I, apparently a homosexual. Wearing powder and lipstick, three Iron Crosses, and many rings, he typifies the absurd individuals Céline encounters frequently. Simmer is found bludgeoned, strangled, and tossed into a patch of weeds.

Count von Leiden (fon LI-dehn), the octogenarian master of the castle in Zornhof. He lets young Polish girls ride and whip him. When he rides off on a white horse to fight the Russian army, a group of prostitutes who run the northern plains grab him, tie him to a tree, and beat him. He dies of his wounds despite Céline's medical treatment.

Baron von Leiden, who has only stumps for legs. He is carried around by a Russian prisoner, who eventually murders him and dumps his body in a huge manure pit.

Inge von Leiden, the baron's wife and the mistress of Harras and Simmer. She attempts to seduce Céline to obtain drugs with which to kill her husband. She eventually succeeds and is carted off to her mother's castle.

Frau Kretzer (KREHT-zuhr), who runs the hotel where Céline, Lili, and Le Vigan stay. Her fits include cursing Adolf Hitler, rolling and kicking on the floor, accusing the French of murdering her two sons, and wallowing in their blood-soaked tunics. She is carted away with Inge.

Herr Kracht, the SS police chief. Stubborn, thickheaded, and hating nearly everyone, including Hitler, he keeps order by firing his pistol in the air. He befriends Céline and has him examine those who die, including an old dog. He helps Harras obtain travel permits for Céline, Lili, and Le Vigan.

Castle to Castle, 1957

Louis-Ferdinand Céline, the precariousness of whose existence is intensified by conditions in Siegmaringen, where more than a thousand other collaborators seek refuge. The voice of the sufferer and seer is ever present, and his frenzied pronouncements mingle with graphic details of bizarre situations.

Madame Niçois, an elderly woman in Meudon suffering from cancer whom Céline patiently and faithfully treats. She is a focal point in the beginning of the book and reappears, dying, after Céline finishes his account of life in Siegmaringen.

Major Hermann von Raumnitz, the chief of police, whom Céline treats for an inflammation, thereby acquiring a degree of protection. Raumnitz's wife, Aisha, keeps order in the town with the use of fierce dogs and a whip.

Frau Frucht, who runs the hotel where Céline's group resides. She also carries a whip, using it on maids, cooks, society women, and prisoners. In a final scene, she begs Céline to bring Lili to sleep with her, but he, wary and uninterested, lets the offer slip.

Rigadoon (1969)

Louis-Ferdinand Céline, who encounters increased danger and chaos under Allied bombing. The narrative shifts constantly between dispassionate objectivity and frenzy. In a group of demented children, Céline sees a spirit of adventure and indifference to the war. Although his misanthropic spirit continues unabated, he confesses that his weakness is optimism. Behind the voice that rails is an indomitable spirit that stands, in the end, as a testament of the human strength to endure.

Le Vigan, who is worn out by danger and hardship; he longs for sunshine and peace. He finally receives permission to travel to Rome and takes leave of Céline and Lili.

Felipe (feh-LEE-peh), an Italian bricklayer working in Germany. When a flying brick leaves Céline bleeding and delirious, Felipe helps find food and makes him new canes before catching a train back to the brickyard.

Odile Pomaré, a consumptive nun and teacher who is taking a group of children to safety. When she becomes too ill to travel any longer, Céline takes charge of the children and eventually turns them over to the Red Cross. Her humanity links her to Céline, and her sacrifice shows evidence of his.

— *Bernard E. Morris*

WASHINGTON SQUARE

Author: Henry James (1843-1916)
First published: 1880
Genre: Novel

Locale: New York City
Time: c. 1850
Plot: Psychological realism

Catherine Sloper, an heiress who remains steadfast to her ideal of loyalty. Irreparably harmed by the harshness of her father and the coldness of a calculating suitor, Catherine reestablishes her life to fill the void of love removed. True to her vision, she neither mopes nor is vindictive; she merely compensates by filling her time with charitable and sociable acts, blending her life into her fashionable but anachronistic Washington Square home. Never one to complain, she does one time cry out against her father's heartlessness, her lover's lack of heart, and her meddling aunt's perverse though romantic indiscretions. She forever after forgives but never really forgets, something of tenderness and devotion having gone out of her, a woman who was, in the beginning, richly endowed with these virtues.

Austin Sloper, her socialite physician father whose unfortunate loss of a beautiful wife and son leaves him with no comfort in his plain, simple-hearted daughter. Brilliant and incisive as he is, Dr. Sloper is unable to ridicule Catherine's love out of existence or to supplant love with surface intellectualism. Although he sees clearly the suitor's contrivance, he can never act unselfishly or with unattached love toward the humble daughter who both dotes on him and fears him. He lives on and by irony, finally falling victim himself to a deeper sarcasm. Although his perspicacity makes him aware of events and their consequences, he never understands their meanings. He dies believing that he has thwarted a lovers' plot to gain his fortune and without knowing he has helped kill that love.

Morris Townsend, the suitor who gives up a small fortune offered with love and devotion for a larger fortune that he cannot manage to earn or contrive. As Catherine thinks, he is a man with charming manners and unrealized intellectual abilities, but he is also a shallow, egoistical, and altogether selfish aging young man who has squandered his own small inheritance, sponged off his poor and widowed sister, and set his cap for a plain heiress whose love he rejects when the larger fortune is withheld by her father. Aging as a caricature of his youthful self, he unsuccessfully offers himself to the heiress as one worth waiting for. Soft-spoken Catherine has forgiven him and feels friendly toward him but never wishes to see again this man whom she accuses only of "having treated me badly."

Lavinia Penniman, the widowed sister of Dr. Sloper and the unremitting confidant of the mercenary suitor. Mrs. Penniman, whose husband was a clergyman, is a hopeless romantic who has taken upon herself the playing of Catherine's love and small inheritance against the handsome Townsend's expectation of the doctor's wealth. Badly frightened by the miscarriage of her conspiracy and aware of the possibility of losing her parasitic position in the household, she becomes circumspect, cautious against her brother's wrath and her niece's mute accusations. Gay and indestructible after her brother's death, she once again attempts the part of duenna for the middle-aged Catherine and Townsend, with results that the narrowness of her vision can never comprehend.

Marian Almond, Catherine Sloper's sensible and observant aunt. Mrs. Almond, aware of her responsibility in the matter, because her niece met Morris Townsend at a party given in the Almond house, dislikes the match but hates the meddling of both her brother and her sister. She thinks more highly of Catherine and her simple virtues than do the others; she wishes Morris were as sympathetic and kind as the proud but humble sister on whom the selfish man lives. Her own deep sympathies make for ease with Catherine and antagonism toward Lavinia, the weak-minded matchmaker. Even she is not able to win the jilted girl's confidence, though she manages to relieve the pain of Dr. Sloper's satiric inquiries and Lavinia's fatuous comments.

Mrs. Montgomery, Morris Townsend's widowed sister. A call on Mrs. Montgomery confirms Dr. Sloper's belief that Townsend is a fortune hunter.

THE WASPS
(Spheēkes)

Author: Aristophanes (c. 450-c. 385 B.C.E.)
First performed: 422 B.C.E.
Genre: Drama

Locale: Athens
Time: The fifth century B.C.E.
Plot: Satire

Philocleon (fih-loh-klee-on), an elderly Athenian citizen and a dicast, one of the six thousand jurors of the Athenian courts. He is completely obsessed with judging and litigation, and to sit in court day after day is the greatest joy he can imagine. He prides himself on his hardness of heart; no appeal from a prisoner can move him, and he always votes for conviction. When his son imprisons him within his own house to prevent his going to court, he attempts to escape by almost every ruse imaginable. He finally allows himself to be persuaded to give up his madness because Bdelycleon convinces him that he is not a pillar of the state, as he had imagined, but a dupe of the Athenian political bosses. He no longer attends court; instead, he sits at home in judgment on his dog, Labes, who has been accused of stealing a Sicilian cheese. At the end of the case, Bdelycleon tricks him into voting for acquittal, for the first time in his life. Later, Philocleon reluctantly allows himself to be dressed in a style becoming to a man of his years and to be taken out into society, where Bdelycleon evidently hopes that he will find interests to replace his extreme fondness for law courts. The old fellow is incorrigible. He staggers home drunk from a banquet after having exhibited there the grossest of manners, carried off the flute girl who entertained the guests, and misused several citizens along the streets. His misbehavior will involve him in several lawsuits, but his previous acrimony has been transformed into the wildest of high spirits.

Bdelycleon (DEH-lih-klee-on), Philocleon's son, determined to break his father's bad habits and to make him over into a model old man. Bdelycleon is evidently a man of substance, and he is clear-sighted enough to know that men like his father are being fooled by a corrupt government, which is using the state revenues for many purposes other than feeding a hungry populace. He is an affectionate son, willing to indulge his father's foibles even to the point of acting as defense counsel for Labes, the accused dog. He speaks for moderation and common sense, but in the end he is no match for Philocleon's buffoonery.

Sosias (SOH-see-uhs) and

Xanthias (ZAN-thee-uhs), house servants of Philocleon who aid Bdelycleon in keeping their master prisoner and complain vigorously about his vagaries. Sosias speaks for the dog that accuses Labes during his mock trial, and Xanthias acts as the prosecuting counsel.

A baker's wife and

an accuser, who are wronged by Philocleon as he reels his way back to his house after the unfortunate banquet. They appear to demand satisfaction for his having ruined the baker's wife's wares and thrown rocks at the accuser. When Bdelycleon tries to smooth matters over, his father adds insult to the previous injuries.

A Chorus of wasps, all old men and Philocleon's fellow dicasts. Like him, they are bewitched by the power they seem to enjoy as jurors, and they rise before daylight to be first on hand for the opening of the tribunals. Their costumes suggest their temperament and their stings the sharpness of their verdicts. When they discover that their colleague has been shut in his house, they attempt to storm the doors but are driven off by Bdelycleon and the servants. Later, they, like Philocleon, are convinced of the error of their way of life by Bdelycleon.

WATCH ON THE RHINE

Author: Lillian Hellman (1905-1984)
First published: 1941
Genre: Drama

Locale: Near Washington, D.C.
Time: 1940
Plot: Melodrama

Fanny Farrelly, the head of a distinguished Washington family. She eagerly awaits the return of her daughter, Sara, who has spent many years abroad with her German husband, rearing a family and helping him in his anti-Fascist efforts. Fanny disapproved of the marriage but is now eager to make amends. She is out of touch with what has been happening in Europe, but she responds well to Kurt's explanation of his activities on behalf of the men and women who have opposed Adolf Hitler. Fanny is so moved by Kurt's humane efforts on behalf of his fellow human beings that she conspires with him in the murder of Teck de Brancovis, who plans to inform on Kurt to the German embassy.

David Farrelly, Fanny's good-looking son, who has struggled under the shadow of a famous father. David falls in love with Marthe de Brancovis and helps Kurt survive Teck's scheme against him.

Marthe de Brancovis, Teck's attractive wife, an American who has tired of her husband's gambling and his generally dissolute life. She is a guest in Fanny's home and falls in love with her son David.

Teck de Brancovis, a Romanian nobleman who gambles away his funds and decides to turn in Kurt Muller to the German embassy, which is sure to pay Teck for his efforts. Teck is suave but contemptuous of Americans, including his hostess, Fanny.

Kurt Muller, Sara's husband and the play's hero, a vulnerable man. His hands have been broken in torture, and he dreads returning to Europe, even though he knows that he must leave to rescue his compatriots who are in jail or are facing imminent extermination by the Nazis. Kurt is eloquent yet modest about his role in history. He impresses Fanny with his sincerity and determination and is instrumental in arousing her awareness of the threat to civilization that Fascism poses.

Sara Muller, Kurt's dedicated wife, who has had to brook her mother's displeasure over her marriage. She wins Fanny over, however, with her dedication to Kurt and her family. Sara, in fact, articulates many of the emotions and opinions that Kurt keeps to himself. In this sense, she is his interpreter, saying in her own words what it has meant to follow him and to dedicate herself to his cause.

Bodo Muller, Kurt and Sara's precocious child. Like Sara, he often expresses in blunt fashion opinions about freedom and democracy that Kurt only implies in his manner and halting speech. Bodo injects some humor into the play with his youthful sense of importance.

Babette Muller, the middle child in the Muller family. She is much like her mother, supporting the family's political commitment and feeling a solidarity with her father.

Joshua Muller, Kurt's son. As the oldest child in the family, he feels a special responsibility for carrying on his father's mission.

— *Carl Rollyson*

THE WATCH THAT ENDS THE NIGHT

Author: Hugh MacLennan (1907-1990)
First published: 1959
Genre: Novel

Locale: Canada, Spain, Leningrad, Germany, and China
Time: Early 1950's, with flashbacks
Plot: Social morality

George Stewart, the self-effacing narrator, a part-time university lecturer and radio journalist, Catherine's husband and Sally's stepfather. George has known and loved the delicate Catherine since they were children together. Separated from Catherine by his aunt's ambitions and then his father's bankruptcy, he does not meet her again until, having put himself through college in Toronto, he returns to Montreal, only to find that she has married Jerome Martell. The unemployed George meets Nora, a Communist nurse. Disillusioned as he is with the politics and economics that produced the "dirty thirties," he attends Communist rallies. Still loving Catherine, and admiring Jerome, he watches the marriage suffer from Jerome's increasing involvement in politics, his affair with Nora, and his departure for Spain. After Jerome's death is reported, George and Catherine marry and are happy until Jerome's reappearance triggers George's memories (which constitute much of the book) and a third embolism that nearly kills Catherine. The autumnal beauty of George and Catherine's life after this is recognized as preparatory to their final separation. George's faithful love for Catherine, his affection (obviously reciprocated) for Sally, and his admiration for and understanding of Jerome indicate that he is both generous and just. His political acumen is evident in his work and in the analysis of his own and the younger generation; it can be seen also in his description of the 1930's and the mores of postwar Canada.

Jerome Martell, a brilliant surgeon, Catherine's first husband and a friend of George. Born the son of a cook in a lumber camp, Jerome escaped at the age of ten from his mother's murderer and was adopted by the Martells, an elderly clerical couple. As a teenager in World War I, he bayonetted eleven men, lost his religious faith, and flung himself into medicine. Knowing that Catherine had a damaged heart, he encouraged her to marry him and have a child, assured that his vitality would enable her to survive. Jerome's differences with the Montreal medical establishment are exacerbated by his appearance at a Communist rally with his mistress. He resigns to join the Spanish loyalists; later, fighting with the maquis, he is captured and tortured by the Nazis and is reported dead. He actually is incarcerated in a concentration camp. Released by the Russians, he works in Siberia and China, then returns to Canada after seventeen years to find his daughter grown and his wife remarried. After healing wounds inflicted seventeen years before and helping Catherine recover, he leaves for a remote medical practice. His vitality, his single-mindedness,

his courage, and his finally successful search for meaning in life make him a force in the lives of others. His names suggest both saint and warrior, and he is a powerful influence for good.

Catherine Stewart, later **Martell**, née **Carey**, the wife of Jerome and then George. She has suffered all of her life from a rheumatic heart, her mother's resentment, and her own inability to lead a normal life. Resenting Jerome's concentration on politics, she is reconciled with him before he leaves and supports herself and her daughter Sally until she remarries. She then becomes a painter, trying to express an enjoyment of living intensified by her acceptance of death.

Sally Martell, Catherine and Jerome's daughter, a university student. She resents her father's defection and is in love with a fellow student, Alan Rowe. Both represent the younger generation.

Nora Blackwell, a Communist, a surgical nurse, the unfaithful wife of Harry, and Jerome's mistress. She dies, leaving a daughter whom Harry rears.

Arthur Lazenby, formerly a Communist and now a successful official who smooths Jerome's return. He owes his start to Jerome.

Giles Martell, an elderly, saintly Anglican clergyman. He and his wife, Josephine, reared Jerome.

Dr. Rodgers, the head surgeon at Beamis Memorial Hospital. He is the medical establishment personified.

— *Jocelyn Creigh Cass*

THE WATCHMAKER OF EVERTON
(L'Horloger d'Everton)

Author: Georges Simenon (1903-1989)
First published: 1954
Genre: Novel

Locale: Everton and elsewhere in New York State, and various locations in the East and Midwest
Time: Mid-1950's
Plot: Psychological realism

Dave Galloway, a watchmaker and repairer with his own small shop in Everton, New York. He is the novel's center of consciousness. Forty-three years old, a good citizen, and an ordinary, happy man not much given to reflection, at the opening of the novel Dave has still to learn the "secret in men" which he hopes to communicate at the novel's close to the grandson who will shortly be born to his imprisoned son. The alienation and purposelessness of the modern hero are registered in the details of his drab small-town existence: his lack of friends, his retreat from women, and his clockworklike home habits and work routines. So contracted is his life that he depends almost entirely for love and recognition—for a very sense of self—on the son to whom he has been both father and mother since his wife Ruth left him fifteen years ago, when Ben was an infant. Dave attempts not simply to understand why Ben has stolen and murdered but also to assert the unbroken continuity and closeness of their relationship. Dave's bewildered attempt to do so comes in the face of the fact that Ben has severed his ties with the past and his father, refusing even to acknowledge his presence in court. As a result of his quest to maintain a relationship with Ben, Dave confronts his own deeply buried desire to rebel (which drove him to marry the town tramp) and that of his long-dead father. Through such a quasi-mystical sense of heredity, he can cling to a sense of identity with Ben.

Ben Galloway, Dave's sixteen-year-old-son, quiet and self-possessed, a good son who has never given any trouble, and (until recently) a good student. One Saturday night Ben packs his suitcase, pockets a pistol bought from a school friend, steals his father's decrepit car, and picks up his girlfriend Miriam. The two head for Illinois, where they can legally be married. On the road, still close to home, Ben shoots a man for his car and a few dollars. Captured after an inconsequential shoot-out with police, tried, and imprisoned for life, Ben regrets nothing. Instead, he seems almost exultant, certainly callous, and suddenly adult: He has slept with Miriam, and he has imposed (if only for twenty-eight hours) his will on life.

Miriam Hawkins (in some versions, **Lillian**), Ben's girlfriend. Small for her fifteen and a half years, and not strikingly attractive, Miriam commits herself to Ben as absolutely and exclusively as he to her, persistently refusing to let him take responsibility for the killing. In the months before their elopement, Dave discovers, Ben has lived more in the shabby Hawkins home—with its horde of badly behaved children, a slatternly mother, and a drunken father—than in his own neat apartment.

Musak, Dave's one close friend, a solitary, middle-aged cabinetmaker. A big man who nevertheless moves with silent grace, taciturn and sometimes cynical, Musak is something of a mystery to Dave even after years of friendship. It is while

Dave is playing his regular Saturday night game of backgammon at Musak's place, over a bottle of rye, that Ben decamps with Miriam. After discovering Dave's loss, Musak comes to Dave's apartment, for the first time. He is unquestioning, knowing how to deal with grief and disillusionment, and helps Dave survive.

Wilbur Lane, the top-notch attorney Dave hires to represent his son. Lane is fat, busy, able, self-important, and well-connected. He dislikes Ben for his obstinate sanity (mental instability being the only plea that could possibly save him from imprisonment) and regards Dave as an insignificant nuisance who knows less about his son than the policemen who arrested him. Significantly, he reminds Dave of his successful businessman stepfather, Musselman, against whom as an adolescent Dave defined himself and because of whom he cut himself off from his mother and his past.

— *Joss Lutz Marsh*

THE WATER HEN: A Spherical Tragedy in Three Acts
(Kurka Wodna)

Author: Stanisław Ignacy Witkiewicz (1885-1939)
First published: 1962
Genre: Drama

Locale: Unspecified
Time: Unspecified
Plot: Absurdist

The Father, **Albert Valpor** (or **Walpor** in some texts), a retired skipper of a merchant ship. He is an unflappable pessimist who does not believe that human beings make much difference in the scheme of things. Still, he is rather impressed when his son Edgar kills Elizabeth Gutzie-Virgeling, who is referred to as the Water Hen, and he thinks that perhaps Edgar can make something important out of his life after all. The revolution that takes place at the end of the play fails to impress Albert.

He, **Edgar Valpor**, Albert's good-looking, if inept, son. He is devoted to the Water Hen but balks at her insistence that he shoot her. He wonders with whom he will be able to talk if he shoots her. He is finally convinced by her arguments and actually kills her. He has no real convictions about life, and the murder does not affect him much. When his son Tadzio questions him about the murder, Edgar is unable to explain his motivations. By the end of act 1, Edgar believes that he has created a family by acknowledging Tadzio and marrying Lady Alice. He is amazed when the Water Hen returns and is puzzled when she denies that Tadzio is her son. Because the Water Hen is convinced that he did not suffer because of her death, Edgar submits to the physical agony of a torture machine to demonstrate the reality of his feelings.

Tadzio, who claims to be Edgar's son and eventually convinces him that this is so. By act 2, Tadzio has forgotten why Edgar is his father. Unlike the other characters, he tends to question why things are the way they are. In act 3, ten years later, Tadzio is much taken with the Water Hen, who is now beautiful and sensuous. Tadzio quarrels with Edgar, who has discovered him and the Water Hen in a violent embrace.

Duchess Alice of Nevermore, also called **Lady Alice**, a blond and beautiful woman, one of the objects of Edgar's affections. Alice is hostile toward the Water Hen because her first husband (also named Edgar) was obsessed with the Water Hen. Now married to Edgar Valpor, a friend of her first husband, Alice counsels Tadzio not to question the nature of things because there are no answers. Alice's main interest seems to be in accumulating capital for the Theosophical Jam Company, her latest enterprise, and she is not much concerned with personal feelings. Like Edgar, she believes that she must come to terms with the influence of the Water Hen on her life. When Edgar shoots the Water Hen a second time, Alice tries to take the blame upon herself, but Edgar will not let her do so.

The Water Hen, **Elizabeth Gutzie-Virgeling**, a confidant of Edgar and the object of Tadzio's affection and Alice's hostility. She dies twice in the play, each time apparently trying to make a difference in people's lives even as she expresses a sense of futility in trying to impress them. The Water Hen tends to think of herself as an illusion, a fiction that other characters, such as Alice's first husband, Edgar, have created. The Water Hen also claims that she is a liar and that she does not really exist. Her Polish name, Elzbieta Flake-Prawacka, is a combination of the words *flaki* (tripe) and *prawiczka* (virgin) and is a fitting humorous name for a woman who is a bizarre combination of the down-to-earth (the guts of things) and the unbesmirched ideal.

The Scoundrel, **Richard de-Korbowa-Korbowski**, also known as **Tom Hoozey**, who resembles Edgar and is devoted to Lady Alice of Nevermore. Korbowski despises Edgar Valpor as a weakling and keeps insisting that Alice abandon him.

— *Carl Rollyson*

THE WATERFALL

Author: Margaret Drabble (1939-   )
First published: 1969
Genre: Novel

Locale: London and Yorkshire, England
Time: The 1960's
Plot: Psychological realism

Jane Gray, the narrator, twenty-eight years old, the wife of Malcolm, mother of Laurie and Bianca, cousin of Lucy, and lover of James. She is a published poet and tells her own story. To evoke the importance and complexity of her love, she alternates between first-person and third-person narratives, telling of her shy and lonely childhood and of her drifting into an unhappy and violent marriage. She acknowledges her sexual beauty but is passive, hard-hearted, selfish, and frigid. Although she rejects her husband, Malcolm, she responds to James's confident persistence. With James, she experienced the "miracle" of orgasm, an experience rendered metaphorically by the "waterfall" of the title. Despite some reservations, she knows that this experience has changed her life. She is with James when he crashes his car but is not hurt. At the end, although she is still technically married to Malcolm, she and James remain lovers.

James Otford, Lucy's husband, a father of three, and Jane's lover. He is part owner of a garage and drives sports cars recklessly both on the road and on the racetrack. His appearance, featuring pale eyes and a hard face, is threatening, yet his soft, gray-blond hair suggests the gentle, loving persistence and kindness by which he awakens Jane's sexuality. He is seriously injured in the automobile crash but recovers almost completely. At the end of the story, although he has not left Lucy, he is still intimate with Jane.

Malcolm Gray, the thirty-one-year-old husband of Jane and the father of Laurie and Bianca. He is a well-trained, ambitious, and successful professional guitarist and singer. Jane falls in love with a song he sings. Their marriage fails in part because of his latent homosexuality. Frustrated with Jane's coldness, he beats her and leaves. After the automobile crash, his telling about Jane and James allows Lucy to find the lovers. He threatens to divorce Jane but does not.

Lucy Goldsmith Otford, James's twenty-eight-year-old wife, a mother of three and Jane's cousin. A Cambridge graduate, forceful and promiscuous, she works for a publisher. She has been a close friend of Jane since they were children, and Jane imitates her steps toward adulthood. After the crash, her

discovery of the truth about Jane and James precipitates a change in all of their relationships. James eventually returns to her.

Laurie Gray, the three-year-old son of Jane and Malcolm. Jane sees him growing up like her, fated to be lonely.

Bianca Gray, a baby, the daughter of Jane and Malcolm. Her birth occasions James's first overnight stay with Jane.

Jane's parents, who are Mrs. Goldsmith's sister and the headmaster of a good but not first-rate boys' preparatory school. Jane describes them both as habitual name-droppers obsessed with social position. Jane says that her father's caustic wit masks a lack of intelligence. Most important, Jane believes that, between them, her parents caused her to retreat within herself—alone, unloved, and unloving. They disapprove of her and prefer Jane's younger, more normal sister, Catherine. At the end, Jane tells the reader that they are not as bad as she has said they are.

Mr. and Mrs. Otford, James's parents. He is a London businessman dealing in perfume. She is a beautiful Norwegian who works for Lucy's employer and has affairs. Although they are not rich, they live lavishly.

Mr. and Mrs. Gray, Malcolm's parents. They are Londoners. He is a tax official, and she is a restless, questioning little woman. They get along well with Jane's parents because they are so obviously from an inferior social class.

Mr. and Mrs. (Bridget) Goldsmith, Lucy's parents. Bridget is Jane's mother's sister.

— *George Soule*

THE WATERFALLS OF SLUNJ
(Die Wasserfälle von Slunj)

Author: Heimito von Doderer (1896-1966)
First published: 1963
Genre: Novel

Locale: Vienna and environs
Time: The 1870's to 1910
Plot: Historical realism

Robert Clayton, an engineer and the industrialist director of the Vienna branch of the British firm of Clayton & Powers, Ltd. At the age of twenty-eight, in 1877, he marries Harriet. They honeymoon in the southeastern part of the old Austro-Hungarian Empire, including the town of Slunj and the waterfalls of the Slunjcica River in this remote area of Croatia. After their return to England, Robert's father informs them that he has arranged to open a branch factory of their agricultural machinery plant in Vienna to serve the southeastern provinces of the British empire. Robert, an efficient director, has a prosperous business established eighteen months later. Robert enjoys the social life of Vienna at the turn of the century after a respectful period of mourning following the death of his wife. He is an active, charming, and extroverted man who continues to bring success to his business and brings a host of people from various social circles into his home. Although he is thirty years older than his son, he is often mistakenly identified as a younger brother. Only a short while after he meets the vivacious Monica Bachler, then Donald's lover, Robert decides to marry her.

Donald Clayton, Robert's son, born in Vienna on May 10, 1878, exactly nine months after his parents visited the waterfalls of Slunj. He is sent to England when he is of school age

to live with his grandfather, a typical Englishman who takes great interest in Donald's education. Donald's personality is the complete opposite of his father's. He is incapable of responding to human emotions and actions and has a deathly fear of water in any form. When Monica Bachler tries to seduce him, he notices that it is raining outside and simply does not respond to her advances. At the age of thirty-two, while on an extended business trip, Donald decides that he should marry Monica, most likely because he thinks that a wife belongs in an orderly and well-appointed home. While in Slunj, a place his father has often praised for its beauty and vitality, Donald receives two unexpected letters. One comes from his father, announcing his intended marriage to Monica. The other letter comes from Monica, telling of her love for his father and her resolve to marry him, with the pernicious suggestion that she and Donald should remain friends. This news drives Donald to the waterfalls, where he climbs out on a rickety walkway. The handrail gives way, and he falls a short distance onto a protruding rock. His would-be rescuers find him dead. It is said that Donald did not die from the fall but from fright of the falling waters.

Monica Bachler (BAKH-lehr), who, at the age of thirty-seven in 1910, is the director and engineer of a Swiss technical publishing firm that has just opened an office in Vienna. She falls in love with Donald immediately after her arrival in the capital and pursues this relationship with unusual vigor. Donald, however, is incapable of responding to her amorous and sexual advances; he merely sits, smokes his pipe, and smiles. While Donald is on a business trip to England, Monica is invited to the Clayton tennis parties, where she meets Chwostik, with whom she spends one evening. There she also meets the "alive Donald," Robert Clayton. They fall in love and make plans to marry before Donald returns from another business trip.

Josef Chwostik (YOH-sehf CHVOS-tihk), who is approximately thirty years old, the office manager and, later, business managing director and deputy director of Clayton & Powers in Vienna. Chwostik is the genius who makes the business a profitable enterprise. Although his educational background is very limited, he quickly learns English, Serbo-Croatian, and numerous other foreign languages that help him in business dealings for the firm in the multilingual and multinational Austro-Hungarian Empire. Even though his background is socially and materially disadvantaged, he learns respect and discretion and is included in the social life of his employer,

serving as a highly trusted and respected member of Viennese society.

Zdenko von Chlamtatsch (ZHDEHN-koh fon KHLAHM-tatsh), who in 1910 is a fourteen-year-old schoolboy in Vienna. He and several school friends imitate the "Clayton Brothers," as Robert and Donald are called. The boys even form the Metternich Club, in which they affect a kind of dandyism not uncommon in Vienna at that time. Through Augustus, Robert Clayton's nephew, Zdenko becomes acquainted with the Claytons and is frequently invited to their tennis parties. His personality and behavior resemble those of Donald Clayton. While on holiday at his aunt's home in Hungary, Zdenko goes riding and arrives at the waterfalls of Slunj just in time to witness Donald's fall and death.

Harriet Clayton, Robert's first wife and Donald's mother. She is an unassertive woman who prefers the rural life of horseback riding at her uncle's estate in England to the social life and engineering world of Vienna. Her husband and son rarely accompany her on these trips to England. She dies of tuberculosis in 1898 and is buried in Chifflington, England.

— Thomas H. Falk

WATERLAND

Author: Graham Swift (1949-   )
First published: 1983
Genre: Novel

Locale: Greenwich, England, and the Fenlands of Norfolk
Time: The 1970's, with flashbacks
Plot: Novel of ideas

Tom Crick, a history teacher at a private secondary school in Greenwich, England, the spot where time can be said to begin. The narrator, in his mid-fifties, has been an instructor of history for thirty years and is being forced to retire because the authorities contend that history has little value in the modern world. As a means of understanding his part in his wife's recent mental breakdown and in the deaths of his half brother Dick and boyhood friend Freddie Parr, and in response to his students' lack of interest in the more orthodox history of the French Revolution, Crick tells his students stories, stories from his own life and the life of his family in the Fen Country of Norfolk.

Mary Metcalf Crick, Tom's wife. Mary, also from the Fenlands, has been married to Tom for as long as he has been a teacher. They have been friends and lovers since childhood. While still in her teens, the sexually precocious Mary becomes pregnant by Tom and has an abortion that renders her permanently sterile. After being a supportive teacher's wife and working with the elderly for many years, Mary, believing that God wants her and Tom to have children, kidnaps a baby from a supermarket. The baby is quickly returned, but Mary no longer has any contact with reality and is admitted to a mental institution.

Dick Crick, Tom's older and retarded half brother. He is the offspring of Tom's mother, Helen Atkinson, from an incestuous relationship with her father, Ernest. Undeveloped both emotionally and intellectually, Dick is like his motorcycle, more machine than human. In the early 1940's, when in his late teens, he becomes attracted to Mary Metcalf and she to him. In his jealousy, he kills sixteen-year-old Freddie Parr with an ale bottle, part of the legacy left to him by his true father.

Fearing arrest, he commits suicide by drowning himself in the Fens' River Ouse.

Henry Crick, Tom's biological father but not Dick's. He is the keeper of a lock on the Fens' River Leem. The Cricks are an old Fenland family, but none of the members are either wealthy or prominent. Injured physically and mentally in World War I, Henry is nursed back to health by Helen Atkinson. Aware of the Atkinson legacy, Henry attempts to spare Dick from the truth, but ultimately without success.

Helen Atkinson, Henry's wife and the mother of Tom and Dick. She is very beautiful, and her father turns to her for emotional and sexual consolation in his own disappointments. She dies when her sons are both young, but she passes on her father's legacy to their son Dick—a trunk filled with Ernest Atkinson's writings and bottles of strong ale.

Ernest Atkinson, Tom's grandfather and Dick's father and grandfather. The Atkinsons, a prominent Fenland family since the eighteenth century, founded their wealth and power on brewing ale. Emotionally affected by his family's history and society's disasters, Ernest fathers a child by his daughter, a child whom he hopes will save the world. That child becomes the retarded Dick. After Helen's marriage to Henry Crick, which Ernest reluctantly accepts, he commits suicide.

Lewis Scott, the headmaster at Tom Crick's Greenwich school. Disturbed that Tom is not following the required curriculum of the French Revolution and fearing the negative publicity created by Mary Crick's kidnapping incident, Scott wants Tom Crick to retire. A scientist by training, Scott sees no value in studying the past; to him, the future is everything, and history has no connection to it.

Price, a sixteen-year-old student in Tom's history class.

Price also doubts the value of history, but, unlike Scott, Price sees no future. The world is threatened with imminent destruction, and Price fears that history cannot influence that end. The bright and challenging Price becomes the focus of Tom's storytelling.

Thomas Atkinson, a brewer and the Fen Country's leading citizen during the first half of the nineteenth century. The Atkinson family reaches its apogee of fame and influence with the career of Thomas Atkinson. At that moment Thomas, in a fit of jealousy, strikes and permanently injures Sarah, his wife.

Sarah Atkinson, Thomas' young and beautiful wife. After being injured by her husband while in her thirties, she never recovers her mental health, although she lives for many years. Her demented presence hangs over the Atkinson family and the town for decades, even after her death.

Frederick Parr, a sixteen-year-old friend of Tom, Mary, and Dick. Something of a braggart, Freddie is killed in 1943 by a jealous Dick after Mary, to spare Tom, intimates to Dick that it was Freddie who made her pregnant.

— *Eugene S. Larson*

THE WATERS OF KRONOS

Author: Conrad Richter (1890-1968)
First published: 1960
Genre: Novel

Locale: Unionville, Pennsylvania
Time: The 1960's, with journeys into the past
Plot: Allegory

John Donner, a prolific author who has written a book about his hometown of Unionville, which is now under the water of Lake Kronos. Donner returns to visit the relocated graveyards holding the bodies of his family: the Donners, the Morgans, and the Scarletts. Perhaps he is secretly trying to find a resting place for himself, perhaps he is trying to go home again, and perhaps he is trying to penetrate the murky waters of memory and find his past.

Elijah S. Morgan, Donner's grandfather, a pastor, a Union supporter, and the father of Aunt Jessie and John's father, Harry.

Great-Grandfather Scarlett, who had helped to name Unionville. This captain in the War of 1812 was a squire, a legislator, and an "oil inspector." He has a 20-foot marble monument and a plot numbered 732.

Great Aunt Teresa, a teacher who has celebrated both Grandfather Morgan and Great-Grandfather Scarlett in poems, many of which were printed in *The Unionville Herald* and the *Lutheran Messenger*. She is in her last years when John returns to Unionville. John remembers how she had fled her home whenever she could. She invites John inside the home, whereas his Aunt Jessie did not.

The Reverend Harry A. Donner, John's father, the only father in town who kisses his boys and loves to sing. John, now an old man, finds his thirty-five-year-old father just after Harry has given up his store and just before he studies for the ministry.

Valerie M. Donner, John's mother. John searches for her in Unionville but does not find her before the guard comes for him.

The horse and driver, who are carrying a cargo of coal from beneath the waters and heading toward Unionville. The mysterious driver allows John to accompany him on his trip.

Aunt Jessie Morgan Ryon, John's lame aunt, who does not recognize him when he returns as an old man to the long-submerged Unionville. She was once a pianist and a singer.

Uncle Dick Ryon, Aunt Jessie's Irish husband who, when he worked, was a railroad conductor.

Palmyra Morgan, the wife of Elijah Morgan and the daughter of Postmaster Williams.

Griff Flail's wife and four children, whom John warns to leave the house before they are killed by Griff.

Joe Heisler, the barber who helps John to look presentable.

Mike, the horse at the stable. Mike is the only character who recognizes John.

Morris Strike, the groomer who curries Mike. He makes the statement that people keep looking for others who cannot come around to them; this message relates well to John.

Mrs. Bonawitz, who takes John into her home when he collapses.

Johnny, the boy whom John recognizes as himself as a child. John realizes that the fear that Johnny faces actually is a sense of dread of the other, older self to come.

Guard, who comes for John at the end of the book.

— *Anita P. Davis*

WATERSHIP DOWN

Author: Richard Adams (1920-   )
First published: 1972
Genre: Novel

Locale: The countryside of southern England
Time: The 1970's
Plot: Fantasy

Hazel, one of the rabbits forced to leave Cowslip Warren when it is destroyed by encroaching civilization. He is a young buck rabbit who eventually matures into a wise leader of his warren at Watership Down. Hazel undertakes to guide the rabbits across country to safety; in the course of their travels, he outwits humans, other beasts, natural disasters, and the evil dictator of Efrafa Warren, General Woundwort. Hazel's character is similar to those of such wily tricksters of myth and

folktale as Brer Rabbit, Coyote, Odysseus, and Robin Hood. Eventually, Hazel establishes another warren on the Belt, made up of rabbits from Watership Down and Woundwort's Efrafa Warren.

Fiver, the runt brother in Hazel's litter. Although he is physically weaker than the others, Fiver can see the future, often clouded in myth, allegory, and allusion. Fiver frequently falls into a troubled fit during which he dreams what will befall his rabbit band; these dreams presage encounters with enemies such as General Woundwort and farmers.

Bigwig, another Cowslip Warren rabbit who travels with Hazel to Watership Down. He is notable primarily for his physical strength, bravery, and willingness to defend his friends, Hazel in particular. Bigwig is instrumental in getting the rabbits of the Mark under General Woundwort's control to cooperate in Hazel's plan to liberate does for his warren at Watership Down. He also saves Hazel from the cat while they are at Nuthanger Farm trying to liberate the domesticated rabbits. It is Bigwig who deals the defeating blow to General Woundwort.

Kehaar, the seagull who, after being helped by Hazel's rabbit band shortly after their arrival at Watership Down, acts as their scout, looking for evidence of trouble, predators, and other rabbits. He periodically departs to go to the ocean but always returns to lend assistance to his friends. His odd accent adds comic relief to the story.

General Woundwort, the dictator rabbit of Efrafa Warren. This rabbit runs his warren like a military garrison. All that occurs there is unnatural behavior for rabbits. The rabbits are not allowed to interact with one another, to feed when they normally would, or to breed and frolic. Woundwort maintains rigid control through a hierarchical system of officers and spies. Hazel and his rabbits fight Woundwort to liberate females for their warren. Woundwort is the personification of all that is unnatural in animal behavior. After Bigwig deals Woundwort a defeat, the rabbit disappears into the underbrush; he remains as a figure in the rabbits' mythology.

Prince El-ahrairah, the mythical founder and protector of the race of rabbits. His actions are recounted in tales that are interwoven throughout the story of Hazel and his band. Prince El-ahrairah is the emblem of all that is quintessentially rabbit: wiliness, cunning, playfulness, and a happy-go-lucky approach to life. The stories told about him by the rabbits mirror the predicaments and perils that Hazel's group faces as it struggles to make its way to Watership Down and establish a new warren there. These rabbit stories are the myths and legends that provide explanations for who they are, how rabbits came to be, and what their relationship is to other races (species) in their universe. Although El-ahrairah gradually takes on the character of the Supreme Being of the rabbit world, the stories that the rabbits tell about him reflect the current status of Hazel's group: If they are in danger, the story is serious; if they are secure, the tale is amusing and light-hearted.

The Black Rabbit of Inlé, a rabbit spirit who counsels El-ahrairah about the white blindness plague when he is in need of help.

Strawberry, a young rabbit who travels with Hazel's group and who eventually becomes an adviser in the Watership Down warren.

Laurel, one of the domesticated black angora rabbits at Nuthanger Farm.

Boxwood, a domesticated black-and-white Himalayan rabbit at Nuthanger Farm and the mate of the female Haystack, also a Himalayan. Hazel and his rabbits rescue these rabbits from their domestic captivity.

Clover, a domesticated black angora rabbit liberated from Nuthanger Farm by Hazel's band.

— *Melissa E. Barth*

WATT

Author: Samuel Beckett (1906-1989)
First published: 1953
Genre: Novel

Locale: Ireland's countryside
Time: Probably between the two world wars
Plot: Absurdist

Watt ("Christian name forgotten"), a servant in the Irish country house of Mr. Knott and subsequently an inmate of a mental institution. He is a "big bony shabby seedy knockkneed" man with a big red nose, rotten teeth, and red hair streaked with gray. The more conspicuous parts of his wardrobe include a hat found by his grandfather at the races, a coat bought by his father from a widow, a brown shoe found at the seashore, and a brown boot bought from a one-legged man with borrowed money. He walks with a swinging gait without bending his knees, his smile seems artificially composed, and he drinks only milk. Before coming to Mr. Knott's, he had no fixed address, though he is described as probably a university man and as an experienced traveler. He mechanically obeyed whatever mysterious message summoned him to Mr. Knott's house and obeys when his successor arrives and signals his departure. He is mostly uncommunicative and inarticulate, but he has had male friends and has even enjoyed some romances, at least one of them consummated. It is Watt's mental life that takes up the greater part of the book. He seeks "semantic succour" in naming accurately the objects around him, though even as commonplace an object as a pot gives him trouble. He seeks within his own mind explanations for the events that take place around him; he apparently solves the mysteries surrounding Mr. Knott's meals but fails to account for the visit of two piano tuners. Even when Watt settles on a hypothesis that satisfies him, he must first consider all the alternatives, however implausible, and later communicate them to Sam.

Mr. Knott, the owner of a country house that has been in his family for generations. His appearance varies daily, being at one time "small fat pale and fair" and at another "tall fat pale and dark," with endless variations. His wardrobe also constantly changes. He is constantly moving about his room and constantly moving its furniture. Otherwise, his life is mechanically repetitive. He always has two live-in servants, one in charge of the ground floor and his meals, one in charge of the first floor and personal services. The meals are always the same. Once a week, Watt cooks a mixture of foods, drinks, and medicines, which is served cold to Mr. Knott for lunch and dinner, the leftovers (if any) being consumed by a famished dog. Mr. Knott sometimes walks in the garden. He apparently never communicates, though he makes mysterious noises and sings songs in an unknown tongue.

Sam, Watt's occasional companion in the mental institution. He is able to report the details of Watt's life with Mr. Knott, even though he sees Watt only when the weather is right for both of them, even though they converse while marching

(Sam forward and Watt backward) between two barbed-wire fences, and even though Watt varies his delivery, sometimes inverting the order of words in the sentence, sometimes inverting the order of the letters in the word, and invoking other variations as well.

Arsene, a servant whom Watt displaces, a "little fat shabby seedy juicy or oily bandylegged man" who gives Watt a pessimistic account of the Knott establishment.

Erskine, a fellow servant, for whose mysterious dashes up and downstairs, and for whose mysterious responses to a bell in the night, Watt can find no satisfactory explanation.

Mrs. Gorman, Mr. Knott's fishwoman, with whom Watt necks every Thursday.

Mr. Graves, the unhappily married gardener, from whom Watt learns something of the Knott history.

Lynch, the name of an unhealthy and incestuous family paid by Mr. Knott to maintain a succession of famished dogs to consume his leftovers. Art and Con are the twin dwarfs who bring the dog to Mr. Knott's house each evening.

— *John C. Sherwood*

THE WAVE

Author: Evelyn Scott (Elsie Dunn, 1893-1963)
First published: 1929
Genre: Novel

Locale: The United States, Portugal, and Germany
Time: April 11, 1861-May 24, 1865
Plot: Historical

Jefferson Davis, the president of the Confederate States of America, a man small enough in stature to belie the authority invested in him and capable of seeing more with his one good eye than most men see with both. Very image-conscious, he is ashamed of his desire to flee once it becomes apparent that the Confederacy is doomed, and his fugitive status is difficult for his vanity to endure. He eventually is found secreted in a farmhouse near Irwinsville, Georgia, and at the end of the novel awaits trial for treason against the United States of America.

Abraham Lincoln, the president of the United States of America. A tall, thin man with much presence, Lincoln is too proud to allow himself to show any humility in public. His determination and belief in predestination have brought him to the presidency, and they carry him through the difficult stance he has taken in his actions against the Confederate States of America. Lincoln is assassinated at Ford's Theatre by John Wilkes Booth, who is captured while attempting to escape.

Robert E. Lee, a Confederate general. General Lee is a calmly tenacious man with a kindly eye and manner. Beloved by officers and enlisted men alike, he struggles with depressions and a love of privacy difficult for a leader to display with dignity. He is deeply religious and earns much of his reputation for kindliness and dignity through his efforts to convince enlisted men of the importance of faith. Lee corresponds with General Ulysses S. Grant during the fighting outside Richmond, and through this correspondence he obtains General Grant's respect. Lee is tricked into surrendering his Confederate Armies of Virginia to Grant after General Philip Henry Sheridan strategically contrives to make the numbers of the Union troops seem far larger than they are.

Ulysses S. Grant, a Union general, commander of the Army of the Potomac, a stocky, full-bearded man with pale eyes. Although he has oratorical abilities, he is laconic in personal conversation. His popularity is a continual surprise to him, for he believes himself to be arrogant and shy. He uses his oratorical abilities to recruit soldiers to the Union cause and later leads these same soldiers against Lee to the eventual surrender of Lee. Grant conducts himself superciliously during the surrender negotiations and formalities, and the whole affair of Lee's surrender leaves him determined never to spend as much energy on the man or the cause again.

Edwin George, a tobacco merchant and a Union spy from Tennessee. A handsome but coarse man with curly, graying hair, he believes himself to be wicked and accordingly distrusts and suspects fellow humans. He is undertaking an attempt to glean some information from a former lover and sister-in-law, Eugenia Gilbert. He is unaware that she has accepted a commission to become an abolitionist informer and hopes to extract similar information from him. Their meeting is warm with old attraction and rife with the inner conflict of their interests.

Eugenia Gilbert, an abolitionist spy, an older woman who appears more tired and haggard than her age should merit. She has become hypocritical and cares only for the money to be earned by spying. Her exploitation of her former lover Edwin George probably will be successful, for she unbalances him at their first meeting and secures a promise for a private meeting the following day.

Dickie Ross, a Confederate volunteer. Dickie is young, aflame with enthusiasm, and tired of his clerking position. He is in a rowboat in Charleston Harbor when the first shot is fired on Fort Sumter and responds with youthful, ignorant enthusiasm.

Percy, an attorney's scribe. Percy is unambitious, tedious, methodical, and fastidious about his health and manners. He is killed in a mob that is protesting the marching of Lincoln's troops through Baltimore.

Henry Clay, a little boy affected by the political pull between his Aunt Amanda's Confederate sympathies and his mother's Union sympathies. Henry is anemic, churlish, and frightened by the conflict between the women. He is unable to reconcile his love for both of them as they struggle to win his affections.

Franklin Rutherford and

Charlie, two Union soldiers. Franklin and Charlie are uneducated poor whites, basically well-meaning and patriotic. They become demoralized and embittered by the terrors of battle.

Mrs. Witherspoon, a member of the Confederate Ladies Aid Society. She is proud and falsely patriotic, reveling in the appearance of the mother worried about her soldier son's welfare. She experiences an awakening and her first real suffering when she receives news that her son George has been killed. Her false concern shows itself in indignity at not being the first to be told, then real grief overcomes her and she swoons.

Josie Kendricks, George Witherspoon's fiancée, a member of the same Confederate Ladies Aid Society as Mrs. Witherspoon. Josie is an emotional yet contained young patriot. She is the first to receive the news that George Witherspoon has been killed.

James Witherspoon, Mrs. Witherspoon's youngest son and the late George Witherspoon's brother. Sensitive and unpatriotic, he is driven insane by the knowledge of his brother's death. He wishes he could have died instead, and he believes George has died a needless, worthless death.

Mose Elder and

Cat Foot Dawsey, two black "dirt-eaters" from Tennessee who shoot two men. They are patriotic and have great feelings of guilt over their failure to enlist. They let these guilt feelings convince them that their patriotic duty is to shoot the soldiers, who might be deserters. They shoot the two men without ever making their presence known.

Albert, a Union soldier. Albert is dutifully patriotic and servile, but he deserts when he is refused a leave of absence. He has received news that his sweetheart, Charlotte, can wait no longer for him, and in his desperation to get to her he becomes a deserter and the murderer of an innocent black man.

Melinda and

Thomas, a couple aboard the *Atlantide*, a blockade runner boat. Melinda and Thomas are wealthy idlers, concerned only with their own comfort; they regard the war as a great inconvenience. They are bound for the northeast coast, where Thomas plans halfheartedly to offer his services as a surgeon to the Confederate cause. They are in continual danger from the blockade searchers, and this danger lends them the only significance their lives contain.

Lee Shuck, a Union soldier. Lee is an average soldier, having enlisted out of a middle-class sense of duty. He is awaiting execution by his own commanders, however, for falling asleep while on sentinel duty, and he is bewildered and frustrated that his laxness is so seriously interpreted.

Samuel Wharton and

Sadie Wharton, a Union couple in conflict about which side to support financially. They are self-righteous and vain about their ability to make financial contributions to any cause. Their son fought for the Confederacy, but Samuel wants to support the more official Union. Mrs. Wharton wants to support the Confederacy in memory of their son, and their arguments and ensuing alienations are terrible.

Gunner Renfield, a sailor aboard the *Itasca* during the assault near Fort Jackson. Gunner is an introspective and delicate individual. He is overcome by the horror of the battles and fails to save his shipmate and friend, Harry Dewey, when the *Itasca* is bombed and sinks.

Harry Dewey, another sailor aboard the *Itasca* during the assault near Fort Jackson. Harry is idealistically dependent on the goodwill of his buddies and sentimentalizes their affections for him. When he is tossed overboard during the bombing of the *Itasca*, he relies on his friend Gunner Renfield and drowns when Gunner is too horrified to save him.

Parker, a Union soldier in New Orleans. Parker is an aggressive, alcoholic, and burly man unable to reconcile his dislike of his station with his sense of duty. He forces some Creole shopkeepers to sell him gin against their will, knowing that the sale of liquor to soldiers is against the law of the federal government.

Hallie and

her lover, two lovers who rendezvous during the young man's desertion. Hallie, a pretty and comely girl of about eighteen years, is jaded and embittered by the war situation. Although she physically enjoys meeting her lover, she believes that the war has cheapened romance and forced her to accept a less romantic sort of involvement and commitment, a clandestine rendezvous instead of a marriage proposal.

Eloise Ducros, a young French girl. Eloise is cunning and poor, with barely attractive features hardened into ugliness by poverty. She has been jilted by her French lover and is forced, with Madame Ducros, her housemate, to take in Union boarders to support herself. Her sympathies are Confederate, and she is filled with self-loathing at the position to which she has sunk. She is particularly repulsed by Lieutenant Fisk, who pays her romantic attentions and whom she cannot afford to anger.

Lieutenant Fisk, a Union soldier who is vain, obese, and self-inflated. He is boarding in the house of Confederate sympathizers Madame Ducros and Eloise Ducros. Fisk is engaged in clandestine relations with Eloise, who despises him but receives his attentions because she and Madame Ducros need the money that Fisk gives to them.

Carrie, a rebel pickpocket. Carrie is twenty-nine years old, still attractive but becoming sullen and desperate, having come down in social station because of the war. Carrie kills a Yankee soldier in a fit of passionate hatred while trying to rob him.

Fanny May, a young Confederate mother. Fanny is dreamy, pale, and distant, living in a world apart since the death of her baby. The baby cost Fanny her health and most of her faculties. Despite Fanny's weak condition and the doctor's orders to stay in bed, Fanny and some friends drive out to the hills of Richmond to see the battle. They are shocked when they are shelled, and Fanny becomes even weaker.

Saunders, a plantation owner and a member of Morgan's cavalry. A short and stolid but agile man, Saunders is determined to hijack a train bearing Union soldiers and supplies to Hampton Junction. He succeeds in stopping the train so that the Confederates can attack it and pilfer the supplies.

Smith, a wounded soldier of unknown loyalties. Smith is thin, slow-witted, and easily bewildered. He has been mortally wounded and dies slowly while crawling through a battlefield strewn with bodies from both armies.

Frazer, a Confederate deserter. Frazer is young, virile, and faithless. He is ashamed of his faithlessness as a pretense only; given the chance to do so undetected, he deserts when he realizes that the Confederates are going to be defeated.

Miss Amanda and

Maude May, two Confederate women. The sisters are proud and disdainful, thin, shrewish, and peaked looking. They have difficulty reconciling their pride with their situation, which requires them to beg for food and sell their belongings for a pittance. As a result, they spend most of their time deploring their situation and mournfully hoping the war will end.

— *Ann L. Postlethweight*

WAVERLEY: Or, 'Tis Sixty Years Since

Author: Sir Walter Scott (1771-1832)
First published: 1814
Genre: Novel

Locale: England and Scotland
Time: 1745
Plot: Historical

Edward Waverley, a young British officer who holds his commission in the army of George II of England during the bloody days in 1745 when Charles Edward, the Pretender, is trying to gain the British throne. Through a set of circumstances, he learns of the young Pretender's cause at first hand; he is Charles's guest, lives for a time with some of his supporters, and swears allegiance to him. Although charged with treason and stripped of his commission, he finally regains favor with the king, inherits his father's fortune, and marries the woman of his choice.

Fergus Mac Ivor Vich Ian Vohr, a famous clan chieftain who supports Prince Charles's bid for the throne. He is bluff and hearty, as well as formal and courtly, a good politician. When the rebellion fails, he is executed for his crimes against the crown, and the power of the Highland clans is broken.

Prince Charles Edward Stuart, the Pretender, who, having arrived in Scotland from his exile in France, rallies Highlanders to his cause. He reflects his French court training in the polished, civil manner he shows all those about him. He is ruined when his forces are scattered at the Battle of Culloden.

Sir Cosmo Comyne Bradwardine, a Scottish nobleman and a Jacobite who introduces Edward to the forces marshaled under Prince Charles. Rose Bradwardine, the baron's daughter, finally marries Edward.

Evan Dhu Maccombich, a Highlander in the service of Fergus Mac Ivor. He guides Edward through the Jacobite

camp and introduces him to the famous Scottish chief. Maccombich is executed when the revolt fails.

Donald Bean Lean, a Highland bandit faithful to Mac Ivor and the Pretender. He rescues Edward from his English captors when the young officer is being taken to Stirling Castle to stand trial for treason.

Flora Mac Ivor, Fergus' sister, who is attracted to Edward but whose ardor for him cools. When the revolt fails, she enters a Catholic convent in France.

Rose Bradwardine, Edward's beloved and Sir Cosmo Comyne Bradwardine's daughter. Like her father, she is an ardent Jacobite. After the defeat at Culloden, she marries Edward.

Richard Waverley, Edward's father, who, for political advantage, swears loyalty to King George II. Unfortunate political maneuvers ruin him. When he dies, Edward inherits the family wealth.

Sir Everard Waverley, a Jacobite who is Edward's uncle and Richard Waverley's brother. It is at Waverley-Honour, the family's ancestral home, that Edward receives much of his education in the political and social issues of the day.

Colonel Gardiner, Edward's military superior while the young man holds a commission in George II's dragoons.

Davie Gellatley, Baron Bradwardine's servant, a good storyteller who helps fire Edward's interest in the Jacobite cause.

Alice, Donald Bean Lean's daughter, who is in love with Evan Dhu Maccombich.

THE WAVES

Author: Virginia Woolf (1882-1941)
First published: 1931
Genre: Novel

Locale: England
Time: Between the two world wars
Plot: Psychological realism

Percival, a childhood friend of the six central characters, who respect, admire, and love him. He is the symbol of the ordinary man, a conventional figure. Rather awkward and bumbling but pleasant and accepted everywhere, Percival forms the light around whom the six-sided flower revolves, as Bernard put it. In love with the natural woman, Susan, he is beloved by Neville, the scholar and brilliant poet. A sportsman, a hale fellow, a poor scholar, and finally a soldier who dies in India, Percival represents a kind of norm in personality and conduct.

Bernard, the phrase maker, the chronicler of the group of childhood friends as they grope toward death, the great adversary of all human life, he thinks. Through Bernard, the rest of the characters see life, because in his attempt to grasp reality, he is able to become whomever he meets or talks with. Although he sees himself as a failure, he does catch essences and makes of these his unfinished stories, tales that Percival once saw through and would not let him finish. Deeply devoted to his best friend, Neville, he nevertheless is all things to all the

characters. A husband, father, provider, and friend, he becomes, finally, a seer who tries to sum up the meaning of experiences all have shared.

Neville, a poet, scrupulous artist, lover of a single man, and sensitive genius who keeps his life carefully wrapped and labeled. He is gaunt and handsome, gifted with the tongue of all great men and able to mimic them from Catullus to William Shakespeare. He finds it difficult to survive the shock of Percival's death. He turns first to reproductions of the man and measures his time by the conversations with young, handsome men to whom he is a kind of Socrates. Lonely and introspective, he finally finds diversion with frivolous Jinny. He has the ability to speak to them all, even Susan, who sees him as her antithesis.

Susan, the elemental woman, nature-loving and natural, a born mother and an implement of life. Disliking the pine and linoleum smells of school and civilization, she endures education, even travel, so that she may replace her dead mother, administer love to her earthy father, marry a farmer, and raise a family amid the natural, lovely, rural English sights, smells, sounds, and feelings. She has long loved Bernard and has been the object of Percival's love, but none know of these things until later. She resists social ways, dress, and attitudes, even to the point of boorishness, though she carries human feelings—love, jealousy, admiration, and disgust—to their meetings.

Louis, the son of a Brisbane banker, a self-conscious outcast of the society of his friends but the most brilliant and egotistical one of the group. Endowed with self-knowledge, the result of fine breeding from the Hebrews in their Egyptian bondage through the present, Louis hides his endowments and very real gifts out of shame of ridicule. He finally becomes assertive and makes of business a romance, false but substantial. He fears all the others except Rhoda, whom he makes his mistress after these two outsiders are drawn together by their loneliness. All recognize his supremacy in subtle ways, and he is respected for this fierce inner being in spite of the discomfort it causes the group.

Rhoda, the plain, clumsy misfit who tries to imitate the world that despises her. Alone with her meager self, she longs for anonymity and retreats from reality early. Tolerated by Susan and avoided by Jinny, she has a kind of ease with Bernard and a negative attraction for Louis. Not gifted in any way, she denies the role life has created for her and commits suicide in middle life.

Jinny, the hedonist, the careful cultivator of externals, the one who causes a rustle wherever she goes. Beautiful with physical vitality, which she burns out in a few brief years, Jinny has the superficial drive of appearances as opposed to the elemental in Susan. Assignations are her business; epicureanism is the method, and weariness is the result.

THE WAY OF ALL FLESH

Author: Samuel Butler (1835-1902)
First published: 1903
Genre: Novel

Locale: England
Time: The nineteenth century
Plot: Social realism

Edward Overton, the narrator. Born in the same year as Theobald Pontifex and in the village whence the Pontifexes sprang, he has known the family all his life. He has an intense dislike for Theobald but greatly admires Alethea Pontifex and takes an interest in Theobald's son Ernest. Alethea makes him the trustee of the money she leaves to Ernest, and it is to Overton that Ernest comes after his release from prison. Overton straightens out Ernest's affairs and helps him to reestablish his life. Overton is also the spokesman for the author's ideas.

Ernest Pontifex, the older son of Theobald Pontifex and the hero of the novel. Because of his repressed childhood under the savage domination of his father, Ernest is a tragic failure. He does poorly at school and emerges from Cambridge unable to face life. He is ordained in the Church of England, not from conviction but from lack of preparation for any other career. He is a failure as a clergyman because he has no understanding of people. Through his extreme naïveté, a friend is able to defraud him of his grandfather's legacy; through his ignorance of the world, he makes improper advances to a young woman and is sentenced to six months at hard labor. Upon his release, he meets Ellen, a former maid in his parents' house who has been discharged for immorality. He insists on marrying her because he wants to drop from his position as a gentleman. They set up a secondhand clothes shop. Ellen proves to be a drunkard, and the marriage fails. Ernest is rescued only by the appearance of John, his father's old coachman, who confesses that he is the father of Ellen's child and had married her after her dismissal. Rid of Ellen, Ernest sends their two children to be reared in the country and devotes himself to writing. At the age of twenty-eight, he comes into his aunt's legacy of seventy thousand pounds.

George Pontifex, the father of Theobald and the grandfather of Ernest. He is a wealthy publisher of religious books who browbeats his children. He forces Theobald into the clergy by threatening to disinherit him.

John Pontifex, his older son and successor in business.

Theobald Pontifex, his younger son, the father of Ernest. Forced into the clergy by his father, he obtains the living of Battersby. Thus, he can marry Christina Allaby, by whom he has three children. He is savagely ill-tempered with them as the result of his own domination by his father. His ill-treatment of Ernest almost ruins the latter's life.

Christina Pontifex, Theobald's wife, one of five marriageable daughters of a clergyman. At their father's suggestion, they play cards to see who shall catch Theobald, and Christina wins. She is a submissive wife, given to piety and romantic daydreaming, with no understanding of her children.

Alethea Pontifex, Theobald's sister. She is more broadminded and humane than he and, being independently wealthy, can help Ernest, whom she makes her heir without his knowledge.

Joey Pontifex, Ernest's younger brother, a clergyman.

Charlotte Pontifex, Ernest's unattractive sister.

Ellen, a pretty maid in the Pontifex home. She is dismissed for immorality and is given money by Ernest. Years later, he meets her by accident and marries her. She is a confirmed drunkard, and the marriage fails. He is able to get rid of her when he discovers that she was already married when she married him.

John, the Pontifex coachman, who defends Ernest against Theobald. He is the father of Ellen's first child.

Dr. Skinner, the tyrannical headmaster of Roughborough School, where Ernest Pontifex was a pupil.

Pryer, a London curate and false friend. He absconds with the twenty-five hundred pounds that Ernest Pontifex had inherited from his grandfather and that had been entrusted to him for investment.

THE WAY OF THE WORLD

Author: William Congreve (1670-1729)
First published: 1700
Genre: Drama

Locale: London, England
Time: The seventeenth century
Plot: Comedy of manners

Mirabell, a man of fashion, intelligent and authentically in love with Mrs. Millamant. He enjoys the favors, either overt or covert, of most of the women in the play, who, either through unrequited love of him or mutual affection, try to affect the course of his fortune. He is presented as a man of genuine parts, not so superficial as to render him without a sense of honor or the genuine ability to experience love, but at the same time a clever schemer. His love for Mrs. Millamant and his hope of legitimate income are the motivating factors in his intrigues. Mirabell is somewhat more in love with Mrs. Millamant than she with him. Although his stake in the marriage is higher than hers, he bears up well under the handicap, never attempting to outmaneuver Mrs. Millamant by feigning indifference. Instead, he rather admirably presses his proposal with candor and plain dealing as to his love. Thus, he keeps a manly station without lowering himself to beg or unduly flatter her, and he impresses her with his devotion. He emerges from the action as a Restoration gentleman who possesses wit, charm, and masculinity and who does not deal in simper, pose, or guile. Although he is a master schemer on occasion, in him the vestiges of sense, honor, and right have not become translated into chicanery, venery, or deception.

Mrs. Millamant, Lady Wishfort's niece, loved by Mirabell and perhaps the most fascinating member of the cast. Mrs. Millamant contains within her personality an attractive haughtiness, and she enjoys making Mirabell's suit appear an even more one-sided affair than it is. She has a frankness that sometimes uncouples her from her train of followers and a glitter that—especially in the famous comic-love scene between herself and Mirabell—approaches radiant wit. For all her practiced arts of conversation and her determination to keep love a game, Mrs. Millamant is levelheaded, and Mirabell's commendable qualities will meet good use in such a wife. Beneath her protests and shams, she has carefully marked a line to follow. She wisely recognizes Mirabell as the man to keep her on it.

Lady Wishfort, a sex-starved old woman. Past the natural flows of passion in her sex, she falls victim to the insatiable demands of false passion. Anxiously casting about for reassurance, she is easy prey for any man who can stomach the odious game of pursuing her. She is more than straight comedy because she carries, though chillingly, a kind of pathos. Her wrath against Mirabell, brought about because he pretended love to her, is averted in the end, and she emerges a wiser woman.

Mrs. Marwood, the consort of Fainall. She is jealous of Mirabell's love for Mrs. Millamant, and her main interest in foiling Mirabell's plans is formulated in bitterness. She wishes Fainall, the lover toward whom she is passive at best and hostile at worst, to gain control not only of his wife's fortune but of Lady Wishfort's as well in order to destroy Mirabell's hopes. In this endeavor, she concocts a plan to reveal the "immoral" nature of Mrs. Fainall, Lady Wishfort's daughter, so that Fainall will have a strong bargaining position from which to demand control of the money. Her deceptions and personal immorality are exposed, and she is defeated by her own envy and malice.

Fainall, an unscrupulous, avaricious man who possesses no morals above or beyond those necessary to his own satisfaction, but whose charm and manner allow him to deceive others. No dupe, he is allied with Mrs. Marwood in an attempt to acquire Lady Wishfort's fortune. While carrying on his affair with Mrs. Marwood, he hypocritically plants and reveals indiscretions on the part of his wife. He represents better than any character in the play the attitude toward societal relationships that appears so perverse outside of the Restoration era—distaste for mate, cultivated love, interest in self best served by interest in the affairs of others, and tedious attention to a reputation that is all the more precious for being morally unstable.

Mrs. Fainall, Fainall's wife, Lady Wishfort's daughter, and at one time Mirabell's mistress. In the end, because of Mirabell's help, she gains the upper hand over her husband.

Foible, Lady Wishfort's resourceful, energetic servant, allied with Mirabell.

Witwoud, an idle, foppish follower of Mrs. Millamant. He represents the effeminate character of the affected "gentlemen" of the period.

Petulant, a man of fashion, much like Witwoud.

Sir Wilful Witwoud, the half brother of Witwoud, quite different from Witwoud because of his blunt, raucous, and honest nature.

Waitwell, Mirabell's serving-man, married to Foible. Mirabell uses him in his plot against Lady Wishfort.

Mincing, Mrs. Millamant's maid.

THE WAY WE LIVE NOW

Author: Anthony Trollope (1815-1882)
First published: 1875
Genre: Novel

Locale: London and Suffolk, England
Time: February-August, 1873
Plot: Social realism

Lady Carbury, an aspiring writer trying to arrange favorable reviews for her book *Criminal Queens*. Since the death of her abusive husband, she has sought literary fame and friends for herself, but she also anguishes over the wasted life of her son Felix, the one human being to whom she is devoted. She also is irritated by her daughter Hetta's insistence on making her own marriage choice. Lady Carbury finally has to accept Felix's failure and Hetta's romantic marriage to Paul Montague, as well as her own inadequacies as an author, but she finds happiness in a second marriage to Mr. Broune, an editor.

Sir Felix Carbury, a dissolute young gentleman who enjoys a run of luck at gambling but reluctantly acquiesces to his mother's urging that he pursue marriage with Marie Melmotte. With little effort, he gets Marie to fall in love with him, but he is able neither to impress Marie's father into acceptance of their engagement nor to follow through on Marie's plan that they elope. His luck at cards changes, and he loses so badly that his friends will no longer play with him. He is beaten by the fiancé of a working-class girl he tries to seduce, and he is forced to leave England and live quietly in Germany.

Hetta Carbury, Lady Carbury's daughter, who is wooed by Roger Carbury. Although she increasingly recognizes and admires his wisdom and probity and thinks she ought to be able to love him, she knows she prefers Paul Montague. Although their engagement is threatened when she learns about Paul's relationship with Mrs. Hurtle, she forgives him and they marry.

Roger Carbury, a country gentleman who wants to marry his cousin Hetta but is unable to persuade her to accept him. Although Roger believes that Paul Montague's relationship with Hetta is a betrayal of their friendship, he works to prevent Paul from a renewed entanglement with Mrs. Hurtle, whom Roger regards as a completely unsuitable match for an English gentleman. He finally becomes reconciled to Paul's marriage to Hetta, and he promises to make their son his heir.

Paul Montague, Roger's friend and his rival for Hetta's love. Paul had met and become engaged to Mrs. Hurtle during a trip from America, where he had worked for a while, back to England. Roger had persuaded him that Mrs. Hurtle's reputedly wild past would make her an unsuitable wife, and Paul had ended the engagement. When Mrs. Hurtle appears again in London hoping to resume their relationship, Paul finds it impossible to stay away from her, even though he believes she is a dangerous woman, capable of violence, and he knows he loves Hetta Carbury. He manages to extricate himself both from his relationship with Mrs. Hurtle and from his involvement with Augustus Melmotte's America-to-Mexico railroad scheme.

Winifred Hurtle, a beautiful American who had become engaged to Paul Montague and who believes her only hope for happiness is to renew their engagement. An independent, spirited woman, she has survived marriage to an abusive former husband and an episode in Oregon in which she found herself forced to shoot a man. Although she dreams of a safer life in England, she also scorns the rigid English code of propriety and regard for family origins that make Roger Carbury oppose Montague's relationship with her.

Augustus Melmotte, an unscrupulous financier who is the talk of upper-class London for what people believe to be his fabulous success at making money. He knows his continued success depends on his ability to maintain this belief in his financial wizardry. Although English aristocrats are repelled by his uncouth arrogance, their need for money to support their own expensive modes of life makes them put their repulsion aside and vie for invitations to his parties. Melmotte aims to move more permanently into upper-class society by entering Parliament and marrying his daughter Marie to an aristocrat, but his ambition makes him take too many risks. When he is discovered to have forged signatures on several documents, he kills himself.

Marie Melmotte, Augustus Melmotte's daughter, whom he assumes he can use as an instrument of his ambition by marrying her to an English lord. Marie's ignorant naïveté at first makes her passively willing to marry her father's choice, Lord Nidderdale, but when she realizes Nidderdale is interested only in her money, she decides she wants to be valued for more than that. Unfortunately, her own romantic choice, Sir Felix Carbury, also is interested only in her money. When Marie is forced to accept this fact, she despairs of love and again agrees to marry Nidderdale, coming to appreciate his honesty about his feelings as he, in turn, has come to admire her spirit. After Augustus Melmotte's financial collapse and death, Nidderdale withdraws his suit, and Marie decides to go to America with money her father had given her and she had refused to give back to him.

— *Anne Howells*

THE WAY WEST

Author: A. B. Guthrie, Jr. (1901-1991)
First published: 1949
Genre: Novel

Locale: Independence, Missouri, and the overland trail to Oregon
Time: 1845
Plot: Historical realism

Lije Evans, the thirty-five-year-old captain of a wagon train. A strong, large man with an easygoing manner, he goes west because of his strong conviction that Oregon should become part of the United States, not of England, and because he thinks that his son deserves a better chance. Although he does not actively seek the post, he is elected captain. Unlike his predecessor, Tadlock, Evans does not enjoy giving speeches, and he is compelled to make special provisions for the weaker members of the company. He feels like a whole man for the first time when he takes a stand against Tadlock, who wants to hang a thieving Indian. His awe of the wilderness culminates in Oregon, which he views as a fitting place for his grandson to be born.

Rebecca Evans, Lije's wife and the strongest of all the women. She reluctantly leaves her comfortable home in Missouri because she thinks that there are more opportunities for her son and husband in Oregon. Stout, assured, and unafraid, she sees it as her duty to suppress her own fears and disappointments and to help the weak women, such as Judith Fairman and Mrs. Byrd. She is an insightful person who can predict how people will act and feel in certain situations, although she is occasionally baffled by the behavior of her men. Because she wants to maintain harmony in her family, she decides not to tell Lije that Brownie is not the father of Mercy's child.

Brownie Evans, the seventeen-year-old son of Lije and

Rebecca. At the beginning of the trip, he daydreams of performing heroic feats because he fears that he will never be as brave as Dick Summers, his idol. He proves himself when he fights off the Indian dogs that are attacking his dog, Rock. Because he is a boy doing the man's job of taking care of the cattle on the journey, he matures quickly. By the end of the trip, he speaks to his father with the self-confidence of an adult as he tells Lije that he is going to marry Mercy and that he should take the lead wagon across the raging river.

Dick Summers, a mountain man and the pilot of the wagon train. His decision to go west with the company marks the end of his life as a farmer after his wife dies, as well as the beginning of his return to the beaver country that he left eight years earlier. He takes a new pleasure at the awakening memory of beaver streams, squaws, and mountain men that he has known. His vast knowledge of frontier lore is indispensable to the pioneers, most of whom are not nearly as skilled in hunting, locating water, and dealing with the Indians. He is also the confidant of Lije and Brownie Evans, who constantly go to him for advice. Summers' fierce independence makes him unpopular with Tadlock, who rankles at his flagrant breaking of rules, such as the prohibition against drinking alcohol on the journey. Even though Summers pilots the company safely to Oregon, he does not share their enthusiasm for settling and returns to the frontier.

Henry McBee, who is dirty, shiftless, and poor. He sides with whoever is in power at the time. Because of his eagerness to carry out Tadlock's order to kill all the dogs in camp, McBee becomes Lije's enemy. Before leaving for California, McBee kills Lije's dog, Rock, so that he can have the "last laugh."

Mercy McBee, a pretty sixteen-year-old. Unlike her parents, she is kind, gentle, and hardworking. Seduced and impregnated by Curtis Mack, she agrees to marry Brownie, but only after telling him of her condition. She feels unworthy of Brownie and hopes that he has forgiven her.

Judith Fairman, the sickly wife of Charlie Fairman. She works to the limits of her strength. She moves to Oregon in the hope that a change of climate will be good for her sickly son, Tod. Devastated by the loss of Tod, she is sustained by the hope that her new baby will be a replacement.

Tod Fairman, the five-year-old son of Judith and Charlie Fairman. He no sooner recovers from the river fever that has plagued him all of his life than he dies from the bite of a rattlesnake.

Higgins, often called **Hig**, Fairman's hired man. Skinny, toothless, and ugly, Hig looks after Tod and entertains the pioneers with his sharp wit and his fiddle playing, although his ironic comments tend to disrupt the council meetings at times. He is also a deep thinker who feels dwarfed by the vastness of the new land.

Curtis Mack, the frustrated husband of Amanda. He quits business and starts west to get things off his mind, namely his troubled marriage. The anger and disappointment that he feels from his wife's refusal to sleep with him drive him to commit the senseless murder of a Kaw Indian and to seduce the innocent, trusting Mercy. Mack tries to atone for his sin by staying behind with the single men and assisting with the dangerous task of driving cattle across the Dalles River.

Weatherby, an old preacher. He decides to go west because he is convinced that he has been chosen to spread the word of God. He forms an unlikely partnership with the hard-drinking Summers, who provides him with food and shelter. The train comes to depend on the words that he speaks during council meetings, funerals, and weddings. He leaves the train shortly before it reaches Oregon so that he can Christianize the Indians, who, he fears, are in danger of being corrupted by the encroaching white settlers.

Tadlock, the Illinois man who organizes the company. More educated than most of the pioneers, he has the skills of a politician and an organizer and is a firm believer in discipline and method. His egotistical desire to lead the first company to reach Oregon becomes intolerable when he refuses to slow the wagon train for the benefit of the fever-stricken Martin. As a result, he is relieved of his command by the council. He joins a wagon train going to California because he believes that he will be more likely to realize his political ambitions there.

Mr. and Mrs. Byrd, a weak, unfit family beset by misfortune. Mr. Byrd is visibly afraid of fording the raging river that causes his pregnant wife to pitch out of the wagon and to deliver her baby prematurely. Incredibly, Mr. Byrd apologizes when his wagon crashes off the mountain, even though Evans is responsible.

— *Alan Brown*

WE
(My)

Author: Yevgeny Zamyatin (1884-1937)
First published: 1927 (corrupt text); 1952 (complete text)
Genre: Novel

Locale: A city-state known as the One State
Time: About a millennium in the future
Plot: Fantasy

D-503, the narrator and the protagonist, a mathematician and builder of the spaceship *Integral*. At first, D-503 is a faithful follower of the Benefactor, the leader of a futuristic society, the One State. D-503 blindly believes that the One State is a just society, that individual freedom is a burdensome remnant of the distant past, and that the numbers, the inhabitants of the One State, live and work best in a collective state of contentment rather than happiness. He is happy to contribute to the export of the One State's ideas, by way of the *Integral*, to other planets. His metamorphosis begins when he meets, and falls in love with, a female number, I-330, who harbors dangerous ideas of individuality and personal freedom. He even promises to place the spaceship at her disposal in her efforts to topple the government of the One State. D-503 discovers, to his horror, that he has developed a soul (anathema in the materialistic, totally rational society of the One State); the hair growth on his hands is another indication of the suppressed, primitive side of his nature. He changes his mind at the last moment, after discovering that I-330 does not really love him but only wants to use him and the spaceship. D-503 is an ironic caricature of an intellectual and a scientist who unquestioningly serves a totalitarian ruler, believing that the ruler is right in creating a collective frame of mind and in basing everything on a rational basis, excluding all emotions and spiritual values. D-503's wavering and an almost complete conversion, or a betrayal of reason, indicate the vulnerability of such convictions and the indestructibility of "the other half" of the human psyche, even after hundreds of years of brainwashing.

I-330, the woman with whom D-503 falls in love, a leader of the revolution. As the letter in her name hints, I-330 stands for individuality, infinity, and irrationality: individuality in protest against the deadening collectivism; infinity, refuting the finite world of the One State as a result of the final revolution that took place a thousand years ago; and irrationality, signifying the rebellion against the atrophying grip of reason based exclusively on mathematics. I-330 demonstrates that some individuals eventually will pierce the crust of conditioning and reject being nameless numbers. A strikingly beautiful woman, she uses her charms to assist the revolutionaries in their rebellion. Her failure in the end is only a temporary setback; eventual success is ensured: If, after a thousand years of strict controls, a revolution was possible, what is to stop it the next time?

O-90, D-503's girlfriend and registered sexual partner. O-90 is assigned to D-503 after a careful examination of their hormones but is supposed to be shared by others. She falls in love with D-503, against the rules and scientific tests. She displays another forbidden sentiment, jealousy of the love relationship between D-503 and I-330. She is a plump and less appealing woman than I-330 but also is capable of genuine feelings. It is significant that during the rebellion, she escapes to freedom across the border of the One State, carrying with her D-503's unborn child, thus ensuring that in the future the numbers will become individuals again and live in freedom.

R-13, D-503's friend, who shares O-90 with him. He is poet laureate of the One State. Showing a striking physical resemblance to the greatest Russian poet, Alexander Pushkin, R-13 ostensibly serves the One State while secretly supporting the rebellion. His position makes it clear that even the officially sanctioned artists cannot escape the lure of individuality and freedom. He dies together with I-330, but his poetry gives hope that free art can never be totally suppressed.

The Benefactor, the authoritarian leader of the One State. Elected "unanimously" for the fortieth time, he is devoid of a normal human countenance and is seldom seen acting like a human being. He is more of a myth or a symbol, almost an idea. He is the quintessential totalitarian leader, commanding total obedience and loyalty.

S-4711, a member of the Guardians. As his snakelike letter indicates, S-4711 is an omnipresent secret police agent who seems to spy on everyone. In the end, he sides with I-330 and the rebels. That his fate at the end of the rebellion is not clear may be another indication of his elusiveness and insincerity.

U, a supervisor of the building in which D-503 lives. The only character without a number (D-503 omits her number lest he say something unflattering about her), she seems to have the sole duty of keeping an eye on D-503 as the builder of the *Integral*. In the course of her duty, she, too, falls in love with him. At the crucial moment of the rebellion, her sense of duty prevails, and she reports D-503's complicity, ostensibly to save him from punishment.

— Vasa D. Mihailovich

THE WEATHER IN THE STREETS

Author: Rosamond Lehmann (1901-1990)
First published: 1936
Genre: Novel

Locale: London, the British countryside, and Austria
Time: Late 1920's or early 1930's
Plot: Psychological realism

Olivia Curtis, a twenty-seven-year-old woman separated from her husband, Ivor Craig. Olivia leads an impoverished semi-bohemian life in London, where she shares a small house with her flighty cousin Etty Somers and works part-time for a pittance in the studio of a photographer and painter named Anna, one of a circle of artists and writers who form Olivia's present world. Called home by the serious illness of her father, Olivia takes a train to Tulverton, where the older Curtises live. In the dining car, she meets Rollo Spencer, whom she has not seen for ten years; they had met briefly at his sister Marigold's coming-out party and later at her wedding. Olivia is immediately and again attracted to Rollo and senses his fascination with her even though he cannot remember her name. The next day, Olivia is invited to attend a small dinner party at the Spencers', after which Rollo drives her home. The beginnings of what is to be an eight-month affair are evident.

Rollo Spencer, the handsome, self-assured, and prosperous son of Sir John and Lady Spencer, in his thirties. He also is the husband of Nicola Maude, a sickly and nervous woman, almost an invalid. Rollo is loving and generous with Olivia. He buys her flowers and jewelry, but they can never go to places where he might be seen and recognized, so their times together are spent in out-of-the-way pubs and small inns in country towns. A few times, Rollo meets some of Olivia's friends and enjoys them; he has a great capacity for pleasure.

Mrs. Curtis, Olivia's mother. Through Mrs. Curtis' questions and remarks, details of Olivia's life and personality are revealed. The reasons that Olivia cannot share her troubles with her mother and her sister Kate, married and with four children, are clear: The gulf between Olivia and her family is seen to be unbridgeable. Their conventional, kindly, superficial, and domestic outlook is in sharp contrast to Olivia's reserved, independent, and proud nature.

Lady Spencer, Rollo's mother, a woman whom Olivia has always loved and admired because of a sense of congeniality of temperament and values. The older woman has always been fond of Olivia, whom she regards as her daughter Marigold's friend, but this relationship changes when Lady Spencer confronts Olivia, having learned from a very discreet source that Rollo and Olivia were seen together in Austria. Lady Spencer is instrumental in making Olivia perceive that the affair must end, yet the older woman also reveals that she is still fond of

Olivia and concerned about her. The two lovers do meet again, but the thought of Lady Spencer, implacable and stern in her determination that her son's marriage to Nicola be preserved, helps Olivia in her anguished realization that Rollo's ability to play the double game is in direct contrast to her own single-minded and jealous love. Shortly afterward, Rollo is seriously hurt in a car crash, and Lady Spencer shows her kindness to Olivia by calling her to tell her about the accident and later to arrange a short and final visit to Rollo's house, where he is recuperating, the family being away for a few hours.

— *Natalie Harper*

THE WEAVERS
(Die Weber)

Author: Gerhart Hauptmann (1862-1946)
First published: 1892
Genre: Drama

Locale: Germany
Time: The 1840's
Plot: Social criticism

Herr Dreissiger (DRI-sih-gehr), a manufacturer who works his weavers for all he can, paying them as little as he can, though he does not think he is a bad man. When the weavers riot, he tries to stand up to them but is forced to flee with his family.

Herr Pfeifer (PFI-fur), Herr Dreissiger's manager, who judges the weavers' work harshly, so that less money must be paid for it. He sides with his master against the weavers.

Moritz Jaeger (MOH-rihts YAY-gehr), a husky young returned soldier. Appalled at the weavers' misery, he leads them to riot. He terms Herr Dreissiger an oppressive villain.

Becker, an impudent young giant of a man who is one of the weavers. He becomes a leader in the riots. After he is captured, his fellow weavers free him from the hands of the police.

Old Baumert (BOW-mehrt), an elderly weaver who kills his pet dog so that his family can have meat.

Old Hilse (HIHL-zeh), an elderly weaver who believes the weavers are wrong to riot. He stays at his loom, only to be killed by a stray bullet.

Gottlieb Hilse (GOT-leeb), Old Hilse's son. His wife shames him into joining the rioters.

Luise Hilse (lew-EE-zeh), Gottlieb's wife. She braves the bayonets of the soldiers.

Mielchen Hilse (MEEL-khehn), Gottlieb and Luise's small daughter.

Emma Baumert and

Bertha Baumert, Old Baumert's two daughters, who wear themselves out at the looms.

William Ansorge (AHN-zohr-geh), the owner of the house in which the Baumerts live.

Pastor Kittelhaus (KIH-tehl-howz), a minister who has no sympathy for the rioting workers.

Herr Welzel (VEHL-tsehl), the keeper of the inn where the leaders of the weavers meet.

Anna Welzel, Herr Welzel's merry, red-haired daughter.

Weinhold (VIN-hohlt), the tutor in Herr Dreissiger's house. He sympathizes with the weavers.

Wiegand (WEE-gahnt), a joiner and coffin maker.

THE WEB AND THE ROCK

Author: Thomas Wolfe (1900-1938)
First published: 1939
Genre: Novel

Locale: North Carolina, New York, and Europe
Time: 1900-1928
Plot: Impressionistic realism

George Webber, a lonely child reared by a family-proud aunt and uncle in the small city of Libya Hill, North Carolina. His childhood is the bleak existence of a youngster taken up by charity. As a youth, he is an omnivorous, voracious reader who yearns to acquire the power of writing great novels, hoping someday to write about the two-sided world he knows, that of the rich and the poor. After attending college, George moves to New York City, only to find that he is as lonely among the big city's millions of people as he was in a small town. Even a trip to Europe gives him no satisfaction, for he is a silent, brooding, and distrustful man. His salvation, ultimately, is a love affair lasting several years, an experience that brings him out of himself. His mistress helps him lose his childish illusions about fame and greatness. His self-knowledge becomes complete when, during a trip to Europe, he awakens in a hospital after a sordid brawl to recognize that life is knowing one's self completely.

Mrs. Esther Jack, a successful, well-known designer of stage sets in New York City. She meets George Webber aboard ship, falls in love with him, and becomes his mistress and counselor for several years, although she is fifteen or twenty years older than her lover. She takes George to meet many well-known people and helps him to realize that life is more than mere fame. She encourages George to write, and with her help his long-sought novel begins to take shape. She dominates George so much, however, that he is forced to leave her, lest her very goodness and love become his undoing as a writer.

Mr. and Mrs. Joyner, George's uncle and aunt, who rear him after his mother's death. They are proud of their family and try to turn the boy against his father.

Mr. Webber, George's father, who deserts his wife and child to run off with another woman. Despite his father's behavior, George loves and admires the man. Mr. Webber's death brings George a small inheritance that enables him to attend college and to travel to Europe.

THE WEDDING

Author: Mary Helen Ponce (1938-   )
First published: 1989
Genre: Novel

Locale: Taconos, a fictional town in Southern California
Time: The 1950's
Plot: Social realism

Blanca Muñoz (BLAHN-kah muhn-YOHZ), a young Mexican American woman who plans her wedding. She is originally determined to stay away from *pachucos*, tough young Latino men, but when she becomes interested in men, she chooses from the available selection. Enjoying the fights and excitement of Saturday night dances, she admires Cricket's physical prowess and status among the Los Tacones gang. On several fronts, Blanca manages her life well. After several rejections in the job market, she gets a highly regarded job at a poultry farm. She is not afraid to talk back to an Anglo-American woman who disparages Mexican Americans. With her mother as a model, she respects her relatives and compliments her aunt on hand-embroidering special kneeling cushions, which Blanca secretly considers "low-class Mexican." Planning the wedding, Blanca manages her money and even crosses Cricket in making advance arrangements for the orchestra to play the fast dance music she loves. When things go wrong, Blanca adopts a passive optimism: If she pretends everything is all right, maybe no one will notice. She takes this attitude toward her pregnancy, which is never mentioned specifically in the novel.

Samuel Lopez, called **Sammy-the-Cricket** or simply **Cricket**, the barely literate leader of Los Tacones who marries Blanca. Engaging in vandalism in grammar school, Cricket aspires to be meaner than any of his tough, mean brothers. His favorite pastime is kicking and stoning dogs. Sullen and given to tantrums, Cricket cannot handle mainstream society. After failing at several jobs involving manual labor, he keeps a job as a garbage worker by smoking marijuana to get the energy that impresses his boss. After buying a bad used car, Cricket retaliates by throwing a brick through the dealership window. Completely selfish, he uses others to enhance his status. With fights and insults, he keeps the gangs on the edge of conflict. Ignoring Blanca, he refuses any financial responsibility for the wedding. Although Los Tacones respect "the chicks" and pay for the bridesmaid's bouquets, Cricket scorns their values. After collecting money from Los Tacones to pay the dance band, he spends it on tailor-made shirts for himself. After the wedding, he cleans his "boppers" (dark glasses) on Blanca's wedding dress and will not let her lean against him lest she wrinkle his "drapes." At the dance, he resents Blanca's dancing ability. He ends the evening securely in his field of expertise, brutally kicking the leader of the rival Planchados gang and passing out, convinced he is winning.

Father Francis Ignatius Ranger, Taconos' parish priest, whose hypocrisy reveals the irony of his name (Francis, presumably for St. Francis of Assissi, and Ignatius, for the founder of the Jesuit order). Father Ranger feels betrayed at being assigned to Taconos amid needy Mexican Americans. He seeks the cultured life of Los Angeles. His fairly innocent pleasures—attending jazz concerts and enjoying the meetings of the parish's teenage girls—betray his spiritual charge. He hates and is hated by the *pachucos*. After calling the police when a fight occurs, he must live down the label of "stool pigeon." Father Ranger is bright enough to characterize the *pachucos* and to see the connection between the women's minimal lives and the life of marriage and children the church advocates for them. Offering no practical help to Blanca and Cricket, he decides that all he can do is pray and prepare the paperwork for the wedding. Disapproving of their marriage, he nevertheless enjoys his center-stage role in the church's mighty event of the wedding mass.

Lucy Matacochis (mah-tah-KOH-chees), Blanca's maid of honor and bossy best friend. She wins the reader's respect because of her energetic ability to survive. Having led a rough life since the age of fourteen, she works in her Aunt Tottie's bar and looks for a man with a steady job and a fine car. Lucy tries to take over the wedding arrangements while shrugging off responsibilities that divert attention from herself. Ignoring the maid of honor's responsibility to provide the kneeling cushions for the wedding mass, Lucy eagerly helps Blanca dress on the wedding morning because that is a status task. Lucy enjoys her position among the bridesmaids as the authority on makeup, men, and birth control. She anticipates the wedding dance as a place to meet men. Beautified by "falsies" that give her skinny figure a spectacular bustline, she enthusiastically fights at the dance. When Blanca miscarries, Lucy, who sees Cricket's viciousness, tells her to leave him. Realistic and tough, Lucy voices the reader's hope that Blanca will free herself from her stereotyped future.

WEEDS

Author: Edith Summers Kelley (1884-1956)
First published: 1923
Genre: Novel

Locale: Rural Kentucky
Time: c. 1910-c. 1920
Plot: Naturalism

Judith Pippinger Blackford, the daughter of a Kentucky sharecropper who becomes another sharecropper's wife. The story begins when she is a little girl. She is a diamond in the rough, a child who stands out—because of her beauty, vitality, and strength of character—among the ignorant, overworked people who surround her. She displays artistic ability at an early age and obviously could have been successful in that field if she had had any opportunities. Instead, she is condemned like all the other girls to marry a poor farmer, with nothing to look forward to but drudgery and childbearing. When the story ends, she has had three children and one self-induced miscarriage. Her beauty has faded, her body is bent and coarsened by poverty and toil, her rebellious spirit has been broken, and she is resigned to her fate.

Jerry Blackford, Judith's sharecropper husband. This farmer's son is a strong and handsome man who loves and admires Judith, although he cannot fully understand her moods, lacking her intelligence and sensitivity. His main interest, like that of most of the men in the area, is raising tobacco and trying to climb out of poverty. A large part of this naturalistic novel deals with the problems of tobacco growers over a period of good and bad years. The price of tobacco is high when weather conditions have caused a small crop; when there is favorable weather, the big yield drives tobacco prices down. The years of endless toil and disappointment gradually erode the Blackfords' affection for each other. At the end of the novel, the near-fatal illness of their youngest child brings them back together, making them realize that their fate is stamped and sealed. Like Adam and Eve in Genesis, their life of toil will be relieved only by whatever comfort they can give each other.

Jabez Moorhouse, an elderly farmhand who plays the fiddle at country socials. This wizened country philosopher is the counterpart of Judith, with whom he maintains a friendship throughout the novel. Jabez is the only other character who can see the beauty and mystery of nature, and he has the creative urge that sensitivity inspires. His main regret in life is that he was never able to learn to play the violin as well as he knows himself to be capable of doing. Like Judith, his higher aspirations have had no chance of flowering in this grim, impoverished environment.

Lizzie May Pippinger Pooler, Judith's older sister, a sharecropper's wife. Lizzie May is also physically attractive, but she lacks the special qualities of her younger sister. When Lizzie May marries and begins bearing children, she accepts her role in life with unquestioning docility, lacking the imagination to see that things could be any different. Her main functions in the novel are to portray the typical farm wife and to serve as a foil to Judith's unique personality.

Dan Pooler, Lizzie May's sharecropper husband, a hardworking, unimaginative man who typifies the character and experiences of the average man in the region.

Luke and

Hat Wolf, a crude sharecropping couple, Judith and Jerry's closest neighbors. They, too, represent the typical farmers of the region. At one point, Judith discovers that Jerry, from whom she has become estranged, is having an affair with Hat. This further embitters her life and makes her feel more spiritually isolated than ever.

The Revivalist, a young traveling preacher. Judith is sexually captivated by this handsome young man because of his soulful eyes. For several months, they have a clandestine love affair. She is ultimately disappointed to realize that he is a creature of surface appearances and does not really share her inexpressible yearnings for some transcendental reality. When she discovers that she is pregnant with his child, she nearly kills herself trying to induce a miscarriage. His function in the story is to highlight her unique spirit and her hopeless predicament in this blighted environment.

— *Bill Delaney*

THE WELL

Author: Elizabeth Jolley (1923-   )
First published: 1986
Genre: Novel

Locale: Western Australia
Time: Early 1980's
Plot: Psychological realism

Hester Harper, an Australian rancher. A thin, flat-breasted, middle-aged woman with a lame leg, she is aware of having been a disappointment to her father, with whom she lives, because she was a girl, and an ugly, crippled one at that, instead of a boy. When she takes an orphaned teenager home with her, Hester feels close to another human being for the first time since the loss of her childhood governess. After her father's death, Hester neglects and then sells her land, planning to spend the money on luxuries for Katherine and for herself and determining never to let Katherine leave her. When the girl, driving fast in the dark, hits some object, presumably a man, Hester throws the body into her well to protect Katherine and to keep her. When she finds her money missing and learns that there has been a thief in the neighborhood, Hester assumes that the money is in the well with the man, but she is willing to lose the money rather than to lose Katherine.

Katherine, an orphan. Almost sixteen years old when Hester meets her, she is a pretty, delicate-looking girl with thin blond hair and a childish voice. Ingratiating and imaginative, she becomes a playmate for her employer, out of whom she can soon wheedle anything she wants. After the automobile accident, Katherine's sexual frustrations turn into an obsession. She is certain that the man in the well is still alive and that he must be released so that he can marry her. Even though Hester has the well covered, believing that the two women can return to their normal life together, it is obvious that Katherine has other plans. She seems to have some of Hester's missing cash. Moreover, she insists on having an unsavory girlfriend come to the ranch. It is obvious that she will not stay indefinitely with Hester.

Mr. Bird, a stock and station agent, a somewhat younger friend of Hester's father. He considers it his obligation to help Hester with business affairs after her father's death. He warns Hester repeatedly about her reckless spending, which he accurately ascribes to her infatuation with Katherine. Although Hester sees him as a bore, after his death she discovers notebooks full of financial advice for her, proving that he has been her only real friend.

Mr. Harper, Hester's father. Although he is ill and dependent on her, in old age he enjoys tyrannizing over his daughter. His lifelong indifference to her is evident in her memory of the events that took place years before, when he heartlessly banished her beloved governess and foster mother, who had had a miscarriage as the result of his seduction.

Mr. Borden, a neighboring rancher, a young, strong man who buys Hester's house and then her land. It is at the party given to celebrate the purchase that Katherine discovers what she has been missing in her life with Hester, and it is after that party that Katherine has her accident.

Rosalie Borden, Mr. Borden's wife, a plump, noisy young woman with an ever-increasing brood of children. To Hester, she symbolizes the life from which her own ugliness has forever barred her. At the party, when Rosalie warns Hester that Katherine will and should leave her, Rosalie betrays her own distaste for the eternal spinster.

— Rosemary M. Canfield Reisman

THE WELL OF LONELINESS

Author: Radclyffe Hall (1880-1943)
First published: 1928
Genre: Novel

Locale: England and France
Time: Early twentieth century
Plot: Social realism

Stephen Gordon, the protagonist. The only daughter of English gentry, Stephen is baptized Stephen Mary Olivia Gertrude but is called Stephen because her father desperately wanted a son. As a child, she loathes dresses, preferring to wear pants and play as a war hero. She develops her muscles through fencing and riding and is more comfortable with her horses than at social gatherings, where she often suspects people of laughing at her. After a failed relationship with Angela Crossby, she leaves her estate, Morton, for London, where she becomes a successful novelist. During World War I, she serves as a driver with the London Ambulance Column and meets Mary Llewellyn. They fall in love and settle in Paris.

Sir Philip Gordon, Stephen's father. Aristocratic, sporting, and scholarly, Sir Philip waited ten years for a son, only to have a daughter instead. He rears Stephen much as a boy would be reared in that Victorian period. Although he is devoted to his daughter, taking her hunting and riding and reading with her in his study, his feelings are often more like pity than love. Early on, he recognizes that his daughter is not like other children, confirming his intuition by reading an influential theory of "inversion" from Richard von Krafft-Ebing. Both Stephen and Lady Anna, his wife, frequently ask him about Stephen's apparent "oddness." Sir Philip, hoping to protect his daughter, dismisses their concerns. He dies before he can tell either one about "what" Stephen is.

Lady Anna Gordon, Stephen's mother. The "archetype of the very perfect woman," Lady Anna is beautiful, graceful, simple, and uneducated. She and her husband love each other passionately. Her aversion to her daughter begins soon after the girl's birth. She is often critical, cold, and distant, unable to love or understand her masculine daughter. Lady Anna finds it difficult to show affection to Stephen, as a big-boned and tempestuous child, and often quarrels with the teenaged Stephen over clothes and social proprieties. When confronted with Stephen's love for Angela Crossby, she instructs her daughter to leave Morton.

Miss Puddleton, Stephen's schoolmistress at Morton and later her companion. Affectionately known as Puddle, this small, round, educated woman arrives at Morton when Stephen is fourteen years old, to see after her education. The author suggests that Puddle's capacity to understand and guide Stephen stems from Puddle's own personal experience. Following the Angela Crossby incident, Puddle inspires Stephen to persevere with courage and honor, working and writing for the sake of those like her. Puddle remains by Stephen's side as a confidant and friend until World War I.

Martin Hallam, who is at first a friend of Stephen but later is a rival. A landowner from British Columbia, Martin meets Stephen at a New Year's dance when Stephen is eighteen years old. Enjoying each other's company, they spend much of their time together until Martin declares his love. Stephen is terrified and repulsed. Martin leaves. After the war, Martin contacts Stephen, visiting her and Mary in Paris. He falls in love with Mary and competes with Stephen for her affection.

Angela Crossby, the neighbor with whom Stephen falls in love. The American wife of an English businessman, Angela is lonely, discontented, bored, and "not overburdened with virtue." Although she does not love Stephen, she finds herself drawn to Stephen's affection and passion, as much out of loneliness as out of curiosity and fascination. She encourages their meetings, with all their kisses and embraces, but she appeals to her honor and to the fact that she is married to keep the relationship from becoming more intimate. Faced with the growing intensity of Stephen's feelings and having found a new, male lover, Angela ends up betraying Stephen.

Mary Llewellyn, the woman Stephen meets during the war and with whom she falls in love. Mary is a young, uneducated, innocent, Welsh orphan when she meets Stephen in the London Ambulance Column at the front. Following the war, she moves to Paris with Stephen. Because Stephen is reluctant to express her feelings, Mary declares her love first, and they settle into a domestic routine. Their life as a couple is difficult. Mary is often lonely while Stephen is writing. They are not accepted in respectable society. As they begin to socialize with more lesbians, Mary starts to coarsen. Martin offers her the possibility of respect.

— Jodi Dean

WESTWARD HO!

Author: Charles Kingsley (1819-1875)
First published: 1855
Genre: Novel

Locale: England and South America
Time: The sixteenth century
Plot: Historical

Amyas Leigh, a handsome blond giant, a hardy adventurer who accompanies Francis Drake around the world and Walter Raleigh to Ireland and who valiantly engages the Spanish in the Old World and the New. Struck blind by lightning during the battle against the Spanish Armada, he retires from the sea and marries Ayacanora.

Frank Leigh, his scholarly older brother, a sometime tutor and courtier. Captured by Don Guzman's men, he refuses to accept Catholicism and is tortured and burned to death.

Sir Richard Grenvile, Amyas' godfather, a famous seaman and explorer.

Sir Francis Drake, the leader of the first English voyage around the world.

Sir Walter Raleigh, an English courtier, navigator, historian, and poet.

Eustace Leigh, the cousin of Amyas and Frank, a Catholic distrusted by his cousins. Spurned by Rose, he vows revenge. Threatening to turn Rose over to the Inquisition, he is attacked by Amyas and Frank. Before escaping and disappearing, he informs the Inquisition that Rose is a Protestant. His villainy is attributed by the author to his Jesuit training.

Rose Salterne, the mayor's beautiful daughter, loved by Amyas and Frank but married to Don Guzman, whom she loves passionately. She is brought before the Inquisition because of her Protestant belief, which she will not renounce. She is tortured and then burned to death.

Salvation Yeo, Amyas' friend, a tall, dark sailor who idolizes Amyas and shares his adventures. Lightning kills him during the storm that aids the English in the destruction of the Armada.

Don Guzman de Soto, a charming but treacherous Spanish nobleman who captures Rose's heart and marries her. Amyas hates him because of Frank's death. In the destruction of the Armada, Don Guzman goes down in a wrecked ship.

Ayacanora, a supposed Indian maiden who falls in love with Amyas. She is really John Oxenham's lost daughter. She dislikes Amyas' brotherly attitude toward her, which finally changes when he becomes her adored, though blind, husband.

Mrs. Leigh, the widowed mother of Amyas and Frank, a devout Protestant made somewhat melancholy by memories of earlier Catholic persecution of English Protestants. Saddened by Frank's death, she is happy at last to have the blind Amyas (Sir Amyas now) home with her.

Lucy, a witch who goes with Rose to Spain and who later reports the deaths of Rose and Frank. Lucy escapes by accepting the Catholic faith.

John Oxenham, Salvation's friend, who is captured by Spanish Inquisitors. He is the father of Ayacanora.

WHAT A BEAUTIFUL SUNDAY!
(Quel beau dimanche)

Author: Jorge Semprun (1923-   )
First published: 1980
Genre: Novel

Locale: The Buchenwald death camp
Time: During World War II
Plot: Social morality

Gerard Sorel, the narrator, also known as **Sanchez**, **Camille Salagnac**, **Rafael Artigas**, **Rafael Bustamante**, **Larrea**, **Ramon Barreto**, and other pseudonyms. He is a Spaniard and Communist Party member who spent time in the Buchenwald concentration camp. He narrates his story and never reveals his real name. From a bourgeois background, yet well known and trusted in the Party underground, Gerard survives the prison camp because of the Party's place in its organization. He is an intellectual, or observer, by temperament. He constantly compares individuals, national groups, and times in history. His prison camp experiences, especially the constant awareness of others' deaths, make him question the reality of his experiences and even of his existence. This sense of unreality is further fostered by his many identity changes and the changes, over the years, in the Communist Party line.

Fernand Barizon, a Communist Party member from France who survives Buchenwald with Gerard and discusses it with him fifteen years later. The meaning of his remark "What a beautiful Sunday!" is never articulated, though Gerard's memory of the statement resonates throughout the novel. Barizon is not an intellectual. He remembers his true and very physical love affair with a French garment union member, Juliette, and he has a zest for food and a desire for comfort. He is an extremely loyal friend. He never fully trusts the Party's insistence on organization because he operates more from the heart.

Willi Seifert, who is assigned by the Nazi SS to be kapo of the Arbeitsstatistik (record-keeping department). He had once been a member of the Communist Youth Movement. With his power in the camp, though he also is a prisoner, he is able to save Party members and others from extermination by assigning them to non-life-threatening jobs. He is a man of great personal authority, yet he is later frightened by Joseph Stalin's purges and eventually disappears.

Henk Spoenay, a Dutch prisoner who acts as liaison between Seifert and the SS. He is the same age as Gerard, and they are friends.

Leon Blum,

Johann Wolfgang von Goethe, and

Johann Peter Eckermann, who are visualized by the narrator, Sorel. Blum, ironically, not only was a leader of the Socialist Party and the Popular Front, and therefore ultimately imprisoned on the premises of Buchenwald, but also was the author of a book of conversations between Goethe and Eckermann. Some of the conversations in Blum's book were supposed to have taken place at Etters Hill, near Weimar, the site of Buchenwald.

Jehovah or **Johann**, one of the much-persecuted Jehovah's Witnesses at Buchenwald. He opens every conversation with Sorel by quoting a passage from the Bible that is appropriate to the moment.

Aleksandr Solzhenitsyn, a Russian dissident who writes of the Stalinist gulag. Sorel eventually realizes the parallel between the institutions of Communist labor camps and those of Nazi internment camps. Consequently, Sorel acknowledges the Russian Revolution as a historical catastrophe.

— *Anna R. Holloway*

WHAT EVERY WOMAN KNOWS

Author: Sir James M. Barrie (1860-1937)
First published: 1918
Genre: Drama

Locale: Scotland and England
Time: Early twentieth century
Plot: Social satire

Maggie Wylie, a wife who knows well what every woman should know—that a wife is the moving force behind any successful husband. At twenty-seven years of age, she is the plain, unmarried sister of David and James Wylie. Neither her curls nor her soft Scottish voice quite compensate for her too-resolute manner. She is married to John Shand after a six-year wait, as the result of a bargain made by David, James, and their father. Maggie proves herself the mistress of her husband's fate, even against the wiles and scheming of Lady Sybil Tenterden.

John Shand, a proud, defiant, and calculating young man of extraordinary promise. Caught by the Wylie men as he prowls their library looking for books, John agrees to marry Maggie in five years in exchange for three hundred pounds to finance his education. With Maggie unobtrusively behind him, he wins a seat in Parliament, boastful that he has not a soul to help him. He would leave Maggie, whom he respects, for Sybil, whom he thinks he loves, but no Scotsman will damage his career. He also has finally found out how he has come to be a success.

David Wylie, Maggie's older brother. He is the moving force of the family, the head of Wylie and Sons, stonemasons. The 600-volume library is actually David's; he has an unsatisfied hunger for education and a deep respect for the learned. He shrewdly sees in John Shand's need for money a means of getting a husband for Maggie. Businessman that he is, he is pleased to see John equally skilled in driving a good bargain. David has the brisk manner of the person who must get everywhere first.

James Wylie, Maggie's second brother. Dominated by David, he has become taciturn and tactless. He is used to having his opinions disregarded, but he offers them nevertheless. Although he has no use for books and education, he is impressed by John's scholarship and drive. He becomes, in spirit, John's humble servant. Observing that Maggie is "queer," James wonders why great writers have failed to notice that all women are thus. His wife's ability would belie this notion.

Alick Wylie, the father of the family, now retired. He is no longer the head except in name. His is a disdainful view of learning, although he says "it's not to riches, it's to scholarship I make my bow." His small, bright blue eyes seem always to be counting costs.

The Comtesse de la Brière (bree-EHR), a rude, calculating person of the world who laughs at the crudeness of the young politician. She sportingly challenges Sybil to conquer John. Over the years, the comtesse sees that Maggie is "the pin Shand picked up to make his fortune," and she becomes Maggie's ally in defending her rights against the younger woman.

Lady Sybil Tenterden, the niece of the comtesse. Beautiful and unscrupulous, she schemes to ensnare John and teach him what he has not found in books, but her charm without intelligence is not enough to hold the ambitious young man.

Mr. Charles Venables, a member of the cabinet. Venables' thirty-year acquaintance with the comtesse serves to develop both these characters in the play. As protégé to Venables, John bumbles some political coups. About to sever relations with John, Venables reconsiders when reminded that it is he who once said, "A man whose second thoughts are good is worth watching." John's second thoughts result from Maggie's influence and a speech she wrote for him.

WHAT I'M GOING TO DO, I THINK

Author: Larry Woiwode (1941-   )
First published: 1969
Genre: Novel

Locale: Madison and Milwaukee, Wisconsin; Pyramid Bluffs, Michigan; and Chicago, Illinois
Time: 1964
Plot: Psychological realism

Christofer (Chris) Van Eenanam, a graduate student in mathematics at the University of Chicago. At the age of twenty-three, he is still deeply unsure of his identity. His inability to resolve the conflicts within his personality, partially caused by the loss of his Catholic faith, undermines his relationship with Ellen Strohe even after their marriage. His feelings about her, and about virtually everything important to him, are deep but inconsistent. Always having to prove himself to himself, he is unable to provide Ellen the attention and understanding that she needs. After a tumultuous three-year relationship, begun when they were university students, they are married when Ellen becomes pregnant. The novel begins as they arrive at her grandparents' lodge in northern Michigan, where they spend their honeymoon. During the summer, as

Chris repairs the lodge, he struggles with his ambivalent feelings about being a husband and prospective father.

Ellen Sidone Anne Strohe Van Eenanam, Chris's pregnant wife. The twenty-one-year-old woman, brought up by her grandparents after the deaths of her parents in an accident, needs reliability and consistency in a lover to bring her out of her shell. She, too, is unsure of her feelings about the marriage and about being a mother. Her pregnancy only increases her self-absorption, and Chris's ambivalence precludes his being sufficiently helpful.

Aloysius James Strohe, Ellen's grandfather, a wealthy brewery owner. A domineering, crafty, possessive, and insightful old man, Strohe recognizes the weakness in Chris but fails in his attempts to get Ellen to renounce him. His virtues are those of the Germanic, self-made, practical man. He has no patience with the equivocal personality of Chris or his interest in the abstractions of mathematics. He lets the young couple stay at the lodge in expectation that the experience will separate them.

Grandma Strohe, Ellen's Christian Scientist grandmother. Her inflexible morality allows no space for human error. She never forgives or forgets. Her rejection of Chris is absolute, and her cruelty to Ellen in the name of religion is reprehensible.

Orin Clausen, a neighboring farmer, a coarse, provincial man with the rural mistrust of the unknown and the urban.

Chris earns Orin's respect by putting in a hard day's work stacking Orin's hay bales, but Orin reminds Chris of the life as a farmer that Chris went to school to escape.

Anna Clausen, Orin's widowed sister-in-law, another example of rural isolation and its subsequent loneliness. Anna lives with her brother-in-law in a state of mutual antipathy as business partners. The young couple could give her pleasure merely by paying her a visit, but, caught up in themselves, they never do so.

— *William J. McDonald*

WHAT MAISIE KNEW

Author: Henry James (1843-1916)
First published: 1897
Genre: Novel

Locale: London, Folkestone, and Boulogne
Time: The 1890's
Plot: Psychological realism

Maisie Farange, the neglected daughter of divorced and irresponsible parents. Shuttled back and forth between her father and mother, Maisie at first lacks moral perception, although she herself is incorruptibly innocent. Then, under the tutelage of Mrs. Wix, she grows in moral and intellectual sense, rejects the immorality of her stepparents, and chooses to live with Mrs. Wix.

Mrs. Wix, a governess employed to replace Miss Overmore. Mrs. Wix alone seems concerned for Maisie's welfare. Refusing to condone the immorality around her, she is the moral influence in the young girl's environment.

Sir Claude, Ida Farange's second husband. Genuinely interested in Maisie, Sir Claude most nearly approaches the fatherly role. He is unable, however, to end his affair with

Mrs. Farange (Miss Overmore), and Maisie refuses to live with them.

Miss Overmore, Maisie's governess, later the second Mrs. Beale Farange. After she tires of her husband, she begins an affair with Sir Claude, who is captivated by her beauty. She does not love Maisie, but she feels that she can hold Sir Claude through his devotion to the girl.

Ida Farange, Maisie's mother. Divorced from Beale Farange, Ida marries Sir Claude but soon loses interest in her daughter and husband. She turns Maisie over to him and goes out of their lives.

Beale Farange, Maisie's father. After his divorce, Beale marries Miss Overmore, but they soon tire of each other. Beale goes to America and out of the story.

WHAT PRICE GLORY?

Authors: Maxwell Anderson (1888-1959) and Laurence Stallings (1894-1968)
First published: 1926
Genre: Drama

Locale: The French countryside
Time: During World War I
Plot: Realism

First Sergeant Quirt, the company's senior noncommissioned officer (NCO). He was Flagg's senior NCO in China when the captain was enlisted, and they had a disagreement over a woman that continues decades later. Quirt is brutal and dangerously self-confident, and he steals Flagg's girlfriend after decking a drunken Irishman. In spite of Flagg's order, he refuses to marry the dishonored woman. At the battlefront, Quirt longs for action, so much so that he is seriously wounded in the foot and must return behind the lines. He escapes from the hospital and confronts Flagg. The two agree to a game of blackjack to decide their fate, but orders calling them back to the front force them to abandon their duel. Quirt serves as the essential soldier: a violent womanizer always ready to answer a call to arms.

Captain Flagg, the company commander. Formally a corporal and a veteran of duty in both China and Cuba, Flagg is an alcoholic, which gets him into considerable difficulties. He does, at least, have some compassion for his girlfriend, Char-

maine, but it is frequently obscured by his drunken brawling, which leads to his imprisonment on a charge of attempted manslaughter at one point in the play. He is also keenly aware of Quirt's abilities as a soldier, as well as Quirt's desire to usurp his command. A particularly touching scene occurs in act 2, when Flagg comforts a shell-shocked lieutenant. When he is sober, Flagg is a creditable leader who seems to be aware of the suffering inherent in war. In spite of these compassionate tendencies, he, like Quirt, does not hesitate when the call to arms is sounded.

Charmaine de la Cognac, described as a "drab," an attractive young woman who is the daughter of Cognac Pete, a local tavern keeper. She is quite liberal with her affections. In the opening scene, she worries over Flagg and his impending journey to Paris. In the next scene, she kisses Quirt passionately. Charmaine is an example of the brutality and the callousness of the common soldier. Quirt and Flagg care quite little about her and her situation. Not even the love of a beautiful woman will keep these men from hearing the call to arms.

Private Lewishon, a young Jewish recruit who demonstrates that war can be brutal to both soldiers and civilians. He first appears in act 1, pleading with Flagg for replacement identification tags. The captain dismisses him with a promise to replace the missing items but laughs at the young soldier's homesickness. The irony in this scene is revealed when Lewishon is mortally wounded in the attack on the wine cellar at the battlefront.

— *Richard S. Keating*

WHAT THE BUTLER SAW

Author: Joe Orton (1933-1967)
First published: 1969
Genre: Drama

Locale: A psychiatric clinic in England
Time: The 1960's
Plot: Farce

Dr. Prentice, a middle-aged psychiatrist. Prentice is an unscrupulous man who does not hesitate to use his position as a doctor to seduce Geraldine Barclay, who is applying for a job as his secretary. He also refuses to tell the truth, despite the trouble this causes Geraldine with Dr. Rance. It was this same lustful lack of scruples that led him to interfere with an unknown chambermaid at the Station Hotel many years before, resulting in her conception of Geraldine and Nick.

Dr. Rance, a psychiatrist sent from the government to check on how psychiatric clinics are being run. He is a brutal, power-mad doctor, and he tries to certify everybody as insane, though it is obvious that he is the only one who is truly mad.

Mrs. Prentice, Dr. Prentice's wife. During a brief stint as a chambermaid at the Station Hotel, she was raped in a linen cupboard during a power outage (hence her inability to recognize her attacker as her fiancé, Dr. Prentice). She is a blasé, disillusioned woman who belongs to a lesbian women's group. The failure of the Prentices' marriage is attributed to the fact that Mrs. Prentice refused to consummate their marriage during their wedding night.

Nicholas (Nick) Beckett, a page boy from the Station Hotel, now an applicant for the job as Dr. Prentice's secretary. Nick is an accomplished typist and blackmailer with an insatiable sexual appetite, exemplified by his attempted rape of Mrs. Prentice (his mother) and the accomplished molestation of "a section of the Priory Road School for girls" on the same night. He turns out to be Geraldine's twin brother and the Prentices' son.

Geraldine Barclay, an applicant for the position as Dr. Prentice's secretary. A young, attractive girl, she is trusting and believes in telling the truth. Although she is the only person with any morals (except, perhaps, for Sergeant Match), she gets the brunt of Dr. Rance's abuse, as when he cuts off all of her hair. Her ignorance of the whereabouts of pieces missing from a statue of Winston Churchill seems symbolic of her purity and naïveté. Ultimately, it is revealed that she is Nick's twin and the Prentices' daughter.

Sergeant Match, a policeman looking for Geraldine Barclay and Nicholas Beckett. His more important mission, however, is to find Geraldine and Sir Winston's missing parts; of lesser interest is his charge to find the molester of the girls from Priory Road School. Having accomplished his main task, which is of national importance, Match has no qualms about forgetting everything else he has witnessed, though this willingness may be related to the large amount of narcotics that Dr. Prentice has given him.

— *T. M. Lipman*

WHAT'S BRED IN THE BONE

Author: Robertson Davies (1913-1995)
First published: 1985
Genre: Novel

Locale: Primarily Canada, England, and Germany
Time: Mid-1800's-1980's
Plot: Psychological

Francis Chegwidden Cornish, a Canadian art expert. The novel purports to tell what has been "bred in the bone" of Francis. Francis, who is from a wealthy but emotionally distant family, is a sensitive, intelligent boy. He teaches himself to observe carefully and to draw what he sees; he later discovers that his affinity in art is for the Old Masters and that he is false to himself when he tries to express himself in modern styles. His skill at observation makes him useful to the British intelligence service before and during World War II. He paints the myth of himself, an expression of what has made him what he is, in Old Master style. When the painting is discovered after the war, art experts dub it *The Marriage at Cana* and attribute it to the Alchemical Master.

The Daimon Maimas, Francis' personal attendant spirit, the guiding force in his life. It is he who has arranged Francis' life to make him what he is, though his control does not mean that Francis lacks freedom of choice.

The Lesser Zadkiel, the recording angel. His records provide the biography of Francis.

James Ignatius McRory (also called **the Senator** and **Hamish**), Francis' maternal grandfather. A Scottish Catholic, McRory has made a fortune in the timber business. His desire to rise socially leads him to debut his daughter at court in London. He is interested in photography and teaches Francis the effects of different angles and types of light on a subject. In his will, he leaves Francis a substantial sum of money and exempts him from entering the family banking business.

Sir Francis Cornish, Francis' father. The younger son in an old family, he agrees to marry the pregnant Mary-Jacobine McRory after certain financial agreements are made. He is appointed president of his father-in-law's bank, a figurehead position. His real work is in intelligence, and he recruits Francis to follow him in that field.

Mary-Jacobine (Mary-Jim or Jacko) Cornish, née

McRory, Francis' mother. Mary-Jacobine, a beautiful young woman, makes her debut at the court of King Edward VII in 1903; on that night, she becomes pregnant with the child of a footman who reminds her of a famous actor. She later becomes the perfect society wife but spends little time with her sons.

Mary-Benedetta (Mary-Ben) McRory, Francis' great-aunt. Mary-Ben has the greatest hand in rearing Francis. She instills in Francis a romantic Catholicism and has him baptized a Catholic at the age of fourteen, even though he already has been baptized a Protestant. Her collection of prints inspires Francis' interest in art.

Francis "the Looner" Cornish, Francis' elder brother. The Looner is mentally and physically handicapped because of Mary-Jacobine's attempts to end the unwanted pregnancy begun on her debut night. Francis' mother and father believe the Looner to be dead; he is kept upstairs in his grandfather's house. His existence instills in Francis a compassion for the unfortunate.

Zadok Hoyle, a groom for the McRory family. Unknown to him and to the McRory family, he is the Looner's father. Zadok also assists the local undertaker by preparing bodies for burial. He allows Francis to watch him in the embalming process, teaching him a respect for individuals and the fragility of life.

Ismay Glasson Cornish, Francis' cousin and later his wife. Francis at first believes her to be his dream woman, the woman who will complement his masculine nature with her feminine nature to make him whole. She tricks him into marriage to cover her pregnancy by another man, then leaves the child with her parents and joins her lover in Spain. The child and

Ismay's family become a drain on Francis' finances. Ismay is a great believer in idealistic, unrealistic causes.

Tancred Saraceni, an art expert. He takes Francis as an apprentice and teaches him the style, physical composition (ingredients of paints), and iconography of Old Master paintings. He is casuistic about restoring paintings to look somewhat better than they did originally. He leaves Francis his fortune and his possessions.

Ruth Nibsmith, Francis' friend and lover. She casts Francis' horoscope seriously, wisely, and perceptively.

Aylwin Ross, a Canadian art critic, Francis' protégé. Ross becomes famous for his explication of *The Marriage at Cana*, unaware of its origin. He commits suicide after Francis refuses to buy the painting for the Canadian National Gallery.

Victoria Cameron, the McRorys' cook. She cares for the Looner and instills some hard, practical Calvinist values in Francis.

Dr. Joseph Ambrosius (J. A.) Jerome, the McRory family physician. Dr. J. A. recommends the false burial of the Looner, believing that knowledge of his existence will harm Francis.

Colonel Jack Copplestone, Francis' contact in British Intelligence. He arranges Francis' positions as a spy to coincide with his art activities.

The Reverend Simon Darcourt, Francis' friend and biographer. In the frame fiction, he complains that he cannot find enough information to write Francis' biography properly.

Arthur Cornish, Francis' nephew and executor, a banker. he is worried by the whiff of scandal about Francis that Simon has brought to him.

— *Karen M. Cleveland*

WHEAT THAT SPRINGETH GREEN

Author: J. F. Powers (1917-   )
First published: 1988
Genre: Novel

Locale: The American Midwest
Time: The 1930's to 1968
Plot: Philosophical realism

Joe Hackett, a Roman Catholic priest. Always at odds with the status quo, Joe has some sexual adventures in his teens but eventually opts for priesthood and celibacy. In his seminary days, Joe practices severe asceticism, including wearing a hair shirt; he also attempts contemplative prayer. At his first Mass, he fights the pastor's custom of taking up a special collection. After assignments as curate at Holy Faith and assistant director at Catholic Charities, Joe is made pastor of St. Francis and Clare Church in Inglenook. He does away with the envelope system of church contributions while building a convent, school, and rectory. He never talks about money from the pulpit. Joe's priestly friends are few, but he and his first curate, Bill Schmidt, form a bond in the midst of many humorous intergenerational conflicts. Joe learns that neither asceticism nor contemplation makes a good priest and that fidelity to Gospel principles, working with people, and completing mundane tasks such as typing—the unheroic life as a priest—is the cross. Joe has traits of a prophet, as well as good sense. Joe drinks heavily, eats well, and is an avid baseball fan. At the age of forty-four, many problems arise for Joe, including the diocese's assessment of a sum beyond Joe's financial assets. Miraculously, Joe receives a bequest from the priest with whom he had fought over funds at his first Mass. At the book's end,

Joe is assigned to Holy Cross Parish.

Bill Schmidt, Joe's first curate, who arrives late wearing jeans and a t-shirt, driving an orange car and lacking typing skills. Bill's 1960's ideals and behaviors mirror Joe's after ordination, but Joe does not see that. In their relationship, Joe coaches compassionately and Bill matures. Joe faces himself more honestly and mellows. Bill's loyalty to Joe is clear when he joins Joe in their unsuccessful efforts to find a way to pay the parish assessment. With Bill, Joe finds priestly fellowship.

Lefty Beeman, a priest ten years older than Joe, known as a problem priest who is frequently reassigned. Over time, Lefty and Joe become good friends as they eat and drink through many conversations on the priestly life.

Cooney,

Mooney, and

Rooney, seminary classmates who are both attracted to and puzzled by Joe's ideas and behaviors. They represent the ordinary run of priests, and by their attitudes they portray what Joe refuses to be.

Michael "Catfish" Toohey, a Catholic school and seminary classmate and enemy of Joe. Toohey obeys all the rules and after ordination serves as the archbishop's spokesman. He uses his power in that position to cause problems for Joe.

Brad, the Inglenook *Universe*'s columnist, whose favorite topic is the town's weather ball. Brad is a conservative and subtly criticizes Joe in his column for Joe's non-support of political causes, including a federal contract for the local defense plant and the Vietnam War. Brad and his wife, Barb, have a son who flees to Canada with Joe's blessing. Another son, Scott, fights in Vietnam. Brad loses his job at the local paper as the result of some controversial writing. He is hired to write his controversial column for the *New Shopper*, a tabloid-style publication of Inglenook's discount supermarket, the Great Badger.

Mr. Barnes, a clerk in the liquor store that Joe patronizes weekly. After Mr. Barnes loses his job, he is hired by the Great Badger, and Joe switches his business to that store. Joe becomes a hero when he accidentally interferes with a robbery at the liquor store.

Father Felix, a monk who comes to St. Francis and Clare every weekend to say Mass. He wears a forest-green habit, dislikes sports, and is the antithesis to Joe's notions of what a monk/priest should be, because he eats heartily and prays little. Father Felix is a bridge between Bill and Joe.

Conklin, a seminary classmate and friend of Bill; he has given up the priesthood. His sexual and alcohol-related escapades get Bill in trouble. Joe intervenes, and Conklin takes his revenge by falsely reporting Joe and Lefty to Public Health for having a sexually transmitted disease. This causes Joe and Lefty to hide their problems from each other. They later realize that this violates their friendship.

Mr. McMaster, a professional fund-raiser hired by the archbishop to assist pastors. His suave manner fails to change Joe's decision not to solicit from the pulpit, and he comes to admire and respect Joe.

— *Francine Dempsey*

WHEN I WHISTLE
(Kuchibue o fuku toki)

Author: Shūsaku Endō (1923-1996)
First published: 1974
Genre: Novel

Locale: Japan
Time: The 1960's
Plot: Social realism

Ozu, an aging Japanese businessman entering his senior years. Ozu is a humble clerk, preoccupied with memories of his youth and greatly troubled by his increasing fear of the different moral vision animating the youth of postwar Japan, as exemplified in the unadorned avarice and ambition of his son, Eiichi. Nostalgic for an older, more disciplined, and even militaristic Japan, he finds in the present a predatory industrial power immune to simple human compassion and idealism. His mental search recalls Nada Middle School and his impish friend Flatfish, who whiled away his youth with Ozu, longing for female companionship. Both had sought the affection of the nubile, beautiful Aiko. Ozu's flashbacks and reveries of his youth and postadolescent contacts with Flatfish come crashing to a halt when he learns of Flatfish's death from a battlefield disease. He determines to search for Aiko to report this bad news. Finding her accidentally, as one of his son's terminal cancer patients, Ozu sees Aiko as merely one laboratory rat, prey to medical science's preoccupation with advanced objective knowledge at the expense of nurturing care and concern for individual persons. While locating Aiko's childhood home, now bulldozed in the name of progress, Ozu sinks into despair as his generation fades into the bleak sunset of Japan's moral resignation in the midst of its economic and technological triumphs.

Flatfish, Ozu's childhood friend and constant companion in the idyllic days before World War II. Flatfish is an undisciplined, unintellectual parody of Japanese manhood, always in trouble at the Nada Middle School, where he and Ozu met, and unconcerned about career advancement in his chosen employment. Irrepressible, frivolous, and hopelessly attracted to the young girls in his class and older ones, Flatfish surrenders any claim to scholastic prowess or responsible citizenship, choosing to remain an adolescent as long as he can. He tempers Ozu's basic reserved nature and teaches him to revel in the spontaneous and childish. Living only in Ozu's flashbacks,

Flatfish is a vivid contrast to Ozu's son, Eiichi, in his free, unpretentious pursuit of joy and immediate fulfillment. Flatfish is the buoyant, unfettered spirit of Japanese manhood that has died in the aftermath of the wars. Ozu's discovery of his death triggers the novel's denouement as Ozu seeks out the lovely Aiko to share his grief, only to discover more.

Eiichi, Ozu's son. Ambitious and without scruples, Eiichi is desperate to rise within the medical profession as a surgeon. He is completely identified with a grim, work-oriented Japan: He is driven, technological, spiritually barren, and the epitome of Western imperialism that his father fought to defeat. He finds his father's basic humanism debilitating and unprogressive, a needless sentimentality that impedes efficiency and his ultimate career goals. His reputation for callousness and insensitivity are well established when father and son are united by the illness of Ozu's beloved Aiko. Here their differing ethics are underscored and foregrounded. As his patient, Aiko represents to Eiichi (an aptly drawn representative of the new generation of Japanese professionals) only a convenient subject for an experimental cancer treatment, not a person deserving care, love, or basic dignity.

Aiko, a patient of Eiichi and the object of Ozu's adolescent infatuation. Aiko is a war widow and the living symbol to Ozu of all that is pure and authentic in the Japanese culture of his youth. She lives in the novel more as a memory or an icon than as a living, breathing human being, trapped as she is in Eiichi's experimental cancer program. Her death signals to Ozu the final victory of technological imperialism over the tenderness and compassion representative of the Japanese character to him in his adolescence in prewar Japan.

Dr. Ii, a malevolent, unscrupulous doctor in the hospital where Eiichi works. Dr. Ii is an imperious, natural product of postwar Japan's rigid determination to rise from the ashes of ignominy and defeat. He is experienced in using people and is perfectly willing to prescribe worthless drugs for his patients if the pharmaceutical company that produces them continues to fund his research. As the dubious role model for Eiichi and other medical personnel, Dr. Ii manifests the greed and indifference to civility that Ozu finds manifested everywhere in the new Japan.

— *Bruce L. Edwards*

WHEN THE MOUNTAIN FELL
(Derborence)

Author: Charles-Ferdinand Ramuz (1878-1947)
First published: 1934
Genre: Novel

Locale: Switzerland
Time: The eighteenth century
Plot: Regional

Séraphin Carrupt (say-rah-FA[N] kah-REWPT), an elderly Swiss shepherd. He is killed when an avalanche slides at night onto the mountain pasture where he is keeping his cattle.

Antoine Pont (ahn-TWAHN poh[n]), a young, newly married Swiss shepherd who is thought dead after the avalanche covers the mountain pasture. Miraculously, he is not killed. Living on cheese, he burrows his way out of the mass of rock and earth after two long months. He courageously wants to go back to rescue Séraphin Carrupt, his companion, but his wife dissuades him, knowing the old man is dead.

Thérèse Pont (tay-REHZ), Antoine's young wife. She realizes on the night when the avalanche falls that she is going to have a child. When her husband returns, she can scarcely believe that she is not seeing a ghost. Only she is courageous enough to follow her husband back to the scene of the avalanche to dissuade him from trying to dig out his companion.

Philomène Maye (fee-loh-MEHN mah-YEH), Thérèse's mother, who tries to shield her daughter from news of her husband's supposed death.

Old Barthélémy (bahr-tay-lay-MEE), a shepherd who lives through the avalanche but dies as he is being carried down the mountain for treatment.

Maurice Nendaz (moh-REES nah[n]-DAHZ), a lame old man, the first villager to realize that what he hears is an avalanche, not a storm in the distance.

Old Plon (ploh[n]), a shepherd who thinks he hears noises under the huge pile of rock and earth left by the avalanche and assumes that he is hearing ghosts.

WHEN WE DEAD AWAKEN
(Naar vi døde vaagner)

Author: Henrik Ibsen (1828-1906)
First published: 1899
Genre: Drama

Locale: A coastal town of Norway
Time: The nineteenth century
Plot: Psychological symbolism

Arnold Rubek, a sculptor. At a mountain resort on the coast of Norway, Rubek and Maia, his wife, see Irene. In his youth, Rubek had found in Irene the perfect model, but he had turned away from her love. After leaving Irene, Rubek had stopped creating beautiful works in marble and made only concealed caricatures, with an animal's face hidden behind the human one. Finding his life of ease with Maia intolerable, he goes with Irene in search of their lost love and finds death with her in the snow at the top of the mountain.

Irene von Satow, the inspiration for Rubek's greatest work, *Woman Awakening from the Dead on the Resurrection Day After the Sleep of Death*. Irene tells Rubek that she is dead. She had meant to kill Rubek with a knife but decides to spare him when he tells her that he too has suffered. Although she tells him that he is already dead, she lures him to the mountaintop where they perish in the snow.

Maia Rubek, Rubek's wife. She finds Ulfheim, a sportsman, intriguing and accompanies him on a hunting trip to the mountains.

Ulfheim, a wealthy sportsman known as a bear-killer. After he and Maia quarrel on the snow-covered mountain, they are reconciled and tell each other of their youthful disappointments. Returning from the mountain, they meet Rubek and Irene going up toward the icy heights. Ulfheim warns them of the approaching storm.

A Sister of Mercy, a symbolic character. She watches Irene in each critical scene. At the end, she appears on the mountain, makes the sign of the cross, and wishes Rubek and Irene peace as they lie buried in the snow.

WHEN YOU COMIN' BACK, RED RYDER?

Author: Mark Medoff (1940-   )
First published: 1974
Genre: Drama

Locale: Southern New Mexico
Time: Late 1960's
Plot: Social criticism

Stephen "Red" Ryder, the graveyard clerk at a restaurant. A small, plain, nineteen-year-old man with brown hair, Stephen dresses in the style of the 1950's and has a tattoo on his arm that reads "Born Dead." Intense and unhappy, he feels stifled by the small New Mexico town in which he lives and has elaborate dreams of leaving, but he feels responsible for his ill mother. His dissatisfaction with his life is reflected in his negative relationships with others. His association with the cowboy hero Red Ryder serves to magnify his inability to mold his own life.

Angel, the daytime waitress. In her early twenties, Angel is overweight and plain. She lives with her mother and grandmother, and her life revolves around them, her job, and nights spent watching television with Lyle. She obviously cares about Stephen, and his departure at the end of the play is a devastating event in her life. Simple, sweet-natured, and vulnerable, she is a sympathetic character in the midst of the violence of the play.

Lyle Striker, the owner of the local gas station and motel. Lyle, who is in his sixties, has a brace on one knee and walks with a crutch as the result of a stroke. None of this is a sign of weakness, however, and he remains an active and attractive man. He engages in a friendly rivalry with Stephen and has some feelings for Angel. Straightforward and likable, he is a sensible man of considerable inner strength who attempts to maintain an even keel, even in the midst of an upsetting situation.

Richard Ethredge, a textile import businessman. Confident and good-looking in his late thirties, Richard is attractive and graceful. Authoritative, manipulative, and somewhat condescending, particularly toward his wife, he is accustomed to being in control and in charge. His money and his attitude make him a primary target of the young man who invades the scene, and the shallowness of his strength makes him easy prey.

Clarisse Ethredge, a violinist and college professor. Also in her late thirties, Clarisse is reserved, shy, and quiet, largely as a result of her husband's dominance. In the action of the play, she reveals a repressed sexuality and strength of character that are not evident in early scenes.

Teddy, a young drifter and drug runner. Thirty years old, Teddy is a former GI with long hair, dressed in an army fatigue jacket. Teddy is intense, insulting, and violent, both physically and psychologically. He despises a world that he finds unacceptable in its weakness. Unpredictable in his behavior, he has an innate ability to reveal people's fears and desires and thereby dominate them. His violence is without apparent purpose and occurs without any evident motivation. His sudden intrusion into the otherwise placid life of the play's characters is the force that motivates self-recognition and change.

Cheryl, Teddy's companion. Cheryl is busty and very attractive, no more than twenty years old, and dressed in jeans and a tank top. Submissive and basically silent through most of the play, she refuses to leave with Teddy at the end, exhibiting an independence and strength not previously revealed.

Mr. Carter, the owner of the restaurant. Mr. Carter is cheap, cantankerous, and totally devoted to his business. He is disdainful of other people and sees them only as tools for his own endeavors.

— *John C. Watson*

WHERE ANGELS FEAR TO TREAD

Author: E. M. Forster (1879-1970)
First published: 1905
Genre: Novel

Locale: England and Italy
Time: Early twentieth century
Plot: Social realism

Lilia Herriton, a young English widow. Unhappy in her life with her late husband's family, she goes to Italy with Caroline Abbott. There she marries Gino Carella, but her life is unhappy. She dies giving birth to a son.

Philip Herriton, Lilia's brother-in-law. As the family messenger, Philip is sent to Italy to bring Lilia home, but he arrives too late to prevent her marriage to Signor Carella. He returns to Italy after her death to retrieve the child, only to fall in love with Miss Abbott and to become friendly with Carella. Although he thinks he understands the world, Philip discovers he knows nothing when the baby is killed and Miss Abbott falls in love with Carella.

Gino Carella, an Italian. Although poor and somewhat vulgar, Signor Carella is a man of splendid physique. Com-

pletely devoted to his son, he is nearly crushed by the child's accidental death.

Harriet Herriton, Lilia's sister-in-law, whose scheme to kidnap the baby from Carella results in the child's death when a carriage overturns.

Mrs. Herriton, the matriarch of the Herriton family in Sawston, England.

Irma Herriton, Lilia's daughter. Left in England to be supervised by Mrs. Herriton, Irma announces to all of Sawston the news of her dead mother's Italian son.

Caroline Abbott, a friend who is responsible for Lilia's marriage. She goes to Italy again to retrieve the child, only to fall in love with Signor Carella.

WHERE HAS TOMMY FLOWERS GONE?

Author: Terrence McNally (1939-   )
First published: 1972
Genre: Drama

Locale: New York City
Time: 1971
Plot: Social satire

Tommy Flowers, a thirty-year-old dropout from St. Petersburg who has become a self-proclaimed urban revolutionary in New York City. Like his idols James Dean and Holden Caulfield, he sees himself as an outsider, defiant in the face of established authority, a confirmed malcontent who makes terrorist raids on an oppressively corrupt society and its stifling conventions. At first, these attacks on conformity are pranks—

shoplifting, defaulting on cab fare or the check for a meal, engaging in sex and drugs at any opportunity, and alarming shoppers by announcing that there is a bomb in Bloomingdale's. The menace becomes less playful after he manufactures a real bomb and carries it around Manhattan with him. He sets up a ménage of misfits with Ben, Nedda, and his dog Arnold, but this surrogate family fails to satisfy his need for a community that allows individual expression. After Ben dies and Nedda flees for the security of the suburbs, Tommy, in a final aggressive (he would say redemptive) act, takes his bomb and wires it to go off in a telephone booth near a policeman.

Nedda Lemon, an aspiring cellist who has fled the suburbs for the promise of a career in New York City. What she finds instead is a mean, cold city that offers, at best, the prospect of being booked to play the Lord's prayer at bar mitzvahs in Brooklyn. Despondent, she meets Tommy in the ladies' room at Bloomingdale's, where he discovers her stowing shoplifted goods in her cello case. She takes Tommy, Ben, and Arnold into her flat in the Village and for a while is content with this domestic arrangement, until Tommy's continued anarchic campaign to overturn the established order leads her to entertain fantasies of pipe-smoking doctors, station wagons, and the rest of the scenario of suburban stability. Arrested when she returns to pay a check that Tommy has failed to pay, Nedda is incarcerated and must resort to her father for her rescue.

Jack Wonder, known as **Ben Delight**, an old has-been stage actor and panhandler. Ben and Tommy share a street corner where Ben rants about having spent his career in the shadow of Paul Muni, claiming that Muni got all the parts that rightfully should have been Ben's. He staunchly defends the stage against the screen. He is ignorant of James Dean but has seen Tommy's disastrous stage performance in a minor Off-Broadway play. Ben precipitates one of Tommy's indictments of old age, but they are reconciled and move into Nedda's Village flat, where Ben passes his evenings endlessly reading *Variety*. He becomes ill and is taken to Bellevue, where he dies. Tommy regards Ben's death as yet another abandonment.

Arnold, Tommy's sheepdog, whom Tommy abandons to follow a sexy seventeen-year-old Californian to her hotel room. Left on the street alone, Arnold soliloquizes on the indecisiveness of his master while assuring the audience that he is not a talking but a thinking dog.

— *Thomas J. Campbell*

WHERE THE AIR IS CLEAR
(La región más transparente)

Author: Carlos Fuentes (1928-   )
First published: 1958
Genre: Novel

Locale: Mexico City, Mexico
Time: 1910-1954
Plot: Allegory

Federico Robles (feh-deh-REE-koh RROH-blehs), a wealthy and powerful business tycoon. Robles is born to peons working on the Ovando hacienda but has the opportunity to go to Morelia with a priest to serve as his sacristan. They go to the Zamacona hacienda, where Robles meets fifteen-year-old Mercedes Zamacona, with whom he begins sexual relations. After the lovers are found out, Robles flees and never again sees Mercedes, whom he made pregnant. Robles fights in the Mexican Revolution and later becomes a wealthy lawyer working for North American companies. Robles finally meets his son, Manuel Zamacona, who is later killed by an unknown assailant. Robles marries the beautiful Norma Laragoiti to complete his success. Robles begins a sexual and emotional relationship with Hortensia Chacón, whose Indian mother was a servant in the Ovando household. Although Hortensia is a typist in Robles' office, they do not meet until he begins to visit her in the hospital, where she is recovering after being beaten by her estranged husband. Robles takes care of Hortensia, who is now blind. She later stands by him when he goes bankrupt as the result of rumors and the dirty dealings of other businessmen. Norma, crazed by the thought of losing her wealth and social position, threatens to leave him. After Norma dies in a fire, Robles marries Hortensia, who is pregnant. The two withdraw to the countryside to grow cotton. Robles represents the corrupt businessman who sheds his false self to return to an authentic existence.

Ixca Cienfuegos (EEH-kah see-ehn-FWEH-gohs), a mysterious Indian who appears everywhere and knows all the characters. As he moves in the various social classes, he listens to the characters' life stories. He performs humanitarian acts but almost lets Norma drown in the ocean. He may have been responsible for her death, a sacrifice demanded by Teódula Moctezuma, his mother. After the fire, Teódula informs Ixca that he can go back to his true life, having performed the

sacrifice. His wife is to be Rosa, Norma's maid and the recent widow of a taxi driver. Ixca disappears for three years but reappears at the end of the novel. He waits for Rodrigo in the latter's car and explains that Teódula believed that Norma's sacrifice was necessary. He forces Rodrigo's foot onto the accelerator but finally allows him to stop the automobile.

Norma Larragoiti de Robles (lahr-rah-goh-EE-tee), Robles' wife, Ixca's lover, and Rodrigo's former girlfriend. Norma pretends to be the daughter of an aristocratic family that lost everything during the revolution, but her mother is a maid and her father had been a small businessman before his suicide. She becomes Ixca's lover while married to Robles. Although she knows that he wants to destroy her, she loves him. After an argument with Robles about his bankruptcy, she locks herself in her room, throws herself on the bed, and laughs hysterically. When the house catches on fire, she is unable to find the key and dies.

Rodrigo Pola (rrohd-REE-goh POH-lah), a failed poet. When his father returned to the revolutionary troops, he left his bride of two weeks pregnant. Rodrigo is reared by his mother, who works hard to educate him. He falls in love with Norma, who later tires of him. He feels unfulfilled and often complains of his bad luck. Toward the end of the book, he begins to write screenplays of little value, but they make him rich. He is now respected and marries the aristocratic Pimpinela de Ovando

Pimpinela de Ovando (peem-pee-NEH-lah deh oh-VAHN-doh), a member of the fallen landed aristocracy. She is innocent, dignified, and well-mannered. She lives reasonably well but tries to get back the family's lands. She falls in love with a young lawyer, Robert Regules, but does not marry him because her mother objects. She later regrets this decision when he becomes rich. She marries Rodrigo after he becomes wealthy.

Teódula Moctezuma (teh-OH-duh-lah mohk-teh-SEW-mah), an Indian woman who represents the great mother figure of Aztec mythology. She keeps the coffins of her dead husband and sons in her house and performs Aztec rites over their cadavers. Believing Norma to be the victim of the sacri-fice she demands from Ixca, she goes to Norma's burning house and throws her ritualistic jewelry into the fire as she gives thanks for the sacrifice.

Gabriel, a border crosser who returns to Mexico with gifts for his family. He is stabbed in the stomach during a party.

WHITE BUTTERFLY

Author: Walter Mosley (1952-   )
First published: 1992
Genre: Novel

Locale: Los Angeles, California
Time: 1956
Plot: Detective and mystery

Ezekiel "Easy" Rawlins, (ee-ZEE-kee-ehl), an African American detective. He finds himself drawn into the investigation of a number of brutal murders of black women at the request of the Los Angeles police department, because he can go places and do things that the police officially cannot. Easy is from Louisiana via Texas and went to Los Angeles during World War II to work in the aircraft plants; he remained there after the war. Easy no longer has his job at the plant but is settled in California. He owns a house and lives off the proceeds of several rental properties he bought with money he obtained illegally and which he keeps secret. Easy is fairly flexible as a detective, but he has one motto that he lives by: As a rule, he will not run down a black man for the law.

Raymond "Mouse" Alexander, Easy's best friend from Texas. Mouse, a psychotic killer, reflects Easy's dark and brutal side and often rescues him from tough situations when quick, violent action is needed. Mouse also expresses the suspicion of some African Americans toward whites. His casual attitude toward killing people provides much of the mordant humor in the novel.

Regina (Gina) Rawlins, Easy's wife of two years and the mother of their baby girl, Edna. She works as a nurse at Temple Hospital. She is a gentle, warm woman who grew up in a desperately poor Southern black family. As well as taking care of her alcoholic father, she reared most of her thirteen younger brothers and sisters after the death of her mother. Her marriage to Easy is in trouble. Midway through the novel, she takes Edna and runs away with Dupree Bouchard, a friend of Easy from his aircraft-working days. Her departure plunges Easy into depression and a fit of self-pity.

Quinton Naylor, an African American police sergeant who approaches Easy to help the department with an investigation. Easy is uncomfortable with him because of Quinton's official position in law enforcement and acquiescence to his white superiors. Easy describes him as having "rage-colored" skin, but he still talks like a white man.

Robin Garnett, also known as **Cyndi Starr** and as **the White Butterfly**. A twenty-one-year-old white woman from a wealthy Los Angeles family who has dropped out of college to work in the black section of town as a stripper, using the stage name of the White Butterfly. She is found murdered. Although she is white and was killed in a different manner, at first she is suspected to have been killed by the same person who killed several black women.

William Wharton, also known as **Mofass**, Easy's business partner in his scam with the apartments he owns. Officially, Easy works as a janitor in his own buildings, and Mofass acts as the owner/manager. A chain smoker of cheap cigars, his most notable characteristics are his wracking cough and his conservative business sense.

Vernon Garnett, Robin's father, a prominent and wealthy man. He kills his daughter when he finds out about her low life. Using his political and economic position, he is able to manipulate the cooperation of the police department to hide his crimes. He also commits additional murders, including that of Phyllis Weinstein (Sylvia Bride), a stripper friend of Robin who is hiding Robin's illegitimate baby, Feather Starr. As he searches for his granddaughter, he finally exposes his culpability. At the novel's end, Easy takes the homeless orphan home to live with him and his adopted son, Little Jesus, a Hispanic mute.

James "J. T." Saunders, a psychopath who preys on young women and is charged with the Los Angeles murders, but not before he is killed in a bar fight in Oakland by a local policeman. The "assassination," as Easy calls it, is part of the broad cover-up Vernon Garnett orchestrates with a corrupt policeman, Captain Violette, to conceal his murder of his daughter.

— *Charles L. P. Silet*

THE WHITE COMPANY

Author: Sir Arthur Conan Doyle (1859-1930)
First published: 1891
Genre: Novel

Locale: England, France, and Spain
Time: The fourteenth century
Plot: Historical

Sir Nigel Loring, an English nobleman. Although he is soft-spoken and slight of build, with squinting eyes, he is a brave man. He leads the White Company of English bowmen. He is captured by the Moors in Spain but released after a period of captivity.

Alleyne Edricson, a young Englishman reared in the Abbey of Beaulieu. He leaves the abbey a timid, unworldly per-son, but he develops into a brave yet gentle knight, becoming the Socman of Minstead. He falls in love with Lady Maude, Sir Nigel Loring's daughter, and finally wins her hand in marriage.

Lady Maude, the daughter of Sir Nigel Loring. She is a beautiful and spirited young aristocrat. When Alleyne proves himself as a knight, she agrees to marry him.

Hordle John, an immensely strong young Englishman who fails to adapt himself to the life in the Abbey of Beaulieu, where he is a novitiate. Leaving the abbey, he becomes a bowman in the White Company. A good soldier, he finally becomes squire to Alleyne after Alleyne is knighted by Prince Edward.

Samkin Aylward, a bowman in the White Company, a companion to Alleyne.

The Socman of Minstead, Alleyne Edricson's brother. A great, yellow-bearded fellow, he is a rascal. He mistreats Lady Maude, who is rescued by Alleyne. He is killed while assaulting Sir Nigel's castle in Sir Nigel's absence.

The Abbot of Beaulieu (boh-LYEW), a stern, unworldly man. He is Alleyne's guardian.

The Seneschal of Villefranche (veel-FRAH[N]SH), a wicked and rapacious French lord who drives his serfs to hatred and violence. When his serfs rebel, he is brutally killed. The rebellion endangers the lives of his English guests, who include Sir Nigel and Hordle John.

THE WHITE DEVIL

Author: John Webster (c. 1577-1580—before 1634)
First published: 1612
Genre: Drama

Locale: Rome and Padua, Italy
Time: The sixteenth century
Plot: Tragedy

Vittoria Corombona (veet-TOH-ree-ah koh-rohm-BOH-nah), the brilliant and beautiful wife of an elderly Florentine official. She becomes the mistress and later the bride of Paulo Giordano Ursini, the duke of Brachiano. She is a woman of tremendous courage and willpower and makes an eloquent and impassioned defense of her honor against the malicious but essentially just accusations of Duke Francisco de Medicis and Cardinal Monticelso. She dies with the same intensity with which she lived, refusing to weep but recognizing in her last moments the depths to which her career has brought her: "My soul, like to a ship in a black storm, is driven, I know not whither."

Flamineo (flah-MEE-nee-oh), her brother, an ironic commentator on his own life and the society in which he moves. He strives for worldly success without scruple, playing pander for his sister, murdering her husband to win favor with his master, Duke Brachiano, and finally killing his own brother in a hasty quarrel. There are in him, however, lingering traces of humanity that make him compassionate at the sight of his mother beside the body of Marcello. He remains an opportunist to the end and dies with an ironic jest on his lips.

The duke of Brachiano (brah-KEE-ah-noh), Vittoria's lover, whose desire for her outweighs every moral consideration. He brutally repudiates his duchess and has both her and Vittoria's husband murdered to make himself free to marry his glamorous mistress. His crimes haunt him in the form of apparitions as he lies dying from Lodovico's poison.

Isabella (ee-zah-BEHL-lah), Brachiano's patient wife, whose devotion to him almost exceeds the bounds of credulity. Deeply injured by Brachiano's harsh repudiation, she takes the blame for their separation to shield him from the wrath of her brother, the duke of Florence. Her death is, ironically, the result of her hopeless love; she is poisoned when she kisses a portrait of her husband.

Count Lodovico (loh-doh-VEE-koh), a nobleman banished for murder after he has squandered his large estate. He secretly loves the duchess and avenges her death by bringing destruction on the heads of Brachiano, Vittoria, and Flamineo.

Francisco (frahn-CHEES-koh), Isabella's brother, the powerful duke of Florence and a clever, subtle politician. No considerations deter him from avenging his sister's murder; he hires Lodovico and two others to kill Brachiano and disguises himself as the Moor, Mulinasser, to watch the success of his plots. He chooses this private revenge in preference to war, recognizing that the citizens of his own state would be the greatest sufferers if he attacked Brachiano.

Cardinal Monticelso (mohn-tee-CHEHL-soh), later Pope Paul IV, a violent enemy of Vittoria, whose husband was his cousin. Less subtle than Francisco, he is in some ways more vicious with his books of Roman sinners, who were undoubtedly blackmail victims. He retains scruples enough to condemn Lodovico's projected murders.

Cornelia (kohr-NEE-lyah), the mother of Vittoria, Flamineo, and Marcello, a ranting old woman in the tradition of William Shakespeare's Queen Margaret. She is shocked and repelled by the sins of her two older children and becomes mad with grief after Flamineo stabs Marcello.

Camillo (kah-MEEL-loh), Vittoria's foolish old husband. He is easily gulled by Flamineo, who convinces him that the best way to keep Vittoria faithful is to deny her the pleasure of his company. He is murdered while on a mission for the state.

Marcello (mahr-CHEHL-loh), Cornelia's loved younger son, who is free from most of the vices of his brother and sister. Disgusted by Flamineo's attentions to Zanche and the insults he directs at their mother, he accepts his brother's challenge but is treacherously stabbed before they can fight.

Zanche (ZAHN-kay), Vittoria's Moorish maid. Like most of the characters, she is loyal only to herself. She reveals the guilt of Vittoria and Flamineo to Mulinasser and offers him Vittoria's jewels as her dowry if he will wed her. She is trapped with her mistress by Flamineo and dies with them by Lodovico's hand.

Giovanni (jee-oh-VAHN-nee), Brachiano and Isabella's precocious young son. He is old enough to recognize evil, and he banishes Flamineo from court as soon as he is made duke.

Antonelli (ahn-toh-NEHL-lee) and
Gasparo (GAHS-pah-roh), Lodovico's companions, who assist in the murder of Brachiano.

Hortensio (ohr-TEHN-syoh), Brachiano's attendant.

Doctor Julio (YEW-lee-oh), an expert in poisoning who contrives Isabella's death.

WHITE-JACKET: Or, The World in a Man-of-War

Author: Herman Melville (1819-1891)
First published: 1850
Genre: Novel

Locale: A vessel of the U.S. Navy
Time: The 1840's
Plot: Adventure

White-Jacket, a common seaman aboard the United States frigate *Neversink* on a voyage from the Pacific around Cape Horn to the eastern seaboard. White-Jacket gets his name aboard the ship when he sews for himself a canvas jacket for protection against the cold of the Cape. He is a sensitive young man and is greatly disturbed by practices common aboard U.S. naval vessels of the nineteenth century; floggings, tyrannical officers, and issuance of liquor to crewmen all draw his fire. White-Jacket's story ends when he falls overboard off the Virginia capes and throws off the canvas coat to be better able to swim for his life. White-Jacket's account was instrumental in abolishing flogging as punishment in the U.S. Navy.

Jack Chase, a Britisher in United States service aboard the USS *Neversink*. He is the educated and civil petty officer under whom White-Jacket serves. His good work in getting privileges for the crew earns him the respect of the coarse seamen with whom he sails.

Captain Claret, a typical commander of naval vessels of the nineteenth century. He, along with his officers, feels that naval officers should drive men, not lead them. The captain is stern and usually fair but sometimes peevish and unpredictable. He never feels that common seamen deserve even a modicum of the respect ordinarily paid human beings.

WHITE NOISE

Author: Don DeLillo (1936-   )
First published: 1985
Genre: Novel

Locale: Blacksmith, a fictional American college town
Time: Early 1980's
Plot: Philosophical realism

Jack A. K. Gladney, the narrator. Fifty years old, Jack enjoys his academic success as founder and chair of the unique Hitler studies department at the College on the Hill in Blacksmith, a pastoral Midwestern town. Not a German speaker, he takes German lessons so that he will not make a fool of himself at a planned international conference on Hitler studies. Jack appears happy with his fifth wife, Babette, and his children and stepchildren, but he suffers an unease in his materialist and consumerist world of shopping malls, supermarkets, and television, all products of technology. In particular, he finds in them no solace for his great fear of death. Jack's obsession with death intensifies when he suffers from a technological disaster that exposes him to Nyodene D., a toxic agent. Jack's concern about death causes him to throw out many of his possessions and search out the inventor of Dylar, a medication that might cure his fear of death. Denied the medication and told that it is a failure, Jack shoots its inventor, Mr. Gray, but also shoots himself. Neither dies.

Babette Gladney, Jack's current wife, the mother by her earlier marriages of Denise and Steffie. In addition to her family roles, Babette is a jogger, reads tabloids to the blind Old Man Treadwell, and lectures adults on good posture. Babette is very forgetful but denies to Jack and Denise that she is taking any medication that causes this. Because of her great fear of death, she commits adultery with Mr. Gray, the inventor of Dylar, so that she take the drug. The drug, however, fails her.

Murray J. Siskind, a former New York sportswriter. Appointed visiting lecturer on living icons at the College on the Hill in the popular culture department, he befriends Jack. Siskind then enlists Jack in his dream of establishing an Elvis studies department, and in their discussions they discover similarities between Hitler and Elvis. Siskind seems to find

meaning in consumerism and enjoys teaching a seminar on car crashes in films. He and Jack take long walks and have long discussions, frequently about death.

Heinrich Gerhardt Gladney, Jack's fourteen-year-old son from his first marriage. Heinrich, named when Jack was beginning his Hitler studies department, is a student of science who talks mostly about environmental hazards. He challenges any statement of certainty and any possibility of knowing any truth.

Denise Gladney, Babette's eleven-year-old daughter from an earlier marriage. Denise is generally critical of her mother's behavior. She confronts Babette about her forgetfulness and conspires with Jack to find out what medication Babette is hiding from them.

Steffie Gladney, Babette's younger daughter from an earlier marriage. When Babette chews gum in place of the cigarettes she has given up, Steffie lectures her on the health dangers of chewing gum. She is obsessed with health.

Wilder, a preschool-age child from Jack's fourth marriage. Wilder's innocence comforts his mother and stepfather. He is large-headed and small of body. He disturbs them with a long crying spell for which they can find no cause. At the book's end, Wilder rides his plastic tricycle safely across a major highway in a miraculous escape from death.

Howard Dunlop, Jack's German teacher. As he gives lessons in his boardinghouse room, his behavior becomes increasingly odd. When he becomes a reminder of death, Jack discontinues his lessons.

Old Man Treadwell, an elderly blind man who lives alone but enjoys being read to from tabloids. He and his sister, Gladys, disappear and are found in the shopping mall, where they have been lost for four days.

Winnie Richards, a secretive young researcher at the College on the Hill. She has a reputation of moving around the campus without being seen on the walkways or in her office. She helps Jack when he is trying to find out what Dylar is.

Mr. Gray, also called **Willie Mink**, a mysterious project manager of Dylar experimentation who seduces Jack's wife before giving her the medication. His office is in the Roadway Motel, in the Germantown area of Iron City, where Jack shoots him.

Vernon Dickey, Babette's father. Dickey, a white-haired man, appears sitting in the yard and seems to Jack to be a figure of death. He gives Jack the German-made gun with which Jack later shoots Mr. Gray.

Bob Pardee, Babette's former husband and Denise's father. He raises funds for the Nuclear Accident Readiness Foundation.

Orest Mercator, Heinrich's snake-handling friend. He trains to set a record sitting with dangerous snakes but fails the test.

— *Francine Dempsey*

WHO HAS SEEN THE WIND

Author: W. O. Mitchell (1914-   )
First published: 1947
Genre: Novel

Locale: A small town in the prairies of Saskatchewan
Time: 1929-1937
Plot: Bildungsroman

Brian Sean MacMurray O'Connal, who ages from four to eleven during the course of the story. A slight, lean, dark "black Scotch" boy, Brian is imaginative and always inquisitive about the rhythms of nature that he witnesses on the sweeping, beckoning, and now drought-ridden Saskatchewan prairie where he lives. By the age of eleven, Brian has experienced the deaths both of cherished pets and of beloved members of his close family, making him mature beyond his years. Always sensitive to the relentless patterns of birth and death around him, Brian perceives aspects of life about which his contemporaries Forbsie Hoffman and Artie Sherry comprehend little. Brian's sturdy independence makes his mother heartsick, but his independence and his extraordinary visionary capacity protect him somewhat from the harsh emotional blows he is dealt so early.

Gerald O'Connal, Maggie's large, auburn-haired husband, Brian and Bobby's father, and the town druggist. A quiet, serious man, as befits his respectable position in the town, Gerald is also gentle and sensitive. It is Gerald who solves the conflict between Brian and his grandmother over Brian's puppy Jappy, who shares Brian's wonder and respects his sorrow over the birth and death of a baby pigeon, who quietly finances his impoverished brother Sean's irrigation project, and who is his wife's model of the kind of person she wants their sons to be. Always concerned for others, he downplays persistent signs of his own ill health and dies suddenly at the age of forty-three of gall bladder disease.

Maggie MacMurray O'Connal, a small, dark, pretty, and intense woman. She loves and admires her husband and cares fiercely about her sons, instilling in them a desire to be strong, worthy, and successful. Ordinarily a person who does not express her emotions, she nevertheless makes them evident on such occasions as the near death of infant Bobby and in her dignified but forceful defense of Brian to his sadistic teacher Miss Macdonald. Although she is devastated by her husband's death, her love and ambition for her sons is undiminished.

Margaret (Maggie) Biggart MacMurray, Maggie O'Connal's mother. Traveling west to homestead with her husband John in 1885, she led the pioneer's hard, challenging life, which she loved, and she delights still to tell her grandchildren about the old days. Now elderly, lame, and increasingly frail, she lives with her daughter's family. At first, she appears an authoritative figure to the small Brian. After Gerald's death, however, a mutual sympathy grows between grandmother and grandson; each appreciates the other's independence and affinity for the natural world. At eighty-two years of age, she dies of pneumonia, seeking the outdoor air at the last.

Sean O'Connal, Gerald's brother and his senior by fifteen years. A huge, profane redhead, never married, Sean loves his brother and his brother's family tenderly, having seen to Gerald's upbringing and education himself. A grain farmer devastated and embittered by the drought of the 1930's, Sean is a man of the future, vainly advocating conservationist plowing, irrigation, and farming methods. After Gerald's death, he encourages Brian's growing interest in agricultural engineering, assuring the boy's future.

Young Ben, the half-wild, wholly unchecked son of the reprobate Old Ben, but really a true child of nature, a noble savage. The shock-haired, gray-eyed, broad-cheeked Young Ben resists all efforts, both sympathetic and vengeful, to tame and educate him, preferring his natural habitat, the broad Saskatchewan prairie. He shares with Brian a compassion for helpless creatures, and he maintains an almost wordless, close, protective relationship with Brian. Young Ben embodies a freedom of spirit that Brian perceives but cannot attain.

Mr. Digby, the elementary school principal, weathered-looking, with a shock of fair hair, very blue eyes, and threadbare clothing. Though improvident, Mr. Digby is a man of compassion and lively intellect, always doing his best to combat the small town's narrowness and bigotry. He releases Young Ben from school, quietly financing the boy's few necessities after Old Ben is jailed, imperiling his own job in the process. He understands the needs of both his students and the many adults to whom he lends a sympathetic ear. Up to now a contented bachelor, he comes to love Ruth Thompson as a kindred spirit as well as a desirable woman.

Ruth Thompson, a dramatically dark-haired and dark-eyed teacher at Digby's school. As compassionate as Digby, she takes overt action against injustice more readily than he does and vanquishes the town bully Mrs. Abercrombie. Breaking for the second time an engagement to the sardonic yet humane town doctor Peter Svarich, she will marry Digby instead.

— *Jill Rollins*

WHO'S AFRAID OF VIRGINIA WOOLF?

Author: Edward Albee (1928-   )
First published: 1962
Genre: Drama

Locale: New Carthage, a small New England college town
Time: The 1960's
Plot: Absurdist

Martha, a middle-aged faculty wife and daughter of the president of a small New England college. Martha is loud, aggressive, and vulgar, secure that her father's position at the college will insulate her from censure. She has a volatile relationship with her husband, George. A crass joke may turn into a vicious insult, followed by a moment of happy intimacy, all smoothed over by constant consumption of liquor. Martha is particularly cruel about George's lack of academic success. She had envisioned him taking over the history department and eventually the college, but because he is only an associate professor at the age of forty-six, she considers him a failure. Martha and George's marriage revolves around a series of games, none more central than the myth that they have a teenage son, a fiction Martha in some strange way has convinced herself to believe despite the fact that they cannot have children. When Martha's continuous attacks on George's professional status and masculinity prove too much for him to bear, he retaliates by revealing before their guests Nick and Honey that his and Martha's son is "dead," effectively shattering Martha's carefully maintained fantasy world and forcing both him and Martha to face the future without the comfort of fantasy and game-playing.

George, Martha's husband, an associate professor in the history department. George is more subdued than Martha, but he participates in Martha's games, becoming especially uninhibited when drinking. George is intelligent and quick-witted, with a gift for wordplay, which he uses against both Martha and Nick. At first, George seems to have an advantage over Nick by virtue of his position at the college, but he soon finds himself threatened by Nick's youth, attractiveness, and professional ambition. As he drinks, he reveals a streak of cruelty by humiliating Honey with the story of her false pregnancy, which Nick had confided to him earlier. Although at first he seems somewhat reticent, even browbeaten by Martha, when the conversation turns to his and Martha's supposed son, he accuses Martha of making incestuous advances toward the boy. He then destroys his wife's illusions in the cruelest way possible, traumatizing Martha and mortifying Nick and Honey at the same time.

Nick, a new faculty member in the biology department. Nick is young, handsome, and ambitious. He is initially willing to play along with Martha and George's strange games because he wants to ingratiate himself with the older faculty member and particularly with the president's daughter. His eagerness to please even extends to going to bed with Martha, practically right in front of George. Nick's inability to satisfy Martha's sexual demands, coupled with his insecure status at the college, leads Martha to humiliate Nick. He acquiesces until George shatters Martha's power by revealing the truth about their imaginary son.

Honey, Nick's young wife. Honey is very timid, especially in contrast to George and Martha. She has neurotic and psychophysiological problems. Nick married her because he thought she was pregnant, but it turned out to be a false pregnancy. Now Honey becomes ill frequently, particularly when drinking or under stress. Honey is cautious and relatively reserved, careful not to mix her drinks and reluctant to become involved with George and Martha's games, yet fearful of offending them. Under the influence of liquor, Honey loses many of her inhibitions. Her actions are mostly childlike, in contrast to the viciousness of the others. Honey is humiliated when George reveals that Nick has confided the story of Honey's hysterical pregnancy to him.

— *Charles Avinger*

WICKFORD POINT

Author: John P. Marquand (1893-1960)
First published: 1939
Genre: Novel

Locale: New York and Wickford Point
Time: The twentieth century
Plot: Social satire

Jim Calder, the narrator, a writer of popular magazine fiction. Observant, ironic, and critical, he is magnetically drawn to Wickford Point by family relationships, early experiences, and pleasant recollections, but he is equally repelled once there by the combined inconsequence, fatuity, and snobbishness of the Brills. Jim bears some resemblance in both experience and personality to the author.

Mrs. Clothilde Wright (née **Brill**), his violet-eyed cousin, a financially irresponsible scatterbrain, charming but foolish.

Bella Brill, her daughter, a divorcée. She is fickle, perpetually dissatisfied, as irresponsible as Clothilde, and attractive to men but beginning to lose her youthful beauty.

Mary Brill, Bella's blue-eyed, yellow-haired, mild, and sweet older sister, conscious of her inferiority to Bella in attracting men.

Patricia (Pat) Leighton, Jim's helpful, understanding, and discreet longtime friend. She is an executive of comfortable means.

Joe Stowe, Bella's former husband, a financially successful writer. He was a close friend of Jim at Harvard and afterward. His brief marriage to Bella was doomed from the start.

Harry Brill, Clothilde's elder son, a snob, ne'er-do-well, and leech on Clothilde.

Sid Brill, his clothes-conscious, do-nothing brother, another leech.

Avery Gifford, Bella's wealthy former sweetheart, an amiable young man now married and the father of three children.

Archie Wright, Clothilde's second husband, a painter.

Allen Southby, Jim's bachelor friend, an ivory-tower Harvard professor of English, author of a celebrated though not widely read study of early American authors. He is an aspiring novelist with no ability to match his aspiration.

Aunt Sarah, Jim's aged, forgetful great-aunt, intelligent, classically trained, and acidulous. She is Jim's principal link with the family past.

John Brill, the Wickford sage, the family poet (possibly modeled on John Greenleaf Whittier and sometimes traced to Edward Everett Hale). Jim thinks of him as an old fraud.

George Stanhope, the literary agent for Jim and Joe.

General Feng, the Chinese commander in whose forces Jim and Joe serve after World War I.

Cousin Sue, the family nurse for Aunt Sarah.

Howard Berg, a man with whom Bella becomes involved.

WIDE SARGASSO SEA

Author: Jean Rhys (Ella Gwendolen Rees Williams, 1894-1979)
First published: 1966
Genre: Novel

Locale: Jamaica, Dominica, and England
Time: The 1830's
Plot: Domestic realism

Antoinette Cosway, later **Bertha Mason Rochester**, whose story constitutes a revisionist treatment of events culminating in her transformation into the famed madwoman in the attic, Bertha Mason Rochester in Charlotte Brontë's *Jane Eyre* (1847). Antoinette, the protagonist and narrator of approximately one-half of the story, reflects on her youth and the loneliness and isolation that she experienced as a white Creole child in the predominantly black West Indies. Having outlived most of her family, she halfheartedly submits to a marriage with the British Mr. Rochester that has been arranged by her stepbrother. In reality, this union is a business deal whereby Antoinette's inheritance is consigned to Rochester in return for his accepting responsibility for her. This latter point proves important as whispers and insinuations spread about Antoinette, her beautiful mother, and her younger brother, individuals thought to have "slept too long in the moonlight," who exhibit the madness supposedly present in all white Creoles. Antoinette's naïveté about life outside the West Indies contrasts sharply with Rochester's comparative worldliness. Her query to her soon-to-be husband reveals her troubled vulnerability—she speaks not of love or even romance but of rest: "Can you give me peace?" This attitude exposes a young woman who has deferred to the decisions of the men in her life—her father, stepbrother, and husband—while depending on old and subservient women for what little emotional support and nurturance she has received. She becomes a woman who cannot act and who is increasingly defined by men, as symbolized by Rochester's arbitrarily changing her name from Antoinette to Bertha. When her husband rejects her because of his growing preoccupation with her possible madness, Antoinette, denying her own resources, consults the black arts for a spell to bring love to their marriage. When this desperate attempt fails, she becomes blank, a shell destined for the profound madness chronicled in *Jane Eyre*.

Mr. Rochester, a young British gentleman, the second son of a proper English family who is forced by the law of primogeniture to secure his own fortune. His narration of the second half of the story recounts his arranged marriage to a beautiful but mysterious West Indian girl who brings to the union the fortune he seeks. Despite certain odd circumstances surrounding their marriage, only after receiving a revealing letter from a black man who claims to be a relative of his bride does Rochester realize why this marriage was so eagerly sought by her stepbrother. He also realizes that everyone but him is aware of the potential for madness that exists in his new wife's family. Sensing that he has been the victim of a duplicitous plot, Rochester expresses hatred for the deceptive beauty of the islands, a quality that he has come to associate with Antoinette as well. Seeking only his own sanity, he returns to England with Antoinette and conceals her with a nurse in the attic of his family home. Also on his return to England, he learns that both his father and his brother have died, thus ironically providing him with the fortune that he already has secured at great cost to himself and at even greater cost to Antoinette.

Annette Cosway Mason, Antoinette's mother, who was widowed at an early age. After her first husband's death, the family was very poor and lonely for five years. Determined to provide for her children and herself, Annette marries Mr. Mason and is happy for a time, but after the natives destroy her home and kill her son, Annette turns against Mason and tries to kill him. He places her in a separate house with servants as attendants. There her daughter witnesses the effects of madness. Vivid impressions burn indelibly into Antoinette's mind.

Christophine Dubois, a native of Martinique given to Annette as a wedding present by her first husband. Christophine becomes Antoinette's nurse and is the only person who consistently supports the lonely young woman. A colorful person given to expressing bromides of conventional wisdom, Christophine receives the news of the terms of Antoinette's marriage with the pronouncement, "All women . . . nothing but fools." A practitioner of voodoo, she refuses to use her black arts on Rochester until Antoinette has told him herself about her family secrets. In the end, Christophine's wisdom is not strong enough to save Antoinette.

Mr. Mason, Annette's second husband and Antoinette's stepfather. After Annette's demise, Mason attempts to care for Antoinette.

Pierre, the younger brother of Antoinette, who is afflicted with the family curse of madness. Their mother dotes on him much more than on Antoinette. Pierre is killed when natives set fire to the Mason home.

Aunt Cora, a relative of the Cosways who tries to protect Antoinette's rights and fortune after learning of Richard's arranged marriage for Antoinette.

Richard Mason, Antoinette's stepbrother, who negotiates the marriage of Antoinette and Rochester.

Daniel Cosway, a black man who claims to be a relative of Antoinette. He writes a letter to Rochester telling him about the taint of madness that follows Antoinette's family.

Sandi Cosway, Daniel's half brother and a relative of Antoinette. Implications persist that Sandi and Antoinette are involved romantically.

Grace Poole,
Mrs. Eff, and
Leah, servants in the house in England in which Rochester confines Antoinette.

— *Lagretta T. Lenker*

THE WIDOWER'S SON

Author: Alan Sillitoe (1928-   )
First published: 1976
Genre: Novel

Locale: Ashfield and elsewhere in England and Europe
Time: Early twentieth century to 1976
Plot: Psychological realism

Colonel William Scorton, the protagonist, a gunner during World War II. A straight-backed career soldier, he is rugged, tall, and authoritative. He is also very self-disciplined and organized, but rather pessimistic and solitary. He was molded into the image of the perfect soldier by a father who never showed him the slightest affection. The military order and discipline of his twenty-five years in the army have carried over into his civilian life, where he attempts to run his marriage and his career as if he were still in the army. Eventually, he realizes that he was never really cut out to be a soldier. Despite the lack of emotion shown to him during his childhood and the blandness of his military career, he is a passionate man who feels things deeply and who yearns for a true, loving relationship. At first glance, he falls head over heels in love with Georgina, but he never really understands that their marriage is doomed because they both are completely unable to express their emotions. Although he truly loves his wife, their marriage leaves them incomplete and yearning for something that neither of them has the emotional experience to comprehend. William's passions rise as he realizes that his wife is having an affair, causing their marriage to become a war zone and climaxing in an intensely emotional scene that results in William's suicide attempt. Rescued once again by his wartime friend Oxton, William finally realizes that there is nothing left of his marriage to save. He returns home to reestablish his relationship with his father and to sort out his thoughts and emotions before beginning his new career as a schoolteacher.

Sergeant Charlie Scorton, the widower of the title and William's father. Every inch the soldier, Charlie is tall, strong, and stubborn, and he has never exhibited any weakness during his eighty-three years. After watching his best friend die in the coal mines, he decides to enter the army, a decision that results in his complete estrangement from his family. Feeling rather bereft of family and friends, he learns to cover his pain with a sort of icy indifference that makes him an excellent soldier. Unfortunately, he carries this coldness into his brief marriage and the rearing of his son. Although he loves his son and wants only the best for him, he has no idea of how to behave with him and so treats William as if he were a child soldier. Never realizing that his son might have needs or desires of his own, Charlie chooses his son's career for him, sending him off to military school as soon as possible. Living vicariously through William and his military career, Charlie does not understand the reasons for William's resentment, nor does he recognize that he might not have done what was really best for his son. Living a rather lonely life, with only his sister Doris as company, he finally learns to accept William as an individual.

Georgina Woods Scorton, William's wife. Tall and fair, with piercing, cold, blue eyes, she too was reared in a military family. Restless in temperament, she attended boarding schools and spent her vacations with her grandmother. Never having seen a good example of married life, she must create her own ideas about marriage. Failing at this, and unhappy with the lack of emotion in her marriage, she is miserable and suffers from an inner despondency. She eventually renews her acquaintance with an old lover as a form of release and rebellion. This, however, only becomes the catalyst for the explosion of her marriage into outright war, and she and William fight almost constantly. Eventually, both she and William run out of passion and anger, and their marriage dissolves.

Sergeant Harold Oxton, William's batman during World War II. An extremely ugly man with false teeth, narrow eyes, a shapeless nose, and a lined face, he is a truly good person. Although he is a menace as a gunner, he is indispensable to William because of his common sense, his infinite stamina, and his blind loyalty. Completely devoted to his mother, he left home only twice, both times to fight against the Germans during the world wars. After his mother's death, he goes to work for William as a bouncer in a bowling alley and eventually meets and marries a nice German lady with whom he lives a happy, well-ordered life.

Brigadier "Jacko" Woods, Georgina's father. Tall, bony, and angular, the white-haired, blue-eyed brigadier is restless, forceful, talented, energetic, and unpredictable. An excellent infantry officer, he is the only soldier in the story who succeeded and became happy by making the army his career.

— *Susan V. Myers*

WIELAND: Or, The Transformation, an American Tale

Author: Charles Brockden Brown (1771-1810)
First published: 1798
Genre: Novel

Locale: Pennsylvania
Time: The eighteenth century
Plot: Gothic

Mr. Wieland, a religious fanatic. He fears a dreadful punishment because he has not answered a "call" to become a missionary. He dies by what seems to be spontaneous combustion: His clothes suddenly burst into flames one night as he meditates. He is Clara and young Wieland's father.

Clara Wieland, the narrator, who writes a long letter telling of the tragedy that is visited upon her family. She is attracted to Carwin, but when he defames her character to drive off a rival suitor, her love ends. Eventually, she marries Henry Pleyel, the brother of her childhood friend.

Mrs. Wieland, Clara's mother. She dies shortly after her husband, leaving Clara and young Wieland to be reared by an aunt.

Wieland, Clara's brother. He, Clara, and his wife, Catharine, live together as friends. He is a somber, melancholy man of a religious turn. When he hears strange voices, he believes he is in communication with some supernatural power. Thinking he is guided by heaven, he sacrifices his wife and their children. Regaining his sanity later and crushed by remorse, he commits suicide by stabbing himself.

Catharine Pleyel, a childhood friend of the Wielands. She marries Wieland and has four children by him. She is killed, along with their children, by her husband, while he is in a fit of madness.

Henry Pleyel, Catharine's brother, a lively young man. Eventually, he and Clara marry, after the death of his first wife, a European baroness.

Carwin, a stranger who appears dressed like a humorous beggar. He loves Clara but defames her to Henry, out of jealousy. He is accused by Clara of being the "voice" that guided Wieland to kill, because he is a ventriloquist. He assures Clara of his innocence and disappears from the area to become a farmer.

WIELOPOLE/WIELOPOLE: An Exercise in Theatre
(Wielopole, Wielopole)

Author: Tadeusz Kantor (1915-1990)
First published: 1984
Genre: Drama

Locale: Poland
Time: Sometime after World War II
Plot: Psychological

Uncle Karol and
Uncle Olek, two of the author's maternal uncles. They are inseparable to the point that one will not go anywhere without the other. They differ, however, in that Karol is very patriotic and believes in fighting (and dying) for one's country, whereas Olek is the type who believes in avoiding conscription at any cost. They serve as a kind of dark comic relief.

Uncle Stas, a Siberian deportee and another of the author's maternal uncles. Karol and Olek are so embarrassed by Stas's appearance—he looks like a busker wearing a tattered army uniform—that they decide to pretend that they do not know him.

Mother Helka (**Helena Berger**), also called **the Bride**, the author's mother. Dressed completely in white, she is dead at the time of the wedding, though in real life she lived long enough to give birth to the author.

Father (**Marian Kantor**), the author's father, a soldier. He is also dead at the time of the wedding, and he is by turns reviled and welcomed by Helka's family.

Mad Aunt Manka, an insane old woman. Another of the author's maternal relatives, she continually quotes biblical passages in a hysterical way, "as she periodically goes through a religious crisis."

Grandma Katarzyna, the author's maternal grandmother. Although she, too, is dead at the beginning of the play, she later comes alive, only to announce the timing of the crucifixion of Adas (a young recruit), the Priest, and Helka.

The Priest, Grandma Katarzyna's brother. Although he is dead, he performs the marriage ceremony for Helka and Marian. At the end, he is led away by the Little Rabbi, a character who appears only briefly.

The Photographer's Widow, the wife of the late town photographer, Ricordo. She serves double duty as the new town photographer and as a harbinger of death. She not only tends the dead bodies but also creates them by killing people with her camera-cum-machine gun.

— *T. M. Lipman*

WIFE

Author: Bharati Mukherjee (1940-　　)
First published: 1975
Genre: Novel

Locale: Calcutta, India; and Queens and Manhattan, New York
Time: The 1950's-the 1970's
Plot: Psychological realism

Dimple Dasgupta, the female protagonist, an ordinary woman from the urban Bengali middle class. She attends Calcutta University, hoping that a college degree will enhance her prospects for finding a good husband. Obsessed with her own physical inadequacies, she entertains vivid, unrealistic fantasies about a glamorous lifestyle after marriage. Her arranged marriage to Amit Basu, an engineer bound for America, leaves her disappointed and disillusioned. She resents Amit and his family, and she hates her subservient role, that expected of a Bengali bride. When she becomes pregnant, she expresses her quiet rebellion by inducing an abortion. She and Amit immigrate to New York. After Amit gets a job, she spends most of her time alone in their apartment, watching television, sleeping, or reading magazines. Her excessive exposure to soap operas and violence on television warps her values and distorts her sense of reality. She frequently plunges into moods of depression, fantasizing about different ways of committing suicide or inflicting pain on her husband. Unable to find love in her arranged marriage, she has an affair with Milt Glasser, an all-American boy. Her cultural values are eroded in Milt's company. Driven by guilt, passion, and revenge, she finally liberates herself by stabbing her husband to death. This act of self-empowerment makes her feel strangely American, like some character in a television show.

Amit Basu, Dimple's husband. He immigrates to the United States with the idea of making a fortune and then returning to his homeland to live in affluence. Insensitive, indifferent, and acquisitive, he slights his wife and fails to win her heart after marriage.

Milt Glasser, an enormous young American who seduces Dimple by treating her with sensitive casualness. To her, he represents America, promising the "glittering alternatives" cut off by her marriage to Amit. Milt lures her to drink vodka, eat hamburgers, wear jeans, and sleep with him.

Ina Mullick, a well-educated, seemingly Americanized and "chillingly sexy" Bengali woman involved in the women's liberation movement. A graduate of Calcutta University, she wanted to be a physicist, but her educational career was cut short when her father married her off to Bijoy Mullick, a rich Bengali entrepreneur living in America. An unhappy wife, she expresses her sense of rebellion against the ideal of Indian womanhood by adopting American attitudes toward sexuality. Presumably, she has had a lesbian relationship with an American woman, Leni Anspach, and is carrying on an affair with Milt Glasser. She is considered a bad influence on Indian expatriate wives.

Jyoti and

Meena Sen, the Bengali couple with whom Dimple and Amit stay when they first arrive in New York.

Marsha Mookerji, Milt Glasser's sister, a professor at Columbia University. She is married to a Bengali professor, Prodosh Mookerji. During their sabbatical, the Mookerjis let Amit and Dimple move into their Manhattan apartment.

— *Chaman L. Sahni*

THE WILD ASS'S SKIN
(La Peau de chagrin)

Author: Honoré de Balzac (1799-1850)
First published: 1830
Genre: Novel

Locale: Paris, France
Time: Early nineteenth century
Plot: Allegory

Raphael de Valentin (rah-fa-EHL deh vah-leh[n]-TA[N]), a reckless young man who learns that one must pay for everything in life. A poor, struggling law student and writer, he finds a wild ass's skin with magic powers in an antique shop in Paris. The skin grants all his wishes but shrinks in size with each wish; when it disappears, the owner dies. Raphael uses the magic powers to find material happiness with money, food, drink, and women. The skin keeps shrinking, however, and as it does he becomes unhappy again. He finds a brief respite when he marries his former landlady's daughter, but death approaches inexorably.

Rastignac (rahs-teen-YAHK), an adventurer and gambler. A friend of Raphael de Valentin, he finds work for Raphael as a hack writer and editor by introducing him to influential friends, including Countess Foedora. On occasion, he gambles on Raphael's account, winning large sums of money for him.

Pauline de Valentin, Raphael's wife, whom he marries shortly before his death. Pauline's first appearance is as the daughter of Raphael's landlady. Pauline admires him and does household chores for him; she even gives him money from her little hoard. When she meets Raphael later, she is rich, her long-lost father, an army captain believed lost in Siberia, having returned home with a fortune. She tries to commit suicide by strangling herself when she sees her husband dying.

Foedora (few-doh-RAH), a mysterious countess. She is a widow but refuses to marry a second time or take a lover, much to the disappointment of Raphael, who loves her passionately.

Emile (ay-MEEL), a friend to whom Raphael tells the story of his unhappy life. Emile merely laughs at his friend's troubles.

Mme Gaudin (goh-DA[N]), Raphael's mother-in-law and erstwhile landlady.

THE WILD DUCK
(Vildanden)

Author: Henrik Ibsen (1828-1906)
First published: 1884
Genre: Drama

Locale: Norway
Time: The nineteenth century
Plot: Social realism

Hjalmar Ekdal, a photographer. After his father's imprisonment for making and using a false map to fell timber on government land, his father's former partner, Werle, a businessman, set Hjalmar up as a photographer. He got Hjalmar a room in a house run by the mother of the Werles' former maid, Gina Hansen, who knows how to retouch photographs, and encouraged the two to marry. They have been married for some years when the play opens, and Hedvig, their fourteen-year-old daughter, is Hjalmar's chief joy. In addition to his photography, Hjalmar is working on an invention. Since old Ekdal's release from prison, he has lived with Hjalmar and his family. Hjalmar and old Ekdal have a strange attic filled with rabbits, doves, and a wild duck wounded by Werle and given to them. Hedvig claims it as a pet. Old Ekdal and his son, who "hunt" in the attic, shoot the rabbits and doves. They do not kill the duck because it is Hedvig's pet. Although Gina's bad grammar annoys Hjalmar, he is happy with her and with his life. Grateful for Werle's aid, he thinks that Werle helped him because he and Werle's son, Gregers, had been boyhood friends. When Gregers, who has been away for many years, returns and realizes that his father has tricked Hjalmar into marrying Gina and caring for Hedvig, who is probably Werle's child, he says that Hjalmar is a wild duck that has been wounded, but that he will cure him. The knowledge he gives Hjalmar wrecks his friend's happiness. Because Gina is not sure who the father of Hedvig is, he cannot bear to talk to the child. When Hedvig kills herself after her father rejects her, Hjalmar is horrified. Over the child's dead body, he and Gina are reconciled. Relling, a skeptical doctor who has known Hjalmar since college days, says that his grief is not very deep and that he will be spouting sentimental poetry about Hedvig in a few months.

Gregers Werle, a son of the merchant Werle, a thwarted idealist disillusioned by his father. He can never convince people that his ideas are valid. After he has enlightened Hjalmar, he expects happiness to follow the truth. He is baffled by Gina's and Hjalmar's reaction; Gina seems indifferent, and Hjalmar is crushed. When Hedvig shoots herself, Gregers feels that she did not die in vain because sorrow has ennobled Hjalmar.

Old Werle, a merchant and manufacturer. Acquitted of implication in the map fraud that sent Ekdal to jail, he continues to pay the Ekdal family, apparently from conscience. About to marry Mrs. Sorby, his present housekeeper, he sends Hedvig a note telling her that he will pay her grandfather a hundred crowns a month for life and that after his death Hedvig will continue to receive that amount for her lifetime. Hedvig has weak eyes, like Werle, and will become blind. Although Werle has put everyone in a situation of vulnerability, he tries to support them. His misguided son hastens their downfall.

Gina Ekdal, Hjalmar's wife. Gina says that she married Hjalmar because she loved him and that she deceived him about old Werle only because she was afraid he would not marry her if he knew of the affair. A good wife, she takes life calmly and apparently has no feeling of guilt for her past misbehavior. After Hedvig's death, she is able to comfort Hjalmar. She is a primitive, uncomplicated, and nearly peasant woman.

Hedvig, the young daughter, a loving child with weak eyes. Always confused by the adult world, she is driven to desperation when her supposed father turns against her. After Gregers has convinced Hedvig that to sacrifice her wild duck to her father would win his approval, Hedvig takes his pistol and goes into the attic. There, she shoots herself. Because there are powder burns on her dress and her grandfather has just told her that the way to kill a duck is to shoot it in the breast, her death is clearly intentional.

Old Ekdal, Hjalmar's father, a picturesque character given to scurrying around at the wrong time, drinking in his room, and game hunting in the attic. Everyone seems to be fond of old Ekdal.

Mrs. Sorby, Werle's housekeeper, a protective, efficient woman. She evidently has a past, but she and Werle have told each other everything and look forward to a happy marriage.

Relling, a doctor with no illusions who lives in Hjalmar's house. He tells Gregers that Hjalmar's sorrow for Hedvig is temporary.

Molvik, a student of theology, Relling's drinking companion.

THE WILD GEESE
(Gan)

Author: Mori Ōgai (Mori Rinatarō, 1862-1922)
First published: 1911-1913
Genre: Novel

Locale: Tokyo, Japan
Time: 1880
Plot: Psychological realism

Okada, a medical student at Tokyo University, a young man who lives a life of balance and order. He is a good but not outstanding student and a solid athlete who is a member of the rowing team (an outlet for his inclination toward the martial arts). He appears to do nothing with passion; he is remarkably free from obsession. In his free time, he takes long walks, and he often visits the local bookstores, where he searches for the Chinese romance novels that are the only books he reads for pleasure. His view of Otama, whom he encounters on one of his walks, is colored by his fantasy of the ideal woman. A true woman, Okada believes, is one who is able to concentrate solely on the traditional womanly virtues and who is able to be concerned primarily with her appearance even on the verge of death. Because he has so little contact with Otama, he is able to keep his fantasies about her intact.

Otama, a virtuous and obedient young woman who, through no fault of her own, becomes a fallen woman in the eyes of society. Although her father had turned down various marriage proposals for Otama, he finally accepted a proposal from a policeman who intimidated him. It turned out that the policeman already had a wife and children; he had simply been using Otama as a plaything. Because her prospects for a good marriage have been ruined by that calamity, Otama agrees to become the mistress of the moneylender Suezo, who plays on Otama's desire to ensure that her father will be well cared for as he grows older. As the novel progresses, Otama discovers that Suezo has deceived her about his career, and she loses her innocence when she resolves that she will never again be tricked on account of her naïveté. In spite of that resolution, however, she begins to have romantic fantasies about Okada. Her thoughts of Okada awaken her sexual desire, which has lain dormant in spite of her sexual relationships with Suezo and her policeman husband.

Suezo, who began his career as a lowly servant who ran errands for medical students but has managed to become wealthy by making loans to students who have temporarily run out of money. Suezo does not care that he and his family are reviled because his is a despised profession; his concerns are almost exclusively financial. As he has become more successful, however, he has come to resent his wife Otsune, who is a good mother but is also ugly and quarrelsome. When he decides that he deserves the companionship of a beautiful, obedient woman, he remembers Otama and realizes that he has the opportunity to turn her misfortune to his own advantage. He makes her his mistress, but afterward he has to deal with his wife's anger and resentment. Although Otsune is dull-witted and is temporarily confused by Suezo's excuses, she knows that he is seeing another woman. As his family situation deteriorates, Suezo becomes more obsessed with Otama, who becomes more beautiful and fascinating in his eyes as she becomes more worldly.

Otama's father, a candy seller who loves his daughter dearly but is too weak and ineffectual to protect her. He stands by helplessly as his daughter is ruined by the bigamist policeman who marries her under false pretenses. Later, he can only watch as Otama, after she becomes Suezo's mistress, changes from an innocent and trusting girl into a sexually aware and worldly woman.

Otsune, Suezo's argumentative and unattractive wife. Initially a good mother, she begins to neglect her children as well as her husband when she becomes consumed by anger and resentment brought on by her awareness of Suezo's relationship with Otama.

— *Shawn Woodyard*

THE WILD PALMS

Author: William Faulkner (1897-1962)
First published: 1939
Genre: Novel

Locale: The United States
Time: 1927 and 1937
Plot: Tragicomedy

Harry Wilbourne, a twenty-seven-year-old intern working in a New Orleans hospital. He meets and falls in love with Charlotte Rittenmeyer, a local socialite and would-be artist. Harry has humble antecedents and has made his way through medical school on a $2,000 legacy left to him by his doctor father. Although he is unaccustomed to going out socially, he accompanies an acquaintance from the hospital to a party. Over the next several weeks, Harry's natural reticence is swept away by Charlotte's vivacity, and he agrees to run away with her. Their short, tempestuous love affair eventually provides Harry with insights into matters of the human heart.

Charlotte Rittenmeyer, a bored, failed artist who latches onto the mild-mannered Harry Wilbourne, an impoverished intern whom she meets at a local artist's salon. She willingly abandons her husband and two daughters to leave New Orleans and live with Harry, at first in Chicago, later in Utah, and finally in Texas, where she dies from a bungled abortion reluctantly performed by Harry. She helps Harry to discover love and the joys of sex, as well as to learn to relish life lived from day to day.

Francis "Rat" Rittenmeyer, Charlotte's husband, a sophisticated man about town. Because he is Catholic, he will not divorce his wife when she decides to elope with Harry; instead, he gives Harry a Pullman check to cover the cost of Charlotte's return trip should she ever decide to come back to him. Although he is deeply hurt by her betrayal, he behaves decently and even gives a cyanide capsule to Harry to spare him the long imprisonment awaiting him for inadvertently causing his wife's death.

The doctor, a short, somewhat fat, untidy, provincial, middle-aged man who appears at the beginning of the story to tend to the dying Charlotte. He functions as a stand-in for what Harry would have become without his experiences in love. He is outraged by Harry's behavior and turns him in to the police when he calls for an ambulance to take Charlotte to the hospital. He owns the beachside cabin Harry and Charlotte rent at the story's conclusion, as well as the cabin next door, where he lives with his childless wife.

The doctor's wife, known as **Miss Martha**, who is as settled and conventional as her husband but shows some compassion for Harry and Charlotte. She suggests that Harry be allowed to run away to avoid prosecution, but she is overruled by her more legalistic husband.

Buck Buckner, who runs a failing mining operation in the mountains of Utah. Harry and Charlotte go there in order to escape falling into a conventional middle-class "marriage" in Chicago. Buck persuades Harry to perform an abortion on his wife, Billie, because they cannot afford to raise a child. The operation is successful, but Harry is worried enough about its outcome that he makes Buck promise to take Billie to a proper doctor once they have fled the mountains.

— *Charles L. P. Silet*

WILD SEED

Author: Octavia E. Butler (1947-   )
First published: 1980
Genre: Novel

Locale: West Africa, New England, and Louisiana
Time: 1690-1840
Plot: Fantasy

Anyanwu, an immortal shape-shifter and healer, the novel's protagonist. By manipulating her physical form, Anyanwu can change her gender, race, and species. She begins the novel in Africa in the guise of an elderly woman living alone, the mother of many children. She leaves her home when she encounters Doro, who promises her a safer existence in a new world (America) and children who will never die. To the powerful and immortal Doro, Anyanwu is "wild seed," a freak of nature whose powers he wishes to use in building an immortal culture of people he will breed and rule. Anyanwu is drawn to Doro and the idea of immortal children. Doro abuses her until a war is begun between them that lasts more than 150 years and spans the course of the novel. Only after Anyanwu's suicide attempt convinces Doro to treat her and all of his people with some respect can she care for him.

Doro, an immortal body-vampire, the novel's antagonist. Doro lives eternally by invading other people's bodies. Late in the novel, it is revealed that he wished to die when he discovered the brutal nature of his powers as a child. He has come to accept his fate and works to build a "superrace" through enslavement of and forced breeding of individuals with extraordinary mental and physical abilities. Although his goals never change, he becomes less brutal through prolonged contact with Anyanwu.

Isaac, Doro's favorite son. Although he is not immortal, Isaac, a man of mixed racial heritage has telekinetic ability, the power to move things with his mind. He is promised Anyanwu as a mate by his father early in the novel, despite Doro's sexual involvement with her. Though he resists at first, over time Anyanwu comes to find Isaac a loving and respectful husband. Isaac dies midway through the novel. His last words are a plea to his wife to forgive Doro for his cruelty; he loves his father and believes only Anyanwu can make him a decent man.

Thomas, a Native American man used by Doro as a breeder. To punish Anyanwu for her resistance to his authority, Doro forces her to have sex with the physically and emotionally ill Thomas. He is a hateful and violent man but learns to care for Anyanwu after she heals him. Doro's merciless response to this bond is to kill Thomas by taking over his body.

Nweke, the daughter of Anyanwu and Thomas. Nweke, a central character during the middle section of the book, has powerful mental and physical abilities. They eventually drive her mad, causing her to attack her adoptive father, Isaac, who unknowingly kills the girl in an attempt to defend himself.

— *Elyce Rae Helford*

WILHELM MEISTER'S APPRENTICESHIP
(Wilhelm Meisters Lehrjahre)

Author: Johann Wolfgang von Goethe (1749-1832)
First published: 1795-1796
Genre: Novel

Locale: Germany
Time: Late eighteenth century
Plot: Bildungsroman

Wilhelm Meister (VIHL-hehlm MIS-tur), the novel's hero, who provides continuity to an otherwise long series of vignettes. He is the son of a wealthy merchant who cannot understand his son's fascination for the theater. Meister, discovering that his first love is unfaithful, travels for his father's firm collecting debts and publicizing the company's wares. He meets actors along the way, joins them, keeps them out of financial difficulties, and learns that a young boy he has been protecting is his own son. Meister finally marries and settles down with a nobleman's sister, a "beautiful Amazon" who once rescued Meister's troupe of actors from bandits. He believes he has served his apprenticeship in life.

Philina (fih-LEE-nah), a gay young actress in love with Meister and around whom a group of unemployed actors forms. Meister, after lending financial aid to the destitute troupe, decides to travel with them. Philina is devoted to Meister, and she nurses him back to health after he is wounded by robbers.

Mariana (mah-ree-AH-nah), Meister's first love, whom he abandons when he learns that she is a kept woman. After her death, it develops that she has born him a child; through a set of coincidences, the boy is with his father in the traveling company of actors.

Mignon (mee-NYOH[N]), a graceful, pretty child whom Meister rescues from a troupe of acrobats who mistreat her. She becomes devoted to Meister and follows him everywhere. She becomes ill and dies. It is learned after her death that she was the daughter of a nobleman priest by an incestuous affair he had had with his sister. The mad priest, turned harpist, ironically had been in the traveling company with Meister and Mignon. He had been expelled from the group and sent to live with a clergyman after he had attacked and nearly killed Meister's illegitimate son, Felix.

Aurelia (ow-RAY-lee-ah), a woman who has lost her husband and been deserted by her nobleman lover. She takes Mariana's child as her ward when Mariana dies of a broken heart. When Meister meets Aurelia on his travels, he, unknowingly, also finds his son. After Aurelia dies, he becomes her ward's protector.

Melina (meh-LEE-nah), a wandering player rescued by Meister when a girl's parents discover that Melina has been indiscreet with their daughter. Meister sees the pair married, and he gives Melina money with which he starts the company that Meister joins.

The prince of ——, an influential nobleman for whom a local count and countess provide entertainment by hiring Melina's company for a series of performances. The prince is pleased by the entertainment; the count and countess are confused by the strange antics of the players generally and of Meister in particular, for he makes love to the countess and convinces the count that in Meister the nobleman sees his own *Doppelgänger*.

Old Barbara, Mariana's maid, who explains to Meister after Mariana's death that Felix is his son by her former mistress.

Natalia (nah-TAH-lee-ah), a beautiful "Amazon," the sister of one of Meister's nobleman friends, who leads a party to rescue Meister's troupe when it is set upon by robbers. It is Natalia whom Meister finally marries.

Serlo (SAYR-loh), an actor-manager and Aurelia's brother. He gives Meister's company a contract.

Lothario (loh-TAH-ree-oh), a nobleman, Natalia's brother, who befriends Meister and introduces him to intellectual circles in Germany. Lothario had loved Aurelia and deserted her.

Norberg, Mariana's wealthy patron, to whom she is unfaithful by making love to Meister.

Laertes (LAYR-tehs), Philina's escort and Meister's carefree friend. He loves to dance and play practical jokes.

Felix, Meister and Mariana's illegitimate son.

Werner (VAYR-nur), Meister's prospective brother-in-law, who warns him that Mariana is a woman of easy virtue.

Countess ——, Lothario and Natalia's sister.

WILHELM MEISTER'S TRAVELS
(Wilhelm Meisters Wanderjahre: Oder, Die Entsagenden)

Author: Johann Wolfgang von Goethe (1749-1832)
First published: 1821, 1829
Genre: Novel

Locale: Germany
Time: Early nineteenth century
Plot: Philosophical

Wilhelm Meister (VIHL-hehlm MIS-tur), a philosophical gentleman who, upon becoming a Renunciant, has pledged to wander the earth, never stopping any one place for more than three days. Meister, having deserted the world of commerce and the stage, is trying to form some spiritual conclusions. The novel's end finds him still on the road, furthering his final purifying sacrifice.

Felix, Meister's son, who travels with his father except for a period of years spent in a school learning the value of labor and art. He injures himself in a fall and is last seen receiving medical attention from his father.

Lenardo (lay-NAHR-doh), Meister's friend, who discovers that part of the money an uncle had given him to use in traveling had come from a farmer and his daughter whom the uncle had found it necessary to dispossess. The Nut-Brown Maid, the farmer's daughter, becomes a point of conscience for Lenardo, and he spends a great deal of time traveling in an effort to learn what has become of her. Meister, fortunately, discovers her and sends word to Lenardo that the girl is well and safe; Lenardo is then free to return home.

Hersilia (hur-SIHL-yah), Lenardo's cousin, much admired by Felix. When Hersilia shoves Felix during some innocent love play, Felix is offended. Dashing off wildly, he injures himself in a fall on some stones beside a stream.

Flavio (FLAH-fee-oh), a young man for whom his father, a major, has arranged a marriage with his sister's daughter, Hilaria. After many misunderstandings—Hilaria wants to marry her uncle instead of the son, for example—Flavio finally marries her and becomes a prosperous merchant.

Makaria (mah-KAH-ree-ah), a wise old woman who keeps a castle from which she dispatches advice that solves the problems of friends and relatives, and in which lives a savant who studies the stars and explains their secrets to Meister.

Joseph (YOH-sehf) and
Mary (mah-REE), a couple with a beautiful baby whom Meister and Felix encounter on the road. Joseph is a woodworker who has done artistic holy panels for a local chapel in which the family resides. He had rescued Mary from a band of robbers who had killed her husband. He married her shortly after her child was born. When Meister and Felix meet him, he is a prosperous rent collector who lives happily with his family.

Jarno (YAHR-noh), often called **Montan** (mohn-TAHN), a geologist friend of Meister whom he encounters on his travels. Jarno had known Meister during their acting days. Like Meister, he has become a Renunciant.

Fitz, a beggar boy and a friend of Felix. He knows the country and serves as a guide for a while for the father and son. Fitz leaves the party when he is able to escape from a beautiful garden in which Meister and Felix are taken captive by men who, it turns out, mean them no harm.

Hilaria (hih-LAHR-ee-ah), a young girl met by Meister as he travels with an artist friend in the Italian lake country, the home of Meister's foster daughter, Mignon. Hilaria travels with a pretty widow. When her education is completed, she marries Flavio.

Julietta (yew-lee-eh-TAH), Hersilia's older, plain sister.

WILLIAM TELL
(Wilhelm Tell)

Author: Friedrich Schiller (1759-1805)
First published: 1804
Genre: Drama

Locale: Switzerland
Time: The fifteenth century
Plot: Historical

William (Wilhelm) Tell, a renowned hunter of the Canton of Uri. Tell, a pacifist, avenges the oppression of the Swiss people by slaying the ruthless governor, the representative of the emperor of Austria. Tell's skill as a marksman is tested when he is ordered by the governor to shoot an apple off the head of his son at seventy paces. Arrested despite his obedience, Tell, in another feat of daring, escapes from the boat that carries him to imprisonment, gets his crossbow, and slays the evil governor, Gessler. Returning to his home, he finds a monk—actually a nobleman in disguise—in hiding because he has murdered the emperor. Removal of the heartless monarch and his brutal governor brings lasting freedom to the Swiss people.

Hermann Gessler (HUR-mahn GEHS-lehr), the governor of Uri and Switz, slain by Tell. Gessler, the youngest son of the

emperor of Austria, sublimates his lack of status by subjugating those under his rule. Undaunted in his mercilessness, he plunders, deceives, and slays.

Ulrich von Rudenz (EWL-reekh fon REW-dehnts), the nephew of the Free Noble of Switzerland. In the spirit of youthful change and the desire for status, he wishes to side with Austria. His contention that old regimes must pass to make way for the new is motivated by his love for a woman he thinks loyal to Austria. Learning his mistake about her loyalty, Ulrich gains the courage to ridicule the governor for his unreasonableness and to prove himself a gallant in defending his own people. He becomes the baron, replacing his deceased uncle, and pronounces the Swiss free.

Bertha von Bruneck (BAYR-tah fon BREW-nak), a rich heiress. Her efforts to lighten the load of the mistreated people are at first misunderstood, the peasants crying that she would pay for injury with gold. She proves her humanitarianism, however, and takes Ulrich as her husband.

Werner Stauffacher (VEHR-nehr SHTOW-fah-kur), a citizen of the Canton of Switz. Lamenting the plight of the downtrodden people, he is spurred to action by his wife. He becomes the organizer of the forces of his canton for the conspiracy.

Walter Fürst (VAHL-tehr fewrst), a citizen of Uri, Tell's father-in-law. Reflecting the sageness of the mature, Fürst tempers the brashness of the young, who would rush headlong to avenge wrongdoing. He organizes the leaders of the three cantons for the conspiracy and serves as the leader of the Uri forces.

Arnold von Melchthal (MEHLKH-tahl), a citizen of Unterwald who slays a representative of the governor who attempts to take Melchthal's oxen. In reprisal, Melchthal's father is barbarously blinded by government order. The atrocity makes Melchthal the likely volunteer as confederacy leader, to mobilize the people of Unterwald.

Werner, Baron von Attinghausen (AHT-tihng-how-zehn), Ulrich's uncle. He is the venerable leader, and in his own goodness he is naïve about the malevolence of others. Despite his rude awakening to reality, his last words are prophetic of the peace to come to his people, and his final admonition, which guides the confederates in their ensuing battle for liberty, is for union among themselves.

Conrad Baumgarten (BOWM-gahr-tehn), a citizen of Unterwald whose escape is the first indication in the play of the government's evil treatment of the people. Baumgarten is fleeing because he has murdered a government agent for an attempted attack on Baumgarten's wife. Baumgarten serves willingly in the confederacy.

Rösselmann (ROOS-sehl-mahn), the priest of Uri, representing the church. He tries, for the sake of peace, to seek a compromise before rising in arms against the government. Seeing the heinous acts of the oppressors, the priest leads the confederates in swearing to death rather than to slavery. He pleads for aggression in defending themselves, rather than delay.

Walter, Tell's son. He displays his bravery when an apple is placed on his head as his father's target.

Hedwig (HEHD-vihg), Tell's wife and the daughter of Fürst. Hers is the plight of the warrior's wife, uncertainty and anxiety filling her days.

Gertrude (gehr-TREW-deh), Stauffacher's wife, who advocates action rather than lamenting if the people are to preserve their liberty.

Friesshardt (FREES-hahrt), a soldier and an attendant to Gessler. With bullying fervor, he binds Tell and drags him away at the governor's orders after the huntsman has shot the apple.

Armgart, a peasant woman. She detains Gessler and derides him for his abuse of the people, after he has been shot from a cliff by Tell.

Rudolph der Harras (HAH-ras), Gessler's master of horse. His declaration that he will carry on after Gessler's death portends further difficulty for the Swiss. His intentions are short-lived, however, when the government forces are disrupted.

THE WIND: Attempted Restoration of a Baroque Altarpiece
(Le Vent: Tentative de restitution d'un rétable baroque)

Author: Claude Simon (1913-   )
First published: 1957
Genre: Novel

Locale: A small town in southern France
Time: The 1950's
Plot: Antistory

Antoine Montès (ahn-TWAHN mohn-TEHZ), age thirty-five, who arrives in a small town to take possession of a vineyard inherited from a father whom he has never known. His mother had left the town and Antoine's father after she discovered him making love to the maid. Montès fires the bailiff, who refuses to uproot his own family from the property. Montès makes the acquaintance of several people in a town that generally rejects him: Rose (with whom he falls in love), Maurice, distant cousins, the notary, and a stranger (the narrator) whom he meets in a photography shop.

Maurice (moh-REES), a pretentious and nosy fertilizer salesman. He tries to befriend Montès and discovers that he is hiding stolen goods for Rose. He steals a note written by Cécile to Montès and tries to blackmail her father with it.

Cécile (say-SEEL), the younger, tomboyish daughter of Montès' distant relative. She breaks off her relationship with her fiancé as she becomes enamored of Montès and writes Montès a note. When she is found out by her older sister, she forces her former fiancé to make love to her.

Hélène (ay-LEHN), the older sister of Cécile. She discovers Cécile's relationship with Montès and is successful in thwarting Maurice's attempts at blackmailing their father. She informs the authorities about the stolen goods and Jep's role in the burglary by going to the prosecutor's house. She tells his wife that Rose had been in her employ. Having discovered Rose and Jep making love in her house, she dismissed Rose, who was then hired by the victims of the latest burglary.

The notary, who would like Montès to sell his property and leave the town. He believes, with the other people in town, that Montès is an imbecile for not doing so.

The social worker, who allows Montès to visit Rose's two orphaned children on the first Thursday of every month but discourages him from trying to adopt them.

The priest, who has received the stolen goods from Montès so that he might return them to the rightful owner.

Rose, a waitress in a very modest hotel. She and her two children are befriended by Montès. She confides in him and places in his care jewelry stolen by her husband.

Jep, a former boxer and Rose's gypsy husband. After Hélène informs on him to the authorities, he thinks that he has been betrayed by his wife, stabs her, and is later killed by the police in a scuffle.

Theresa, the older of Rose's daughters. She goes on a walk with Montès, during which they meet her father, who knocks him out in a fight.

The bailiff, an older man who lives on Montès' property with his wife and children. He does not want to leave the property when Montès returns to claim it. One of his daughters had been the father's mistress. In the lawsuit that ensues, the bailiff is awarded the property because of outstanding debts.

The prosecutor's wife, who is irate that she should be disturbed during dinner by Hélène. She believes that Hélène should have gone to her husband's office to inform him.

The narrator, a teacher and writer who becomes Montès' friend after they meet in a photography shop.

— *Peter S. Rogers*

WIND FROM AN ENEMY SKY

Author: D'Arcy McNickle (1904-1977)
First published: 1978
Genre: Novel

Locale: The northwestern United States
Time: First half of the twentieth century
Plot: Historical realism

Bull, the chief of the fictional Little Elk tribe. He has kept his band in the mountains, isolated from the white men who have invaded the land below. At the novel's beginning, Bull takes his grandson to see a hydroelectric dam that has been constructed in a meadow that was sacred to the Little Elk people. When he realizes that the white men have "killed the water," he shoots, ineffectually, at the dam. Bull knows that talking to the white men is of no use—the two cultures cannot understand each another, even when they know the meaning of the individual words.

Henry Jim, Bull's brother, who decided to live among the white men thirty years earlier. He believed that assimilating into their culture was the way to survive. In an effort to lead the people away from the old ways, he gives the Featherboy bundle, the Little Elks' most sacred object, to a "dog-faced" minister who sells it to a museum. As a result, he and Bull have not talked to one another for three decades. By the novel's end, he has moved out of the nice house the white men had built for their "prize Indian" and is living in a tipi on his farm. He has even forgotten the English language, an indication of his total rejection of the white culture.

Louis, Bull's other brother, who has stayed in the mountain camp with Bull. He distrusts white men completely, although he can tolerate Rafferty, whom The Boy says "talks pretty good," which means that he listens as well as speaking, a quality Louis appreciates.

Antoine, Bull's grandson, who has just returned from the Indian boarding school in Oregon. In coming back to the mountains, he is returning to his traditional heritage, but he comes back knowing the English language. This means that he will become an interpreter, allowing interaction between his grandfather's people and the white people below, an important element in the novel. At the novel's end, only Antoine holds any hope for a future, but it is a future his grandfather would not have wished.

Adam Pell, the man who designed the dam. He has made a "hobby" of Indians and has traveled the world "helping" Indian people. For example, he went to Peru to help descendants of the Incas, who he says were the world's greatest engineers, build a dam. He also is the director of the Americana Institute, the museum that purchased the Featherboy bundle and allowed it to be chewed to pieces in the museum's basement. He thinks he knows "these people," but he eventually is stunned by his own lack of understanding. When Pock Face kills Pell's nephew, Pell begins to understand the enormity of his own actions, but he still does not understand all that he believes he does. He attempts to give Bull and his people a sacred object from another culture, one made of "valuable" gold, in lieu of the destroyed Featherboy bundle. Later, when Bull shoots him, he dies with a surprised look on his face.

Rafferty, the Indian agent, the one white man in the novel for whom the Indians have any regard. He tries to help them and to understand them, and he tries to let Pell and his nephew know why the Indians are upset by the desecration of their sacred objects and the land. When the meeting he arranged turns into a fiasco as a result of Pell's ignorance, Rafferty, along with Pell, is shot by Bull.

The Boy, whose Indian name is **Son Child**, the tribal police for the area. He is torn between worlds. He loves and respects Bull and his people, but he lives in a white man's world and is a cog in the machinery of the white world. His Indian name was translated into English as The Boy, a significant change. He is a strong, understanding man, not a "boy," as the white world would have it. When Bull shoots Pell and Rafferty, Son Child does his duty and shoots the chief. He says, "Brother! I have to do this!" before putting a bullet into Bull's heart, a bullet Bull does nothing to resist.

Pock Face, an angry young man caught between worlds. He wears cowboy boots and "can talk about horses like a white man." He listens to what the elders say, but without hearing. His shooting of Pell's nephew is the result of a misunderstanding on both sides.

— *N. Jacquelyn Kilpatrick*

THE WIND FROM THE PLAIN TRILOGY
(Ortadirek; Yer demir, gök bakir; *and* Ölmez otu)

Author: Yashar Kemal (Yaşar Kemal Gökçeli, 1922-   )
First published: 1960-1968
Genre: Novels

Locale: Turkey
Time: c. 1955-1965
Plot: Social realism

The Wind from the Plain, 1960

Halil Taşyürek, called **Old Halil**, a village elder, born in 1884. He argues with Meryemdje for the right to ride an old horse. The horse falls dead before the argument is resolved. He disappears for a time and is thought dead.

Iron Earth, Copper Sky, 1963

Meryemdje, the widowed mother of Long Ali, grandmother of Hassan and Ummahan, and oldest woman in the village of Yalak, born in 1886. She denies that Old Halil, who had disappeared the previous fall, is dead and refuses to participate in the funeral service. She is proven right when he reappears. She takes an oath of silence. To prevent Adil Effendi, the moneylender, from seizing her belongings, she bundles them up and hides them under a log. She keeps watch for Effendi, but he never comes. Like all the cattle in the village, her family's calf is hidden in a cave. Meryemdje visits the calf and breaks her oath of silence to give it soothing words. When another woman is hurt in a fight, Meryemdje prepares a healing ointment. She leads a mob of women against Sefer Effendi, the village Muhtar (headman), when they learn that he betrayed them. She backs down when the Muhtar brings out his rifle.

The Undying Grass, 1968

Meryemdje, whose son leaves her behind, alone, when villagers descend to the Chukurova Valley for the cotton harvest. She is too weak to make the journey. Her family leaves her enough food to survive until their return. At first, she spends much of her time trying to catch a stray rooster. When she finally traps him, she lets him go. She is lonely and bored in the village. When Omer arrives with instructions from the Muhtar to kill her for money, she greets him so affectionately that he relents.

Halil Taşyürek, who, having survived the blizzard to reach a neighboring village, spends the winter in the home of a friend. When harvest time arrives, he searches the valley for the Yalak villages. When he finds them, he joins in the harvest. He tries to help Long Ali, who is in trouble for abandoning his

Long Ali, who undertakes a treacherous journey with his family through rugged mountains because he thinks he can find work picking cotton.

Halil Taşyürek, who has his son hide him in a grain crib when he returns to the village. The villagers learn where he is hiding and come to the grain crib as a group. They force him to come out and persuade him they will not harm him. When they leave, he leaves the village despite a blizzard.

Hassan, the son of Long Ali and grandson of Meryemdje. He makes matches. He gives some to Taşbaş before the local police take Taşbaş to jail.

Memet Taşbaş Effendi, called **Taşbaş**, an old man and venerated elder of the village. The villagers acclaim him a saint with mystical powers, which he comes to accept. When he is first arrested by the local police, he is let off with a warning to desist from assuming the role of a saint. The villagers decide that his release is further proof of his saintliness. After the police arrest him a second time, he escapes during a blizzard.

mother. He persuades Long Ali to get up in the middle of the night to pick extra cotton. After the villagers beat Long Ali, Halil leaves them, followed by a large yellow sheepdog. He tries to steal some cotton but is caught. His captors make a halter around his neck with a rope and force him to carry the sack of cotton through four villages. He is stoned and spat on. Finally, someone forces his captor to put him in a cart and return him to the Yalak villagers.

Memet Taşbaş Effendi, who survives the blizzard thanks in part to Hassan's matches. He returns to the villagers while they are picking cotton. His mystical powers disappear, so he walks into the sea and drowns.

— Tom Feller

THE WIND IN THE WILLOWS

Author: Kenneth Grahame (1859-1932)
First published: 1908
Genre: Novel

Locale: England
Time: Early twentieth century
Plot: Allegory

Mole, an introvert. He is introduced to the world about him by Water Rat, who takes him on various excursions and becomes his friend. Mole learns to swim, to row, and to find the meaning of the wind in the willows. He even learns to see Him who brings Life and Death to all creatures.

Water Rat, an extrovert. He becomes Mole's friend and shows him the world of stream and forest.

Toad, a wealthy playboy. He lives at Toad Hall, the most magnificent residence in animal land. He becomes addicted to every fad. He takes Mole and Water Rat on a short-lived trip in a gypsy caravan and then becomes an automobile owner, driv-

ing the fastest and gaudiest of cars. He gets into and out of all sorts of scrapes.

Badger, a recluse who lives in the Wild Wood. No one dares bother him. He likes People but hates Society. Even so, he helps other animals, including Toad. When Toad Hall is taken over by the stoats and weasels, he helps the other animals drive out the intruders.

Otter, who joins Mole and Water Rat on their first picnic.

Sea-Farer, a seagoing rat who visits Water Rat and tries to tempt him into traveling about the Wide World.

WIND, SAND, AND STARS
(Terre des hommes)

Author: Antoine de Saint-Exupéry (1900-1944)
First published: 1939
Genre: Novel

Locale: The Pyrenees, the Sahara, and the Andes
Time: The 1920's and 1930's
Plot: Autobiographical

Antoine de Saint-Exupéry (sah[n]-tayg-zew-pay-ree), a French pioneer of early aviation. Beginning in 1926, when he began to fly the mails across the Pyrenees, the author had many adventures. In this random novelistic account of eight years as a pilot, Saint-Exupéry tells of some of his experiences, without a trace of melodrama or pride. Planes still had open cockpits when he began to fly, and in low visibility, pilots often would thrust their heads out because they could not see through the windscreen. Without radio, becoming lost was not uncommon. Once, a thick cloud cover forced the pilot lower and lower, until he crashed at 170 miles per hour into a gentle slope at the top of a barren plateau. Miraculously, the pilot and mechanic survived the crash, but they nearly died in their 124-mile trek across a blazing desert, to be saved at last by a camel-riding Bedouin. Another time, the pilot was caught in a cyclone and was sucked down to earth at 150 miles per hour. He battled to stay airborne, 60 feet above water, against a headwind of more than 100 miles per hour. During a heroic twenty-minute struggle, he managed to advance only 100 yards. Nearly exhausted, he finally succeeded in escaping the storm. The author writes of these and other such ordeals with a grace, beauty, and sensitivity that heightens the experiences into a poetry of wisdom. In 1944, Saint-Exupéry failed to return while on a reconnaissance mission over the Mediterranean in World War II.

Mermoz, a friend and fellow aviator. He surveyed the Casablanca-Dakar line across the Sahara, the South American line between Buenos Aires, Argentina, and Santiago, Chile, and was the first to cross the South Atlantic in a hydroplane. He was also the first, in 1931, to carry the mails from Toulouse, France, to Buenos Aires. He survived a dozen crashes, capture by the Moors in the Sahara, and getting caught by the tails of tornadoes. Once, he and his mechanic were forced down at an altitude of 12,000 feet on a mesa in the Andes that had sheer drops on all sides. To escape, they rolled the plane down an incline until it reached the precipice, went off into the air, picked up enough speed to respond to the controls, and swept down to the valley below. Mermoz cleared the desert, the mountains, the sea, and the night for safer air travel. After a dozen years of such pioneering, he went down one night over the South Atlantic and did not return.

Guillamot (gee-yah-mah), the author's closest friend and mentor. Guillamot taught the author the secrets of flying and finding one's way that no text or map could. He flew the routes surveyed by Mermoz. On one flight, he became lost in a snowstorm over the Andes. Forced down when his fuel ran out, he made himself a shelter, in which he stayed for two days and two nights until the storm blew over. He then walked for five days and four nights across the treacherous Andes without an ice-ax, ropes, or provisions, his hands and feet and knees bleeding in a temperature of twenty degrees below zero. When he finally emerged from that world of crags and ice and snow, he was near death, his face blotched and swollen, hands numb and useless, and feet frozen into mere deadweights. In the author's eyes, Guillamot was a friend of extraordinary courage and moral greatness.

— Henry J. Baron

THE WINDS OF WAR

Author: Herman Wouk (1915-   )
First published: 1971
Genre: Novel

Locale: Washington, D.C., and major sites of World War II
Time: 1938-1941
Plot: Historical

Victor "Pug" Henry, a career U.S. Navy officer. A short, physically fit man in his late forties, slightly graying, Henry has aspirations of becoming an admiral, perhaps even chief of naval operations. He is a family man, though relations with his wife sometimes are strained. He takes an active interest in the lives of his three children. On the way to his post as naval attaché in Berlin, he meets the Tudsburys, father and daughter, leading to his developing a fondness for Pamela Tudsbury. His assignment in Berlin and the patronage of President Franklin Delano Roosevelt give him the opportunity to meet Adolf Hitler and Winston Churchill and to be present in Europe at the outbreak of World War II. Visiting Great Britain shortly thereafter, he finds himself taken along as an observer on a bombing run over Berlin. After completing his assignment in Berlin and returning to Washington, D.C., Henry carries out several important missions for the president. He is present at Roosevelt's historic meeting with Churchill in the North Atlantic and is posted to Moscow, where he meets Joseph Stalin. Throughout, Henry repeatedly attempts to get assigned to sea duty; he is granted his wish, only to reach Pearl Harbor the day after the Japanese raid that sinks the battleship he was to have commanded.

Rhoda Henry, a Navy wife approaching fifty and still attractive. She is growing tired of the demands placed on the wife of a career officer and is suffering from a middle-age depression. Rhoda accompanies her husband to Berlin, where she meets Palmer Kirby, with whom she ultimately has an affair after the Henrys return to Washington. She attempts to hold the family together despite her own transgressions, keeping her infidelity a secret. She establishes a fine household in Washington that serves as a home for Victor Henry and the three children when they are not off serving abroad or working away from Washington.

Natalie Jastrow, a research assistant for her uncle, Aaron

Jastrow, a noted historian. A lissome woman of thirty who has renounced her Jewish ancestry, she led a wild life before settling down with her uncle in Siena, Italy. Initially devoted to Leslie Slote, she gradually falls in love with Byron Henry. With Byron, she visits Slote in Warsaw and witnesses German atrocities there, but she has difficulty convincing her uncle to leave Italy. Separated from Byron, who has gone to submarine school in the United States, she finally begins a trek toward freedom, but the Germans block her way. She manages to meet Byron in Lisbon. They marry there but are quickly separated again. Natalie, now pregnant, tries even more earnestly to get her uncle to leave Italy, but nothing is successful. After giving birth to Louis Henry, she makes further attempts to evade the grasp of the Germans. She is caught in Axis-occupied territory when the United States enters the war.

Byron Henry, a handsome, red-haired young man in his mid-twenties, unsure of his goals in life but ultimately pressed into military service just as the United States enters the world-wide conflict. Openly rebelling against his father, Byron travels to Europe to pursue a career in art. He secures a job as secretary to Aaron Jastrow and falls in love with coworker Natalie Jastrow. Even though he and Natalie see the horrors of Hitler's invasion of Poland, he is unable to persuade her to leave her uncle as World War II breaks out in Europe. They both go to Warren Henry's wedding in Florida, but Natalie returns to Siena when Byron goes to submarine school. Byron manages to be reunited with Natalie in Lisbon, where his submarine docks briefly, and the two are married. The war separates them again, however, and Byron goes to the Pacific theater to serve aboard a submarine there.

Pamela Tudsbury, a personal assistant to her father, Alistair Tudsbury. A woman approaching thirty, of decent figure and wholesome if not stunning beauty, she has devoted her life to aiding her father in promoting British nationalism through his newspaper and radio work. She accompanies him on worldwide trips and meets Victor Henry aboard a ship bound for Berlin. She also travels with her father to the United States, Germany, Russia, and the Far East, crossing paths with Henry. She is captivated by the older man and falls deeply in love with him. She is present with Victor at the bombing of London and is with her father in Singapore when the Japanese invade and capture it.

Aaron Jastrow, a prominent American Jew and an internationally known historian. Nearly sixty-five years old, Jastrow has authored numerous scholarly works. He is in Siena completing a study of the Roman emperor Constantine and believes his renown as a writer will keep him safe from German harassment. Only reluctantly does he agree to leave Italy with daughter Natalie. His fame proves a stumbling block, however: His movements are monitored by German Gestapo agents, who track him to France and to Switzerland and who reach him just as he and Natalie are to leave clandestinely, aboard a tramp steamer, for Palestine. He returns to his villa in Siena to wait out the war.

Leslie Slote, a junior American diplomat. Once Natalie Jastrow's lover, Slote plays the role of jilted suitor as his assignments with the U.S. State Department take him to Berlin and then to Warsaw, where he assists in evacuating Americans when the Germans invade Poland. He is posted briefly to Moscow, then to Switzerland, where he is presented early evidence of Hitler's systematic extermination of the Jews. Slote tries to get his superiors in the State Department to pay attention to this information but repeatedly meets roadblocks.

Alistair "Talky" Tudsbury, a highly respected British radio and newspaper correspondent. Corpulent and aging, Tudsbury nevertheless commands a large audience in his native England and has the respect of journalists and politicians internationally. He travels throughout Europe, the United States, the Middle East, and the Far East, reporting on British preparations for all-out combat and on the conduct of operations in the various combat zones.

Madeline Henry, the Henrys' nineteen-year-old daughter, who leaves college to take a job in New York City as an assistant to radio celebrity Hugh Cleveland. She drifts into an amorous relationship with Cleveland, ignoring her family's repeated warnings. Concurrently, she rises in the entertainment world as a junior executive.

Warren Henry, the Henrys' oldest son. A Naval Academy graduate in his mid-twenties, handsome and committed to a career in the Navy, he enrolls in flight school and while there meets Janice LaCouture, the daughter of a Florida politician. They marry shortly before Warren gets his pilot's wings. He is then assigned to an aircraft carrier based at Pearl Harbor, Hawaii. Warren is considered a promising aviator by the higher-ups in the Navy. He is on patrol away from Pearl Harbor when the Japanese attack on December 7, 1941, but manages to return in time to engage in a dogfight over the island of Oahu.

General Armin von Roon, a German military professional and member of the German general staff. Roon's account of World War II from the Germans' perspective is interspersed throughout the narrative of the Henry family saga. Roon gives both a sweeping assessment of Hitler's strategic campaigns and personal observations about Hitler and his closest associates as the Germans sweep through western and central Europe and eastward into the Soviet Union.

Franklin Delano Roosevelt, the president of the United States. Although disabled by polio, Roosevelt is a keen observer of world events and a shrewd political dealer. He calls on Victor Henry several times to gain the naval officer's assistance in dealing first with the Germans, then with the Russians. Roosevelt maneuvers carefully to satisfy both the American Congress (especially the isolationist elements) and the British, especially Churchill; he is clearly on the side of the Allies, though he manages to maintain a façade of neutrality. Throughout, the president moves the United States into a wartime posture, anticipating the country's inevitable entry into the worldwide conflict.

Janice LaCouture, a young, blond Florida beauty who marries Warren Henry. Although she comes from a wealthy family and is the daughter of a prominent politician, she cheerfully accompanies Warren to Pearl Harbor, Hawaii, and adapts to being a Navy wife. She bears a son, Victor, to carry on the Henry line. She is a witness at first hand to the Japanese attack on Pearl Harbor on December 7, 1941.

Hugh Cleveland, a well-known American radio personality. Middle-aged and going to seed physically, he nevertheless commands a large listening public. His shows allow prominent political figures to give American listeners a sense of the growing tensions in Europe. At Madeline Henry's suggestion, he begins a touring amateur talent show that features American servicemen. Cleveland's failing marriage drives him to chase other women, including the Henrys' daughter.

Palmer Frederick (Fred) Kirby, an engineer and manufacturer of technological equipment, a widower approaching fifty years of age. Kirby meets the Henrys in Berlin and falls in love with Rhoda. His travels to New York and Washington give him opportunity to pursue his friendship with her, a friendship that culminates in their having an affair while Victor Henry is overseas. Business with the government and his expertise in manufacturing specialty items lead to Kirby being recruited to work with the Manhattan Project to produce the atom bomb.

Berel Jastrow, a cousin of Aaron Jastrow, a Polish Jew residing outside Warsaw. Although he is in his sixties, Jastrow is able-bodied and adept at a number of occupations; he is also skilled at manipulating local government administrators. He manages to get his family out of Warsaw when the Germans invade, but eventually he is captured by the Nazis and placed in a concentration camp.

Avram Rabinovitz, a Jewish organizer who helps Jews wishing to escape the Nazis. He arranges for the Jastrows to leave Italy via a transport steamer and is disappointed when Aaron and Natalie refuse to go through with their escape. He continues to work with them to help return them to U.S. custody.

Ted Gallard, a British fighter pilot engaged to Pamela Tudsbury. He participates in several dangerous missions and eventually is shot down over Germany. Wounded, he languishes in prison for a time and eventually dies of his injuries.

Carter "Lady" Aster, a U.S. Navy executive officer on Byron Henry's submarine in the Atlantic. Aster proves to be highly competent but ruthless. He drives Byron to become a qualified submariner.

Ernst Grobke, a German submarine officer about Victor Henry's age. Grobke becomes friends with Henry during the latter's journey to Berlin. He takes Henry to visit German submarine bases and introduces him to influential political figures within the Nazi regime.

Isaac LaCouture, a Florida politician. An isolationist who opposes Roosevelt's various programs to aid England and Russia against Germany, he is nevertheless pleased when his daughter marries Warren Henry and becomes a service wife. He uses what influence he has with the State Department to try to get Natalie Jastrow and her uncle out of Italy.

Wolf Stöller, a German businessman who supports Hitler. After inviting Victor Henry to several social affairs, he tries to recruit the American officer as a German spy.

— *Laurence W. Mazzeno*

WINDSOR CASTLE

Author: William Harrison Ainsworth (1805-1882)
First published: 1843
Genre: Novel

Locale: England
Time: The sixteenth century
Plot: Historical

Henry VIII, the king of England, married to Catherine and later to Anne. After Anne's execution, he is free to marry again. True to history, Henry is presented as a combination of both good and evil.

Catherine of Aragon (EHR-uh-gon), the queen of England, whose marriage to Henry is annulled so that he may marry Anne.

Anne Boleyn (boh-LIHN), Catherine's successor, unfaithful to Henry but jealous of Henry's attentions to Jane Seymour. She is executed for her affair with Norris.

Cardinal Wolsey (WOOL-zee), the Lord High Chancellor, who uses Wyat and later Mabel in attempts to overthrow Anne. Henry removes him from office, publicly disgraces him, and later has him arrested. He dies on the way to London.

The earl of Surrey, a member of the court, imprisoned after a duel with Richmond over Geraldine. Released, he joins the pursuers of Herne.

The duke of Richmond, Henry's natural son.

Lady Elizabeth Fitzgerald, the fair Geraldine, loved by both Surrey and Richmond.

Mabel Lyndwood, the granddaughter of Lyndwood, a royal forester. She is the unacknowledged daughter of Wolsey and is loved by both Herne and Fenwolf. She dies after being abducted by Herne.

Morgan Fenwolf, a gamekeeper who saves Anne from attack by a stag. He joins Herne's midnight huntsmen and is imprisoned after the huntsmen attack Henry and Suffolk, but he escapes. He fails in an attempt to murder Herne and is later burned in a forest fire while pursuing Herne.

Herne the Hunter, a spectral demon seeking to destroy Henry. He is vaguely symbolic of humanity's dual nature.

Sir Thomas Wyat, who is in love with Anne and bewitched by Herne.

Lady Mary Howard, Surrey's sister, who marries Richmond.

Lady Frances Vere, who is wed to Surrey after Henry refuses him permission to marry Geraldine.

Princess Elizabeth, the young daughter of Henry and Anne.

Jane Seymour, who is loved by Henry after Anne becomes queen. Later, she becomes Henry's third wife.

Sir Henry Norris, who is in love with Anne. He is sent to the Tower of London for intrigue with Anne.

THE WINE OF ASTONISHMENT

Author: Earl Lovelace (1935-   )
First published: 1982
Genre: Novel

Locale: Bonasse, a village in Trinidad
Time: The 1930's to 1951
Plot: Social realism

Bee, a Spiritual Baptist preacher and a farmer. A dedicated, conscientious, and responsible leader, he struggles for years to keep his church alive despite a law prohibiting his sect's religious practices. He is strong, dignified, righteous, and long-suffering. Faced with increased official repression, the disintegration of his congregation, and the loss of his children's respect, he bravely but reluctantly breaks the law and endures the brutal consequences. Hopeful that black political representation will change the law, he works tirelessly for the election of Ivan Morton only to feel trapped, humiliated, and despairing when his trust is betrayed. Challenged by Bolo to restore the integrity of the community, Bee decides on violent, redemptive action but is circumvented when the police intervene. As the novel closes, religious freedom has been restored, but Bee is unable to recall the Spirit to his church. He feels that the Spirit still lives in the steel band.

Eva, Bee's wife, the dialect-speaking narrator of the novel. A self-sacrificing, middle-aged black woman, she is devoted to her religion, her five children, and her husband, for whom she is a supportive confidante and moderating influence. Relatively uneducated but observant and worldly-wise, she believes that God has afflicted black people with tribulations but given them the strength to bear and overcome their sufferings. She views brown-skinned people as tools of the whites while trying to understand and excuse Ivan Morton for betraying his past and his race. Despite Morton's example, she advocates education for her children as a way to escape poverty and powerlessness.

Bolo, a famous stickfighting champion and an estate laborer. Tall and slim, with a broad nose, high cheekbones, and full lips, he is the strongest and bravest man in Bonasse. A favorite of the village, he is good-natured, humorous, helpful, and sympathetic but begins to change when the war starts and ritual stickfighting is banned. With the arrival of American soldiers and easy money, many Trinidadians become hustlers and prostitutes, traditional values are forgotten, and Bolo becomes increasingly bitter and unimportant. Looking to Bee and his church to maintain the people's identity and integrity, Bolo tries to protect the congregation from police brutality, is badly beaten, and is jailed for three years. After his release,

Bolo is appalled and heartbroken by the church's acquiescence in the ban on its traditional practices and by the general moral and political corruption. Enraged by their weakness, he deliberately antagonizes and terrorizes the villagers, hoping to provoke them into reclaiming their dignity and self-respect. He fails in his aim when he abducts two village girls and is fatally shot by the police.

Ivan Morton, a minister in the Legislative Council. The son of a poor black estate worker, he is respected as a teacher before turning to politics. He is ambitious, insensitive, self-serving, and cynical. Always seen as the hope of the village, he assumes the trappings of the old white "plantocracy." He forgets his promises and rejects his past and the values of those who elected him. As a young man, he impregnates and then abandons a local black girl and soon afterward marries a light-skinned woman who speaks correct English. He further reveals his sense of social and racial inferiority when he urges the Spiritual Baptists to become "civilized" and states, "We can't change our colour . . . but we can change our attitude. We can't be white but we can act white." To ensure black support, Morton has religious freedom granted just before the election.

Clem, later known as **Lord Trafalgar**, Bolo's friend. Lively, gregarious, and adaptable, he keeps his self-respect while taking advantage of the changes in Trinidad. Formerly a leader in traditional stickfight chants and bongo songs, he satisfies the demands of a new audience and becomes a calypso singer known as Lord Trafalgar.

Corporal Prince, a policeman. Tall, thickset, and powerful, he follows orders and zealously scourges Spiritual Baptist churches around the island. Hungry for promotion and taking pleasure in brutality, he ruthlessly persecutes other black people, including Bee and his congregation, without compassion or understanding.

Mitchell, a laborer for the Americans, a snackette owner and political organizer. Loud-mouthed, dishonest, and corrupt, he is a thief, black marketeer, and moneylender who boasts of his wealth. He treats Bolo with disrespect and is punished as a result. He turns his talents to working for Ivan Morton.

— *Douglas Rollins*

WINESBURG, OHIO: A Group of Tales of Ohio Small Town Life

Author: Sherwood Anderson (1876-1941)
First published: 1919
Genre: Novel

Locale: Winesburg, Ohio
Time: Late nineteenth century
Plot: Psychological realism

George Willard, the young reporter who learns about life from confessions and observations of townspeople. The son of an insensitive man and a sensitive mother, young Willard accepts the practical help of his father but follows the inclinations of his mother in accepting his job. Living as he does in the family hotel, which has seen better days, he runs alone and thinks long thoughts. Something about him draws the weak, the insecure, and the hopeless as well as the clever and strong. His loyalties to those who give him their confidences are unflinching. He takes advantage of a lonely farm girl, but only at her insistence, and then secretly. On the other hand, he has an exaggerated sense of chivalry concerning the girl whom he has long admired. He is searching for the truth. This search

finally, after his mother's death, takes him away from the town that formed him.

Elizabeth Willard, his mother, whose hotel and life savings never benefit anyone, but whose spirit serves as a bond and inspiration to two men. Promiscuous in her youth, though in search of spirituality, Mrs. Willard had married on the hearsay of village wives expressing contentment. Never in love with her husband, she cherishes a beautiful memory of a lover who murmured to her, "Oh, the dear, the dear, the lovely dear." The two who loved her most, her son and Dr. Reefy, repeat these words to her dead but seemingly young and uncorrupted body. She lives and dies in quiet desperation and in search of loveliness.

Dr. Reefy, a poet of obscurity who writes great truths on scraps of paper that he throws away in wads and with a laugh. True to a vision of greatness, the doctor loved twice in his life. One love was a pregnant girl who miscarried, then married the understanding doctor and died, leaving him a comfortable income. The other, Elizabeth Willard, he befriends in her last days of a ravaging disease; he was never her lover.

Helen White, the banker's daughter with a college complex but small-town disposition. Lovely and gracious, Helen is an inspiration to three Winesburg boys, though only George Willard arouses a like response in her. Like the other main characters, she is unconsciously in quest of beauty and truth.

Kate Swift, a schoolteacher who burns inwardly with a deep desire to live and to pass along the passion of living. Attracted as she is to her former student George Willard, Kate cannot finally cast aside her small-town prudery. Always confusing the physical and the spiritual in her effort to awaken her protégé, spinsterish Kate is secretly worshiped in a like way by the Presbyterian minister, who considers her a messiah of sorts (having seen her naked and praying from his clerical window).

The Reverend Curtis Hartman, the Presbyterian minister, Kate's admirer.

Wing Biddlebaum, a fugitive teacher who ran from unfair accusations of homosexuality to become the restless-fingered berry picker and handyman of the town. Only once in the many years of his hiding out in Winesburg does Wing attempt to pass along his fervor for knowledge, which made him a great teacher. George is on the verge of discovering the man's tragic secret and is moved by the aging man's eloquence.

Jesse Bentley,

Louise Hardy, his daughter, and

David Hardy, his grandson. These people reveal the deterioration of the pioneering spirit in northern Ohio. Jesse, the lone surviving brother of a farm family, turns from the ministry to farm management with religious zeal. He neglects his frail wife, who dies in childbirth, and he resents the daughter who should have been his son David. When his neurotic but brilliant daughter turns to a village boy and has a son by him, the old man takes this birth as his omen and names the son David. In a moment of fright when the obsessed old man is about to offer up a lamb as a sacrifice to God, the boy strikes his grandfather, leaves him for dead, and runs away, never again to see the old man, his mother, or the town.

WINGS

Author: Arthur Kopit (1937-　　　)
First published: 1978
Genre: Drama

Locale: A hospital and a convalescent hospital
Time: The 1970's
Plot: Expressionism

Emily Stilson, a retired aviator in her seventies. She suffers a stroke and is taken to a hospital, where she recovers over a two-year period. The play presents both her internal thoughts and her external behavior. Internally, she remains intact, though she is extremely confused as to what has happened to her and where she is. Thrown back on her memories, she reaches the conclusion that, following an aviation accident, she is being held prisoner by unknown forces in a Romanian farmhouse disguised to look like a hospital. She interprets the doctors' questions as attempts to pump her for information. Although she believes herself to be lucid, nothing but gibberish emerges when she speaks. At moments when her thinking becomes jumbled, she returns to memories of flying and walking on the wings of airplanes. When she realizes that her ability to express herself does not match her ability to generate thought within herself, she becomes angry and reacts violently. This reaction, indicative of a desire to communicate with others, brings her out of herself somewhat and advances her therapy. She essentially learns to speak all over again. As her condition improves, more of her memories become conscious. Her son takes her to an aircraft museum, where she finds that her hands automatically manipulate the controls even though she cannot recall how to use them and forgets again as soon as she is no longer in physical contact with the plane. Talking with her therapist, she recounts an out-of-body experience in which she felt herself to be floating on the ceiling. As she speaks, the therapist disappears from her consciousness, which is taken over by a memory in which she is flying blind and lost, but nevertheless enjoying a feeling of freedom. The recollection ends with her walking out onto the wing of the aircraft, courageously facing the unknown—presumably her own death.

Billy, a stroke patient in his thirties. Billy is a member of Emily Stilson's therapy group. He owns a farm and is an expert cook, although he is not always clearly aware of his past. His response to the disabilities resulting from his stroke is to keep up a barrage of semicoherent chatter that prevents the therapist from pointing out deficiencies in his language skills and memory. During a therapy session, for example, he accuses the therapist of not having paid him for a cheesecake recipe he gave her, in an effort to put her on the defensive and make her the focus of the session.

Amy, the therapist who works with Emily Stilson, Billy, and other patients. She is extremely patient with and affectionate toward her patients. She encourages them to work through their disabilities and cheers each breakthrough. She negotiates Billy's efforts to deflect the therapy she offers him good-humoredly, and she gives Emily much personal attention, taking her outside and talking with her about her family and her past.

— *Philip Auslander*

THE WINGS OF THE DOVE

Author: Henry James (1843-1916)
First published: 1902
Genre: Novel

Locale: London and Venice
Time: c. 1900
Plot: Psychological realism

Mildred (Milly) Theale, "the dove" who goes to Europe to learn to live and to die there of an incurable disease. A handsome young woman of great means, inherited through the deaths of her entire family of six, this New Yorker with her Bostonian writer friend and a companion her own age tries to extend her experiences so as to encompass a lifetime in a few short months. Although Milly seems never to suffer, she is the first to know that her sickness will be fatal, and she needs only the strength and subtlety of an eminent physician to confirm this fact. Her fine manners and sensitivity to others' needs make her a delightful companion to all, even when the truth of her condition would otherwise make others pity her. Bright, vivacious, and charming in all ways, she finally wins a heart and ironically loses both hers and his to the tragic situation. Her generosity in remembering her two closest friends (whom she forgives for plotting a scheme of marriage) is unacceptable finally. The wings meant for sheltering then become symbols of religious purity.

Kate Croy, the young woman who befriends Milly Theale in England and seeks through her a solution to her own problems. A victim of her father's bad reputation and her uncompromising aunt's machinations, Kate is a beautiful, stylish, and acute observer of the society in which her aunt, Mrs. Lowder, has placed her. Her hopeless love for a young newspaper reporter only makes her decisions more poignant, for she decides he must marry the rich and doomed Milly for their own marriage finally to be realized. Sparkling and perceptive as she is, Kate fails to live the lie so calmly planned and must live out her existence in her aunt's entourage.

Merton Densher, Kate Croy's unacceptable lover and Milly Theale's beloved. Densher, just returned from a journalistic assignment in America to a secret engagement with Kate, finds that his charms, good looks, and good manners are the pawns to two separate schemes. He is rejected as her niece's fiancé by Mrs. Lowder but encouraged as a suitor of Milly Theale, whom he had met briefly in America. His fine perceptions and sensitivities are so keenly balanced that he can neither propose nor reject, neither have nor hold. He binds Kate as his lover to an agreement, only to find at last that he loves Milly, but he cannot break off his engagement to Kate. Both he and Kate suffer.

Lord Mark, a nobleman encouraged by Mrs. Lowder as a suitor for her niece. He is attentive to both Kate and Milly, and both reject him. He then gains an unconscious revenge by informing the dying girl of the relationship between Kate and Densher. Neither young nor old-appearing, Lord Mark is supercilious to the point of caricature. Without intending malice, he manages to do harm more efficiently than if he had intended it. He is considered a good catch by older matchmakers and abhorred by the objects of his attentions.

Mrs. Lowder, a managing woman who succeeds in convincing everyone that her own will is the strongest and that her judgments are infallible. Although Mrs. Lowder intimidates more than she inspires, her nature is not altogether cold. She simply sees the world as it is and tries to fit those nearest her into the mold.

Mrs. Stringham, a schoolmate and longtime friend of Mrs. Lowder and the companion to Milly Theale. Her warm nature and compassionate responses offset the calculating forces of the highborn English. As a writer, she observes and comments wisely on human character and manners.

Susan Shepherd, the younger American companion to Milly and a sweetly sympathetic friend to all the troubled young lovers. Susan suffers more than emphatically and comforts the stricken compassionately.

Sir Luke Strett, the distinguished physician who involves himself more than professionally to make of Milly Theale's living death an experience in vivid life. Although there is nothing he can do for her, he extends his great humanity to the young and lovely American so desirous of life and so tragically doomed.

THE WINNERS
(Los premios)

Author: Julio Cortázar (1914-1984)
First published: 1960
Genre: Novel

Locale: Buenos Aires and aboard a cruise ship
Time: The 1950's
Plot: Satire

Gabriel Medrano (meh-DRAH-noh), a dentist and a womanizer who is dissatisfied with life on board the *Malcolm*. He allies himself with a group that does not accept the official explanation of why the passengers have not been given complete access to the ship, that of an outbreak of typhus among the crew's members. When Claudia Lewbaum's son Jorge becomes ill, Medrano decides that the unsatisfactory response of the ship's authorities requires forcible entry into the restricted areas of the ship. He storms the radio room and forces the operator to send a message to Buenos Aires about Jorge's condition. The radio operator then kills Medrano. The passengers are asked to sign a statement that Medrano died of typhus instead of gunshot wounds.

Carlos López, a leftist high school Spanish teacher who refuses to believe that the passengers are being denied access to the entire ship because of an outbreak of typhus. He threat-

ens one of the ship's officers that he will storm the other side of the ship if the restrictions on passenger movement are not lifted. He agrees with Medrano about the need to send a radio message because of Jorge's illness. He is struck unconscious in the assault on the sailors' quarters and is returned to his room. He refuses to sign the official statement about the cause of Medrano's death.

Persio (pehr-SEE-oh), a short, bald, eccentric proofreader and aspiring writer. He is a dreamer who lives in a world of philosophical speculation. He is so engrossed in his own thoughts that he does not involve himself in the controversy among the passengers about their treatment on the ship.

Raúl Costa (rrah-EWL KOHS-tah), a homosexual architect who tries to seduce Felipe Trejo. During his secret exploration of the other side of the ship, he steals three guns and ammunition from the sailors' quarters and then divides it among Medrano, López, and himself. He helps Medrano and López storm the other side of the ship and, after shots are fired, finds Medrano dead in the radio room. Like López, he refuses to sign the official statement about the cause of Medrano's death.

Paula Lavalle (lah-VAH-yeh), an attractive redhead who writes poems and stories. Although she is Costa's close friend and traveling companion, she is courted by López. She also denies the official version of events on the ship.

Claudia Lewbaum, the divorced mother of Jorge. Her son's high fever precipitates the assault on the other side of the ship. Her budding friendship with Medrano ends abruptly with his death.

Felipe Trejo (feh-LEE-peh TREH-hoh), a high school student learning to deal with his sexual feelings. His fantasies of sexual conquest remain unfulfilled because there are no young ladies his age on board. Although he is contemptuous of ho-mosexuality, it intrigues him. He rejects Costa's advances, only to be raped by a sailor, an incident he represses by fabricating a tale in which he seduced an insatiable Paula.

Dr. Restelli (rreh-STEH-yee), a conservative colleague of López who teaches Argentine history. He speaks up for the passengers who accept the restrictions imposed by the ship's authorities. He organizes a passenger talent show to lift everyone's spirits and take their minds off the alleged outbreak of typhus among the ship's staff. He accuses those who challenge the authorities of trying to ruin the cruise for the others.

Don Galo Porriño (GAH-loh poh-RREEN-yoh), a successful Galician businessman confined to a wheelchair. He speaks in defense of the authorities and considers those who are unwilling to submit to the crew's demands to be guilty of insubordination and anarchy.

— Evelyn Toft

WINTER IN THE BLOOD

Author: James Welch (1940-   )
First published: 1974
Genre: Novel

Locale: Northern Montana
Time: Early 1970's
Plot: Family

The narrator, an American Indian of Blackfeet and Gros Ventre ancestry. He remains nameless throughout the novel. As the story begins, he has returned to his family's home on the reservation after years of drifting from place to place. The familiar sights there stir painful memories of his dead father and brother, the only people he ever loved. Their deaths triggered his wandering. He spends much of the novel searching for Agnes, a young Cree woman who ran away from him soon after he took her home to his mother and grandmother, who mistakenly believed her to be his wife. He follows her into a dismal world of tawdry bars, casual violence, and drunken sexual encounters, meeting a succession of strange men and lonely women. He finds Agnes and pleads with her to settle down with him, hoping that she can bring him enough warmth and happiness to crowd out his insistent memories. Instead, her friends beat him. When he returns home to the reservation, as much tired of himself as he is of squalid town life, he learns that his grandmother died while he was gone. Beaten down by events, he nevertheless experiences an emotional epiphany, prompted by an unlikely event. During a tremendous struggle to free a cow trapped in mud, his grief for his father and brother lessens because he realizes how much he mourns them. At the novel's end, he begins to plan for the future. He will finally allow a doctor to examine the leg he injured at the time of his brother's death, and he will propose properly to Agnes.

Teresa First Raise, the narrator's mother, a handsome, bitter Blackfeet woman of fifty-five years. The death of John First Raise, her husband and the narrator's father, left her a prosperous widow, but prosperity does not bring her happiness. Even before her husband died, she was discontented and prone to making the nagging remarks that drove away first her husband and then the narrator. Soon after the narrator's arrival at the family home, she disappears inexplicably for three days. When she reappears, she is hung over and accompanied by a new husband.

Mose First Raise, the narrator's dead brother, who appears in flashbacks. The two brothers were close, working happily together on their parents' farm. One evening at dusk, a calf strayed from the cattle they were herding. Distracted by the calf, Mose rode into the path of an oncoming car. He was struck and killed.

Agnes, a young Cree woman who, although barely out of high school, already has acquired a reputation for drunkenness, thievery, and promiscuity. Both Teresa and the narrator's grandmother despise her because she is Cree; the Cree are traditional enemies of the Blackfeet. Her thoughts and feelings are not explored in the novel; she is seen through the mostly disapproving eyes of the narrator.

Lame Bull, the narrator's new stepfather. He masks his ambition with geniality. His marriage to Teresa First Raise makes him a successful cattleman, and although the narrator sees him as a fortune hunter, he proves his worth through his hard work and shrewdness.

The airplane man, a mysterious white man who befriends the narrator in a bar. The airplane man gets his name from one of the conflicting stories he tells about himself, a story that involves airline tickets torn into pieces and the desertion of his wife and children. When he later claims to be pursued by the Federal Bureau of Investigation, he asks the narrator to drive him to refuge in Canada. The airplane man is last seen in handcuffs, captured by the police for an unknown crime.

Yellow Calf, an old Blackfeet man who is blind, wise, and more than he first appears to be. After listening to Yellow Calf's stories of Blackfeet history, the narrator believes that Yellow Calf was not only his grandmother's secret protector many years ago, when she was abandoned by her tribe, but also her illicit lover. The timing of these events coincides with the birth of Teresa First Raise. If the story is true, Yellow Calf is the narrator's maternal grandfather.

The grandmother, Teresa's mother, who is ailing and near death. Once the wife of a Blackfeet chief, she and Yellow Calf are the narrator's links to a traditional Indian identity. Her funeral ends the novel.

— Kelly Fuller

THE WINTER OF OUR DISCONTENT

Author: John Steinbeck (1902-1968)
First published: 1961
Genre: Novel

Locale: New Baytown, Long Island
Time: 1960
Plot: Social realism

Ethan Allen Hawley, a storekeeper, the protagonist. As his name suggests, he is descended from a line of early pioneering Americans, but he has descended, too, into lower-class circumstances. The family fortune has been lost, and although he is a Harvard graduate and a veteran of World War II, he has been consigned to a clerkship in a grocery store. Like his ancestors, Ethan is an independent spirit, discontented with his lot but trying to keep a philosophical spirit about it. He resorts to delivering apostrophes—some learned, some ridiculous—to the shelves of canned goods, and he celebrates his love for his wife, Mary, by making funny faces at her or answering her in puns or circumlocutions. These verbal exercises are a way for Ethan to come to terms with his low fortunes and serve as a contradictory impulse to his real, half-buried ambition to succeed. At first, this desire takes the form of his instructing his son on the old-fashioned virtues of honesty and independence; he even turns down a bribe by a salesman. Ethan's discontent and the pressures exerted by a materialistic society eventually lead him to corruption.

Joe Morphy, a bank clerk and friend of Ethan. A good-natured but mediocre man, Joe suffers from a form of discontent with his job and his social life. Unmarried and with little chance of advancement, Joe has made the most of his situation. He is friendly, knows everyone in town, and is a kind of factotum, a source of information and advice on life and love. He is a catalyst in human affairs, influencing the formation of schemes but taking no real part in them. He innocently gives Ethan information on how to rob a bank and provides the impetus for Ethan's plan.

Alfio Marullo, Ethan's employer. Like Ethan, Marullo is defined by contradictions. Hardworking and cautious with money, Marullo is proud of his success and in consequence constantly supplies Ethan with heavy doses of advice on how to achieve it. For all of his criticism of Ethan as being too "soft," too concerned with making friends rather than money, Marullo is not the ogre that years of work and arthritis seem to have made him. He has taken a liking to Ethan and admires his honesty and his ways as a family man. By the end of the novel, he turns over the store to Ethan.

Mr. Baker, the town banker. Shrewd and opportunistic, Baker represents those materialistic values Ethan wants to repudiate. Superficially gracious, Baker talks mostly about money, investments, and schemes for making more of both. He may have been responsible for the ruin of Ethan's father. Baker's advice to Ethan about investing Mary's money seems an attempt to advance his own interests more than Ethan's. His scheme to swindle land from Danny Taylor by getting him drunk makes him all the more odious to Ethan, who declares that he "hates" Baker.

Margie Young-Hunt, a divorcée attracted to Ethan. A card reader and self-proclaimed witch, Margie is part fraud and part confidant. As her name suggests, she is a huntress of men, though not so young any longer. She survives on alimony checks and has been casually intimate with a number of men, including Joe Morphy. She is not particularly malicious, but her will to survive keeps her on the edge of opportunity. She predicts that Ethan will come into money and tries to seduce him near the end of the novel.

Danny Taylor, the town drunk, a boyhood friend of Ethan. He wills Ethan his land in exchange for Ethan giving him a thousand dollars.

Mary Hawley, Ethan's wife, a trusting, loving, rather superficial figure who shines only in Ethan's light. She trusts him implicitly.

— *Edward Fiorelli*

THE WINTER'S TALE

Author: William Shakespeare (1564-1616)
First published: 1623
Genre: Drama

Locale: Sicilia and Bohemia
Time: The legendary past
Plot: Tragicomedy

Leontes (lee-ON-teez), the king of Sicilia. For many years a close friend of King Polixenes of Bohemia, Leontes, curiously, becomes insanely jealous of him. Afraid of becoming a cuckold, he imprisons Hermione, wrests her son away from her, and attempts to murder Polixenes. When he learns that Hermione is pregnant, he rails; he calls his daughter a bastard and forces Antigonus to leave the child alone in a deserted area. Finally, coming to his senses, he realizes the awful truth. Through his jealousy, he loses his child, wife, and friends.

Polixenes (poh-LIHKS-eh-neez), the king of Bohemia. The innocent victim of Leontes' wrath, he flees to his kingdom, bewildered by his friend's outburst. Many years later, he is to meet Leontes under much happier circumstances.

Hermione (hur-MI-uh-nee), the queen to Leontes and one of the noblest women in Shakespearean drama. Like Polixenes, she is baffled by Leontes' jealousy. Imprisoned, with her children snatched away from her, she remains in hiding with Paulina, his devoted friend, until she is reunited with her family after sixteen years.

Perdita (PUR-dih-tuh), the daughter of Leontes and Hermione. Luckily for her, after she is abandoned she is found by an old shepherd, who protects her as his own child until she is of marriageable age. Meeting young Prince Florizel of Bohemia, she falls in love with him. Later, she and her repentant father are reunited.

Paulina (poh-LEE-nuh), the wife of Antigonus and lady in waiting to Hermione. Realizing the absurdity of Leontes' accusations, the courageous woman upbraids him unmercifully for his blind cruelty to Hermione, whom she keeps hidden for sixteen years. Finally, through her efforts, husband and wife meet on a much happier note.

Camillo (ka-MIHL-oh), a lord of Sicilia and Leontes' trusted adviser, who realizes that Hermione is completely innocent of adultery. When ordered by Leontes to kill Polixenes, loyal, steadfast Camillo cannot murder a good king. Instead, he sails with Polixenes and serves him well for many years. Later, he returns to his beloved Sicilia.

Antigonus (an-TIHG-uh-nuhs), a lord of Sicilia and Paulina's husband. Much against his will, this unhappy man is forced to abandon Perdita in a deserted wasteland. Unfortunately for this good man, who is aware of the king's irrationality, he is killed and eaten by a bear; hence, the fate and whereabouts of Perdita remain unknown for many years.

Autolycus (oh-TOL-ih-kuhs), a rogue. A ballad-monger, he is a delightful scoundrel. Quick with a song, he is equally adept at stealing purses and, in general, at living by his quick wit.

Florizel (FLOR-ih-zehl), the prince of Bohemia. In love with Perdita, he refuses to give her up, even though, in so doing, he angers his hot-tempered father, who does not want to see his son marry a girl of apparent low birth.

An old shepherd, the reputed father of Perdita.

A clown, his oafish son.

Dion (DI-on) and

Cleomenes (klee-OM-eh-neez), lords of Sicilia.

Mamillius (ma-MIHL-ee-uhs), the young prince of Sicilia, the son of Leontes and Hermione.

WINTERSET

Author: Maxwell Anderson (1888-1959)
First published: 1935
Genre: Drama

Locale: New York
Time: The twentieth century
Plot: Tragedy

Esdras, a kindly and philosophical old rabbi who is troubled because of his son's guilt in withholding testimony in the Romagna case. Convinced of his past error in trying to protect Garth, Esdras decides to tell of Shadow's murder.

Garth, his son, a witness to a murder committed years ago by Trock. His fear of Trock has kept him silent.

Miriamne (mih-ree-AM-nee), Esdras' fifteen-year-old daughter, who is in love with Mio but, like Esdras, hopes to protect Garth. Rushing to Mio after he has been shot, she is killed when she runs into the line of fire of Trock's machine gun. Like William Shakespeare's Juliet, Miriamne is a virtuous, intense young girl whose love for her sweetheart conflicts with her loyalty to her family, and who chooses to die with the man she has loved.

Bartolomeo Romagna (BAHR-toh-loh-MEH-oh roh-MAHN-nyah), called **Mio** (MEE-oh), the classically tragic young son of Romagna, who was innocent of murder but condemned and executed because of prejudice against his being an anarchist. Mio lives only to prove Romagna's innocence. He witnesses the shooting of Shadow. Torn between loyalty to his father and love for Miriamne, whose brother will be killed if Mio informs on Trock, Mio hesitates too long and is at last gunned down.

The doomed Mio may be compared with Hamlet and other sons in earlier literature who sought to avenge a father's murder and thereby brought on not only their own deaths but those of others as well.

Trock, a coldhearted murderer released from prison and dying of tuberculosis. With only six months to live, he is willing, if necessary, to protect his past guilt with additional murders. He resembles American gangsters and professional murderers of the 1920's.

Shadow, his henchman, who is murdered by two other followers of Trock. He lives long enough to confront and accuse Trock.

Judge Gaunt, the elderly judge who sentenced Romagna to death. He is intermittently insane from brooding over his part in Romagna's death.

Carr, a cynical teenage friend of Mio.

Lucia, a street-piano man.

Piny, an apple-woman.

Herman, a shoe salesman.

A radical, a symbolic character who complains of capitalistic oppression.

WISE BLOOD

Author: Flannery O'Connor (1925-1964)
First published: 1952
Genre: Novel

Locale: The American South
Time: The 1940's
Plot: Psychological realism

Hazel Motes, the protagonist, the twenty-two-year-old grandson of a backwoods preacher. He is driven to find Christ in the city. Hazel tested his grandfather's religion in the Army and goes to the city of Taulkinham to test that religion again. He both distrusts and is haunted by it. Everything about Hazel, from his black hat to the look in his eyes, identifies him as a preacher to those who see him, but he devotes much of his stay in the city to trying to escape his religious destiny. Hazel is a loner whose only human contacts emerge from his attempts to escape Christ. He needs no friends (even though Enoch Emery

tries to establish a friendship with him) or sexual relationships (although Sabbath Lily tries to seduce him). As a religious man who denies religion, he is a misfit in a secular world.

Enoch Emery, a lonely young man who becomes Hazel Motes's "prophet." From his early life with a father who later abandoned him and through the rest of his eighteen years, Enoch has found little love in his world. Even at the Rodemill Boys' Bible Academy, Enoch was unable to find a friend. He seeks friendship with Hazel, seeing in him a loner like himself. Perhaps Enoch's "wise blood" causes him to sense Hazel's determination to discover real truths about the human condition. Enoch spends his time working at the zoo (he hates the animals) and secretly watching the women at the public swimming pool. As is true of many of Flannery O'Connor's characters, his personality is almost a caricature.

Asa Hawks, Sabbath Lily's father, a hypocritical preacher who claims to have blinded himself as a test of faith. He carries with him news clippings that detail both his intended blinding and his failure to carry through. He is threatened by Hazel's presence and leaves, abandoning his daughter.

Sabbath Lily Hawks, Asa Hawks's seductive teenage daughter. She too recognizes Hazel's insistent need for God, but she has her own agenda. Suspecting that her father is about to leave her, she attempts to seduce Hazel, first during an excursion in his car and later in his room. She reads Hazel the answer she received to a letter she wrote to an advice column.

The columnist's answer embodies much of what O'Connor thought was wrong with the world, expressing that religion should not be taken too seriously. Sabbath Lily offers to help Hazel enjoy sin, but he refuses her.

Hoover Shoates, an evangelist con man who uses the name **Onnie Jay Holy**. He tries to cut in on what he supposes is Hazel's scam, sidewalk preaching. When Hazel rejects him, he tries to drive him out of business with a man he calls the "True Prophet," Solace Layfield.

Mrs. Flood, Hazel's landlady. Stupid and dishonest, she steals from Hazel after he has blinded himself, but dimly she senses that Hazel is seeking truths she knows nothing about. At the end, she thinks he may have found them.

Solace Layfield, a preacher hired by Hoover Shoates to offer a false message. Hazel kills him.

—Ann Davison Garbett

WISE VIRGIN

Author: A. N. Wilson (1950-   )
First published: 1982
Genre: Novel

Locale: London, Cambridge, and Wiltshire
Time: Early 1980's
Plot: Love

Giles Fox, a blind scholar and librarian, forty-eight years old. His life already is dictated by habit: Every day he wears a gray suit, white shirt, and silk blue tie, and each dinner is a variation of cold meat, noodles, olives, and fresh fruit. He is obsessed by *A Tretis of Loue Heuenliche*, a medieval tract on virginity, and labors to produce the definitive edition of the text. Ironically, the content of the discourse concerns spiritual love, but by focusing solely on philology and linguistics, Giles fails to acknowledge the work's applicability to his own life.

Tibba Fox, Giles's daughter. An attractive, clever teenager with searching green eyes, Tibba leads two lives: At home, she assumes adult responsibilities by managing the house and caring for her blind father; at school, she is a popular but elusive coquette. Her favorite authors are Harold Pinter and Virginia Woolf, but she reads to Giles every evening from Sir Walter Scott and Anthony Trollope. To her, time is divided into B.C., before Mary's death, and A.D., All Desolation. Giles remarries when Tibba is thirteen years old. Carol, his second wife, is perceived by Tibba as a rival. Tibba puts a curse on her stepmother, asking God to kill her; within twenty-four hours, Carol is run over by a taxicab. Tibba is both shocked and pleased by this apparent power, but she never attempts to exercise it again.

Mary Hargreaves Fox, Giles's late first wife and Tibba's mother. Already deceased when the novel opens, Mary is remembered by Tibba as having hazel eyes, an oval face, and Vidal Sassoon hair. Her relationship with Giles is based primarily on physical attraction, and when she becomes pregnant out of wedlock, they feel forced into marriage. Resentment quickly arises on both sides, and Mary seeks, through numerous affairs, the attention and love she needs. After eight painful years of marriage, she and Giles develop a deeper love for each other, only to face Mary's death in childbirth.

Carol Fox, Giles's late second wife and nurse. Although described simply as beautiful, her Liverpudlian accent reveals her lower-class origins and explains why she marries Giles after knowing him only for a few weeks. A strong rivalry

develops between Carol and Tibba for Giles's affection, but the tension is short-lived: Carol is hit and killed by a taxicab less than a year after being married to Giles.

Louise Agar, Giles's research assistant. Described as lumpish, with unshapely and columnar legs and a poor complexion, she has soft, thick hands and abundant long hair. In her mid-twenties, she still lives with her mother, her teddy bear, and her Winnie the Pooh poster. Although her research in diphthongs failed to produce a doctorate, she is one of the few individuals familiar enough with Giles's linguistic research to be of any use to him. Tibba hires her to serve as Giles's professional assistant. Eventually, Louise and Giles fall in love.

Meg Gore, Giles's older sister, with a rosy complexion and bright blue eyes. She tends to face her problems with determination and optimism. A bit of a busybody, she serves as a good support for Monty Gore, her husband, but tends to annoy Giles and Tibba by mothering them.

Monty "Ruddy G." Gore, Meg's husband and a housemaster of Pangham. A stereotypical teacher, Monty has short hair, glasses, and a caricatured Roman nose. Although in his fifties, he lusts for teenage girls, especially his niece Tibba. Until Piers Peverill, an unruly student, challenges his authority, he views life as an amusing joke.

Piers Peverill, Tibba's boyfriend and one of Monty's students. Charming, arrogant, and handsome, Piers is spoiled by his rich, divorced parents. He deliberately breaks Pangham's school rules, and Monty attempts to have him expelled on numerous occasions. Piers's parents make sizable contributions to the proper people, and he is promptly reinstated.

Captain de Courcy, Tibba's fraudulent speech therapist. Having been court-martialed in the army and failing in theater work, he falsely proclaims to have a degree from the Royal Academy of Dramatic Art so that he can give voice lessons. Although Tibba's stammer does not improve, she spends numerous hours fantasizing about a life with de Courcy.

— Coleen Maddy

THE WITCHES OF EASTWICK

Author: John Updike (1932-)
First published: 1984
Genre: Novel

Locale: Eastwick, Rhode Island
Time: The 1960's
Plot: Psychological symbolism

Alexandra Spofford, a large, gray-blonde divorcée and mother. She and two fellow divorcées are convinced they have magic powers and explore witchcraft as a form of women's liberation. Together they form an alliance in rebellion against the small-town conventions they believe have inhibited them. Their magic powers, however, not only have a liberating effect but also create mischief. Alexandra turns her former husband into polychrome dust and keeps him in a jar in the cupboard, and the witches raise a thunderstorm to punish some youngsters who call Alexandra a hag. Alexandra is the leader of the coven of three witches because she is the oldest and the earthiest, and she relates most strongly to nature, from which the witches believe they derive their special powers. She is also a sculptor, working in the earthy medium of clay to make figures of female sensuality she calls "bubbies." The powers that she and the other witches develop eventually lead to mayhem and even murder. They pursue the satanic Darryl Van Horne, and when he chooses Jennifer, a younger woman, they conjure her death. Chastened and guilty, Alexandra marries an art instructor who takes her to Taos, New Mexico.

Jane Smart, the second witch. She is dark and short, and her special talent is music, especially the cello. Like her two friends, she neglects her children in favor of the powerful sisterhood of the witches, and she uses her magic powers in dubious ways. For example, she transforms her former husband into a dried herb hanging in the cellar. In addition, she and the other two women perform such tricks as breaking an old woman's string of pearls, turning tennis balls into bats and toads, and killing innocent puppies and squirrels. The coven of witches disbands after they compete for the attentions of Darryl Van Horne and place a death curse on Jennifer, a young unmarried woman whom Darryl selects over them. Ultimately, Jane uses her powers to attract a new husband, a staid scion of an old Boston family.

Sukie Rougemont, a redhead, the youngest and most recently divorced of the three witches. She also neglects maternal responsibilities to pursue her talents as a writer and to develop her magical powers, which she already has used to transform her former husband into a placemat. Free from patriarchal structures and traditional puritan controls, Sukie has a love affair with Felicia's husband, Clyde; participates with the other two witches in orgies with Darryl Van Horne; and uses her magic powers to inflict illness on her rival, Jennifer. Demoralized, Sukie attracts a salesman of word processors. She writes rather mechanical romantic novels.

Darryl Van Horne, a mysterious, wealthy bachelor who is new to Eastwick. A manipulative psychopath, he entices the witches to his mansion, which he has decorated with black sheets, couches, and walls and where they frolic together, including engaging in an orgy in a hot tub on Halloween. Although he prides himself on his skills as a critic, unlike the witches he is neither creative nor procreative. He may be a metaphysical fantasy created by the witches themselves. Whether imaginary or real, Van Horne is the devil. He may have murdered Jennifer for her money. He runs off to New York afterward with both her fortune and her brother. Unlike the witches, Van Horne has no sympathy for the natural world. He is surrounded by artificial creations such as tennis courts, stereos, and vinyl hamburgers. He denounces nature and all of its works in a sermon he gives at the Unitarian Church titled "This Is a Terrible Creation." Because of his existential emptiness, he cannot appreciate, for all their moral ambiguity, the beauties of nature, art, or the women of Eastwick.

Brenda Parsley, a married woman and critic of the witches. She takes over the Unitarian Church, running it more efficiently than her husband, but in the process becomes a dreadful woman. She receives her comeuppance when bumblebees and butterflies come out of her mouth as she denounces the witches from her pulpit.

Felicia Gabriel, the mother of Christopher and Jenny Gabriel and ill-tempered wife of the editor of the local newspaper. When she is especially outraged, parrot feathers, dried wasps, and bits of eggshell spew from her mouth. A critic of the witches, she considers herself a virtuous woman devoted to good causes, but she has reserves of malicious energy.

Jennifer Gabriel, an unmarried X-ray technician who rivals the witches for the affections of Darryl Van Horne. Soon after marrying Darryl, she dies of cancer, which may have been caused by the witches, who stick her facsimile with pins.

— *Margaret Boe Birns*

WITH FIRE AND SWORD
(Ogniem i mieczem)

Author: Henryk Sienkiewicz (1846-1916)
First published: 1884
Genre: Novel

Locale: Poland and the Ukraine
Time: The seventeenth century
Plot: Historical

Pan Yan Skshetuski (sksheh-TEW-skih), a young lieutenant and the valiant hero of this romance dramatizing the seventeenth century struggle for Polish unity. Courageous, loyal to his prince, magnanimous to his defeated enemy, and faithful to his beloved, Pan Yan is a conventional heroic figure.

Princess Helena Kurtsevich (kewrt-TSEH-vihch), his beloved. In love with Pan Yan but constantly pursued by a jealous lover, she is alternately a captive and a fugitive from capture. Ultimately, she is saved by Pan Yan's followers.

Princess Kurtsevich, the widow of Prince Constantine Kurtsevich. She is the mother of five sons and the aunt of Helena, whose estate is in her hands. She promises to help Pan

Yan with Helena if he will not interfere with the ownership of the estate.

Bogun (BOH-gewn), Princess Kurtsevich's adopted sixth son and an aspirant for Helena's hand. Learning of the princess' plan to help Pan Yan with Helena, he kills her and two of her sons, burns the estate, and pursues Helena relentlessly. At last, he is captured and turned over to Pan Yan, who generously spares his life.

Prince Yeremi Vishnyevetski (yeh-REH-mih vihsh-nyeh-VEHTS-skih), a Polish national hero and Pan Yan's general. He engages in a long struggle against the marauding Cossacks and is finally victorious.

Hmelnitski (khmehl-NIHTS-skih), the hetman of the Zaporojian Cossacks. Assisted as an unknown traveler by Pan Yan, he pledges friendship to him; afterward, he has occasion to save Pan Yan's life. He plays a double game against Prince Yeremi by seeming to hold the truce while some of his followers oppose the prince. Finally, the prince defeats him in a heroic stand.

Tugai Bey (TEW-gay bay), the hetman of the Tartars and an ally of Hmelnitski, who persuades him not to order the death of the captured Pan Yan.

Zagloba (zah-GLOH-bah), a jovial and kindhearted nobleman. At first he is Bogun's ally, but he turns against him and rescues Helena.

Horpyna (khohr-PEW-nah), a witch who holds Helena captive.

Jendzian (YEHN-dzyan), Pan Yan's faithful servant, who learns that Helena is Horpyna's captive and assists in her rescue.

Prince Karl, a disputant in the election for king. He finally withdraws in favor of Prince Kazimir.

Prince Kazimir (kah-ZEE-mihr), later King Kazimir.

Prince Dominik Zaslavski Ostrogski (zahs-LAHV-skih ohs-TROHG-skih), the commander in chief of the Commonwealth armies.

Pan Kisel (KIH-sehl), the leader of the government faction that wishes to negotiate with Hmelnitski.

Pototski (poh-TOT-skih), a leader of the armies of the king.

WITHIN THE GATES

Author: Sean O'Casey (John Casey, 1880-1964)
First published: 1933
Genre: Drama

Locale: A park in London
Time: The twentieth century
Plot: Morality

Jannice, a young and dying prostitute. The streetwalker is a modern Everywoman who turns, in her final days on Earth, to family, church, social agency, lover, and finally poet. Of all those to whom she turns, including her father, the Bishop, none sustains her with love and compassion except the poet.

The Dreamer, a young poet. Sensitive to the impoverished spirit of modern people, weighed down by mass conformity, he protests and urges the Down-and-Outs to throw off their worldly bonds. As Jannice dies, he sings his song of praise to the independent spirit who is dying within the gates.

The Bishop (**Gilbert**), Jannice's father. Limited only to conventional responses, the guilty lover and irresponsible father cannot admit his guilt in spite of Jannice's mockery.

Worship of self has replaced compassion, and he can only utter Latin comfort as she dies.

The Old Woman, Jannice's mother, a drunkard steeped in sin and hatred. Her only happy memory is of a week spent with a long-dead Irish soldier.

The Atheist, the foster father of Jannice. Deserted by both the mother and the daughter, he is now too much interested in his rabble-rousing, speechifying, and pamphleteering to take Jannice back.

The Down-and-Outs, the victims of dead traditions, bowed by the master classes.

The Gardener, a man in love with physical love who rejects Jannice.

The Salvation Army Officer, Jannice's lover.

WIVES AND DAUGHTERS

Author: Elizabeth Gaskell (1810-1865)
First published: 1864-1866
Genre: Novel

Locale: Hollingford, a country town in England
Time: Mid-nineteenth century
Plot: Domestic realism

Molly Gibson, the only daughter of the town doctor. When the story opens, Molly is twelve years old, eagerly anticipating the annual garden festival on the grounds of the Towers, the grand home of Lord and Lady Cumnor. Sadly, Molly is disillusioned by the behavior and words of the aristocrats and those who serve them, particularly Clare Kirkpatrick, their former governess, who is now a widow. The scene introduces some of the people who will have a considerable influence on Molly's life. Molly is devastated when Mrs. Kirkpatrick becomes her stepmother through a marriage arranged by Lady Cumnor. Molly is a steady, sensible girl, however, and she does her best to be a dutiful daughter to the woman who has usurped her

place in the doctor's home. She has much to put up with from her silly, pretentious, and snobbish stepmother, but she makes friends with her stepsister, Cynthia Kirkpatrick. Molly lives by her principles, which are to do what is right, even when it is painful to do so. She thus never reveals her love for Osborne Hamley, and later for his younger brother Roger, as Cynthia flirts with both of the young men though she loves neither of them. Later, Molly compromises herself by meeting with the overseer, Mr. Preston, who is blackmailing Cynthia over a foolish indiscretion that occurred several years earlier. When Osborne's secret marriage to a poor Frenchwoman is revealed, it is Molly who helps to heal the breach between the dying man and his father, Squire Hamley. Molly is an unselfish young woman who bears her own suffering in silence. Her marriage to Roger Hamley is clearly foretold at the end of the novel, and her happiness is well deserved.

Cynthia Kirkpatrick, the daughter of the new Mrs. Gibson. A lively, pretty young woman, Cynthia captures the heart of every man she meets. She is fond of Molly, who is her direct opposite in relations with others, but they are alike in that Cynthia, too, has a sense of reserve and does not often reveal her feelings. The author shows unusual psychological insight, for her time, in subtly creating a puzzling young woman who flirts with every man in sight but is unable to give love because she has never experienced it. Reared in poverty and insecurity, Cynthia was unwanted by her vain and shallow mother. Like Molly, she is sensible and practical, and her marriage to Walter Henderson, a young lawyer, is eminently suitable and appropriate.

Mr. Gibson, the town doctor, Molly's father. An honest, selfless, dedicated physician, he does his best to do what is right for his young motherless daughter. Outwardly unemotional and reserved, Mr. Gibson is the principal observer in the narrative. He and Molly complement each other, and it is through their eyes that the reader sees and feels. Mr. Gibson is intelligent, logical, and slightly sarcastic. He has provided Molly with a stable, affectionate upbringing, and his concern for her led him to marry Mrs. Kirkpatrick, at the prompting—

without his realization—of the meddlesome Lady Cumnor. Mr. Gibson shows understanding sympathy for his daughter, and their devotion to each other strengthens and sustains both of them.

Roger Hamley, the younger son of Squire Hamley and Mrs. Hamley. Roger has not received the parental attention and adulation bestowed on his brother Osborne. This emotional neglect apparently has not affected the development of the younger son, who quietly and earnestly becomes an eminent scientist, whereas Osborne languishes without any strong sense of purpose or serious pursuits. Roger soon realizes the folly of his infatuation for Cynthia, and his love for Molly is as steady and deep as he himself is.

Squire Hamley, the owner of a large estate. He is from an ancient family whose wealth depends on advantageous marriages. He represents an aspect of the country society that is in strong contrast to the feudalistic earl and duchess.

Clare Hyacinth Kirkpatrick Gibson, the second wife of Mr. Gibson. In exchange for material security and social standing, she provides what Mr. Gibson was seeking for his daughter, protection and teaching in social matters. Her pretensions to learning and her snobbery make her appear supercilious. She is an unlikable character whose faults are largely the result of her circumstances.

— *Natalie Harper*

A WIZARD OF EARTHSEA

Author: Ursula K. Le Guin (1929-   )
First published: 1968
Genre: Novel

Locale: The imaginary world of Earthsea
Time: Unspecified
Plot: Fantasy

Ged, or **Sparrowhawk**, the title character. Over the course of the novel, he learns the true meaning of wizardry, its limits as well as its capabilities. As a youth on the Isle of Gont, Ged shows potential as a wizard. He also displays overconfidence and a willingness to try magic beyond his skill. Earthsea is a world of widely scattered islands, some sophisticated and some modest and plain. When Ged goes to the school for wizards on Roke Island, he feels that he does not fit in. His home island is isolated and backward, and many of the students on Roke are from wealthy and sophisticated families on important islands. Because he feels inferior, Ged attempts wizardry for which he is not yet prepared. Jasper, a fellow student, taunts Ged into attempting a dangerous summoning of a dead spirit. Ged's attempt fails; he summons a mysterious shadow. Ged's release of the shadow upsets the balance of Earthsea, which wizards are charged to preserve. The shadow pursues Ged across Earthsea. Ged must deal with it or die. In his desperate efforts to deal with the shadow, Ged matures, eventually becoming the most powerful wizard on Earthsea.

Ogion, Ged's first tutor in wizardry. Living as a hermit on the Isle of Gont, Ogion teaches Ged wizardry, but not as much as Ged would like to learn. Ogion has to straighten up the messes Ged makes while trying to guide him toward maturity. When Ged releases a malign spirit unintentionally, Ogion must dispel it. Ogion insists that a wizard should use his powers sparingly and never for selfish reasons.

Vetch, Ged's best friend. Vetch and Ged meet at the school for wizards on Roke. In contrast to Ged, Vetch is calm and easygoing. He has neither the sheer natural ability of Ged nor Ged's pride and ambition. Like Ged, Vetch comes from an island outside the main centers of trade and culture on Earthsea, but unlike Ged, Vetch does not feel inferior to the wizards from the larger and more sophisticated islands. When Ged begins pursuing the shadow, rather than fleeing it, he meets Vetch in the East Reach, on Iffish. Vetch insists on accompanying Ged on his voyage to a final confrontation with the shadow. Even though Ged has to face the shadow alone, Vetch's friendship gives him needed support in his quest.

Jasper, a student, from the important island of Havnor, at the school for wizards. He expresses contempt for Ged, whom he considers crude and ill-mannered. Jasper seems also to envy Ged's powers and goads him into using them on several occasions. On the last occasion, Ged frees the shadow. Jasper spurs Ged on his way to maturity by taunting and provoking him.

Nemmerle, the warder of the school for wizards and an archmage. Nemmerle frees Ged from the initial attack of the shadow, but he loses his life in the process. Because of the guilt he feels over Nemmerle's death, Ged leaves Roke for Low Torning to be the people's wizard and, eventually, to confront the shadow.

Serret, who tries to use Ged for her own ends. As a girl, she provokes Ged into summoning the spirit that Ogion must dispel. As a woman, she welcomes Ged to the Court of the Terrenon on the island of Osskil, hoping he will free a spirit trapped in a stone. Ged, who is becoming wiser, recognizes this spirit as a terrible danger and refuses.

Pechvarry, a boatmaker who becomes Ged's friend. After loosing the shadow, Ged flees to Low Torning, one of the Ninety Isles, where he meets Pechvarry. Ged's time on this island helps him recover from the trauma of releasing the shadow. Ged again encounters the shadow while trying to heal Pechvarry's dying son. This encounter motivates Ged to try to deal with the force he has set loose. Ged learns boatmaking from Pechvarry, a skill that stands him in good stead in his voyages, first to flee the shadow and then to pursue it.

Yevaud, a dragon whom Ged confronts after leaving Low Torning. Ged masters Yevaud because he knows the dragon's name. Yevaud offers him the boons of treasure or knowledge of the shadow's name. Instead, Ged binds Yevaud and his kin not to raid humans any more. In protecting others from the dragons, Ged shows his increased maturity.

— *Gene Doty*

WOLF SOLENT

Author: John Cowper Powys (1872-1963)
First published: 1929
Genre: Novel

Locale: Devon, England
Time: The twentieth century
Plot: Psychological realism

Wolf Solent, a history master hired by Squire Urquhart. Wolf returns to Ramsgard and meets Gerda Torp. Yielding to his animal nature, he seduces her, but he later makes her his wife. Forced by financial necessity to assist the squire on a pornographic project, Wolf is then forced by Gerda to cash a check for his degrading work with the squire. The existence of his spiritual love for Christie Malakite confuses his life, but this love refuses to become physical, and he remains with his wife.

Gerda Torp, Wolf's beautiful wife, still attractive to men. Gerda loses her loyalty to Wolf and has an affair with Bob Weevil when Wolf refuses to cash the check.

Christie Malakite, Wolf's spiritual mate. Unable to arouse physical love in Wolf, she moves away with Olwen after her father dies.

Squire Urquhart, the Ramsgard squire engaged in writing a history of all the salacious stories of Dorset.

Ann Solent, Wolf's mother.

Selena Gault, Wolf's father's former mistress.

Albert Smith, a hatter.

Mattie Smith, Wolf's illegitimate half sister, later Darnley's wife.

Olwen, the product of an incestuous relationship between Mr. Malakite and his oldest daughter.

Bob Weevil, Gerda's flashy young lover.

Mr. Torp, Gerda's father, a stonecutter.

Lob Torp, his son.

Darnley Otter, Wolf's friend and Mattie's husband.

Jason Otter, Darnley's brother, a poet.

Mr. Malakite, a bookseller, Christie's father.

THE WOMAN FROM SARAJEVO
(Gospodjica)

Author: Ivo Andrić (1892-1975)
First published: 1945
Genre: Novel

Locale: Sarajevo and Belgrade
Time: 1900-1936
Plot: Psychological

Rajka Radaković (RI-kah rah-DA-koh-vihch), a woman from Sarajevo. Rajka is the quintessential miser. Her miserliness derives from a sense of insecurity, which came about primarily from her father's failure in business. Her father dies from grief, but not before advising his daughter to save at every step and to distrust people, because trusting people allows concern for others to govern one's life, which, in turn, makes one dangerously vulnerable. Rajka's bitter childhood experience stays with her all of her life. After taking over her father's business, she makes sure never to allow others to take advantage of her. Moreover, she denies herself every pleasure and isolates herself from people, even relatives. Eventually, her thrift and avarice become an obsession and grow to monstrous proportions. The excessive egotism, selfishness, miserliness, and lack of normal human drives in the end ruin her, along with everyone with whom she associates. The author offers some plausible explanations for Rajka's behavior. In addition to insecurity, a desire to avenge and redeem her father contributes heavily to her behavior. The remembrance of the past shapes her view of the world as basically evil, selfish, insensitive, and even cruel. Such a cruel world crushes soft and emotional people, like her father, but it bows before hard and resolute people, like herself. The only security people like Rajka can find is in money, and money becomes a god to which she is willing to sacrifice everything.

Obren Radaković, Rajka's father, a rich merchant from Sarajevo who goes bankrupt. In a very brief role (Rajka is only fourteen years old when he dies), Obren leaves his daughter a weighty and even dangerous legacy, contained in a few guidelines: Do not trust people, depend only on your own strength and resoluteness, save as much as possible, and never allow emotions to govern your life. Another lesson Rajka learns from her father's experience is that honest work alone is not enough for a successful life. Rajka's allegiance to her father borders almost on an Oedipus complex, all the more so because her mother is a very weak person.

Radojka Radaković (rah-DOY-kah), Rajka's mother. The exact opposite of her husband, Radojka is a harmless, good-natured, and meek woman, weak in spirit and in body. As such, she is unable to offer Rajka any support, not even love, no matter how much she tries. She simply cannot comprehend her daughter and therefore stays out of her life, powerless to influence Rajka in any way.

Vladimir Hadži-Vasić (HAHD-zhee VAH-sihch), Rajka's favorite uncle, only four years her senior. Vladimir enjoys life, likes beautiful things, loves to give expensive gifts, and spends everything he can. Essentially a good-for-nothing, he stands for everything Rajka does not, and that is probably why she likes him better than any of her other relatives. She even has

motherly feelings and is exceptionally sentimental toward him, especially after his early death of tuberculosis at the age of twenty-three.

Rafo Konforti, a merchant from Sarajevo. A helpful and honest business partner, he helps Rajka learn the trade business without taking advantage of her inexperience. He is swept away by the profound changes during World War I.

— *Vasa D. Mihailovich*

THE WOMAN HATER

Authors: Francis Beaumont (c. 1584-1616) and John Fletcher (1579-1625)
First published: 1607
Genre: Drama

Locale: Milan
Time: Early seventeenth century
Plot: Comedy

Gondarino (gohn-dah-REE-noh), a widower, so disillusioned by his late wife's infidelity that he despises all women. Plagued by Oriana's teasing, he retaliates by accusing her of wantonness. When his lies are discovered, he is ordered to kiss a dozen ladies in waiting, a fate worse than death in his eyes.

Oriana (oh-ree-AH-nah), a merry, virtuous young noblewoman who makes a game of Gondarino's well-known misogyny, succeeding only in strengthening his prejudices while she wins the love and admiration of the duke.

Count Valore (vah-LOH-reh), her brother. Bored with court life, he finds amusement in Lazarillo's search for a feast and in tricking the intelligencers who prey on those around them. He remains loyal to Oriana and helps to prove Gondarino's accusations false.

The duke of Milan, a young ruler who is attracted by Oriana's beauty. He plans a test to prove or disprove Gondarino's slander and rejoices at the vehemence with which

Oriana refuses Arrigo's staged advances. He claims her for his bride.

Lazarillo (lah-zah-REEL-loh), a gourmet who yearns only to feast on the head of the fish umbrana.

Julia, a prostitute whom he marries to achieve his wish.

Francissina (frahn-CHEES-see-nah), her colleague. She is married, through the wiles of the pander, to a well-to-do mercer.

A mercer, her naïve husband-to-be, who longs to be a scholar. Deceived when he takes the pander's black robes as a mark of the academic profession, he accepts his irregular marriage philosophically.

A pander, a clever opportunist who sees two of his clients wed at considerable profit to himself.

Lucio (LEW-chee-oh) and

Arrigo (ahr-REE-goh), ambitious and rather corrupt officials of the duke's court.

WOMAN HOLLERING CREEK AND OTHER STORIES

Author: Sandra Cisneros (1954-   )
First published: 1991
Genre: Short fiction

Locale: The borderlands of the United States and Mexico
Time: The 1910's-the 1980's
Plot: Social

Lucy Anguiano (ahn-gee-AH-noh), a lively, dark-skinned Texas girl. She inspires the young female protagonist and narrator in "My Lucy Friend Who Smells Like Corn" to depict their experiences of growing up. Lucy's voice joins those of the narrator and others, re-creating a childhood world full of smells, sounds, and colors. Lucy and her many sisters fulfill the narrator's desire to experience intimate sisterhood and true friendship.

Salvador, a boy in "Salvador Late or Early" who experiences poverty and the hardships of life at an early age. He is always busy helping his mother and his younger brothers.

Micaela (mee-kah-EH-lah), a young and playful Mexican American girl, the protagonist and narrator in "Mericans." Her Mexican "awful grandmother," who embodies severe religious piety, makes Micaela and her brothers Alfredito and Enrique wait at the entrance of a church while she prays. Micaela depicts with innocence and humor the world of penitents around her and the people's devotion to the Virgin of Guadalupe.

Rachel, the young narrator of "Eleven," who expresses the painful feelings of growing up. On her eleventh birthday, Rachel's teacher unjustly humiliates her in class, causing her distress. Rachel wants to leave childhood behind, hoping to become older and wiser; she realizes, however, that the child within remains forever.

Chaq Uxmal Paloquín (chahk ewj-MAHL pah-loh-KEEN), **Boy Baby**, a thirty-seven-year-old Mexican man who initiates the protagonist and narrator of "One Holy Night" into the mysteries of female sexuality. In a confidential tone, the eighth-grade narrator reveals how the mysterious man, claiming to be a descendant of Mayan kings, seduces her and makes her believe that she is his queen Ixchel. When her grandmother discovers her pregnancy, she is sent to Mexico to live with a witch woman and female cousins. Her innocent cousins dream about love and the perfect man, but the narrator has experienced sexual coming-of-age under the most sordid circumstances.

Cleófilas Enriqueta DeLeón Hernández (kleh-OH-fee-lahs ehn-ree-KEH-tah deh-leh-OHN ehr-NAHN-dehs), a Mexican in "Woman Hollering Creek" who dreams about a romantic future, as seen in television, movies, and magazines. She leaves her father and six brothers to marry Juan Pedro Martínez Sánchez in Texas. As the happy bride travels to her new home, she expresses curiosity about Woman Hollering Creek. Her dreams of romance and passion are shattered when she finds herself a victim of domestic violence. Fearing for her life and protective of her son Juan Pedrito and her unborn child, she decides to escape back to Mexico. She succeeds with the help of Felicia, a Chicana driver who hollers and laughs when they drive across the creek named after the wailing woman of mestizo folklore. Felicia and Cleófilas transform the lament of the victimized into the triumphant laughter of the liberated woman.

Carmen Berriozabal (beh-rree-oh-sah-BAHL), a secretary in a San Antonio law firm. In "*La Fabulosa*: A Texas Operetta," she represents the woman who drives men crazy with her seductive ways.

Rudy Cantú (kahn-TEW), also called **Tristán** (trees-TAHN), the male protagonist and narrator of "Remember the Alamo," who dares to be different by performing as a dancer with female impersonators. He fulfills childhood dreams and escapes the ordinary world by entertaining others.

Clemencia (kleh-mehn-see-ah), a vindictive Mexican American painter who, disappointed with marriage, seduces men and makes them be unfaithful to their wives. The protagonist and narrator of "Never Marry a Mexican," she depicts race and class discrimination in Mexico and in the United States.

Inés Alfaro (ee-NEHS AHL-fah-roh), the protagonist and narrator of "Eyes of Zapata." She reveals lyrically her lifelong relationship with the legendary Mexican hero Emiliano Zapata. Her memories and imagination re-create her bittersweet past as well as the individual and collective hardships during the Mexican Revolution. The mother of two of Zapata's children, she is painfully aware of his infidelities. As do other women in her family, she survives through magical powers and fantasies.

Lupe Arredondo (LEW-peh ah-rreh-DOHN-doh), a passionate Chicano painter from California who moves to Texas. The protagonist and narrator in "*Bien* Pretty," she describes humorously her ill-fated love affair with Flavio Munguía. Lupe survives heartbreaks while exploring herself and sexuality, edifying and destructive ways of loving, and issues of gender, class, race, and ethnicity. Art and the return to the religious beliefs of her ancestors allow her the expression of emotions, spiritual survival, and the coming to terms with the intertwined cultures of a Mexican American.

Rosario (Chayo) De Leon (roh-SAHR-ee-oh CHI-yoh deh leh-OHN), a Chicana artist who, following the religious folk custom of inscribing petitions and promises, leaves a note and a braid of her hair for the Virgin of Guadalupe in "Little Miracles, Kept Promises." She finds strength in female ancestors and religious figures to battle predetermined sex roles. As the new mestiza who straddles several borders, she celebrates a universal female identity.

— *Ludmila Kapschutschenko-Schmitt*

THE WOMAN IN THE DUNES
(Suna no onna)

Author: Kōbō Abe (1924-1993)
First published: 1962
Genre: Novel

Locale: A Japanese seaside village
Time: 1955-1962
Plot: Allegory

Niki Jumpei, a Japanese schoolmaster and amateur collector of insects. Thirty-one years old and ordinary looking, Niki is a rather commonplace member of the conformist urban Japanese populace. He lives in the city with a woman who is not a wholly fulfilling sexual partner. He is a creature of regular habits, appears to derive his sense of identity from the way that his society and his colleagues define him, and is not particularly individualistic or imaginative. Beneath this team-player exterior, however, Niki does harbor a few sparks of desire for individual difference and distinction; hence, he collects insects as a hobby. He took up this hobby in the hope that he would find a rare or hitherto unknown specimen of some insect and thereby earn for himself renown as an amateur entomologist. Niki also likes to toy with abstract theories about the nature of reality; he is attracted to notions such as the speculation that sand moves in waves like water (except that unlike water, sand desiccates). The novel opens on an August weekend in 1955 when Niki is out alone on an insect-gathering trip among some sand dunes by the sea. What begins as a weekend outing eventually becomes a seven-year adventure as he becomes a guest of a village in the dunes, particularly of one woman in the dunes.

The Woman in the Dunes, who remains unnamed throughout the novel. About thirty years of age, she is small in build and pleasant in temperament. She is a widow and lives alone, having lost her husband and only daughter to a sand slide during a typhoon the previous year. She is a down-to-earth, sensual woman (she sleeps nude, with only a towel to cover her face) and seems to have an intuitive, almost primal, grasp of the life force and a tenacious will to survive. Poor, unprepossessing, and unsophisticated though she is, she is not without dignity and spiritual beauty. Like the other inhabitants of this Kafkaesque dune village, the woman lives in a house at the bottom of a sand pit, and her only access to the outside world is a rope ladder suspended from the pit mouth, a ladder that can be retracted by the villagers. The village supplies her with a sense of community and the necessities of life, chief of which is water. An indefatigable and loyal worker, she in turn supplies the village council with quantities of the local salt-laced sand, which is sold illegally to dubious construction companies in the city. Niki is lured to her house by the villagers, who assign him to be her helpmeet. Through their life together, Niki learns to derive meaning from his existence— not by discovering an obscure insect but by realizing through their interaction a new sense of manhood, humanity, and community.

The Woman in the City, who also remains nameless and contrasts with the one in the dunes. The city woman probably is Niki's lover and possibly is his wife. Sex between Niki and this woman is made uneasy by twinges of psychological rape and rendered discomfiting by feelings akin to a psychological venereal disease. Their coitus is deficient in libido and excessive in self-consciousness. Niki compares it to punching off on some season ticket, and it is always performed through the prophylactic screening of a condom.

The Villagers of the Dunes, also anonymous, resembling a Greek chorus, Niki's captors and arbiters of his fate. They are motivated by the need of their community to survive; hence,

they provide Niki as a mate to their woman. They are insular and uncaring about the larger society beyond their community, yet they have the redeeming qualities of peasantlike good humor, wisdom, and pragmatism. For example, when Niki escapes from the woman's pit only to become trapped in quicksand, the villagers rescue him ungrudgingly. Indirectly through the villagers and more directly through the woman, Niki learns to appreciate the differences between the bestial and the beautiful in sexuality, between the illusion of freedom and the true freedom in choice exercised, and between rote conformity and individual meaningfulness in responsible human activity.

— C. L. Chua

THE WOMAN IN WHITE

Author: Wilkie Collins (1824-1889)
First published: 1860
Genre: Novel

Locale: England
Time: The 1850's
Plot: Detective and mystery

Walter Hartright, the primary narrator. Engaged as an art instructor to Laura Fairlie, he endears himself to his student, who is betrothed to an older man of rank. Laura decides to complete her wedding plans, and Hartright leaves to go to Central America. When he returns, he learns of Laura's unhappy marriage. Hartright then gathers facts to incriminate the conspirators who have plotted to take Laura's money. He marries Laura, who is now penniless, during the investigation.

Laura Fairlie, who becomes Lady Glyde. In her husband's conspiracy to secure her fortune, Laura is concealed for a time in her room. Meanwhile, the woman in white is held incommunicado, dies, and is buried as Laura, Lady Glyde. Laura, committed by the conspirators to the asylum from which the woman in white has escaped, is abducted and hidden until Hartright completes his investigation.

Marian Halcombe, Laura's half sister, who works with Hartright as a protector of the frail Laura. Strong and courageous, she combats Laura's adversaries during Hartright's absence. Although she is in love with Hartright, Marian, absorbed in feminism, is willing to remain unmarried and to live with the Hartrights.

Sir Percival Glyde, Laura's husband, who resorts to conspiracy, involving his wife's incarceration, to get money to pay his debts. Knowing of Hartright's investigation of his parentage, Sir Percival sets fire to the vestry to destroy church records that would establish his illegitimacy; he dies in the fire.

Count Fosco, his Italian accomplice in the conspiracy. Identified as a foreign spy by Hartright, Fosco exposes his own and Sir Percival's villainy.

Countess Fosco, his wife, the former **Eleanor Fairlie**, a gay and socially prominent woman dispossessed by her family when she married the count. Cold and impenetrable because of the secrets sealed up during six years of marriage, she obeys her husband's orders in the conspiracy.

Anne Catherick, the woman in white, committed as a young girl to an asylum by Sir Percival because he feared she

knew his secret. She is the illegitimate daughter of Philip Fairlie, Laura's father—hence the marked resemblance to Laura. Anne is buried as Lady Glyde. Because of Mrs. Fairlie's attention to Anne as a child, Anne always dresses in white.

Mrs. Catherick, her mother, who lives on income from Sir Percival for her part in forging a marriage entry in the church records.

Professor Pesca, Hartright's longtime friend. Pesca's Italian background helps to identify Fosco as a spy.

Mrs. Elizabeth Clements, Anne's guardian, who reveals Sir Percival's past attentions to Mrs. Catherick, pointing to the supposition that Anne is Percival's child.

Frederick Fairlie, Laura's uncle. An artistic hypochondriac, he lives in seclusion on the family estate.

Mrs. Vesey, Laura's former governess.

Hester Pinkorn, Fosco's cook. She narrates the description of the mysterious young woman hidden in Fosco's house, her behavior during her illness, and the incidents of her death.

Alfred Goodricke, a doctor who tells of his attendance to the young woman. He attributes her death to heart disease.

Mrs. Eliza Michelson, the housekeeper at Sir Percival's estate. She acts as an informant between Marian and Anne Catherick, when Anne calls secretly in her effort to save Laura from Sir Percival's wiles.

Margaret Porcher, a slatternly, obstinate housemaid, hired by Sir Percival to keep Marian away from Laura.

Fanny, Laura's maid, discharged by Sir Percival to rid the house of servants faithful to Laura and Marian.

Mrs. Rubelle, Fosco's friend, hired as a nurse to Marian to prevent her from foiling the conspiracy.

Major Donthorne, the owner of a resort who writes Hartright about Philip Fairlie's and Mrs. Catherick's early affair at his place. This information establishes Anne Catherick's parentage.

A WOMAN KILLED WITH KINDNESS

Author: Thomas Heywood (c. 1573-1641)
First published: 1607
Genre: Drama

Locale: Yorkshire, England
Time: Early seventeenth century
Plot: Tragedy

John Frankford, a well-to-do gentleman. Generous and just to his whole household, he wins undying loyalty from his servants. He finds his trust betrayed by his beloved wife and his friend Wendoll, whom he had taken into his home. Although he is reluctant to accept his servant Nick's revelation of their guilt, he forces himself to try to learn the truth. Too merciful to take the bloody revenge demanded by convention from an injured spouse, he satisfies himself by banishing his wife to his manor in the country, where she dies heartbroken.

Anne Frankford, his wife. She seems at the time of her marriage the epitome of gracious, chaste womanhood, but she cannot resist the persistent advances of Wendoll, whom her husband leaves alone with her. After the discovery of her infidelity, she is so overcome by her sense of guilt and by her husband's generosity that she starves herself and dies, forgiven on her deathbed, in Frankford's arms.

Wendoll, her lover, Frankford's protégé. Although his conscience rebels at his base betrayal of Frankford's hospitality, he gives in to passion and persuades Anne to return his love, shamelessly baiting her husband with double entendres as they play cards. Once discovered, he repents and sees that he must wander, like Cain, to escape the report of his ingratitude.

Charles Mountford, an impulsive country squire. In a heated quarrel over his hawk's prowess, he kills two of the servants of his friend Sir Francis Acton and makes a bitter enemy of their master. Freed from prison at the cost of his entire fortune, he lives in the country with his sister, contented with their simple life, until he is again arrested, this time at the request of a creditor whom he trusted. Released by Acton's intercession, he feels obligated to repay his debt to his enemy and offers him his only remaining treasure, his sister, a gesture understandable only in terms of his rigid code of honor.

Susan, his loyal sister, who shares his misfortunes. She is appalled at first by her brother's proposal that she give herself to Sir Francis, but she finally accepts his view of the matter enough to explain his offer to their enemy, swearing at the same time that she will kill herself rather than stain her honor. Relieved of this grim choice by Sir Francis, she accepts his proposal of marriage.

Sir Francis Acton, Anne Frankford's brother. The slaying of his servants makes him Charles Mountford's implacable enemy until he sees Susan and falls in love with her. Unable to purchase her favors, he resolves to win them by his kindness in freeing her brother. He is so overcome by Charles's offer that he refuses to dishonor their house and asks for the young woman as his bride.

Malby and

Cranwell, friends of Sir Francis.

Shafton, a greedy opportunist who offers Charles a large loan under the cover of friendship, then has him imprisoned for debt.

Nicholas, Frankford's watchful manservant. He distrusts Wendoll from the moment of his entrance into the house and later reveals his villainy to his master.

Jenkin,

Cicely, and

Spigot, good-humored members of Frankford's household who are devoted to their master and well aware of what goes on in his home.

Jack Slime and

Roger Brickbat, country men who dance to celebrate Frankford's marriage.

Old Mountford,

Sandy,

Roger, and

Tidy, hard-hearted relatives and former friends of Charles. They refuse Susan's plea for money to free her brother, who had been their benefactor in better times.

THE WOMAN OF ROME
(La romana)

Author: Alberto Moravia (1907-1990)
First published: 1947
Genre: Novel

Locale: Rome, Italy
Time: The 1930's
Plot: Naturalism

Adriana (ah-dree-AH-nah), a prostitute. She is a heroically proportioned woman, even at sixteen years of age. She first augments her income as a seamstress by working as an artist's model; next, she tries to become a dancer. When her lover puts off marrying her, she easily drifts into prostitution because she likes men and the indolent life her new profession affords her. She becomes pregnant by a murderer but persuades a young anti-Fascist that the unborn child is his.

Gino (JEE-noh), Adriana's first lover. He promises to marry Adriana, but she discovers that he already has a wife. As her lover, he is soft-spoken and gentle.

Astarita (ahs-tah-REE-tah), Adriana's first customer, brought to her by her friend Gisella. He is a police official and is friendly to Adriana, even to keeping her lover Mino out of prison. Astarita is killed by Sonzogno in revenge for a slap.

Sonzogno (sohn-ZOHN-nyoh), a hoodlum. Adriana admires his strength, takes him as a lover, and becomes pregnant. Sonzogno, seeking revenge for a slap, seeks out Astarita at the ministry where he works and throws the man over a balcony to his death.

Mino (MEE-noh), a nineteen-year-old student and an anti-Fascist. He is a weak young man. When he is questioned by the police, he betrays his fellow conspirators and later commits suicide in remorse. He is convinced by Adriana that he is the father of her unborn child.

Gisella (jee-ZEHL-lah), Adriana's friend and fellow prostitute. Gisella acts as procuress to start Adriana in her career.

Adriana's mother, a poor woman who sells her daughter's physical charms as an artist's model and then is bitterly angry when the girl accepts a lover. When Adriana's prostitution brings in money and offers promise of an easy life, the mother is quite content.

A WOMAN OF THE PHARISEES
(La Pharisienne)

Author: François Mauriac (1885-1970)
First published: 1941
Genre: Novel

Locale: Bordeaux, France
Time: Early 1900's to mid-1910's
Plot: Social realism

Louis Pian (lwee pyah[n]), the elderly narrator of the story, a landowner, the illegitimate son of Marthe Pian and her first cousin, Alfred Moulis. He is thirteen years old when the story begins. He lost his beloved mother when he was seven years old, in a suicide "accident." When his sister, Michèle, and his best friend, Jean, fall in love, he is jealous of both of them and tries to keep them apart. He betrays a confidence by showing his stepmother a letter from his teacher M. Puybaraud to Octavie Tronche. Deprived of intimacy and sexual satisfaction himself (being self-centered and dispassionate, he never marries), he resents and affects to despise intimacy in others.

Brigitte Pian (bree-ZHEET), Louis' stepmother and his mother's cousin, a pillar of the church. She has dark eyes, big ears, a double chin, and long, yellow teeth with gold fillings. Although unlike Louis in her passionate temperament, she resembles him in being deprived of intimacy and sexual satisfaction and in reacting resentfully by trying to spoil love for others, including Léonce Puybaraud and Octavie Tronche, Michèle Pian and Jean de Mirbel, and Octave and Marthe Pian. She also delights in crushing opponents, such as Abbé Calou. Self-righteous, proud, and hypocritical, she convinces herself that she is God's mouthpiece and enjoys the sadistic manipulation of people's lives. She overcompensates for feelings of sexual inferiority through an attitude of superiority and her will to power. She persecutes the Puybaraud family and reduces them to dependence on her handouts, and she contributes to Octavie's miscarriage and death.

Marthe Pian (mahrt), Louis' mother, who committed suicide when her lover, first cousin Alfred Moulis, terminated their affair.

Octave Pian (ohk-TAHV), Louis' supposed father, a landowner. He wears a long mustache and is fond of eating and of hunting on his country estate. He is kind but weak and hesitant, except on rare occasions, and frequently has been paralyzed into impotence by his love for his first wife, Marthe. He probably drank himself to death after reading the letters revealing his wife's affair with her cousin and Louis' probable illegitimacy. He loves his children, especially Michèle.

Michèle Pian (mee-SHEHL), Louis' sister and only sibling, a year older than he. She has dark skin, a heavy lower jaw, white teeth, and pretty legs that she shows off whenever possible. She hates her stepmother for her domineering ways and her interference between herself and Jean de Mirbel. Brigitte succeeds in separating them with her vicious insinuations.

M. Rausch (rohsh), a schoolmaster and a former member of the papal guard. He has a scarred upper lip, a walleye,

and yellow hair. He dresses carelessly, often wearing slippers rather than shoes, and is dirty. A harsh disciplinarian to his pupils, he is obsequious toward those in authority.

Abbé Calou (kah-LEW), the parish priest of Baluzac, near the Pian estate. He has blue eyes, a large nose, good teeth, and big, hairy hands, and he is a head taller than Count Mirbel. He specializes in reforming rebellious boys, reputedly by harsh discipline but really through understanding, kindness, and trust. He tries particularly hard to help Jean de Mirbel but is punished for allowing Michèle to write to him.

Jean de Mirbel (zhahn deh meer-BEHL), a future landowner of noble family, fifteen years old at the novel's beginning. He is handsome and dark-haired, and he has pointed white canine teeth, badly set. He adores his beautiful but selfish and indifferent mother and is bitterly disappointed at her using her visit to him to spend the night with a lover. He steals money from Abbé Calou and runs away with Hortense Voyod, the anticlerical lesbian wife of the local pharmacist.

Countess de Mirbel, Jean's mother. Slim, beautiful, and youthful, she has a slightly snub nose, heavy eyelids, sea-green eyes, and a charming contralto voice. She is hedonistic, insincere, manipulative, and self-centered. She lies about her adulterous activities. At odds with her husband, she wrote indiscreet letters that fell into the hands of her brother-in-law Count Adhémar de Mirbel. She uses the pretext of a visit to Jean to spend the night with her dramatist lover.

Count Adhémar de Mirbel (ah-day-MAHR), a retired colonel, seventy years old at the beginning of the story, Jean's uncle and guardian. He is tall, stout, and blue-eyed. He wants Jean to be disciplined harshly.

Léonce Puybaraud (lay-OHNS pwee-bah-ROH), one of the twenty teachers at Louis' school of two hundred pupils. He is also general secretary of the local Catholic charities. His lack of qualifications makes him dependent on Brigitte Pian, who resents his love for Octavie Tronche and bullies him mercilessly. He marries Octavie and buys a piano for her, which infuriates Brigitte, who is supporting them. He shares Octavie's dream of rearing children of their own.

Octavie Tronche (ohk-tah-VEE trohnsh), a teacher at a Catholic school sponsored by Brigitte Pian. She is flat-chested and has sparse, dull hair; small, colorless eyes; and pale lips. She is graceful, charming, and saintly. Brigitte hates her for enjoying the sexual fulfillment and (prospectively) the motherhood Brigitte herself has been denied. Thanks partly to Brigitte's persecution, Octavie loses her baby and dies in childbirth.

Hortense Voyod (vwoy-YOH), a landowner and the lesbian wife of a local pharmacist. She is blonde, freckled, and unattractive. Her private life runs afoul of Abbé Calous' interventions, so she joins with a local schoolteacher and his wife to plot against the priest. She runs away with Jean, who is young enough to be her son, to spite Calou.

— *Patrick Brady*

WOMAN ON THE EDGE OF TIME

Author: Marge Piercy (1936-   )
First published: 1976
Genre: Novel

Locale: New York City and environs, and Mattapoisett, Massachusetts
Time: 1976 and 2137
Plot: Utopian

Consuelo (Connie) Camacho Ramos (kohn-SWEH-loh kah-MAH-choh RRAH-mohs), a thirty-seven-year-old Mexican American woman whose early beauty has been erased by hard times and tragedy. Her first husband was killed, and her daughter was taken from her by the state's child welfare agency, but she is determined to survive. Once she used her mind at college; now she uses it to live with crushing poverty. She is fiercely loyal to what she has left of her family, a niece, and it is a fight with her niece's pimp that results in her entering a mental hospital. From there, Connie discovers a unique talent: She can commune with the future. With the help of Luciente, a woman from the future, she visits Mattapoisett, Massachusetts, in the year 2137 and is amazed by the utopian life that she finds there. Meanwhile, back in 1976, she battles the doctors who wish to perform neuroelectric experiments on her in a struggle that is fueled by the social consciousness that she is developing under Luciente's tutelage.

Luciente of Mattapoisett (lew-see-EHN-teh), a woman in her thirties with sleek black hair, black eyes, and bronze skin. She is from the year 2137 and, as a "sender," is able to contact receptive people from the past, such as Connie. Luciente works primarily as a plant geneticist, although, like everyone in her village, she shares in a number of other tasks. She is energetic, kind, and sensitive. She acts as Connie's guide and ambassador during Connie's visits to Mattapoisett. In many ways, Luciente represents what Connie is capable of becoming but could never hope to be in the racist, sexist, class-conscious society of 1976.

Jackrabbit of Mattapoisett, an artist and one of Luciente's current lovers. He is a slender young man with curly, light brown hair. His long legs and a boundless appetite for life and love prompted him to choose the name Jackrabbit. He went mad as a teenager and was strengthened by the healing process. This bout with mental illness and the caring way in which his community responded stand in powerful contrast to Connie's predicament. Jackrabbit can be careless and irresponsi-

ble, but his silly, curious nature makes him a pleasure to know. Jackrabbit is killed while serving a voluntary six-month stint on defense.

Bee of Mattapoisett, a big-boned black man with a bald head. He is a chef and another of Luciente's current lovers. He reminds Connie of Claud, the boyfriend she had after she left her second, abusive husband. Connie and Bee make love one night in Mattapoisett.

Dolores (Dolly) Campos, Connie's twenty-two-year-old niece, a prostitute addicted to drugs. Unlike Connie, she is unable to see beyond a life of easy money and quick highs.

Geraldo (hehr-AHL-doh), Dolly's handsome pimp and boyfriend. Geraldo commits Connie to Bellevue Hospital after she hits him over the head with a bottle in an attempt to stop him from attacking Dolly.

Luis (Lewis) Camacho (lew-EES), Connie's older brother and the owner of a plant nursery in New Jersey. Upwardly mobile, he has left his heritage behind by adopting the Anglicized name Lewis and marrying women who are successively more light-skinned and Anglo-looking. He has no sympathy for Connie's plight.

Gildina 547-921-45-822-KBJ, a young woman from the future, but a future that is vastly different from Luciente's. A series of operations and shots have given her a tiny waist, oversized hips and buttocks, and enormous, pointed breasts. She is a contract girl, assigned to a mid-level officer for two years of sexual services. Her existence is a stark reminder of what the future might bring.

Cash, the mid-level officer to whom Gildina is contracted. He has superneurotransmitters in his brain that are capable of turning him into a fighting machine. This technology is a refinement of the experiments planned for Connie.

Sybil, a practicing witch and Connie's friend at the mental hospital. She is tall, haughty, and strong.

— *Liz Marshall*

THE WOMAN WHO OWNED THE SHADOWS

Author: Paula Gunn Allen (1939-   )
First published: 1983
Genre: Novel

Locale: Albuquerque, New Mexico; San Francisco, California; and Oregon
Time: The 1970's and 1980's
Plot: Psychological realism

Ephanie Atencio (EHF-uhn-ee ah-TEHN-see-oh), a woman who grew up among the Guadalupe Indians in New Mexico learning tribal stories from her grandmother. Because of her mixed racial background, she was never fully accepted by either whites or Native Americans. Her childhood friend Elena feels guilty about their closeness and deserts her. Ephanie's other childhood friend, Stephen, also betrays her by invalidating her capabilities and her memories. It takes Ephanie a lifetime to remember the particular incident that sparked her change to a fearful, unhappy existence. When she was twelve years old, Stephen dared her to swing from a high tree, and the branch broke. She fell, breaking both her ribs and her spirit. Without understanding what she is doing, she acquiesces to the voices around her who urge her to be more ladylike, to be passive and silent. Ephanie's first husband abuses and deserts her, leaving her with two children, Ben and Agnes. She moves to San Francisco, marries a Japanese American, suffers the loss of an infant son, and is divorced. She becomes absorbed in the history of the Native Americans and their systematic slaughter by whites. She sees that even those who romanticize or pity Native Americans perpetuate divisiveness and victimization. Increasingly, she feels isolated, fragmented, hopeless, and suicidal. What helps Ephanie regain a sense of self-worth and purpose are the old songs and stories from the women of the past. They show her that she is not alone and that she must do her part to pass on what she has learned.

Shimanna, called **Sylvia** by the whites, Ephanie's maternal grandmother. She attended a mission school in Albuquerque and a school for Indians in Pennsylvania. She married a white man, and although she returned to the Guadalupe pueblo, she was not entirely welcome. Ephanie's mother and Ephanie both inherited the label "half-breed." Shimanna teaches Ephanie Indian mythology, including songs and stories about the spider woman who created all the worlds. Even after she dies, she appears to Ephanie at various times as a presence who cares for her and encourages her by reminding her of the old stories.

Elena, a Chicana neighbor, Ephanie's childhood friend and true love. They grow and play together and share their dreams. In early adolescence, on the day they daringly climb Picacho Peak, Elena announces that she cannot see Ephanie again. Absorbing the homophobic prejudices of those around her,

Elena had asked a nun at school about hugging and giggling with Ephanie, and the nun had pronounced that it was a sin. Thus Ephanie is betrayed and denied love before she even recognizes it as love. She never sees Elena again, but she thinks of their early years together as the only time she was truly happy.

Teresa, a white woman Ephanie meets in a therapy group in San Francisco. Teresa does a psychic reading and tells Ephanie that an older woman who wears a spider pin is watching over her, but that Ephanie needs to investigate something from her past that still troubles her. Ephanie recognizes the woman as her grandmother, who told her stories of the spider woman and her daughters. Teresa introduces Ephanie to some women in a lesbian commune. Ephanie likes them, but she cannot seem to make them or Teresa understand her anxieties and her problematic status as an Indian in a white-dominated culture.

Stephen, an older Indian friend, as close as a cousin or brother, who worked in the trading store run by Ephanie's father. He sees himself as Ephanie's teacher and guide; she sees him as bright and self-assured. He hovers around her over the years, helping out when her first husband abandons her and again when her infant son Tommy dies. Stephen is psychologically abusive, telling Ephanie that she needs him because she is helpless, saying he would marry her if he were not so much older, and denying her memories of the past. Ephanie has love/hate feelings toward him without understanding why.

Thomas Yoshuri, Ephanie's second husband and father of their twin sons, Tommy and Tsali. Tommy dies when he is a few weeks old, and they wrap his body in the Japanese flag that Thomas' sister Sally had given to Ephanie. Thomas is bitter and isolated, a heavy drinker never able to overcome his childhood years in a relocation camp to which the U.S. government had sent Japanese Americans during World War II. The marriage soon ends in divorce.

— *Lois Marchino*

A WOMAN'S LIFE
(Une Vie)

Author: Guy de Maupassant (1850-1893)
First published: 1883
Genre: Novel

Locale: Normandy and Corsica
Time: Early nineteenth century
Plot: Naturalism

Jeanne de Lamare (zhahn deh lah-MAHR), the woman whose life is recounted from young womanhood to the time she becomes a grandmother. As an innocent young girl, just out of a convent, she goes to live in the country with her parents. There, she marries a man whom she soon discovers to be parsimonious and unfaithful to her. Jeanne bears a child, on whom she lavishes all of her affection. She then discovers that her husband is unfaithful to her again, this time with the wife of a neighboring count. The count kills his wife and Julien, and the rest of Jeanne's life is spent catering to the extravagant whims of her son.

Julien de Lamare (zhew-LYAN), Jeanne's thoroughly reprehensible husband. He manages the estate in a penurious manner, and he fathers a child by the maid. Later, he takes Countess de Fourville as his mistress. He is killed when the count discovers him with the countess.

Paul de Lamare, Jeanne's son, whom she spoils completely. He runs away from school and spends the next few years asking for and getting money from his mother. He writes to ask her permission to marry his mistress. When she does not approve, he marries the girl anyway, and they have a child. After his wife dies, he returns home with his daughter.

Baron Simon-Jacques Le Perthuis des Vauds (see-MOH[N] zhahk leh pehr-TWEE day voh), Jeanne's father, whose liberal style of living reduces his family to living quietly in the country. He finally dies of apoplexy caused by worry over his grandson and his property.

Rosalie, the maid, who is also Jeanne's foster sister. She has an illegitimate child by Julien, and she and the child are sent away. After Julien's death, she returns to look after Jeanne.

The Countess Gilberte de Fourville (zheel-BEHRT deh fewr-VEEL), a neighbor with whom Julien goes riding almost every day and with whom he is having an affair.

The Count de Fourville, Gilberte's husband, who loves her passionately. When he learns that she and Julien are in a shepherd's hut together, he pushes the hut over a cliff and kills them both.

Abbé Tolbiac (ah-BAY tohl-BYAHK), the village priest, very much concerned with his parishioners' morals. When he finds out about the affair between Gilberte and Julien, he tells the count.

THE WOMAN'S PRIZE: Or, The Tamer Tamed

Author: John Fletcher (1579-1625)
First published: 1647
Genre: Drama

Locale: Italy
Time: The sixteenth century
Plot: Farce

Petruchio (peh-TREW-kee-oh), a widower, famous as the tamer of his shrewish first wife, Kate. Angered and confused by the various husband-taming tricks of Maria and beaten at every point, he at last surrenders to her and is rewarded with a generous love.

Maria, Petruchio's second wife. A lesser Lysistrata, she is determined to win a signal victory for her sex over the man most famous for conquering a member of it. She is clever and witty, turning Petruchio's angry bull-like sallies with affected mildness and concern or with passionate displays of her own temper. After she overwhelms him completely, she graciously promises to make him a perfect wife.

Livia (LIHV-ee-uh), Maria's sister, in love with Rowland. She succeeds in fooling her father and her ridiculous elderly suitor, and after several complications she succeeds in marrying her sweetheart.

Bianca (bee-AHN-kah), their cousin. Also showing kinship with Lysistrata, she is active and resourceful on behalf of both

sisters in the battle of the sexes.

Petronius (peh-TROH-nee-ews), the father of the sisters. A well-meaning but somewhat tyrannical father, he rages furiously but impotently at his daughters' independence. He accepts their eventual triumphs with good grace.

Rowland, Livia's sweetheart. Misunderstanding Livia's behavior toward him and Moroso, he renounces her, but when the misunderstanding is clarified, he marries her joyfully.

Moroso (moh-ROH-soh), a foolish, wealthy old man in love with Livia. He is tricked into witnessing and approving her marriage contract with Rowland without realizing what he is signing.

Sophocles (SOF-oh-kleez), a friend of Petruchio. He is used by Maria, who flirts with him, to arouse Petruchio's jealousy.

Tranio (TRAH-nee-oh), another of Petruchio's friends.

Jacques (zhahk), Petruchio's servant. He is bewildered by his master's reversal of marital fortune.

THE WOMEN AT THE PUMP
(Konerne ved vandposten)

Author: Knut Hamsun (Knut Pedersen, 1859-1952)
First published: 1920
Genre: Novel

Locale: A small coastal town in northern Norway
Time: Late nineteenth century
Plot: Satire

Oliver Andersen, a man who lost a leg and possibly (the villagers speculate) something more in a mysterious shipboard accident. Lazy, self-seeking, and full of guile, Oliver is nevertheless charming and sympathetic. He drifts from job to job, never failing to capitalize on his handicap. With his wife, Petra, he rears a large family (though his paternity is questionable) and is much like a self-indulgent, boastful child himself. Fortune and misfortune alike leave Oliver unfazed for long; he squanders the gains from his spectacular salvage of a wrecked ship and from his discovery of the loot from a mail robbery, but his resiliency and cunning enable him time after time to turn misfortune to his advantage.

Petra Andersen, an attractive woman who is engaged to Oliver before his accident but who rejects him for Mattis the Carpenter when Oliver returns disabled. Later, she reconsiders and marries him, and shortly thereafter she bears a son. Her repeated "visits" to Scheldrup Johnsen, the wealthy double consul's son, and to lawyer Fredriksen, who holds the Andersens' mortgage, often save the family from financial ruin.

Frank Andersen, Petra's eldest son, who is introverted and academically brilliant. He studies languages at the university and eventually returns to the village as headmaster of

the local senior school.

Abel Andersen, Petra's second son, a blacksmith. Called **the Squirrel** as a child, he is lively, industrious, and straightforward. His infatuation with Little Lydia and his unswerving determination to marry her despite her equally determined refusals offer some of the novel's more touching comic scenes. When she refuses his offer of a gold engagement ring that he has forged himself, he quickly and pragmatically gets engaged to a local farm girl, Louise, whom he soon marries.

C. A. (Double Consul) Johnsen, known as the **First Consul** until he becomes the town's only double consul. Wealthy and socially ascendant, Johnsen busies himself with more ponderous (though less concrete) duties than the running of his successful mercantile and shipping business, which he happily leaves to his clerk and his son. When his steamship sinks and is discovered to be uninsured, Johnsen is crushed by the prospect of financial ruin; when his son Scheldrup arrives and mysteriously manages to pay off the creditors, however, Johnsen revives and reassumes his role as unchallenged patriarch of the village.

Scheldrup Johnsen, the double consul's son. Frank, businesslike, and thoroughly "modern," Scheldrup travels extensively to foreign ports to learn the shipping business. Brown-eyed, amorous Scheldrup once got his ears boxed by Petra over something he whispered to her at a dance hall; not a few villagers suspect that he might have something to do with the surprising number of brown-eyed babies born in the village.

Fia Johnsen, the double consul's daughter, called **the Countess** because of her her refinement and artistic temperament. Attractive and accomplished, Fia prefers a life of moderation and calm to one of passion and rejects all of her several suitors, whom she rightly suspects of wooing her dowry as much as her. A talented but not brilliant artist, she is content to paint, travel, and act as a cultured hostess to her artist friends.

Fredriksen, a pompous and aspiring lawyer. Fredriksen is elected to the Storting (the Norwegian legislature), where he makes a name for himself by sponsoring a bill in direct conflict with the interests of his wealthy constituents. He energeti-cally but unsuccessfully courts the daughters of the wealthiest villagers, thinking to win them with the suggestion that he may soon be appointed a government minister.

The Doctor, a rational, humorless, and suspicious man. He takes vindictive pleasure in baiting others and fomenting trouble. In expounding genetic theory, he hints broadly that Scheldrup is the father of the inexplicable number of brown-eyed children in the village.

The Postmaster, a long-winded philosopher. He bores others with his interminable ramblings on human thought, enlightenment, and God. The trauma of the post office robbery leaves him a childlike, babbling madman.

Little Lydia, a childhood friend of Abel. Lighthearted and changeable, she resists his determined efforts to win her heart.

— *Catherine Swanson*

WOMEN BEWARE WOMEN

Author: Thomas Middleton (1580-1627)
First published: 1657
Genre: Drama

Locale: Florence, Italy
Time: Early seventeenth century
Plot: Tragedy

The duke of Florence, a lecherous, ruthless ruler. Capturing Leantio's wife with the aid of Livia and Guardiano, he takes her partly by force and partly by seduction. Later, having sworn an oath to his brother, the Lord Cardinal, that he will no longer live with her in adultery, he carries out his promise by having her husband killed and marrying her immediately thereafter. There is poetic justice in his death, for his new wife prepares poison for the good brother and a servant mistakenly serves it to the duke. He dies in agony.

The Lord Cardinal, the duke's brother. He preaches morality with vehemence and at length but has little or no effect on the multipresent evils of the corrupt court. He remains alive to deliver a last blast of morality after the holocaust at the play's end.

Fabricio (fah-BREE-chee-oh), the father of Isabella. A foolish, ineffectual man, he insists on marrying his daughter to the rich ward of Guardiano. He is stunned with horror in the final scene but is alive at the play's end.

Hippolito (eep-POH-lee-toh), Fabricio's brother. Devoured by incestuous lust, with the aid of his sister Livia he corrupts his niece. He kills Leantio for family pride after the duke has let him know that Leantio and Livia are having an illicit affair. Just before his own death, he speaks lines that give the tone of the play: "Lust and forgetfulness has been amongst us,/ And we are brought to nothing."

Livia (LEE-vee-ah), the sister of Fabricio and Hippolito. The essence of evil in a play crawling with evil, she aids the duke in his plan to ravish Bianca. She lies to Isabella, telling her that she is not the daughter of Fabricio and therefore not the niece of Hippolito. She is swept away by obsessive lust for Leantio, whom she takes as a lover and showers with wealth. Her rage at his death is boundless. She has Hippolito and Isabella shot with poisoned arrows in a wedding masque for the duke and Bianca; she is herself slain by poison fumes that Isabella has planted in a censer she carries in the masque.

Guardiano (gwahr-dee-AH-noh), the uncle of the Ward. Unscrupulous, depraved, and ambitious, he aids Livia and the duke in entangling Bianca. He also is enthusiastic about the marriage of his ward with Isabella, but after the marriage, when he finds out that she has been corrupted by her uncle, he plots the death of Hippolito. Through the Ward's stupidity, Guardiano is killed instead of his intended victim.

The Ward, a rich, stupid heir. He is brought to marriage with Isabella only after much labor and persuasion by Guardiano. After the marriage, even his stupidity is insufficient armor against the horror of the disclosure of her sins.

Leantio (lee-AHN-tee-oh), a merchant's agent. He steals away from her family a beautiful girl, Bianca, whom he marries and adores immoderately. When he returns from a business venture to find her the duke's arrogant and contemptuous mistress instead of the submissive and loving wife he left behind, he is swept by helpless fury. Partly for revenge, he takes evil Livia as his mistress and indiscreetly boasts of this affair to his wife. She tells the duke, who informs Hippolito to have him kill Leantio and thus make way for Bianca's second marriage.

Bianca (bee-AHN-kah), Leantio's wife. A beautiful and innocent girl when she runs away with Leantio, she rouses keen pity during her betrayal and helplessness. After her seduction, however, instead of being a Lucrece, she becomes as evil as her corrupters or nearly so. Like Herodias, she decides to kill her critic, the Lord Cardinal. Her passion for the evil duke has become so great that when her poisoning plot miscarries and he is killed, she takes the remaining portion of the poison and dies with him.

Isabella (ee-zah-BEHL-lah), the daughter of Fabricio. Finding the Ward repulsive, she resists her father's efforts to bring about her marriage to him. When her aunt Livia convinces her that her passion for her handsome and accomplished uncle is not incestuous, however, she decides to marry the Ward as a cover for her affair with Hippolito. When Livia, in her agony over the loss of Leantio, tells the truth about the whole situation, Isabella plans revenge on Livia and murders her with the poisoned censer; she herself dies the victim of her victim.

The mother of Leantio, a well-meaning, gullible old woman. She plays into Livia's hands by having Bianca come to Livia's house and plays chess with her hostess, all the time unaware that her daughter-in-law is being violated in another room in the house. She and the Lord Cardinal are exempt from the horror or contempt that the other principal characters arouse, but they are not calculated to arouse much sympathy in a beholder or reader.

Sordido (sohr-DEE-doh), the servant of the Ward.

WOMEN IN LOVE

Author: D. H. Lawrence (1885-1930)
First published: 1920
Genre: Novel

Locale: England and Austria
Time: Early twentieth century
Plot: Psychological realism

Rupert Birkin a school inspector in the mining district of Beldover. As the novel opens, he has become disenchanted with Hermione Roddice and, in terminating their stultifying, prolonged affair, is finding his way toward a new mode of living. With some hesitation, he falls in love with Ursula Brangwen. After Hermione tries to kill him, he moves into his own lodgings at "the Mill" and struggles to reach an understanding with Ursula that will enable a marriage in which they can respect and preserve their separate identities. Impatient with conventions and the older generation, he argues fiercely with Ursula's father when he asks for his daughter's hand. Though sickly, he is essentially robust, and though his strong will and dogmatic pronouncements sometimes make him comical, he inspires Gerald Crich and the Brangwen sisters. His convictions ultimately are vindicated by events. He forms a deep friendship with Gerald and wants to swear blood brotherhood with him because he feels a need for a lasting friendship with a man in addition to marriage to a woman.

Ursula Brangwen, a primary school teacher in Beldover. She falls in love with Rupert Birkin, is initially put off by his demands, but ultimately reaches an understanding with him. Sensitive and thoughtful, she is horrified by Gerald's treatment of his horse and retains a measure of distrust of Gerald throughout the novel. She has greater faith in traditional ideas of love and marriage than does Birkin, but she refuses to compromise her own soul and insists on speaking her mind. After learning that Birkin intends to see Hermione before she leaves for Italy, she impulsively throws away the rings he gave her. She relents, however, and they are reconciled. After her father forbids her marriage and strikes her, she immediately elopes with Birkin. It is the fact that she retains full possession of herself in the face of Birkin's forceful personality that makes their relationship possible.

Gudrun Brangwen (GEW-druhn), an aspiring artist who has just returned home from art school in London when the novel opens. Immediately attracted to Gerald Crich, she is inclined to take a somewhat detached point of view. Her infatuation never becomes true love because, on a certain level, she always despises him. Sensitive and at times superior, she is nauseated by the squalor of the mining town of Beldover and the stares of the miners' families. Gerald's father employs her to tutor Gerald's sister, Winifred, in drawing. She accepts Gerald's advances, but in the alpine hostel she meets Loerke, whose corrupt aesthetics fascinate and ultimately seduce her. In the absence of Birkin and Ursula, her hatred for Gerald blooms, and she barely escapes being murdered.

Gerald Crich (krikh), the operator of the coal mine in Beldover and the son of Thomas Crich, the owner. Athletic, handsome, and a womanizer, he is also an efficient manager who imposes order, rejecting his father's more benevolent methods. Although capable of brutality in his treatment of those in his power, whether they are animals or workers, he ultimately is unable to control events. His suicide is only the last in a series of tragedies that befall him. He has "worn the mark of Cain" since he accidentally killed his brother as a child. His valiant attempt to save his drowning sister Diana at the water-party comes to naught, and his father's death and mother's insanity precipitate his affair with Gudrun. The affair never involves deep understanding, and it inevitably sours. After almost strangling Gudrun to death, he commits suicide by wandering into the snow, and he succumbs to exhaustion beside a crucifix in a mountain shrine.

Hermione Roddice, a wealthy, clever intellectual. At the outset, her relationship with Rupert Birkin is hopelessly frayed. Their bitter quarrels stem from her essential falseness. She plays hostess to the four principal characters at Breadalby, her country estate, yet at best the others admire rather than like her. Her violent, even murderous, nature emerges when she tries to break Birkin's skull with a lapis lazuli paperweight, and at least unconscious malice is involved when she drops Gudrun's sketchbook into the water and when she later advises Ursula not to marry Birkin. Her role ends when she leaves for Italy, just as Ursula and Birkin seal their commitment.

Loerke (LEHR-keh), a German sculptor who is staying at the lodge in the Tyrolean alps with his young companion, Leitner. Although amoral and physically unattractive, he fascinates the Brangwen sisters and exerts a profound and disastrous influence over Gudrun, appealing to her tendency to draw a sharp distinction between art and life. His homosexual relationship with his companion already has soured. He disdains Gerald, who knocks him over before he starts to strangle Gudrun. When he revives and strikes Gerald, the blow brings Gerald to turn from murder to suicide.

— *Matthew Parfitt*

THE WOMEN OF BREWSTER PLACE: A Novel in Seven Stories

Author: Gloria Naylor (1950-   )
First published: 1982
Genre: Novel

Locale: An urban neighborhood in the North
Time: The 1930's-the 1960's
Plot: Social realism

Mattie Michael, a strong, elderly, unmarried black woman who reared a son before moving to Brewster Place. Mattie is the pivotal character in the novel. It is her own personal tragedies—her father's shame and rejection when he learns that she is pregnant; the loss of her son, Basil, whom she loves dearly; the loss of her worldly possessions—that make her sensitive to the tragedies of others. She is the character who breathes life and hope into the dismal atmosphere of Brewster Place. At the end of the novel, Mattie is the first to begin tearing down the wall that makes Brewster Place a literal and figurative dead end for its residents. In their symbolic protest and rage, she and the other women in the community join together to fight their condition instead of being ruled by it.

Etta Mae Johnson, Mattie's closest friend, an attractive woman who carries herself with pride. In Rock Vale, the town in which Mattie and Etta grew up, there was no place for a woman with Etta's rebellious, independent spirit. She refused to play by society's rules and spent most of her life moving to one major city after another, from one promising black man to another, in the hope that one of them would take care of her. Upon her return to Brewster Place, Etta learns that her friend Mattie can give her what she is searching for, things that no man has ever given her: love, comfort, and friendship.

Kiswana Browne, formerly **Melanie**, a young black woman who rejects her parents' middle-class values, changes her name, and boasts of her African heritage. She is also an activist who organizes a tenants' association at Brewster Place. Kiswana, in her naïveté, believes that her mother is ashamed of being black because she leads a middle-class existence. Finally realizing that she and her mother are not so different, that they are both women who are proud of their heritage and who desire to improve the lot of future generations, Kiswana learns to be more tolerant to those whose lifestyles are different from hers.

Luciela Louise Turner, a young married woman, the granddaughter of Eva Turner, the woman who befriended and sheltered Mattie years earlier. She constantly makes excuses for her husband's frequent absences from her and their month-old baby. When her husband learns that she is pregnant again, he threatens to leave her. In an attempt to prevent his leaving once more, she gets an abortion. When her daughter dies in a household accident, however, Luciela loses her connection with life and the ability to feel. She slowly begins to waste away. Mattie refuses to accept her friend's gradual suicide and rocks Luciela in her arms until Luciela is able to feel, to express her sorrow, and to return to life again.

Cora Lee, a young, unmarried high school dropout who continues to have babies because she loves children. After reluctantly agreeing to attend a performance of a William Shakespeare play with her children at Kiswana's insistence, Cora Lee begins to change her outlook on life and motherhood. She realizes that her children are more than playthings, more than her baby dolls; they are human beings with needs and desires of their own.

Theresa, a lesbian who is Lorraine's lover. She has been with men (some of whom were kind, others cruel), but she is drawn naturally to women. In her direct and outspoken manner, she insists that being a lesbian means being different, by nature, from other people. It means being outside society, because society punishes those who are different in such an intense way. She prefers to ignore the straight world and socializes only with lesbians. She is jealous of Lorraine's friendship with Ben, the janitor.

Lorraine, a teacher who fears society's condemnation of her lesbian relationship with Theresa. Her view of what it means to be a lesbian is very different from Theresa's. She detests the word "lesbian" and insists that she is not different from other people. In the past, however, she has suffered more than Theresa for her choice. Her father disowned her, and she lost her teaching job in Detroit and fears that she could be fired again. She and Theresa have moved many times because of her fears. She craves social acceptance and cannot accept being cut off from the community. Ben is the only one in the community who does not view her as being different. Becoming a scapegoat for the entire community's fears and prejudices, near the end of the novel she is brutally raped by a group of gang members.

Ben, the elderly, alcoholic janitor of Brewster Place. He is a kind, gentle, and nonjudgmental man who sees some of his own daughter in Lorraine and who comforts her when she is rejected and ridiculed by the women of Brewster Place. Ben is killed by Lorraine when he appears in the alley where she has just been raped.

— *Genevieve Slomski*

WOMEN OF MESSINA
(Le donne di Messina)

Author: Elio Vittorini (1908-1966)
First published: 1949
Genre: Novel

Locale: A village in Italy and various railroad cars
Time: 1945-1949
Plot: Social realism

The narrator, who is never named. His father worked for the railroad company, but this information is the only distinctive point about the narrator. He is an ordinary Italian who mourns for the past and discusses the changes wrought by the Fascist regime and World War II.

Uncle Agrippa, Siracusa's wandering father, an older man who is retired from the railroad company. For years, he has traveled throughout Italy, searching for his daughter. After many years of journeying, however, the object of his travels is no longer finding Siracusa but what he calls "the reunion": a perfect dimension in which human beings will understand one another without conflict. In addition, Agrippa's travels underline the subplot of the novel, which can be divided into three themes: the need for knowledge, the role of the individual in society, and the utopian "reunion."

Ventura, also known as **Ugly Mug**, a former Fascist officer who lives anonymously in the village. He cannot forget the past, however, even while he is trying to adapt to the present. After Siracusa undergoes her "Teresa" transformation, Ventura is identified merely as "Teresa's husband."

Siracusa (see-rah-KEW-zah), Ventura's lover and Uncle Agrippa's daughter. She ran away during the war to search for a better world. Siracusa knows about Ventura's past and has forgiven him. With him, she undergoes a symbolic metamorphosis, acquiring a new identity as **Teresa**.

Carlo the Bald, a former Fascist who is now working for the Italian government and who represents the new law. Carlo the Bald forces the addressing of the postwar moral dilemma regarding the punishment of former Fascists. His softer side is revealed when he listens sympathetically to Uncle Agrippa's tale of his search for his missing daughter while the two men are on a train together.

— Rosaria Pipia

THE WOMEN OF TRACHIS
(Trachinai)

Author: Sophocles (c. 496-406 B.C.E.)
First performed: 435-429 B.C.E.
Genre: Drama

Locale: Trachis
Time: Mythic Hellenic prehistory
Plot: Tragedy

Daianeira (day-an-EH-rah), also known as **The Day's Air** or **Daysair**, the daughter of Oineus and wife of the great hero Herakles. Powerfully alluring and aware of her beauty ("looks are my trouble"), she is unhappy as the action begins because her husband has been away from his family for some time. She admires him and finds him very attractive, but her love is tested when she learns that Herakles has sent a young female captive to their home. In an attempt to remove any possibility of competition, she sends Herakles a love charm given to her by a centaur. When the potion turns out to be a deadly poison, she is driven mad with grief, and when her son criticizes her, she feels completely deserted and decides to destroy herself.

Herakles (HEHR-uh-kleez), the son of Zeus, one of the greatest of the Greek heroes, who has been condemned by the gods to carry out a series of labors that keep him away from his wife and son. Headstrong, impulsive, and very passionate, he is unbeatable by any man in combat but is susceptible to the lures of Eros. When the potion his wife sends him turns out to be a lethal mixture, he is driven mad with pain and anger. He appears for the first time late in the play, dressed in a "mask of divine agony," seeking a dignified death but too furious to be able to control himself. Ultimately, he is able to regain his heroic stature in his final instruction to his son.

Hyllos (HI-lohs), the son of Herakles and Daianeira. He is loving and dutiful, obedient, and respectful. He shares his mother's desire to see Herakles return home. When his father is poisoned, he blames his mother for the betrayal; when he learns the truth, he is shattered by grief. Struggling against the overpowering emotion caused by the loss of his parents, he resolves to carry out his father's last request, to marry Iole, and to prove his devotion to his parent's legacy.

Iole (I-oh-lay), the daughter of Eurytus, a king. Her name literally means "tomorrow," or the future. She caught Herakles' eye, and he destroyed her father's capital city to get her. In his dying speech, Herakles commands his son to marry her. She does not speak during the play, but her gestures register her sadness at her situation when Daianeira observes and questions her.

Likhas (LI-kuhs), the family herald for Herakles and Daianeira. An honest, reliable, determined, and persistent man, he is totally faithful but not particularly sharp-witted. He is killed by Herakles, who blames him for the work of the potion.

A messenger, a figure who is aware of the palace gossip and able to provide information beyond the official sources. He often disagrees with and chides the somewhat pompous Likhas. He is snide and cynical, even with the queen.

A nurse, or **housekeeper**, an old and tottery woman who is physically smaller than Daianeira. She provides information about actions (such as the suicide of Daianeira) that occur offstage.

— Leon Lewis

THE WOMEN'S ROOM

Author: Marilyn French (1929-   )
First published: 1977
Genre: Novel

Locale: A New Jersey suburb and Cambridge, Massachusetts
Time: The 1950's and 1960's
Plot: Social realism

Mira, a graduate student in the English department at Harvard who is the divorced mother of two sons. She is older than most of the other graduate students, having gone back to school at the age of thirty-eight, yet the younger women seem much more comfortable with themselves. It is not until she becomes part of a small circle of friends at Harvard that she begins to see her personal life in terms of feminist politics: Her consciousness is raised. From that perspective, she looks back at her earlier self with scorn. Although intelligent and a voracious reader, Mira accepted, almost without question, the limits put on her behavior and aspirations, first by her parents and later by her husband. Married to a wealthy man, living in a beautiful house, and dressed in lovely clothes, she considered herself successful until her husband asked her for a divorce. At Harvard, she makes friends who help her learn to trust herself and to challenge the limits others place on her.

Val, a graduate student in social science at Harvard and the divorced mother of a daughter. A year or so older than Mira, Val is tall, big-boned, flamboyant, and fleshy. She is known for her collection of capes from around the world. She talks loudly and authoritatively. At times, it seems as if Val has transformed every one of her experiences into theory. Val is more politically involved than the others. Eventually, her politics force her to take an uncompromising stand on women's rights, and she is killed as a result.

Isolde, a graduate student in English at Harvard. She is a lesbian in her mid-twenties, tall, and very thin, with pale green eyes. She is central to the group, providing its source of creative energy. Iso is able to see the positive side of everyone. Mira and others often go to her when they need someone with whom to talk.

Ava, Isolde's lover for four years. Very shy, tall, and willowy, Ava leaves Iso to study dance in New York City.

Clarissa, an English graduate student at Harvard in her early twenties. Reared by liberal and educated parents, happy, and content with herself, Clarissa seems to be the embodiment of that for which the others strive, yet clouds appear on her horizon: Her husband expects her to do all the housework even as she is studying for her doctoral orals.

Kyla Forrester, an English graduate student at Harvard in her early twenties. She is short, with long, straight red hair, wide blue eyes, and an oval face. A perfectionist, she smokes incessantly when nervous. Her husband's lack of support for her studies causes her to doubt herself, to drink too much, and to succumb to hysteria and weeping.

Christine (Chris) Truax, Val's teenage daughter. She is very close to her mother. Chris's rape and her harsh treatment by the police and the courts transform Val's politics irrevocably.

Ben Voler, Mira's lover, an expert on the (fictional) African country Lianu. Ben is in his mid-thirties, with a dark complexion and a large, round face. He is extremely supportive of Mira's work until he gets the opportunity to return to Lianu.

Tadziewski (Tad), Val's lover. In his mid-twenties, Tad is fair, blue-eyed, gangly, and sensitive. He falls madly in love with Val. When she informs him that she will continue to have other lovers, he throws a hysterical jealous fit that ends the relationship.

Norm, Mira's husband, a physician. He is handsome but unfeeling and shallow.

Martha, Mira's friend during her years of marriage. Foulmouthed and refreshingly honest, Martha brags about her "built-in shit detector." She has returned to college and intends to go to law school. When her affair with her French professor ends, she attempts suicide and is never the same afterward.

— *Liz Marshall*

THE WONDER-WORKER

Author: Dan Jacobson (1929-   )
First published: 1973
Genre: Novel

Locale: London and Switzerland
Time: c. 1950-1970
Plot: Psychological symbolism

Timothy Fogel, a psychotic individual who parallels the narrator. Beginning with his conception and ending with the murder of Susie, the narrative traces Timothy's development as a strange, isolated boy into a profoundly disturbed young man. As a child, Timothy believes he can transform himself into any inanimate form. Rejected by a young girl named Susie, young Timothy retreats into his subjective world, reveling in his meditative "power." As Timothy matures, so does his obsession with his "gift" and Susie until, in an effort to possess Susie completely, he murders her and her unborn child.

Gerhard Fogel, Timothy's father, a Jew who fled from Nazi Germany to settle in England. Gerhard is a commercial artist who leads a quiet, nondescript life. Although he is tortured by the possibility that Timothy is really Mr. Truter's son, Gerhard accepts the "arrangement" between his wife and the landlord because of financial necessity. After his wife's death, Gerhard attempts to understand and help his son, to no avail. An underdog, Gerhard contrasts to his counterpart in the novel, the narrator's successful father.

Maureen Sullivan Fogel, Timothy's mother, a large Irishwoman with copper-colored hair and large, crooked teeth. She works as a salesclerk in a tobacco shop. Maureen appears to be mentally handicapped in some way. She tells Timothy that, ever since she was rescued from the remains of a hotel destroyed by a German bomber, her mind has been damaged. Gerhard, attracted to her helplessness, married her. After their marriage, Maureen continued working as a clerk, and, one day, unaware of her condition, Maureen gave birth to Timothy on the floor of Robinson's tobacco shop. Apparently for reasons of convenience, Maureen has a sexual relationship with the

landlord, Mr. Truter. Maureen falls ill and dies when Timothy is a teenager.

Susie Sendin, a young woman with whom Timothy is obsessed. Susie's appearance seems average—light brown hair, hazel eyes, and a smattering of freckles on her nose—as does her personality, yet she becomes Timothy's entire world. Irritated and flattered by Timothy's attentions, she shuns his strange affection and dates other boys, which Timothy sees as betrayal. Susie falls in love with a married man. While pregnant with that man's child, she is murdered by Timothy.

Laurence Sendin, Susie's brother and Timothy's friend. Laurence, an adolescent thief, confides in Timothy, and the two become partners of sorts. Through Laurence, Timothy develops a fascination for jewels, which, in his warped imagination, he ties into his "gift" and his desire for Susie. It appears that Timothy uses Laurence to become closer to his sister.

Mr. Truter, the Fogels' landlord. Mr. Truter, Maureen's lover, is possibly Timothy's father. It is implied that Mr. Truter exchanges reductions in rent for sexual favors from Maureen. Timothy, who witnesses the two making love, is shunned by Susie and others because of his mother's scandalous relationship with the landlord.

Mabel, Susie's friend. At Susie's insistence, Mabel becomes Timothy's unlikely girlfriend. Although he despises the homely, overweight Mabel, Timothy courts her to spite Susie.

Elsie Brody Fogel, Gerhard's second wife. Heavily made up, with dyed-black hair, Elsie is a tacky, garrulous, and dullwitted woman who shows great curiosity in Timothy's peculiarities.

The narrator, Timothy's counterpart, who discovers that he is a patient in a mental institution. Paranoid and self-absorbed, the narrator harbors deep resentment toward his doctor and father. Fascinated with his own psyche, he creates his autobiography, the story of Timothy Fogel. According to the narrator's father, however, the pages of his book contain only scribbling.

The narrator's father, Gerhard's counterpart, who visits the narrator in the sanatorium. Unlike Gerhard, the narrator's father seems to be a successful, self-confident businessman, ashamed of his son's condition.

Dr. Wuchs, a psychiatrist treating the narrator. Dr. Wuchs is an immaculately dressed, well-respected professional. The narrator, however, suspects that he was a Nazi during the war and that his skills and motives are questionable.

— *Lisa S. Starks*

WONDERFUL FOOL
(Obaka san)

Author: Shūsaku Endō (1923-1996)
First published: 1959
Genre: Novel

Locale: Tokyo, Japan
Time: The 1950's
Plot: Wit and humor

Gaston (Gas) Bonaparte, a native of the Savoy region in France and a descendant of Emperor Napoleon I. Having failed to qualify as a missionary priest in France, he has followed an inner call to journey to Japan to act out some nebulous missionary role despite his limited knowledge of Japanese. A gigantic man resembling a sumo wrestler, he has a long, horselike face, with sad eyes. Despite his size and his obvious strength, he is a coward who will not even defend himself against an attacker. Moreover, he is both a simpleton and a bungler. He is a man of peace, love, and compassion who seeks to aid any creature he sees suffering from misfortune, oppression, or a physical handicap, whether it is a man, woman, or a dog; he is the "wonderful fool" of the novel's title.

Takamori Higaki, a young bachelor and university graduate who works in a bank in the Otemachi district of Tokyo and is a former pen pal of Bonaparte. He lives in the residential district of Kyōdō in Setagaya Ward, quite removed from the heart of Tokyo, with his mother and younger sister, who, to his annoyance, is in the habit of "policing" him. Although he takes his position at the bank seriously, after work he likes to make merry with friends in the amusement district of the city. He is a spendthrift and always lacking in funds. When Bonaparte arrives in Japan, the Higakis invite him into their home as a guest.

Tomoe Higaki, Takamori's sister, six years his junior. She is strong-minded, shrewd, a bad loser, and independent. She saves her money and invests it in the stock market. A university graduate, she studied Italian as well as typing and shorthand. She works for the Disanto Trading Company, located in the Marunouchi Building across the street from Tokyo Station. Although she is very attractive, she resembles in her character the Japanese Amazon Tomoe Gozen of *The Tale of Heiki*, who rode to battle with her lord, Yoshinaka Kiso.

Takuhiko Osako, a business associate of Tomoe at the Italian trading company where she works. A grandson of Baron Osako, a member of the prewar nobility, he is a very thin man who wears rimless glasses and dresses with sartorial splendor, being unusually careful of his personal appearance. He is, however, effeminate in voice and manner. Although he courts Tomoe, she regards him strictly as a friend whom she dates on occasion.

Chōtei Kawaii, an old, emaciated Oriental diviner, formerly a teacher and school principal, who makes a meager living telling people's fortunes and writing love letters for women. He befriends Bonaparte.

Endō, a tubercular gangster with a face like General Tojo. A lone wolf and a "hit man" for the Hoshino gang of Tokyo, he is a pitiless killer who does what he likes without rancor or lament. A sniper in the army during World War II, he lost faith in people entirely and became a nihilist after his brother was executed at the end of the war for a war crime of which he was innocent. He trusts nobody and nothing but his Colt pistol. A university graduate, he speaks French.

Major Kobayashi, a land surveyor in the small city of Yamagata and a former army officer of the battalion in which Endō's brother served. A thin man in his early fifties, he has a ratlike face and very round eyes, and he looks mean.

— *Richard P. Benton*

WONDERLAND

Author: Joyce Carol Oates (1938-   )
First published: 1971
Genre: Novel

Locale: Upstate New York; Ann Arbor, Michigan; Chicago; Wisconsin; New York City; and Toronto
Time: 1939-1971
Plot: Psychological realism

Jesse Harte, later **Vogel**, and then **Pedersen**, a high school student who survives his distraught father's murder of the remaining Harte family, during the Depression, in upper New York State. When his grandfather Vogel pays his hospital bills, he agrees to be called Jesse Vogel and to live on the old man's remote farm, until he is placed in an orphanage. Dr. Karl Pedersen adopts him when he is sixteen years old, on condi-

tion that he now be known as Jesse Pedersen and prepare for a medical career. After a few years, however, Jesse cannot recognize his face as his own any longer and leaves to work his own way through medical school. By the age of twenty-four, he has fallen under the influence of instructor Talbot Waller Monk, whose callous treatment of patients' bodies further confuses his sense of identity and worth. He breaks his engagement with nurse Anne-Marie Seton and, to be close to the distinguished doctor Benjamin Cady, marries Cady's daughter Helene. Remembering his own lost childhood, he can weep over hospitalized battered children. Busily furthering his career and becoming involved with the mysterious Reva Denk, however, he ignores his two daughters' need for a father. As a result, one daughter, Michelle, joins a drug commune in Canada. Awakened at last to how he has failed his family, Jesse follows her and buys her back from Noel, her onetime lover.

Dr. Karl Pedersen, a mystic and physician famous for instinctual diagnoses. He adopts Jesse as a substitute for his own children, both of whom are considered geniuses but neither of whom shows any promise in the field of medicine. As head of his own clinic as well as of his family, he is a completely domineering figure. What he considers necessary discipline his children maintain is an attempt to devour them. When Jesse finally runs away from the destructive demands of his adoptive father, Dr. Pedersen pronounces him dead.

Mary Pedersen, an ordinary woman who has become obese and addicted to alcohol because she cannot live up to her husband's standards of perfection. She enjoys Jesse because he alone is willing to talk to her. She joins him when, having seen his own face in a mirror as that of a fat stranger, he flees to Buffalo. Mary is weak-willed, however, and returns to Dr. Pedersen and to imprisonment within her widening flesh.

Hilda Pedersen, a brilliant thirteen-year-old who feels ugly in the eyes of her father. Knowing that she is a mathematical prodigy is little comfort to her in the face of his unconcealed rejection and her mother's reference to her as a freak. She is often on the verge of unconsciousness, torn between their dislike for her and the mystery of her wizardry.

Frederich Pedersen, Hilda's seventeen-year-old brother, who feels that his music composes itself. Unfortunately, his gift of special sensitivity is considered of no use to the world of medicine, and his father goes looking for a truer son in Jesse.

Talbot "Trick" Waller Monk, a thirty-year-old laboratory section man for Dr. Cady. He is capable of such bizarre insensitivities as eating a boiled portion of human flesh. He also writes poems in which no people appear. Although he suffers from a rheumatic heart condition, he attacks Jesse physically as if suicidal. He tells Helene that he is in love with her but, at the same time, says that love is illusory. He reappears in New York City, now a famous poet (author of the title poem, which prefaces the novel, and of another on the body's central nervous system, titled "Vietnam"). He has become a pathetic, unpredictable drug addict.

Dr. Roderick Perrault, the chief resident at La Salle Hospital and a specialist in brain cancers. He takes Jesse as his apprentice, with expectations that Jesse will become his junior partner. He is interested in the possibility that a brain might be transplanted and, with it, the original mind still intact and operative. The issue, though a scientific one, affects Jesse's personal sense of shifting identity as well as the struggle within him between fate and free will.

Dr. Benjamin Cady, Helene's father, who argues that a mind, having memory and personality, is distinguishable as separate from the brain. He and Dr. Perrault seriously debate these differences and whether, after the body's death, certain brains should be preserved by the government for the good of the nation. His second marriage, at the age of sixty-seven, helps liberate Helene from a lifelong fixation on her father.

Helene Cady, a daughter who has been extremely close to her father since childhood. She wants Jesse to promise they will have at most one child. Later, she is tempted to abort their first daughter. After Michelle, their second daughter, is born, she weeps, feeling that she is a failure because she cannot have more children. With men other than her father, she has always felt uncomfortable, and at times she is hostile toward the inner workings of her body.

Reva Denk, a stranger whom Jesse meets accidentally in 1956. He is immediately attracted to her. She resists him until she requires an abortion. He refuses but offers to act as father to her unborn child because he likes to think that he is dedicated to life. He follows her to the commune where she lives with the father of that child and his wife. When Reva says that Jesse's attention is suffocating, Jesse begins to slash himself with a razor blade.

Michelle (Shelley) Vogel, Jesse's daughter, who calls herself an unadopted baby in a letter written after she deserts her family. In 1969, she is bailed out of a county jail in Toledo, only to wander off again to Florida, Texas, and Toronto. She is with Noel, a draft dodger on drugs, who has reduced her to a state of degradation in their Canadian commune. When Jesse finds her, she seems to be suffering from hepatitis and hunger. He refuses to let her die and rows her back to the United States in a fifteen-foot boat.

Noel, Shelley's companion in Canada. He finally agrees to sell her body back to Jesse at the same price he would pay for a corpse: five hundred dollars. He says that he once saved her from jumping off a bridge but that he has no personal feeling for her.

— *Leonard Casper*

WOODCUTTERS
(Holzfällen: Eine Erregung)

Author: Thomas Bernhard (1931-1989)
First published: 1984
Genre: Novel

Locale: Vienna, Austria
Time: The 1980's
Plot: Social realism

The narrator, a writer who has recently returned to Vienna after twenty-five years in London. He is disgusted with himself for having accepted an invitation from the Auersbergers, met by chance in the street and well known to him in the 1950's. He had hoped to make a clean break with his artistic past, which drove him to a nervous breakdown. He observes his fellow guests, many of whom he already had seen at the funeral of a suicide, Joana, that afternoon, while they were all waiting for the guest of honor, a famous actor. On leaving the Mozarteum in the 1950's, the narrator had had close emotional and artistic ties with Jeannie Billroth, also present and now a celebrated writer, before turning to the Auersbergers and Joana. He feels hatred for them all now for setting him on the artistic path through life. The narrator is asleep when the actor arrives, and his behavior is ungracious throughout, but by the end he takes a kinder view of Vienna.

Jeannie Billroth, a celebrated writer. She is the Austrian Virginia Woolf, according to the narrator, a writer of trash who has sold herself for state subsidies. In her youth, she was the first to take the narrator's poetry seriously, so that inevitably they now loathe each other, and he can note that she has grown fat and ugly. At Joana's funeral, she takes a collection to help with expenses but is generally abused for tastelessness. That evening, she addresses a naïve question to the actor and has to endure further insults.

Elfriede Slukal, professionally known as **Joana**, an unsuccessful choreographer, dancer, and actress from Kilb, Lower Austria, who has hanged herself. A country girl, pampered by her parents, she had set her sights on Vienna and was a member of the artistic circles attended by the narrator after he left Jeannie. She married a tapestry weaver, Fritz, and her beauty helped to make his studio world famous. Seventeen years ago, Fritz ran away to Mexico with Joana's best friend, and she became bloated and drunken, trying for a time to earn a living with a "movement studio." Her last years were spent with a seedy former actor who tried in vain to cure her alcoholism.

Mr. Auersberger, a talented pianist and composer, a close friend of the narrator in the 1950's and now his host. Of humble origins, he is a social climber who likes to impress people with coarsely ill-mannered scenes (for example, complaining about the goulash after the funeral and removing his dentures in public) and embarrassing remarks. His evenings have often ended with broken glass and furniture. Now he is a bloated alcoholic with a taste for young male writers.

Mrs. Auersberger, the woman who invites the narrator to the supper party. She is a social climber from the minor aristocracy; she and her husband live off their dwindling estates. Her artistic gatherings of twenty-five years ago horrify the narrator. Once a singer, she now has a grating voice and a shabby appearance, and she quarrels in public with her husband.

Actor from Vienna Burgtheater, a performer enjoying success as Ekdal in Henrik Ibsen's *The Wild Duck*. As the guest of honor at the Auersbergers, he appears well after midnight for supper. He behaves in the manner of a self-centered celebrity, insulting Jeannie brutally when she asks him a question. The narrator describes him as a mindless ham, which is perhaps partly true. He departs, wishing he could live in peace like a woodcutter.

John, whose real name is **Friedrich**, a former actor turned commercial traveler. He has a chronic cough and was Joana's constant companion for the last eight years of her life. He gives a grisly account of Joana's death while the narrator is eating goulash. He met Joana at her foolish "studio" and attempted without success to cure her alcoholism. The narrator recognizes good qualities in John despite his appearance.

— *W. Gordon Cunliffe*

THE WOODLANDERS

Author: Thomas Hardy (1840-1928)
First published: 1887; serial form, 1886-1887
Genre: Novel

Locale: Rural England
Time: The nineteenth century
Plot: Social realism

Grace Melbury, a young Englishwoman whose expensive education sets her apart from her family and neighbors in the village of Little Hintock. She returns to find that she is intended by her father to be the bride of Giles Winterborne, until that young man loses his little fortune. Later, she is courted by a young physician, Edgar Fitzpiers, whom she marries without love at her father's urging. As she begins to mature, Grace realizes that she has been mistaken in her marriage. When her husband turns to a rich, young widow, Grace is surprised at her lack of feeling until she realizes that as she has outgrown an external view of life she has come for the first time to appreciate her rural neighbors. Although her pride is hurt by her husband's philandering, she takes joy in discovering what love can be, for she truly falls in love with Giles Winterborne. Only later, as Winterborne lies dying, having sacrificed himself for her, does she really mature as a woman. Some months later, she and her husband become reconciled and prepare to start life anew in another part of England.

Edgar Fitzpiers, a young physician of good family. Although he is an excellent doctor, he also is a vain and shallow young man who wastes his skill and his time in all sorts of romantic studies. Living alone in Little Hintock village, he is attracted to Grace Melbury and marries her, although he feels he is marrying beneath his station. Soon afterward, he drifts into an affair with Felice Charmond, a wealthy widow of the neighborhood. Through this unhappy passion, he loses his wife, his practice, and almost his life. After the scandalous death of his mistress abroad, he realizes his selfishness and courts his wife anew, winning a new start in marriage and in his profession.

George Melbury, a timber merchant. Conscience-stricken because he had stolen a friend's fiancée years before, he proposes to make amends by marrying his daughter Grace to the friend's son, Giles Winterborne, but he finds that he cannot bring himself to enforce the marriage after the young man has lost his lands. He then marries Grace to the local doctor, who he believes is the only man in the community suitable for her. Throughout the story, until Grace matures enough to take her life into her own hands, George Melbury dominates his daughter, several times plunging her into grief through his decisions, even though he means well by her.

Giles Winterborne, a young timberman and landowner, a natural gentleman. He loves Grace Melbury devotedly and sacrifices his health and life for her happiness and good name. He endures many embarrassments at the hands of the Melburys, even to being jilted when, through no fault of his own, he loses his lands and is forced to become an itinerant worker. His noble nature is a great factor in helping Grace Melbury achieve emotional maturity.

Felice Charmond, a rich young widow and a former actress who has inherited a great estate, including the local manor house, from her deceased husband. A creature of sensual passion, she readily begins an affair with Dr. Fitzpiers. The affair, the last of a long series for her, is no mere flirtation, for she learns truly to love the young physician and follows him to the Continent after he and his wife separate. There, her death at the hands of an earlier lover, an American from South Carolina, frees the doctor from his passion.

Marty South, a poor young woman in love with Giles Winterborne. Her letter to Dr. Fitzpiers causes an argument between the physician and Felice Charmond. The argument takes Fitzpiers away from the widow shortly before her death and saves him from being involved in scandal when she is shot and killed by a former lover.

Suke Damson, a pretty, amoral young village girl who has an affair with Dr. Fitzpiers before his marriage. Although it is a passing relationship for him, Suke falls deeply in love. After her marriage, she reveals unwittingly to her husband that her affections lie elsewhere.

Tim Tang, Suke Damson's husband, a sawyer employed by Mr. Melbury. Bitter because his wife still loves Dr. Fitzpiers rather than himself, he sets a mantrap, such as is used to catch poachers, for the physician. The jealous husband's plan goes wrong and the trap almost gives serious injury to innocent Grace Melbury. The incident turns out to be the unintended catalyst that brings Grace and her husband together once more. Tang and his wife emigrate to New Zealand.

Robert Creedle, an old servant loyal to Giles Winterborne in both prosperity and adversity.

John South, Marty South's father. His death influences the careers of Giles Winterborne and the others because Giles's leases to his lands are written to expire at the death of the old man.

THE WOODS

Author: David Mamet (1947-   )
First published: 1979
Genre: Drama

Locale: A summer cottage in the woods
Time: The 1970's
Plot: Psychological realism

Ruth, a young woman seeking a romantic commitment from her reluctant lover. Spending a weekend at a cabin with Nick, trying to escape the pressures of the city, their jobs, and their obviously deteriorating relationship, she speaks incessantly in fragmented sentences and incomplete narratives. Fear of abandonment, loss, and decay are the central themes running through her conversation. What emerges is the gradual revelation of her psychological state: She is having problems controlling her rising hysteria and her need to make contact. After Nick's attack on her, she is able to withdraw emotionally from him and offer him a kind of a sexual nurturing for his childlike need.

Nick, an intensely troubled young man. For much of the play, he speaks very little, in contrast to Ruth and her flood of language. His few comments contain the themes of fear of entrapment, fear of death, and fear of meaninglessness. When he feels the need to break through Ruth's romantic imaginings, he explodes and attacks her physically and sexually. When the assault fails and Ruth acknowledges the impossibility of her desires for a warm, committed relationship, Nick becomes increasingly vulnerable, frightened, and willing to express his emotional neediness. At the end, he comes to her arms as a child, and they cling to each other out of necessity, united by their mutual fears.

— *Lori Hall Burghardt*

WOODSTOCK

Author: Sir Walter Scott (1771-1832)
First published: 1826
Genre: Novel

Locale: England
Time: 1651
Plot: Historical

Sir Henry Lee, a Royalist forced by the soldiers of Cromwell to move from the royal lodge, Woodstock, with his daughter. After they move back to the lodge, he helps to hide Prince Charles until the young prince can make his escape from England. Finally, as an old man, he lives just long enough to see the prince crowned as King Charles II.

Alice Lee, the daughter of Sir Henry, in love with Markham Everard, Sir Henry's nephew. Her father will not allow the marriage because Everard is a Puritan. Because of her love for Everard, she spurns Charles's advances when he stays at the lodge disguised as a page. When Charles escapes, he asks Sir Henry to withdraw his objections to her marriage to Everard.

Albert Lee, Sir Henry's son. He helps to keep Charles hidden and makes arrangements for his escape. He disguises himself as the prince and decoys Cromwell's soldiers while Charles escapes. When Albert is captured, Cromwell sentences him to death, but Cromwell later relents and changes the sentence to banishment. Albert finally is killed in battle.

Colonel Markham Everard, Sir Henry's nephew and a Puritan. In spite of his beliefs, he refuses to betray Charles and even helps him to escape. He is in love with and marries Alice.

Roger Wildrake, Everard's friend and a Royalist. He also refuses to betray the king and sends a message to Woodstock warning that Cromwell is coming.

Joceline Joliffe, the lodgekeeper at Woodstock. He is a Royalist, and he kills the Roundhead steward Tomkins for making advances to Phoebe Mayflower, the woman Joliffe loves. He finally marries Phoebe.

Louis Kerneguy, a churlish and mischievous young page, really Prince Charles Stuart in disguise. He has been rescued from the Puritans and is in hiding until he can get out of the country. He cannot understand why his advances to Alice are repulsed, and he readily accepts Everard's challenge to a duel. He finally returns to England, after many years, and is crowned king.

Joseph Tomkins, a steward for the Puritans, killed by Joliffe.

Dr. Anthony Rochecliffe, the Royalist chaplain of Woodstock who helps to rescue Charles from the Puritans.

Oliver Cromwell, Lord Protector of the Commonwealth, who is pursuing and trying to capture Charles before he can leave the country.

A WORD CHILD

Author: Iris Murdoch (1919-   )
First published: 1975
Genre: Novel

Locale: London, England
Time: Early 1970's
Plot: Psychological

Hilary Burde, a linguist, former don, and minor bureaucrat, the brother of Crystal and lover of Thomasina. A big, hairy, dark man, Hilary, now guarded and remorseful, irresistibly attracts the three women on whom the plot turns. He is an angry, unloved orphan who was separated from his younger sister, Crystal, who represents goodness to him. Hilary escapes delinquency and despair only because of his talent for languages: He is a "word child," created by language, not love. Uninterested in what words mean, he seeks to learn the rules of grammar, which represent law to him. His fellowship at Oxford promises a decent life for him and his sister until he becomes obsessed with Anne, the wife of Gunnar Jopling, another don. Gunnar and Hilary both leave Oxford, the first to a successful career, the second to become a government clerk. In London, Hilary carefully limits his involvements. The rigid routine that mirrors his emotional state reserves an evening a week for each of his friends and two evenings for Crystal. Gunnar's second wife asks Hilary to see her husband so that the past will no longer poison the present. Again, however, Hilary destroys both the woman he loves and Jopling's happiness. Hilary realizes that he is not solely responsible; all are in some degree victims of chance. He ceases to identify guilt and despair with penitence, and his new understanding means escape from the past. The measure of Hilary's growth is that this time he does not burden Crystal with what he has done but suffers alone. He also relinquishes his grip on Crystal so that she may marry.

Crystal Burde, Hilary's younger sister, self-sacrificing, simple, and instinctively good. Crystal cares for Hilary after

Anne's death, follows him to London, and warns him not to continue seeing Gunnar's wife. Gunnar had slept with Crystal on the night Anne died. She still cares for him but marries Arthur Fisch and plans a happy life in rural Yorkshire.

Gunnar Jopling, an Oxford don, a career civil servant, and Hilary's alter ego. Jopling is successful and happily married but equally obsessed by the past. Both of his wives die in accidents resulting from their attraction to Hilary, and both deaths are precipitated by Gunnar's knowledge. Both Biscuit and Crystal love Jopling, and his relation to Hilary is not solely one of hatred. Jopling conceals Hilary's part in both deaths, and both tragedies lead Gunnar to further public success.

Lady Kitty Jopling, Gunnar's second wife, the beautiful daughter of an Irish peer. She wants the child Jopling cannot give her and wishes Hilary to father a child, which she will claim is Gunnar's. Jopling appears as Hilary is refusing, and Kitty is killed accidentally.

Thomasina Uhlmeister, a minor Scottish actress who is Hilary's jealous mistress, determined to marry him. She tells Jopling of Hilary's relationship with Kitty, thus precipitating the tragedy. It is unclear whether she and Hilary will ever marry.

Arthur Fisch, an unprepossessing, good man who is a minor civil servant. He rescues drug addicts. He loves Crystal and eventually marries her.

Biscuit, Lady Kitty's Eurasian maid, a follower of Hilary who is devoted to Jopling. Appearing as a mysterious agent of change in Hilary's life, she actually is gathering information and delivering messages for Kitty.

— *Jocelyn Creigh Cass*

WORDS AND MUSIC

Author: Samuel Beckett (1906-1989)
First published: 1962
Genre: Drama

Locale: Unspecified
Time: Indeterminate
Plot: Absurdist

Croak, a character addressed as "lord" by Words; Croak, in turn, refers to Words and Music as his "balms" and "comforts" and, more familiarly, as Joe and Bob. Wearing carpet slippers and carrying a club, Croak arrives late, asks them to forgive his delay, and then announces the performance's first theme: love. He communicates his desires and, more often and more demonstrably, his displeasure, less by means of words than by means of sighs, groans, exclamations of anguish, and the peremptory thumping of his club. Disappointed by Words's disquisition on love, he calls on Music. Then (either because the playing does not please him or because Words repeatedly interrupts Music), Croak changes the subject, first to age and later

to "the face." His early gentleness soon gives way to tyrannical demands and ultimately to anguish as Words's speech conjures up for him the face of Lily (presumably the same face he saw earlier and that had caused him to be late). As the performance gains momentum, and as Words and Music finally do play together as bidden, Croak becomes more and more their helpless, perhaps enraptured audience. At the end of this radio play, Croak is heard haltingly shuffling away, back to the tower—back into the silence—from which he first came.

Words, a character who is deferential toward his master, Croak, but imperious toward Music, with whom he is cooped up in the dark. Interested as he may be in pleasing the master who commands them to play together, Words appears more interested in gaining his master's sole favor by silencing Music, as if Words assumes that the two are at odds and thus in competition with each other. Before the master's arrival, Words rehearses his speech on "sloth." When Croak announces that the theme is "love," Words simply repeats the same speech, substituting the word "love" for the word "sloth" wherever necessary. Neither his speech on love nor the next on age pleases Croak; however, with Music's help, the persistent Words, although still disdainful of his partner, does improve. His ragged speech turns into tentative song; consequently, and concurrently, his early imperiousness turns into gentleness. The earlier antagonism gives way to faltering cooperation and eventually to success. Working at last in concert with Music, Words composes the poem that silences the pair's demanding audience, Croak. Words, however, is shocked by Croak's sudden departure and unsuccessfully implores him to stay.

Music, played by a small orchestra. As the play begins, Music is tuning up, only to be peremptorily silenced by Words.

Here and through much of the play, Music appears conciliatory, even imploring. When Words's initial performances fail to please Croak, Music tries to help, suggesting possible directions, gently leading as well as unobtrusively accompanying a partner to whom Music is willing to grant ascendancy, or perhaps the illusion of ascendancy. Where Words appears cold, Music seems warm. Just at the point where Words begins to succeed, however, Music suddenly takes over, though whether in a sudden burst of enthusiasm or in retaliation for past wrongs is not at all clear. Less ambiguous and also more characteristic is Music's "brief rude retort" very near the end of the play; it may be the reason Croak departs. Its effect on the now "imploring" Words is more pronounced, as Music achieves this ironic triumph over his counterpart and nemesis.

Pause, the absence of sound and sense that Words and Music attempt to fill for Croak.

Lily, the woman whose face Croak saw on the stairs and that he now recalls as he listens to Words and Music.

— *Robert A. Morace*

THE WORDS UPON THE WINDOW-PANE

Author: William Butler Yeats (1865-1939)
First published: 1934
Genre: Drama

Locale: Dublin, Ireland
Time: The 1920's
Plot: Naturalism

Jonathan Swift, the eighteenth century satirist and poet, here a spirit called up in a séance. The ghost of Swift resembles the man at a more or less recognizable point in his life, during old age but before his descent into madness. In his two dialogues with the spirit forms of the women whom he loved, the satirist's wry cynicism has turned to bitterness and paranoia. In countering Vanessa's passionate offer of marriage, he describes his own "disease of the blood" and the more general malaise of a debased humanity. Swift is caught at that point in his late life where intellectual arrogance is waging a losing struggle with the social chaos that he believes is about to engulf him. His ghostly encounter with Stella, whose poem provides the "words" of the title, represents, however, a brief recurrence of the younger Swift, capable of redemption through intellectual grace and courage.

John Corbet, a graduate student at the University of Cambridge, a specialist in Swift's life and work. Corbet's initial skepticism about contact with the spirit world dissolves as the play progresses; the ghostly colloquies between Swift and Vanessa and between Swift and Stella convince him that he has discovered the "mystery" behind Swift's celibacy. Although the revelation affords Corbet a measure of intellectual exaltation for its own sake, he also clearly views the discovery as a stepping-stone in his own scholarly advancement. To an extent, Corbet also serves as provider of literary background. His historical and critical asides to Dr. Trench and to Mrs. Henderson supply the audience with facts about Swift's life and his relationships with Vanessa and Stella, insights crucial to an understanding of the play.

Dr. Trench, an elderly scholar, president of the Dublin Spiritualists' Association. Trench serves as the play's moral and intellectual pivot; like Corbet, he is an intellectual, a man of reason. He also has become convinced of more ghostly realities, enabling him to glimpse the boundary between rea-

son and passion. At the same time that he holds the overly emotional and superstitious impulses of the other séance participants in check, he lends credibility to the séance's central action, the calling up of ghosts. As Corbet acts as dramatic channel for literary and historical information about Swift, Trench serves as an interpreter of spiritualist practice and Dublin legend.

Ester Vanhomrigh, called **Vanessa**, Swift's lover and protégé. Vanessa appears in the first of Swift's two dialogues with the women he loved. She describes her loyalty and passion to an obdurate Swift and rationally demands a reason for his refusal to marry. Why, she asks, has he raised her from her humble station, educating and "refining" her, if he does not love her? When Swift counters that he feels disgust at the prospect of siring children, she leaves him to his solitude.

Esther Johnson, called **Stella**, Swift's lover. The second of the women in Swift's life, Stella is more nearly his equal than Vanessa. In his brief scene with her, he describes his admiration for her intellectual excellence and specifically praises her poem to him. She is the representative of those women who are able to love "according to the soul," and, at least according to Swift, thereby possess greater happiness than those who experience bodily love. During the opening scenes of the play, Trench informs Corbet that the house in which the séance takes place originally was Stella's.

Mrs. Henderson, a simple Irishwoman, a medium through whom the spirits of Swift, Vanessa, and Stella pass. Mrs. Henderson's role is largely passive. She serves first as a conduit for the exchanges between Swift and his lovers, then as ignorant reflector of Corbet's scholarly knowledge. In a very real sense, she is the stock figure of "old Ireland," the peasant woman to whom the movement of history and the rise of great individuals are nonsense. By the same token, she is both literally and metaphorically possessed by Ireland's past and by its madness. As the play ends, she is left alone. While she modestly goes about making tea, she simultaneously serves as the mouthpiece for Swift's tragic ravings.

Cornelius Patterson, a gambler. Bent only on the materialistic benefits of his contact with the "Other World," Patterson is the stereotype of the twentieth century materialist interested only in his own gain.

Abraham Johnson, an evangelist. Johnson futilely seeks to reconcile the reality of the spirit world with the teachings of Christianity. As ignorant as Mrs. Henderson is of Swift's importance, he is able to see the writer only as an embodiment of

evil and must be restrained from disrupting the séance.

Mrs. Mallet, an experienced spiritualist. Like Patterson and Johnson, Mrs. Mallet's interest in spiritual contact comes from self-interest; unlike the two men, however, she is free from selfishness. Her principal aim is to contact her drowned husband. Her longing for the beloved dead thus mirrors, in miniature, the larger themes of the play.

Miss Mackenna, another veteran spiritualist, secretary of the association.

— *John Steven Childs*

THE WORKHOUSE WARD

Authors: Lady Augusta Gregory (1852-1932) with Douglas Hyde (1860-1949)
First published: 1909
Genre: Drama

Locale: A ward in Cloon Workhouse, Ireland
Time: c. 1900's
Plot: Comedy

Michael Miskell, a pauper and current resident of the Cloon Workhouse. Michael is an old and disputatious peasant who spends his time talking to his former neighbor, Mike McInerney, who is now his fellow workhouse inmate. Michael seems determined to have the last word, to suffer the most, and to come from the greatest family. In short, he is in a continual battle to defend his position against his old neighbor and fellow pauper. He is cunning and has the verbal skills to question the value of another's possessions or family while inflating his own situation. He rehashes old grudges and charges such as being bitten by Mike's dogs after returning from a fair day. Apparently that incident happened many years earlier, but Michael claims that it caused his downfall because he has been "wasting from then till now." Although their lives have been so closely tied together, his dearest wish is to be buried at a distance from his old neighbor. Although he dismisses all troubles and obstacles with words, however, he is vulnerable to not having an opponent with whom to contend. When Mike McInerney indicates that he is to leave with his sister, Michael poignantly asks if Mike is going "to leave me with rude people and with townspeople . . . and they having no respect for me or no wish for me at all." He needs someone to talk to because his life is talk, and, "with no conversable person," he is miserable.

Mike McInerney, an old farmer who has lost his land and been reduced to pauper status in the Workhouse. He spends his time defending himself against the assaults of Michael Miskell and making countercharges against his adversary. He does seem to have been better off in earlier years than Michael, but his strategies of attack and defense are quite similar to those of

his opponent. He claims, for example, that the banshee cries for the famous family of the McInerneys but never for the low Miskells. Their equal battle is turned in his favor by the arrival of his sister, Honor Donohue, with the invitation to join her in her seaside home. His victory does not lead to a final cry of triumph, however, and he softens his attitude to his old adversary by first offering him his pipe and then taking the unusual step of asking his sister to take Michael into the household. When she refuses, he is content to remain where he is; for all of its difficulties, a workhouse of continual verbal battles is preferable to a more regular but boring life without talk and the constant excitement of verbal battle. At the end of the play, they return to the battle that has been going on for so many years as Mike defends against Michael's attacks the house he has just rejected. Their battle finally exhausts words, and they resort to a final barrage of pillows, mugs, and whatever is within reach. Their relationship is a marriage of enemies that only death can dissolve.

Honor Donohue, an elderly woman, Mike's sister. She masks her need for a man in her home with a newfound charity to her impoverished brother. Although she is eager to have her brother help out in the house, she is not an obliging fool. When she is faced with the prospect of having two quarreling old men with her day and night, she proves as resilient as they are stuck in their ways. She immediately leaves them and goes off by herself with the clothes she had offered to Mike, to seek "a man for my own." She is not interested in living through words and roles; the practical business of living comes first in the life of which she takes charge.

— *James Sullivan*

WORKS AND DAYS
(Erga kai Ēmerai)

Author: Hesiod (fl. c. 700 B.C.E.)
First transcribed: c. 700 B.C.E.
Genre: Poetry

Locale: The village of Ascra in central Greece
Time: Hesiod's lifetime
Plot: Moral

Hesiod (HEE-see-uhd), an honest and hardworking Greek farmer. His father, a seafaring trader (and presumably a farmer as well), had emigrated from his homeland on the coast of Asia

Minor (modern Turkey) in a state of poverty and had sailed across the Aegean Sea to mainland Greece in search of a better livelihood. There, he settled in the district of Boeotia, in the meager village of Ascra on the lower slopes of Mount Helicon, which was sacred to the Muses of poetry. He acquired land, achieved middle-class status and a measure of prosperity, and was able to bequeath an estate of some value to his sons, Hesiod and Perses. A bitter dispute about the inheritance, however, led to litigation and to charges by Hesiod that Perses had attempted to get the better of him by bribing the corrupt barons who functioned as judges. Hesiod, in fact, treats this litigation as the immediate occasion of this thoroughly didactic poem, which is addressed to Perses. Hesiod speaks in the first person and exhorts his brother to forsake his lazy, scheming, and contentious habits and to devote himself to honest living and hard work; these general exhortations are accompanied by explicit instructions about proper conduct, managing a farm, and seafaring. The poem concludes with a straightforward list of propitious and unpropitious days. Hesiod's advice to Perses is grounded in a firm belief that this is a hard but moral universe in which Zeus, the ruler of the gods, rewards industry and integrity and punishes those who cheat and rob. Inspired by the ever present Muses of Mount Helicon, Hesiod, as he informs Perses (and his readers), already was a prize-winning poet before he composed this poem.

Perses (PUR-sees), Hesiod's brother, who figures prominently as the person to whom the poem is immediately addressed and whose moral reformation it seeks to effect. Perses is always merely the addressee and is never allowed to speak for himself or to defend himself against his brother's charges of fraud, sloth, and troublemaking; he might have given a different account of his personal conduct and of the dispute over the inheritance. He is, however, implicitly treated by Hesiod as capable of amendment and of becoming a man who is honest and industrious; otherwise, there would have been no justification for addressing him didactically in such a poem.

Zeus (zews), "the father of gods and men," who demands of human beings hard labor and honest dealings. He governs Hesiod's universe according to a standard of strict and absolute justice. In a mythological account of the origin of work, sorrow, and disease, Hesiod tells the story of Zeus's conflict with Prometheus (proh-MEE-thee-uhs) and his creation of Pandora ("Allgifts"). To punish Prometheus, the patron and protector of humankind, for stealing fire from the Olympian gods and giving it to humans, Zeus had the gods create the seductress Pandora and confer on her all charms, graces, and deceits; he then sent her into the world with a jar in which were stored all human miseries and arranged for her to open it and release them, only Hope remaining trapped inside.

— *Hubert M. Martin, Jr.*

THE WORKS OF LOVE

Author: Wright Morris (1910-   )
First published: 1952
Genre: Novel

Locale: Nebraska, California, and Chicago
Time: The 1880's-the 1930's
Plot: Regional

Will Jennings Brady, a hardworking man who holds a number of jobs, but none for very long. A onetime handyman, night clerk in a hotel, hotel manager, chicken farmer, egg entrepreneur, and waybill sorter, he finally ends up as a department store Santa Claus. The son of Nebraska pioneers, orphaned at an early age, he lacks culture and education. A taciturn and kind but naïve man who does not drink, smoke, gamble, or swear, he embarks on a quest that takes him from the desolate western plains to Omaha, then to California, and on to Chicago in search of his airy dreams of wealth, happiness, and love. He attains none of these. Along the way, his fortunes briefly rise but mainly fall. As a husband and father, he is inept and incapable of understanding the needs of his family. After repeated failures, both as a businessman and as a family man, he turns Will, Jr., over to foster parents and heads for Chicago, where he dies penniless and alone, after falling into a sewage canal.

Ethel Czerny Bassett, a widow who marries Will Brady. A Bohemian immigrant, quiet and somewhat religious, she relies on Will's help after the death of her husband, owner of the hotel where Brady works. After marrying Brady, she goes with him on a honeymoon to Colorado Springs, but she spends her nights there rolled up in a sheet, afraid to consummate the marriage. After returning to Nebraska, she still experiences sexual problems. Although Brady provides her with many domestic amenities, including a large house, she does not sleep with him. After discovering Brady's affair with a cigar-counter girl in Omaha, she leaves.

Will Brady, Jr., a baby adopted by Will Brady after a runaway prostitute abandoned him on Brady's doorstep. Despite his father's ineptitude as a parent, Will, Jr., does well in school, joins the Boy Scouts, and cultivates a love for nature. Often perplexed by his father's odd behavior, he spends much of his time living elsewhere, mostly in foster homes.

Gertrude Long, Will Brady's second wife, a cigar-counter girl and a prostitute. The young and immature daughter of vaudevillian actors, she first meets Brady in a hotel in Omaha. Attracted initially by his good looks and unusual behavior, she lets the relationship develop and marries him, only to discover that he is no more able to fulfill her needs than he was able to fulfill those of his first wife. Brady, preoccupied with his dreams of riches and power, spends all of his energy tending to business. Meanwhile, she spends her time idly listening to phonograph records and going to cheap films. Although she pities Brady, she does not love him, and their relationship slowly disintegrates after she joins him in California and begins again to work as a prostitute.

T. P. Luckett, an egg producer and the person in charge of the Union Pacific commissary in Omaha. He persuades Will Brady to give up his hotel job in Calloway and lends him money to move to Murdock to raise chickens for the carriage trade.

— *Rodney P. Rice*

THE WORLD ACCORDING TO GARP

Author: John Irving (1942-   )
First published: 1978
Genre: Novel

Locale: Boston; Steering, a preparatory school; Vienna; and New York City
Time: 1942 through the early 1970's
Plot: Picaresque

T. S. Garp, a writer. Because his father dies before he is born, Garp grows up in a world created by his mother. As a result, he spends most of his life trying to create his own identity and never fully achieves one separate from that of his mother. He is educated at a private boys' school, where his mother is the head nurse. He goes to Europe after graduation and becomes closely involved in the darker side of life in Vienna. He returns home and marries the daughter of his wrestling coach, and while she teaches, he stays home and cares for the children and writes. He indulges in a series of affairs with other women but does little to hide the fact from his wife. He writes three books and loses a son in a bizarre car accident that maims his other son and emasculates his wife's lover. He becomes the wrestling coach at Steering School, buys the Percy mansion, and, at the age of thirty-three, is shot to death by the youngest Percy daughter, who is now hopelessly insane.

Jenny Fields, a nurse. Jenny believes in evidence and results rather than emotions. Determined to have a child but having no desire to have a husband or to have anything to do with a man, Jenny has a very clinical one-night encounter with a brain-damaged soldier, who dies shortly thereafter, and produces Garp. She subsequently takes a position at the Steering School so that Garp will have a proper education and goes about attending classes and reading voraciously so that Garp will have the benefit of her knowledge. After Garp graduates, she goes to Vienna with him and there writes her autobiography, which becomes a feminist sensation. Her family home in Vermont becomes a haven for distressed women, and, eventually, she decides to enter politics. At a political rally, she is killed by a man dressed as a deer hunter.

Helen Holm, an English professor. Abandoned by her mother, Helen is brought up by her father, a wrestling coach. She becomes introverted and somewhat shy and is given to reading books. When her father takes a position at Steering School, Helen momentarily mistakes Jenny for her mother, who also was a nurse. She earns a Ph.D. at the age of twenty-three, becomes a college professor, marries Garp, and has two children. She has a number of affairs, the last being with Michael Milton, whom she accidentally emasculates in a car accident. Eventually, she takes a position at Steering and outlives Garp by many years, dying in old age.

Ernie Holm, a wrestling coach. A small, neat man who is nearly blind, Ernie takes the position of wrestling coach at Steering School so that his daughter will have a good education. He does not realize that Steering School is a boys' school until it is too late. He is the first friend Jenny Fields ever has, and it is because of him that Garp finds a sport in which he excels, a very important part of a Steering boy's life. He dies of a heart attack while masturbating at home, at nearly the same time that Jenny is murdered, although the events of his death are kept quiet. He is buried at Steering School the same day as Stewart Percy.

Dean Bodger, the dean of Steering School. A short-haired, muscular man, he is a brave and kindhearted individual who becomes a friend of Jenny Fields. His grasp of reality is a little off, but he means well, and it is he who rearranges the scene of Ernie Holm's death so that his daughter will not know what actually happened. Bodger dies while a spectator at a wrestling match.

Stewart "Fat Stew" Percy, a Steering School history instructor. A large, florid man, he is noted for putting on a good appearance and doing nothing. Although he holds the title of secretary of Steering School, the only work he does for fifteen years is to teach a course titled "My Part in the Pacific," which is nothing more than personal reminiscences of the war and how he met his wife, Midge Steering. Because his wife is the last member of a very wealthy family, the marriage gave Stewart the leisure to do nothing. He develops a fierce antagonism toward Garp and even blames him for the death of his daughter Cushman. He dies the same day as Ernie Holm.

Cushman (Cushie) Pierce, a student. A pretty girl, she quickly develops disciplinary problems at school and is transferred to five different private girls' schools. Her problem is that she likes sex and is more than willing to participate in it. She seduces Garp and is his first sexual experience. She dies in childbirth with her first child.

Tinch, an English teacher, a frail man with a stutter. Tinch's only reputation with the student body of Steering School is for his bad breath. He encourages Garp to write, and it is he who recommends that Garp and his mother go to Vienna. He fails to realize that his memories of the city are based on a visit in 1913 and that the city has changed. He freezes to death after a fall in the winter coming home from a faculty party.

Charlotte, a prostitute. A tall, sad-faced woman, Charlotte tries to answer Jenny Fields's questions on lust and eventually develops a friendly, not always professional relationship with Garp. She plans to retire with the money that she has saved and move to Munich, where she hopes to marry a doctor who will take care of her. Instead, she becomes sick and enters an expensive private hospital outside Vienna. She dies at the age of fifty-one, and her parting gift to Garp is two free encounters with the prostitutes who were her friends.

Harrison Fletcher, an English professor, Helen's colleague at the state university. Harrison has an affair with a student and then quickly drops her to have an affair with Helen. He is denied tenure because of his affair with the student, and he and his wife both move away, though they remain friends of Garp and Helen. He dies in an airplane crash while on vacation.

Alice Fletcher, a writer suffering from a severe speech impediment. Alice is aware of her husband's affair with his student. She appeals to Garp for help, with the results that her husband transfers his attentions to Helen and that Alice has an affair with Garp. She writes, but she cannot finish her novels. She wants the affair to continue, but Garp ends it after Helen ends her affair. Even after Alice and her husband move away, she still tries to rekindle her affair with Garp. She dies in an airplane crash with her husband.

Michael Milton, a graduate student. At the age of twenty-five, he is bright, thin, and tall. He takes a course from Helen because he has decided to have an affair with her. Helen finally succumbs, but she is overwhelmed with guilt and decides to end it. While consoling Michael over this decision, she accidentally bites off most of his penis when Garp's car plows into the one in which they are sitting. He loses the remainder of it during his subsequent hospitalization.

Roberta Muldoon, a former football player. A six-foot, four-inch former tight end, Roberta has had a sex change operation and becomes a fast friend of Jenny Fields. She lives in Jenny's house and acts as something of a bodyguard. Un-

able to maintain a relationship with a man, she still manages to become Garp's friend. When Jenny is murdered, she blames herself for not acting quickly enough. After Jenny's death, she becomes the resident administrator of the Fields Foundation, which uses the money Jenny left to help women. She dies after running on the beach.

Ellen James, a woman whose name is used by a group of radical feminists. As an eleven-year-old child, she was raped by two men who cut out her tongue so that she could not describe them. Instead, she wrote careful descriptions that led to their arrest and conviction. She meets Garp on an airplane after his mother's funeral and moves in with the family; her own family has recently died. She grows up to be a writer. At first, she hates the Ellen Jamesians, who have their own tongues cut out to sympathize with her, but she eventually befriends them.

— *C. D. Akerley*

WORLD ENOUGH AND TIME

Author: Robert Penn Warren (1905-1989)
First published: 1950
Genre: Novel

Locale: Kentucky
Time: 1801-1826
Plot: Philosophical realism

Jeremiah Beaumont (jeh-reh-MI-uh BOH-mont), a man betrayed by his idealism as well as by the compromises and realities of life. An earnest young lawyer, he first becomes disillusioned with his benefactor, Colonel Cassius Fort, a famous lawyer and politician, on learning that Fort has seduced an innocent girl. He renounces his benefactor, becomes involved in politics, and marries the betrayed girl. Jeremiah loses a bitter election. He gives up his intention of killing his wife's seducer, but a scurrilous political handbill, giving a false account of the seduction, enrages him. He kills his former benefactor and is convicted on the basis of false evidence. An old friend helps him to escape from prison. While hiding out, Jeremiah learns that this friend had been responsible for the libelous handbill. Jeremiah's wife commits suicide, and he is murdered when he attempts to go back to tell the real story. Jeremiah's story is a reworking of that of a historical figure, Jeroboam Beauchamp.

Colonel Cassius Fort, Jeremiah's benefactor, a frontier politician. Although he did seduce the girl whom Jeremiah marries, he is not the author of the handbill that bears his name and that drives Jeremiah to kill him. This character is based on Colonel Solomon P. Sharp, who, like Fort, was assassinated in 1825.

Rachael Jordan, the daughter of a planter. She is seduced by Fort and later marries Jeremiah, on the condition that he kill Fort. Later, she dissuades him from fulfilling his promise. When Jeremiah sees the scurrilous handbill, however, he kills Fort. After her husband's conviction, Rachael also is arrested. Both are freed by Jeremiah's false friend. Later, Rachael kills herself.

Wilkie Barron, Jeremiah's opportunistic and false friend, whom he has known since their days as law students together.

Barron and several others break into jail and free Jeremiah shortly before his execution date, but Jeremiah learns that Barron was responsible for the handbill that made him kill Fort. After Jeremiah is killed by one of Barron's men, Barron goes on to become rich and successful. Finally, he shoots himself. Among his papers is found Jeremiah's manuscript, revealing the whole story.

Jasper Beaumont, Jeremiah's bankrupt father. Jeremiah inherits his father's moodiness, and he develops the feeling that he must work hard to settle his father's score.

Dr. Leicester Burnham, young Jeremiah's teacher, who is a loyal friend. He recommends his pupil to Fort and remains loyal to Jeremiah during his trial.

Mrs. Beaumont (née Marcher), Jeremiah's mother, who is disinherited by her wealthy father. Her final illness postpones Jeremiah's law studies.

Thomas Barron, Wilkie's uncle. While visiting him, Jeremiah meets Rachael.

Percival Scrogg, a fanatic liberal newspaper editor. He and Wilkie Barron together print and distribute the handbill attributed to Fort.

Josh Parham, a rich landowner with whom Jeremiah forms a partnership. Their land speculation falls through when the Relief Party comes to power. Parham, an Anti-Relief man, swears not to open up Kentucky land while the Relief Party is in office.

Felix Parham, Josh's son.

Desha, the Relief candidate, elected governor in 1824.

Sellars, the candidate who defeats Jeremiah in their election contest.

La Grand' Bosse, a river pirate. After escaping from prison, Jeremiah and Rachael take refuge with him.

THE WORLD MY WILDERNESS

Author: Rose Macaulay (1881-1958)
First published: 1950
Genre: Novel

Locale: A village in the south of France and London
Time: The years immediately following World War II
Plot: Social realism

Helen Michel, the handsome and sensuous widow of Maurice Michel and former wife of Sir Gulliver Deniston. In her early forties, curvaceous, with tawny eyes, dark hair, and classical features, she is highly sexed and quite attractive. Intelligent but indolent, well-educated, artistic, and unconventional, she lives in a secluded seaside villa in France, for amusement translating Greek, playing chess, and occasionally gambling compulsively. Maurice Michel mysteriously drowned a few months earlier, and Helen is stepmother to his son Raoul. Her own children are Richie and Barbary Deniston and the infant Roland Michel, on whom both she and Barbary dote. Because Maurice had for a time been considered a "collaborator" of sorts, attempting to coexist with the Germans after they occupied France, Helen is shunned by many neighbors. Much preferring her own company and that of Maurice's cousin Lucien Michel, a married man who becomes her lover after Maurice's death, she is grateful for their distance. As the novel begins, she seems detached from Barbary, sending her to spend time with Sir Gully in England. After Barbary's true parentage is revealed, Helen reclaims her, taking her back to France for the good of both mother and daughter.

Barbary Deniston, Helen's seventeen-year-old daughter by her second lover, a fact that is revealed at the end of the story. Small and young-looking, with olive skin, full lips, dark hair, and gray, slanting eyes, she always appears watchful and ill at ease. Although she trusts nobody, she worships Helen and has inherited her artistic ability. Caught in the tumult of World War II, she has joined the resistance, engaging in anarchy almost casually and continuing to do so after the need has passed, accompanied always by her stepbrother Raoul. Barbary prefers wilderness to civilization because it provides better places of refuge. Her name is indicative of her innocently barbarian nature. In London, she gravitates toward its "wilderness" of bombed-out ruins, teaming up again with Raoul, who has been sent by his grandmother to live with an uncle. After setting up a flat in the shell of an apartment building, she is drawn to a ruined church, where she performs daily penance. Although her father is wealthy, she steals as an act of rebellion against his conventional ways and his conventional new wife. As the story ends, the mystery of her penitence is solved: Her friends had drowned Maurice Michel. Unwilling or unable to prevent the murder (she was evidently tortured into providing

information), she has suffered her own and Helen's grief. Her brush with death enables Helen to forgive and be reunited with her. Because Barbary is illegitimate, Helen feels that only Barbary is really all hers.

Raoul Michel, Barbary's stepbrother, a boy in his mid-teens. Born of a marriage of convenience, he is small and olive-skinned, with large brown eyes and an often furtive air. Like Barbary, Raoul has joined the resistance; unlike her, he appears not to suffer from having been allied with his father's murderers, although at the end of the story he truly grieves. Having been sent to London by his grandmother, who heartily disapproves of Helen Michel, he joins Barbary in the "wilderness" of London's ruins. After her accident, he decides to settle down and learn how to live in civilization.

Richmond (Richie) Deniston, Helen's eldest son, a man in his early twenties. Slim, well-educated, and elegant, he sees most of the world as Philistines, and he relishes civilization, fearing the encroachment of chaos. Although he had escaped from a prisoner-of-war camp and been smuggled back to England by the very resistance of which Barbary is a part, he disapproves of his "wild" sister; his stilted worship of civilization contrasts with her fear of it. An admitted intellectual snob, he practices Catholicism only because he likes tradition.

Sir Gulliver Deniston, Helen's former husband, a somewhat cynical lawyer who is still in love with her but is now married to the much younger Pamela. He is intelligent and distinguished looking but pale. He considers honor his guiding principle and is crushed to learn that Barbary is not really his child. Partly because he cannot fathom Barbary and partly because of his hurt, he agrees to let Helen take her back to her "wild" life in France; because of his honor, he promises not to tell Richie of Barbary's parentage.

Pamela Deniston, Sir Gulliver's young second wife, the mother of his son and expecting another child. She is handsome and athletic, with clear skin and brown hair. She resents Barbary's invasion of her life and disapproves of her "barbarian" ways. Barbary senses her dislike and returns it in full measure, refusing to acknowledge her young half brother's existence.

— *Sonya H. Cashdan*

A WORLD OF LOVE

Author: Elizabeth Bowen (1899-1973)
First published: 1955
Genre: Novel

Locale: County Cork, Ireland
Time: Two summer days in the early 1950's
Plot: Psychological

Antonia Montefort, a photographer in her early fifties, the owner of the dilapidated Montefort manor in the south of Ireland. Antonia inherited the manor from Guy Montefort, her cousin, who was killed in action in World War I at the age of

twenty. Antonia lives in London but occasionally visits the manor, where she is served by the Danbys: Fred runs the manor farm, and Lilia, his wife, manages the housework in a dilatory way. Antonia, having arranged their marriage, keeps them on the manor out of a sense of responsibility. Capricious and demanding, Antonia is indolent, caustic, and fearful of old age.

Jane Danby, the twenty-year-old daughter of Fred and Lilia. She is the favorite of her father and of Antonia, who has paid for her education. Exploring the attic one day, Jane finds a beautiful Edwardian dress and a packet of letters signed by Guy and tied in white ribbon. The recipient of the letter is not named, but they clearly are love letters and inspire Jane to speculate obsessively about the writer and the woman to whom he was writing. She even imagines that his ghost is present on a few occasions. She suspects that it was her mother, Lilia, to whom the letters were addressed, and Lilia does not deny it but does not read the letters. The mystery is solved at the end of the novel, when Jane burns the letters after discovering that they were not written to her mother. Jane tells Antonia of her discovery, but not Lilia. She then goes off to Shannon Airport to meet Richard Priam, who is coming to visit Lady Latterly, a neighbor. As the passengers descend from the plane, Richard and Jane see each other and immediately fall in love.

Lilia Danby, a woman who was engaged to Guy Montefort when she was seventeen and beautiful. She is now overweight, discontented, lazy, and ill-tempered. She has been a burden to Antonia since Guy's death because, but for that mischance,

she would have inherited the manor instead of Antonia. She continues to dream of escaping but has long since lost the will to do so. She knows that Guy was unfaithful to her, as is her husband Fred, but, at the end of the novel, she seems to have undergone a kind of change, a renewal of energy, and is making an effort to reestablish a closer relationship with Fred.

Fred Danby, the illegitimate cousin of Guy Montefort and Antonia who was persuaded by Antonia to marry Lilia. He runs the manor farm with uncomplaining diligence but not much success for his efforts. His favorite daughter is Jane, but he is fair and civil to Maud, his younger daughter, and to his wife. He is reserved and slow to speak, resigned to his life and accepting of his obligations.

Maud Danby, the twelve-year-old daughter of Fred and Lilia. Maud lives in her own world, like each of the other characters, but whereas Jane's world is inhabited by romantic notions and the ghost of Guy Montefort, Maud's contains an imaginary playmate named Gay David, a parody of Guy. Maud teases and torments everyone in the household with considerable ingenuity, thus provoking responses that help to reveal the thoughts and feelings of the other persons in the novel. She contributes a tone of humor without in any way intending to do so.

— *Natalie Harper*

A WORLD OF STRANGERS

Author: Nadine Gordimer (1923-)
First published: 1958
Genre: Novel

Locale: Johannesburg, South Africa
Time: Early 1950's
Plot: Social satire

Tobias (Toby) Hood, a publisher's agent. He has come from London to Johannesburg, South Africa, to work for a time in his family's publishing firm, Aden Parrot. Brown-haired and stocky, the Oxford-educated, twenty-six-year-old Toby is the first-person narrator of the novel. At odds with the liberal politics of his family, Toby comes to South Africa determined to see and do what interests him and not to be guided by social conscience. Through Hamish and Marion Alexander, he meets a group of privileged and luxury-loving white South Africans, including Cecil Rowe. He has an affair with Cecil, though he fails to make a serious commitment to her. Through Anna Louw, with whom he has a very brief affair, he meets Indians and Africans, including the black Steven Sitole, who becomes his closest friend. Toby finds himself slipping between two untouching worlds, the segregated white world and the world of the black townships. The death of Steven makes him face the changes that have shaped him since arriving in South Africa, where he now plans to stay indefinitely.

Steven Sitole (see-TOH-lay), formerly a journalist, then an insurance agent. Tall, thin, and elegantly dressed, Steven attracts many admirers. He has little stability, always moving from room to room and always pitting his wits against authority. A man of varied experience, he spent a year in England after the war and also earned a bachelor's degree from a correspondence college. Toby is drawn to him for his vitality and for the strength of his desire for a private life. Anna Louw

and Sam Mofokenzazi regret his lack of political concerns. Steven introduces Toby to the black townships and to his drinking companions. Steven dies tragically in a car accident while fleeing from a police raid on a club.

Cecil Rowe, a former model who now rides show horses. The twenty-eight-year-old Cecil is slim and vividly attractive. Born in South Africa of English parents, she is the divorced and inattentive mother of a three-year-old son. Uncommitted and lacking direction, she often seems lost and fearful. She has an affair with Toby but is unaware of his friendship with Steven. Eventually, she plans to marry Guy Patterson.

Anna Louw (loh), a lawyer who works for the Legal Aid Bureau, taking up African causes. A short, dark-haired, young Afrikaans woman, she is divorced from her Indian husband. Bravely refusing to live according to the segregations imposed by white South African society, she is abandoned by her conventional family. She takes Toby to a party, where he meets Steven Sitole. Later, Toby sleeps with Anna out of friendship rather than desire. Finally, Anna is arrested for political action. Toby visits her while she is out on bail.

Sam Mofokenzazi (moh-foh-kehn-ZAH-zee), a journalist for an African newspaper. Sam, who is very short, is described by Toby as having a "Black Sambo" face. A writer, jazz pianist, and composer, Sam is politically aware and also a responsible, stable family man. Toby is a frequent guest at the house of Sam and his wife, Ella, often sleeping there. He becomes even closer to Sam after the death of Steven.

Hamish Alexander, one of the most powerful gold-mining millionaires in South Africa. Bald, red-faced, and advanced in years, he relishes the privileges of his position. He and his wife, Marion, live at High House, an estate with a swimming pool, a tennis court, paddocks, and exquisite gardens. He also breeds horses, and Cecil Rowe rides show horses for him.

Marion Alexander, Hamish Alexander's wife. Although Toby's mother and his great-uncle Faunce once knew her, they would now disapprove of her self-indulgent and exclusive way of life. Disguising her advancing age with elaborate dress and makeup, she is a fashionable and expert hostess to the large groups of people regularly gathered at High House.

John Hamilton, a regular guest at High House. He helps Toby find his first flat in Johannesburg. An avid hunter, he takes Toby on a bird hunt into the bush.

Guy Patterson, a senior official in Hamish Alexander's mining group. A large man, thickened and lined with age, he is still handsome. A war hero who was educated at Cambridge, he joins the hunting party organized by John Hamilton. He shares Cecil's racial prejudice and will be able to offer her a life of material satisfactions.

— Susan Kress

THE WORLD OF THE THIBAULTS
(Les Thibault)

Author: Roger Martin du Gard (1881-1958)
First published: 1922-1940
Genre: Novel

Locale: France
Time: Early twentieth century
Plot: Social realism

M. Thibault (tee-BOH), an eminent Catholic social worker who has no time for the problems of his own disturbed family. When his son Jacques runs away in revolt against the smug respectability of his father and the dull Thibault household, the bigoted father suspects him, wrongly, of unnatural relations with his companion, a Protestant boy named Daniel de Fontanin. He gets the boy back and puts him into a reformatory that he has founded. M. Thibault is mercifully killed, during an incurable illness, when Antoine and Jacques give him an overdose of morphine.

Jacques Thibault (zhahk), an active youngster whose spirit is nearly broken by the cruel guards at the reformatory. His older brother Antoine, a doctor, helps in his gradual recuperation. Later, repulsed by Jenny de Fontanin, he disappears for three years. He spends part of that time in England. He then goes to Geneva, where he becomes an international socialist and an influential writer working to prevent the outbreak of World War I. Traced through his writing, he is called back as his father is dying. There, he again sees Jenny, and they are lovers until his pacifist duties call him back to Geneva. His plane is wrecked while he is trying to shower pamphlets on the workers and soldiers of France and Germany calling for peace through a general strike and refusal to bear arms. Badly injured and suspected of being a spy, he is shot by an orderly while he is being carried to headquarters for investigation.

Antoine Thibault, the older son, a doctor. He recognizes biographical and family details in a story published by Jacques in a Swiss magazine and summons his brother home during M. Thibault's last illness. He falls in love with one of his patients, an adventurer named Rachel, the former mistress of Hirsch, a sadistic libertine. Rachel eventually deserts Antoine to follow Hirsch to Africa. A necklace comes back to Antoine to announce her death. Antoine, gassed during the war, dies just before the signing of the armistice.

Gise (zheez), an orphan girl living with the Thibaults. After Jacques disappears, she is the only one confident that he is still alive.

Daniel de Fontanin (dahn-YEHL deh fohn-tah-NA[N]), a young Protestant who has an innocent and boyish affection for Jacques Thibault. Later, he finds success as an artist and leads a bohemian life. Desexed by a shell fragment during the war, he afterward spends much of his time assisting at a military hospital and playing with his nephew, young Jean-Paul, the son of his sister Jenny and his dead friend, Jacques Thibault.

Rachel (rah-SHEHL), Antoine Thibault's mistress, who tries unsuccessfully to end her affair with Hirsch. Eventually, she deserts Antoine and goes to Africa with her former lover.

Jenny de Fontanin, the daughter of a staunch Protestant family and the sister of Jacques Thibault's friend. A shy, frigid girl, she cannot bear to be touched by Jacques. After Antoine Thibault detects that she is suffering from meningitis, she experiences a miraculous faith cure through Pastor Gregory. Later, she meets Jacques, now a mature and self-assured pacifist, and falls in love with him. Her mother, coming home, finds them sleeping together. She plans to go to Geneva with him but gives him up when she realizes that he is dedicated to the pacifist cause. After his death, she bears his son, Jean-Paul.

Madame de Fontanin, the mother of Daniel and Jenny. Deserted by her husband, she occupies herself in war work as a hospital administrator in Paris.

Jérome de Fontanin (zhay-ROHM), her husband, who runs away with Noemie, his cousin. He dies in Vienna, suspected of embezzlement.

Nicole (nee-KOHL), the daughter of Noemie, who comes to live with Madame de Fontanin after her mother goes off with Jérome. Daniel tries in vain to seduce her.

Hirsch, a lecherous, brutal fifty-year-old man who has incestuous relations with his daughter Clara. To protect himself from disgrace, after Clara's husband learns her secret, Hirsch strangles both and throws their bodies into an Italian lake. He then flees to Africa and sends for Rachel, his former mistress.

Clara Hirsch, who marries Rachel's brother. When she sends for her father to join her and her husband in Italy, she creates a situation that results in her death.

Meynestrel (may-nehs-TREHL), an international Socialist leader burned to death when the plane from which he and Jacques are distributing antiwar leaflets crashes in France.

THE WORLD'S ILLUSION
(Christian Wahnschaffe)

Author: Jakob Wassermann (1873-1934)
First published: 1919
Genre: Novel

Locale: Europe
Time: Prior to World War I
Plot: Social realism

Christian Wahnschaffe (VAHN-shahf-feh), the son of a rich German capitalist, a young man of great physical courage. He lives and travels in the best European society. Through his association with a refugee Russian revolutionary, Christian becomes convinced of the futility of his idle life. Despite family opposition, he gives up his inheritance to become a poor man, going about helping the unfortunates of the world.

Bernard Crammon, Christian's aristocratic friend and traveling companion in his luxurious and leisurely life.

Eva Sorel (AY-vah soh-REHL), a dancer of whom Christian becomes enamored. She finally gives herself to him, but by this time his growing idealism has dulled his sensual interests, and the affair does not last long.

Ivan Becker (EE-vahn), a Russian revolutionary. He introduces Christian to the problems of poverty.

Amadeus Voss (ah-mah-DAY-ews fos), a young man who once studied for the priesthood. He adds to Christian's conviction that his life is futile. Voss expects to gain wealth from the association, and he proves disloyal when Christian actually goes about giving his fortune back to the family.

Karen Engelschall (EHN-gehl-shahl), a prostitute whom the liberalized Christian befriends. She also expects to profit handsomely from the association, and she thinks Christian mad when he gives up his wealth.

Denis Lay, an English nobleman and Christian's rival for Eva's affections. Lay dares Christian to compete in a swimming contest with him. He drowns despite Christian's efforts to save him.

The Grand Duke Cyril, of St. Petersburg, who wishes to lay everything he can command at Eva's feet. She refuses him and returns to Western Europe to become Christian's mistress.

THE WOULD-BE GENTLEMAN
(Le Bourgeois Gentilhomme)

Author: Molière (Jean-Baptiste Poquelin, 1622-1673)
First published: 1671
Genre: Drama

Locale: Paris, France
Time: The seventeenth century
Plot: Comedy of manners

Monsieur Jourdain (zhohr-DAHN), a rich, forty-year-old tradesman. Ashamed of and denying his father's occupation, he tries to pass as a gentleman through elaborate spending of his wealth. He has a "sweet income and visions of nobility and grandeur," says his music master, "though he is an ignorant cit." In addition to his music master, he has also in attendance a dancing master, a fencing master, and a philosophy master, and through their instructions he hopes to ape persons of quality. He wants concerts every week but would add a marine trumpet to the chamber music strings. He stages elaborate serenades and fireworks to impress a marchioness. He sends her his diamond ring through a count who uses the ring and money borrowed from Jourdain to court the marchioness for himself. He is vain and childish about his fine clothes, even though he is uncomfortable in them, and he has two lackeys in attendance whom he keeps busy putting on and taking off his gown so that he can show off his new breeches and vest underneath. He is completely befuddled by the philosophy master's explanation of—and rejects instruction in—logic (he wants something prettier), morality (he wants passion whenever he wants it), and Latin, but he is entranced to learn of the placing of tongue and lips in the pronunciation of vowels and consonants and is delighted to hear that he has been speaking prose all his life. After he has heard some speech supposed to be Turkish, he apes the flowery Oriental manner in his own discourse, to the amusement of all. Because his wife realizes how ridiculous he is, he calls her names and damns her impertinence.

Madame Jourdain, his wife, a woman of rare good sense who knows that her husband is making a fool of himself and scolds him accordingly. She dislikes his parties and his guests. Her ideas concerning her daughter's marriage to Cleonte are sensible. She does not want her son-in-law to be able to reproach his wife for her parents or her grandchildren to be ashamed to call her grandmother. By taking literally the statements of the count and by replying to them, she shows a keen sense of humor. She holds the marchioness in scorn and scolds her for making a fool of Jourdain. She makes her maid her confidante and partner in her efforts to bring sense into the house.

Nicole (nee-koh-LEH), the maid, also a sensible woman and trusted by her mistress. She ridicules and laughs at Jourdain's clothes; when she cannot stop laughing, despite his commands, she requests a beating rather than choke herself trying to stop. Her bold, frank comments on Jourdain's guests earn for her blows and evil epithets from her master. Her witty gaiety is her fine quality.

Dorante (doh-RAHNT), a count who flatters Jourdain and calls him his friend. He offers to get Jourdain admitted to court entertainments. These attentions enable him to borrow money from Jourdain, pay his numerous bills, and make gifts to the marchioness he is wooing, even to the point of using Jourdain's diamond ring as a gift to the lady from himself. He is a clever trickster who avails himself of every opportunity that Jourdain's foolishness provides.

Cleonte (klay-OHNT), a young man in love with Jourdain's daughter but despised by her father because of his ordinary birth, though favored by her mother as a sensible fellow eminently suitable as a son-in-law. With noble frankness, he admits his army service and his working parents, and he says that he neither is nor pretends to be a gentleman. He is sincere in his love, and after a lovers' misunderstanding is upset until both he and his servant, with whom he is friendly, are reconciled with their loves.

Covielle (koh-VYEHL), a servant to Cleonte, in love with and loved by Nicole. When he and Cleonte make up an amusing inventory of their beloveds' qualities and shortcomings, Covielle speaks out boldly to his master on the subject. It is Covielle who plans and stages the farcical "Son of the Great Turke" masquerade that unites the lovers. Even Dorante is impressed by his cleverness and subtlety.

Lucile (lew-see-LYAH), the daughter of the Jourdains. Because of her love for Cleonte, she refuses to marry her father's choice of a husband, a real gentleman. Her happy turn of wit is shown in her clever play with Nicole about their feelings for Cleonte and Covielle.

Dorimène (doh-ree-MEHN), a marchioness and a widow, loved by Dorante. Although she has accompanied him to Jour-

dain's house, she does not favor going because she knows nobody there. Although Madame Jourdain, on her surprise entrance at a dinner Monsieur Jourdain is giving to impress the nobility, rails at her, she blames Dorante for the unpleasantness. She finally and sensibly decides to marry Dorante before he ruins himself with the many gifts he brings her.

A music master,

a dancing master,

a fencing master, and

a philosophy master, Jourdain's tutors, who rail at and ridicule one another. At the same time, they ridicule Jourdain and similar dupes. All are vain of their own arts.

A master tailor, who is clever at turning aside Jourdain's complaints about the clothes made for him by saying that the colors and patterns, as well as the tight shoes, are the fashion among gentlemen.

A journeyman tailor, who is clever at getting money from Jourdain by raising him in rank with each remark addressed to him.

WOYZECK

Author: Georg Büchner (1813-1837)
First published: 1879
Genre: Drama

Locale: Germany
Time: Early nineteenth century
Plot: Psychological realism

Friedrich Johann Franz Woyzeck (FREE-drihkh YOH-hahn frahnts VOY-tsehk), a superstitious, slow-witted peasant conscripted as a fusilier in the German army. He is devoted to his sweetheart and their small son. To earn money to support them, he does many menial jobs, including shaving the Captain. He attributes his low moral standards to his poverty and lack of education. He has strange visions and is driven out of his mind by his mistress' infidelity. He kills her and then drowns accidentally while trying to get rid of the murder weapon.

Andres (AHN-drehs), a matter-of-fact soldier and Woyzeck's friend.

Marie, Woyzeck's mistress and the mother of his little boy. A hearty, earthy person, she takes the Drum Major as her second lover, defying Woyzeck when he discovers her infidel-

ity. She is murdered by Woyzeck after he sees her dancing with the Drum Major at an inn.

The Drum Major, Marie's second lover. A swaggering, powerful man, he beats Woyzeck badly in a fight over Marie.

The Captain, Woyzeck's commander. He teases Woyzeck about being a cuckold, thereby arousing Woyzeck's suspicions about Marie.

The Doctor, an eccentric. He pays Woyzeck to submit to absurd medical experiments. He finds Woyzeck laughable and makes the man appear ridiculous in front of others.

Karl, a loafer in the garrison town. He says, before Marie's murder, that he smells blood on Woyzeck.

Kaethe (KAY-teh), a girl at the inn in the garrison town. She is the first to notice that Woyzeck has blood on his hands after he has murdered Marie.

A WREATH FOR UDOMO

Author: Peter Abrahams (1919-   )
First published: 1956
Genre: Novel

Locale: London, southern France, and the country Panafrica
Time: The 1950's
Plot: Political realism

Michael Udomo (ew-DOH-moh), a Panafrican who leads his country's opposition to colonialism. A central characteristic of Udomo is that, even while a doctoral student in England, he is devoted to his country's liberation. A major part of Udomo's character is his leadership of the rebel African People's Party on returning to Panafrica. As party leader and later as prime minister, Udomo reveals his personality as a political rebel: He is opposed to tribalism, associating it with factionalism and colonialism; he is in favor of modernization of Africa; and he feels that to achieve this goal, help from the colonialists will be needed. These views are important in moving the plot along to other Panafricans' opposition to them.

Udomo is shown to be a charismatic leader who meets with conflict in his ideas of how to build Panafrica after the end of colonialism.

Tom Lanwood, a veteran revolutionary and political theorist from Panafrica who is nearing sixty years of age. While Udomo is in England, Lanwood is his idol for his dedication to revolution. After Udomo's rise to power in Panafrica, when Lanwood returns, it is clear to Udomo that thirty years in England have made Lanwood woefully out of touch with the reality of the Panafrican situation. Lanwood, for example, believes that total Africanization of workers is needed, whereas Udomo and Mhendi both believe that European know-how is necessary, because the Panafrican people have not been adequately educated or prepared for total Africanization. Lanwood serves at least two purposes in advancing the plot: in showing Udomo's growth from idol worshiper to leader who figuratively leaves his idol behind, and in making clear yet another difference of opinion Udomo faces with one of his Panafrican colleagues.

Selina (say-LEE-nah), a powerful Panafrican revolutionary. Selina is central in being able to sway women to the side of the revolutionary forces. She opposes Udomo on the questions of tribalism and Africanization. She is a staunch and uncompromising believer in both and believes that Udomo is moving much too slowly. Her disagreement with Udomo on this matter ultimately leads her to be in opposition to him.

David Adebhoy (ah-DEHY-boy), a Panafrican revolutionary who, like Selina, initially supports Udomo but who agrees with Selina's views on tribalism and Africanization. Like Selina, Adebhoy ends up being opposed to Udomo because of these matters.

Davis Mhendi (MAYN-dee), a revolutionary from Pluralia. Exiled in London as a result of a failed revolution, Mhendi returns to Africa after Udomo's rise to power in Panafrica. Mhendi is a staunch revolutionary, believing that until colonialism leaves Pluralia, he and the revolutionaries with him should do everything possible to disrupt everyday life in Pluralia, cutting power lines and derailing trains, for example. Mhendi represents the dedicated subversive. The author makes it clear that the time has not yet come for this kind of revolutionary: Udomo leads the Pluralian colonists to kill Mhendi as a means to maintain whites' support of Panafrica. Mhendi's presence both reveals the author's ideas of revolution and later shows that Udomo has been co-opted, to a degree, by white colonialists.

Paul Mabi (MAH-bee), a Panafrican artist and revolutionary. Mabi becomes especially important to Udomo because Udomo needs the support of the Panafrican mountain people, of which Mabi is one. Mabi thus comes to work quite closely with Udomo and is sympathetic to the pressures Udomo is under as a revolutionary leader.

Lois Barlow, Udomo's thirty-five-year-old white lover. At first haunted by her dead husband, Lois comes to fall in love with Udomo. During their relationship, Lois illustrates the tension between Udomo's private and political lives. Although Lois has a dream of being with Udomo forever, she realizes that his political work is more important to him and that someday she will have to let him go. Still, even as Udomo rises to power in Panafrica, he continues to be nostalgic about his interlude with her. Lois' presence in the novel helps to portray the emotional aspect of Udomo's life, in contrast to his political interests.

Maria, Mhendi's Panafrican lover. Her resemblance to his wife, who was killed after the revolution attempt in Pluralia, expedites his falling in love with her. As with Lois and Udomo, Maria's presence illustrates the importance of a political leader's private life.

Jo Furse, Lois' roommate. She briefly has an affair with Udomo, resulting in her pregnancy and abortion. This latter incident is the catalyst in Lois leaving Udomo.

— *Jane Davis*

A WREATH OF ROSES

Author: Elizabeth Taylor (1912-1975)
First published: 1949
Genre: Novel

Locale: Abingford, England
Time: A summer in the mid-1940's
Plot: Character study

Camilla Hill, an unmarried school secretary in her late thirties who usually makes no effort to enhance her pleasant-enough, blue-eyed looks and good figure. After years of lazy, serene summer holidays with her two closest friends and confidantes, Camilla is confronted this summer with their separate preoccupations: Frances Rutherford's with old age and despair, and Liz Nicholson's with marriage and new motherhood. Resentful, alienated, and increasingly aware of her own encroaching middle age and her life's sterility, Camilla is quickly becoming waspish and bitter. Casting about for stimulation, she begins a curiously unpleasant, desultory near-affair with Richard Elton, whom she meets on the train to her holiday. Camilla is violently shaken from her emotional lethargy by Richard's revelation of his horrible secret, but it is not a happy awakening.

Frances Rutherford, in her seventies, once Liz's governess, now a painter and sometime pianist. Advancing old age, worsening rheumatism, and approaching death have all darkened Frances' vision; violence and inhumanity are now the subjects of her paintings, which once delicately reflected simpler, more pleasant details of life. Frances now feels that she has wasted her life. Her resentment is expressed in her brusque treatment of Camilla and particularly Liz, to whom she devoted much of her younger life. Her anger is somewhat softened by Morland Beddoes' sympathetic, devoted admiration, so that she can finally accept her increasing need to depend on the others.

Elizabeth (Liz) Nicholson, who is girlish in appearance in her thirties. She is restless and insecure as a married woman and mother. Absorbed in the care of her baby, Harry, she is nevertheless acutely aware of Frances' testiness, Camilla's jealousy, and the impulses that compel Camilla to pursue Richard Elton, whom Liz instinctively loathes. During the holiday, Liz reconciles herself to the compromises demanded in marriage and relaxes somewhat into motherhood, gaining maturity and becoming less self-absorbed.

Richard Elton, who is probably in his mid-thirties, movie-star handsome but perceptibly weak in character. Richard is able to overcome Camilla's initial indifference to him, first when they are drawn together by their mutual witnessing of a suicide at the train station, then later with the image he creates of himself out of stories of wartime heroics, literary aspirations, and a brutal childhood—all false. He benefits from Camilla's loneliness and yearning for a romantic relationship. In reality a sadist who has recently murdered a young woman, Richard desperately tries to hold self-knowledge and horror at bay, reaching out to Camilla as a woman too strong to harm. Having lost Camilla and increasingly unnerved by Morland Beddoes' scornful scrutiny, Richard finally commits suicide, leaping into the path of an approaching train as he and Camilla had seen the stranger do.

Morland Beddoes, in his fifties, rumpled and plump, a well-established film director with a distinguished wartime military career. Captivated as a younger man by a painting of Liz by Frances, Morland has subsequently built a collection of Frances' work and has corresponded with her for years. Now he comes at last to meet Frances and stays to admire, to sympathize with, and to encourage her. Concerned for the

happiness of all three women, Morland is especially disturbed by Camilla's reckless pursuit of Richard, whom he instantly recognizes as a man with something to hide. There is hope that Morland's own attraction to Camilla may bring an end to the isolation they have both felt to varying degrees.

The Reverend Arthur Nicholson, Liz's husband and Harry's father. Both the aura of his clerical authority and his overbearing masculinity have hemmed Liz in, provoking her petulance with him. He learns to accept her growth as an individual, no longer girlish and submissive as she was when he first knew and loved her.

— *Jill Rollins*

THE WRECK OF THE "GROSVENOR"

Author: W. Clark Russell (1844-1911)
First published: 1877
Genre: Novel

Locale: The Atlantic Ocean
Time: The nineteenth century
Plot: Adventure

Mr. Coxon, the captain of the *Grosvenor*. He is a tough skipper who is hard on his crew to the point of cruelty. He even refuses to pick up survivors from one shipwreck. Later, he is forced to allow his second mate to rescue people from another wreck the *Grosvenor* meets, but he puts the mate in irons after the rescue. The crew of the ship mutinies and kills the captain.

Mr. Duckling, first mate of the *Grosvenor*. He always sides with the captain and is killed by the mutineers.

Mr. Royle, second mate of the *Grosvenor*. He is a compassionate man who does what he can for the mistreated crew. He, with the crew's help, forces the captain to permit the rescue of two survivors of a wrecked ship. After the mutiny, the muti-

neers force the mate to navigate for them. He finally rescues himself, Mary Robertson, the steward, and one loyal sailor from the ship, which sinks in a storm.

Mary Robertson, a young woman saved by Mr. Royle after a shipwreck. She and the mate fall in love and are married after they reach the shore and safety. The girl is the daughter of a wealthy owner of a shipping firm.

Mr. Robertson, Mary's father, rescued with her by Mr. Royle. He dies of natural causes aboard the *Grosvenor*.

Stevens, a sailor who leads the mutiny aboard the *Grosvenor*. He is unsuccessful in carrying out his plan to scuttle the ship with Mr. Royle and the Robertsons aboard.

THE WRECKAGE OF AGATHON

Author: John Gardner (1933-1982)
First published: 1970
Genre: Novel

Locale: Sparta, in ancient Greece
Time: The sixth century B.C.E.
Plot: Philosophical

Agathon (AG-uh-thon), a philosopher and seer, originally a native of Athens but now living in exile in Sparta. Old, fat, and balding, Agathon is considered by some a wise man; by most, he is dismissed as a public nuisance who bothers decent citizens in the streets and rails at the established order of things. A philosopher in the Socratic mode, Agathon questions all conventions and refuses to accept the prevalent systems in society, politics, and thought. His sympathy with the oppressed Helots brings him into connection with their revolt against the Spartan tyranny, but in the end, Agathon is unable to translate his moral and philosophical feelings into practical, political applications. Still, the Spartan tyrant Lykourgos realizes that Agathon is implacably opposed to his own rigid and demanding system and imprisons the seer, hoping to break his will and demonstrate the supremacy of Spartan law. Agathon is reduced to remembering the events of his past, commenting on the problem of the present, and trying to pass along what wisdom he commands to his young Helot disciple, Demodokos. Aided by the Helot rebels, Agathon escapes but soon dies of the plague while in hiding.

Demodokos, called **Peeker** by Agathon, a twenty-year-old Helot who was picked out by Agathon one day in the street to

be his follower. Although Peeker finds much that is irritating, even despicable, about his master, he is unable to break away from Agathon and travels with him loyally, even into the midst of the Helot conspiracy and then into prison. Peeker is young, skinny, and often embarrassed to be in Agathon's company; he is shamed by his master's deliberately rude, often boorish behavior, and he cannot grasp many of the philosophical meanings of Agathon's baffling riddles. Still, as the novel progresses, Peeker matures, growing in strength as Agathon weakens and becoming more compassionate as Agathon sickens. In the end, Peeker travels to Athens to seek out Agathon's wife, Tuka, and to continue his master's philosophical quest.

Tuka, Agathon's wife. Now in her sixties, she was once a beautiful woman and Agathon's childhood sweetheart. When Agathon becomes embroiled in the Helot conspiracy and his ongoing struggle against Lykourgos, Tuka returns to her native Athens, unwilling to become part of Agathon's destruction. She is strong-willed and obsessive to the point of madness, a jealous woman whose fits of anger and fury alternate strangely with gentle, harp-playing behavior.

Iona, Agathon's mistress, a leader of the Helot revolt and wife of Dorkis. In her sixties, she is a clever, determined woman, still holding to the intense beauty she had when younger. For years, she and Tuka conducted a running battle over control of Agathon; it has ended with neither of them winning. Although Iona has been Agathon's lover for years, she remains deeply devoted to her husband and to the cause of Helot freedom.

Dorkis, a Helot, friend to Agathon and husband of Iona. He is a pleasant, easygoing man in late middle age, seemingly mild in nature and perhaps even weak in character. He knows of Agathon's long-standing affair with his wife and seems to ignore it. Trusted by the Spartans as a loyal servant, Dorkis is actually a key leader in the Helot revolt and is known by the code name of Snake. When the Spartans finally discover and capture him, he is tortured and killed. He shows great bravery in his death.

Lykourgos, a tyrant and lawgiver of Sparta. A severe, one-eyed man in late middle age, he is remolding the Spartan state to be a military garrison devoid of artistic frills and intellectual curiosity. His set of laws is strict and inflexible, and his view of human society and the world leads inevitably to conflict with Agathon.

— *Michael Witkoski*

A WRINKLE IN TIME

Author: Madeleine L'Engle (Madeleine Camp, 1918-   )
First published: 1962
Genre: Novel

Locale: The northeastern United States and the planets Camazotz and Uriel
Time: The future
Plot: Fantasy

Meg Murry, the protagonist. At the age of thirteen, Meg is going through an awkward phase. Her figure is gangly and her hair stringy; she wears both braces and glasses. Moreover, she has a quick temper that marks her as "unfeminine." Because Meg is not a conventionally "good" student, her teachers assume that she is "slow." They are sadly mistaken; Meg has mastered short-cuts in mathematics. Understandably, her ability makes her stubborn and frustrated when she is asked to work problems in the traditional, roundabout way. Meg is ashamed of her faults, but as the story progresses, she learns that these "faults" are her greatest assets.

Charles Wallace Murry, Meg's younger brother. Like Meg, Charles is considered to be "slow." He seldom talks around people outside his family and did not speak at all until the age of four. When he does talk, however, his vocabulary and syntax are those of an adult. Besides being highly intelligent, Charles Wallace is thoughtful beyond his five years. In the first chapter, for example, he rises from bed during a storm to make cocoa and sandwiches for his mother and sister, who have been awakened by the thunder.

Dr. (Mr.) Murry, Meg and Charles's father. A brilliant scientist, Dr. Murry has been sent by the federal government to the planet Camazotz to rectify the wrongs in its society. When the novel begins, he has been missing for nearly a year.

Dr. (Mrs.) Murry, his wife and the children's mother. A biologist and bacteriologist, she exemplifies women who suc-cessfully combine scholarship, homemaking, and motherhood. While she conducts experiments in the laboratory affixed to her house, a stew simmers on a nearby Bunsen burner. She also shows concern over Meg's bruises and enjoys cozy moments with her family.

Sandy Murry and

Dennys Murry, the Murrys' ten-year-old twin sons. Good students and athletes, the twins fit the stereotype of "well-rounded" children.

Mrs. Whatsit, one of three supernatural beings who commission and enable the Murry children to journey to Camazotz. She assumes the guise of an elderly bag lady.

Mrs. Who, another of the supernatural beings, who appears as a plump little matron.

Mrs. Which, the third supernatural being, who materializes as a shimmer of light.

Calvin O'Keefe, Meg's friend, who accompanies her to Camazotz.

Aunt Beast, a furry, tentacled creature who nurtures Meg back to health after she passes through the near-lethal chill of the Dark Thing, an extraterrestrial embodiment of evil.

It, a huge, disembodied brain that controls the thinking of all the people on Camazotz.

— *Rebecca Stingley Hinton*

WRITTEN ON THE BODY

Author: Jeanette Winterson (1959-   )
First published: 1992
Genre: Novel

Locale: London and Yorkshire, England
Time: Late twentieth century
Plot: Picaresque

The narrator, unnamed and of unspecified gender. Significantly a professional translator, the narrator also acts as sole interpreter, through whose perspective all other characters and events are viewed. The character of the narrator is unfolded through revelations of his/her romantic and sexual exploits, which are relayed in retrospective meditations alternating among despair, cynicism, humorous self-mockery, and romantic lyricism. Although the narrator often is flippant and cynical in recalling past loves, the context within which these are related is a mournful, obsessive, and sincere account of the most recent and traumatically ended affair, with the adored Louise, who is later discovered to be dying of leukemia. The self-portrait is a mixture of romantic and sexual renegade with selfless and devoted lover. There are the other aspects of the narrator's character implicit in the narrative, rather than self-acknowledged; among these less sympathetic qualities is the casualness with which former lovers are abandoned. The narrator admits to an addiction to passion and to dismissing comfortable or contented relationships, specifically marriage, as hypocritical and deadening.

Louise, the central focus of the narrator's monologue, discussed or addressed *in absentia*. Revealed through this impassioned perspective, she is described as a pre-Raphaelite beauty with flaming red hair. The Australian is unhappily married to Elgin, a physician and cancer researcher. She is the only one of a series of married lovers of the narrator who immediately decides to leave her husband to be with her/him. Halfway through the novel, it is revealed that Louise is dying of lymphocytic leukemia. Her absence results from the fact that the narrator reluctantly has abandoned her to ensure her return to Elgin's expert care.

Elgin, Louise's husband, a physician who specializes in the treatment of cancer. Portrayed through the narrator's eyes, he appears boring, clinical, and cold. This characterization is supplemented by references to Louise expressing her disappointment in Elgin who, when she had married him, had more humane ambitions for his medicine but, seduced by fame, abandoned his original intention of practicing in the Third World in favor of research. He is the son of poor Jewish shopowners, Esau and Sarah Rosenthal. It was his mother Sarah's death from cancer that inspired Elgin to choose his particular field of medical research.

Jacqueline, the most recent of the narrator's former lovers. Jacqueline is abandoned in favor of Louise. Jacqueline works as an animal psychologist at the zoo, helping the animals to adjust to their unnatural surroundings. Physically unprepossessing, Jacqueline is portrayed as a kind and practical but unexciting person. The affair with her is presented in direct (and unflattering) contrast to the subsequent heady, obsessional passion with Louise. On being confronted with the affair with Louise, Jacqueline tears up the apartment she shared with the narrator in an uncharacteristic rage, then leaves.

Esau and
Sarah Rosenthal, Elgin's parents, Jewish shopowners.

Inge, a Dutch "anarcha-feminist," a former lover of the narrator.

Bathsheba, a married dentist, a former lover of the narrator.

Crazy Frank, the giant son of midgets, a former lover of the narrator.

Bruno, a furniture mover who finds Jesus while trapped under a wardrobe. He is a former lover of the narrator.

Gail, the manager of a Yorkshire wine bar in which the narrator temporarily works. She is both lascivious and maternal toward the narrator, encouraging him/her to search for Louise.

— *Susan Chainey*

WUTHERING HEIGHTS

Author: Emily Brontë (1818-1848)
First published: 1847
Genre: Novel

Locale: The moors of northern England
Time: 1757-1803
Plot: Love

Heathcliff, a dark-visaged, violently passionate, black-natured man. A foundling brought to the Earnshaw home at an early age, he is subjected to cruel emotional sufferings during his formative years. His chief tormentor is Hindley Earnshaw, who is jealous of his father's obvious partiality toward Heathcliff. Heathcliff endures his torment with the sullen patience of a hardened, ill-treated animal, but just as the years add age his suffering adds hatred in Heathcliff's nature, and he becomes filled with an inhuman, almost demonic, desire for vengeance against Hindley. This ambition, coupled with his strange, transcendent relationship with Catherine, Hindley's sister, encompasses his life until he becomes a devastatingly wasted human. He evaluates himself as a truly superior person who, possessing great emotional energies and capabilities, is a creature set apart from the human. Some regard him as a fiend, full of horrible passions and powers. In the end, he dies empty, his will gone and his fervor exhausted, survived by Cathy and Hareton, the conventionalists, the moralists, the victims of his vengeful wraths.

Catherine Earnshaw, the sister of Hindley, later the wife of Edgar Linton and mother of young Cathy Linton. Catherine is spirited as a girl, selfish, wild, saucy, provocative, and sometimes even wicked. She can be sweet of eye and smile, and she is often contrite for causing pain with her insolence. In childhood, she and Heathcliff form an unusually close relationship, but as her friendship with Edgar and Isabella Linton grows,

she becomes haughty and arrogant. In spite of her devotion to Heathcliff, she rejects him for fear that marriage to him would degrade her. Instead, she accepts Edgar Linton's proposal. Her deep feeling for Heathcliff remains; he is her one unselfishness, and she insists that Edgar must at least tolerate him so that her marriage will not alter her friendship with Heathcliff. Her marriage is a tolerably happy one, possibly because Catherine becomes dispirited after Heathcliff's departure as a result of her rejection. Upon his return, they become close friends again, despite his apparent vile character and foul treatment of her family. In their inhuman passion and fierce, tormented love they are lost to each other, each possessing the other's spirit as if it were his or her own. Her mind broken and anguished, Catherine finally dies in childbirth.

Hindley Earnshaw, the brother of Catherine Earnshaw, husband of Frances, and father of Hareton. As a child, he is intensely jealous of Heathcliff and treats the boy cruelly. After the death of Frances, Hindley's character deteriorates rapidly; he drinks heavily and finally dies in disgrace, debt, and degradation as the result of Heathcliff's scheme of vengeance.

Edgar Linton, the husband of Catherine and father of Cathy. A polished, cultured man, he is truly in love with Catherine and makes her happy until Heathcliff returns to Wuthering Heights. He is a steady, unassuming person, patient and indulgent of both his wife and his daughter.

Cathy Linton, the daughter of Edgar and Catherine and wife of Linton Heathcliff. A bright, spirited, and affectionate girl, she pities Linton, becomes his friend, and through the trickery and bribery of Heathcliff is forced to marry the sickly young man. She becomes sullen and ill-tempered in Heathcliff's household, but she finds ultimate happiness with Hareton Earnshaw.

Hareton Earnshaw, the son of Hindley and Frances and the object of Heathcliff's revenge against Hindley. Under Heathcliff's instruction, or rather neglect, Hareton grows into a crude, gross, and uneducated young man. Cathy, after Heathcliff's death, takes him under her charge and begins to improve his mind and manners. The two fall in love and marry.

Linton Heathcliff, the son of Heathcliff and Isabella and the husband of Cathy Linton. He is a selfish boy indulged and spoiled by his mother. After her death, he returns to live with Heathcliff and at Wuthering Heights sinks into a weak-willed existence, a victim of his father's harsh treatment. Sickly since infancy, he dies at an early age, shortly after his marriage to Cathy Linton.

Isabella Linton, the sister of Edgar, Heathcliff's wife, and mother of Linton. A rather reserved, spoiled, and often sulking young woman, she becomes infatuated with Heathcliff. In spite of her family's opposition and warnings, she runs away with him. Later, regretting her foolish action, she leaves him and lives with her son Linton until her death.

Frances Earnshaw, the wife of Hindley. She dies of consumption.

Mr. Earnshaw, the father of Catherine and Hindley. He brings Heathcliff to Wuthering Heights after a business trip to Liverpool.

Mrs. Earnshaw, his wife.

Mrs. Ellen Dean, called Nelly, the housekeeper who relates Heathcliff's history to Mr. Lockwood and thereby serves as one of the book's narrators. A servant in the household at Wuthering Heights, she goes with Catherine to Thrushcross Grange when the latter marries Edgar Linton. Some years later, she returns to live at Wuthering Heights as the housekeeper for Heathcliff. She is a humble, solid character, conventional, reserved, and patient. Although Hindley's disorderly home and Heathcliff's evil conduct distress and often appall her, she does little to combat these unnatural personalities, perhaps through lack of imagination but certainly not from lack of will, for in the face of Heathcliff's merciless vengeance she is staunch and strong.

Mr. Lockwood, the first narrator, a foppish visitor from the city and Heathcliff's tenant. Interested in his landlord, he hears Mrs. Dean relate the story of the Earnshaw and Linton families.

Joseph, a servant at Wuthering Heights. He is forever making gloomy observations and predictions about other people and offering stern reprimands for their impious behavior.

Zillah, a servant at Wuthering Heights.

Mr. Green and

Mr. Kenneth, lawyers in Gimmerton, a neighboring village.

X

XALA

Author: Ousmane Sembène (1923-   )
First published: 1973
Genre: Novel

Locale: Dakar, Senegal
Time: Early 1970's
Plot: Social realism

Abdou Kader Beyè (ah-BEW KAY-dehr BAY-yay), called **El Hadji**, a prosperous Senegalese businessman in his fifties. He is a Muslim and a polygamist, with two wives and eleven children. Ousted from his first career as schoolteacher because of his union activities under the colonial regime, he prospers with the coming of independence, moving through a succession of business ventures, not always honest and sometimes exploiting the poor. Part of the rising native bourgeoisie, he is a member of the select Group of Businessmen of Dakar, as well as of several boards. Confident, ostentatious, and pompous, he spends money lavishly on a Mercedes-Benz automobile and a chauffeur, villas for each of his spouses, European clothes, and, finally, the showy, elaborate celebration of his third marriage. Someone has cast on him a spell, the *xala*, that makes him impotent, a disgrace in his society. Only at the end, when he has tried every means to remove the spell and correct his condition, when he has lost everything—wealth, reputation, two of his wives, colleagues and friends, and property—does he learn that the spell was cast by a relative with whom he had dealt dishonestly years earlier.

The beggar, who is unrecognized as a member of Abdou Kader Beyè's clan. In spite of being picked up by the police frequently at El Hadji's request, the beggar returns consistently to the same spot opposite El Hadji's office, sitting cross-legged at the street corner and chanting in an annoying, piercing voice. It is he who finally brings about the downfall of El Hadji, to avenge his clan, which El Hadji had robbed of property years earlier.

Adia Awa Astou (ah-DEE-ah AH-wah ah-STEW), the first wife of El Hadji. An attractive woman approaching forty, Awa habitually has dressed in white since her visit to the Kaaba with her husband, as the devout Muslim she became at her marriage. In manner and speech, she is reserved, dignified, and straightforward. Fidelity to her responsibility as spouse and as mother of her six children imposes restraint and self-denial as she copes with her husband's foolishness and her children's questions. A woman of great inner strength, she refuses the solution of divorce suggested by Rama, her oldest daughter. It is Awa, with Rama, who stands beside El Hadji in his final moment of humiliation.

Oumi N'Doye (EW-mee ihn-DOH-yay), the second wife of El Hadji. She is younger than and completely different from Adia Awa Astou. Dominated by Westernized tastes, she thrives on French fashion magazines, a superficial social life, and extravagant spending. She resents her position as second wife. Jealousy and hatred of Awa motivate her demands for material advantages for her children and the elaborate measures she takes to keep El Hadji in her villa longer than the allotted time for polygamous marriage under Muslim law. When she realizes that El Hadji's bankruptcy will entail seizure of her villa, she removes everything to her parents' house before the creditors' agents arrive.

N'Gone (ihn-GOH-nay), the third wife of El Hadji. At the age of nineteen, N'Gone is pretty and pleasure-loving but has twice failed her examinations and cannot get a job. Her aunt proposes to find for her a wealthy husband. She is really a pawn, married off to El Hadji. Because he cannot consummate the marriage as a result of the *xala*, N'Gone returns eventually to her parents and associates with a young man of her own generation.

Yay Bineta (bee-NAY-tah), the twice-widowed paternal aunt of N'Gone. Physically unattractive and with a malicious expression in her eyes, this unfortunate busybody brings misfortune to others through her mischief. Through flattery, cunning, and manipulation, she inserts N'Gone into the life and attentions of El Hadji, finally succeeding in arranging the marriage that precipitates his ruin.

Rama (RAH-mah), the oldest daughter of El Hadji and Awa. A university undergraduate active in movements to conserve African values and culture, such as the Wolof language, she also reveals modern revolutionary attitudes toward what should be changed. Close to her mother by affection and respect, she advises divorce but accepts her mother's decision against it.

— *Mary Henry Nachtsheim*

XENOGENESIS

Author: Octavia E. Butler (1947-   )
First published: 1989
Genre: Novels

Locale: Chkahichdahk, a living Oankali "spaceship," and Earth
Time: Indeterminate future
Plot: Science fiction

Dawn, 1987

Lilith Iyapo, a survivor of a nuclear war that almost completely destroys Earth. Terrified to learn that her captors are aliens, Lilith gradually becomes used to the Oankali, but her fear is renewed when she realizes that they intend to breed with humans in a genetic "trade" and will no longer allow humans to breed among themselves. Lilith reluctantly agrees to awaken other humans and acclimatize them to their fate. Although she eventually cares for the Oankali, Lilith feels guilty and wonders whether she has betrayed humanity.

Nikanj, an ooloi (the Oankali third sex) specifically bred to live with humans. When Lilith's human mate, Joseph, is killed, Nikanj uses Joseph's sperm to impregnate Lilith with the first human-Oankali child.

Tate Marah, the first human awakened by Lilith. Initially Lilith's friend, Tate does nothing to prevent Joseph's death when the humans rebel against the Oankali, thus choosing to side against Lilith.

Gabriel (Gabe) Rinaldi, a human awakened by Lilith. Gabe distrusts the Oankali and convinces other humans to rebel against them.

Curt Loehr, a human who is unable to accept the Oankali. Believing that Lilith is Oankali rather than human, Curt irrationally kills Joseph, reasoning that Lilith's mate also must be an enemy.

Jdahya, the Oankali male who makes initial contact with Lilith. Jdahya helps Lilith overcome her fear of the Oankali.

Joseph Shing, Lilith's lover and mate, who is killed by Curt Loehr.

Adulthood Rites, 1988

Akin, the first human-Oankali male born to a human mother. When Akin is kidnapped by Resisters because he looks like a human baby, he begins to understand the Resisters' motivation in fighting the Oankali. Akin eventually speaks on the Resisters' behalf, asking the Oankali to restore the Resisters' fertility and allow them to settle on Mars, even though he believes humans are genetically predisposed to destroy themselves.

Tate Marah, a Resister in the village of Phoenix. Tate encourages the village to buy Akin from his kidnappers and becomes the child's closest friend. When Akin's family comes for him, Tate is tempted to join the Oankali but chooses to go to the Mars colony out of loyalty to Gabe.

Gabriel (Gabe) Rinaldi, a Phoenix Resister who treats Akin with kindness but who continues to hate the Oankali.

When Tate is severely injured, Gabe only reluctantly allows Akin to heal him because the healing necessitates intimate contact with the Oankali.

Lilith Iyapo, Akin's mother. Although she has borne and loved many human-Oankali children, Lilith still experiences moments of tremendous bitterness toward the Oankali.

Augustino (Tino) Leal, Akin's human father and a former Resister. Although Tino feels guilty about leaving his Resister village, he believes it is better to have children with the Oankali than to live a sterile, pointless existence.

Tiikuchahk, Akin's paired sibling. Because Akin and Tiikuchahk are deprived of the sibling bonding process, Tiikuchahk develops as a male instead of a female as expected, and he and Akin are not able to mate, as do most Oankali siblings.

Imago, 1989

Jodahs, the first human-Oankali ooloi. Jodahs is considered dangerous by the Oankali because it has trouble controlling its shape-changing and regenerative abilities. Jodahs finds its own human mates, proving that it has a special ability to win over humans, even those who have resisted the Oankali for more than a century.

Aaor, Jodahs' paired sibling, who also becomes ooloi. At first unable to find the human mates it needs so desperately, Aaor becomes disconsolate and almost dies, but with Jodahs' help it eventually finds human mates.

Jesusa, Jodahs' human female mate, who is part of a small hidden group of still-fertile humans. Jesusa believes that it is her duty to bear human children, even though she is afflicted with a dangerous genetic condition and most of her children will die horribly. Jodahs and its family convince Jesusa that her people's suffering can end if they accept the Oankali.

Tomás, Jesusa's brother and Jodahs' human male mate. He is almost blind and crippled from his genetic afflictions until Jodahs heals him. Tomás accepts Jodahs more readily than does Jesusa.

Lilith Iyapo, Jodahs' mother. Lilith longs to warn Jesusa and Tomás that their mating with Jodahs will be permanent whether or not they want it to be. She keeps silent, however, because she loves Jodahs and knows that unless he finds human mates he will face exile or death.

Nikanj, Jodahs' ooloi parent, who is dismayed when Jodahs becomes ooloi. Nikanj fears that its own desire for a same-sex child has caused it to turn Jodahs into an ooloi before the Oankali are ready to face this challenge.

— *Amy Sisson*

THE YEAR OF LIVING DANGEROUSLY

Author: C. J. Koch (1932-   )
First published: 1978
Genre: Novel

Locale: Indonesia, primarily Jakarta
Time: 1965
Plot: Political

Guy Hamilton, a correspondent for ABS, an Australian news agency. Tall and handsome, Hamilton was born in England but grew up in Singapore and Australia. He becomes one of the best newsmen in Jakarta, Java. He and Billy Kwan have a successful partnership as well as a friendship. He falls in love with Jill Bryant but nearly betrays her, a lapse that causes Billy to break off their friendship.

Jill Bryant, a secretary at the British embassy. Emotionally vulnerable because of a failed marriage and a destructive affair, she is close to Billy, who is supportive but nonthreatening. She loves Guy and has become pregnant by him, but she believes Billy when he tells her that Guy has betrayed her.

Billy Kwan, a freelance cameraman. A half-Chinese, half-Australian dwarf, Billy, though intelligent and caring, is obsessive, controlling, and emotionally unstable. He chooses Guy as a friend and partner, helping him to get started in Jakarta. He idealizes Guy and Jill and believes that he has arranged their love affair; perhaps he has. He also idealizes President Sukarno, believing him to be the savior of his people. When Billy's delusion becomes apparent, he stages a political protest during which he is killed. He keeps dossiers on subjects and people. The narrator uses these to fill in the gaps in his own knowledge.

Wally O'Sullivan, a correspondent for a Sydney newspaper. The unofficial head of the press corps in Jakarta, the overweight Wally presides over the gatherings in the hotel bar. When Wally is deported because of his taste for Indonesian young men, it is generally believed that Billy betrayed him.

Pete Curtis, a Canadian journalist who works for *The Washington Post*. Curtis is Hamilton's main competition, and they are friendly rivals. Curtis is not very sensitive to others and often visits Indonesian prostitutes.

Colonel Ralph Henderson, a military attaché at the British embassy. His *pukka sahib* demeanor suggests the remnants of the British Empire. He, too, is attached to Jill.

Kumar, Hamilton's Indonesian assistant, a member of the PKI, the Indonesian Communist Party. Kumar arranges a meeting between Guy and Vera Chostiakov. Kumar acutely perceives the Western advantages that his country lacks.

Vera Chostiakov, a cultural attaché at the Soviet embassy. She uses her sexual attractiveness to try to get information from Guy about a Chinese arms shipment to the PKI. Her play for Guy leads Billy to believe Guy to be false.

Sukarno, the Indonesian president. A charismatic man, he attempts to build a powerful Indonesian self-image but eventually loses touch with his people and lets political schemes overtake him.

Ibu, an Indonesian woman. Ibu (which means "mother" in Indonesian) represents the poor for Billy, and her fate impels Billy to undertake his rebellion against Sukarno.

R. J. Cook, the narrator, a correspondent for a news agency. A divorced, lapsed Catholic, he becomes confessor, or confidant, to the members of the press corps. His knowledge of his colleagues, combined with information from Billy's files, allows him to write this account.

— Karen M. Cleveland

THE YEAR OF THE DRAGON

Author: Frank Chin (1940-   )
First published: 1981
Genre: Drama

Locale: San Francisco's Chinatown
Time: The 1970's
Plot: Social

Fred Eng, a Chinese American travel agent and tourist guide, head of Eng's Chinatown Tour 'n Travel. Fred, the eldest son of Pa Eng, is in his forties, unmarried, and balding. Born in China and brought by Pa to San Francisco when an infant, Fred feels neither Chinese nor fully assimilated American Chinese. His job, which he despises, makes him conform to the American stereotype of the Chinese American, epitomized in the play by the American film character Charlie

Chan. Although he must live and work in San Francisco's Chinatown, Fred hates the place. When in school, he apparently had promise as a writer, but he has lost sight of his dream to become one. Torn between his desire for his own life and his responsibilities to his family, Fred hates himself and the life he feels compelled to live. In the play's main action, the family members have gathered at their Chinatown home in San Francisco to celebrate the Chinese New Year, which is likely to be the dying Pa's last. Fred wants to get Ma and Johnny to leave San Francisco's Chinatown after Pa's death and move to Boston with Sis. He tries to get Pa to tell them to go, but the old man refuses and dies during a struggle with Fred. Fred remains in Chinatown, even though he hates it, because the San Francisco Chinatown is the only place he feels he belongs.

Wing Eng, called **Pa**, the father of Fred, Sis, and Johnny, and the honorary mayor of San Francisco's Chinatown. A stylish but conservative dresser, Pa is a China-born Chinese man in his sixties. He has been in the United States since 1935 and regards San Francisco's Chinatown as his home. He is dying of a lung disease. As the play's action demonstrates, Pa is at times brutally autocratic and selfish, but he is loved by his children and wife. Pa clearly depends on Fred but also abuses him and considers him a failure. He refuses to see Fred as an individual and spurns Fred's request that he tell Johnny and Ma to move to Boston. Pa's love-hate relationship with Fred dramatizes the play's central conflict.

Hyacinth Eng, called **Ma**, a Chinese American in her middle or late fifties. Ma is Pa's second wife (his American wife) and the mother of Sis and Johnny. She is proud of being born and reared American and of her mission-school education. Ma loves her home and family. She fears change but is aware that her family is drifting apart. Maniacally efficient, practical, and irrational, Ma attempts to escape moments of stress by going to the bathroom or bursting into song and dance. For Pa, whom she loves, she plays the role of a Chinese woman, though not successfully. Through Ma, the audience discerns historical discrimination against Chinese in the United States.

Johnny Eng, the younger brother of Fred, a Chinese American in his late teens. Johnny is a Chinatown street kid, on probation for carrying a gun. Although he is an alienated youth, Johnny believes in the Chinese family. He wants to stay in Chinatown and help Fred with his tour business. He therefore resists Fred's attempts to make him move to Boston and live with his sister, Sis.

Mattie, called **Sis**, a Chinese American, the married daughter of Ma and Pa Eng. Sis is middle class in dress and manners. She has married a white American, has moved out of Chinatown, and is having commercial success in Boston as a Chinese cook, under the pseudonym **Mama Fu Fu**. She has just published a cookbook that promises to be a success. She hates Chinatown and has returned only at the request of her dying father. Sis is a fully assimilated Chinese American.

Ross, Mattie's Caucasian husband. A sincerely interested and admiring student of all things Chinese, Ross is aesthetic, supercilious, and pleasant. Unlike Ma, Fred, Sis, and Johnny, Ross reads Chinese. In the play's main action, Ross represents the majority white culture in the United States, which admires the Chinese culture yet does not understand the difficulties of the Chinese adjustment to life in the United States.

China Mama, an old woman, Pa Eng's China-born Chinese wife. She is Fred's biological mother, whom Pa left behind when he immigrated with Fred to the United States. Pa has brought China Mama to America so that he may die "Chinese." Near the end of the play, her presence incites Ma to try to act like a Chinese-born woman to please Pa Eng.

— *James W. Robinson, Jr.*

YEAR OF THE UNICORN

Author: Andre Norton (1912-   )
First published: 1965
Genre: Novel

Locale: Another world
Time: After the war with Alizon
Plot: Science fiction

Gillan, the protagonist and narrator. An orphan reared in Abbey Norstead, Gillan is about twenty years old and without a home or social status. She elects to become a bride of a Were-Rider, a member of an efficient but strange group of men from a magical and threatening land called the Waste. The Were-Riders fought for High Hallack, where Gillan lived, and claimed thirteen brides for their services if they won the war against Alizon. Gillan discovers many secrets of the group she enters and discovers myriad unknown strengths in herself and her husband.

Kildas, a bride of the Were-Riders who is slightly more aware and kind than the others. Generally, the brides are a passive, mindless group who are easily controlled by the Weres, who employ magic to manage them.

Herrel, the Wronghanded, a Were-Rider who takes on

animal shapes. He is the future husband of Gillan. He has a low standing with the Were-Riders at the start of the novel, but it apparently improves as he learns to accept himself and to love Gillan. He reveals his "animal" persona to Gillan, but to his surprise he does not lose her love.

Halse, the Strongarmed, an enemy of Herrel who was not claimed as a husband by a young maid. He is arrogant, physically strong, a powerful sorcerer, and a leader of many Were-Riders. He despises and envies Herrel, who has a growing self-possession and respect within the Weres.

Hyron, the captain of the Were-Riders, who grudgingly includes Herrel within the group. He appears to enforce the rules of the Weres, but he is frustrated by the laws and the demands for justice made by Gillan and Herrel.

— *Mary Jo Deegan*

THE YEARLING

Author: Marjorie Kinnan Rawlings (1896-1953)
First published: 1938
Genre: Novel

Locale: Florida scrub country
Time: Late nineteenth century
Plot: Regional

Jody Baxter, a young Florida boy. A lover of animals, of play, and of the excitement of hunting, Jody is a child at the

beginning of the story. Matured by the experiences of one year—his father's illnesses, the death of Fodder-wing, and the killing of Flag—Jody is at the end of the novel ready to accept the responsibilities that come with growing up. One of the most appealing and believable boys in American fiction, Jody deserves comparison with Tom Aldrich, Tom Sawyer, Huck Finn, and Stephen Crane's Whilomville boys.

Ezra "Penny" Baxter, his father, a friend and companion to his son, who idolizes him. Penny's diminutive size only increases Jody's admiration of his father's ability to hunt and work hard for a plain living. Penny possesses scrupulous honesty and a simple philosophy of life that he attempts to pass on to his son. Both father and son are drawn to the beauty of the rich and varied natural world about them.

Ora "Ma" Baxter, Jody's mother, a bulky woman considerably larger than her husband. She loves Jody but is annoyed by his "wasting" time and is unwilling to forgive Flag for his depredations.

Fodder-wing Forrester, Jody's crippled friend, a frail boy who loves and has a way with animals, especially those that, like himself, have been crippled through no fault of their own. He dies shortly after naming Flag for Jody.

Oliver Hutto, Penny's friend, whose courtship of Twink causes him to be beaten by the Forrester boys and whose marriage results in the vengeful burning of his mother's home.

Grandma Hutto, his mother, a friend of the Baxters.

Twink Weatherby, Oliver's yellow-haired sweetheart and later his wife.

Lem Forrester, the older brother of Fodder-wing. He is jealous and fiercely resentful of Oliver's love for and marriage to Twink.

Buck Forrester, another Forrester brother who helps the Baxters after Penny is bitten by a rattlesnake.

Flag, Jody's beautiful but mischievous and destructive pet fawn. He is wounded when Mrs. Baxter, in anger, shoots him because of the destruction he has caused. Jody sorrowfully shoots him again to end his suffering. Flag's growing up partly parallels Jody's. Flag fails to adapt his irresponsible ways to life with the Baxters and dies as a result. Jody rebels at first against life's ways but at last submits and learns to accept the sorrows of life with its joys.

Pa and

Ma Forrester, rough but good-hearted parents of the exclusively male Forrester brood.

Mill-Wheel,

Gabby,

Pack, and

Arch Forrester, four of their sons.

Doc Wilson, the physician who attends Penny during his illnesses.

Old Slewfoot, a giant black bear that raids the Baxter hogs. He is finally killed by Penny.

Nellie Ginright, the owner of the canoe in which Jody flees after Flag's death.

THE YEARS

Author: Virginia Woolf (1882-1941)
First published: 1937
Genre: Novel

Locale: London, England
Time: 1880-1937
Plot: Domestic realism

Colonel Abel Pargiter, a solid, middle-class, retired army officer, father of the family whose progress through the years is traced in fragmentary episodes from 1880 to 1937. Lonely and purposeless, he sits in his club, goes to the city, visits his mistress, Mira, and returns to his genteel but rather shabby home on Abercorn Terrace, where his wife lies ill of a lingering illness and his children are gathered for tea. Mrs. Pargiter dies that night. All his children but one leave for lives of their own. The exception is Eleanor, with whom the colonel lives in the same pattern until his death some thirty years later.

Eleanor Pargiter, Colonel Abel Pargiter's eldest daughter. Naturally cheerful, efficient, and given to social work, she is, at the age of twenty-two, the mainstay of the family during her mother's lingering illness. After her mother's death, she continues to live with her father as his housekeeper and companion, staying with him until he dies when she is fifty-five years old. She sells the house on Abercorn Terrace and goes to live alone between her travels abroad. When she is over seventy, she still finds life a continual discovery and enjoys the prospects of a bright new day.

Edward Pargiter, Abel's scholarly son. As a student at Oxford, he is in love with Kitty Malone, who refuses him. He later becomes a Greek scholar of considerable distinction.

Morris Pargiter, Abel's not-too-successful barrister son.

Delia Pargiter, Abel's daughter. Rebellious and resentful of the restrictions imposed by her mother's illness, she longs to escape the ties of home. She dreams of herself on the political platform with her hero, Charles Parnell. Later, under the illusion that he is a wild Irish rebel, she marries handsome, conventional Patrick.

Milly Pargiter, Abel's daughter. She marries Hugh Gibbs, with whom she lives on an estate in the country. Obese and unimaginative in their later years, they appear gross and tiresome to the younger generation.

Rose Pargiter, Abel's youngest daughter. Always a firebrand with a love for causes, she joins the suffragette movement and is imprisoned for the cause. With the years, she grows stout and deaf but never loses her air of independence.

Martin Pargiter, Abel's youngest son. As a young man, he joins the army, which he detests. He retires as a captain and returns to London to live alone in a flat.

North Pargiter, Morris Pargiter's son. After service in World War I, he lives in lonely isolation on a sheep farm in Africa. He returns to the greater loneliness of crowded London and ponders what it is that so separates human beings from one another.

Peggy Pargiter, Morris Pargiter's daughter, who lives in loneliness as a doctor.

Sir Digby Pargiter, Colonel Abel Pargiter's brother, a public servant.

Maggie Pargiter, Sir Digby Pargiter's elder daughter, who becomes happily married to a Frenchman named René.

Sara Pargiter, Sir Digby Pargiter's sensitive, crippled

younger daughter. After her sister Maggie's marriage, she lives alone in a shabby flat.

Kitty Malone, a cousin of the Pargiter family. As a young girl, she is loved by Edward Pargiter but marries her mother's choice, the wealthy, fashionable Lord Lasswade. As the years go by, she reflects on the changes they bring and wonders who is right and who is wrong in the choices people make. She finds a measure of peace when she escapes, alone, to the country, where time seems to stand still.

Crosby, the Pargiters' faithful servant at the house on Abercorn Terrace.

Mira, Colonel Abel Pargiter's lower-class mistress.

Eugenie, Sir Digby Pargiter's handsome, frivolous wife.

Hugh Gibbs, Milly Pargiter's husband.

Lord Lasswade, Kitty Malone's husband.

Celia, Morris Pargiter's wife.

Patrick, Delia Pargiter's Irish husband.

René (Renny), Maggie Pargiter's French husband.

Nicholas Pomjalovsky, the Polish friend of Eleanor, Sara, and Maggie Pargiter.

Miss Craddock, Kitty Malone's eccentric history teacher.

YELLOW BACK RADIO BROKE-DOWN

Author: Ishmael Reed (1938-   )
First published: 1969
Genre: Novel

Locale: Yellow Back Radio (a town in the Old West) and Washington, D.C.
Time: 1801-1809
Plot: Satire

The Loop Garoo Kid, a black circus cowboy, an American Hoo-Doo manifestation of Lucifer. His evil reputation, however, is unwarranted: He identifies himself as "the cosmic jester," an eternal pleasure principle. A member of the divine family, he is now sought by the Christian God as the only one who can prevent the unhealthy domination of the eternal goddess, who appears variously as his former girlfriend Diane (the Roman goddess Diana) and the Virgin Mary.

Drag Gibson, a wealthy and powerful rancher, Loop Garoo's nemesis. He started with nothing, riding drag (hence his name, though it also implies transvestitism) for other cattlemen, but he amassed a fortune through his cunning and ruthlessness. Drag also is a supernatural character: The explorers Lewis and Clark appear near the middle of the novel and reveal that Drag has escaped from hell. His struggle with Loop Garoo is therefore a form of the eternal struggle between good and evil.

Mustache Sal, Drag's wife, formerly Loop Garoo's girlfriend. Sal marries Drag in answer to a personal ad, motivated by the opportunity to inherit his wealth. She crawls before Loop on the night before her wedding, begging to have sex with him. Instead, Loop brands a hell's bat on her abdomen.

Chief Showcase, an American Indian, Drag's lackey. A cousin of Cochise, Showcase is the last surviving Crow Indian and so is kept by Drag as a literal "Showcase." Although he plays the defeated primitive or noble savage before Drag, he first appears in a high-tech helicopter, rescuing Loop Garoo from Drag's minions. Chief Showcase is the first to recognize

Loop as Lucifer, and he expresses the essential unity of the black and Native American causes and identities. His secret revenge on the white man is tobacco: With feigned civility, he offers a cigar to every enemy he encounters.

Field Marshall Theda Doompussy Blackwell, an army general. He is identified as President Thomas Jefferson's secretary of defense, though no such title existed in Jefferson's time. With Pete the Peek, he develops a plan to conquer the American West and set himself up as emperor. Theda is depicted as a stereotypical Pentagon hawk: He wheedles money from Congress through Pete the Peek and lavishes it on scientists (Harold Rateater and Dr. Coult) who develop new weapons for him.

Pete the Peek, a congressman, Theda's lover. He is called "The Peek" because he is a voyeur. Theda treats him as a stooge, apparently interested only in the federal appropriations Pete brings him.

Pope Innocent, putatively Loop Garoo's rival, to whom Drag appeals for help. Innocent recalls the days before Loop's estrangement from the Judeo-Christian God and pleads for him to return. The novel ends with Loop's reunion with Innocent on his ship bound for Europe. There were no popes named Innocent in the nineteenth century, so this character is one of the many anachronisms in the novel. He represents the ageless church as partner/nemesis of Loop Garoo, rather than a historical individual.

— John R. Holmes

A YELLOW RAFT IN BLUE WATER

Author: Michael Dorris (1945-1997)
First published: 1987
Genre: Novel

Locale: The Pacific Northwest
Time: Late 1980's
Plot: Family

Rayona Taylor, the fifteen-year-old daughter of American Indian Christine George Taylor and African American Elgin Taylor. After Rayona's parents separate, she is brought up by her alcoholic mother. When Christine becomes seriously ill as a result of her drinking, she is committed to a detoxification ward. Rayona helps her to escape, and they drive to the Montana reservation where Christine was reared. When they arrive,

Christine deserts Rayona and leaves her with Ida. Father Tom, a young Catholic priest new to the reservation, recruits Rayona into a parish youth group known as the "God Squad." He invites her to a weekend youth rally in Helena, and on the way they stop for a swim in Bearpaw Lake. Tom feigns drowning. Rayona rescues him and drags him onto a yellow raft in the middle of the lake. He makes sexual advances toward her and blames her for his actions. Appalled at his own behavior, Tom deserts Rayona, and she finds herself homeless and alone. She wanders into Bearpaw State Park and meets Sky and Evelyn. She stays with them during the summer and works on the maintenance crew at the park. At the end of the season, Evelyn and Sky drive Rayona back to the reservation to find Christine. They arrive on the day of the annual rodeo. Rayona meets her cousin, Foxy Cree. He is scheduled to ride but is too drunk. He convinces Rayona to impersonate him and ride in his place. Rayona accepts the challenge and rides Dayton Nichols' feisty horse, Babe. She is thrown three times but refuses to admit defeat and remounts. Her determination and courage win the admiration of the crowd, and the judges award her a prize. When she steps to the podium to accept, she reveals her true identity. Evelyn and Sky leave her in the care of Dayton, who takes her home to be reunited with Christine.

Christine George Taylor, Rayona's mother and the supposed daughter of Ida. Feeling unloved by Ida, craving attention, and living in the shadow of her talented brother Lee, Christine turns to men and alcohol for solace in her teenage years. Although she admires Lee, she is intimidated by him. She realizes that his reputation as an up-and-coming member of the Indian community enhances her own social position. When Lee and Dayton protest against the Vietnam War draft, Christine believes that Lee's reputation will be damaged, thereby diminishing her own social status; she convinces him to join the service. Later, Christine moves to Seattle, meets Elgin Taylor, becomes pregnant by him, and marries him. After a rocky marriage of fifteen years, Elgin leaves Christine for the last time while she is in the hospital recovering from her latest binge. Sick, hurt, and afraid, Christine drives to the Montana reservation with Rayona and leaves her with Ida. Still unwelcome at Ida's home, she moves in with Dayton.

Ida George, the mother of Lee and foster mother of Christine. Although Ida is thought to be Christine's mother and Rayona's grandmother, she actually is Christine's half-sister and cousin. When Ida's aunt Clara (her mother's sister) became pregnant by Ida's father, the family agreed to conceal the scandal by claiming that Ida was the one who was pregnant. Ida accompanied Clara, who posed as Ida's guardian, to a Catholic home for unwed mothers in Denver. After giving birth, Clara remained in Denver and Ida returned to the reservation with Christine and reared her as her own child. After the death of her parents several years later, Ida lived for a short time with disabled Korean War veteran Willard Pretty Dog, Lee's father. Ida and he separated, and she refused to acknowledge him or anyone else as Lee's father. Ida reared Lee and Christine as brother and sister, never revealing to them the truth about their parentage.

Lee George, Christine's foster brother and cousin. An accomplished rodeo rider and performer of traditional Indian dances, he is well thought of on the reservation and is expected to be a strong tribal leader. He is killed in the Vietnam War and is given a hero's burial.

Dayton Nichols, Lee's best friend. Christine, envious of his friendship with Lee, tries to seduce Dayton as a means of breaking up their relationship. He rebuffs her, and she resents him even more. Years later, after Lee's death, her illness and their common memories of Lee heal and bring them together.

Evelyn and

Sky, Rayona's surrogate parents when she works at Bearpaw State Park. Their home is the first stable environment she has known.

Father Hurlbert, a Catholic priest who becomes Ida's best friend and only confidant.

— *Pegge Bochynski*

THE YELLOW WALLPAPER

Author: Charlotte Perkins Gilman (1860-1935)
First published: 1892
Genre: Novella

Locale: New England
Time: Late nineteenth century
Plot: Social realism

The narrator, unnamed, who also is the protagonist. She is an imaginative, creative woman living in a society that views women who exhibit artistic and intellectual potential as anomalies, misfits, or, as in this story, ill. The narrator, having recently borne a child, apparently suffers from an ailment now identified as postpartum depression. Her husband, John, who is a doctor, misidentifies her condition and prescribes a "rest cure" made popular by the well-respected physician Weir Mitchell. The rest cure assumes that intellectual stimulation damages a woman physically and psychologically, so John requires the narrator to stop all writing, all reading, and essentially, all higher-level thinking. The narrator, however, cannot deny her creative imagination, so she writes in secret the document that is the novella, through which readers can trace the harmful psychological effects of the rest cure. She develops a fascination with the yellow wallpaper in their room. Her mental illness becomes more pronounced, until, finally, she openly displays madness.

John, the narrator's husband, a physician. He differs from his imaginative wife in that he believes only in what he can see

and touch. In his physical evaluation of his wife, he finds nothing wrong, so he believes she creates her own illness, that she is a hypochondriac. He enforces restrictions on his wife's conduct in an attempt to end her disturbing behavior and cure her "nervous condition." He seems to enjoy this control over her life, for his efforts extend far beyond limiting her intellectual stimulation. He chooses in which room she will live, whom she may see, and how she spends her time. He counters every desire his wife expresses with a measure keeping her from fulfilling her wish. He places himself in a superior, paternal position from which he denies the validity of the narrator's perception of her own experiences and well-being. His medical practice keeps him away from home for sufficient time to allow the narrator to develop a subversive routine of writing and, eventually, obsessive rituals centered on the yellow wallpaper in their room.

Jennie, John's sister, who serves as housekeeper and helps John observe and limit the narrator's behavior. Jennie appears bound by her brother's concrete view of the world, though she is the only person in the story besides the narrator who actually looks at the wallpaper, seemingly in an attempt to understand the fascination it holds for the narrator. Although Jennie ultimately aligns herself with her more rational brother, her willingness to explore the possibility of irrational explanations for the narrator's behavior makes her a slightly more sympathetic character than John.

Weir Mitchell, the doctor who popularized the rest cure, only briefly referred to in the story but significant nevertheless. This character was not a literary invention but a real figure in the author's life. In 1887, S. Weir Mitchell treated the author for a "nervous condition" at his Philadelphia sanatorium; the treatment was unsuccessful and harmful.

— *Amy E. Hudock*

THE YEMASSEE: A Romance of Carolina

Author: William Gilmore Simms (1806-1870)
First published: 1835
Genre: Novel

Locale: South Carolina
Time: Early eighteenth century
Plot: Adventure

Gabriel Harrison (Governor Charles Craven), a young man of commanding presence and gay, worldly manner. A stranger looked on with suspicion by some of the South Carolina frontiersmen, he wins them over through his valiant leadership in defending the colony against the Yemassee uprising. He then reveals that he is the new governor of the province in disguise.

Parson Matthews, who dislikes Harrison until won over by his heroism. Matthews' insistence on the friendliness of the Indians, in spite of Harrison's warnings, results in his and his daughter's capture and in their subsequent rescue by Harrison.

Bess Matthews, the parson's daughter, who is in love with and loved by Harrison. The parson finally gives permission for their marriage.

Hector, Harrison's devoted slave and constant companion. After undergoing various ordeals on behalf of or with his master, he refuses Harrison's offer to give him his freedom.

Sanutee, the last great Yemassee chief. Proud and suspicious of the increasing encroachments of the colonists on Yemassee territory, he rouses his people to cast out the land-selling chiefs and to make war on the settlers. He is killed in battle.

Occonestoga, Sanutee's son, a drunkard. He is friendly with the whites, an alliance that forces him to flee his tribe. He

saves Bess Matthews' life and is consequently befriended by Harrison. Returning to the Indian stronghold to spy for Harrison, he is discovered by his father.

Matiwan, Sanutee's wife, who is torn between loyalty to her husband and devotion to her son. Finally, to prevent the carrying out of Sanutee's order that Occonestoga have the tribal mark cut from his skin and be executed, she kills her son.

Hugh Grayson, a rival of Harrison for the affections of Bess Matthews. He, too, is finally won to friendship by Harrison's bravery. After revealing himself as the governor, Harrison makes Hugh Grayson commander of the garrison forces.

Walter Grayson, Hugh's brother, an honorable young farmer.

Dick Chorley, a sailor whom Harrison discovers to be a Spanish agent come to arm the Indians against the English settlers.

Ishiagaska, another Yemassee chief.

Enoree Mattee, an Indian prophet who aids Sanutee in rousing his people against the settlers.

Granger, a trader.

Mrs. Granger, his brave and quick-witted wife.

Dugdale, Harrison's strong and faithful dog.

YONNONDIO: From the Thirties

Author: Tillie Olsen (1913-   )
First published: 1974
Genre: Novel

Locale: A Wyoming mining town, a South Dakota farm, and Omaha, Nebraska
Time: The 1920's
Plot: Realism

Anna Holbrook, who is married to Jim and is the mother of Mazie, Will, Ben, the baby Jim, and baby Bess, born later in the story. Early in her life, Anna is as strong as a bull, with black eyes and black hair. After a move to a Dakota farm, she gives birth in March to Bess and develops health problems, culminating in a severe miscarriage when Bess is four months old, after they have moved back to town in Colorado. She eventually feels better and is again in command of her children and her life. She tries to achieve a better life for her children, wanting them to secure an education and getting a library card for them. When she learns of the importance of hygiene and good diet, she attempts to provide these. She and the family enjoy good times in the country summer and out walking in Denver. At the end of the book, after a heat wave with the temperature in the hundreds for days, she notices that the "air's

changen" and sees that tomorrow it will become tolerable. The title is taken from the poem "Yonnondio" by Walt Whitman, which refers to those, like Anna, of whom eventually nothing remains, no picture or poem.

Jim Holbrook, Anna's blue-eyed husband and the father of the five children. He works in the dangerous coal mines in Wyoming. The hard life leads him to drink occasionally, but finally he takes his family to a Dakota farm. After a year of hard work, they get nothing and lose their animals. They then take the train to Denver, their hometown, from which they have been away seven years. Here Jim hopes for a job in the slaughterhouses, but first he works in the sewers, eventually getting a fine forty-five-cent-an-hour position. To him, a job is God, and praying is not enough. Because of his difficult circumstances, he is at times harsh to his wife and children, yet basically he is a loving husband and father.

Mazie Holbrook, the oldest of five children, between six and a half and nine years old during the story. A thin, now rather homely child, not doing well in school and often with sadness in her heart, she is nevertheless effective at mothering the younger children, both at the beginning of the story and later, when her mother is not well. Later in the story, she is more independent, enjoying play and exploring the neighborhood. Partly because a crazed, drunken man almost kills Mazie, her father decides that the family will leave in the spring to be tenant farmers in South Dakota. There, Mazie shares the delights of clean, beautiful country life and begins school in the fall. Less happy in Denver, she eventually adjusts.

Will Holbrook, who is five years old at the opening of the story. Later, he is defiant to his mother and disrespectful to Mazie. Near the end of the book, he has, as does Mazie, a lust for sensation.

Alex Bedner and

Else Bedner, old friends of the Holbrooks in Denver. Alex has attained the high-skill job of a tool and die maker and thereby a considerable rise in living standard. A piano in the living room and a stained-glass window are evidence of the Bedners' status. Unfortunately, they have no children. The Bedners serve as foils to the prolific but impoverished Holbrooks.

— *E. Lynn Harris*

YOU CAN'T GO HOME AGAIN

Author: Thomas Wolfe (1900-1938)
First published: 1940
Genre: Novel

Locale: New York, England, and Germany
Time: 1929-1936
Plot: Autobiographical

George Webber, a young writer in the first flush of success as a novelist. He learns that success brings enemies and that success is sometimes empty of meaning. His great aim in life, idealist that he is, is to write the truth, to portray people as they are, the great and small, the rich and poor. He faces disillusionment at every turn. He finds that his fellow men are greedy after the world's goods; he finds, too, that they do not relish his truthful portrayal of them. George visits Germany, a place he loves, only to find that country filled with fear and persecution in the 1930's, during the Nazi regime. He returns home to the United States to preach, in new novels, against selfishness and greed, hoping he can awaken the people of his own land to arise and defeat the forces threatening the freedom of humankind.

Foxhall Edwards, an editor for a publishing house who becomes George Webber's friend and trusted adviser for a time. He is a genius at encouraging young writers to find themselves and acquire the confidence they need to produce literary art. He is also a skeptical person who believes that if

humans are not destined for freedom, they must accept this fact. Edwards' fatalism is at odds with George's idealistic desire to better the lot of humankind by working to change conditions. These divergent attitudes cause a break in the friendship between the two men.

Lloyd McHarg, a successful American novelist who has won worldwide fame based on a number of excellent novels. He has found fame to be empty and searches for something; he knows not what. McHarg's disillusionment is a bitter lesson for young, idealistic George Webber, for whom McHarg has been a symbol of greatness as a man of letters.

Esther Jack, an older woman who has been George's mistress in the past and becomes so again for a time after he has achieved success. He leaves her a second time when he decides that to find himself, he must leave Esther's sophisticated set and get to know the common people of the world.

Else von Kohler, a beautiful, intelligent young German woman with whom George has a tender romance while revisiting Germany during the 1930's.

YOU CAN'T TAKE IT WITH YOU

Authors: George S. Kaufman (1889-1961) and Moss Hart (1904-1961)
First published: 1937
Genre: Drama

Locale: New York City
Time: 1936
Plot: Farce

Penelope (Penny) Vanderhof Sycamore, a mother in her mid-fifties, the matriarch of a comic household, carefree and easygoing. Penny clearly loves her family and life itself. After a typewriter is mistakenly delivered to her, she drops her old hobby of painting and begins to write plays. She does both very badly, but with style and good humor.

Paul Sycamore, Penny's husband and father of the Sycamore brood. Paul has given up ordinary work to construct fireworks in his basement. He often tries them out in the center of the living room. He intends to market them, but his plans never quite work out. Paul is less involved than his wife in the lives of the children because he spends so much time in the basement.

Grandpa Martin Vanderhof, the patriarch and founder of the family's unconventional lifestyle. The Sycamore family clearly revolves around Grandpa, and his eccentric clear-sightedness saves the day more than once. One day, Grandpa left work and never returned; he spends his life now in a more productive manner, throwing darts, attending commencements, and enjoying his family.

Essie Sycamore Carmichael, the elder daughter, who is married. Essie splits her time between making new kinds of candy (successfully) and practicing to become a ballerina (unsuccessfully).

Ed Carmichael, Essie's husband. Ed plays the xylophone, operates an amateur printing press in the living room, and occasionally peddles Essie's candies.

Alice Sycamore, the younger daughter, in her early twenties. Alice is the only normal person in the Sycamore family. She works in an office on Wall Street and has no unusual hobbies. She is devoted to her outlandish family, however, and generally approves of their lifestyles. Alice is in love with Tony Kirby but is afraid that their families will never get along.

Anthony (Tony) Kirby, Jr., Alice's fiancé, fresh out of college and the new vice president of his father's business, where Alice works. Tony finds the Sycamores delightful, in contrast to his stodgy family, although, like Alice, he is basically a normal person.

Anthony Kirby, Sr., Tony's father. Mr. Kirby is a stereotypical Wall Street mogul: tired, worried, stiff, and bothered by indigestion. He is at first appalled by the antics of the Sycamores but comes to appreciate their "seize the day" attitude.

Rheba, the black maid. Entertaining in her own right, Rheba provides fairly objective commentary on the doings of the Sycamores.

Donald, Rheba's boyfriend. Donald is on relief and wanders around the Sycamore house in his bathrobe, but he, too, appears more normal than the white people around him.

Mr. De Pinna, an iceman who came to make a delivery eight years earlier, fell under the Sycamores' spell, and has stayed ever since. Mr. De Pinna is Paul's assistant in the basement fireworks factory and models for Penny's paintings.

— *Evelyn Romig*

YOU KNOW ME AL: A Busher's Letters

Author: Ring Lardner (1885-1933)
First published: 1916
Genre: Novel

Locale: Chicago, Illinois
Time: c. 1915
Plot: Satire

Jack Keefe, a right-handed White Sox pitcher. In his letters to Al, Jack gives a full account of his adventures; he also reveals himself to be a shameless braggart and chronic self-excuser. With complete lack of reticence, he discusses his foolish episodes with his girlfriends, his troubles with his baseball career, and later his marital misadventures and his in-law troubles. Jack is a powerful pitcher, but his laziness, alibis, stinginess, and egotistical gullibility make him the rather pathetic hero of this satire.

Al Blanchard, Jack Keefe's correspondent, patronized and used by Jack. Al is the recipient of the letters that elaborate every detail of the pitcher's life. Apparently, Al never does see through Jack.

Florrie, Jack's wife and Allen's sister-in-law. Disgusted with Jack's stinginess, Florrie leaves him when he is sold to Milwaukee. She rejoins him when she learns she is pregnant. She names the baby after Allen.

Allen, Jack's brother-in-law, also a pitcher.

Marie, Allen's wife.

Violet, a girlfriend who abandons Jack when he is sent back to the minor league.

Hazel, another girlfriend, who marries a boxer.

Al, Jack's son.

YOU MUST REMEMBER THIS

Author: Joyce Carol Oates (1938-   )
First published: 1987
Genre: Novel

Locale: A city in upstate New York
Time: The 1950's
Plot: Psychological realism

Enid Maria Stevick, the youngest daughter of Hannah and Lyle Stevick. Although only fifteen years old, she embarks on a clandestine love affair, with her father's half brother Felix. This secret, obsessional relationship undermines her already precarious sense of self, which is split into two parts. The first self is Enid Maria, the "A" student, obedient daughter, and talented musician; the second self is called "Angel-face" and is a wild, daring sensualist whose erotic wishes draw her closer and closer to madness and death. As a result of her split personality, Enid is drawn to the charismatic Felix as if by powers beyond her control. It is Angel-face who is attracted to transgression, criminality, and sneaky thrills. She grows in power and knowledge during the affair with the dangerous, violent Felix. This is an intense sexual relationship from which cruelty is inseparable and that overcomes Enid as a kind of sickness. She is thrown into even greater turmoil when she discovers that she is pregnant and must undergo an abortion. When Felix breaks off the relationship, Enid attempts suicide. Enid Maria emerges from this traumatic episode determined to flee her small town and is admitted into a prestigious Roches-ter music school. It is the Angel-face side of herself who keeps various memories of the dark side of life in Port Oriskany and who tells Enid what must be remembered from the world she leaves behind.

Felix Stevick, the younger half brother of Lyle. A former professional prizefighter, Felix has a history of aggression and criminality. He had to quit the ring because he could not master his fear of death, and his character has been shaped by his experience as a boxer. For Felix, boxing means living on a purely instinctual, physical level and allowing all of his impulses to crush and to dominate to come into play. His incestuous relationship with his niece Enid, a teenage girl half his age, also is informed by the values of the boxing ring. His predatory instincts allow no room for sympathetic feeling, and he feels that he is above the demands of conventional morality. His is a love/hate relationship with Enid, begun impulsively when he was intoxicated and excited by her youthful sensuality. It takes on a life of its own that neither can control. Even outside the ring, whether with Enid or as a shady businessman whose dealings are largely with the underworld, Felix carries with him an aura of violence and is surrounded by brutality and death. His protégé, Jo-Jo Pearl, is killed in the ring because of the influence of Felix's underworld business interests. His partner, Al Samson, also becomes a victim of the mob, and Felix himself beats a pimp and in turn is savagely beaten by Jo-Jo's father. Like Enid, Felix leaves Port Oriskany, settling down with a wife somewhere else.

Lyle Stevick, a furniture dealer, husband, and father of four. He is stable, kind, and gentle but also ineffectual, even a failure. He is a great reader. When he notes that the land mass of the communist countries is larger than that of the United States, he is branded a communist sympathizer by his conservative community. Although he builds a bomb shelter in his basement to defend against the threat of nuclear warfare, Lyle ironically is unable to protect his family from what happens to them as they grow up in changing times. Although he is mild-mannered and weak, he and his wife are a model of comfortable domestic happiness, in contrast with the insanity of Enid's love affair with her Uncle Felix.

Warren Stevick, Enid's brother. He undergoes physical and mental trauma while serving in Korea and emerges as an early protester against nuclear weapons. In his idealistic devotion to Mahatma Gandhi and Henry David Thoreau, and in his unalloyed goodness, he is another counterweight to the violent Felix.

Jo-Jo Pearl, a tough young prizefighter, and protégé of Felix. Trusting in Felix, he dies in the ring as a result of underworld manipulation.

Al Samson, Felix's increasingly erratic business partner. Together they engage in sundry shady deals. Living by the law of the underworld jungle, the increasingly weak and sickly Samson becomes the prey of other mobsters.

Hannah Stevick, Enid's mother. She organizes her life around her church, home, and children, but as a busy mother of four, she is not always in touch with her fragile youngest daughter, Enid.

— *Margaret Boe Birns*

YOUMA: The Story of a West-Indian Slave

Author: Lafcadio Hearn (1850-1904)
First published: 1890
Genre: Novel

Locale: Martinique
Time: The 1840's
Plot: Psychological realism

Youma (yew-MAH), a slave in Martinique. She is a personification of loyalty. When her childhood playmate, her mistress' daughter, asks Youma to take care of her child, Youma grants the dying woman's request. Although she finds the child irksome at times, she steadfastly cares for the little girl, even giving up marriage to fulfill her promise. At last, in a slave riot in 1848, she refuses to save her own life when her fellow slaves will not let her save the life of the child by taking it out of a burning building.

Aimée Desrivières (ay-MAY day-reev-YEHR), a white girl reared with Youma. The two love each other almost as sisters. Aimée, as she lies dying, asks Youma to become her little daughter's nurse, and the slave agrees to do what she can for the child.

Marie Desrivières, nicknamed Mayotte. She is the little child placed in Youma's care.

Gabriel (gah-BRYEHL), a field hand and slave. He loves Youma and wants to marry her. When Youma's owner refuses to permit the marriage, he offers to elope with Youma and seek freedom, but Youma refuses to abandon her care of little Mayotte.

Madame Peyronette (pay-roh-NEHT), Mme Desrivières' mother and Youma's owner. Although she intends to free Youma when the slave marries, she will not let Youma marry a field hand such as Gabriel.

Monsieur Desrivières, the husband of Aimée Desrivières. He is Gabriel's owner. At his wife's death, he is happy to see Youma take over the care of his child, for he is grief-stricken.

THE YOUNG LIONS

Author: Irwin Shaw (1913-1984)
First published: 1948
Genre: Novel

Locale: The Bavarian Alps, New York City, North Africa, England, France, and Germany
Time: 1937-1945
Plot: War

Christian Diestl (DEES-tehl), a former ski instructor, now a sergeant in the German army. Handsome, rugged, and cynical, he is determined to enjoy and to survive the war. Too worldly-wise to accept Nazi ideology but eager to prosper, he enthusiastically fights in Germany's early victories and tastes the spoils of war. As the tide of battle turns against the Nazis, Diestl prepares to save himself rather than die for a lost cause. Trapped in a concentration camp by a mutiny, he disguises himself as an inmate and kills a German officer to escape. As he flees toward Switzerland, he fatefully crosses the paths of two American soldiers.

Noah Ackerman, a university student drafted into the American infantry after the attack on Pearl Harbor. Born poor, physically slight, and Jewish, he is a target of suspicion and contempt. At boot camp, he must fight his own platoon mates, who want a scapegoat for their prejudice and an outlet for their aggression. He emerges a tough, hardened soldier who performs heroically and skillfully in combat. He fights not so that one nation can defeat another but so that ordinary citizens can live free of ideology. He is one of the soldiers whom Diestl ambushes and kills.

Michael Whitacre, a successful film and stage writer with easy duty in a photography battalion. Well off, and accustomed to comfortable living and cultured acquaintances, Whitacre enlists after a messy divorce but finds infantry life too demanding. Feeling only slight guilt, he uses his influence to secure a safer billet in the war effort. He is content to play soldier behind the lines in London while others fight and die. After being injured in an air raid because he is drunk, he meets Ackerman and is moved by the man's loyalty to his platoon. Following Ackerman to France, Whitacre experiences real combat for the first time. After Diestl kills Ackerman in the ambush, Whitacre stalks and slays the stormtrooper.

Hope Plowman, Ackerman's wife. She is a sensitive, sensible, and sensuous woman attracted by Ackerman's sincerity and intelligence. Over the objections of her Protestant parents, she marries him. Through her, Ackerman learns to express his passionate, poetic nature. After his unit departs for Europe, she gives birth to their child.

Laura Whitacre, a beautiful actress married to Michael Whitacre for several years. Like her husband before the war, she cares more for private pleasures than for politics. She regards the war as a rude intrusion into a comfortable life.

During Whitacre's absence, she readily finds another man and files for divorce.

Gretchen Hardenburg, the wife of Diestl's commanding officer. Left alone in Berlin, she lives a frantic life of self-indulgence; her beauty, sophistication, and availability quickly attract the attention of politicians and officers stationed in the capital. When Diestl visits her to report that her husband has been seriously wounded, she takes him as a lover.

Johnny Burnecker, Ackerman's best friend in the platoon. A simple Midwestern farm boy, Burnecker yearns only to go home and till the soil, as his ancestors have done. Admiring Burnecker's sense of family and land, Ackerman treats him as his spiritual brother and fights fiercely to protect him. Burnecker's death makes Ackerman bitter and reckless.

Colonel Colclough, Ackerman's superior. An officer by virtue of his birth and a stickler for rank, he is in charge of his men, but he does not lead them. Concerned neither for patriotism nor for his men, Colclough wants only for his unit to obey orders and perform well so that his own career will be enhanced.

— *Robert M. Otten*

YOUNG TÖRLESS
(Die Verwirrungen des Zöglings Törless)

Author: Robert Musil (1880-1942)
First published: 1906
Genre: Novel

Locale: A boarding school in the Austrian Empire
Time: Mid- or late nineteenth century
Plot: Philosophical realism

Törless (TEHR-lehs), a young boy at the celebrated military boarding school "W" in a remote eastern town of the Austrian Empire. When Törless first arrives at the boarding school, he is homesick and writes letters home almost daily. Although a friendship with the youthful cadet Prince H. helps him to overcome this early personal problem, it is only when Törless becomes acquainted with two older classmates, Beineberg and Reiting, that he begins to resolve this crisis in his psychological development. Beineberg indirectly helps Törless to overcome the attendant and painful experiences of his awakening sexuality. Most important in the coming to adolescent consciousness, however, is his difficult and ambivalent homosexual relationship with his classmate Basini. Even though Törless is physically present during the torture of Basini and even receives some vicarious pleasure from the events, he seems to be intellectually separated from them. He is trying to come to terms with a confusion that does not allow him to reconcile the events he observes and feels with the intellectual world he is developing. No one on the faculty seems able to help him to articulate this dilemma. It is not until later, while under questioning about the Basini affair, that Törless suddenly recognizes the conundrum that has plagued him. He explains that there are things that are on some occasions seen with the eyes and at other times with the eyes of the soul. Having attained this insight, Törless decides to leave the boarding school.

Basini (bah-SEE-nee), another student. Basini has all the personal characteristics of the physically and intellectually weak person. He is caught stealing money from the lockers of other students by Beineberg and Reiting, who take it upon themselves to punish him. Törless is involuntarily included in this conspiracy. For Törless, a period of immense confusion

ensues, because he believes that the theft should be reported. Even more troublesome is the response of his parents, who are not outraged by the theft and suggest that Basini be given the opportunity to mend his ways in the future. The punishment takes place in a secret attic room where the three boys carry out a systematic plan of enslaving Basini. Each boy conducts a personal experiment with his slave, submitting Basini to brutality, humiliation, and egregious sexual demands. Basini is incapable of defending himself against his tyrannizers. As a final form of brutalization, it is decided to turn him over to the entire student body, so that the masses will have the opportunity to annihilate Basini. Törless tries to warn him, but it is too late. Fearing the mass of tormentors, Basini turns himself in to the school authorities, who undertake an extensive inquest that results in his dismissal.

Beineberg (BI-neh-behrg), a young baron and student, two years older than Törless. He is a dictatorial conspirator in the Basini affair. Beineberg's father served as an officer in the British military in India, whence he returned with a somewhat perverted understanding of the Buddhist philosophy. The son attempts to apply these teachings by trying to wield spiritual powers over Basini. Through hypnosis, Beineberg hopes to initiate contact with Basini's lost soul and thereby cure him of his crime. Basini, however, rejects Beineberg's hypnotic suggestions and defeats the experiment, leading Beineberg to give him a wrathful beating. Beineberg's activities are not discovered by the school authorities, and he is able to remain in and be graduated from the military boarding school.

Reiting (RI-tihng), who also is two years older than Törless and is the other dictatorial conspirator in the Basini affair. Reiting is the instigator who promotes physical punishment of

Basini. He rejects any suggestion from Törless that alternate means should be found to deal with the thief. In the secret attic room, Reiting takes considerable pleasure in torturing Basini and, after some time, proposes that Basini should be turned over to the entire school to suffer from the attacks of the masses. While Beineberg is conducting his spiritual experi-

ments, Reiting's behavior produces an example of how large groups can effect mindless physical terror. Like his friend Beineberg, Reiting goes unpunished and completes his studies at the school.

— *Thomas H. Falk*

YOUR BLUES AIN'T LIKE MINE

Author: Bebe Moore Campbell (1950-   )
First published: 1992
Genre: Novel

Locale: Rural Mississippi and Chicago, Illinois
Time: The 1950's through the 1980's
Plot: Social realism

Armstrong Todd, a fifteen-year-old African American boy from Chicago who is sent to stay temporarily with his grandmother in Hopewell, Mississippi. Armstrong is a good-looking, outgoing boy whose only fault, an adolescent tendency to show off, is enough to get him murdered.

Delotha Todd, his mother, a vibrant, ambitious woman who has left Hopewell for Chicago to better herself. After Armstrong's death, she is determined to replace him with another son. This obsession wrecks her marriage and nearly ruins the life of her younger boy.

Wydell Todd, Armstrong's father, an attractive man who loves Delotha but is overwhelmed by her. Whenever she shows more interest in her ambitions or her children than in him, Wydell drowns his sorrows in drink. When Delotha turns to him for help, as she does at the end of the novel, he can be a nurturing and responsible father.

Lily Cox, a young white woman from a poor family who quit school at the age of sixteen to marry Floyd Cox. After the murder, she becomes the target of her husband's frustrations, and eventually she is sent to a mental institution. She finally takes refuge with her daughter Doreen.

Floyd Cox, Lily's husband, the owner of a pool hall patronized by African Americans. Floyd is a coward and a bully, governed by his fear of the whites who run his community, of his black customers, and, above all, of his father and his brother. After killing Armstrong, he loses his business and spends the rest of his life picking fights, stealing, serving time in prison, and blaming everyone but himself for his misfortunes.

Clayton Pinochet, the publisher of the Hopewell newspaper and the son of Stonewall Pinochet of Pinochet Plantation. A well-meaning, decent man, Clayton disapproves of his father's rapaciousness but can defy him only by secretly aiding those he knows are right. Although he finally offers to marry his black mistress, she rejects him because she knows that he is too weak to live with his decision.

Ida Long, a small, young black woman who shares with Lily the dream of escaping from Hopewell. Ida is a woman of strong convictions who stays in Hopewell only to care for her foster father. She finally demands and gets her rightful share of her white father's property.

— *Rosemary M. Canfield Reisman*

YVAIN: Or, The Knight with the Lion
(Yvain: Ou, Le Chevalier au lion)

Author: Chrétien de Troyes (c. 1150-c. 1190)
First transcribed: c. 1170
Genre: Drama

Locale: Britain
Time: The sixth century
Plot: Arthurian romance

Yvain (ee-VAH[N]), a knight of the Round Table. After hearing of Calogrenant's misadventure at the magic spring, Yvain avenges him and kills the Knight at the spring. Yvain marries the Knight's widow, Laudine de Landuc, and lives happily until lured away by promised adventures. When he fails to return, Laudine renounces him, and grief drives Yvain mad. After his wits are restored, he is ashamed to admit his identity. Accompanied by a lion he has befriended, he becomes known as the Knight with the Lion. After countless adventures, Yvain finally is reconciled with his lady.

Laudine de Landuc (loh-DEEN deh lah[n]-DEWK), Yvain's wife. Made a widow by Yvain, she marries him after he has begged her forgiveness. When he fails to return from his adventures as promised, she renounces him; she accepts him back only after Lunete intercedes for him.

Lunete (lew-NEHT), a damsel serving Laudine. Lunete befriends Yvain and brings about his marriage to Laudine. She is

sentenced to die when Yvain does not return; however, as the Knight with the Lion, Yvain rescues her. Thus reinstated, she is able to reconcile the estranged pair.

Sir Gawain (ga-WA[N]), Yvain's friend and King Arthur's nephew.

King Arthur, of the Round Table.

Guinevere, his queen.

Sir Kay, the cynical seneschal, humbled by Yvain.

Harpin of the Mountain (ahr-PA[N]), a giant slain by Yvain.

Calogrenant (kah-loh-greh-NAH[N]), Yvain's cousin, whose tale of the Knight of the Magic Spring begins Yvain's adventures.

Lady Noroison (noh-rwah-ZOH[N]), who is championed by Yvain.

Count Alier (ahl-YAY), the knight who is plundering Lady Noroison's lands. He is defeated by Yvain.

Z

ZADIG: Or, The Book of Fate
(Zadig: Ou, La Destinée, histoire orientale)

Author: Voltaire (François-Marie Arouet, 1694-1778)
First published: 1748
Genre: Novel

Locale: Babylon
Time: Remote antiquity
Plot: Social satire

Zadig (zah-DEEG), a wealthy young man. Educated and sensible, he rises to the position of prime minister of Babylon, only to be forced to flee after his supposed affair with Queen Astarte. Enslaved by the Egyptians, he serves Setoc and then King Nabussan. Finally, he finds Astarte and rescues her from Ogul. In a tournament of wits and arms, he wins Astarte as his bride. He rules Babylon justly and compassionately.

Astarte (ah-stahr-TAY), the queen of Babylon. After Zadig flees, she also escapes, with Cador's aid. She is captured by the prince of Hyrcania, escapes from him, is captured by Arbogad, and is sold to Ogul. Zadig rescues her and then wins her hand.

Moabdar (moh-ahb-DAHR), the king of Babylon. Suspicious that Zadig and Astarte are lovers, he forces Zadig to flee. When Astarte also escapes, he marries Missouf. Later, he goes mad and is killed in a revolt.

Cador (kah-DOHR), Zadig's best friend, who helps Astarte escape.

Jesrad (zhehs-RAHD), an angel who helps Zadig.

Itobad (ee-toh-BAHD), an evil lord, Zadig's rival for Astarte's hand.

Semire (say-MEER), Zadig's first betrothed. He loses an eye while rescuing her from kidnappers. She then refuses to marry a one-eyed man.

Hermes (ehr-MEHS), the doctor who predicts that Zadig's eye cannot heal.

Orcan (ohr-KAH[N]), the noble who marries Semire.

Azora (ah-zoh-RAH), Zadig's first wife, who becomes too difficult to live with.

Arimaze (ah-ree-MAHZ), called The Envious, Zadig's enemy.

Missouf (mee-SEWF), an Egyptian woman whose lover is killed by Zadig. She marries King Moabdar.

Setoc (say-TOHK), Zadig's Arabian master.

Almona (ahl-moh-NAH), a widow, later Setoc's wife.

Nabussan (nah-bews-SA[N]), the king of Serendib, who has only one faithful wife out of one hundred.

Arbogad (ahr-boh-GAHD), a happy brigand who sells Astarte to Ogul.

Ogul (oh-GEWL), a voluptuary cured by Zadig.

ZAÏRE

Author: Voltaire (François-Marie Arouet, 1694-1778)
First published: 1733
Genre: Drama

Locale: Jerusalem
Time: During the reign of Orosmane, sultan of Jerusalem
Plot: Tragedy

Zaïre (zah-EER), a slave of the sultan Orosmane, captured in infancy. Zaïre finds that she can love the Muslim ruler in spite of his religion. She discovers, however, that the Christian leader, Lusignan, is her father and Nerestan is her brother. She then vows to become a Christian and, counseled by her brother, postpones her nuptials. Torn between her love for Orosmane and her loyalty to her family, Zaïre goes to meet her brother and is killed by the jealous Orosmane.

Nerestan (nay-reh-STAH[N]), Zaïre's brother. A prisoner of the Muslims since the age of four, Nerestan escaped to fight against the Turks, only to be captured at Damas. Because of his bravery, he is released to secure the ransom of the Christian prisoners. He learns that Lusignan is really his father and that Zaïre is his sister. A devout Christian, Nerestan attempts to persuade Zaïre to abandon her plans to marry the sultan.

Orosmane (oh-rohs-MAH[N]), also called **Osman**, the sultan of Jerusalem. Captivated by his slave Zaïre, he decides to make her his sultana. Ignorant of the relationship between Zaïre and Nerestan, he thinks they are lovers and murders her in a fit of jealousy.

Lusignan (lew-zeen-YAH[N]), a French prince in the line of the kings of Jerusalem. Because of Lusignan's title, Orosmane refuses to ransom him, but Zaïre is able to secure his release.

After he is liberated, he learns that Nerestan and Zaïre are his long-lost children.

Chatillon (shah-tee-YOH[N]), a French captive ransomed by Nerestan.

Fatima (fah-TEE-mah), a slave of the sultan, captured in adulthood. Fatima is a devout Christian who exerts her influence on Zaïre.

Corasmin (koh-rahs-MA[N]) and
Meledor (may-lay-DOHR), officers of the sultan.

EL ZARCO, THE BANDIT
(El zarco: Episodias de la vida mexicana en 1861-1863)

Author: Ignacio Manuel Altamirano (1834-1893)
First published: 1901
Genre: Novel

Locale: The province of Morelos, Mexico
Time: 1861-1863
Plot: Historical

Nicolas (nee-koh-LAHS), a Mexican blacksmith of Indian descent. Nicolas, who is infatuated by Manuela, realizes while he is imprisoned for accusing an officer of shirking his duties that Pilar is his true love. Released from jail, he joins Martín Sánchez and assists in El Zarco's capture. When the bandit is finally executed, Nicolas and Pilar pass by on the way to their wedding.

El Zarco (SAHR-koh), a bandit. Taking advantage of the troubled times during the War of Reform, El Zarco leads his cutthroats through the countryside, murdering and plundering. Flattered by her devotion, he takes Manuela as his bride.

Manuela (mah-NWEH-lah), Doña Antonia's impetuous daughter. In love with the bandit El Zarco, she refuses to believe the stories of his cruelty. After she runs away with him, she sees his sordid side, but she still remains true to him. When he is executed, she falls to the ground dead.

Martín Sánchez (mahr-TEEN SAHN-chehs), a rancher. Enraged by the death of his father and his son at the hands of El Zarco, Martín swears to track down the bandits. At Calavera, he captures El Zarco, but the outlaw is rescued. Undaunted, Martín again captures the bandits and executes them.

Pilar (pee-LAHR), Doña Antonia's godchild, in love with Nicolas.

El Tigre (TEE-gray), El Zarco's bestial lieutenant.

Doña Antonia (ahn-TOH-nyah), Manuela's mother.

ZAZIE IN THE METRO
(Zazie dans le métro)

Author: Raymond Queneau (1903-1976)
First published: 1959
Genre: Novel

Locale: Paris, France
Time: Shortly after World War II
Plot: Farce

Zazie Lalochère (zah-ZEE lah-loh-SHEHR), a preteenage girl who is nasty, precocious, clever, and vulgar. She has come to Paris for the sole purpose of riding the subway. Unfortunately, the subway workers are on strike. Zazie spends her entire stay griping about life, causing havoc, and setting the people with whom she comes in contact at loggerheads, especially her uncle, Gabriel, whom she suspects of being a homosexual. When, finally, the subway resumes operation, Zazie is so exhausted from her escapades and partying that she misses the entire adventure, although her Paris weekend has nevertheless been a thrilling, eye-opening, and maturing experience.

Gabriel, who works under the stage name of **Gabriella** as a female impersonator and dancer in a gay nightclub. Tall and muscular, yet graceful, the thirty-two-year-old Gabriel considers his act art and himself an artist. Although he lacks sophistication, at times he waxes philosophical about life's transience. Alternately severe and indulgent with his niece Zazie, he plays his part in the madcap and unbridled events of tourism gone wild by inviting friends, acquaintances, and a busload of foreigners to share in the Paris-by-night activities.

Trouscaillon (trews-ki-YOH[N]), also known as **Pedro-Surplus, Bertin Poirée** (pwah-RAY), and **Haroun al-Rations**, a man of many names and many callings, among them plainclothes policeman, traffic officer, flea-market vendor, and child molester. For the middle-aged and still attractive Trouscaillon, forgetting his current name and putting on his disguises are done for fun and merriment. He is ineffectual in his police functions, because he has neither police presence nor command of police jargon. He enjoys women of all ages, including young Zazie, but is at heart too fickle to remain faithful to any.

Marceline (mahr-seh-LEEN), Gabriel's wife. A soft-spoken woman, she is very handsome and always well dressed, yet she never goes out, even to the neighborhood café. When she has trouble with Trouscaillon, however, she flees out her apartment window. Upon returning Zazie to her home, Marceline is called Marcel by Zazie's mother.

Charles, a taxi driver. He is Gabriel's best friend and serves as Zazie's guide, despite his very sketchy knowledge of the French capital. At the age of forty-five, he is still looking for the ideal woman, not realizing that she is right there in his favorite bar. Finally, he and Mado, the barmaid, marry, the cause for Gabriel and his guests to enjoy the carnival feast.

Madeleine (Mado) Ptits-pieds (mahd-LEEN ptee-PYAY), a pretty and pleasant barmaid. She marries Charles at last. Thereafter, she is seldom called by her diminutive and nickname, but by her given name, Madeleine.

Turandot (tew-rahn-DOH), a bar owner and Gabriel's landlord. He is gullible, good-hearted, and easily impressed.

Gridoux (gree-DEW), a cobbler, probably in his fifties. He is nosy and arrogant. Along with Laverdure, he is the neighborhood philosopher.

Laverdure (lah-vehr-DEWR), Turandot's parrot. Acting as a Greek chorus, he punctuates (and often deflates) the bar patrons' speech. His most famous one-line rejoinder is "Talk, talk, that's all you can do."

Madame Mouaque (mew-AHK), a middle-aged and homely but rich and snobbish widow who finds Gabriel, then Trouscaillon, irresistible. She joins the wedding party and, being too cantankerous and noisy, is gunned down by the riot police.

Jeanne Lalochère (zhahn), Zazie's mother. She murdered her husband, allegedly because he tried to rape Zazie; more likely, she wanted to be free of him to pursue other men. She leaves her daughter with Gabriel to reconcile with her current lover.

Fyodor Balanovitch (FYOH-dohr bah-LAH-noh-vihch), a tour guide and friend of Gabriel. He has become blasé over Pigalle nightclub acts and disinterested in the city's celebrated sights.

— *Pierre L. Horn*

ZERO

Author: Ignácio de Loyola Brandão (1936-   )
First published: 1974
Genre: Novel

Locale: A large city in Latin America
Time: Late 1960's
Plot: Political

José Gonçalves (gohn-SAHL-vehz), also called **Zé**, a vagabond worker at odd jobs and later an assassin and subversive. At twenty-eight years of age, he is small and unattractive, with a limp caused by a deformed foot. Though lacking the requisite self-assurance and drive, he once dreamed of being a singer. An avid reader, he is attracted to grotesques and oddities. Although seemingly apathetic, he is violent, feeling trapped and conscious of systematic oppression and his own mundane, captive life. José is relatively content as long as he retains his solitude, but when he marries, he is thrust into a confusing world that both beckons him and rejects him, threatening his individuality. In an atmosphere of rising political turmoil and violence, he is picked up and questioned regarding various small crimes. Bombarded by his wife Rosa, advertisements, and the government, he is pressured for material comforts. He begins robbing, then killing, and he gets what he wants, but it seems not to be worth it, especially when Rosa becomes estranged and ill and loses their child. After being harassed and brutalized by government officials, he finally joins the Communs, an antigovernment terrorist group. As the fight escalates, he wants only to escape everything. Betrayed and arrested, he is to be executed but escapes. He finally realizes that the group threatens his identity as much as does the oppressive government that he is fighting.

Rosa Maria, Jose's wife. Short and plump, she is seen as unattractive by José's friends. She was reared as a good Catholic. She answers José's personal advertisement and they marry, though her people do not approve. Immediately, she begins to pressure him for material comforts for them and their unborn child, especially for a house of their own. The difficulties they encounter render her sick and apathetic. She aborts the child, then hemorrhages and returns to her parents, because José spends much time away as a terrorist. She is abducted by members of a cult and, in a grotesque ritual, is sacrificed as a means of ridding the earth of evil.

Gê, the leader of the Communs, a terrorist group. Self-sacrificing and charismatic, he is a well-known fighter with an obscure background, apparently a medical school graduate turned rebel. Surviving all attempts to capture or kill him, he walks into José's house one day and provides José with a possible outlet for his frustrations. With Gê's persuasion, José joins the group. Gê takes José under his wing and lectures him on the necessity of living for the group cause and not for individual action, a necessity that José never accepts.

Atila, José's friend and fellow subversive. His nickname derives from his tendency toward violence when drinking. His teaching degree proved useless when he refused to bribe officials for a position. He drives a bus until José goes to join the Communs; he accompanies José for the fun of it. He joins in robbing and killing, is eventually caught and brutally tortured, but will not divulge information on the group and is finally released.

Malevil, José's friend and fellow subversive. A twenty-one-year-old student and a neighbor of José and Rosa, he is out of school because of military intervention there. Atila tells José that Malevil is the first case of reanimation after having been frozen. He works at a nightclub. When he is framed by the police and imprisoned, he joins the Communs and the fight against oppression. When he becomes disillusioned with this as well, he betrays and identifies José in a scene much like that of Judas at Gethsemane.

Ige-Sha, a female African shaman. Searching for a person as a sacrifice for purifying the world from evil, she finds Rosa and executes her in a brutal ritual.

Carlos Lopez, a textile worker. A patriot with a sick son, he keeps running up against a bureaucratic government as he tries to find treatment. He is faithful, persevering in the face of all apathy, but when his son finally dies without care, he, too, turns against the system.

— *John S. Nelson*

THE ZONE: A Prison Camp Guard's Story
(Zona: Zapiski nadziratelia)

Author: Sergei Dovlatov (1941-1990)
First published: 1982
Genre: Novel

Locale: A labor camp in Komi, in the northern Soviet Union
Time: 1963-1965 and 1982
Plot: Social morality

Sergei Dovlatov (sehr-GAY dov-LAH-tov), the author not only of *The Zone* but also of a series of letters to its Russian émigré publisher, Igor Yefimov, reprinted at intervals throughout the novel. The letters act in part as a frame story but chiefly as a vehicle for direct comment by the author on the Soviet labor camp "archipelago" in which he served as an army guard from 1963 through 1965. His most important conclusion is that there is no fundamental difference between guards and prisoners (*zeks*).

Boris Alikhanov (ah-lih-KHA-nov), a labor camp guard for special punishment cells, the fictional counterpart to Dovlatov. Tough and strong, standing more than six feet tall, he attended college for three years and reads books. He is also part Jewish, but he does not advertise this fact. His friendships with a variety of guards and *zeks*, representing twenty Soviet nationalities, gradually teach him that even in the vast remoteness of a northern camp, life offers all that one needs to know about human existence. Alikhanov, the hard-drinking guard, suffers as much as do the prisoners. One night, horribly drunk on *zek* moonshine, he starts a big fight in the barracks and has to be tied up with telephone wire. In the morning, he is escorted (by his best friend) into one of the very cells he has been guarding. Thus, the guard who has sympathized with the prisoners becomes a prisoner himself.

Lance Corporal "Fidel" Petrov, Alikhanov's best friend. He is called Fidel because at a political lesson once, when asked to name a member of the Politburo, he said, "Fidel Castro." It is he who is told to escort Alikhanov to the stockade. On the way, Alikhanov simply walks off into the snow.

Petrov threatens to shoot him, but Alikhanov keeps walking. Finally, Petrov begins to weep and tells Alikhanov that he can do what he wants, whereupon Alikhanov returns to his escort, accepts his punishment, and saves Petrov from a similar fate.

Boris Kuptsov, a *zek* who refuses to work, an extreme individualist. One day, in front of Alikhanov, Kuptsov chops off his own hand with an ax. Alikhanov sees something of himself in Kuptsov.

Captain Pavel Romanovich Egorov (PAH-vehl roh-MAH-noh-vihch yeh-GOH-rov), a twelve-year veteran of the camps. He goes on leave to Sochi and brings back a bride, who suffers much in the married officers' quarters. When the barking from the kennels nearly brings her to hysteria, the captain goes out with his rifle and shoots Harun, the dog making the most noise. He returns proudly with the corpse.

Katya, Captain Egorov's wife. A graduate student sick of intellectuals, she found Egorov's honesty and bluntness refreshing. She is ashamed of herself for not being able to tolerate the freezing filth of the officers' quarters, but she cannot accustom herself to life in the far north.

Captain Tokar, an old veteran of the camps who loves only one living thing, his dog Brooch. The dog is killed, cooked, and eaten by the *zeks* one night at a party, to which Alikhanov, ambling along through "the zone," is invited. When Alikhanov learns the truth about the "cutlets" that the *zeks* are eating, he honorably informs Captain Tokar of the fate of his dog. Later, when Alikhanov is sent to the stockade, Captain Tokar cannot bring himself to rescind the order.

— *Donald M. Fiene*

ZOO: Or, Letters Not About Love
(Zoo: Ili, Pis'ma ne o lyubvi)

Author: Viktor Shklovsky (1893-1984)
First published: 1923
Genre: Novel

Locale: A Russian émigré colony in Berlin
Time: The 1920's
Plot: Epistolary

Viktor Shklovsky (VIHK-tohr SHKLOV-skee), the narrator, a Russian novelist, literary critic, and political émigré living in Berlin after the consolidation of Bolshevik power in the Soviet Union. The narrator is in love with the woman to whom he writes the letters that form the novel; she does not reciprocate the narrator's feelings. She does, however, allow him to write to her as long as he does not write about his love. Because he cannot write what he wishes, he writes about what interests him: the theory of literature; literary friends in Berlin and in Russia whom he has left; descriptions of places; cars and the effect of technology on the world; the contrast between the life of bourgeois Europe, which Alya comes to represent, and the revolutionary culture to which he has become accustomed; and his bitter experience of exile. These topics reveal a man who values talent, wisdom, compassion, and magnanimity. He is ironic, witty, and imaginative, though he says that he is sick of wit and irony. He says that he is "sentimental" because he "takes life seriously." It gradually becomes clear that the narrator's passion for Alya is not so great as his passion for literature, as she is surely aware. In the last letter, he reveals his deep and enduring patriotism, asking his country to allow him to return home.

Elsa Triolet, also called **Alya**, a Russian woman and a writer. She has actually written the letters that bear her signature, but much of her characterization comes through Shklovsky's letters to her. She has been married to a Frenchman, André Triolet; they lived in Tahiti, a description of which (from one of her letters) she turns into a book somewhat later, authenticating her literary talent. The couple has parted, however, with him returning to Paris, her to Berlin. She refuses to love the narrator and says that she is "no *femme fatale* [but] . . . Alya, pink and fluffy." The narrator thinks that she treats men like toys and in letter 11 calls her an "utter woman." Her attitude toward clothes and buying things, however, leads him to call her "alien." He identifies her with the consumer-oriented, bourgeois European culture, entirely foreign to the cataclysmic experience of Civil War Russia from which she has escaped. He reasons, therefore, that she cannot understand and love the roughness of Russians with their unpressed pants in contrast to the European men in their tuxedos. In Alya's letter 19, however, she contradicts his characterization of her as alien with her description of her old nurse Stesha, who "loves the male sex," as a gentle and "completely warm" woman. Alya believes that she herself is like Stesha, whom the narrator realizes is profoundly Russian. The narrator calls

Alya a "woman with no vocation," and she defines herself in letter 16 as "good for nothing." She has the ability to do many things, but she leaves the possibilities unused, like a package she has bought, brought home, and left unopened. She agrees with the narrator that wherever she goes, she knows "immediately what goes with what and who with whom," and she knows that she does not go with him. She shows him that he does not know how to write love letters and that he is more interested in his love and his art than in her. This rejection precipitates their break and the narrator's letter asking permission to return to Russia.

— *Martha Manheim*

THE ZOO STORY

Author: Edward Albee (1928-   )
First published: 1959
Genre: Drama

Locale: Central Park, New York City
Time: A Sunday afternoon in summer, late 1950's
Plot: Absurdist

Peter, an executive for a publishing house. An average-sized and nearsighted man in his early forties, Peter has Catholic tastes and dresses conservatively; he is an upper-class representative of the Eisenhower years. His family life is predictably normal: a good wife, two daughters, two cats, two parakeets, and a nice apartment in the East Seventies of Manhattan. His attitude reflects his status: He is naïve, complacent, passive, proper, and a bit bored. His intention on this afternoon was to read quietly in Central Park. A stranger, Jerry, interrupts him with talk and then aggression. Although Peter is slow to anger, Jerry's incessant prodding eventually drives him to pick up Jerry's knife. After Jerry impales himself, Peter exits the now-ending play with his previously established character destroyed by this chance and absurd encounter.

Jerry, an emotionally disturbed man in his late thirties. Anxious and angry about his bisexuality, poverty, and alienation, Jerry tries to make sense of his pain by walking from the New York Zoo looking for another human to confront. Finding Peter, he talks in a rambling yet intelligent way about the miseries of his life. His autobiography reveals his inability to relate to others, including the fellow residents of his rooming house on the upper West Side. In a final and suicidal attempt to give his life meaning, Jerry has on this day set out intent on creating the suicidal encounter that ends the play. By impaling himself on a knife held by Peter, the paragon of the normal, Jerry at once makes contact with another human and challenges the bourgeois sense of social and moral order.

The Landlady, the caretaker of Jerry's rooming house. A lustful, obese, ignorant, and drunken woman, she, like her dog, makes unwanted advances toward Jerry. Presented in one of his narratives, she is the emblem of his disgust with humanity and the repulsiveness of his experiences.

The Dog, the landlady's canine friend. This black beast with a constant erection snarls and attempts to bite Jerry every time he enters or leaves his room. In an attempt to placate the monster, Jerry feeds it hamburgers and finally poisons the dog. When the dog recovers, Jerry is strongly drawn to the now-calmer animal. For a moment, he feels empathy for the dog that he has hurt. This violent love/hate foreshadows the play's final encounter between Jerry and Peter.

The queen, a black homosexual who occupies a flat in Jerry's building. This gay man lives with his door always open, never leaving except to go to the bathroom; he does nothing but model his Japanese kimono and tweeze his eyebrows. In Jerry's eyes, he becomes the image of an indifferent and supercilious god.

— *Daniel D. Fineman*

ZOOT SUIT

Author: Luis Miguel Valdez (1940-   )
First published: 1978
Genre: Drama

Locale: Los Angeles, California
Time: Early 1940's
Plot: Historical

El Pachuco (pah-CHEW-koh), a mythical figure, the zoot-suited spirit of the Pachucos, alienated gangs of Mexican American youth living in the Los Angeles area. A rebellious, street-smart, young Chicano, El Pachuco is master of ceremonies of this play set in the World War II years, as well as a leading figure, chorus, and the alter ego of Hank Reyna. In his "cool" outfit (long jacket, baggy trousers, and lengthy watch chain), El Pachuco preaches, with bitter humor, fidelity to one's own culture and language and defiance of the Anglos. It is the Anglos, Americans not of Mexican origin, who seek to control the lives of his people (la Raza), robbing them of ethnic pride and manhood while exploiting them and discriminating against anyone with a brown skin.

Henry (Hank) Reyna (RRAY-nah), a twenty-one-year-old Chicano with Indian features, the gang leader of the Thirty-eighth Street Pachucos. Hank is arrested on the eve of joining the Navy, along with a number of other gang members, for the alleged murder of a Chicano one summer night in 1943 at a lakeside gathering spot. He is convicted in a rigged trial. Rebellious, angry, and resentful of authority, which represents for him discrimination against Chicanos, Hank does nothing to placate those in control of his fate. Although he presents an impenetrable façade to his persecutors and jailers, Hank is extremely confused about his own identity as an American in a country at war that regards him, too, as a foreign enemy. In his puzzled state, Hank seeks guidance from El Pachuco, who urges rejection of America and faith in his own heritage. After a successful appeal and release from prison, Hank remains uncertain whether integration into American life or rejection of it is the answer for himself and his people.

George Shearer, a dedicated yet realistic young public service lawyer. George volunteers to defend the Pachucos in their murder trial, convinced that they are victims of racial prejudice and irrational war hysteria. He finds, however, that before he can help them he must first overcome Chicano mistrust of him; he is, in their eyes, just another "gringo." During a ludicrously one-sided trial, the judge badgers George mercilessly, making no effort at impartiality, while the Press convicts the young Chicanos in the pages of Los Angeles newspapers. When a guilty verdict is handed down despite his best efforts, George plans an appeal but is drafted into the Army before he can proceed.

Alice Bloomfield, an attractive young Jewish activist and leftist reporter who organizes the Pachucos' defense effort after their original conviction by raising funds and enlisting the support of American liberals, including prominent Hollywood figures. An uncertain relationship begins between her and Hank in the months she works in behalf of his cause. The gap between their backgrounds, Hank's alienation and anger, and his commitment to Della, a Mexican American girl, make it unclear whether the two young people have a future together.

Rudy Reyna, Henry Reyna's hero-worshiping younger brother, who longs to don his own zoot suit, which for him is the symbol of manhood and defiance of Anglo hegemony. A marauding band of servicemen strip Rudy of his flamboyant zoot suit and his dignity as they rampage through the streets looking for brown-skinned "foreigners" who, they believe, do not sufficiently respect the American way of life in wartime.

Enrique Reyna (ehn-REE-keh),

Dolores Reyna,

Lupe Reyna (LEW-peh), and

Della Barrios (DEH-yah BAH-rree-ohs), Hank's family and girlfriend, who support and sustain him.

The Press, the malevolent forces of yellow journalism that perpetuate feelings of Anglo racial superiority against Chicanos and incite injustices.

— *James E. Devlin*

ZORBA THE GREEK
(Vios kai politela tou Alexe Zormpa)

Author: Nikos Kazantzakis (1883-1957)
First published: 1946
Genre: Novel

Locale: Crete
Time: Mid-twentieth century
Plot: Psychological realism

Zorba, the central figure of the novel. He is about sixty years old but feels that, ironically, his desires becomes more pronounced as he grows older. When he goes to the city to buy tree-harvesting equipment, he easily becomes sidetracked and spends most of his boss's money on women and wine. He has a huge appetite for earthly pleasures. He is loud, crude, and larger than life. He believes in the primacy of the senses over moral and intellectual faculties. His pagan theology is rooted in nature and his own senses. He carries his *senturi*—the Greek counterpart of an American hammer dulcimer—everywhere, but he plays only when he is in the right mood and in the right company. Music is sacred to him. He dances whenever he is so full of emotion that he can no longer contain it. At his own child's funeral, he was filled with grief and had to express it in dancing. He is a free spirit guided by his senses rather than his intellect. He laughs at his own shortcomings and is honest and open, like a child. Zorba practices his paganism to the last days of his life while wandering in Serbia.

The Narrator, who goes to Crete to experience the world by engaging in a capitalist venture but takes all of his books and bookishness with him. By chance, he and Zorba meet and become friends. The Narrator tells the story and analyzes the incidents. He observes Zorba with fascination. His sterile intellectual sensibility, however, is slowly transformed by his novel experiences. He begins to see the value of sensual pleasures. Zorba guides and encourages him. When the Narrator meets the beautiful, young Widow, he is attracted to her, but Zorba must coax him to pursue the relationship. Zorba's ecstatic dancing and pagan theology, Madam Hortense's musings about love, and Crete's wine and atmosphere transform the Narrator to the point where he wants to partake of the sensual life. The death of the Widow shakes him to his soul and transforms him further. He learns how to dance, drink wine, and worship nature and its promptings. A Zorbatic, pagan theology that celebrates life takes root deep inside him. He eventually leaves the island but is entirely imbued with the spirit of Crete and of Zorba.

Madam Hortense, who had a wild and colorful life as a courtesan. She was a mistress to many important men of her time. Now she is an aging, broken woman who has nothing but her memories. Upon meeting Zorba, she comes alive again. She experiences affection and intimacy through Zorba's vibrant paganism. Her life is brightened by some brief moments of happiness in the company of Zorba, but then, tired of her long and dreary life, she begins to fade away with illness. She dies in Zorba's arms with a satisfied smile on her face.

The Widow, a melancholy woman who prefers a lonely life to a desperate attempt to bring men into her life to fill the void her husband left behind. She is young and beautiful. Men of the village lust after her and wish they could have her, even for one night. She rejects them all with disdain. The men resort to harassing and ostracizing her. When the narrator and Zorba arrive, things begin to change for her. Zorba gives her protection and support, and the Narrator fills her mind and imagination. After much procrastination, the Narrator finally goes to her, and she welcomes him to her bed. This one-night affair marks her. Jealous women whip up stories and instigate a frenzied mob attack in front of the church. She is stoned and beheaded.

Pavli, a sensitive young man who dares to express his love for the Widow. Other young men tease him and laugh at his melancholy, lovesick disposition. Pavli's father disapproves of his son's choice of a love object and tries to dissuade him. One night, Pavli writes a love letter and delivers it to the Widow personally. His father finds the letter and punishes Pavli further. Finding no sympathy for his misery and feeling despised by the woman he adores, he drowns himself in the ocean.

— *Chogollah Maroufi*

ZUCKERMAN UNBOUND

Author: Philip Roth (1933-   )
First published: 1981
Genre: Novel

Locale: New York City
Time: 1969
Plot: Comic realism

Nathan Zuckerman, an American Jewish novelist who has to cope with fame following the publication of his first successful novel. The novel, titled *Carnovsky*, is based enough on Nathan's own experience that his family and friends become angry at his depiction of Jews in what they see as a peep-show atmosphere of perversion. The book has made Nathan both rich and famous, but he still struggles with the conflicts that result from the book's relationship to life, for he is taken to be the model of his lecherous protagonist Carnovsky, and his wife and family see themselves unflatteringly portrayed in his fiction.

Alvin Pepler, a former television quiz-show winner from a 1950's game show called *Smart Money*. He was caught up in the scandal that resulted when the show's producers persuaded him to lose so that a non-Jew, who had been given the answers, could win. Pepler is a former Marine, a nonstop talker, and an expert in trivia, with a photographic memory. As the novel progresses, he increasingly becomes Nathan's double, or "secret sharer." Pepler "attaches" himself to Nathan, pesters him with talk about his own writing, and finally urges him to read his review of Nathan's own book. In its discussion of the complex relationship between life and art, the review reflects Nathan's own conflicts. Pepler argues that Nathan stole the character of Carnovsky from him, and that he, Pepler, is the model for Carnovsky.

Laura Zuckerman, Nathan's wife, a quiet and kind lawyer who aids and defends young men who escape the military draft by going to Canada. Nathan calls her a goody-good Pollyanna WASP who never says what is on her mind. Nathan no longer loves her and moves out after the publication of his novel, but he feels guilty that he does not love her.

Selma Zuckerman, Nathan's mother. She lives in Miami and is being threatened implicitly by an anonymous caller, who Nathan suspects is Alvin Pepler.

Caesara O'Shea, a glamorous film star from Ireland with a sad and seductive air. According to the gossip magazines, Nathan is dating her. Actually, Nathan met her only once, at a dinner party, and has spent one evening with her. She leaves Nathan to have an affair with Fidel Castro.

Victor Zuckerman, Nathan's father, a podiatrist who has been disappointed in Nathan because of what he sees as Nathan's demeaning depiction of Jews. Victor is in a nursing home suffering from the effects of a stroke. His last word to Nathan before he dies is "Bastard."

Henry Zuckerman, Nathan's brother, a successful dentist. Nathan sees his brother as the tallest and most handsome of all the Zuckerman men. Because of Henry's kindly, gentle, and doctorly manner, all of his patients fall in love with him, and he falls in love with his patients. Henry accuses Nathan of killing his father with his best-selling book.

Essie Metz, Nathan's cousin, an elderly woman who lives across the hall from Nathan's mother. Essie tells Nathan about Alvin Pepler, whom the family knew when Nathan was younger.

Gilbert Carnovsky, the central character in Nathan's controversial best-seller, a double for Nathan himself.

André Schevitz, Nathan's literary agent. André's gallant continental manner, his silver hair, and his European accent have earned for him the appellation "the Headwaiter." In addition to being an agent, he is an adviser, confessor, and handholder to Nathan and a stable of film stars and novelists.

Rosemary Ditson, an elderly retired schoolteacher who lives alone in a basement apartment next door to Nathan's wife, Laura. Laura looks after Rosemary, and Rosemary loves her. Rosemary hates Nathan for his treatment of Laura.

— *Charles E. May*

ZULEIKA DOBSON: Or, An Oxford Love Story

Author: Max Beerbohm (1872-1956)
First published: 1911
Genre: Novel

Locale: Oxford, England
Time: Early twentieth century
Plot: Satire

Zuleika Dobson, a bewitching young woman with whom all the Oxford undergraduates fall in love. She can love only a man who will not love her. After all the young Oxonians have committed suicide for love of her, Zuleika takes a train for Cambridge and another try for a man she can love. She earns her living as a magician.

The Duke of Dorset, a rich young English aristocrat in love with Zuleika. When she pours a pitcher of water on his head, he believes he is released from his vow to commit suicide for her. When a strange bird sings, heralding a death in his family, he commits suicide anyway, rather than break a

tradition. He throws himself in the river and drowns.

Noaks, an impecunious student. Zuleika thinks she can love him, because he does not love her. Noaks, however, commits suicide by jumping out a window because he thinks Katie Batch does not love him.

Katie Batch, the pretty daughter of the Duke of Dorset's landlady. She tells Zuleika that the duke committed suicide out of respect for tradition, not love for Zuleika.

The Warden of Judas College, Zuleika's grandfather. Her visit to see him at Oxford sets off the whole absurd chain of events.

Cyclopedia
of
LITERARY
CHARACTERS

TITLE INDEX

AUTHOR INDEX

CHARACTER INDEX

Bains, Mr. (Miss Peabody's Inheritance), 1259

Baird, Jennifer, 545

Bajazeth (Tamburlaine the Great), 1891

Bakayoko, Ibrahima, 745

Baker, Dr. (Rebecca), 1604

Baker, Harry, 512

Baker, Jordan, 776

Baker, Miss (A Voyage Round My Father), 2078

Baker, Miss Hermione, 377

Baker, Mr. (The Nigger of the "Narcissus"), 1349

Baker, Mr. (The Winter of Our Discontent), 2149

Baker, Rena, 208

Bakewell, Tom, 1422

Bakul (Clear Light of Day), 355

Balaban, Daniel, 752

Balafré, Le (The Prairie), 1549

Balafré, Le (Quentin Durward), 1575

Balaguet, emir of (The Song of Roland), 1810

Balamir (The Cannibal), 285

Balan (Idylls of the King), 906

Balance, Justice (The Recruiting Officer), 1608

Balance, Sylvia, 1608

Balanovitch, Fyodor, 2204

Balcairn, Baron (Vile Bodies), 2060

Balcar, Dr. Anna, 929

Balcárcel de Moral, Jorge, 755

Balderstone, Caleb, 241

Baldissera, General (Fontamara), 667

Baldo (Jubiabá), 988

Baldock (Edward II), 560

Baldridge, Alpha, 1646

Baldridge, Brack, 1646

Baldridge, Euly, 1646

Baldry, Chris, 1626

Baldry, Kitty, 1626

Balducci, Liliana, 1915

Balduíno, Antônio, 988

Balduque, Serafín, 1476

Baldwin (Tamburlaine the Great), 1892

Baldwin, Cecily, 1189

Baldwin, George, 1188

Baldwin of Flanders (Hereward the Wake), 839

Baldy (Midnight's Children), 1245

Bale, Simon, 1348

Balfour, Amelie, 1797

Balfour, David, 1009

Balfour, Ebenezer, Esquire, of Shaws, 1009

Balfour of Burley, John (Old Mortality), 1401

Balia (The Pretenders), 1553

Balibari, Chevalier (Barry Lyndon), 150

Baligant (The Song of Roland), 1810

Baligny (The Revenge of Bussy d'Ambois), 1628

Balin (Idylls of the King), 906

Balin le Sauvage (Le Morte d'Arthur), 1282

Baliol (Doctor Faustus), 510

Ball, Ian, 1606

Ball, Professor (Night Rider), 1354

Ballard, Horatio, 2011

Ballard, Lester, 330

Ballas, Jan, 1229

Balli, Stephano, 99

Ballinger, Drew, 481

Ballio (Pseudolus), 1567

Balliol, Lady Matilda de, 1036

Balliol, Messer Roussel de, 1035

Ballon, Monsieur (Peer Gynt), 1477

Balmori (Gazapo), 718

Baloo (The Jungle Books), 994

Baloum, Samba, 1587

Baloyne, Yvor, 845

Balsamo, Joseph, 1227

Balsomo, Joseph, 404

Baltazar (The Issa Valley), 956

Balthasar (Much Ado About Nothing), 1304

Balthasar (Romeo and Juliet), 1661

Balthazar (Ben-Hur), 176

Balthazar (The Spanish Tragedy), 1827

Balthazar, Frère (Roderick Random), 20

Balthazar, S., 35, 37

Balthus, Father (The Crystal World), 427

Baltram, Bettina, 754

Baltram, Edward, 753

Baltram, Ilona, 754

Baltram, Jesse, 753

Baltram, May, 754

Balu (The Financial Expert), 644

Balwhidder, Reverend Micah, 76

Bama (In the Wine Time), 926

Bambaev, Rostislav, 1791

Bamberger (The Cruise of the Cachalot), 424

Bambi (Bambi), 137

Bambil, Gloria, 155

Bambridge, Mr. (Middlemarch), 1244

Banahan, Catherine, 1861

Banat (Journey into Fear), 982

Bancroft, Barney, 2039

Band, George "Brass," 1928

Bandar-Log (The Jungle Books), 994

Bandele (The Interpreters), 943

Bandit (Miracle of the Rose), 1253

Bandol, Sharli, 1598

Banford, Jill, 685

Banford, Mr. (The Fox), 686

Bangham, Mrs. (Little Dorrit), 1101

Bangles, Mr. Peter, 1046

Banjo (Banjo), 139

Banjo (The Man Who Came to Dinner), 1180

Bank Clerk, A London (Moll Flanders), 1268

Banker (Operetta), 1420

Bankes, William, 1963

Banks, Ethel, 142

Banks, Joseph, 265

Banks, Rosie M., 937

Banks, Sir Gerald, 1448

Banks, Sir Joseph, 1309

Banks, Zora, 502

Banner, Judge Goodwill, 1332

Bannie, Miss (This Child's Gonna Live), 1932

Bannister, Guy, 1079

Bannon, Horace, 1443

Bannon, Nora, 1008

Banquo (Macbeth), 1154

Bantam, Angelo Cyrus, Esq., 1505

Banter (Roderick Random), 20

Bantison, Squire (Monsieur Beaucaire), 1273

Banzin, Eberhard, 1879

Baptista (The Taming of the Shrew), 1892

Baptiste (Natives of My Person), 1331

Baptistin (The Count of Monte-Cristo), 401

Bar madam (No Longer Human), 1362

Barabas (The Jew of Malta), 971

Barabbas (Barabbas), 140

Barach, Elie, 1538

Baraglioul, Geneviève de, 1040

Baraglioul, Julius de, 1040

Baraglioul, Juste-Agénor de, 1040

Baraglioul, Marguerite de, 1040

Barb (The Great Valley), 778

Barban, Tommy, 1908

Barbara (The Book of Laughter and Forgetting), 225

Barbara (Major Barbara), 1170

Barbara (The Old Curiosity Shop), 1397

Barbara (The Survivor), 1875

Bárbara, Doña (Doña Bárbara), 525

Barbara, Old (Wilhelm Meister's Apprenticeship), 2137

Barbara, Sister (The Madman and the Nun), 1160

Barbarka (The Issa Valley), 956

Barbary, Miss (Bleak House), 203

Barbassou, Captain (Tartarin of Tarascon), 1897

Barbemuche (The Bohemians of the Latin Quarter), 218

Barber (The Sunken Bell), 1870

Barber, Victor the, 1272

Barber, village (The Three-Cornered World), 1937

Barberini, Cardinal (Galileo), 708

Barbette (The Chouans), 342

Barbie (Pigs in Heaven), 1509

Barbillus (Claudius the God and His Wife Messalina), 354

Beaufort, Fanny, 28
Beaufort, Henry, 834
Beaufort, Julius, 28
Beaufort, Mary, 1914
Beaufort, Mrs. (The Age of Innocence), 28
Beaufort, Thomas, 834
Beaugard, Captain (The Soldier's Fortune), 1799
Beaugosse, Daouda, 745
Beauharnais, Rose-Josef-Marie de, 1327
Beaujo (Geography of a Horse Dreamer), 722
Beaujolais, comte de (Monsieur Beaucaire), 1273
Beaulieu, Michel, 1146
Beaumanoir, Lucas de (Ivanhoe), 958
Beaumont (Edward II), 560
Beaumont, Jasper, 2178
Beaumont, Jeremiah, 2178
Beaumont, Liz, 448
Beaumont, Mrs. (Evelina), 599
Beaumont, Mrs. (World Enough and Time), 2178
Beaumont, Ned, 737
Beaumont, Thad, 447
Beaumont, Wendy, 448
Beaumont, William, 448
Beauséant, Madame de (Père Goriot), 1484
Beauty (Everyman), 600
Beauvais, Marquis Henri de, 1967
Beaver, John, 806
Beaver, Mrs. (A Handful of Dust), 806
Beavers, Wesley, 1113
Beavis, Anthony, 607
Beavis, James, 608
Beavis, John, 607
Bebb, Babe, 223
Bebb, Bertha (Bert), 223
Bebb, Leo, 222-223
Bebb, Lucille, 222-223
Bebb, Sharon, 222-223
Bebe, Uncle (On Heroes and Tombs), 1409
Bebelo, Zé, 492
Bébert (Journey to the End of the Night), 983
Bebra, Mr. (The Tin Drum), 1954
Becerra, Carmen, 638
Bechstein, Art, 1318
Bechstein, Joseph "Joe the Egg," 1319
Beck, Madame (Villette), 2061
Beck, Mr. (The Increased Difficulty of Concentration), 929
Beck, Werner, 2092
Beckendorff, Mr. (Vivian Grey), 2073
Becker (The Weavers), 2113
Becker, Friedrich, 1373
Becker, Ivan, 2182
Becket, Thomas, 1306
Becket, Thomas à, 162
Beckett, Nicholas (Nick), 2120

Beckoff, Arnold, 1974
Beckoff, Mrs. (Torch Song Trilogy), 1974
Beckwith, Seth, 1293
Becky (The Conjure Woman), 388
Becky Lou (The Tooth of Crime), 1973
Bécu (Earth), 550
Becuccio (Among Women Only), 59
Beddoes, Morland, 2185
Bede, Adam, 14
Bede, Adam, Jr., 15
Bede, Lisbeth, 15
Bede, Matthias, 15
Bede, Mrs. Lisbeth, 14
Bede, Seth, 14
Bedford, Duchess of (The Last of the Barons), 1049
Bedford, duke of (Henry VI, Part I), 834
Bedford, Duncan, 1797
Bedford, Frances, 1797
Bedford, John, 1600
Bedford, Malcolm, 1796
Bedford, Middleton, 1797
Bedford, Sarah Tait, 1796
Bedford, Valette, 1797
Bedivere (Brut), 256
Bedivere (Idylls of the King), 906
Bedloe, Agatha, 1683
Bedloe, Daphne, 1683
Bedloe, Ian, 1683
Bedloe, Lucy Dean, 1683
Bedloe, Thomas, 1683
Bednar, Captain (The Man with the Golden Arm), 1184
Bedner, Alex, 2197
Bedner, Else, 2197
Bedouin workers at Harran (Cities of Salt), 348
Bedoya, Cristóbal (Cristo), 344
Beduer (Brut), 256
Bedwell, Jonathan, 186
Bedwin, Mrs. (Oliver Twist), 1406
Bee (The Wine of Astonishment), 2145
Bee of Mattapoisett (Woman on the Edge of Time), 2161
Beebe, Reverend Arthur, 1665
Beech, Abner, 394
Beech, Jeff, 394
Beecham, Curtis, 1127
Beecham, Dolphus, 1127
Beecham, Harold Augustus (Harry), 1312
Beecham, Nathan, 1126
Beecham, Noah Webster, 1127
Beecham, Percy, 1127
Beeder, Sir William, 866
Beeler, Sheryl, 1907
Beelzebub (Paradise Lost), 1455
Beeman, Lefty, 2121
Beevers, Ernest, 1950
Beevor, Beatrice, 683
Beezer-Iremonger (God on the Rocks), 744

Beffa (The Mill on the Po), 1250
Begbick, Leocadia, 1642
Beggar (The Balcony), 134
Beggar (The Radiance of the King), 1587
Beggar (Xala), 2189
Beggs, Dixie, 1700
Beggs, Joan, 1700
Beggs, Judge Austin, 1700
Beggs, Mrs. (Save Me the Waltz), 1700
Begley, John, 1524
Begpick, Ladybird, 1642
Begpick, Leokadia, 1642
Begriffenfeldt, Professor (Peer Gynt), 1477
Beguildy, Jancis, 1552
Beguildy, Mrs. (Precious Bane), 1552
Beguildy, Wizard, 1552
Begum (Heat and Dust), 826
Behan, Mary, 189
Behana, Madame (The Tree Climber), 1988
Behemoth (The Master and Margarita), 1210
Behrens, Hofrat, 1164
Behrman, S., 1383
Beineberg (Young Törless), 2200
Beiters, Konrad, 1128
Beizmenne, Erwin, 1128
Bel-Ami, 168
Bel-Imperia (The Spanish Tragedy), 1827
Bela (A Hero of Our Time), 840
Bela (Holy Place), 855
Belacqua (The Divine Comedy), 505
Belakane (Parzival), 1460
Belarius (Cymbeline), 432
Belcampo, Pietro, 494
Belch, Sir Toby, 2012
Belcher (Doctor Faustus), 510
Belcovitch, Bear, 335
Belcovitch, Becky, 335
Belcredi, Baron Tito, 832
Bele, King (Frithiof's Saga), 697
Belen (Brut), 255
Belfast (The Nigger of the "Narcissus"), 1349
Belfield, Henrietta, 307
Belfield, Mr. (Cecilia), 307
Belflor, Count de (The Devil upon Two Sticks), 492
Belford, John, 353
Belgae (The Faerie Queene), 612
Belgrano, General Manuel, 901
Belhôtel, Dominique, 143
Belhôtel, Saturnin, 143
Belial (Paradise Lost), 1455
Belial (Paradise Regained), 1456
Belinda (Fiskadoro), 656
Belinda (The Old Bachelor), 1395
Belinda (The Rape of the Lock), 1595
Belinda (Season of Adventure), 1719
Béline (The Hypochondriac), 896
Belize (Angels in America), 70
Belknap, Alvin, 58

Boy (Six Characters in Search of an Author), 1781
Boy (A Taste of Honey), 1899
Boy (Triptych), 1997
Boy (A Voyage Round My Father), 2078
Boy (Waiting for Godot), 2080
Boy (Wind from an Enemy Sky), 2140
Boy, Brack's Oldest (River of Earth), 1646
Boy, Gravedigger's (Lear), 1063
Boy, Persian (Henderson the Rain King), 831
Boy, Pilot's (The Rime of the Ancient Mariner), 1639
Boy age fifteen (Incident at Vichy), 928
Boy Baby (Woman Hollering Creek and Other Stories), 2156
Boy Blue (In the Castle of My Skin), 920
Boy from the Island (The Quare Fellow), 1572
Boy of nine (The Deputy), 487
Boyan (The Lay of Igor's Campaign), 1059
Boyce, Deighton, 253
Boyce, Humphrey, 1880
Boyce, James, 1880
Boyce, Rupert, 333
Boyce, Selina, 253
Boyce, Silla, 253
Boyd, Gordon, 311, 637
Boye, Mr. (Runner Mack), 1674
Boyer (The Kingdom of This World), 1022
Boyet (Love's Labour's Lost), 1141
Boykin, Dallas, 1653
Boykin, Edie Bell, 1982
Boykin, Lindsay Lee, 1653
Boykin, Lorene, 1653
Boykin, Mac, 1654
Boykin, Mrs. Mac, 1654
Boylan, Blazes, 2025
Boyle, "Captain" Jack, 994
Boyle, Chick, 421
Boyle, Fru (Niels Lyhne), 1349
Boyle, Juno, 994
Boyle, Master (Philadelphia, Here I Come!), 1496
Boyle, Mr. (The Apple of the Eye), 88
Boyle, Mrs. (The Apple of the Eye), 88
Boyle, Mrs. (The Mousetrap), 1293
Boys, Mack and the (Cannery Row), 283
Boys, young (Triptych), 1997
Boysie (A Brighter Sun), 246
Boythorn, Lawrence, 203
Brabantio (Othello), 1430
Brabner, Janice, 1573
Brace, Eloisa, 1174
Brace, Jerome, 1174
Bracebridge, Mrs. Henry, 970
Bracegirdle, Mary, 422
Braceweight, Mr. (Born in Captivity), 230
Braceweight, Walter, 230
Brachiano, duke of (The White Devil), 2127

Bracidas (The Faerie Queene), 612
Brack, Judge (Hedda Gabler), 828
Brack's Oldest Boy (River of Earth), 1646
Bracken, Matilda, 1619
Brackenburg, Fritz, 561
Brackenbury, Sir Robert, 1634
Brackenshaw, Lady (Daniel Deronda), 444
Brackenshaw, Lord (Daniel Deronda), 444
Brackley, Sir Daniel, 194
Bracknel, Alfred, 235
Bracknel, Amy, 235
Bracknel, Denis, 235
Bracknel, May, 235
Bracknel, Mr. (The Bracknels), 235
Bracknel, Mrs. (The Bracknels), 235
Bracknell, Lady Augusta, 916
Bracy, Maurice de, 958
Brad (My Amputations), 1309
Brad (Wheat That Springeth Green), 2122
Bradamant (Orlando furioso), 1424
Bradamant (Orlando innamorato), 1425
Bradamante (The Non-existent Knight), 1366
Braddock, General Edward, 842
Bradley (Buried Child), 262
Bradley (Sea Glass), 1711
Bradley, Dr. (The Man Who Came to Dinner), 1180
Bradley, Jackson, 301
Bradmond (Bevis of Hampton), 182
Bradshaw, Bennett T., 498
Bradshaw, Jemima, 1676
Bradshaw, Mr. (Ruth), 1676
Bradshaw, Richard, 1676
Bradshaw, Sir William, 1302
Bradwardine, Rose, 2107
Bradwardine, Sir Cosmo Comyne, 2107
Brady, Caithleen (Kate), 405, 406
Brady, Cecilia, 1054
Brady, Mathew, 352
Brady, Mick, 150
Brady, Mr. "Dada" (The Country Girls Trilogy and Epilogue), 405
Brady, Mrs. (Barry Lyndon), 150
Brady, Mrs. "Mama" (The Country Girls Trilogy and Epilogue), 405
Brady, Nora, 150
Brady, Nurse (The Pornographer), 1537
Brady, Pat, 1054
Brady, Susan, 1523
Brady, Uncle (Barry Lyndon), 150
Brady, Will Jennings, 2176
Brady, Will, Jr., 2176
Bragado, Doña Ramona, 852
Bragard, Count F. A. de (The Enormous Room), 582
Bragelonne, vicomte de (The Vicomte de Bragelonne), 2057
Bragg, Clinton, 1849
Braggadocio (The Faerie Queene), 611

Brague (The Vagabond), 2047
Bragwell (Roderick Random), 20
Brahe, Dr. Tycho, 1007
Brainworm (Every Man in His Humour), 599
Braithwaite, Cecil Otis, 894
Braithwaite, Edwin, 1573
Braithwaite, Ellen, 659
Braithwaite, Esther Brown, 894
Braithwaite, Geoffrey, 659
Braithwaite, Maurice, 1934
Bramber, Earl of (Handley Cross), 807
Bramble, Matthew, 604
Bramble, Tabitha, 605
Bramimond (The Song of Roland), 1810
Bramson, Mrs. (Night Must Fall), 1353
Branch, Nicholas, 1079
Brancovis, Marthe de, 2098
Brancovis, Teck de, 2098
Brand (Brand), 236
Brand, Abbot (Hereward the Wake), 839
Brand, Sir Denys, 231
Branden, Philip, 1715
Brander, George Sylvester, 970
Brandimart (Orlando furioso), 1424
Brandini, Carleto, 528
Brandini, Estrela Vésper, 529
Brandir, Lord Alan, 1125
Brandon, Colonel (Sense and Sensibility), 1730
Brandon, Constancia, 1418
Brandon, David, 335
Brandon, George, 1418
Brandon, Sir William, 1634
Brandt, Margaret, 357
Brandt, Peter, 357
Brandy (The Search for Signs of Intelligent Life in the Universe), 1716
Brandybuck, Meriadoc (Merry), 1123
Brangene (Tristan and Isolde), 1998
Branghton, Mr. (Evelina), 598
Brangwaine (Le Morte d'Arthur), 1283
Brangwen, Gudrun, 1590, 2165
Brangwen, Tom, 1589
Brangwen, Ursula, 1589, 2165
Brangwen, William (Will), 1589
Branly, Comte de (Distant Relations), 503
Brannon, Biff, 819
Branom, Dr. (A Clockwork Orange), 356
Brant, Captain Adam, 1293
Brant, Joseph, 541
Brant, Stephen, 677
Brantley, Ethelred T., 384
Branwen (The Mabinogion), 1153
Brasher, Phil, 141
Brashford, Jake, 1606
Brask, Hans, 692
Brasowitsch, Athalie, 1267
Brasowitsch, Athanas, 1267
Brasowitsch, Mrs. (A Modern Midas), 1267

Centuri (Right You Are (If You Think So)), 1638

Centurio (Celestina), 307

Ceparius (Catiline), 303

Céphise (Andromache), 67

Cepparello, Ser, 475

Cerda, Amalia, 393

Cereno, Don Benito, 176

Ceres (The Centaur), 309

Ceres (Proserpine and Ceres), 1566

Cérès, M. Hippolyte, 1480

Cerimon (Pericles, Prince of Tyre), 1487

Cervantes, Luis, 2034

Cervantes, Miguel de, 1912

Cervier, Le Loup (The Deerslayer), 477

César, Don (Fortune Mends), 678

Cesare (V.), 2046

Césarine (César Birotteau), 312

Cesira (Two Women), 2019

Cespedes, Don Luis de, 492

Cespedes, Leonora de, 492

Cethegus, Caius, 303

Ceyssac, Madame (Dominique), 520

Ceyx (Book of the Duchess), 227

Chabalier, Bernard, 261

Chabouly, Monsieur (Paradox, King), 1458

Chactas (Atala), 110

Chadband, The Reverend Mr. (Bleak House), 203

Chaddha, Mr. (The Householder), 885

Chad's Bess, 15

Chadwick (The Warden), 2095

Chaerea (The Eunuch), 593

Chaerestratus (The Arbitration), 90

Chaffanbrass, Mr. (Orley Farm), 1427

Ch'ai Chin, 43

Chaikin, Freddy, 1523

Chainbearer (The Chainbearer), 314

Chainmail, Mr. (Crotchet Castle), 423

Chairman (Season of Anomy), 1719

Chairman of the City Council (The Bedbug), 164

Chaka (Chaka), 315

Chalk, Bobby, 1719

Chalk, Esther, 577

Chalk, Vera, 577

Challenge (Sundown), 1869

Chalmers, Irene, 760

Chalmers, Lawrence (Larry), 760

Chalmers, Nicholas (Nick), 760

Chaly, Maxim Petrovich, 281

Chamberlain (Dirty Linen), 502

Chamberlain, Art, 1105

Chamberlain, Brice, 1713

Chamberlayne, Edward, 363

Chamberlayne, Lavinia, 363

Chamberlin, Anne, 1203

Chamberlin, Colonel (Marse Chan), 1203

Chamberlin, Miss Lucy, 1203

Chambers, Frank, 1544

Chamcha, Saladin, 1696

Chamois Hunter (Manfred), 1188

Chamont (The Orphan), 1428

Chamorro, Juan, 1751

Champ (The Island of Crimea), 953

Champion-Cheney, Arnold, 346

Champion-Cheney, Clive, 347

Champion-Cheney, Elizabeth, 346

Champion-Cheney, Lady Catherine (Kitty), 347

Champmathieu (Les Misérables), 1258

Chan, Marse, 1203

Chan, Rainsford, 856

Chan Shih-yin (Dream of the Red Chamber), 536

Chancellor, Miss (The Madras House), 1162

Chancellor, Olive, 232

Chancery Prisoner (Pickwick Papers), 1505

Chandal, Channah, 454

Chandal, Ilana Davita, 454

Chandal, Michael, 454

Chandal, Sarah, 454

Chandler, Annie, 1623

Chandler, George, 1623

Chandler, James, 1622

Chandler, Karen, 1623

Chandler, Little (Dubliners), 541

Chandler, Marie, 1623

Chandler, Rose, 1623

Chandler, Susan, 1623

Chandlers (The Street), 1858

Chaney, Tom, 2006

Chang (Lost Horizon), 1129

Chang, Colonel (The Martyred), 1206

Chang Fei, 1658

Chang, Helen, 2021

Chang, Ralph, 2021

Chang Ta-kung, 1149

Chang, Theresa, 2021

Chang-hi-tang (The Circle of Chalk), 347

Chang-ling (The Circle of Chalk), 347

Chani (The Great Dune Trilogy), 772

Channing, Christina, 720

Channing, Mr. (Marse Chan), 1203

Channing, Mrs. (Marse Chan), 1203

Chant, Mercy, 1913

Chantal (The Balcony), 133

Chantal (The Sunday of Life), 1868

Chantal, Mlle (The Diary of a Country Priest), 496

Chantelouve (Down There), 531

Chantelouve, Hyacinthe, 531

Chanticleer (Reynard the Fox), 1630

Chantrapa (The Temple of Dawn), 1712

Chantry-Pigg, Father Hugh, 1978

Chantyman (Mourning Becomes Electra), 1293

Chao, Henry, 2021

Ch'ao Kai, 43

Chao Mao-ts'ai, 2007

Chao T'ai-yeh, 2006

Chao Wu-niang, 1148

Chao Yi-niang (Dream of the Red Chamber), 535

Chao Yün, 1659

Chap, First (Largo Desolato), 1045

Chap, Second (Largo Desolato), 1045

Chapdelaine, Maria, 1198

Chapdelaine, Mrs. (Maria Chapdelaine), 1198

Chapdelaine, Samuel, 1198

Chapin, Ann, 1905

Chapin, Edith Stokes, 1905

Chapin, Joseph (Joby), Jr., 1905

Chapin, Joseph Benjamin (Joe), 1905

Chapin, Marcus, 1288

Chapin, Merle Meekins, 1288

Chaplain, military (Mother Courage and Her Children), 1289

Chaplain, prison (Tattoo the Wicked Cross), 1899

Chaplain, prison (The Trial), 1992

Chaplitsky (The Queen of Spades), 1574

Chapuys (A Man for all Seasons), 1178

Chapy, Mr. (The Villagers), 2061

Char Nyuk Tsin, 815

Character Man, Old (Tonight We Improvise), 1971

Character Woman (Tonight We Improvise), 1971

Charcoal burner (Molloy), 1269

Chardon, Eve, 1129

Chardon, Lucien, 1129

Charinus (Andria), 65

Charisius (The Arbitration), 90

Charisma (V.), 2045

Charissa (The Faerie Queene), 610

Charites (The Golden Ass), 748

Charity (The Pilgrim's Progress), 1511

Charlebois, Odette, 1213

Charlemagne (Huon of Bordeaux), 893

Charlemagne (Orlando innamorato), 1425

Charlemagne (The Pilgrimage of Charlemagne), 1510

Charlemagne (The Song of Roland), 1809

Charles (As You Like It), 102

Charles (The Call of the Wild), 276

Charles (Dombey and Son), 519

Charles (Firstborn), 654

Charles (Henry VI, Part I), 834

Charles (The Hunchback of Notre Dame), 892

Charles (The Immoralist), 916

Charles (The MacGuffin), 1156

Charles (Quentin Durward), 1575

Charles (Zazie in the Metro), 2203

Charles I (John Inglesant), 977

Charles I (The Memoirs of a Cavalier), 1226

Charles I (Twenty Years After), 2014

Charles II (Old Saint Paul's), 1402

Clavering, Sir Francis, 850
Claverton, Lord (The Elder Statesman), 564
Claverton-Ferry, Michael, 564
Claverton-Ferry, Monica, 564
Clawson, Cliff, 97
Clay (Dutchman), 546
Clay, Ambrose, 2065
Clay, Collis, 1908
Clay, Georgette "Granny," 2065
Clay, Henry, 729, 2105
Clay, Lady Leocadia, 1236
Clay, Liza Lee, 2065
Clay, Marion, 70
Clay, Mrs. (Persuasion), 1490
Clay, Sir Robert, 1237
Clay, Violet, 2065
Clayhanger, Clara, 354
Clayhanger, Darius, 354
Clayhanger, Edwin, 354, 355
Clayhanger, George Edwin Cannon, 355
Clayhanger, Hilda, 355
Clayhanger, Maggie, 354, 355
Claypole, Noah, 1406
Claypool, Tom, 2070
Clayton, Donald, 2101
Clayton, Harriet, 2102
Clayton, Robert, 2101
Cleander (The Pretenders), 1553
Cléante (The Hypochondriac), 896
Cléante (The Miser), 1256
Clèante (Tartuffe), 1898
Cleary, John, 1862
Cleary, Nettie, 1862
Cleary, Timmy, 1862
Cleaver, Fanny, 1437
Cleaver, Harold, 997
Cleaver, M. (Our Mutual Friend), 1437
Clegg, Fredrick, 367
Cleghorn, Ma (Grey Granite), 1708
Clegthorpe, Samuel, 993
Clelia (The Borough), 231
Clem (The Wine of Astonishment), 2145
Clémence (Death on the Installment Plan), 472
Clemence (The Grandissimes), 767
Clemencia (Woman Hollering Creek and Other Stories), 2157
Clemens (The Last Athenian), 1045
Clemens, Brother (The Holy Sinner), 855
Clement (Hiding Place), 859
Clement, Father (The Fair Maid of Perth), 615
Clement, Justice (Every Man in His Humour), 599
Clement, Karen Hansen, 604
Clement, Sir James, 632
Clemente, Don (The Saint), 1681
Clementina, Maria, 2048
Clementine (The Poor Christ of Bomba), 1533

Clements, Laurence G., 1527
Clements, Mrs. Elizabeth, 2158
Clena, Viscount (Penguin Island), 1480
Clennam, Arthur, 1100
Clennam, Mrs. (Little Dorrit), 1100
Cleomenes (The Winter's Tale), 2150
Cleon (The Bondman), 218
Cleon (The Knights), 1028
Cleon (The Maid's Tragedy), 1169
Cleon (Pericles, Prince of Tyre), 1487
Cléone (Andromache), 67
Cleonice (The Castle of Fratta), 296
Cleonice (Lysistrata), 1151
Cleonte (The Would-Be Gentleman), 2182
Cleontius (The Forced Marriage), 674
Cleopatra (All for Love), 40
Cleopatra (Antony and Cleopatra), 83
Cleopatra (Caesar and Cleopatra), 271
Cleopatra (Dombey and Son), 520
Cleopatra (The Ides of March), 905
Cleopatra (The Legend of Good Women), 1067
Cleopatra-Semiramis (Back to Methuselah), 131
Cleora (The Bondman), 218
Clepper, Viney, 325
Cleremont (Philaster), 1498
Clergy (King Johan), 1017
Clergyman, A (Moll Flanders), 1268
Cleric, Gaston, 1311
Clerici, Giulia, 387
Clerici, Marcello, 386
Clerimont, Ned, 1768
Clerk (The Garden Party), 712
Clerk, Chief (The Metamorphosis), 1236
Clerk, young (Hunger), 893
Clerk of Inquiries (The Trial), 1992
Clerk of Oxford (The Canterbury Tales), 285
Clerricot, Miss (The Boarding-House), 216
Clerval, Henry, 689
Cleto (Sotileza), 1817
Cleveland (The Mysteries of Pittsburgh), 1319
Cleveland, Frederick, 2073
Cleveland, Hugh, 2143
Clèves, Prince de (The Princess of Clèves), 1558
Clèves, Princess de (The Princess of Clèves), 1558
Clevinger (Catch-22), 300
Clewes, Leland, 962
Clifford, Jane, 1384
Clifford, Tom, 531
Clifton, Tod, 947
Cligés (Cligés), 356
Climal, M. de (Marianne), 1090
Clinia (The Self-Tormentor), 1729
Clinias (Arcadia), 91
Clinker, Humphry, 605

Clinton, Henry (Harry), 668
Clinton, Mrs. (Evelina), 599
Clinton, Reverend E., 1612
Clipstone, Pete, 531
Clisthenes (Thesmophoriazusae), 1924
Clitandre (The Misanthrope), 1256
Clitheroe, Jack, 1524
Clitheroe, Nora, 1524
Clitipho (The Self-Tormentor), 1729
Cliton (The Liar), 1078
Clitophon (Arcadia), 91
Clive (Cloud Nine), 359
Cloche, Madame Sidonie, 143
Clock, E. A., 215
Clocklan, Percy, 731
Clodius (The Last Days of Pompeii), 1047
Cloe (The Faithful Shepherdess), 617
Clonbrony, Lady, 6
Clonbrony, Lord, 6
Clora (Family), 619
Cloridan (Orlando furioso), 1424
Clorin (The Faithful Shepherdess), 617
Clorinda (Jerusalem Delivered), 971
Close, Mister (Down from the Hill), 531
Closerstil, Mr. (Doctor Thorne), 512
Clotaldo (Life Is a Dream), 1087
Clotel (Clotel), 358
Cloten (Brut), 255
Cloten (Cymbeline), 432
Clothru (Deirdre), 478
Clotilde (Doctor Pascal), 511
Clotyn (Gorboduc), 762
Clout, Colin, 612, 1753
Clov (Endgame), 577
Clover (Animal Farm), 74
Clover (Watership Down), 2104
Clover, Charles, 1485
Clovis (Mont-Oriol), 1274
Clovis, Esther, 601, 1072
Clown (Antony and Cleopatra), 83
Clown (Botchan), 233
Clown (Doctor Faustus), 510
Clown (Othello), 1430
Clown (Triptych), 1997
Clown (The Winter's Tale), 2150
Clowns (Hamlet, Prince of Denmark), 806
Cloyd, Clem, 1014
Cloyne (Purple Dust), 1568
Clubin, Sieur, 1966
Clumly, Esther, 1871
Clumly, Fred, 1870
Clumsey, Sir Tunbelly, 1617
Clunch (The Old Wives' Tale), 1403
Cluny, Abbot of (Huon of Bordeaux), 893
Cluppins, Mrs. Betsey, 1505
Clutter, Bonnie, 918
Clutter, Herbert (Herb), 918
Clutter, Kenyon, 918
Clutter, Nancy, 918
Cluveau, Albert, 119

CHARACTER INDEX

CHARACTER INDEX

Hamille, Ironman, 709
Hamilton, Alexander, 267
Hamilton, Berry, 1835
Hamilton, Charles, 753
Hamilton, Doctor (Mutiny on the Bounty), 1309
Hamilton, Duke of (Henry Esmond), 848
Hamilton, Fannie, 1835
Hamilton, Freddy, 1187
Hamilton, Guy, 2191
Hamilton, Jack, 2068
Hamilton, Jenico, 490
Hamilton, Joe, 1835
Hamilton, John, 2181
Hamilton, Kit, 1835
Hamilton, Liza, 552
Hamilton, Milo, 2065
Hamilton, Rose, 767
Hamilton, Samuel, 552
Hamilton, Will, 552
Hamish (What's Bred in the Bone), 2120
Hamlet (Hamlet, Prince of Denmark), 805
Hamlet, ghost of King (Hamlet, Prince of Denmark), 805
Hamley, Roger, 2154
Hamley, Squire (Wives and Daughters), 2154
Hamm (Endgame), 577
Hamm, Frances, 1654
Hamm, Gene, 1654
Hammer, Marietta, 259
Hammer, Paul, 258
Hammer, Uncle (Roll of Thunder, Hear My Cry), 1656
Hammerdown, Mr. (Vanity Fair), 2051
Hammersley, Captain (Charles O'Malley, the Irish Dragoon), 321
Hammerton, William, 1028
Hammond (The Shoemaker's Holiday), 1757
Hammond, David, 1875
Hammond, Joyce Emily, 1555
Hammond, Old (News from Nowhere), 1343
Hammond, Richard (Dick), 1343
Hammond, Valerie, 1933
Hamond (The Vagabond), 2047
Hamondsson, Gunnar, 1850
Hamondsson, Kolskegg, 1850
Hampel, Alexander, 1486
Hamps, Aunt Clara, 354, 355
Hampton, Claudine, 1144
Hampton, Freddy, 348
Hampton, Hope, 945
Hampton, Reverend M., 1763
Hampton, Skip, 1048, 1144
Hananiah (In the Heart of the Seas), 921
Hana-no-suke (Hizakurige), 852
Hancock, Alexandra Finch, 1962
Hancock, Dr. (Pilgrimage), 1510

Hancock, Len, 1448
Hancock, Vee, 1448
Hand, Laurel McKelva, 1420
Hand, Robert, 603
Hand, Wilson, 1408
Handford, Julius, 1437
Hands, Georgie, 1743
Hands, Israel, 1987
Handsome (The Questionnaire), 1579
Handy, Abel, 2095
Handy, Old (The Bull from the Sea), 258
Hanema, Angela, 410
Hanema, Nancy, 410
Hanema, Piet, 410
Hanema, Ruth, 410
Hangman (The Quare Fellow), 1572
Hangman (The Spanish Tragedy), 1827
Hank (In the Heart of the Valley of Love), 923
Hank (The Boys in the Band), 234
Hanka (The Peasants), 1473
Hanks, Ruby, 490
Hann, Mr. (The Martyred), 1206
Hanna (The Sleepwalkers), 1784
Hannah (Clarissa), 353
Hannah (Jane Eyre), 966
Hannay, Richard, 1931
Hannibal (Casuals of the Sea), 298
Hannigan, Daisy, 191
Hanno (Salammbô), 1686
Hans (The King of the Golden River), 1020
Hans (The Kitchen), 1025
Hans (Luther), 1149
Hans (The Shoemaker's Holiday), 1757
Hansa, Per, 726
Hansel (The Rat), 1597
Hansen, Arne, 1755
Hansen, Mr. (After Many a Summer Dies the Swan), 25
Hansen, Peder, 726
Hansine (The Promised Land), 1565
Hanson, Minnie, 1779
Hanson, Sven, 1779
Hansted, Emanuel, 1565
Hansted, Mr. (The Promised Land), 1565
Hanuman (The Ramayana), 1593
Hanz, Gottfried, 677
Hapgood, Celia, 809
Hapgood, Elizabeth, 809
Hapgood, Penn, 427
Haphazard, Sir Abraham, 2095
Hapsburg, Duchess of (Funnyhouse of a Negro), 704
Har Dayal (Esmond in India), 589
Harald Sigurdsson the Stern (Heimskringla), 829
Harald the Fairhaired (Heimskringla), 829
Haraldsson, Mattias, 125
Harapha (Samson Agonistes), 1688
Harappa, Iskander, 1748

Harappa, Rani, 1748
Harcamone (Miracle of the Rose), 1253
Harcourt, Mr. (The Country Wife), 408
Harcourt-Reilly, Sir Henry, 363
Hard Case (The Quare Fellow), 1572
Hard Heart (The Last of the Mohicans), 1051
Hard-Heart (The Prairie), 1549
Hardacanute (Heimskringla), 829
Hardcaster, Percy, 1627
Hardcastle, Kate, 1750
Hardcastle, Miss (That Hideous Strength), 1825
Hardcastle, Mr. (She Stoops to Conquer), 1750
Hardcastle, Mrs. (She Stoops to Conquer), 1750
Harden, Jane, 1938
Harden, Lucia, 506
Hardenburg, Gretchen, 2200
Harder, T. Stedman, 1278
Hardibrás (Paradox, King), 1458
Hardihood (Odyssey), 1388
Hardin, Salvor, 682
Harding, Captain Cyrus, 1320
Harding, Dale, 1414
Harding, Eleanor, 2094
Harding, Hester, 1728
Harding, René, 1728
Harding, Reverend Septimus, 141, 1046, 2094
Härdtl, Anna, 378
Hardwigg, Professor (Journey to the Center of the Earth), 983
Hardy (Local Anaesthetic), 1108
Hardy, Benedict (Ben), 1230
Hardy, David, 2146
Hardy, François, 2087
Hardy, Lord (The Funeral), 703
Hardy, Louise, 2146
Hardy, Michael, 807
Hare, Jenny, 1303
Hare, Mary, 1635
Hare-Lip (Darkness at Noon), 449
Haredale, Emma, 144
Haredale, Geoffrey, 144
Hargrave, Millicent, 1906
Hargrave, Walter, 1906
Hargreaves, Sir John, 891
Hari (The Siege of Krishnapur), 1763
Harish, Noga, 569
Harish, Reuven, 569
Härjanson, Gistre, 1990
Hark (The Confessions of Nat Turner), 384
Harkavy, Daniel, 2058
Harker (Dessa Rose), 490
Harker, Jonathan, 532
Harkness, Gary, 577
Harkness, George, 925
Harkonnen, Baron Vladimir, 772

Nettles, Professor Leopold, 1044
Nettleship, Charlotte, 721
Nettleship, Horace, 721
Nettleship, Lionel, 721
Nettleship, Maudie, 721
Neubauer (Horacker), 865
Neuenburg, duke of (The Devil's Elixirs), 494
Neuenburger, Herr (Bluebeard), 214
Neumann, Baruch David, 1970
Neumiller, Alpha, 229
Neumiller, Augustina, 183
Neumiller, Charles, 183, 229
Neumiller, Charles John Christopher, 183
Neumiller, Jerome, 183, 229
Neumiller, Katherine, 230
Neumiller, Marie, 183, 184
Neumiller, Martin, 183, 229
Neumiller, Otto, 182
Neumiller, Susan, 184
Neumiller, Timothy "Tim," 184
Neuvillette, Christian de, 434
Neuwirth (Temptation), 1904
Nevada (A Photograph), 1502
Nevels, Amos, 517
Nevels, Cassie, 517
Nevels, Clovis, 517
Nevels, Clytie, 517
Nevels, Enoch, 517
Nevels, Gertie, 517
Nevels, Reuben, 517
Neves, Lobo, 585
Nevil, Colonel Sir Thomas, 368
Nevil, Lydia, 368
Nevile, Marmaduke, 1049
Neville (The Waves), 2107
Neville, Constance, 1750
Neville, George, 1021
Neville, Major (The Antiquary), 82
Neville, Philip, 869
Neville, Reverend Mr. A. J., 320
Nevins, John, 2003
New Orleans, Governor of (Manon Lescaut), 1190
Newberg, Jep, 1869
Newby family (The Chant of Jimmie Blacksmith), 321
Newcomb, Bee, 325
Newcome, Barnes, 1341
Newcome, Clive, 1341
Newcome, Colonel Thomas, 1340
Newcome, Ethel, 1341
Newcome, Hobson, 1341
Newcome, Jason, 314, 1696
Newcome, Lady Ann, 1341
Newcome, Mrs. Hobson, 1341
Newcome, Opportunity, 1614
Newcome, Rosa, 1341
Newcome, Seneca, 1614
Newcome, Sir Brian, 1341

Newcome, Sophia Althea, 1341
Newcome, Susan, 1341
Newcome, Thomas, Esq., 1341
Newman, Christopher, 55
Newman, James, 497
Newsome, Chadwick, 52
Newsome, Howie, 1439
Newson, Elizabeth-Jane, 1217
Newson, Richard, 1218
Newspaperman (The Man Who Would Be King), 1183
Newt (Lonesome Dove), 1113
Newton, Isaac, 1503
Neyarky, Alik, 263
Nezhdanov (Virgin Soil), 2067
Nezvanova, Anna "Netochka," 1335
N'Gone (Xala), 2189
Ngugi, Jim, 1024
Nguyen Thi Tuyet Suong, 1408
Niagara (Paul Bunyan), 1471
Niam (Finn Cycle), 645
Nibs (Peter Pan), 1492
Nibsmith, Ruth, 2121
Nicanor (Coriolanus), 395
Nicanor (The Cutter), 430
Niceros (The Satyricon), 1699
Nicholas (A High Wind Rising), 842
Nicholas (The Kitchen), 1026
Nicholas (A Nest of Simple Folk), 1335
Nicholas (A Woman Killed with Kindness), 2159
Nicholas, Cardinal (Heimskringla), 830
Nicholas, Saint (The Castle of Otranto), 297
Nicholas I (Hadji Murad), 801
Nicholas II (Oktiabr' Shestnadtsatogo), 1394
Nicholas III (The Divine Comedy), 505
Nicholas of Morimondo (The Name of the Rose), 1324
Nichols, Brigadier General (Guard of Honor), 793
Nichols, Dayton, 2195
Nicholson, Elizabeth (Liz), 2184
Nicholson, Reverend Arthur, 2185
Nicholson, Richard, 1209
Nicholson, Terry O., 839
Nicias (The Knights), 1028
Nick (The Handmaid's Tale), 807
Nick (The Knight of the Burning Pestle), 1028
Nick (The Time of Your Life), 1952
Nick (Who's Afraid of Virginia Woolf?), 2130
Nick (The Woods), 2172
Nicke (The Death of a Beekeeper), 466
Nickelmann (The Sunken Bell), 1870
Nickleby, Kate, 1345
Nickleby, Mrs. (Nicholas Nickleby), 1345
Nickleby, Nicholas, 1345
Nickleby, Ralph, 1345
Nickles (J. B.), 960

Nicodemon, Rabbi (The Nazarene), 1333
Nicodemus, King (The Mother), 1285
Niçois, Madame (Castle to Castle), 2096
Nicol, Brenda, 601
Nicola (Arms and the Man), 94
Nicola, Don (The Foreign Girl), 674
Nicola, Father (The Italian), 957
Nicolas (El Zarco, the Bandit), 2203
Nicolás, Fray (House Made of Dawn), 874
Nicolás, Master (Don Quixote de la Mancha), 524
Nicole (Memoirs of a Physician), 1227
Nicole (62: A Model Kit), 1781
Nicole (The World of the Thibaults), 2181
Nicole (The Would-Be Gentleman), 2182
Nicolette (Aucassin and Nicolette), 112
Nicoll (Fruits of the Earth), 702
Nicolo (To Have and to Hold), 1961
Nicopompus (Argenis), 93
Niece (Colours in the Dark), 370
Niece (Manhunt), 1189
Niece, Edward's (Edward II), 560
Nielsen, Marie, 1478
Niemand, Fritz Jemand von, 1815
Niessen, Lola, 2002
Nièvres, Madeleine de, 520
Nièvres, Monsieur de (Dominique), 520
Nifty Louis (The Man with the Golden Arm), 1184
Nigel (Kindred), 1013
Nigel (Quartet in Autumn), 1573
Night (The Faerie Queene), 610
Night Brother (Sour Sweet), 1821
Night Swan (Ceremony), 310
Nightgall, Lawrence, 1977
Nightingale (Bartholomew Fair), 151
Nightingale, Mr. (Tom Jones), 1969
Nightingale, R. E. A., 1857
Nightingale, Ronald, 1214
Nightshade, Jim, 1805
Nightshade, Mr. (Headlong Hall), 818
Nijo, Lady (Top Girls), 1973
Nikanj (Dawn), 2190
Nikanj (Imago), 2190
Nikila, Benjamin, 1222
Nikila, Maja, 1222
Nikita (Under Western Eyes), 2033
Nikka (The Bride), 240
Nikolaevna, Zinaida (Zina), 657
Nikolavna, Mary, 75
Nikolayevna, Anna, 106
Nikolayevna, Natalya, 331
Nikulaussön, Erlend, 1031
Niles, Bruce, 1367
Niles, Captain Peter, 1293
Niles, Hazel, 1293
Nils (Arne), 94
Nilsa (The Boy Without a Flag), 234
Nilssen, Peter, 1580
Nilsson, Axel, 615

Pearson, Bruce William, Jr., 1823

Pearson, Hattie Tyson, 978

Pearson, John, 978, 1238

Pearson, Judge Alf, 978

Pearson, Lucy Potts, 978

Pearson, Matey, 514

Pearson, Mr. (The Hoosier Schoolmaster), 863

Pearson, Mr. and Mrs. Walter (Angel Pavement), 69

Pearson, Sally Lovelace, 978

Pearson, Tub, 514

Peasant (Brand), 236

Peasant (Simplicissimus the Vagabond), 1774

Peasants (The Garden of Earthly Delights), 711

Peaseblossom (A Midsummer Night's Dream), 1246

Pechorin, Grigoriy Aleksandrovich, 840

Pechvarry (A Wizard of Earthsea), 2155

Peck, Georgiana, 359

Peck, Old Man (Green Grow the Lilacs), 782

Peck, Reverend John, 359

Peckem, General (Catch-22), 300

Peckham, Charlotte Thom, 1281

Peckham, Lewis, 1720

Pecksniff, Charity, 1204

Pecksniff, Mercy, 1204

Pecksniff, Seth, 1204

Pecksuot (The Courtship of Miles Standish), 412

Pécuchet (Bouvard and Pécuchet), 233

Pedal, Lady (Malone Dies), 1269

Pedant (The Taming of the Shrew), 1893

Pedant, Sir Avarice, 1903

Pedant, Young (The Temple Beau), 1903

Peddler (Green Grow the Lilacs), 782

Peder (The People of Juvik), 1481

Pedersen, Dr. Karl, 2170

Pedersen, Frederich, 2170

Pedersen, Hilda, 2170

Pedersen, Jesse, 2169

Pedersen, Mary, 2170

Pedigree, Sebastian, 449

Pedlar, 981

Pedlar, John Abner, 149

Pedlar, Nathan, 149

Pedrick, Reverend Horace, 411

Pedrico (The Old Man and the Sea), 1400

Pedrillo (Don Juan), 523

Pedringano (The Spanish Tragedy), 1827

Pedro (The Changeling), 318

Pedro (Macho!), 1156

Pedro (Victory), 2059

Pedro, Don (The Devil upon Two Sticks), 492

Pedro, Don (Much Ado About Nothing), 1304

Pedro, Master (Don Quixote de la Mancha), 525

Pedro, Prince (Ignes de Castro), 910

Pedro-Surplus (Zazie in the Metro), 2203

Pedrugo, Pedrillo, 1069

Peecher, Emma, 1438

Peeker (The Wreckage of Agathon), 2185

Peel, Margaret, 1146

Peel, Maureen, 215

Peel, Parson Daniel, 1469

Peel-Swynnerton, Matthew, 1403

Peep, Mother (The Killer), 1010

Peep-Bo (The Mikado), 1248

Peeperkorn, Mynheer (The Magic Mountain), 1164

Peet (The Whole Armour), 799

Peet, Reverend (Spoon River Anthology), 1834

Peety, Nanny, 572

Pegeen Mike (The Playboy of the Western World), 1523

Peggotty, Clara, 452

Peggotty, Daniel, 452

Peggotty, Ham, 452

Peggy (At Swim-Two-Birds), 108

Peggy (The Dining Room), 499

Peggy (Lucy), 1147

Peggy (Monkey Grip), 1271

Peggy (Mutiny on the Bounty), 1309

Peggy (The Taking of Miss Janie), 1887

Peggy (Turvey), 2011

Peggy, Aunt (The Conjure Woman), 388

Pegler, Mrs. (Hard Times), 811

Peider (Andorra), 65

Peiksva, Father (The Issa Valley), 956

Peiraeus (Odyssey), 1387

Peisistratus (Odyssey), 1387

Pekuah (Rasselas), 1596

Pelagia (Hypatia), 895

Pelagio, Don (The Satin Slipper), 1697

Pelasgus (The Suppliants), 1872

Pelayo (Paradox, King), 1457

Pelayo (The King, the Greatest Alcalde), 1021

Peleg, Captain (Moby Dick), 1265

Pelele (El Señor Presidente), 1729

Pelet, M. (The Professor), 1561

Pelet, Mme (The Professor), 1562

Peleus (Andromache), 66

Pelham, Hannah, 50

Pelham, Major John, 1875

Pelham, Morris, 1875

Pelias (Jason and the Golden Fleece), 967

Pell, Adam, 2140

Pell, Solomon, 1505

Pellam, King (Idylls of the King), 907

Pelleas (Idylls of the King), 906

Pelléas (Pelléas and Mélisande), 1478

Pellegrinotto, Don Eligio, 1056

Pellerin (Night Flight), 1351

Pellerin (A Sentimental Education), 1731

Pelles, King (Le Morte d'Arthur), 1282

Pellinore (Le Morte d'Arthur), 1283

Pelops (Thyestes), 1945

Peloux, Charlotte, 323, 324

Peloux, Frédéric, 323, 324

Pelumpton, Mr. (Angel Pavement), 69

Pelumpton, Mrs. (Angel Pavement), 69

Pelzer, Walter, 792

Pemberton, Lady Honoria, 307

Pembroke (Edward II), 560

Pembroke, Agnes, 1118

Pembroke, earl of (King John), 1018

Pembroke, Herbert, 1118

Pembroke, Lord (The Tower of London), 1977

Pembroke, Ralph, 551

Pena, Fausta, 1910

Peña, Manuel, 1435

Pénable, Renée de, 514

Peñaloza, Humberto, 1381

Peñas, Sabas, 1479

Pencroft, Jack, 1320

Penda (Brut), 256

Pendennis, Arthur (The Newcomes), 1342

Pendennis, Arthur (Pendennis), 849

Pendennis, Helen, 849

Pendennis, Laura, 849, 1342

Pendennis, Major Arthur, 849

Penderton, Captain Weldon, 1614

Penderton, Leonora, 1614

Pendleton, Jill, 1584

Pendola, Father (The Castle of Fratta), 296

Pendomer, Mrs. Clarice, 1647

Pendrake, Mrs. (Little Big Man), 1099

Pendyce, George, 406

Pendyce, Horace, 406

Pendyce, Margery, 406

Penelope (The Moonstone), 1280

Penelope (Odyssey), 1386

Penfeather, Lady Penelope, 1684

Penfold, Mark, 1072

Pengilly, Reverend Andrew, 569

Penguillan, Benjamin, 1515

Peniculus (The Menaechmi), 1231

Peniston, Darthea, 889

Peniston, Mrs. (The House of Mirth), 878

Penn, Winston, 1131

Pennett, Mr. (Memoirs of a Fox-Hunting Man), 1226

Penniman, Lavinia, 2097

Pennsylvania (Captains Courageous), 291

Penny, Gilbert, 1936

Penny, Howat, 1936

Penny, Jasper, 1936

Penny Whistle (Tonight We Improvise), 1971

Pennyfeather, Paul, 476

Penrose, Jocelyn, 555

Penrose, Julius, 269

Penrose, Marjorie, 269
Pentacost, Candida (Candy), 1011
Pentacost, Jarcey, 1377
Pentecost, Martha Loomis, 974
Pentheus (The Bacchae), 128
Pentland, Bascom, 1391
Pentstemon, Uncle (Mr. Polly), 849
Peona (Endymion), 578
People in and around Sirancy, France (The Inquisitory), 939
Pepa, Mari, 1479
Pepablo (Stone Desert), 1847
Pepe (He Who Searches), 816
Pépé, Don (Nostromo), 1370
Pepel, Vaska, 1142
Pepel, Vassily, 1142
Pepeta (The Cabin), 270
Pepita (The Bridge of San Luis Rey), 242
Pepito (The Great Galeoto), 775
Pepler, Alvin, 2208
Pepper (Great Expectations), 774
Pepper (The Snail on the Slope), 1791
Pepper, Harry, 142
Pepperill, Dan, 427
Peppino (The Count of Monte-Cristo), 401
Peps, Dr. Parker, 520
Per (The People of Juvik), 1481, 1482
Peralta, Don (The Purple Land That England Lost), 1569
Peran-Wisa (Sohrab and Rustum), 1797
Peranzules, Don Álvaro, 602
Perault (The Call of the Wild), 276
Perceval (The Quest of the Holy Grail), 1577
Perceval, Sibyl, 982
Perceval of Wales (Cligés), 356
Perch, Mr. (Dombey and Son), 520
Perch, Mrs. (Dombey and Son), 520
Perch, Mrs. (If Winter Comes), 910
Percival (The Waves), 2107
Percival, Bettina, 1
Percival, Dr. Emmanuel, 890
Percival, Eglantine "Tina," 1405
Percival, Harry, 1405
Percival, Lady Anne, 169
Percival, Mr. (Belinda), 169
Percival, Sir. See also Parzival
Percival, Sir (Le Morte d'Arthur), 1282
Percivale, Sir (Idylls of the King), 906
Percy (The Wave), 2105
Percy, Captain Ralph, 1961
Percy, Henry, 1633
Percy, Henry, Jr., 832
Percy, Henry, Sr., 832
Percy, Stewart "Fat Stew," 2177
Percy, Thomas, 832
Perdican (No Trifling with Love), 1365
Perdicas (Tamburlaine the Great), 1892
Perdikkas (Funeral Games), 704
Perdita (The Winter's Tale), 2149

Perdorff, Dr. (Kings Row), 1024
Peredur (The Mabinogion), 1153
Peregil (Legend of the Moor's Legacy), 1068
Peregil's wife (Legend of the Moor's Legacy), 1069
Peregrina, Loyd, 73
Peregrine (Volpone), 2075
Pereira, Alfonso, 2061
Pereira, Chico, 1521
Pereira, Lindinalva, 988
Pereira, Mary, 1245
Peret, Louise, 426
Peretola, Zoroastro da, 1657
Perez, Catalena, 799
Perez, Colonel (The Honorary Consul), 861
Perez, Dominic, 799
Pérez, Dora, 1458
Pérez, General (Paradox, King), 1458
Pérez, Gil, 729
Perez, Michael, 1672
Pérez, Mortal, 698
Pérez, Pedro, 524
Perez, Pito, 705
Perez Zambullo, Don Cleophas Leandro, 492
Peribáñez, Don Platón, 271
Périchole, La (The Bridge of San Luis Rey), 242
Pericles (Pericles, Prince of Tyre), 1487
Pericles, Captain (The King of the Mountains), 1020
Periebanou (The Arabian Nights' Entertainments), 90
Perigot (The Faithful Shepherdess), 617
Perillo, Nikolai Gorimirovich, 1704
Perine, Effie, 1175
Perión of Gaul, King, 52
Periplecomenus (The Braggart Soldier), 236
Periquillo (The Itching Parrot), 957
Perissa (The Faerie Queene), 610
Peritas (The Persian Boy), 1488
Perithous (The Two Noble Kinsmen), 2016
Perken (The Royal Way), 1669
Perker, Mr. (Pickwick Papers), 1505
Perkins, Corporal Thankful, 1559
Perkins, Madge, 908
Perkins, Noddy, 462
Perkins-Cooke, Sammie Jo, 462
Permaneder, Alois, 257
Permaneder, Frau (Buddenbrooks), 257
Pernalete, Ño, 526
Perne, Misses (Pilgrimage), 1510
Pernelle, Madame (Tartuffe), 1898
Pero (Bussy d'Ambois), 268
Pérouse, La (The Counterfeiters), 402
Perpetua, Rose, 970
Perraj, Rito, 1861
Perrault, Dr. Roderick, 2170
Perrault, Father (Lost Horizon), 1129
Perrin (The Doctor in Spite of Himself), 511
Perron, Guy, 1592

Perrot, Bastian, 737
Perry (Peregrine Pickle), 1485
Perry, Ida, 1075
Perry, Matthew, 733
Perseda (The Spanish Tragedy), 1827
Persephone (The King Must Die), 1019
Perses (Works and Days), 2176
Perseus (The Metamorphoses), 1236
Persial, Mr. (In the Ditch), 921
Persio (The Winners), 2147
Persky, Simon, 1749
Person, Thin (Peer Gynt), 1477
Perth (Moby Dick), 1265
Perturber, Professor John R., Jr., 1909
Pervading Fragrance (Dream of the Red Chamber), 536
Pesah, Rabbi (In the Heart of the Seas), 922
Pesca, Professor (The Woman in White), 2158
Pescara, marquis of (The Duchess of Malfi), 542
Pescatore, Romilda, 1056
Pestalozzi, Corporal (That Awful Mess on Via Merulana), 1915
Pestov, Marfa Timofyevna, 877
Pet (Little Dorrit), 1100
Pet (Little House on the Prairie), 1103
Petacci, Claretta, 608
Pete (Blues for Mister Charlie), 214
Pete (City of Night), 352
Pete (A Clockwork Orange), 356
Pete (Maggie), 1163
Pete (Requiem for a Nun), 1621
Pete (Saved), 1701
Pete (The Universal Baseball Association, Inc., J. Henry Waugh, Prop.), 2039
Pete the Peek (Yellow Back Radio Broke-Down), 2194
Peter (The Apostle), 86
Peter (Badenheim 1939), 131
Peter (The Edible Woman), 558
Peter (The Floating World), 663
Peter (The Kitchen), 1025
Peter (The Last Athenian), 1045
Peter (My Ántonia), 1311
Peter (Pincher Martin), 1513
Peter (Porgy), 1535
Peter (The Romance of the Forest), 1658
Peter (Romeo and Juliet), 1661
Peter (Shuttlecock), 1761
Peter (A Tale of a Tub), 1887
Peter (The Zoo Story), 2206
Peter, Father (The Mysterious Stranger), 1320
Peter, Friar (Measure for Measure), 1220
Peter, Saint (The Divine Comedy), 506
Peter, Saint (Jurgen), 995
Peter, Saint (Sand Mountain), 1690
Peter Innocent Bon, 2053
Peter of Pomfret (King John), 1018

Philip III (Funeral Games), 704
Philip, Duke (Monsieur d'Olive), 1273
Philip the Bastard (King John), 1017
Philip the Fair (The Lion of Flanders), 1097
Philipot, Henri, 371
Philippa (The Lion of Flanders), 1097
Philippe (Memoirs of a Physician), 1227
Philippe (The Vicomte de Bragelonne), 2057
Philiste (The Liar), 1078
Phillip (A Generous Man), 719
Phillip, Jackson, 1453
Phillips, Ceinwen, 886
Phillips, Gilbert, 459
Phillips, Grace Renfrew, 1694
Phillips, Joe, 1951
Phillips, Matthew, 1694
Phillips, Maud Martha Brown, 1215
Phillips, Paul, 1215
Phillips, Paulette, 1216
Phillips, Queenie, 683
Phillips, Reverend James Forrest, 1694
Phillips, Sarah, 1694
Phillotson, Richard, 990
Philo (Antony and Cleopatra), 83
Philoclea (Arcadia), 91
Philocleon (The Wasps), 2097
Philocomasium (The Braggart Soldier), 236
Philocrates (The Captives), 292
Philoctetes (Philoctetes), 1498
Philoetius (Odyssey), 1386
Philogano (The Pretenders), 1553
Philomela (The Legend of Good Women), 1067
Philomen (Minty Alley), 1253
Philomena (Kwaku), 1032
Philomène (Mouchette), 1290
Philomène, Sister (Sister Philomène), 1780
Philopolemus (The Captives), 291
Philosophe, Palmyre, 767
Philosopher (Rasselas), 1596
Philosopher, Old (The Crock of Gold), 422
Philosophy master (The Would-Be Gentleman), 2183
Philostrate (A Midsummer Night's Dream), 1246
Philotime (The Faerie Queene), 611
Philotis (Marriage à la Mode), 1202
Philotis ('Tis Pity She's a Whore), 1956
Philotus (Timon of Athens), 1953
Philoxenus (Arcadia), 91
Philpot, Dudley, 1840
Philtera (The Faerie Queene), 612
Philumena (Andria), 65
Phineas (A Separate Peace), 1732
Phineus (Jason and the Golden Fleece), 968
Phipps, Denis, 1822
Phipps, Gillian (Jill), 1627
Phipps, Tristram (Tristy), 1627
Phlegyas (The Divine Comedy), 504

Phoebe (Daniel Martin), 445
Phoebus (The Metamorphoses), 1235
Phoedime (Mithridates), 1262
Phoenicium (Pseudolus), 1567
Phoenicopterus (The Birds), 192
Phoenix (Andromache), 67
Phoenix (Dream of the Red Chamber), 535
Phoibee, Pollo, 1912
Phokus (Bend Sinister), 175
Pholus (The Divine Comedy), 505
Phormio (Phormio), 1501
Phosphoridos (Romulus the Great), 1663
Photini (The King of the Mountains), 1020
Photographers (The Balcony), 134
Phraortes, Prince (Artamenes), 97
Phrygia (The Brothers), 251
Phrygia (The Pot of Gold), 1546
Phrynia (Timon of Athens), 1953
Phunky, Mr. (Pickwick Papers), 1505
Phuong (The Quiet American), 1580
Phylax (Romulus the Great), 1663
Phyllis (Coonardoo), 394
Phyllis (Iolanthe), 950
Phyllis (The Legend of Good Women), 1067
Physical Training (Chips with Everything), 339
Physician (No One Writes to the Colonel), 1364
Physician, old (The Menaechmi), 1231
Pi, Dr. Omicron, 141
Pia, La (The Divine Comedy), 505
Pia, Lady Emilia, 226
Pian, Brigitte, 1042, 2160
Pian, Louis, 2160
Pian, Marthe, 2160
Pian, Michèle, 2160
Pian, Octave, 2160
Piani (A Farewell to Arms), 627
Pianura, duke of (The Valley of Decision), 2048
Piatt, Oliver, 1772
Picardia (The Return of Martín Fierro), 717
Piccarda (The Divine Comedy), 506
Piccolino (The Dwarf), 546
Piccolomini, Max, 2085
Piccolomini, Prince Octavio, 2085
Pich, Miss (Paradox, King), 1458
Pichana (Black Valley), 199
Pickard, Sarah, 325
Pickerbaugh, Dr. Almus, 97
Pickerbaugh, Orchid, 97
Pickering, Colonel (Pygmalion), 1569
Pickett, Clarence, 1075
Pickle, Gam, 1485
Pickle, Gamaliel, 1485
Pickle, Grizzle, 1485
Pickle, Julia, 1485
Pickle, Peregrine, 1485
Pickpocket, black (Mr. Sammler's Planet), 1297

Pickpockets (Operetta), 1420
Pickwick, Mr. Samuel, 1504
Pickwort, Hedgepinshot Mandeville, 86
Picrochole (Gargantua and Pantagruel), 714
Piedad, Santa Sofía de la, 1416
Pierce (The Basic Training of Pavlo Hummel), 152
Pierce of Exton, Sir (Richard II), 1633
Pierce, Cushman (Cushie), 2177
Pierce, Joel, 1391
Pierce, Mitchell, 482
Pierce, Tam, 482
Piero (The Revenger's Tragedy), 1629
Piero da Medicina, 505
Pierpoint (The Apes of God), 85
Pierpoint, Ethel Drayson, 1241
Pierpoint, Mrs. (Mid-Channel), 1241
Pierquin (The Quest of the Absolute), 1577
Pierre (The Flanders Road), 658
Pierre (Invitation to a Beheading), 948
Pierre (The Madwoman of Chaillot), 1162
Pierre (Natives of My Person), 1331
Pierre (Possessing the Secret of Joy), 1543
Pierre (Venice Preserved), 2054
Pierre (Wide Sargasso Sea), 2131
Pierre, Maître (Quentin Durward), 1575
Pierrot (Don Juan), 523
Pierrot (Miracle of the Rose), 1253
Piers (The Shepheardes Calendar), 1753
Piers the Plowman (Piers Plowman), 1508
Pietersen, Morris, 206
Pietersen, Zachariah, 206
Pietra, Venceslau Pietro, 1158
Pietranera, Gina, 322
Pietro (The Cloister and the Hearth), 357
Pietro (A Quality of Mercy), 1571
Piety (The Pilgrim's Progress), 1511
Pigasov, Afrikan Semyonych, 1671
Pigeon (Alice's Adventures in Wonderland), 38
Pigeon, Cecily, 1384
Pigeon, Gwendolyn, 1384
Pigeon, Nicholas, 1747
Pigeonnier, Madame (The Bark Tree), 143
Pigg (Handley Cross), 807
Pigg, James, 843
Piggott, Agnes, 1718
Piggott, Fola, 1718
Piggott, Police Commissioner "Piggy," 1718
Piggy (Lord of the Flies), 1122
Pigsie (Griever), 789
Pigsy (Monkey), 985
Pihl, Rud, 1478
Pilar (El Zarco, the Bandit), 2203
Pilar (For Whom the Bell Tolls), 672
Pilar, Abbess Madre Maria del (The Bridge of San Luis Rey), 242
Pilar the Black (I, the Supreme), 901
Pilate (Song of Solomon), 1810
Pilate, Pontius, 1210

CHARACTER INDEX

Prothero, Mary "Pokey," 791

Protiste, Abbé (Journey to the End of the Night), 983

Protopopov (The Three Sisters), 1940

Protos (Lafcadio's Adventures), 1040

Proudfit, Willie, 1354

Proudfute, Oliver, 615

Proudie, Bishop Thomas, 1046

Proudie, Dr. (Barchester Towers), 140

Proudie, Mrs. (Barchester Towers), 140

Proudie, Mrs. (Doctor Thorne), 512

Proudie, Mrs. (Framley Parsonage), 688

Proudie, Mrs. (The Last Chronicle of Barset), 1046

Proudie, Olivia, 141, 688

Proudlock (Mr. Facey Romford's Hounds), 1296

Prouheze, Doña (The Satin Slipper), 1697

Prouty, Squire (The Green Mountain Boys), 785

Prouza, Jan, 582

Provedoni, Antonio, 296

Provedoni, Aquilina, 296

Provedoni, Leopardo, 296

Provincial (Brother Ass), 251

Provis, Mr. (Great Expectations), 774

Provo, Lois, 719

Provo, Selma, 719

Provocación (A Meditation), 1221

Provost (Measure for Measure), 1220

Prozorov, Andrey, 1940

Prozorov, Irina, 1940

Prozorov, Olga, 1940

Prst, Veronika, 581

Prudence (Caught), 305

Prudence (The Pilgrim's Progress), 1511

Prudence, Mme (Camille), 279

Prue (The Gentleman Dancing Master), 720

Prulliére (Nana), 1325

Prunesquallor, Alfred, 764

Prunesquallor, Irma, 764

Prushevsky (The Foundation Pit), 681

Pryanchikov, Valentine (Valentulya) Martynich, 653

Pryderi (The Mabinogion), 1153

Pryer (The Way of All Flesh), 2108

Prynne, Amanda, 1560

Prynne, Hester, 1702

Prynne, Mrs. (Da), 436

Prynne, Ms. (A Month of Sundays), 1276

Prynne, Ruth, 1189

Prynne, Victor, 1560

Pryor, Mrs. (Shirley), 1757

Prytanis (Thesmophoriazusae), 1924

Przyballa, Lina, 179

Pseudartabas (The Acharnians), 11

Pseudolus (Pseudolus), 1567

Psmith, Ronald Eustace, 1064

Psyche (Cupid and Psyche), 427

Psyche (The Golden Ass), 749

Psyche (The Princess), 1557

Psyche (Till We Have Faces), 1948

Ptits-pieds, Madeleine (Mado), 2203

Ptolemy (Fire from Heaven), 648

Ptolemy (Funeral Games), 704

Ptolemy (The Persian Boy), 1488

Publisher (The Left-Handed Woman), 1066

Publius (Julius Caesar), 991

Publius (Titus Andronicus), 1959

Publius Porphyrius (The Death of the Gods), 471

Publius Vergilius Maro (The Death of Virgil), 471

Pucci, Giannozzo, 1662

Puccio (The Divine Comedy), 505

Pucelle, Joan la (Henry VI, Part I), 834

Pucinski, Murray "The Goose," 1070

Puck (A Midsummer Night's Dream), 1246

Puddleton, Miss (The Well of Loneliness), 2116

Puente, Lourdes, 539

Puente, Pilar, 539

Puentes, Isidro, 1847

Puff, Mr. (The Critic), 421

Puget, Lieutenant Peter, 265

Pugh, Mr. (Under Milk Wood), 2029

Puig (Man's Hope), 1192

Pujaree (The Shadow Bride), 1745

Pukhov, Andrey, 1917

Pukhov, Vladimir "Volyoda" Andreyevich, 1917

Pulcher, Clodia, 905

Puli (Nectar in a Sieve), 1334

Pullet, Mr. (The Mill on the Floss), 1249

Pullet, Mrs. Sophy, 1249

Pulleyn, Lady Clara, 1341

Pulleyn, Lady Henrietta, 1342

Pullman, James, 889

Pultoric, Tiger, 1336

Pulver, Ensign (Mister Roberts), 1261

Pumblechook, Uncle (Great Expectations), 774

Pumpkin (Portnoy's Complaint), 1538

Pumpkin, Jewish (Portnoy's Complaint), 1538

Pums, Herr (Berlin Alexanderplatz), 179

Punt, Larry, 1551

Punt, Mrs. Amy, 849

Puntarvolo (Every Man out of His Humour), 600

Puntschu (Pandora's Box), 1453

Pup (Leaf Storm), 1062

Pupil (The Lesson), 1073

Puppy (Alice's Adventures in Wonderland), 38

Puppy (Bartholomew Fair), 151

Purdie, Jack, 461

Purdie, Mabel, 461

Purdy, Colonel (The Teahouse of the August Moon), 1900

Pureco, Father (The Futile Life of Pito Perez), 705

Purecraft, Dame (Bartholomew Fair), 151

Purefoy, Mrs. (Ulysses), 2025

Purgon, Dr. (The Hypochondriac), 896

Purkeet, Rick, 229

Purple Cuckoo (Dream of the Red Chamber), 536

Pursewarden, Percy, 35-37

Purvis, Captain (A Bell for Adano), 170

Pusey, Iris, 868

Pusey, Jennifer, 868

Pushkin (Boris Godunov), 229

Puta, Roger, 983

Putana ('Tis Pity She's a Whore), 1956

Putbus, Count Malte Moritz von, 1830

Putnam, Abbie, 489

Putnam, Thomas, 423

Puttbutt, Benjamin "Chappie," III, 966

Puttbutt, George Eliott, 966

Puyat, Pauline, 1980

Puybaraud, Léonce, 2160

Puysange, Felise de, 995

Pwyll (The Mabinogion), 1153

Pye, Albert, 305

Pyetukh (Dead Souls), 460

Pygmalion (Back to Methuselah), 131

Pyke (Nicholas Nickleby), 1347

Pylade (Andromache), 67

Pylades (*Euripides'* Electra), 566

Pylades (*Sophocles'* Electra), 567

Pylades (Iphigenia in Tauris), 952

Pylaszczkiewicz (Ferdydurke), 635

Pyle (The Petrified Forest), 1494

Pyle, Alden, 1580

Pym (Adam Bede), 15

Pym, Arthur Gordon, 1328

Pym, Della, 172

Pym, Magnus Richard, 1486

Pym, Mary (Mabs), 1487

Pym, Richard Thomas "Rick," 1486

Pym, Thomas Richard "Tom," 1487

Pymsent, Mr. (Pendennis), 851

Pyncheon, Clifford, 879

Pyncheon, Colonel (The House of the Seven Gables), 879

Pyncheon, Hepzibah, 880

Pyncheon, Jaffrey, 879

Pyncheon, Phoebe, 880

Pyne (Volunteers), 2076

Pynsent, Amanda, 1557

Pyramus (The Legend of Good Women), 1067

Pyramus (Romulus the Great), 1663

Pyrgopolinices (The Braggart Soldier), 235

Pyrochles (The Faerie Queene), 611

Pyrocles (Arcadia), 91

Pyrot (Penguin Island), 1480

Pyrrhot (Bussy d'Ambois), 268

Pyrrhus (Andromache), 67

Ronald (Hopscotch), 864
Ronberry, Miss (The Corn Is Green), 395
Rondò, Battista di, 146
Rondò, Corradino di, 146
Rondón, Dolores, 698
Ronnie (Getting Out), 723
Ronno (Bambi), 137
Rönnow, Captain (The Family at Gilje), 620
Ronny, Mr. (Marse Chan), 1203
Roo, Aunt (Harland's Half Acre), 812
Rookwood, Barberina, 654
Roon, Armin von, 2092
Roon, General Armin von, 2143
Rooney (Streamers), 1857
Rooney (Wheat That Springeth Green), 2121
Rooney, Andy, 808
Rooney, Mr. (All That Fall), 46
Rooney, Mrs. (All That Fall), 46
Rooney, Mrs. (Handy Andy), 808
Rooney, Raglan "Pappy," 2039
Roos, Anneliese (Rose), 121
Roosevelt, Franklin Delano, 2143
Root, Arnold, 738
Root, Esther, 1590
Root, Mr. (Raintree County), 1590
Rooth, Miriam, 1981
Rootham, Margaret Matthews, 1360
Roper, Amelia, 1787
Roper, Edwin, 1991
Roper, Jim, 701
Roper, Mrs. (The Small House at
    Allington), 1787
Roper, William, 1178
Ropes, Silas, 427
Roque, Louise, 1731
Roque, M. (A Sentimental Education), 1731
Roquentin, Antoine, 1332
Rörlund, Doctor (The Pillars of Society),
    1512
Rory (Roderick Random), 19
Rosa (Bleak House), 203
Rosa (Independent People), 929
Rosa (The Line of the Sun), 1097
Rosa, Doña (The Hive), 851
Rosa Maria (Zero), 2204
Rosalba (Love in the Time of Cholera),
    1136
Rosalba, Ellena di, 956
Rosales, Romeo (Orlando), 517
Rosalie (A Woman's Life), 2162
Rosalind (As You Like It), 101
Rosalind (Green Card), 780
Rosalinde (The Shepheardes Calendar),
    1753
Rosaline (Love's Labour's Lost), 1141
Rosamond (The Robber Bridegroom), 1651
Rosamund (The Fountain Overflows), 683
Rosamund, Queen (Ubu Roi), 2023
Rosanette (A Sentimental Education), 1731

Rosario (The Cabin), 270
Rosario (Coronation), 397
Rosario (Doña Perfecta), 527
Rosario (The Family of Pascual Duarte), 622
Rosario (The Lost Steps), 1131
Rosario, Wanda, 1786
Rosas, Concha, 306
Rosas de Vives, Josefina, 1934
Rosasharn (The Grapes of Wrath), 768
Rosaura (Life Is a Dream), 1087
Rose (Brighton Rock), 247
Rose (Earth), 550
Rose (The Lost Flying Boat), 1127
Rose (The Magus), 1167
Rose (The Recruiting Officer), 1608
Rose (A Room on the Hill), 1664
Rose (Through the Looking-Glass), 1944
Rose (The Wind), 2139
Rose, Arthur, 345
Rose, Billy, 172
Rose, Caroline, 372
Rose, Dessa, 489
Rose, Frau Lina, 1503
Rose, Gregory, 1849
Rose, M. James Sandy, 1352
Rose, Ma (A Chain of Voices), 313
Rose, Müller, 383
Rose, Oskar, 1503
Rose of Provence (Tom Burke of "Ours"),
    1967
Rose of Sharon Rivers, 768
Rosebloom, Janey, 1522
Roseboro, Virgil, 89
Rosedá, Rosenda, 988
Rosedale, Mr. (The House of Mirth), 878
Rosemarie (To the Land of the Cattails),
    1962
Rosemary (A Rat's Mass), 1599
Rosemary (A Severed Head), 1744
Rosemonde, Madame de (Dangerous
    Acquaintances), 442
Rosen, Duke of (Kings in Exile), 1023
Rosen, Fernie May, 283
Rosen, Gabriel, 225
Rosen, Keith, 2010
Rosen, Lucy, 2010
Rosenbaum, Haim, 1636
Rosenbaum, Scoop, 828
Rosenberg, Dr. Proinsias, 964
Rosencrantz (Hamlet, Prince of Denmark),
    805
Rosencrantz (Rosencrantz and Guildenstern
    Are Dead), 1666
Rosencranz, Lieutenant (The Raid), 1589
Rosenfeld, Toni, 1962
Rosenkrantz, Lulu, 189
Rosenthal, Esau, 2187
Rosenthal, Sarah, 2187
Rosenthurm, Prince von (The Devil's
    Elixirs), 494

Roseta (The Cabin), 270
Rosetree, Harry, 1636
Rosetta (Two Women), 2020
Rosette (Mademoiselle de Maupin), 1160
Rosette (No Trifling with Love), 1365
Rosewater, Eliot, 743
Rosewater, Fred, 743
Rosewater, Lister Ames, 743
Rosewater, Sylvia Du Vrais Zetterling, 743
Rosey (The Newcomes), 1341
Rosie (The Guide), 796
Rosie (A Painter of Our Time), 1447
Rosie, Auntie (The Coffin Tree), 364
Rosier, Edward, 1539
Rosina (Bearheart), 157
Rosina (The Foreign Girl), 675
Rosine (The Barber of Seville), 140
Rosine, The Penitent (The Balcony), 134
Rosita, Madame (Malcolm), 1174
Roskus (The Sound and the Fury), 1818
Rosmer, Beata, 1667
Rosmer, Johannes, 1667
Ross (Black Boy), 195
Ross (Macbeth), 1155
Ross (The Year of the Dragon), 2192
Ross, Aylwin, 2121
Ross, Colonel Norman, 793
Ross, Constable Neville, 1620
Ross, Cora, 793, 1857
Ross, Dickie, 2105
Ross, Lady Sara, 1914
Ross, Leo, 508
Ross, Lethe, 1313
Ross, Lord (Richard II), 1633
Ross, Mattie, 2005
Ross, Mr. and Mrs. Tom, 2095
Ross, Robert, 2095
Ross, Samuel E., 970
Rosselli, Emilio, 1976
Rosselli, Gemma, 1976
Rösselmann (William Tell), 2139
Rosseter, Lady (Mrs. Dalloway), 1302
Rossi, Herr (Bluebeard), 214
Rossignol (Marat/Sade), 1195
Rossignol, Jean-Pierre le, 1072
Rossiter, Clare Elizabeth, 677
Rossiter, Emily, 1405
Rossiter, Jonathan, 1405
Rossiter, Miss Mehitable, 1405
Rosskam, Old (Ironweed), 952
Rossman, Karl, 58
Rosso (The Courtesan), 411
Rostenkowski, Steffi, 1336
Rostov, Count Ilya, 2090
Rostov, Count Nikolay, 2090
Rostov, Count Petya, 2090
Rostova, Countess Natalya, 2090
Rostova, Countess Vera, 2090
Rostova, Princess Natasha, 2090
Rostovitch, Philomena, 1780

Thorfinn, Bishop, 125

Thorgeir of Lightwater (The Story of Burnt Njal), 1850

Thorgerda (The Story of Burnt Njal), 1850

Thorir (Grettir the Strong), 1680

Thorir of Gard (Grettir the Strong), 1680

Thorkill (The Ceremony of Innocence), 312

Thorl, Thomas, 76

Thorlakson, Thor, 647

Thorne, Arabella, 1259

Thorne, Dr. Thomas (Doctor Thorne), 512

Thorne, Dr. Thomas (Framley Parsonage), 687

Thorne, Dr. Thomas (The Last Chronicle of Barset), 1046

Thorne, Freddy, 410

Thorne, Georgene, 410

Thorne, Mary, 512

Thorne, Mrs. Martha Dunstable, 1046

Thorne, Wilfred, 141

Thornhill, Squire (The Vicar of Wakefield), 2056

Thornton, Ewart, 129

Thornton, Gerald, 1950

Thornton, John, 276, 1368

Thornton, Mrs. (North and South), 1368

Thornton, Sir Frederick, 319

Thorodd (Grettir the Strong), 1680

Thorodsson, Skapti, 1850

Thorold, Earl Tresham (A Blot in the 'Scutcheon), 210

Thorpe, Dr. Randall, 981

Thorpe, Hilary, 1357

Thorpe, Isabella, 1369

Thorpe, Joe (Beppino), 982

Thorpe, John, 1369

Thorpe, Lady (The Nine Tailors), 1357

Thorpe, Lossie, 981

Thorpe, Nolly, 982

Thorpe, Sir Henry, 1357

Thorpe, Violet, 982

Thorthur of Nitherkot (Independent People), 929

Those Who Came (A School for Fools), 1704

Thousandacres (The Chainbearer), 314

Thoux, Madame de (Uncle Tom's Cabin), 2028

Thragnar, King (Jurgen), 995

Thrainsson, Hauskuld, 1850

Thrand (Grettir the Strong), 1680

Thrasilene (Philaster), 1498

Thrasillus (The Golden Ass), 748

Thraso (The Eunuch), 593

Three, Mr. (The Adding Machine), 15

Three, Mrs. (The Adding Machine), 16

Three Shining Ones (The Pilgrim's Progress), 1511

Threepwood, Honorable Freddie (Full Moon), 703

Threepwood, Honorable Freddie (Leave It to Psmith), 1064

Threepwood, Hon. Galahad, 702

Throbbing, Lord (Vile Bodies), 2060

Throssel, Phoebe, 1571

Throssel, Susan, 1572

Thrush, old (The Hobbit), 853

Thugat, Lotario, 1136

Thulja (The Ceremony of Innocence), 311

Thumb, Deacon (A Mirror for Witches), 1255

Thumb, Labour, 1255

Thumb, Mrs. (A Mirror for Witches), 1255

Thumb, Sorrow, 1255

Thumb, Titus, 1255

Thumb, Tom, 1969

Thunder-Ten-Tronckh, Baron (Candide), 283

Thunderjet, Patrick, 263

Thurio, Sir (The Two Gentlemen of Verona), 2015

Thurley, Robert, 735

Thurn and Taxis, Prince Anselm Franz von, 1547

Thursby, Floyd, 1175

Thursley, Joan, 607

Thurston (King Horn), 1016

Thurston, Cora, 201

Thwackum, Reverend Roger, 1969

Thwaite, Arthur, 425

Thwaite, Celia, 425

Thwaites, Mrs. (Morte d'Urban), 1283

Thwaites, Sally Hopgood, 1283

Thyestes (Thyestes), 1944

Thyreus (Antony and Cleopatra), 84

Thyrsis (Orfeo), 1423

Ti Pao, 2007

Tib (Every Man in His Humour), 599

Tibbald, Lewis, 544

Tibe, Pemmer Harge rem ir, 1066

Tiberge (Manon Lescaut), 1190

Tiberius (I, Claudius), 898

Tiberius (Sejanus His Fall), 1727

Tiberius Caesar (Terra Nostra), 1913

Tiberius Claudius Drusus Nero Germanicus (Claudius the God and His Wife Messalina), 353

Tiberius Claudius Drusus Nero Germanicus (I, Claudius), 898

Tibert (Reynard the Fox), 1630

Tick (The Great White Hope), 779

Ticket taker (Manhunt), 1189

Tickit, Mrs. (Little Dorrit), 1101

Ticklepenny, Austin, 1308

Tickler, Reverend Tobias, 688

Tides, Virgil, 854

Tidy (A Woman Killed with Kindness), 2159

T'ieh Pu-ts'an, 1986

Tiera (The Kalevala), 998

Tieta (Tieta, the Goat Girl), 1946

Tietjens, Christopher, 1454, 1455

Tietjens, Sir Mark, 1454, 1455

Tietjens, Sylvia, 1454, 1455

Tiffauges, Abel, 1392

Tiffey, Mr. (David Copperfield), 453

Tiflin, Carl, 1611

Tiflin, Jody, 1611

Tiflin, Mrs. (The Red Pony), 1611

Tigellinus (Quo Vadis), 1582

Tiger (A Brighter Sun), 246

Tiger (Mother Hubberd's Tale, 1289

Tiger, Brother (Anancy's Score), 62

Tiger Lily (Peter Pan), 1492

Tiger Lily (Through the Looking-Glass), 1944

Tigg, Montague, 1205

Tigler, Kathleen Fleisher, 891

Tigranes (A King and No King), 1015

Tigre (Dream on Monkey Mountain), 537

Tigre, El (El Zarco, the Bandit), 2203

Tiikuchahk (Adulthood Rites), 2190

Tikhomirov, Leonid, 1171

Tilden (Buried Child), 262

Tilden, Samuel, 562

Tilford, Amelia, 336

Tilford, Mary, 336

Tilley, Mr. (The Country of the Pointed Firs), 407

Tillie (Alice's Adventures in Wonderland), 38

Tilling, Sophia, 2040

Tillotson, Blake, 1788

Tilly (The Rainbow), 1589

Tilly (A Simple Honorable Man), 1773

Tilney, Captain Frederick, 1369

Tilney, Eleanor, 1369

Tilney, General (Northanger Abbey), 1369

Tilney, Henry, 1369

Tilson, Lester, 1096

Tiltwood, Dick, 1226

Tim (The Knight of the Burning Pestle), 1027

Tim (Strike the Father Dead), 1860

Tim, Uncle (Sea Glass), 1711

Timagoras (The Bondman), 218

Timandra (The Bondman), 218

Timandra (Timon of Athens), 1953

Timar, Michael, 1267

Timautus (Arcadia), 91

Timberlane, Blanche, 293

Timberlane, Cass, 293

Timberman, Aaron, 314

Timberman, Lowiny, 314

Timberman, Zephanaiah, 314

Timbo (Philadelphia Fire), 1496

Time Traveler (The Time Machine), 1950

Timéa (A Modern Midas), 1267

Timewell, Ruth, 1237

Timewell, Stephen, 1237

Timias (The Faerie Queene), 611

Timoclea (Argenis), 93